get with the programming

Through the power of practice and immediate personalized feedback, MyProgrammingLab improves your performance.

Java™

An Introduction to
Problem Solving & Programming

Java™

6th edition

An Introduction to
Problem Solving & Programming

Walter Savitch
University of California, San Diego

Contributor
Kenrick Mock
University of Alaska Anchorage

Prentice Hall

Boston Columbus Indianapolis New York San Francisco Upper Saddle River
Amsterdam Cape Town Dubai London Madrid Milan Munich Paris Montreal Toronto
Delhi Mexico City São Paulo Sydney Hong Kong Seoul Singapore Taipei Tokyo

Editorial Director: *Marcia Horton*
Editor-in-Chief: *Michael Hirsch*
Acquisitions Editor: *Matt Goldstein*
Editorial Assistant: *Chelsea Bell*
Director of Marketing: *Patrice Jones*
Marketing Manager: *Yezan Alayan*
Marketing Coordinator: *Kathryn Ferranti*
Managing Editor: *Jeff Holcomb*
Production Project Manager: *Heather McNally*
Senior Operations Supervisor: *Alan Fischer*
Operations Specialist: *Lisa McDowell*
Art Director: *Kristine Carney*

Text Designer: *Jerilyn Bockorick, Nesbitt Graphics, Inc.*
Cover Designer: *Rachael Cronin*
Manager, Rights and Permissions: *Michael Joyce*
Text Permission Coordinator: *Jennifer Kennett*
Cover Art: *Aron Jungermann / Getty Images*
Media Director: *Daniel Sandin*
Media Project Manager: *Wanda Rockwell*
Full-Service Project Management: *Rose Kernan, Nesbitt Graphics, Inc.*
Composition: *Glyph International Ltd.*
Interior Printer/Bindery: *Edwards Brothers*
Cover Printer: *Coral Graphics*

Credits and acknowledgments borrowed from other sources and reproduced, with permission, in this textbook appear on appropriate page within text.

Microsoft® and Windows® are registered trademarks of the Microsoft Corporation in the U.S.A. and other countries. Screen shots and icons reprinted with permission from the Microsoft Corporation. This book is not sponsored or endorsed by or affiliated with the Microsoft Corporation.

Many of the designations by manufacturers and sellers to distinguish their products are claimed as trademarks. Where those designations appear in this book, and the publisher was aware of a trademark claim, the designations have been printed in initial caps or all caps.

Library of Congress Cataloging-in-Publication Data On File

10 9 8 7 6 5 4 3 —EB—15 14 13 12

Prentice Hall
is an imprint of

www.pearsonhighered.com

ISBN 10: 0-13-216270-9
ISBN 13: 978-0-13-216270-8

Preface for Instructors

Welcome to the sixth edition of *Java: An Introduction to Problem Solving & Programming*. This book is designed for a first course in programming and computer science. It covers programming techniques, as well as the basics of the Java programming language. It is suitable for courses as short as one quarter or as long as a full academic year. No previous programming experience is required, nor is any mathematics, other than a little high school algebra. The book can also be used for a course designed to teach Java to students who have already had another programming course, in which case the first few chapters can be assigned as outside reading.

Changes in This Edition

The following list highlights how this sixth edition differs from the fifth edition:

- Updates have been made for Java version 7, including strings in `switch` statements and the use of type inference in generic instance creation.

- Additional case studies including unit testing, use of the `Comparable` interface, processing comma-separated value files, and others.

- Chapter 5 now begins with a simpler class to more gradually introduce how classes are constructed.

- Chapter 8 has been reorganized with a greater emphasis and more examples on polymorphism and interfaces.

- Chapter 2 describes how to create a Swing application using the `JFrame` class so thereafter students have the option of implementing graphics in applets or in an application.

- Chapter 12 includes an overview of the Java Collections Framework and examples using the `HashMap` and `HashSet` classes.

- A description of `System.out.printf` has been added to Chapter 2.

- A description of `Math.random` has been added to Chapter 6.

- Twenty new programming projects have been added.

- New VideoNotes added throughout the text to enhance student understanding of programming concepts and techniques.

Latest Java Coverage

All of the code in this book has been tested using a pre-release version of Oracle's Java SE Development Kit (JDK), version 7.0. Any imported classes are standard and in the Java Class Library that is part of Java. No additional classes or specialized libraries are needed.

Flexibility

If you are an instructor, this book adapts to the way you teach, rather than making you adapt to the book. It does not tightly prescribe the sequence in which your course must cover topics. You can easily change the order in which you teach many chapters and sections. The particulars involved in rearranging material are explained in the dependency chart that follows this preface and in more detail in the "Prerequisites" section at the start of each chapter.

Early Graphics

Graphics supplement sections end each of the first ten chapters. This gives you the option of covering graphics and GUI programming from the start of your course. The graphics supplement sections emphasize applets but also cover GUIs built using the JFrame class. Any time after Chapter 8, you can move on to the main chapters on GUI programming (Chapters 13 through 15), which are now on the Web. Alternatively, you can continue through Chapter 10 with a mix of graphics and more traditional programming. Instructors who prefer to postpone the coverage of graphics can postpone or skip the graphics supplement sections.

Coverage of Problem-Solving and Programming Techniques

This book is designed to teach students basic problem-solving and programming techniques and is not simply a book about Java syntax. It contains numerous case studies, programming examples, and programming tips. Additionally, many sections explain important problem-solving and programming techniques, such as loop design techniques, debugging techniques, style techniques, abstract data types, and basic object-oriented programming techniques, including UML, event-driven programming, and generic programming using type parameters.

Early Introduction to Classes

Any course that really teaches Java must teach classes early, since everything in Java involves classes. A Java program is a class. The data type for strings of characters is a class. Even the behavior of the equals operator (==) depends on whether it is comparing objects from classes or simpler data items. Classes cannot be avoided, except by means of absurdly long and complicated "magic formulas." This book introduces classes fairly early. Some exposure to using classes is given in Chapters 1 and 2. Chapter 5 covers how to define classes. All of the basic information about classes, including inheritance, is presented by the end of Chapter 8 (even if you omit Chapter 7). However, some topics regarding classes, including inheritance, can be postponed until later in the course.

Although this book introduces classes early, it does not neglect traditional programming techniques, such as top-down design and loop design techniques. These older topics may no longer be glamorous, but they are information that all beginning students need.

Generic Programming

Students are introduced to type parameters when they cover lists in Chapter 12. The class ArrayList is presented as an example of how to use a class that has a type parameter. Students are then shown how to define their own classes that include a type parameter.

Language Details and Sample Code

This book teaches programming technique, rather than simply the Java language. However, neither students nor instructors would be satisfied with an introductory programming course that did not also teach the programming language. Until you calm students' fears about language details, it is often impossible to focus their attention on bigger issues. For this reason, the book gives complete explanations of Java language features and lots of sample code. Programs are presented in their entirety, along with sample input and output. In many cases, in addition to the complete examples in the text, extra complete examples are available over the Internet.

Self-Test Questions

Self-test questions are spread throughout each chapter. These questions have a wide range of difficulty levels. Some require only a one-word answer, whereas others require the reader to write an entire, nontrivial program. Complete answers for all the self-test questions, including those requiring full programs, are given at the end of each chapter.

Exercises and Programming Projects

Completely new exercises appear at the end of each chapter. Since only you, and not your students, will have access to their answers, these exercises are suitable for homework. Some could be expanded into programming projects. However, each chapter also contains other programming projects, several of which are new to this edition.

Support Material

The following support materials are available on the Internet at www.pearsonhighered.com/irc:

For instructors only:

- Solutions to most exercises and programming projects
- PowerPoint slides
- Lab Manual with associated code.

Instructors should click on the registration link and follow instructions to receive a password. If you encounter any problems, please contact your local Pearson Sales Representative. For the name and number of your sales representative, go to pearsonhighered.com/replocator.

For students:

- Source code for programs in the book and for extra examples
- Student lab manual
- VideoNotes: video solutions to programming examples and exercises.

Visit www.pearsonhighered.com/savitch to access the student resources.

Online Practice and Assessment with MyProgrammingLab

MyProgrammingLab helps students fully grasp the logic, semantics, and syntax of programming. Through practice exercises and immediate, personalized feedback, MyProgrammingLab improves the programming competence of beginning students who often struggle with the basic concepts and paradigms of popular high-level programming languages.

A self-study and homework tool, a MyProgrammingLab course consists of hundreds of small practice problems organized around the structure of this textbook. For students, the system automatically detects errors in the logic and syntax of their code submissions and offers targeted hints that enable students to figure out what went wrong—and why. For instructors, a comprehensive gradebook tracks correct and incorrect answers and stores the code inputted by students for review.

MyProgrammingLab is offered to users of this book in partnership with Turing's Craft, the makers of the CodeLab interactive programming exercise system. For a full demonstration, to see feedback from instructors and students, or to get started using MyProgrammingLab in your course, visit www.myprogramminglab.com.

VideoNotes

VideoNotes are Pearson's new visual tool designed for teaching students key programming concepts and techniques. These short step-by-step videos demonstrate how to solve problems from design through coding. VideoNotes allow for self-placed instruction with easy navigation including the ability to select, play, rewind, fast-forward, and stop within each VideoNote exercise.

Margin icons in your textbook let you know when a VideoNote video is available for a particular concept or homework problem.

Integrated Development Environment Resource Kits

Professors who adopt this text can order it for students with a kit containing seven popular Java IDEs (the most recent JDK from Oracle, Eclipse, NetBeans, jGRASP, DrJava, BlueJ, and TextPad). The kit also includes access to a website containing written and video tutorials for getting started in each IDE. For ordering information, please contact your campus Pearson Education representative or visit www.pearsonhighered.com.

Contact Us

Your comments, suggestions, questions, and corrections are always welcome. Please e-mail them to savitch.programming.java@gmail.com.

Preface for Students

This book is designed to teach you the Java programming language and, even more importantly, to teach you basic programming techniques. It requires no previous programming experience and no mathematics other than some simple high school algebra. However, to get the full benefit of the book, you should have Java available on your computer, so that you can practice with the examples and techniques given. The latest version of Java is preferable, but a version as early as 5 will do.

If You Have Programmed Before

You need no previous programming experience to use this book. It was designed for beginners. If you happen to have had experience with some other programming language, do not assume that Java is the same as the programming language(s) you are accustomed to using. All languages are different, and the differences, even if small, are large enough to give you problems. Browse the first four chapters, reading at least the Recap portions. By the time you reach Chapter 5, it would be best to read the entire chapter.

If you have programmed before in either C or C++, the transition to Java can be both comfortable and troublesome. At first glance, Java may seem almost the same as C or C++. However, Java is very different from these languages, and you need to be aware of the differences. Appendix 6 compares Java and C++ to help you see what the differences are.

Obtaining a Copy of Java

Appendix 1 provides links to sites for downloading Java compilers and programming environments. For beginners, we recommend Oracle's Java JDK for your Java compiler and related software and TextPad as a simple editor environment for writing Java code. When downloading the Java JDK, be sure to obtain the latest version available.

Support Materials for Students

- Source code for programs in the book and for extra examples
- Student lab manual
- VideoNotes: video solutions to programming examples and exercises.

Visit www.pearsonhighered.com/savitch to access the student resources.

Learning Aids

Each chapter contains several features to help you learn the material:

- The opening overview includes a brief table of contents, chapter objectives and prerequisites, and a paragraph or two about what you will study.
- Recaps concisely summarize major aspects of Java syntax and other important concepts.
- FAQs, or "frequently asked questions," answer questions that other students have asked.
- Remembers highlight important ideas you should keep in mind.
- Programming Tips suggest ways to improve your programming skills.
- Gotchas identify potential mistakes you could make—and should avoid—while programming.
- Asides provide short commentaries on relevant issues.
- Self-Test Questions test your knowledge throughout, with answers given at the end of each chapter. One of the best ways to practice what you are learning is to do the self-test questions *before* you look at the answers.
- A summary of important concepts appears at the end of each chapter.

Online Practice with MyProgrammingLab

A self-study and practice tool, a MyProgrammingLab course consists of hundreds of small practice problems organized around the structure of this textbook. The system automatically detects errors in the logic and syntax of your code submissions and offers targeted hints that enable you to figure out what went wrong—and why. Visit www.myprogramminglab.com for more information.

VideoNotes

These short step-by-step videos demonstrate how to solve problems from design through coding. VideoNotes allow for self-placed instruction with easy navigation including the ability to select, play, rewind, fast-forward, and stop within each VideoNote exercise. Margin icons in your textbook let you know when a VideoNote video is available for a particular concept or homework problem.

This Text Is Also a Reference Book

In addition to using this book as a textbook, you can and should use it as a reference. When you need to check a point that you have forgotten or that you hear mentioned by somebody but have not yet learned yourself, just look in the index. Many index entries give a page number for a "recap." Turn to that page. It will contain a short, highlighted entry giving all the essential points on that topic. You can do this to check details of the Java language as well as details on programming techniques.

Recap sections in every chapter give you a quick summary of the main points in that chapter. Also, a summary of important concepts appears at the end of each chapter. You can use these features to review the chapter or to check details of the Java language.

Acknowledgments

We thank the many people who have made this sixth edition possible, including everyone who has contributed to the first five editions. We begin by recognizing and thanking the people involved in the development of this new edition. The comments and suggestions of the following reviewers were invaluable and are greatly appreciated. In alphabetical order, they are:

Asa Ben-Hur—*Colorado State University*
Joan Boone—*University of North Carolina at Chapel Hill*
Dennis Brylow—*Temple University*
Billie Goldstein—*Temple University*
Helen H. Hu—*Westminster College*
Tammy VanDeGrift—*University of Portland*

Many other reviewers took the time to read drafts of earlier editions of the book. Their advice continues to benefit this new edition. Thank you once again to:

Gerald Baumgartner—*Louisiana State University*
Jim Buffenbarger—*Idaho State University*
Robert P. Burton—*Brigham Young University*
Mary Elaine Califf—*Illinois State University*
Steve Cater—*Kettering University*
Martin Chelten—*Moorpark Community College*
Ashraful A. Chowdhury—*Georgia Perimeter College*
Ping-Chu Chu—*Fayetteville State University*
Michael Clancy—*University of California, Berkeley*
Tom Cortina—*State University of New York at Stony Brook*
Prasun Dewan—*University of North Carolina*
Laird Dornan—*Sun Microsystems, Inc.*
H. E. Dunsmore—*Purdue University, Lafayette*
Adel Elmaghraby—*University of Louisville*
Ed Gellenbeck—*Central Washington University*
Adrian German—*Indiana University*
Gobi Gopinath—*Suffolk County Community College*
Le Gruenwald—*University of Oklahoma*
Gopal Gupta—*University of Texas, Dallas*
Ricci Heishman—*North Virginia Community College*
Robert Herrmann—*Sun Microsystems, Inc., Java Soft*
Chris Hoffmann—*University of Massachusetts, Amherst*

Robert Holloway—*University of Wisconsin, Madison*
Charles Hoot—*Oklahoma City University*
Lily Hou—*Carnegie Mellon University*
Richard A. Johnson—*Missouri State University*
Rob Kelly—*State University of New York at Stony Brook*
Michele Kleckner—*Elon College*
Stan Kwasny—*Washington University*
Anthony Larrain—*Depaul University*
Mike Litman—*Western Illinois University*
Y. Annie Liu—*State University of New York at Stony Brook*
Michael Long—*California State University*
Blayne Mayfield—*Oklahoma State University*
Drew McDermott—*Yale University*
Gerald H. Meyer—*LaGuardia Community College*
John Motil—*California State University, Northridge*
Michael Olan—*Stockton State*
Richard Ord—*University of California, San Diego*
James Roberts—*Carnegie Mellon University*
Alan Saleski—*Loyola University Chicago*
Dolly Samson—*Hawaii Pacific University*
Nan C. Schaller—*Rochester Institute of Technology*
Arijit Sengupta—*Raj Sion College of Business, Wright State University*
Ryan Shoemaker—*Sun Microsystems, Inc.*
Liuba Shrira—*Brandeis University*
Ken Slonneger—*University of Iowa*
Donald E. Smith—*Rutgers University*
Peter Spoerri—*Fairfield University*
Howard Straubing—*Boston College*
Navabi Tadayon—*Arizona State University*
Boyd Trolinger—*Butte College*
Tom Van Drunen—*Wheaton College*
Subramanian Vijayarangam—*University of Massachusetts, Lowell*
Stephen F. Weiss—*University of North Carolina, Chapel Hill*
Richard Whitehouse—*Arizona State University*
Michael Young—*University of Oregon*

Last but not least, we thank the many students in classes at the University of California, San Diego (UCSD), who were kind enough to help correct preliminary versions of this text, as well as the instructors who class-tested these drafts. In particular, we extend a special thanks to Carole McNamee of California State University, Sacramento, and to Paul Kube of UCSD. These student comments and the detailed feedback and class testing of earlier editions of the book were a tremendous help in shaping the final book.

W. S.
K. M.

Dependency Chart

This chart shows the prerequisites for the chapters in the book. If there is a line between two boxes, the material in the higher box should be covered before the material in the lower box. Minor variations to this chart are discussed in the "Prerequisites" section at the start of each chapter. These variations usually provide more, rather than less, flexibility that what is shown on the chart.

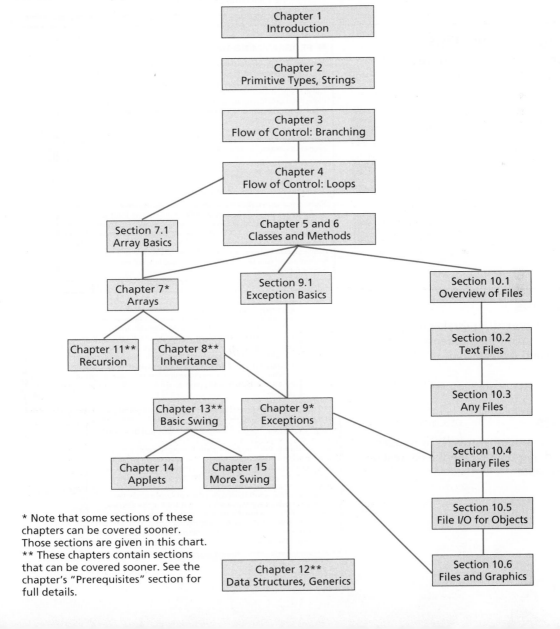

* Note that some sections of these chapters can be covered sooner. Those sections are given in this chart.
** These chapters contain sections that can be covered sooner. See the chapter's "Prerequisites" section for full details.

Features of This Text

Recaps
Summarize Java syntax and other important concepts.

Remembers
Highlight important ideas that students should keep in mind.

RECAP Bytes and Memory Locations

A computer's main memory is divided into numbered units called bytes. The number of a byte is called its address. Each byte can hold eight binary digits, or bits ... piece of data that is too l... uses several adjacent byte... single, larger memory loc... of the adjacent bytes.

REMEMBER Syntactic Variables

When you see something in this book like *Type*, *Variable_1*, or *Variable_2* used to describe Java syntax, these words do not literally appear in your Java code. They are **syntactic variables,** which are a kind of blank that you fill in with something from the category that they describe. For example, *Type* can be replaced by int, double, char, or any other type name. *Variable_1* and *Variable_2* can each be replaced by any variable name.

Programming Tips
Give students helpful advice about programming in Java.

■ PROGRAMMING TIP   Initialize Variables

A variable that has been declared, but that has not yet been given a value by an assignment statement (or in some other way), is said to be **uninitialized**. If the variable is a variable of a class type, it literally has no value. If the variable has a primitive type, it likely has some default value. However, your program will be clearer if you explicitly give the variable a value, even if you are simply reassigning the default value. (The exact details on default values have been known to change and should not be counted on.)

One easy way to ensure that you do not have an uninitialized variable is to initialize it within the declaration. Simply combine the declaration and an assignment statement, as in the following examples:

```
int count = 0;
double taxRate = 0.075;
char grade = 'A';
int balance = 1000, newBalance;
```

Note that you can initialize some variables and not initialize others in a declaration.

Sometimes the compiler may complain that you have failed to initialize a variable. In most cases, that will indeed be true. Occasionally, though, the compiler is mistaken in giving this advice. However, the compiler will not compile your program until you convince it that the variable in question is initialized. To make the compiler happy, initialize the variable when you declare it, even if the variable will be given another value before it is used for anything. In such cases, you cannot argue with the compiler. ■

Gotchas
Identify potential mistakes in programming that students might make and should avoid.

GOTCHA   Hidden Errors

Just because your program compiles and runs without any errors and even produces reasonable-looking output does not mean that your program is correct. You should always run your program with some test data that gives predictable output. To do this, choose some data for which you can compute the correct results, either by using pencil and paper, by looking up the answer, or by some other means. Even this testing does not guarantee that your program is correct, but the more testing you do, the more confidence you can have in your program. ■

FAQs
Provide students answers to frequently asked questions within the context of the chapter.

FAQ[11] FAQ stands for "frequently asked question." **Why just 0s and 1s?**

Computers use 0s and 1s because it is easy to make an electrical device that has only two stable states. However, when you are programming, you normally need not be concerned about the encoding of data as 0s and 1s. You can program as if the computer directly stored numbers, letters, or strings of characters in memory.

There is nothing special about calling the states *zero* and *one*. We could just as well use any two names, such as *A* and *B* or *true* and *false*. The important thing is that the underlying physical device has two stable states, such as on and off or high voltage and low voltage. Calling these two states *zero* and *one* is simply a convention, but it's one that is almost universally followed.

Listings

Show students complete programs
with sample output.

LISTING 1.2 Drawing a Happy Face

```
import javax.swing.JApplet;
import java.awt.Graphics;
public class HappyFace extends JApplet
{
    public void paint(Graphics canvas)
    {
        canvas.drawOval(100, 50, 200, 200);
        canvas.fillOval(155, 100, 10, 20);
        canvas.fillOval(230, 100, 10, 20);
        canvas.drawArc(150, 160, 100, 50, 180, 180);
    }
}
```
Applet Output

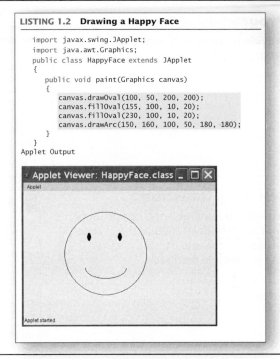

Case Studies

Take students from problem statement
to algorithm development to Java code.

CASE STUDY Unit Testing

So far we've tested our programs by running them, typing in some input, and visually checking the results to see if the output is what we expected. This is fine for small programs but is generally insufficient for large programs. In a large program there are usually so many combinations of interacting inputs that it would take too much time to manually verify the correct result for all inputs. Additionally, it is possible that code changes result in unintended side effects. For example, a fix for one error might introduce a different error. One way to attack this problem is to write **unit tests**. Unit testing is a methodology in which the programmer tests the correctness of individual units of code. A unit is often a method but it could be a class or other group of code.

The collection of unit tests becomes the **test suite**. Each test is generally automated so that human input is not required. Automation is important because it is desirable to have tests that run often and quickly. This makes it possible to run the tests repeatedly, perhaps once a day or every time code is changed, to make sure that everything is still working. The process of running tests repeatedly is called **regression testing**.

Let's start with a simple test case for the Species class in Listing 5.19. Our first test might be to verify that the name, initial population, and growth rate is correctly set in the setSpecies method. We can accomplish this by creating

VideoNotes

Step-by-step video solutions to
programming examples and homework
exercises.

VideoNote
Writing arithmetic
expressions and statements

Programming Examples

Provide more examples of Java programs that solve specific problems.

PROGRAMMING EXAMPLE Nested Loops

The body of a loop can contain any sort of statements. In particular, you can have a loop statement within the body of a larger loop statement. For example, the program in Listing 4.4 uses a while loop to compute the average of a list of nonnegative scores. The program asks the user to enter all the scores followed by a negative sentinel value to mark the end of the data. This while loop is placed inside a do-while loop so that the user can repeat the entire process for another exam, and another, until the user wishes to end the program.

Self-Test Questions

Provide students with the opportunity to practice skills learned in the chapter. Answers at the end of each chapter give immediate feedback.

SELF-TEST QUESTIONS

28. Given the class Species as defined in Listing 5.19, why does the following program cause an error message?

```java
public class SpeciesEqualsDemo
{
public static void main(String[] args)
{
    Species s1, s2; s1.
    setSpecies("Klingon ox", 10, 15);
    s2.setSpecies("Klingon ox", 10, 15);
    if (s1 == s2)
        System.out.println("Match with ==.");
    else
        System.out.println("Do Notmatchwith ==.")
}
}
```

29. After correcting the program in the previous question, what output does the program produce?

30. What is the biggest difference between a parameter of a primitive type and a parameter of a class type?

31. Given the class Species, as defined in Listing 5.19, and the class

Asides

Give short commentary on relevant topics.

ASIDE Use of the Terms *Parameter* and *Argument*

Our use of the terms *parameter* and *argument* is consistent with common usage. We use *parameter* to describe the definition of the data type and variable inside the header of a method and *argument* to describe items passed into a method when it is invoked. However, people often use these terms interchangeably. Some people use the term *parameter* both for what we call a *formal parameter* and for what we call an *argument*. Other people use the term *argument* both for what we call a *formal parameter* and for what we call an *argument*. When you see the term *parameter* or *argument* in other books, you must figure out its exact meaning from the context.

Brief Table of Contents

Chapter 1   **Introduction to Computers and Java**   1

Chapter 2   **Basic Computation**   47

Chapter 3   **Flow of Control: Branching**   137

Chapter 4   **Flow of Control: Loops**   195

Chapter 5   **Defining Classes and Methods**   261

Chapter 6   **More About Objects and Methods**   373

Chapter 7   **Arrays**   479

Chapter 8   **Inheritance, Polymorphism and Inheritance**   575

Chapter 9   **Exception Handling**   657

Chapter 10   **Streams and File I/O**   725

Chapter 11   **Recursion**   799

Chapter 12   **Dynamic Data Structures and Generics**   847

Appendices
   1 **Getting Java**   917
   2 **Running Applets**   918

3 Protected and Package Modifiers 920

4 The DecimalFormat Class 921

5 javadoc 925

6 Differences between C++ and Java 928

7 Unicode Character Codes 932

Index 933

The following chapters and appendices, along with an index to their contents, are on the book's website:

Chapter 13 Window Interfaces Using Swing

Chapter 14 Applets and HTML

Chapter 15 More Swing

Appendices

8 The Iterator Interface

9 Cloning

Table of Contents

Chapter 1 **Introduction to Computers and Java** **1**

1.1 COMPUTER BASICS 2
Hardware and Memory 3
Programs 6
Programming Languages, Compilers, and Interpreters 7
Java Bytecode 9
Class Loader 11

1.2 A SIP OF JAVA 12
History of the Java Language 12
Applications and Applets 13
A First Java Application Program 14
Writing, Compiling, and Running a Java Program 19

1.3 PROGRAMMING BASICS 21
Object-Oriented Programming 21
Algorithms 25
Testing and Debugging 27
Software Reuse 28

1.4 GRAPHICS SUPPLEMENT 30
A Sample Graphics Applet 30
Size and Position of Figures 32
Drawing Ovals and Circles 34
Drawing Arcs 35
Running an Applet 37

Chapter 2 **Basic Computation** **47**

2.1 VARIABLES AND EXPRESSIONS 48
Variables 49
Data Types 51

Java Identifiers   53
Assignment Statements   55
Simple Input   58
Simple Screen Output   60
Constants   60
Named Constants   62
Assignment Compatibilities   63
Type Casting   65
Arithmetic Operators   68
Parentheses and Precedence Rules   71
Specialized Assignment Operators   72
Case Study: Vending Machine Change   74
Increment and Decrement Operators   79
More About the Increment and Decrement Operators   80

2.2 THE CLASS String   81
String Constants and Variables   81
Concatenation of Strings   82
String Methods   83
String Processing   85
Escape Characters   88
The Unicode Character Set   89

2.3 KEYBOARD AND SCREEN I/O   91
Screen Output   91
Keyboard Input   94
Other Input Delimiters *(Optional)*   99
Formatted Output with printf *(Optional)*   101

2.4 DOCUMENTATION AND STYLE   103
Meaningful Variable Names   103
Comments   104
Indentation   107
Using Named Constants   107

2.5 GRAPHICS SUPPLEMENT   109
Style Rules Applied to a Graphics Applet   110
Creating a Java GUI Application with the JFrame Class   110
Introducing the Class JOptionPane   113
Reading Input as Other Numeric Types   123

Programming Example: Change-Making Program
with Windowing I/O   124

Chapter 3   **Flow of Control: Branching   137**

3.1 THE `if-else` STATEMENT   138
The Basic if-else Statement   139
Boolean Expressions   145
Comparing Strings   150
Nested if-else Statements   155
Multibranch if-else Statements   157
Programming Example: Assigning Letter Grades   159
Case Study: Body Mass Index   162
The Conditional Operator *(Optional)*   165
The exit Method   165

3.2 THE TYPE `boolean`   166
Boolean Variables   167
Precedence Rules   168
Input and Output of Boolean Values   171

3.3 THE `switch` STATEMENT   173
Enumerations   179

3.4 GRAPHICS SUPPLEMENT   180
Specifying a Drawing Color   181
A Dialog Box for a Yes-or-No Question   184

Chapter 4   **Flow of Control: Loops   195**

4.1 JAVA LOOP STATEMENTS   196
The while Statement   197
The do-while Statement   200
Programming Example: Bug Infestation   205
Programming Example: Nested Loops   211
The for Statement   213
Declaring Variables within a for Statement   219
Using a Comma in a for Statement *(Optional)*   220
The for-each Statement   222

4.2 PROGRAMMING WITH LOOPS 222

The Loop Body   223

Initializing Statements   224

Controlling the Number of Loop Iterations   225

Case Study: Using a Boolean Variable to End a Loop   227

Programming Example: Spending Spree   229

The break Statement and continue Statement in Loops
   (Optional)   232

Loop Bugs   235

Tracing Variables   237

Assertion Checks   239

4.3 GRAPHICS SUPPLEMENT 241

Programming Example: A Multiface Applet   241

The drawstring Method   247

Chapter 5   Defining Classes and Methods   261

5.1 CLASS AND METHOD DEFINITIONS 263

Class Files and Separate Compilation   265

Programming Example: Implementing a Dog Class   265

Instance Variables   266

Methods   269

Defining void Methods   272

Defining Methods That Return a Value   273

Programming Example: First Try at Implementing a Species Class   278

The Keyword this   282

Local Variables   284

Blocks   286

Parameters of a Primitive Type   287

5.2 INFORMATION HIDING AND ENCAPSULATION 293

Information Hiding   294

Precondition and Postcondition Comments   294

The public and private Modifiers   296

Programming Example: A Demonstration of Why Instance
   Variables Should Be Private   299

Programming Example: Another Implementation of a Class
   of Rectangles   300

Accessor Methods and Mutator Methods   302

Programming Example: A Purchase Class   306
Methods Calling Methods   310
Encapsulation   316
Automatic Documentation with javadoc   319
UML Class Diagrams   320

5.3 OBJECTS AND REFERENCES   321
Variables of a Class Type   322
Defining an equals Method for a Class   327
Programming Example: A Species Class   331
Boolean-Valued Methods   334
Case Study: Unit Testing   336
Parameters of a Class Type   338
Programming Example: Class-Type Parameters Versus
   Primitive-Type Parameters   342

5.4 GRAPHICS SUPPLEMENT   346
The Graphics Class   346
Programming Example: Multiple Faces, but with a Helping
   Method   348
The init Method   352
Adding Labels to an Applet   352

Chapter 6   **More About Objects and Methods   373**

6.1 CONSTRUCTORS   375
Defining Constructors   375
Calling Methods from Constructors   384
Calling a Constructor from Other Constructors *(Optional)*   387

6.2 STATIC VARIABLES AND STATIC METHODS   389
Static Variables   389
Static Methods   390
Dividing the Task of a main Method into Subtasks   397
Adding a main Method to a Class   398
The Math Class   400
Wrapper Classes   403

6.3 WRITING METHODS   409
Case Study: Formatting Output   409
Decomposition   415

Addressing Compiler Concerns   416
Testing Methods   418

6.4 OVERLOADING   420
Overloading Basics   420
Overloading and Automatic Type Conversion   423
Overloading and the Return Type   426
Programming Example: A Class for Money   428

6.5 INFORMATION HIDING REVISITED   435
Privacy Leaks   435

6.6 ENUMERATION AS A CLASS   439

6.7 PACKAGES   441
Packages and Importing   441
Package Names and Directories   443
Name Clashes   446

6.8 GRAPHICS SUPPLEMENT   447
Adding Buttons   447
Event-Driven Programming   449
Programming Buttons   449
Programming Example: A Complete Applet with Buttons   453
Adding Icons   456
Changing Visibility   458
Programming Example: An Example of Changing Visibility   458

Chapter 7   Arrays   479

7.1 ARRAY BASICS   481
Creating and Accessing Arrays   482
Array Details   485
The Instance Variable length   488
More About Array Indices   491
Initializing Arrays   494

7.2 ARRAYS IN CLASSES AND METHODS   495
Case Study: Sales Report   495
Indexed Variables as Method Arguments   503
Entire Arrays as Arguments to a Method   505

Arguments for the Method main 507
Array Assignment and Equality 508
Methods That Return Arrays 511

7.3 PROGRAMMING WITH ARRAYS AND CLASSES 515
Programming Example: A Specialized List Class 515
Partially Filled Arrays 523

7.4 SORTING AND SEARCHING ARRAYS 525
Selection Sort 525
Other Sorting Algorithms 529
Searching an Array 531

7.5 MULTIDIMENSIONAL ARRAYS 532
Multidimensional-Array Basics 533
Multidimensional-Array Parameters and Returned Values 536
Java's Representation of Multidimensional Arrays 539
Ragged Arrays *(Optional)* 540
Programming Example: Employee Time Records 542

7.6 GRAPHICS SUPPLEMENT 548
Text Areas and Text Fields 548
Programming Example: A Question-and-Answer Applet 548
The Classes JTextArea and JTextField 551
Drawing Polygons 553

**Chapter 8   Inheritance, Polymorphism and
                      Interfaces 575**

8.1 INHERITANCE BASICS 576
Derived Classes 578
Overriding Method Definitions 582
Overriding Versus Overloading 583
The final Modifier 583
Private Instance Variables and Private Methods of a Base Class 584
UML Inheritance Diagrams 586

8.2 PROGRAMMING WITH INHERITANCE 589
Constructors in Derived Classes 589
The this Method—Again 591
Calling an Overridden Method 591

Programming Example: A Derived Class of a Derived Class   592
Another Way to Define the equals Methods in Undergraduate   597
Type Compatibility   597
The Class Object   602
A Better equals Method   604

8.3 POLYMORPHISM   606
Dynamic Binding and Inheritance   606
Dynamic Binding with toString   609

8.4 INTERFACES AND ABSTRACT CLASSES   611
Class Interfaces   611
Java Interfaces   612
Implementing an Interface   613
An Interface as a Type   615
Extending an Interface   618
Case Study: Character Graphics   619
Case Study: The Comparable Interface   632
Abstract Classes   636

8.5 GRAPHICS SUPPLEMENT   638
The Class JApplet   639
The Class JFrame   639
Window Events and Window Listeners   642
The ActionListener Interface   644
What to Do Next   644

Chapter 9   Exception Handling   657

9.1 BASIC EXCEPTION HANDLING   658
Exceptions in Java   659
Predefined Exception Classes   669

9.2 DEFINING YOUR OWN EXCEPTION CLASSES   671

9.3 MORE ABOUT EXCEPTION CLASSES   681
Declaring Exceptions (Passing the Buck)   681
Kinds of Exceptions   684
Errors   686
Multiple Throws and Catches   687
The finally Block   693

Rethrowing an Exception *(Optional)*   694
Case Study: A Line-Oriented Calculator   695

9.4 GRAPHICS SUPPLEMENT   707
Exceptions in GUIs   707
Programming Example: A JFrame GUI Using Exceptions   707

Chapter 10   Streams and File I/O   725

10.1 AN OVERVIEW OF STREAMS AND FILE I/O   727
The Concept of a Stream   727
Why Use Files for I/O?   728
Text Files and Binary Files   728

10.2 TEXT-FILE I/O   730
Creating a Text File   730
Appending to a Text File   736
Reading from a Text File   738

10.3 TECHNIQUES FOR ANY FILE   741
The Class File   741
Programming Example: Reading a File Name
  from the Keyboard   741
Using Path Names   743
Methods of the Class File   744
Defining a Method to Open a Stream   746
Case Study: Processing a Comma-Separated Values File   748

10.4 BASIC BINARY-FILE I/O   751
Creating a Binary File   751
Writing Primitive Values to a Binary File   753
Writing Strings to a Binary File   756
Some Details About writeUTF   757
Reading from a Binary File   759
The Class EOFException   764
Programming Example: Processing a File of Binary Data   766

10.5 BINARY-FILE I/O WITH OBJECTS AND ARRAYS   771
Binary-File I/O with Objects of a Class   771
Some Details of Serialization   775
Array Objects in Binary Files   776

10.6 GRAPHICS SUPPLEMENT   779
Programming Example: A JFrame GUI for Manipulating Files   779

Chapter 11   Recursion   799

11.1 THE BASICS OF RECURSION   800
Case Study: Digits to Words   803
How Recursion Works   808
Infinite Recursion   812
Recursive Methods Versus Iterative Methods   814
Recursive Methods That Return a Value   816

11.2 PROGRAMMING WITH RECURSION   820
Programming Example: Insisting That User Input Be Correct   820
Case Study: Binary Search   822
Programming Example: Merge Sort—A Recursive Sorting Method   830

Chapter 12   Dynamic Data Structures and Generics   847

12.1 ARRAY-BASED DATA STRUCTURES   849
The Class ArrayList   850
Creating an Instance of ArrayList   850
Using the Methods of ArrayList   852
Programming Example: A To-Do List   856
Parameterized Classes and Generic Data Types   859

12.2 THE JAVA COLLECTIONS FRAMEWORK   859
The Collection Interface   860
The Class HashSet   861
The Map Interface   862
The Class HashMap   862

12.3 LINKED DATA STRUCTURES   865
The Class LinkedList   865
Linked Lists   866
Implementing the Operations of a Linked List   869
A Privacy Leak   876
Inner Classes   877
Node Inner Classes   878
Iterators   878

The Java Iterator Interface   890
Exception Handling with Linked Lists   890
Variations on a Linked List   892
Other Linked Data Structures   894

12.4 GENERICS   895
The Basics   895
Programming Example: A Generic Linked List   898

APPENDICES
1 **Getting Java**   917
2 **Running Applets**   918
3 **Protected and Package Modifiers**   920
4 **The DecimalFormat Class**   921
Other Pattern Symbols   922
5 **Javadoc**   925
Commenting Classes for Use within javadoc   925
Running javadoc   926
6 **Differences Between C++ and Java**   928
Primitive Types   928
Strings   928
Flow of Control   928
Testing for Equality   929
main Method (Function) and Other Methods   929
Files and Including Files   929
Class and Method (Function) Definitions   930
No Pointer Types in Java   930
Method (Function) Parameters   930
Arrays   930
Garbage Collection   931
Other Comparisons   931
7 **Unicode Character Codes**   932

INDEX   933

Introduction to Computers and Java

1.1 COMPUTER BASICS   2
Hardware and Memory   3
Programs   6
Programming Languages, Compilers, and
    Interpreters   7
Java Bytecode   9
Class Loader   11

1.2 A SIP OF JAVA   12
History of the Java Language   12
Applications and Applets   13
A First Java Application Program   14
Writing, Compiling, and Running a Java
    Program   19

1.3 PROGRAMMING BASICS   21
Object-Oriented Programming   21
Algorithms   25
Testing and Debugging   27
Software Reuse   28

1.4 GRAPHICS SUPPLEMENT   30
A Sample Graphics Applet   30
Size and Position of Figures   32
Drawing Ovals and Circles   34
Drawing Arcs   35
Running an Applet   37

Chapter Summary   38   **Programming Projects**   41   **Answers to Self-Test Questions**   42

It is by no means hopeless to expect to make a machine for really very difficult mathematical problems. But you would have to proceed step-by-step. I think electricity would be the best thing to rely on.

—CHARLES SANDERS PEIRCE *(1839–1914)*

INTRODUCTION

This chapter gives you a brief overview of computer hardware and software. Much of this introductory material applies to programming in any language, not just to programming in Java. Our discussion of software will include a description of a methodology for designing programs known as object-oriented programming. Section 1.2 introduces the Java language and explains a sample Java program.

Section 1.4 is the first of a number of graphics supplements that end each of the first ten chapters and provide an introduction to the graphics capabilities of the Java language. These graphics supplements are interdependent, and each one uses the Java topics presented in its chapter.

OBJECTIVES

After studying this chapter, you should be able to

- Give a brief overview of computer hardware and software
- Give an overview of the Java programming language
- Describe the basic techniques of program design in general and object-oriented programming in particular
- Describe applets and some graphics basics

PREREQUISITES

This first chapter does *not* assume that you have had any previous programming experience, but it does assume that you have access to a computer. To get the full value from the chapter, and from the rest of this book, you should have a computer that has the Java language installed, so that you can try out what you are learning. Appendix 1 describes how to obtain and install a free copy of the Java language for your computer.

1.1 COMPUTER BASICS

The Analytical Engine has no pretensions whatever to originate anything. It can do whatever we know how to order it to perform. It can follow analysis; but it has no power of anticipating any analytical relations or truths. Its province is to assist us in making available what we are already acquainted with.

—ADA AUGUSTA, COUNTESS OF LOVELACE (1815–1852)

Computer systems consist of hardware and software. The **hardware** is the physical machine. A set of instructions for the computer to carry out is called a **program.** All the different kinds of programs used to give instructions to the computer are collectively referred to as **software.** In this book, we will discuss software, but to understand software, it helps to know a few basic things about computer hardware.

Hardware and software make up a computer system

Hardware and Memory

Most computers available today have the same basic components, configured in basically the same way. They all have input devices, such as a keyboard and a mouse. They all have output devices, such as a display screen and a printer. They also have several other basic components, usually housed in some sort of cabinet, where they are not so obvious. These other components store data and perform the actual computing.

The **CPU,** or **central processing unit,** or simply the **processor,** is the device inside your computer that follows a program's instructions. Currently, one of the better-known processors is the Intel®Core™i7 processor. The processor can carry out only very simple instructions, such as moving numbers or other data from one place in memory to another and performing some basic arithmetic operations like addition and subtraction. The power of a computer comes from its speed and the intricacies of its programs. The basic design of the hardware is conceptually simple.

The CPU, or central processing unit, or processor, performs the instructions in a program

A computer's **memory** holds **data** for the computer to process, and it holds the result of the computer's intermediate calculations. Memory exists in two basic forms, known as main memory and auxiliary memory. **Main memory** holds the current program and much of the data that the program is manipulating. You most need to be aware of the nature of the main memory when you are writing programs. The information stored in main memory typically is **volatile,** that is, it disappears when you shut down your computer. In contrast, the data in **auxiliary memory,** or **secondary memory,** exists even when the computer's power is off. All of the various kinds of disks—including hard disk drives, flash drives, compact discs (CDs), and digital video discs (DVDs) are auxiliary memory.

Main memory is volatile; auxiliary memory is not

To make this more concrete, let's look at an example. You might have heard a description of a personal computer (PC) as having, say, 1 gigabyte of RAM and a 200-gigabyte hard drive. **RAM**—short for **random access memory**—is the main memory, and the hard drive is the principal—but not the only—form of auxiliary memory. A byte is a quantity of memory. So 1 gigabyte of RAM is approximately 1 billion bytes of memory, and a 200-gigabyte hard drive has approximately 200 billion bytes of memory. What exactly is a byte? Read on.

The computer's main memory consists of a long list of numbered bytes. The number of a byte is called its **address.** A **byte** is the smallest addressable unit of memory. A piece of data, such as a number or a keyboard character, can be stored in one of these bytes. When the computer needs to recover the data later, it uses the address of the byte to find the data item.

A byte, by convention, contains eight digits, each of which is either 0 or 1. Actually, any two values will do, but the two values are typically written as 0 and 1. Each of these digits is called a **binary digit** or, more typically, a **bit.** A byte, then, contains eight bits of memory. Both main memory and auxiliary memory are measured in bytes.

Data of various kinds, such as numbers, letters, and strings of characters, is encoded as a series of 0s and 1s and placed in the computer's memory. As it turns out, one byte is just large enough to store a single keyboard character. This is one of the reasons that a computer's memory is divided into these eight-bit bytes instead of into pieces of some other size. However, storing either a string of characters or a large number requires more than a single byte. When the computer needs to store a piece of data that cannot fit into a single byte, it uses several adjacent bytes. These adjacent bytes are then considered to be a single, larger **memory location,** and the address of the first byte is used as the address of the entire memory location. Figure 1.1 shows how a typical computer's main memory might be divided into memory locations. The addresses of these larger locations are not fixed by the hardware but depend on the program using the memory.

Sidebar notes (left margin):
Main memory consists of addressable eight-bit bytes

Groups of adjacent bytes can serve as a single memory location

FIGURE 1.1   Main Memory

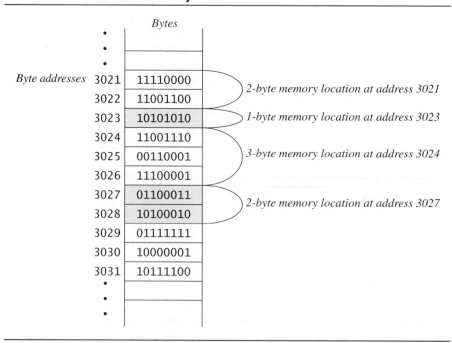

Recall that main memory holds the current program and much of its data. Auxiliary memory is used to hold data in a more or less permanent form. Auxiliary memory is also divided into bytes, but these bytes are grouped into much larger units known as **files**. A file can contain almost any sort of data, such as a program, an essay, a list of numbers, or a picture, each in an encoded form. For example, when you write a Java program, you will store the program in a file that will typically reside in some kind of disk storage. When you use the program, the contents of the program file are copied from auxiliary memory to main memory.

A file is a group of bytes stored in auxiliary memory

You name each file and can organize groups of files into **directories,** or **folders.** *Folder* and *directory* are two names for the same thing. Some computer systems use one name, and some use the other.

A directory, or folder, contains groups of files

FAQ[1] Why just 0s and 1s?

Computers use 0s and 1s because it is easy to make an electrical device that has only two stable states. However, when you are programming, you normally need not be concerned about the encoding of data as 0s and 1s. You can program as if the computer directly stored numbers, letters, or strings of characters in memory.

There is nothing special about calling the states *zero* and *one*. We could just as well use any two names, such as *A* and *B* or *true* and *false*. The important thing is that the underlying physical device has two stable states, such as on and off or high voltage and low voltage. Calling these two states *zero* and *one* is simply a convention, but it's one that is almost universally followed.

RECAP Bytes and Memory Locations

A computer's main memory is divided into numbered units called bytes. The number of a byte is called its address. Each byte can hold eight binary digits, or bits, each of which is either 0 or 1. To store a piece of data that is too large to fit into a single byte, the computer uses several adjacent bytes. These adjacent bytes are thought of as a single, larger memory location whose address is the address of the first of the adjacent bytes.

---

[1] FAQ stands for "frequently asked question."

Programs

A program is a
set of computer
instructions

You probably have some idea of what a program is. You use programs all the time. For example, text editors and word processors are programs. As we mentioned earlier, a program is simply a set of instructions for a computer to follow. When you give the computer a program and some data and tell the computer to follow the instructions in the program, you are **running**, or **executing**, the program on the data.

Figure 1.2 shows two ways to view the running of a program. To see the first way, ignore the dashed lines and blue shading that form a box. What's left is what really happens when you run a program. In this view, the computer has two kinds of input. The program is one kind of input; it contains the instructions that the computer will follow. The other kind of input is the data for the program. It is the information that the computer program will process. For example, if the program is a spelling-check program, the data would be the text that needs to be checked. As far as the computer is concerned, both the data and the program itself are input. The output is the result—or results—produced when the computer follows the program's instructions. If the program checks the spelling of some text, the output might be a list of words that are misspelled.

This first view of running a program is what really happens, but it is not always the way we think about running a program. Another way is to think of the data as the input to the program. In this second view, the computer and the program are considered to be one unit. Figure 1.2 illustrates this view by surrounding the combined program–computer unit with a dashed box and blue shading. When we take this view, we think of the data as input to the program and the results as output from the program. Although the computer is understood to be there, it is presumed just to be something that assists the program. People who write programs—that is, **programmers**—find this second view to be more useful when they design a program.

Your computer has more programs than you might think. Much of what you consider to be "the computer" is actually a program—that is, software—

FIGURE 1.2   **Running a Program**

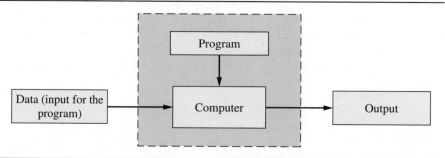

rather than hardware. When you first turn on a computer, you are already running and interacting with a program. That program is called the **operating system.** The operating system is a kind of supervisory program that oversees the entire operation of the computer. If you want to run a program, you tell the operating system what you want to do. The operating system then retrieves and starts the program. The program you run might be a text editor, a browser to surf the World Wide Web, or some program that you wrote using the Java language. You might tell the operating system to run the program by using a mouse to click an icon, by choosing a menu item, or by typing in a simple command. Thus, what you probably think of as "the computer" is really the operating system. Some common operating systems are Microsoft Windows, Apple's (Macintosh) Mac OS, Linux, and UNIX.

An operating system is a program that supervises a computer's operation

---

FAQ What exactly is software?

The word *software* simply means programs. Thus, a software company is a company that produces programs. The software on your computer is just the collection of programs on your computer.

Programming Languages, Compilers, and Interpreters

Most modern programming languages are designed to be relatively easy for people to understand and use. Such languages are called **high-level languages.** Java is a high-level language. Most other familiar programming languages, such as Visual Basic, C++, C#, COBOL, Python, and Ruby, are also high-level languages. Unfortunately, computer hardware does not understand high-level languages. Before a program written in a high-level language can be run, it must be translated into a language that the computer can understand.

Java is a high-level language

The language that the computer can directly understand is called **machine language. Assembly language** is a symbolic form of machine language that is easier for people to read. So assembly language is almost the same thing as machine language, but it needs some minor additional translation before it can run on the computer. Such languages are called **low-level languages.**

Computers execute a low-level language called machine language

The translation of a program from a high-level language, like Java, to a low-level language is performed entirely or in part by another program. For some high-level languages, this translation is done as a separate step by a program known as a **compiler.** So before you run a program written in a high-level language, you must first run the compiler on the program. When you do this, you are said to **compile** the program. After this step, you can run the resulting machine-language program as often as you like without compiling it again.

Compile once, execute often

Compilers
translate source
code into object
code

The terminology here can get a bit confusing, because both the input to the compiler program and the output from the compiler program are programs. Everything in sight is a program of some kind or other. To help avoid confusion, we call the input program, which in our case will be a Java program, the **source program,** or **source code.** The machine-language program that the compiler produces is often called the **object program,** or **object code.** The word **code** here just means a program or a part of a program.

RECAP Compiler

A compiler is a program that translates a program written in a high-level language, such as Java, into a program in a simpler language that the computer can more or less directly understand.

Interpreters
translate and
execute portions
of code at a time

Some high-level languages are translated not by compilers but rather by another kind of program called an **interpreter.** Like a compiler, an interpreter translates program statements from a high-level language to a low-level language. But unlike a compiler, an interpreter executes a portion of code right after translating it, rather than translating the entire program at once. Using an interpreter means that when you run a program, translation alternates with execution. Moreover, translation is done each time you run the program. Recall that compilation is done once, and the resulting object program can be run over and over again without engaging the compiler again. This implies that a compiled program generally runs faster than an interpreted one.

RECAP Interpreter

An interpreter is a program that alternates the translation and execution of statements in a program written in a high-level language.

One disadvantage of the processes we just described for translating programs written in most high-level programming languages is that you need a different compiler or interpreter for each type of language or computer system. If you want to run your source program on three different types of computer systems, you need to use three different compilers or interpreters. Moreover, if a manufacturer produces an entirely new type of computer system, a team of programmers must write a new compiler or interpreter for that computer system. This is a problem, because these compilers and interpreters are large programs that are expensive and time-consuming to write. Despite this cost, many high-level-language compilers and interpreters work this way. Java, however, uses a slightly different and much more versatile approach that combines a compiler and an interpreter. We describe Java's approach next.

Java Bytecode

The Java compiler does not translate your program into the machine language for your particular computer. Instead, it translates your Java program into a language called **bytecode.** Bytecode is not the machine language for any particular computer. Instead, bytecode is a machine language for a hypothetical computer known as a **virtual machine.** A virtual machine is not exactly like any particular computer, but is similar to all typical computers. Translating a program written in bytecode into a machine-language program for an actual computer is quite easy. The program that does this translation is a kind of interpreter called the **Java Virtual Machine,** or **JVM.** The JVM translates and runs the Java bytecode.

A compiler translates Java code into bytecode

To run your Java program on your computer, you proceed as follows: First, you use the compiler to translate your Java program into bytecode. Then you use the particular JVM for your computer system to translate each bytecode instruction into machine language and to run the machine-language instructions. The whole process is shown in Figure 1.3.

The JVM is an interpreter that translates and executes bytecode

It sounds as though Java bytecode just adds an extra step to the process. Why not write compilers that translate directly from Java to the machine language for your particular computer system? That could be done, and it is what is done for many other programming languages. Moreover, that technique would produce machine-language programs that typically run faster. However, Java bytecode gives Java one important advantage, namely, portability. After you compile your Java program into bytecode, you can run that bytecode on any computer. When you run your program on another computer, you do not need to recompile it. This means that you can send your bytecode over the Internet to another computer and have it run easily on that computer regardless of the computer's operating system. That is one of the reasons Java is good for Internet applications.

Java bytecode runs on any computer that has a JVM

Portability has other advantages as well. When a manufacturer produces a new type of computer system, the creators of Java do not have to design a new Java compiler. One Java compiler works on every computer. Of course, every type of computer must have its own bytecode interpreter—the JVM—that translates bytecode instructions into machine-language instructions for that particular computer, but these interpreters are simple programs compared to a compiler. Thus, Java can be added to a new computer system very quickly and very economically.

FIGURE 1.3 Compiling and Running a Java Program

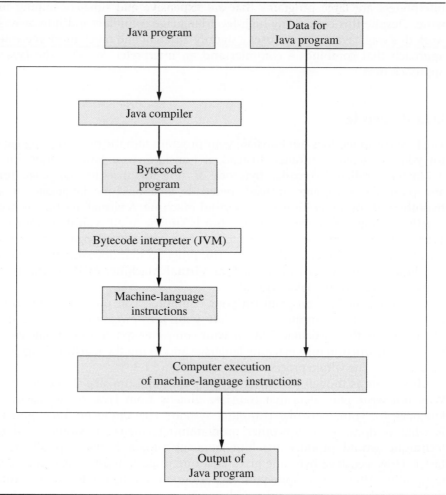

RECAP Bytecode

The Java compiler translates your Java program into a language called bytecode. This bytecode is not the machine language for any particular computer, but it is similar to the machine language of most common computers. Bytecode is easily translated into the machine language of a given computer. Each type of computer will have its own translator—called an interpreter—that translates from bytecode instructions to machine-language instructions for that computer.

Knowing about Java bytecode is important, but in the day-to-day business of programming, you will not even be aware that it exists. You normally will give two commands, one to compile your Java program into bytecode and one to run your program. The **run command** tells the bytecode interpreter to execute the bytecode. This run command might be called "run" or something else, but it is unlikely to be called "interpret." You will come to think of the run command as running whatever the compiler produces, and you will not even think about the translation of bytecode to machine language.

FAQ Why is it called bytecode?

Programs in low-level languages, such as bytecode and machine-language code, consist of instructions, each of which can be stored in a few bytes of memory. Typically, one byte of each instruction contains the operation code, or opcode, which specifies the operation to be performed. The notion of a one-byte opcode gave rise to the term *bytecode*.

Class Loader

A Java program is seldom written as one piece of code all in one file. Instead, it typically consists of different pieces, known as **classes.** We will talk about classes in detail later, but thinking of them as pieces of code is sufficient for now. These classes are often written by different people, and each class is compiled separately. Thus, each class is translated into a different piece of bytecode. To run your program, the bytecode for these various classes must be connected together. The connecting is done by a program known as the **class loader.** This connecting is typically done automatically, so you normally need not be concerned with it. In other programming languages, the program corresponding to the Java class loader is called a *linker*.

For now, think of a class as a piece of code

 SELF-TEST QUESTIONS

myprogramminglab

Answers to the self-test questions appear at the end of each chapter.

1. What are the two kinds of memory in a computer?

2. What is software?

3. What data would you give to a program that computes the sum of two numbers?

4. What data would you give to a program that computes the average of all the quizzes you have taken in a course?

5. What is the difference between a program written in a high-level language, a program in machine language, and a program expressed in Java bytecode?

6. Is Java a high-level language or a low-level language?

7. Is Java bytecode a high-level language or a low-level language?

8. What is a compiler?

9. What is a source program?

10. What do you call a program that translates Java bytecode into machine-language instructions?

1.2 A SIP OF JAVA

> **Java** *n. An island of Indonesia, 48,842 square miles in area, lying between the Indian Ocean and the Java Sea.*
> **java** *n. Informal. Brewed coffee. [From Java.]*
>
> —THE AMERICAN HERITAGE DICTIONARY OF THE ENGLISH LANGUAGE, FOURTH EDITION*

In this section, we describe some of the characteristics of the Java language and examine a simple Java program. This introduction is simply an overview and a presentation of some terminology. We will begin to explore the details of Java in the next chapter.

History of the Java Language

Java is widely viewed as a programming language for Internet applications. However, this book, and many other people, views Java as a general-purpose programming language that can be used without any reference to the Internet. At its birth, Java was neither of these things, but it eventually evolved into both.

The history of Java goes back to 1991, when James Gosling and his team at Sun Microsystems began designing the first version of a new programming language that would become Java—though it was not yet called that. This new language was intended for programming home appliances, like toasters and TVs. That sounds like a humble engineering task, but in fact it's a very challenging one. Home appliances are controlled by a wide variety of computer processors (chips). The language that Gosling and his team were designing had

---

*Full and partial dictionary entries from THE AMERICAN HERITAGE DICTIONARY OF THE ENGLISH LANGUAGE. Copyright © 2010 by Houghton Mifflin Harcourt Publishing Company. Adapted and reproduced by permission from THE AMERICAN HERITAGE DICTIONARY OF THE ENGLISH LANGUAGE, Fourth Edition.

to work on all of these different processors. Moreover, a home appliance is typically an inexpensive item, so no manufacturer would be willing to invest large amounts of time and money into developing complicated compilers to translate the appliance-language programs into a language the processor could understand. To solve these challenges, the designers wrote one piece of software that would translate an appliance-language program into a program in an intermediate language that would be the same for all appliances and their processors. Then a small, easy-to-write and hence inexpensive program would translate the intermediate language into the machine language for a particular appliance or computer. The intermediate language was called bytecode. The plan for programming appliances using this first version of Java never caught on with appliance manufacturers, but that was not the end of the story.

In 1994, Gosling realized that his language—now called Java—would be ideal for developing a Web browser that could run programs over the Internet. The Web browser was produced by Patrick Naughton and Jonathan Payne at Sun Microsystems. Originally called WebRunner and then HotJava, this browser is no longer supported. But that was the start of Java's connection to the Internet. In the fall of 1995, Netscape Communications Corporation decided to make the next release of its Web browser capable of running Java programs. Other companies associated with the Internet followed suit and have developed software that accommodates Java programs.

FAQ Why is the language named Java?

The question of how Java got its name does not have a very interesting answer. The current custom is to name programming languages in pretty much the same way that parents name their children. The creator of the programming language simply chooses any name that sounds good to her or him. The original name of the Java language was Oak. Later the creators realized that there already was a computer language named Oak, so they needed another name, and Java was chosen. One hears conflicting explanations of the origin of the name Java. One traditional, and perhaps believable, story is that the name was thought of during a long and tedious meeting while the participants drank coffee, and the rest, as they say, is history.

Applications and Applets

This book focuses on two kinds of Java programs: applications and applets. An **application** is just a regular program. An **applet** sounds as though it would be a little apple, but the name is meant to convey the idea of a little application. Applets and applications are almost identical. The difference is that an application is meant to be run on your computer, like any other program, whereas an applet is meant to be sent to another location on the Internet and run there.

Applications are regular programs

Applets run
within a Web
browser

Once you know how to design and write one of these two kinds of programs, either applets or applications, it is easy to learn to write the other kind. This book is organized to allow you to place as much or as little emphasis on applets as you wish. In most chapters the emphasis is on applications, but the graphics supplements at the ends of the first ten chapters give material on applets. Applets are also covered in detail in Chapter 14, which is on the book's Web site. You may choose to learn about applets along the way, by doing the graphics supplements, or you may wait and cover them in Chapter 14. If you want just a brief sample of applets, you can read only the graphics supplement for this first chapter.

A First Java Application Program

A user runs and
interacts with a
program

Our first Java program is shown in Listing 1.1. Below the program, we show a sample of the screen output that might be produced when a person runs and interacts with the program. The person who interacts with a program is called the **user.** The text typed in by the user is shown in color. If you run this program—and you should do so—both the text displayed by the program and the text you type will appear in the same color on your computer screen.

The user might or might not be the programmer, that is, the person who wrote the program. As a student, you often are both the programmer and the user, but in a real-world setting, the programmer and user are generally different people. This book is teaching you to be the programmer. One of the first things you need to learn is that you cannot expect the users of your program to know what you want them to do. For that reason, your program must give the user understandable instructions, as we have done in the sample program.

At this point, we just want to give you a feel for the Java language by providing a brief, informal description of the sample program shown in Listing 1.1. *Do not worry if some of the details of the program are not completely clear on this first reading.* This is just a preview of things to come. In Chapter 2, we will explain the details of the Java features used in the program.

The first line

```
import java.util.Scanner;
```

A package is a
library of classes

tells the compiler that this program uses the class Scanner. Recall that for now, we can think of a class as a piece of software that we can use in a program. This class is defined in the package java.util, which is short for "Java utility." A **package** is a library of classes that have already been defined for you.

The remaining lines define the class FirstProgram, extending from the first open brace ({) to the last close brace (}):

```
public class FirstProgram
{
    . . .
}
```

LISTING 1.1   A Sample Java Program

```
import java.util.Scanner;
```
Gets the **Scanner** *class from the package (library)* `java.util`

```
public class FirstProgram
```
Name of the class—your choice

```
{
    public static void main(String[] args)
    {
        System.out.println("Hello out there.");
```
Sends output to screen

```
        System.out.println("I will add two numbers for you.");
        System.out.println("Enter two whole numbers on a line:");

        int n1, n2;
```
Says that **n1** *and* **n2** *are variables that hold integers (whole numbers)*

Readies the program for keyboard input

```
        Scanner keyboard = new Scanner(System.in);
        n1 = keyboard.nextInt();
```
Reads one whole number from the keyboard

```
        n2 = keyboard.nextInt();

        System.out.println("The sum of those two numbers is");
        System.out.println(n1 + n2);
    }
}
```

Sample Screen Output

```
Hello out there.
I will add two numbers for you.
Enter two whole numbers on a line:
12 30
The sum of those two numbers is
42
```

Within these braces are typically one or more parts called **methods.** Every Java application has a method called `main`, and often other methods. The definition of the method main extends from another open brace to another close brace:

A class contains methods

```
    public static void main(String[] args)
    {
        . . .
    }
```

Every application has a main method

The words `public static void` will have to remain a mystery for now, but they are required. Chapters 5 and 6 will explain these details.

Any **statements,** or instructions, within a method define a task and make up the **body** of the method. The first three statements in our main method's body are the first actions this program performs:

```
System.out.println("Hello out there.");
System.out.println("I will add two numbers for you.");
System.out.println("Enter two whole numbers on a line:");
```

Each of these statements begins with `System.out.println` and causes the quoted characters given within the parentheses to be displayed on the screen on their own line. For example,

```
System.out.println("Hello out there.");
```

causes the line

```
Hello out there.
```

to be written to the screen.

For now, you can consider `System.out.println` to be a funny way of saying "Display what is shown in parentheses." However, we can tell you a little about what is going on here and introduce some terminology. Java programs use things called **software objects** or, more simply, **objects** to perform actions. The actions are defined by methods. `System.out` is an object used to send output to the screen; `println` is the method that performs this action for the object `System.out`. That is, `println` sends what is within its parentheses to the screen. The item or items inside the parentheses are called **arguments** and provide the information the method needs to carry out its action. In each of these first three statements, the argument for the method `println` is a string of characters between quotes. This argument is what `println` writes to the screen.

Objects perform actions when you call its methods

An object performs an action when you **invoke,** or **call,** one of its methods. In a Java program, you write such a **method call,** or **method invocation,** by writing the name of the object, followed by a period—called a **dot** in computer jargon—followed by the method name and some parentheses that might or might not contain arguments.

Variables store data

The next line of the program in Listing 1.1,

```
int n1, n2;
```

A data type specifies a set of values and their operations

says that `n1` and `n2` are the names of variables. A **variable** is something that can store a piece of data. The `int` says that the data must be an integer, that is, a whole number; `int` is an example of a **data type.** A data type specifies a set of possible values and the operations defined for those values. The values of a particular data type are stored in memory in the same format.

The next line

```
Scanner keyboard = new Scanner(System.in);
```

enables the program to accept, or **read,** data that a user enters at the keyboard. We will explain this line in detail in Chapter 2.[2]

Next, the line

```
n1 = keyboard.nextInt();
```

A program gets, or reads, data from a user

reads a number that is typed at the keyboard and then stores this number in the variable n1. The next line is almost the same except that it reads another number typed at the keyboard and stores this second number in the variable n2. Thus, if the user enters the numbers 12 and 30, as shown in the sample output, the variable n1 will contain the number 12, and the variable n2 will contain the number 30.

Finally, the statements

```
System.out.println("The sum of those two numbers is");
System.out.println(n1 + n2);
```

display an explanatory phrase and the sum of the numbers stored in the variables n1 and n2. Note that the second line contains the **expression** n1 + n2 rather than a string of characters in quotes. This expression computes the sum of the numbers stored in the variables n1 and n2. When an output statement like this contains a number or an expression whose value is a number, the number is displayed on the screen. So in the sample output shown in Listing 1.1, these two statements produce the lines

```
The sum of those two numbers is
42
```

Notice that each invocation of println displays a separate line of output.

The only thing left to explain in this first program are the semicolons at the end of certain lines. The semicolon acts as ending punctuation, like a period in an English sentence. A semicolon ends an instruction to the computer.

Of course, Java has precise rules for how you write each part of a program. These rules form the **grammar** for the Java language, just as the rules for the English language make up its grammar. However, Java's rules are more precise. The grammatical rules for any language, be it a programming language or a natural language, are called the **syntax** of the language.

Syntax is the set of grammatical rules for a language

---

[2] As you will see in the next chapter, you can use some other name in place of keyboard, but that need not concern us now. Anyway, keyboard is a good word to use here.

RECAP Invoking (Calling) a Method

A Java program uses objects to perform actions that are defined by methods. An object performs an action when you invoke, or call, one of its methods. You indicate this in a program by writing the object name, followed by a period—called a dot—then the method name, and finally a pair of parentheses that can contain arguments. The arguments are information for the method.

EXAMPLES:

```
System.out.println("Hello out there.");
n1 = keyboard.nextInt();
```

In the first example, System.out is the object, println is the method, and "Hello out there." is the argument. When a method requires more than one argument, you separate the arguments with commas. A method invocation is typically followed by a semicolon.

In the second example, keyboard is the object and nextInt is the method. This method has no arguments, but the parentheses are required nonetheless.

FAQ Why do we need an `import` for input but not for output?

The program in Listing 1.1 needs the line

```
import java.util.Scanner;
```

to enable keyboard input, such as the following:

```
n1 = keyboard.nextInt();
```

Why don't we need a similar import to enable screen output such as

```
System.out.println("Hello out there.");
```

The answer is rather dull. The package that includes definitions and code for screen output is imported automatically into a Java program.

SELF-TEST QUESTIONS

11. What would the following statement, when used in a Java program, display on the screen?

    ```
    System.out.println("Java is great!");
    ```

12. Write a statement or statements that can be used in a Java program to display the following on the screen:

    ```
    Java for one.
    Java for all.
    ```

13. Suppose that mary is an object that has the method `increaseAge`. This method takes one argument, an integer. Write an invocation of the method `increaseAge` by the object mary, using the argument 5.

14. What is the meaning of the following line in the program in Listing 1.1?

    ```
    n1 = keyboard.nextInt();
    ```

15. Write a complete Java program that uses `System.out.println` to display the following to the screen when the program is run:

    ```
    Hello World!
    ```

    Your program does nothing else. Note that you do not need to fully understand all the details of the program in order to write it. You can simply follow the model of the program in Listing 1.1. (You do want to understand all the details eventually, but that may take a few more chapters.)

Writing, Compiling, and Running a Java Program

A Java program is divided into smaller parts called classes. Each program can consist of any number of class definitions. Although we wrote only one class—FirstProgram—for the program in Listing 1.1, in fact, the program uses two other classes: System and Scanner. However, these two classes are provided for you by Java.

Writing a Java program

You can write a Java class by using a simple text editor. For example, you could use Notepad in a Windows environment or TextEdit on a Macintosh system. Normally, each class definition you write is in a separate file. Moreover, the name of that file must be the name of the class, with .java added to the end. For example, the class FirstProgram must be in a file named FirstProgram.java.

Each class is in a file whose name ends in .java

Before you can run a Java program, you must translate its classes into a language that the computer can understand. As you saw earlier in this chapter, this translation process is called compiling. As a rule, you do not need to compile classes like Scanner that are provided for you as part of Java. You normally need compile only the classes that you yourself write.

Compiling a Java program

To compile a Java class using the free Java system distributed by Oracle® for Windows, Linux, or Solaris, you use the command javac followed by the name of the file containing the class. For example, to compile a class named MyClass that is in a file named MyClass.java, you give the following command to the operating system:

Use the command javac to compile

```
javac MyClass.java
```

Thus, to compile the class in Listing 1.1, you would give the following command:

```
javac FirstProgram.java
```

Bytecode is in a file whose name ends in .class

When you compile a Java class, the translated version of the class—its bytecode—is placed in a file whose name is the name of the class followed by .class. So when you compile a class named MyClass in the file MyClass.java, the resulting bytecode is stored in a file named MyClass.class. When you compile the file named FirstProgram.java, the resulting bytecode is stored in a file named FirstProgram.class.

VideoNote
Compiling a Java program

Although a Java program can involve any number of classes, you run only the class that you think of as the program. This class will contain a main method beginning with words identical to or very similar to

```
public static void main(String[] args)
```

These words will likely, but not always, be someplace near the beginning of the file. The critical words to look for are public static void main. The remaining portion of the line might use somewhat different wording.

Use the command java to execute

You run a Java program by giving the command java, followed by the name of the class you think of as the program. For example, to run the program in Listing 1.1, you would give the following one-line command:

```
java FirstProgram
```

Note that you write the class name, such as FirstProgram, not the name of the file containing the class or its bytecode. That is, you omit any .java or .class ending. When you run a Java program, you are actually running the Java bytecode interpreter on the compiled version of your program.

The easiest way to write, compile, and run a Java program is to use an **integrated development environment,** or **IDE.** An IDE combines a text editor with menu commands for compiling and running a Java program. IDEs such as BlueJ, Eclipse, and NetBeans are free and available for Windows, Mac OS, and other systems. Appendix 1 provides links to these IDEs and other resources for writing Java programs.

> **FAQ I tried to run the sample program in Listing 1.1. After I typed two numbers on a line, nothing happened. Why?**
>
> When you type a line of data at the keyboard for a program to read, you will see the characters you type, but the Java program does not actually read your data until you press the Enter (Return) key. Always press the Enter key when you have finished typing a line of input data at the keyboard.

SELF-TEST QUESTIONS

myprogramminglab

16. Suppose you define a class named YourClass in a file. What name should the file have?

17. Suppose you compile the class YourClass. What will be the name of the file containing the resulting bytecode?

1.3 PROGRAMMING BASICS

'The time has come,' the Walrus said,
'To talk of many things:
Of shoes–and ships–and sealing wax–
Of cabbages–and kings . . .'

—LEWIS CARROLL, *THROUGH THE LOOKING GLASS*

Programming is a creative process. We cannot tell you exactly how to write a program to do whatever task you might want it to perform. However, we can give you some techniques that experienced programmers have found to be extremely helpful. In this section, we discuss some basics of these techniques. They apply to programming in almost any programming language and are not particular to Java.

Object-Oriented Programming

Java is an **object-oriented programming** language, abbreviated **OOP**. What is OOP? The world around us is made up of objects, such as people, automobiles, buildings, trees, shoes, ships, sealing wax, cabbages, and kings. Each of these objects has the ability to perform certain actions, and each action can affect some of the other objects in the world. OOP is a programming methodology that views a program as similarly consisting of objects that can act alone or

Software objects act and interact

interact with one another. An object in a program—that is, a software object—might represent a real-world object, or it might be an abstraction.

For example, consider a program that simulates a highway interchange so that traffic flow can be analyzed. The program would have an object to represent each automobile that enters the interchange, and perhaps other objects to simulate each lane of the highway, the traffic lights, and so on. The interactions among these objects can lead to a conclusion about the design of the interchange.

The values of an object's attributes define its state

Object-oriented programming comes with its own terminology. An object has characteristics, or **attributes.** For example, an automobile object might have attributes such as its name, its current speed, and its fuel level. The values of an object's attributes give the object a **state.** The actions that an object can take are called **behaviors.** As we saw earlier, each behavior is defined by a piece of Java code called a method.

A class is a blueprint for objects

Objects of the same kind are said to have the same data type and belong to the same class. A **class** defines a kind of object; it is a blueprint for creating objects. The data type of an object is the name of its class. For example, in a highway simulation program, all the simulated automobiles might belong to the same class—probably called Automobile—and so their data type is Automobile.

All objects of a class have the same attributes and behaviors. Thus, in a simulation program, all automobiles have the same behaviors, such as moving forward and moving backward. This does not mean that all simulated automobiles are identical. Although they have the same attributes, they can have different states. That is, a particular attribute can have different values among the automobiles. So we might have three automobiles having different makes and traveling at different speeds. All this will become clearer when we begin to write Java classes.

As you will see, this same object-oriented methodology can be applied to any sort of computer program and is not limited to simulation programs. Object-oriented programming is not new, but its use in applications outside of simulation programs did not become popular until the early 1990s.

RECAP Objects, Methods, and Classes

An object is a program construction that has data—called attributes—associated with it and that can perform certain actions known as behaviors. A class defines a type or kind of object. It is a blueprint for defining the objects. All objects of the same class have the same kinds of data and the same behaviors. When the program is run, each object can act alone or interact with other objects to accomplish the program's purpose. The actions performed by objects are defined by methods.

FAQ What if I know some other programming language?

If Java is your first programming language, you can skip the answer to this question. If you know some other programming language, the discussion here may help you to understand objects in terms of things you already know about. If that other programming language is object oriented, such as C++, C#, Python, or Ruby, you have a good idea of what objects, methods, and classes are. They are basically the same in all object-oriented programming languages, although some other languages might use another term to mean the same thing as *method*. If your familiarity is with an older programming language that does not use objects and classes, you can think of objects in terms of other, older programming constructs. For example, if you know about variables and functions or procedures, you can think of an object as a variable that has multiple pieces of data and its own functions or procedures. Methods are really the same thing as what are called *functions* or *procedures* in older programming languages.

Object-oriented programming uses classes and objects, but it does not use them in just any old way. There are certain design principles that must be followed. The following are three of the main design principles of object-oriented programming:

> OOP design principles

    Encapsulation
    Polymorphism
    Inheritance

Encapsulation sounds as though it means putting things into a capsule or, to say it another way, packaging things up. This intuition is basically correct. The most important part of encapsulation, however, is not simply that things are put into a capsule, but that only part of what is in the capsule is visible. When you produce a piece of software, you should describe it in a way that tells other programmers how to use it, but that omits all the details of how the software works. Note that encapsulation hides the fine detail of what is inside the "capsule." For this reason, encapsulation is often called **information hiding.**

> Encapsulation packages and hides detail

The principles of encapsulation apply to programming in general, not just to object-oriented programming. But object-oriented languages enable a programmer not only to realize these principles but also to enforce them. Chapter 5 will develop the concept of encapsulation further.

Polymorphism comes from a Greek word meaning "many forms." The basic idea of polymorphism is that it allows the same program instruction to mean different things in different contexts. Polymorphism commonly occurs in English, and its use in a programming language makes the programming language more like a human language. For example, the English instruction "Go play your favorite sport" means different things to different people. To one person, it means to play baseball. To another person, it means to play soccer.

Polymorphism also occurs in everyday tasks.[3] Imagine a person who whistles for her pets to come to dinner. Her dog runs, her bird flies, and her fish swim to the top of their tank. They all respond in their own way. The come-to-dinner whistle doesn't tell the animals how to come to dinner, just to come. Likewise when you press the "on" button on your laptop, your iPod, or your toothbrush, each of them responds appropriately. In a programming language such as Java, polymorphism means that one method name, used as an instruction, can cause different actions, depending on the kinds of objects that perform the action. For example, a method named showOutput might display the data in an object. But the number of data items it displays and their format depend on the kind of object that carries out the action. We will explain polymorphism more fully in Chapter 8.

Polymorphism enables objects to behave appropriately

Inheritance is a way of organizing classes. You can define common attributes and behaviors once and have them apply to a whole collection of classes. By defining a general class, you can use inheritance later to define specialized classes that add to or revise the details of the general class.

Inheritance organizes related classes

An example of such a collection of classes is shown in Figure 1.4. At each level, the classifications become more specialized. The class Vehicle has certain properties, like possessing wheels. The classes Automobile, Motorcycle, and Bus "inherit" the property of having wheels, but add more properties or restrictions. For example, an Automobile object has four wheels, a Motorcycle object has two wheels, and a Bus object has at least four wheels. Inheritance enables the programmer to avoid the repetition of programming instructions for each class. For example, everything that is true of every object of type Vehicle, such as "has wheels," is described only once, and it is inherited by the classes Automobile, Motorcycle, and Bus. Without inheritance, each of the classes Automobile, Motorcycle, Bus, SchoolBus, LuxuryBus, and so forth would have to repeat descriptions such as "has wheels." Chapter 8 will explain inheritance more fully.

RECAP Object-Oriented Programming

Object-oriented programming, or OOP, is a programming methodology that defines objects whose behaviors and interactions accomplish a given task. OOP follows the design principles of encapsulation, polymorphism, and inheritance.

---

[3] The examples here are based on those by Carl Alphonce in "Pedagogy and Practice of Design Patterns and Objects First: A One-Act Play." *ACM SIGPLAN Notices* 39, 5 (May 2004), 7–14.

FIGURE 1.4   An Inheritance Hierarchy

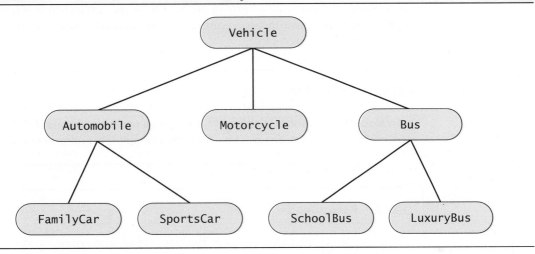

Algorithms

Objects have behaviors that are defined by methods. You as a programmer need to design these methods by giving instructions for carrying out the actions. The hardest part of designing a method is not figuring out how to express your solution in a programming language. The hardest part is coming up with a plan or strategy for carrying out the action. This strategy is often expressed as something called an algorithm.

An **algorithm** is a set of directions for solving a problem. To qualify as an algorithm, the directions must be expressed so completely and so precisely that somebody can follow them without having to fill in any details or make any decisions that are not fully specified in the instructions. An algorithm can be written in English, a programming language such as Java, or in **pseudocode,** which is a combination of English and a programming language.

An example may help to clarify the notion of an algorithm. Our first sample algorithm finds the total cost of a list of items. For example, the list of items might be a shopping list that includes the price of each item. The algorithm would then compute the total cost of all the items on the list. The algorithm is as follows:

An algorithm is like a recipe

Algorithms are often written in pseudocode

Algorithm to compute the total cost of a list of items

1. Write the number 0 on the blackboard.
2. Do the following for each item on the list:

   - Add the cost of the item to the number on the blackboard.
   - Replace the old number on the blackboard with the result of this addition.

3. Announce that the answer is the number written on the blackboard.

VideoNote
Writing an algorithm

Most algorithms need to store some intermediate results. This algorithm uses a blackboard to store intermediate results. If the algorithm is written in the Java language and run on a computer, intermediate results are stored in the computer's memory.

RECAP Algorithm

An algorithm is a set of directions for solving a problem. To qualify as an algorithm, the directions must be expressed completely and precisely.

RECAP Pseudocode

Pseudocode is a mixture of English and Java. When using pseudocode, you simply write each part of the algorithm in whatever language is easiest for you. If a part is easier to express in English, you use English. If another part is easier to express in Java, you use Java.

---

myprogramminglab   ## SELF-TEST QUESTIONS

18. What is a method?

19. What is the relationship between classes and objects?

20. Do all objects of the same class have the same methods?

21. What is encapsulation?

22. What is information hiding?

23. What is polymorphism?

24. What is inheritance?

25. What is an algorithm?

26. What is pseudocode?

27. What attributes would you want for an object that represents a song?

28. Write an algorithm that counts the number of values that are odd in a list of integers.

Testing and Debugging

The best way to write a correct program is to carefully design the necessary objects and the algorithms for the objects' methods. Then you carefully translate everything into a programming language such as Java. In other words, the best way to eliminate errors is to avoid them in the first place. However, no matter how carefully you proceed, your program might still contain some errors. When you finish writing a program, you should test it to see whether it performs correctly and then fix any errors you find.

A mistake in a program is called a **bug.** For this reason, the process of eliminating mistakes in your program is called **debugging.** There are three commonly recognized kinds of bugs or errors: syntax errors, run-time errors, and logic errors. Let's consider them in that order.

A **syntax error** is a grammatical mistake in your program. You must follow very strict grammatical rules when you write a program. Violating one of these rules—for example, omitting a required punctuation mark—is a syntax error. The compiler will detect syntax errors and provide an error message indicating what it thinks the error is. If the compiler says you have a syntax error, you probably do. However, the compiler is only guessing at what the error is, so it could be incorrect in its diagnosis of the problem.

Syntax errors are grammatical mistakes

RECAP Syntax

The syntax of a programming language is the set of grammatical rules for the language—that is, the rules for the correct way to write a program or part of a program. The compiler will detect syntax errors in your program and provide its best guess as to what is wrong.

An error that is detected when your program is run is called a **run-time error.** Such an error will produce an error message. For example, you might accidentally try to divide a number by zero. The error message might not be easy to understand, but at least you will know that something is wrong. Sometimes the error message can even tell you exactly what the problem is.

Run-time errors occur during execution

If the underlying algorithm for your program contains a mistake, or if you write something in Java that is syntactically correct but logically wrong, your program could compile and run without any error message. You will have written a valid Java program, but you will not have written the program you wanted. The program will run and produce output, but the output will be incorrect. In this case, your program contains a **logic error.** For example, if you were to mistakenly use a plus sign instead of a minus sign, you would make a logic error. You could compile and run your program with no error messages, but the program would give the wrong output. Sometimes a logic error will lead to a run-time error that produces an error message. But often a logic error will not give you any error messages. For this reason, logic errors are the hardest kind of error to locate.

Logic errors are conceptual mistakes in the program or algorithm

GOTCHA   Coping with "Gotchas"

Don't let a gotcha get you

Any programming language has details that can trip you up in ways that are surprising or hard to deal with. These sorts of problems are often called pitfalls, but a more colorful term is *gotchas*. A gotcha is like a trap waiting to catch you. When you get caught in the trap, the trap has "got you" or, as it is more commonly pronounced, "gotcha."

In this book, we have "Gotcha" sections like this one that warn you about many of the most common pitfalls and tell you how to avoid them or cope with them.   ∎

GOTCHA   Hidden Errors

VideoNote
Recognizing a hidden error

Just because your program compiles and runs without any errors and even produces reasonable-looking output does not mean that your program is correct. You should always run your program with some test data that gives predictable output. To do this, choose some data for which you can compute the correct results, either by using pencil and paper, by looking up the answer, or by some other means. Even this testing does not guarantee that your program is correct, but the more testing you do, the more confidence you can have in your program.   ∎

myprogramminglab

SELF-TEST QUESTIONS

29. What is a syntax error?

30. What is a logic error?

31. What kinds of errors are likely to produce error messages that will alert you to the fact that your program contains an error?

32. Suppose you write a program that is supposed to compute the day of the week (Sunday, Monday, and so forth) on which a given date (like December 1, 2011) will fall. Now suppose that you forget to account for leap years. Your program will then contain an error. What kind of program error is it?

Software Reuse

When you first start to write programs, you can easily get the impression that you must create each program entirely from scratch. However, typical software is not produced this way. Most programs contain some components that already exist. Using such components saves time and money. Furthermore, existing components have probably been used many times, so they likely are better tested and more reliable than newly created software.

For example, a highway simulation program might include a new highway object to model a new highway design but would probably model automobiles by using an automobile class that was already designed for some other program. To ensure that the classes you use in your programs are easily reusable, you must design them to be reusable. You must specify exactly how objects of that class interact with other objects. This is the principle of encapsulation that we mentioned earlier. But encapsulation is not the only principle you must follow. You must also design your class so that the objects are general and not specific to one particular program. For example, if your program requires that all simulated automobiles move only forward, you should still include a reverse in your automobile class, because some other simulation may require automobiles to back up. We will return to the topic of reusability after we learn more details about the Java language and have some examples to work with.

Besides reusing your own classes, you can and will use classes that Java provides. For example, we have already used the standard classes Scanner and System to perform input and output. Java comes with a collection of many classes known as the **Java Class Library**, sometimes called the **Java Application Programming Interface**, or **API**. The classes in this collection are organized into packages. As you saw earlier, the class Scanner, for example, is in the package java.util. From time to time we will mention or use classes within the Java Class Library. You should become familiar with the documentation provided for the Java Class Library on Oracle® Web site. At this writing, the link to this documentation is http://download-llnw.oracle. com/javase/7/docs/api//. Figure 1.5 gives an example of this documentation.

Java provides a library of classes for you

FIGURE 1.5   **The Documentation for the Class Scanner**

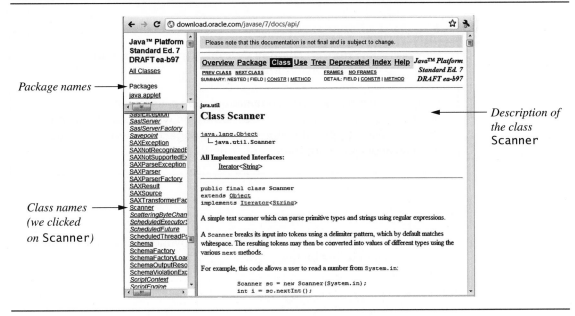

1.4 GRAPHICS SUPPLEMENT

Have a nice day.

—COMMON FAREWELL

Each of Chapters 1 through 10 has a graphics section like this one that describes how to write programs that include various kinds of graphics displays. We typically will display the graphics inside of an applet because it is easier to do, especially for beginners. However, sometimes we will use a windowing interface within an application program to display the graphics. Chapter 2 will introduce you to this approach.

Since some people prefer to delay coverage of graphics until after a programmer, such as yourself, has mastered the more elementary material, you may skip these supplements without affecting your understanding of the rest of the book. In order to cover graphics this early, we will have to resort to some "magic formulas"—that is, code that we will tell you how to use but not fully explain until later in the book. These graphics supplements do build on each other. If you want to cover the graphics supplement in one chapter, you will need to first read all or most of the graphics supplements in previous chapters.

The material on applets and graphics presented here uses classes, objects, and methods. You know that objects are entities that store data and can take actions. In this section, we will use objects only for taking actions, and we will use only one kind of object. Our objects will usually be named canvas and will have various methods that can draw figures—such as ovals—inside an applet display.

REMEMBER You Can Display Graphics in Applets and Application Programs

Whether you write an applet or an application program to display graphics depends on your objective. You would write an applet if you want to have a graphical feature on a Web page. Otherwise, you would write an application program.

A Sample Graphics Applet

Listing 1.2 contains an applet that draws a happy face. Let's examine the code by going through it line by line.

The line

```
import javax.swing.JApplet;
```

LISTING 1.2   Drawing a Happy Face

```
import javax.swing.JApplet;
import java.awt.Graphics;
public class HappyFace extends JApplet
{
    public void paint(Graphics canvas)
    {
        canvas.drawOval(100, 50, 200, 200);
        canvas.fillOval(155, 100, 10, 20);
        canvas.fillOval(230, 100, 10, 20);
        canvas.drawArc(150, 160, 100, 50, 180, 180);
    }
}
```
Applet Output

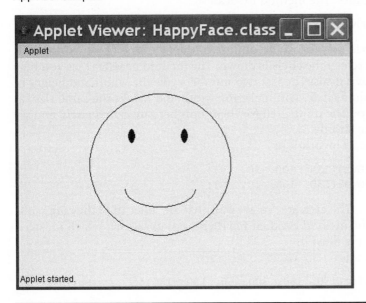

says that this applet—like all applets—uses the class JApplet that is in the Swing library (package). The line

    import java.awt.Graphics;

says that this applet also uses the class Graphics from the AWT library (package). Applets often use classes in the AWT library in addition to classes in the Swing library.

    The next line

    public class HappyFace extends JApplet

Applets use the packages Swing and AWT

begins the class definition for the applet. It is named `HappyFace`. The words `extends JApplet` indicate that we are defining an applet, as opposed to some other kind of class. Although you need not worry about further details yet, we are using inheritance to create the class `HappyFace` based upon an existing class `JApplet`.

The applet contains one method—paint—whose definition begins with

```
public void paint(Graphics canvas)
```

An applet's paint method draws its graphics

The `paint` method specifies what graphics are drawn in the applet. Each of the four statements within the body of the method is an instruction to draw a figure. The paint method is invoked automatically when the applet is run.

We will not discuss the details of method definitions until Chapter 5, but we will tell you enough here to allow you to define the method `paint` to do some simple graphics. The method invocation

```
canvas.drawOval(100, 50, 200, 200)
```

draws the big circle that forms the outline of the face. The first two numbers tell where on the screen the circle is drawn. The method `drawOval`, as you may have guessed, draws ovals. The last two numbers give the width and height of the oval. To obtain a circle, you make the width and height the same size, as we have done here. The units used for these numbers are called *pixels*, and we will describe them shortly.

The two method invocations

```
canvas.fillOval(155, 100, 10, 20);
canvas.fillOval(230, 100, 10, 20);
```

draw the two eyes. The eyes are "real" ovals that are taller than they are wide. Also notice that the method is called `fillOval`, not `drawOval`, which means it draws an oval that is filled in.

The last invocation

```
canvas.drawArc(150, 160, 100, 50, 180, 180);
```

draws the mouth. We will explain the meaning of all of these arguments next.

Size and Position of Figures

All measurements within a screen display are given not in inches or centimeters but in pixels. A **pixel**—short for picture element—is the smallest length your screen is capable of showing. A pixel is not an absolute unit of length like an inch or a centimeter. The size of a pixel can be different on different screens, but it will always be a small unit. You can think of your computer screen as being covered by small squares, each of which can be any color. You cannot show anything smaller than one of these squares. A pixel is one of these squares, but when used as measure of length, a pixel is the length of the side of one of these squares.[4] If you have shopped for a digital camera, you have undoubtedly heard the term *pixel* or *megapixel*. The meaning of the word *pixel* when used in Java applets is the same as its meaning when describing pictures from a digital camera. A **megapixel** is just a million pixels.

A pixel is the smallest length shown on a screen

Figure 1.6 shows the **coordinate system** used to position figures inside of an applet or other kind of Java window-like display. Think of the large rectangle as outlining the drawing area that is displayed on the screen. The coordinate system assigns two numbers to each point inside the rectangle. The numbers are known as the **x-coordinate** and the *y*-coordinate of the point. The **x-coordinate** is the number of pixels from the left edge of the rectangle to the point. The **y-coordinate** is the number of pixels from the top edge of the rectangle to the point. The coordinates are usually written within parentheses and separated by a comma, with the *x*-coordinate first. So the point marked with a blue dot in Figure 1.6 has the coordinates (100, 50); 100 is the *x*-coordinate and 50 is the *y*-coordinate.

A coordinate system positions points on the screen

Each coordinate in this system is greater than or equal to zero. The *x*-coordinate gets larger as you go to the right from point (0, 0). The *y*-coordinate gets larger as you go down from point (0, 0). If you have studied *x*- and *y*-coordinates in a math class, these are the same, with one change. In other coordinate systems, the *y*-coordinates increase as they go *up* from point (0, 0).

You position a rectangle in this graphical coordinate system at coordinates (*x*, *y*) by placing its upper left corner at the point (*x*, *y*). For example, the rectangle given by the dashed blue lines in Figure 1.7 is positioned at point (100, 50), which is marked with a black X. You position a figure that is not

FIGURE 1.6   Screen Coordinate System

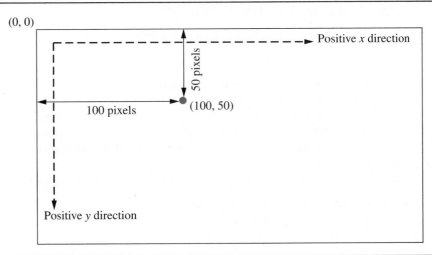

---

[4] Strictly speaking, a pixel need not be a square but could be rectangular. However, we do not need to go into such fine detail here.

FIGURE 1.7   The Oval Drawn by canvas.drawOval(100, 50, 90, 50)

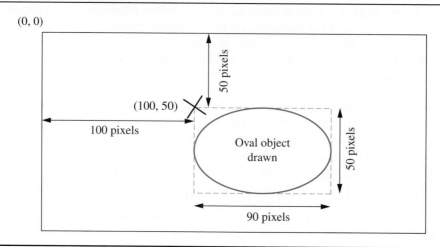

a rectangle at point (x, y) by first enclosing it in an imaginary rectangle that is as small as possible but still contains the figure and then by placing the upper left corner of this enclosing rectangle at (x, y). For example, in Figure 1.7 the oval is also positioned at point (100, 50). If the applet contains only an oval and no rectangle, only the oval shows on the screen. But an imaginary rectangle is still used to position the oval.

Drawing Ovals and Circles

The oval in Figure 1.7 is drawn by the Java statement

```
canvas.drawOval(100, 50, 90, 50);
```

The first two numbers are the x- and y-coordinates of the upper left corner of the imaginary rectangle that encloses the oval. That is, these two numbers are the coordinates of the position of the figure drawn by this statement. The next two numbers give the width and height of the rectangle containing the oval (and thus the width and height of the oval itself). If the width and height are equal, you get a circle.

Now let's return to the statements in the body of the method paint:

```
canvas.drawOval(100, 50, 200, 200);
canvas.fillOval(155, 100, 10, 20);
canvas.fillOval(230, 100, 10, 20);
```

drawOval and fillOval draw ovals or circles

In each case, the first two numbers are the x- and y-coordinates of the upper left corner of an imaginary rectangle that encloses the figure being drawn. The first statement draws the outline of the face at position (100, 50). Since the width and height—as given by the last two arguments—have the same value, 200, we get a circle whose diameter is 200. The next two statements draw filled ovals for the eyes positioned at the points (155, 100) and (230, 100). The eyes are each 10 pixels wide and 20 pixels high. The results are shown in Listing 1.2.

RECAP **The Methods drawOval and fillOval**

SYNTAX

```
canvas.drawOval(x, y, Width, Height);
canvas.fillOval(x, y, Width, Height);
```

The method drawOval draws the outline of an oval that is *Width* pixels wide and *Height* pixels high. The oval is placed so that the upper left corner of a tightly enclosing rectangle is at the point (*x, y*).

The method fillOval draws the same oval as drawOval but fills it in.

Drawing Arcs

Arcs, such as the smile on the happy face in Listing 1.2, are specified as a portion of an oval. For example, the following statement from Listing 1.2 draws the smile on the happy face:

```
canvas.drawArc(150, 160, 100, 50, 180, 180);
```

The first two arguments give the position of an invisible rectangle. The upper left corner of this rectangle is at the point (150, 160). The next two arguments specify the size of the rectangle; it has width 100 and height 50. Inside this invisible rectangle, imagine an invisible oval with the same width and height as the invisible rectangle. The last two arguments specify the portion of this invisible oval that is made visible. In this example, the bottom half of the oval is visible and forms the smile. Let's examine these last two arguments more closely.

The next-to-last argument of drawArc specifies a start angle in degrees. The last argument specifies how many degrees of the oval's arc will be made visible. The rightmost end of the oval's horizontal equator is at zero degrees. As you move along the oval's edge in a counterclockwise direction, the degrees increase in value. For example, Figure 1.8a shows a start angle of 0 degrees; we measure 90 degrees along the oval in a counterclockwise direction, making one quarter of the oval visible. Conversely, as you move along the oval in a clockwise direction, the degrees decrease in value. For example, in Figure 1.8b, we start at 0 and move −90 degrees in a clockwise direction, making a different quarter of the oval visible. If the last argument is 360, you move counterclockwise through 360 degrees, making the entire oval visible, as Figure 1.8c shows.

Finally, Figure 1.8d illustrates an arc that begins at 180 degrees, so it starts on the left end of the invisible oval. The last argument is also 180, so the arc is made visible through 180 degrees in the counterclockwise direction, or halfway around the oval. The smile on the happy face in Listing 1.2 uses this same arc.

drawArc draws part of an oval

FIGURE 1.8 Specifying an Arc

(a) `canvas.drawArc(x, y, width, height, 0, 90);`

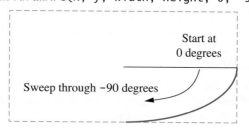

(b) `canvas.drawArc(x, y, width, height, 0, -90);`

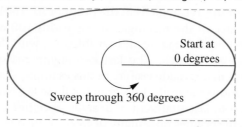

(c) `canvas.drawArc(x, y, width, height, 0, 360);`

(d) `canvas.drawArc(x, y, width, height, 180, 180);`

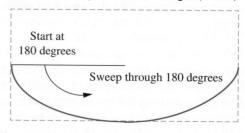

RECAP drawArc

SYNTAX

```
canvas.drawArc(x, y, Width, Height, StartAngle, ArcAngle);
```

Draws an arc that is part of an oval placed so the upper left corner of a tightly enclosing rectangle is at the point (x, y). The oval's width and height are *Width* and *Height,* both in pixels. The portion of the arc drawn is given by *StartAngle* and *ArcAngle,* both given in degrees. The rightmost end of the oval's horizontal equator is at 0 degrees. You measure positive angles in a counterclockwise direction and negative angles in a clockwise direction. Beginning at *StartAngle,* you measure *ArcAngle* degrees along the oval to form the arc. Figure 1.8 gives some examples of arcs.

FAQ What is canvas?

The identifier canvas names an object that does the drawing. Note that canvas is a "dummy variable" that stands for an object that Java supplies to do the drawing. You need not use the identifier canvas, but you do need to be consistent. If you change one occurrence of canvas to, say, pen, you must change all occurrences of canvas to pen. Thus, the method paint shown in Listing 1.2 could be written as follows:

```
public void paint (Graphics pen)
{
    pen.drawOval(100, 50, 200, 200);
    pen.fillOval(155, 100, 10, 20);
    pen.fillOval(230, 100, 10, 20);
    pen.drawArc(150, 160, 100, 50, 180, 180);
}
```

This definition and the one given in Listing 1.2 are equivalent.

Running an Applet

You compile an applet in the same way that you compile any other Java class. However, you run an applet differently from other Java programs. The normal way to run an applet is as part of a Web page. The applet is then viewed through a Web browser. We will discuss this means of viewing an applet in Chapter 14 (on the book's Web site).

You need not know how to embed an applet in a Web page to run it, however. Instead, you can use an **applet viewer,** a program designed to run applets as stand-alone programs. The easiest way to do this is to run the applet from an

An applet viewer
will run an applet

integrated development environment (IDE), such as the ones mentioned earlier in this chapter. Every IDE has a menu command such as Run Applet, Run, Execute, or something similar. Appendix 2 explains how to use Oracle's applet viewer.

Ending an applet

The way to end an applet depends on how you are running it. If you are using an IDE or other applet viewer, you end the applet display by clicking the close-window button with your mouse. The close-window button will likely be as shown in Listing 1.2, but it might have a different location or appearance, depending on your computer and operating system. In that case, the close-window button will probably be like those on other windows on your computer. If you are running the applet from a Web site, the applet stays until you close or navigate away from the page it is on.

myprogramminglab

VideoNote
Another applet example

SELF-TEST QUESTIONS

33. How would you change the applet program in Listing 1.2 so that the eyes are circles instead of ovals?

34. How would you change the applet program in Listing 1.2 so that the face frowns? (*Hint:* Turn the smile upside down by changing the arguments in the call to the method drawArc.)

CHAPTER SUMMARY

- A computer's main memory holds the program that is currently executing, and it also holds many of the data items that the program is manipulating. A computer's main memory is divided into a series of numbered locations called bytes. This memory is volatile: The data it holds disappears when the computer's power is off.

- A computer's auxiliary memory is used to hold data in a more or less permanent way. Its data remains even when the computer's power is off. Hard disk drives, flash drives, CDs, and DVDs are examples of auxiliary memory.

- A compiler is a program that translates a program written in a high-level language like Java into a program written in a low-level language. An interpreter is a program that performs a similar translation, but unlike a compiler, an interpreter executes a portion of code right after translating it, rather than translating the entire program at once.

- The Java compiler translates your Java program into a program in the byte-code language. When you give the command to run your Java program, this bytecode program is both translated into machine-language instructions and executed by an interpreter called the Java Virtual Machine.

- An object is a program construct that performs certain actions. These actions, or behaviors, are defined by the object's methods. The characteristics, or attributes, of an object are determined by its data, and the values of these attributes give the object a state.

■ Object-oriented programming is a methodology that views a program as consisting of objects that can act alone or interact with one another. A software object might represent a real-world object, or it might be an abstraction.

■ Three of the main principles of object-oriented programming are encapsulation, polymorphism, and inheritance.

■ A class is a blueprint for the attributes and behaviors of a group of objects. The class defines the type of these objects. All objects of the same class have the same methods.

■ In a Java program, a method invocation is written as the object name, followed by a period (called a dot), the method name, and, finally, the arguments in parentheses.

■ An algorithm is a set of directions for solving a problem. To qualify as an algorithm, the directions must be expressed so completely and precisely that somebody could follow them without having to fill in any details or make any decisions that are not fully specified in the directions.

■ Pseudocode is a combination of English and a programming language. It is used to write an algorithm's directions.

■ The syntax of a programming language is the set of grammatical rules for the language. These rules dictate whether a statement in the language is correct. The compiler will detect errors in a program's syntax.

■ You can write applets that display pictures on the computer screen. Applets are meant to be sent over the Internet and be viewed in a Web browser. However, you can use an applet viewer, which is a stand-alone program, instead.

■ The method `drawOval` draws the outline of an oval. The method `fillOval` draws the same oval as `drawOval` but fills it in. The method `drawArc` draws an arc that is part of an oval.

Exercises

1. How does a computer's main memory differ from its auxiliary memory?

2. After you use a text editor to write a program, will it be in main memory or auxiliary memory?

3. When a computer executes a program, will it be in main memory or auxiliary memory?

4. How does machine language differ from Java?

5. How does bytecode differ from machine language?

6. What would the following statements, when used in a Java program, display on the screen?

```
int age;
age = 20;
System.out.println ("My age is");
System.out.println(age);
```

7. Write a statement or statements that can be used in a Java program to display the following on the screen:

   3
   2
   1

8. Write statements that can be used in a Java program to read your age, as entered at the keyboard, and display it on the screen.

9. Given a person's year of birth, the Birthday Wizard can compute the year in which the person's *n*th birthday will occur or has occurred. Write statements that can be used in a Java program to perform this computation for the Birthday Wizard.

10. Write statements that can be used in a Java program to read two integers and display the number of integers that lie between them, including the integers themselves. For example, four integers are between 3 and 6: 3, 4, 5, and 6.

11. A single bit can represent two values: 0 and 1. Two bits can represent four values: 00, 01, 10, and 11. Three bits can represent eight values: 000, 001, 010, 011, 100, 101, 110, and 111. How many values can be represented by

    a. 8 bits?   **b.** 16 bits?   **c.** 32 bits?

12. Find the documentation for the Java Class Library on the Oracle® Web site. (At this writing, the link to this documentation is http://download-llnw.oracle .com/javase/7/docs/api/.) Then find the description for the class `Scanner`. How many methods are described in the section entitled "Method Summary"?

13. Self-Test Question 27 asked you to think of some attributes for a song object. What attributes would you want for an object that represents a play list containing many songs?

14. What behaviors might a song have? What behaviors might a play list have? Contrast the difference in behavior between the two kinds of objects.

15. What attributes and behaviors would an object representing a credit card account have?

16. Suppose that you have a number x that is greater than 1. Write an algorithm that computes the largest integer k such that 2^k is less than or equal to x.

17. Write an algorithm that finds the maximum value in a list of values.

18. Write statements that can be used in a Java applet to draw the five interlocking rings that are the symbol of the Olympics. (Don't worry about the color.)

Graphics

19. Find the documentation for the class Graphics in the Java Class Library. (See Exercise 12.) Learn how to use the method `drawRect`. Then write statements that can be used in a Java applet to draw a square containing a circle. The circle's diameter and the square's side should be equal in size.

Graphics

20. Write statements that can be used in a Java applet to draw the outline of a crescent moon.

Graphics

PROGRAMMING PROJECTS

Visit www.myprogramminglab.com to complete many of these Programming Projects online and get instant feedback.

myprogramminglab

1. Obtain a copy of the Java program shown in Listing 1.1 from the Web at the location given in the preface. Name the file `FirstProgram.java`. Compile the program so that you receive no compiler error messages. Then run the program.

2. Modify the Java program described in Programming Project 1 so that it adds three numbers instead of two. Compile the program so that you receive no compiler error messages. Then run the program.

3. Write a Java program that displays the following picture. (*Hint:* Write a sequence of `println` statements that display lines of asterisks and blanks.)

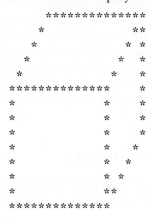

VideoNote
Writing an algorithm for
Project 5

Graphics

Graphics

Graphics

4. Write a complete program for the problem described in Exercise 9.

5. Write a complete program for the problem described in Exercise 10.

6. Write an applet program similar to the one in Listing 1.2 that displays a picture of a snowman. (*Hint:* Draw three circles, one above the other. Make the circles progressively smaller from bottom to top. Make the top circle a happy face.)

7. Write an applet program for the problem described in Exercise 18.

8. Write an applet program that displays the following pattern:

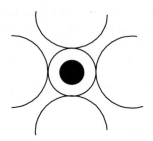

Answers to Self-Test Questions

1. Main memory and auxiliary memory.

2. Software is just another name for programs.

3. The two numbers to be added.

4. All the grades on all the quizzes you have taken in the course.

5. A high-level-language program is written in a form that is easy for a human being to write and read. A machine-language program is written in a form the computer can execute directly. A high-level-language program must be translated into a machine-language program before the computer can execute it. Java bytecode is a low-level language that is similar to the machine language of most common computers. It is relatively easy to translate a program expressed in Java bytecode into the machine language of almost any computer.

6. Java is a high-level language.

7. Java bytecode is a low-level language.

8. A compiler translates a high-level-language program into a low-level-language program such as a machine-language program or a Java bytecode

program. When you compile a Java program, the compiler translates your Java program into a program expressed in Java bytecode.

9. A source program is the high-level-language program that is input to a compiler.

10. The Java Virtual Machine is a program that translates Java bytecode instructions to machine-language instructions. The JVM is a kind of interpreter.

11. `Java is great!`

12.
```
System.out.println("Java for one.");
System.out.println("Java for all.");
```

13. `mary.increaseAge(5);`

14. The statement reads a whole number typed in at the keyboard and stores it in the variable `n1`

15.
```
public class Question15
{
    public static void main(String[] args)
    {
        System.out.println("Hello World!");
    }
}
```

Some details, such as identifier names, may be different in your program. Be sure you compile and run your program.

16. The file containing the class `YourClass` should be named `YourClass.java`.

17. `YourClass.class`.

18. A method defines an action that an object is capable of performing.

19. A class is a blueprint for creating objects. All objects in the same class have the same kind of data and the same methods.

20. Yes, all objects of the same class have the same methods.

21. Encapsulation is the process of hiding all the details of an object that are unnecessary to using the object. Put another way, encapsulation is the process of describing a class or object by giving only enough information to allow a programmer to use the class or object.

22. Information hiding is another term for encapsulation.

23. In a programming language, such as Java, polymorphism means that one method name, used as an instruction, can cause different actions, depending on the kind of object performing the action.

24. Inheritance is a way of organizing classes. You can define a general class having common attributes and behaviors, and then use inheritance to define specialized classes that add to or revise the details of the general class.

25. An algorithm is a set of directions for solving a problem. To qualify as an algorithm, the directions must be expressed so completely and precisely that somebody could follow them without having to fill in any details or make any decisions that are not fully specified in the directions.

26. Pseudocode is a mixture of English and Java that you can use to write the steps of an algorithm.

27. A song object could have the following attributes: title, composer, date, performer, album title.

28. Algorithm to count the odd integers in a list of integers:

    1. Write the number 0 on the blackboard.

    2. Do the following for each odd integer on the list:

       • Add 1 to the number on the blackboard.

       • Replace the old number on the blackboard with the result of this addition.

    3. Announce that the answer is the number written on the blackboard.

29. A syntax error is a grammatical mistake in a program. When you write a program, you must adhere to very strict grammatical rules. If you violate one of these rules by omitting a required punctuation mark, for example—you make a syntax error.

30. A logic error is a conceptual error in a program or its algorithm. If your program runs and gives output, but the output is incorrect, you have a logic error.

31. Syntax errors and run-time errors.

32. A logic error.

33. Change the following lines

    ```
    canvas.fillOval(155, 100, 10, 20);
    canvas.fillOval(230, 100, 10, 20);
    ```

    to

    ```
    canvas.fillOval(155, 100, 10, 10);
    canvas.fillOval(230, 100, 10, 10);
    ```

    The last two numbers on each line are changed from 10, 20 to 10, 10. You could also use some other number, such as 20, and write 20, 20 in place of 10, 10.

34. Change the following line

```
canvas.drawArc(150, 160, 100, 50, 180, 180);
```

to

```
canvas.drawArc(150, 160, 100, 50, 180, -180);
```

The last number is changed from positive to negative. Other correct answers are possible. For example, the following is also acceptable:

```
canvas.drawArc(150, 160, 100, 50, 0, 180);
```

You could also change the first number 150 to a larger number in either of the above statements. Other correct answers are similar to what we have already described.

Basic Computation 2

2.1 VARIABLES AND EXPRESSIONS 48
Variables 49
Data Types 51
Java Identifiers 53
Assignment Statements 55
Simple Input 58
Simple Screen Output 60
Constants 60
Named Constants 62
Assignment Compatibilities 63
Type Casting 65
Arithmetic Operators 68
Parentheses and Precedence Rules 71
Specialized Assignment Operators 72
Case Study: Vending Machine Change 74
Increment and Decrement Operators 79
More About the Increment and Decrement
    Operators 80

2.2 THE CLASS `String` 81
String Constants and Variables 81
Concatenation of Strings 82
String Methods 83
String Processing 85

Escape Characters 88
The Unicode Character Set 89

2.3 KEYBOARD AND SCREEN I/O 91
Screen Output 91
Keyboard Input 94
Other Input Delimiters (*Optional*) 99
Formatted Output with `printf` (*Optional*) 101

2.4 DOCUMENTATION AND STYLE 103
Meaningful Variable Names 103
Comments 104
Indentation 107
Using Named Constants 107

2.5 GRAPHICS SUPPLEMENT 109
Style Rules Applied to a Graphics Applet 110
Creating a Java GUI Application with the `JFrame`
    Class 110
Introducing the Class `JOptionPane` 113
Reading Input as Other Numeric Types 123
Programming Example: Change-Making Program
    with Windowing I/O 124

Chapter Summary 126   **Programming Projects 130**   **Answers to Self-Test Questions 133**

Computers can figure out all kinds of problems, except the things in the world that just don't add up.

—JAMES MAGARY

In this chapter, we explain enough about the Java language to allow you to write simple Java programs. You do not need any programming experience to understand this chapter. If you are already familiar with some other programming language, such as Visual Basic, C, C++, or C#, much that is in Section 2.1 will already be familiar to you. However, even if you know the concepts, you should learn the Java way of expressing them.

OBJECTIVES

After studying this chapter, you should be able to

- Describe the Java data types that are used for simple data like numbers and characters
- Write Java statements to declare variables and define named constants
- Write assignment statements and expressions containing variables and constants
- Define strings of characters and perform simple string processing
- Write Java statements that accomplish keyboard input and screen output
- Adhere to stylistic guidelines and conventions
- Write meaningful comments within a program
- Use the class JFrame to produce windowing interfaces within Java application programs
- Use the class JOptionPane to perform window-based input and output

PREREQUISITES

If you have not read Chapter 1, you should read at least the section of Chapter 1 entitled "A First Java Application Program" to familiarize yourself with the notions of class, object, and method. Also, material from the graphics supplement in Chapter 1 is used in the section "Style Rules Applied to a Graphics Applet" in the graphics supplement of this chapter.

2.1 VARIABLES AND EXPRESSIONS

Once a person has understood the way variables are used in programming, he has understood the quintessence of programming.

—E. W. DIJKSTRA (1930–2002), *NOTES ON STRUCTURED PROGRAMMING (1969)*

primitive *adj. 1. Not derived from something else; primary or basic.*

In this section, we explain how simple variables and arithmetic expressions are used in Java programs. Some of the terms used here were introduced in Chapter 1. We will, however, review them again.

Variables

Variables in a program are used to store data such as numbers and letters. They can be thought of as containers of a sort. The number, letter, or other data item in a variable is called its **value**. This value can be changed, so that at one time the variable contains, say, 6, and at another time, after the program has run for a while, the variable contains a different value, such as 4.

> A variable is a program component used to store or represent data

For example, the program in Listing 2.1 uses the variables numberOfBaskets, eggsPerBasket, and totalEggs. When this program is run, the statement

```
eggsPerBasket = 6;
```

sets the value of eggsPerBasket to 6.

In Java, variables are implemented as memory locations, which we described in Chapter 1. Each variable is assigned one memory location. When

> Variables represent memory locations

LISTING 2.1   A Simple Java Program

```java
public class EggBasket
{
    public static void main(String[] args)
    {
        int numberOfBaskets, eggsPerBasket, totalEggs;        ← Variable declarations

        numberOfBaskets = 10;    ← Assignment statement
        eggsPerBasket = 6;

        totalEggs = numberOfBaskets * eggsPerBasket;

        System.out.println("If you have");
        System.out.println(eggsPerBasket + " eggs per basket and");
        System.out.println(numberOfBaskets + " baskets, then");
        System.out.println("the total number of eggs is " + totalEggs);
    }
}
```

Sample Screen Output

```
If you have
6 eggs per basket and
10 baskets, then
the total number of eggs is 60
```

the variable is given a value, the value is encoded as a string of 0s and 1s and is placed in the variable's memory location.

Choose
meaningful
variable names

You should choose variable names that are helpful. The names should suggest the variables' use or indicate the kind of data they will hold. For example, if you use a variable to count something, you might name it count. If the variable is used to hold the speed of an automobile, you might call the variable speed. You should almost never use single-letter variable names like x and y. Somebody reading the statement

```
x = y + z;
```

would have no idea of what the program is really adding. The names of variables must also follow certain spelling rules, which we will detail later in the section "Java Identifiers."

Before you can use a variable in your program, you must state some basic information about each one. The compiler—and so ultimately the computer—needs to know the name of the variable, how much computer memory to reserve for the variable, and how the data item in the variable is to be coded as strings of 0s and 1s. You give this information in a **variable declaration.** Every variable in a Java program must be declared before it is used for the first time.

A variable declaration tells the computer what type of data the variable will hold. That is, you declare the variable's data type. Since different types of data are stored in the computer's memory in different ways, the computer must know the type of a variable so it knows how to store and retrieve the value of the variable from the computer's memory. For example, the following line from Listing 2.1 declares numberOfBaskets, eggsPerBasket, and totalEggs to be variables of data type int:

```
int numberOfBaskets, eggsPerBasket, totalEggs;
```

A variable declaration consists of a type name, followed by a list of variable names separated by commas. The declaration ends with a semicolon. All the variables named in the list are declared to have the same data type, as given at the start of the declaration.

If the data type is int, the variable can hold whole numbers, such as 42, –99, 0, and 2001. A whole number is called an **integer.** The word int is an abbreviation of *integer*. If the type is double, the variable can hold numbers having a decimal point and a fractional part after the decimal point. If the type is char, the variables can hold any one character that appears on the computer keyboard.

Declare variables
before using
them

Every variable in a Java program must be declared before the variable can be used. Normally, a variable is declared either just before it is used or at the start of a section of your program that is enclosed in braces { }. In the simple programs we have seen so far, this means that variables are declared either just before they are used or right after the lines

```
public static void main(String[] args)
{
```

RECAP **Variable Declarations**

In a Java program, you must declare a variable before it can be used. A variable declaration has the following form:

SYNTAX

```
Type Variable_1, Variable_2, ...;
```

EXAMPLES

```
int styleNumber, numberOfChecks, numberOfDeposits;
double amount, interestRate;
char answer;
```

Data Types

As you have learned, a data type specifies a set of values and their operations. In fact, the values have a particular data type because they are stored in memory in the same format and have the same operations defined for them.

A data type specifies a set of values and operations

REMEMBER **Syntactic Variables**

When you see something in this book like *Type*, *Variable_1,* or *Variable_2* used to describe Java syntax, these words do not literally appear in your Java code. They are **syntactic variables,** which are a kind of blank that you fill in with something from the category that they describe. For example, *Type* can be replaced by int, double, char, or any other type name. *Variable_1* and *Variable_2* can each be replaced by any variable name.

Java has two main kinds of data types: class types and primitive types. As the name implies, a **class type** is a data type for objects of a class. Since a class is like a blueprint for objects, the class specifies how the values of its type are stored and defines the possible operations on them. As we implied in the previous chapter, a class type has the same name as the class. For example, quoted strings such as "Java is fun" are values of the class type String, which is discussed later in this chapter.

Class types and primitive types

Variables of a **primitive type** are simpler than objects (values of a class type), which have both data and methods. A value of a primitive type is an indecomposable value, such as a single number or a single letter. The types int, double, and char are examples of primitive types.

FIGURE 2.1 Primitive Type

Type Name	Kind of Value	Memory Used	Range of Values
byte	Integer	1 byte	−128 to 127
short	Integer	2 bytes	−32,768 to 32,767
int	Integer	4 bytes	−2,147,483,648 to 2,147,483,647
long	Integer	8 bytes	−9,223,372,036,8547,75,808 to 9,223,372,036,854,775,807
float	Floating-point	4 bytes	$\pm 3.40282347 \times 10^{+38}$ to $\pm 1.40239846 \times 10^{-45}$
double	Floating-point	8 bytes	$\pm 1.79769313486231570 \times 10^{+308}$ to $\pm 4.94065645841246544 \times 10^{-324}$
char	Single character (Unicode)	2 bytes	All Unicode values from 0 to 65,535
boolean		1 bit	True or false

Figure 2.1 lists all of Java's primitive types. Four types are for integers, namely, byte, short, int, and long. The only differences among the various integer types are the range of integers they represent and the amount of computer memory they use. If you cannot decide which integer type to use, use the type int.

A number having a fractional part—such as the numbers 9.99, 3.14159, −5.63, and 5.0—is called a **floating-point number.** Notice that 5.0 is a floating-point number, not an integer. If a number has a fractional part, even if the fractional part is zero, it is a floating-point number. As shown in Figure 2.1, Java has two data types for floating-point numbers, float and double. For example, the following code declares two variables, one of type float and one of type double:

> A floating-point number has a fractional part

```
float cost;
double capacity;
```

As with integer types, the differences between float and double involve the range of their values and their storage requirements. If you cannot decide between the types float and double, use double.

The primitive type char is used for single characters, such as letters, digits, or punctuation. For example, the following declares the variable symbol to be of type char, stores the character for uppercase *A* in symbol, and then displays *A* on the screen:

```
char symbol;
symbol = 'A';
System.out.println(symbol);
```

In a Java program, we enclose a single character in single quotes, as in `'A'`. Note that there is only one symbol for a single quote. The same quote symbol is used on both sides of the character. Finally, remember that uppercase letters and lowercase letters are different characters. For example, `'a'` and `'A'` are two different characters.

Single quotes enclose a character

The last primitive type we have to discuss is the type `boolean`. This data type has two values, true and false. We could, for example, use a variable of type `boolean` to store the answer to a true/false question such as "Is `eggCount` less than 12?" We will have more to say about the data type `boolean` in the next chapter.

All primitive type names in Java begin with a lowercase letter. In the next section, you will learn about a convention in which class type names—that is, the names of classes—begin with an uppercase letter.

Although you declare variables for class types and primitive types in the same way, these two kinds of variables store their values using different mechanisms. Chapter 5 will explain class type variables in more detail. In this chapter and the next two, we will concentrate on primitive types. We will occasionally use variables of a class type before Chapter 5, but only in contexts where they behave pretty much the same as variables of a primitive type.

Java Identifiers

The technical term for a name in a programming language, such as the name of a variable, is an **identifier.** In Java, an identifier (a name) can contain only letters, digits 0 through 9, and the underscore character (_). The first character in an identifier cannot be a digit.[1] In particular, no name can contain a space or any other character such as a dot (period) or an asterisk (*). There is no limit to the length of an identifier. Well, in practice, there is a limit, but Java has no official limit and will accept even absurdly long names. Java is **case sensitive.** That is, uppercase and lowercase letters are considered to be different characters. For example, Java considers `mystuff`, `myStuff`, and `MyStuff` to be three different identifiers, and you could have three different variables with these three names. Of course, writing variable names that differ only in their capitalization is a poor programming practice, but the Java compiler would happily accept them. Within these constraints, you can use any name you want for a variable, a class, or any other item you define in a Java program. But there are some style guidelines for choosing names.

Java is case sensitive

---

[1] Java does allow the dollar sign $ to appear in an identifier, treating it as a letter. But such identifiers have a special meaning. It is intended to identify code generated by a machine, so you should not use the $ symbol in your identifiers.

Our somewhat peculiar use of uppercase and lowercase letters, such as `numberOfBaskets`, deserves some explanation. It would be perfectly legal to use `NumberOfBaskets` or `number_of_baskets` instead of `numberOfBaskets`, but these other names would violate some well-established conventions about how you should use uppercase and lowercase letters. Under these conventions, we write the names of variables using only letters and digits. We "punctuate" multiword names by using uppercase letters—since we cannot use spaces. The following are all legal names that follow these conventions:

Legal identifiers

`inputStream YourClass CarWash hotCar theTimeOfDay`

Notice that some of these legal names start with an uppercase letter and others, such as `hotCar`, start with a lowercase letter. We will always follow the convention that the names of classes start with an uppercase letter, and the names of variables and methods start with a lowercase letter.

The following identifiers are all illegal in Java, and the compiler will complain if you use any of them:

Illegal identifiers

`prenhall.com go-team Five* 7eleven`

The first three contain illegal characters, either a dot, a hyphen, or an asterisk. The last name is illegal because it starts with a digit.

Some words in a Java program, such as the primitive types and the word `if`, are called **keywords** or **reserved words**. They have a special predefined meaning in the Java language and cannot be used as the names of variables, classes, or methods, or for anything other than their intended meaning. All Java keywords are entirely in lowercase. A full list of these keywords appears on the inside cover of this book, and you will learn them as we go along. The program listings in this book show keywords, such as `public`, `class`, `static`, and `void`, in a special color. The text editors within an IDE often identify keywords in a similar manner.

Java keywords have special meanings

Some other words, such as `main` and `println`, have a predefined meaning but are not keywords. That means you can change their meaning, but it is a bad idea to do so, because it could easily confuse you or somebody else reading your program.

RECAP Identifiers (Names)

The name of something in a Java program, such as a variable, class, or method, is called an identifier. It must not start with a digit and may contain only letters, digits 0 through 9, and the underscore character (_). Uppercase and lowercase letters are considered to be different characters. (The symbol $ is also allowed, but it is reserved for special purposes, and so you should not use $ in a Java name.)

Although it is not required by the Java language, the common practice, and the one followed in this book, is to start the names of classes with uppercase letters and to start the names of variables and methods with lowercase letters. These names are usually spelled using only letters and digits.

GOTCHA   Java Is Case Sensitive

Do not forget that Java is case sensitive. If you use an identifier, like `myNumber`, and then in another part of your program you use the spelling `MyNumber`, Java will not recognize them as being the same identifier. To be seen as the same identifier, they must use exactly the same capitalization.   ■

FAQ Why should I follow naming conventions? And who sets the rules?

By following naming conventions, you can make your programs easier to read and to understand. Typically, your supervisor or instructor determines the conventions that you should follow when writing Java programs. However, the naming conventions that we just gave are almost universal among Java programmers. We will mention stylistic conventions for other aspects of a Java program as we go forward. Sun Microsystems provides its own conventions on its Web site. While the company suggests that all Java programmers follow these conventions, not everyone does.

Assignment Statements

The most straightforward way to give a variable a value or to change its value is to use an **assignment statement.** For example, if answer is a variable of type `int` and you want to give it the value 42, you could use the following assignment statement:

```
answer = 42;
```

The equal sign, =, is called the **assignment operator** when it is used in an assignment statement. It does not mean what the equal sign means in other contexts. The assignment statement is an order telling the computer to change the value stored in the variable on the left side of the assignment operator to the value of the **expression** on the right side. Thus, an assignment statement always consists of a single variable followed by the assignment operator (the equal sign) followed by an expression. The assignment statement ends with a semicolon. So assignment statements take the form

An assignment statement gives a value to a variable

```
Variable = Expression;
```

The expression can be another variable, a number, or a more complicated expression made up by using **arithmetic operators,** such as + and -, to combine variables and numbers. For example, the following are all examples of assignment statements:

```
amount = 3.99;
firstInitial = 'B';
score = numberOfCards + handicap;
eggsPerBasket = eggsPerBasket - 2;
```

All the names, such as amount, score, and numberOfCards, are variables. We are assuming that the variable amount is of type double, firstInitial is of type char, and the rest of the variables are of type int.

When an assignment statement is executed, the computer first evaluates the expression on the right side of the assignment operator (=) to get the value of the expression. It then uses that value to set the value of the variable on the left side of the assignment operator. You can think of the assignment operator as saying, "Make the value of the variable equal to what follows."

For example, if the variable numberOfCards has the value 7 and handicap has the value 2, the following assigns 9 as the value of the variable score:

```
score = numberOfCards + handicap;
```

In the program in Listing 2.1, the statement

* means multiply

```
totalEggs = numberOfBaskets * eggsPerBasket;
```

is another example of an assignment statement. It tells the computer to set the value of totalEggs equal to the number in the variable numberOfBaskets multiplied by the number in the variable eggsPerBasket. The asterisk character (*) is the symbol used for multiplication in Java.

Note that a variable can meaningfully occur on both sides of the assignment operator and can do so in ways that might at first seem a little strange. For example, consider

The same variable can occur on both sides of the =

```
count = count + 10;
```

This does not mean that the value of count is equal to the value of count plus 10, which, of course, is impossible. Rather, the statement tells the computer to add 10 to the *old* value of count and then make that the *new* value of count. In effect, the statement will increase the value of count by 10. Remember that when an assignment statement is executed, the computer first evaluates the expression on the right side of the assignment operator and then makes that result the new value of the variable on the left side of the assignment operator. As another example, the following assignment statement will decrease the value of eggsPerBasket by 2:

```
eggsPerBasket = eggsPerBasket - 2;
```

RECAP **Assignment Statements Involving Primitive Types**

An assignment statement that has a variable of a primitive type on the left side of the equal sign causes the following action: First, the expression on the right side of the equal sign is evaluated, and then the variable on the left side of the equal sign is set to this value.

SYNTAX

```
Variable = Expression;
```

EXAMPLE

```
score = goals - errors;
interest = rate * balance;
number = number + 5;
```

■ **PROGRAMMING TIP** Initialize Variables

A variable that has been declared, but that has not yet been given a value by an assignment statement (or in some other way), is said to be **uninitialized.** If the variable is a variable of a class type, it literally has no value. If the variable has a primitive type, it likely has some default value. However, your program will be clearer if you explicitly give the variable a value, even if you are simply reassigning the default value. (The exact details on default values have been known to change and should not be counted on.)

One easy way to ensure that you do not have an uninitialized variable is to initialize it within the declaration. Simply combine the declaration and an assignment statement, as in the following examples:

You can initialize a variable when you declare it

```
int count = 0;
double taxRate = 0.075;
char grade = 'A';
int balance = 1000, newBalance;
```

Note that you can initialize some variables and not initialize others in a declaration.

Sometimes the compiler may complain that you have failed to initialize a variable. In most cases, that will indeed be true. Occasionally, though, the compiler is mistaken in giving this advice. However, the compiler will not compile your program until you convince it that the variable in question is initialized. To make the compiler happy, initialize the variable when you declare it, even if the variable will be given another value before it is used for anything. In such cases, you cannot argue with the compiler. ■

RECAP Combining a Variable Declaration and an Assignment

You can combine the declaration of a variable with an assignment statement that gives the variable a value.

SYNTAX

```
Type Variable_1 = Expression_1, Variable_2 = Expression_2,
. . .;
```

EXAMPLES

```
int numberSeen = 0, increment = 5;
double height = 12.34, prize = 7.3 + increment;
char answer = 'y';
```

Simple Input

In Listing 2.1, we set the values of the variables `eggsPerBasket` and `numberOfBaskets` to specific numbers. It would make more sense to obtain the values needed for the computation from the user, so that the program could be run again with different numbers. Listing 2.2 shows a revision of the program in Listing 2.1 that asks the user to enter numbers as input at the keyboard.

Use the standard class Scanner to accept keyboard input

We use the class `Scanner`, which Java supplies, to accept keyboard input. Our program must import the definition of the `Scanner` class from the package `java.util`. Thus, we begin the program with the following statement:

```
import java.util.Scanner;
```

The following line sets things up so that data can be entered from the keyboard:

```
Scanner keyboard = new Scanner(System.in);
```

This line must appear before the first statement that takes input from the keyboard. That statement in our example is

```
eggsPerBasket = keyboard.nextInt();
```

This assignment statement gives a value to the variable `eggsPerBasket`. The expression on the right side of the equal sign, namely

```
keyboard.nextInt()
```

reads one `int` value from the keyboard. The assignment statement makes this `int` value the value of the variable `eggsPerBasket`, replacing any value that the variable might have had. When entering numbers at the keyboard, the user must either separate multiple numbers with one or more spaces or place each number on its own line. Section 2.3 will explain such keyboard input in detail.

LISTING 2.2   A Program with Keyboard Input

```java
import java.util.Scanner;              Gets the Scanner class from
                                       the package (library) java.util
public class EggBasket2
{
    public static void main(String[] args)
    {
        int numberOfBaskets, eggsPerBasket, totalEggs;
                                                              Sets up things so the program
        Scanner keyboard = new Scanner(System.in);            can accept keyboard input
        System.out.println("Enter the number of eggs in each basket:");
        eggsPerBasket = keyboard.nextInt();                   Reads one whole number
        System.out.println("Enter the number of baskets:");   from the keyboard
        numberOfBaskets = keyboard.nextInt();

        totalEggs = numberOfBaskets * eggsPerBasket;

        System.out.println("If you have");
        System.out.println(eggsPerBasket + " eggs per basket and");
        System.out.println(numberOfBaskets + " baskets, then");
        System.out.println("the total number of eggs is " + totalEggs);

        System.out.println("Now we take two eggs out of each basket.");

        eggsPerBasket = eggsPerBasket - 2;
        totalEggs = numberOfBaskets * eggsPerBasket;

        System.out.println("You now have");
        System.out.println(eggsPerBasket + " eggs per basket and");
        System.out.println(numberOfBaskets + " baskets.");
        System.out.println("The new total number of eggs is " + totalEggs);
    }
}
```

Sample Screen Output

```
Enter the number of eggs in each basket:
6
Enter the number of baskets:
10
If you have
6 eggs per basket and
10 baskets, then
the total number of eggs is 60
Now we take two eggs out of each basket.
You now have
4 eggs per basket and
10 baskets.
The new total number of eggs is 40
```

Simple Screen Output

Now we will give you a brief overview of screen output—just enough to allow you to write and understand programs like the one in Listing 2.2. `System` is a class that is part of the Java language, and `out` is a special object within that class. The object `out` has `println` as one of its methods. It may seem strange to write `System.out.println` to call a method, but that need not concern you at this point. Chapter 6 will provide some details about this notation.

So

```
System.out.println(eggsPerBasket + "eggs per basket.");
```

displays the value of the variable `eggsPerBasket` followed by the phrase *eggs per basket*. Notice that the + symbol does not indicate arithmetic here. It denotes another kind of "and." You can read the preceding Java statement as an instruction to display the value of the variable `eggsPerBasket` and then to display the string `"eggs per basket."`

Section 2.3 will continue the discussion of screen output.

Constants

A variable can have its value changed. That is why it is called a variable: Its value *varies*. A number like 2 cannot change. It is always 2. It is never 3. In Java, terms like 2 or 3.7 are called **constants,** or **literals,** because their values do not change.

A constant does not change in value

Constants need not be numbers. For example, `'A'`, `'B'`, and `'$'` are three constants of type `char`. Their values cannot change, but they can be used in an assignment statement to change the value of a variable of type `char`. For example, the statement

```
firstInitial = 'B';
```

changes the value of the char variable `firstInitial` to `'B'`.

There is essentially only one way to write a constant of type `char`, namely, by placing the character between single quotes. On the other hand, some of the rules for writing numeric constants are more involved. Constants of integer types are written the way you would expect them to be written, such as 2, 3, 0, −3, or 752. An integer constant can be prefaced with a plus sign or a minus sign, as in +12 and −72. Numeric constants cannot contain commas. The number 1,000 is *not* correct in Java. Integer constants cannot contain a decimal point. A number with a decimal point is a floating-point number.

Floating-point constant numbers may be written in either of two forms. The simple form is like the everyday way of writing numbers with digits after the decimal point. For example, 2.5 is a floating-point constant. The other, slightly more complicated form is similar to a notation commonly used in mathematics and the physical sciences, **scientific notation.** For instance, consider the number 865000000.0. This number can be expressed more clearly in the following scientific notation:

Java's e notation is like scientific notation

$$8.65 \times 10^8$$

Java has a similar notation, frequently called either **e notation** or **floating-point notation.** Because keyboards have no way of writing exponents, the 10 is omitted and both the multiplication sign and the 10 are replaced by the letter e. So in Java, 8.65×10^8 is written as 8.65e8. The e stands for *exponent,* since it is followed by a number that is thought of as an exponent of 10. This form and the less convenient form 865000000.0 are equivalent in a Java program. Similarly, the number 4.83×10^{-4}, which is equal to 0.000483, could be written in Java as either 0.000483 or 4.83e-4. Note that you also could write this number as 0.483e-3 or 48.3e-5. Java does not restrict the position of the decimal point.

VideoNote
Another sample program

    The number before the e may contain a decimal point, although it doesn't have to. The number after the e cannot contain a decimal point. Because multiplying by 10 is the same as moving the decimal point in a number, you can think of a positive number after the e as telling you to move the decimal point that many digits to the right. If the number after the e is negative, you move the decimal point that many digits to the left. For example, 2.48e4 is the same number as 24800.0, and 2.48e-2 is the same number as 0.0248.

FAQ What is "floating" in a floating-point number?

Floating-point numbers got their name because, with the e notation we just described, the decimal point can be made to "float" to a new location by adjusting the exponent. You can make the decimal point in 0.000483 float to after the 4 by expressing this number as the equivalent expression 4.83e-4. Computer language implementers use this trick to store each floating-point number as a number with exactly one digit before the decimal point (and some suitable exponent). Because the implementation always floats the decimal point in these numbers, they are called floating-point numbers. Actually, the numbers are stored in another base, such as 2 or 16, rather than as the decimal (base 10) numbers we used in our example, but the principle is the same.

FAQ Is there an actual difference between the constants 5 and 5.0?

The numbers 5 and 5.0 are conceptually the same number. But Java considers them to be different. Thus, 5 is an integer constant of type int, but 5.0 is a floating-point constant of type double. The number 5.0 contains a fractional part, even though the fraction is 0. Although you might see the numbers 5 and 5.0 as having the same value, Java stores them differently. Both integers and floating-point numbers contain a finite number of digits when stored in a computer, but only integers are considered exact quantities. Because floating-point numbers have a fractional portion, they are seen as approximations.

GOTCHA   Imprecision in Floating-Point Numbers

Floating-point numbers are stored with a limited amount of precision and so are, for all practical purposes, only approximate quantities. For example, the fraction one third is equal to

```
0.3333333 . . .
```

where the three dots indicate that the 3s go on forever. The computer stores numbers in a format somewhat like the decimal representation on the previously displayed line, but it has room for only a limited number of digits. If it can store only ten digits after the decimal, then one third is stored as

```
0.3333333333 (and no more 3s)
```

This number is slightly smaller than one third and so is only approximately equal to one third. In reality, the computer stores numbers in binary notation, rather than in base 10, but the principles are the same and the same sorts of things happen.

Not all floating-point numbers lose accuracy when they are stored in the computer. Integral values like 29.0 can be stored exactly in floating-point notation, and so can some fractions like one half. Even so, we usually will not know whether a floating-point number is exact or an approximation. When in doubt, assume that floating-point numbers are stored as approximate quantities. ■

Named Constants

Java provides a mechanism that allows you to define a variable, initialize it, and moreover fix the variable's value so that it cannot be changed. The syntax is

Name important constants

```
public static final Type Variable = Constant;
```

For example, we can give the name PI to the constant 3.14159 as follows:

```
public static final double PI = 3.14159;
```

You can simply take this as a long, peculiarly worded way of giving a name (like PI) to a constant (like 3.14159), but we can explain most of what is on this line. The part

```
double PI = 3.14159;
```

simply declares PI as a variable and initializes it to 3.14159. The words that precede this modify the variable PI in various ways. The word public says that there are no restrictions on where you can use the name PI. The word static will have to wait until Chapter 6 for an explanation; for now, just be sure to include it. The word final means that the value 3.14159 is the final value assigned to PI or, to phrase it another way, that the program is not allowed to change the value of PI.

The convention for naming constants is to use all uppercase letters, with an underscore symbol _ between words. For example, in a calendar program, you might define the following constant:

```
public static final int DAYS_PER_WEEK = 7;
```

Although this convention is not required by the definition of the Java language, most programmers adhere to it. Your programs will be easier to read if you can readily identify variables, constants, and so forth.

RECAP Named Constants

To define a name for a constant, write the keywords `public static final` in front of a variable declaration that includes the constant as the initializing value. Place this declaration within the class definition but outside of any method definitions, including the `main` method.

SYNTAX

```
public static final Type Variable = Constant;
```

EXAMPLES

```
public static final int MAX_STRIKES = 3;
public static final double MORTGAGE_INTEREST_RATE = 6.99;
public static final String MOTTO =
                          "The customer is right!";
public static final char SCALE = 'K';
```

Although it is not required, most programmers spell named constants using all uppercase letters, with an underscore to separate words.

Assignment Compatibilities

As the saying goes, "You can't put a square peg in a round hole," and you can't put a `double` value like 3.5 in a variable of type `int`. You cannot even put the `double` value 3.0 in a variable of type `int`. You cannot store a value of one type in a variable of another type unless the value is somehow converted to match the type of the variable. However, when dealing with numbers, this conversion will sometimes—but not always—be performed automatically for you. The conversion will always be done when you assign a value of an integer type to a variable of a floating-point type, such as

```
double doubleVariable = 7;
```

Slightly more subtle assignments, such as the following, also perform the conversion automatically:

```
int intVariable = 7;
double doubleVariable = intVariable;
```

More generally, you can assign a value of any type in the following list to a variable of any type that appears further down in the list:

byte → short → int → long → float → double

For example, you can assign a value of type long to a variable of type float or to a variable of type double (or, of course, to a variable of type long), but you cannot assign a value of type long to a variable of type byte, short, or int. Note that this is not an arbitrary ordering of the types. As you move down the list from left to right, the types become more precise, either because they allow larger values or because they allow decimal points in the numbers. Thus, you can store a value into a variable whose type allows more precision than the type of the value allows.

In addition, you can assign a value of type char to a variable of type int or to any of the numeric types that follow int in our list of types. This particular assignment compatibility will be important when we discuss keyboard input. However, we do not advise assigning a value of type char to a variable of type int except in certain special cases.[2]

If you want to assign a value of type double to a variable of type int, you must change the type of the value using a type cast, as we explain in the next section.

RECAP Assignment Compatibilities

You can assign a value of any type on the following list to a variable of any type that appears further down on the list:

byte → short → int → long → float → double

In particular, note that you can assign a value of any integer type to a variable of any floating-point type.

It is also legal to assign a value of type char to a variable of type int or to any of the numeric types that follow int in our list of types.

---

[2] Readers who have used certain other languages, such as C or C++, may be surprised to learn that you cannot assign a value of type char to a variable of type byte. This is because Java reserves two bytes of memory for each value of type char but naturally reserves only one byte of memory for values of type byte.

Type Casting

The title of this section has nothing to do with the Hollywood notion of typecasting. In fact, it is almost the opposite. In Java—and in most programming languages—a **type cast** changes the data type of a value from its normal type to some other type. For example, changing the type of the value 2.0 from `double` to `int` involves a type cast. The previous section described when you can assign a value of one type to a variable of another type and have the type conversion occur automatically. In all other cases, if you want to assign a value of one type to a variable of another type, you must perform a type cast. Let's see how this is done in Java.

Suppose you have the following:

```
double distance = 9.0;
int points = distance;  ⟵——————— This assignment is illegal.
```

As the note indicates, the last statement is illegal in Java. You cannot assign a value of type `double` to a variable of type `int`, even if the value of type `double` happens to have all zeros after the decimal point and so is conceptually a whole number.

In order to assign a value of type `double` to a value of type `int`, you must place `(int)` in front of the value or the variable holding the value. For example, you can replace the preceding illegal assignment with the following and get a legal assignment:

```
intpoints = (int)distance;  ⟵——————— This assignment is legal.
```

A type cast changes the data type of a value

The expression `(int)distance` is called a type cast. Neither `distance` nor the value stored in `distance` is changed in any way. But the value stored in `points` is the "int version" of the value stored in `distance`. If the value of `distance` is 25.36, the value of `(int)distance` is 25. So `points` contains 25, but the value of `distance` is still 25.36. If the value of `distance` is 9.0, the value assigned to `points` is 9, and the value of `distance` remains unchanged.

An expression like `(int) 25.36` or `(int)distance` is an expression that *produces* an `int` value. A type cast does not change the value of the source variable. The situation is analogous to computing the number of (whole) dollars you have in an amount of money. If you have $25.36, the number of dollars you have is 25. The $25.36 has not changed; it has merely been used to produce the whole number 25.

For example, consider the following code:

```
double dinnerBill = 25.36;
int dinnerBillPlusTip = (int)dinnerBill + 5;
System.out.println("The value of dinnerBillPlusTip is " +
    dinnerBillPlusTip);
```

Truncation discards the fractional part

The expression `(int)dinnerBill` produces the value 25, so the output of this code would be

```
The value of dinnerBillPlusTip is 30
```

But the variable `dinnerBill` still contains the value 25.36.

Be sure to note that when you type cast from a `double` to an `int`—or from any floating-point type to any integer type—the amount is not rounded. The part after the decimal point is simply discarded. This is known as **truncating**. For example, the following statements

```
double dinnerBill = 26.99;
int numberOfDollars = (int)dinnerBill;
```

set `numberOfDollars` to 26, not 27. The result is *not rounded*.

As we mentioned previously, when you assign an integer value to a variable of a floating-point type—`double`, for example—the integer is automatically type cast to the type of the variable. For example, the assignment statement

```
double point = 7;
```

is equivalent to

```
double point = (double)7;
```

The type cast `(double)` is implicit in the first version of the assignment. The second version, however, is legal.

RECAP **Type Casting**

In many situations, you cannot store a value of one type in a variable of another type unless you use a type cast that converts the value to an equivalent value of the target type.

SYNTAX

```
(Type_Name)Expression
```

EXAMPLES

```
double guess = 7.8;
int answer = (int)guess;
```

The value stored in answer will be 7. Note that the value is truncated, not rounded. Note also that the variable *guess* is not changed in any way; it still contains 7.8. The last assignment statement affects only the value stored in *answer*.

■ PROGRAMMING TIP   Type Casting a Character to an Integer

Java sometimes treats values of type char as integers, but the assignment of integers to characters has no connection to the meaning of the characters. For example, the following type cast will produce the int value corresponding to the character '7':

```java
char symbol = '7';
System.out.println((int)symbol);
```

You might expect the preceding to display 7, but it does not. It displays the number 55. Java, like all other programming languages, uses an arbitrary numbering of characters to encode them. Thus, each character corresponds to an integer. In this correspondence, the digits 0 through 9 are characters just like the letters or the plus sign. No effort was made to have the digits correspond to their intuitive values. Basically, they just wrote down all the characters and then numbered them in the order they were written down. The character '7' just happened to get 55. This numbering system is called the Unicode system, which we discuss later in the chapter. If you have heard of the ASCII numbering system, the Unicode system is the same as the ASCII system for the characters in the English language. ■

SELF-TEST QUESTIONS

myprogramminglab

1. Which of the following may be used as variable names in Java?

   rate1, 1stPlayer, myprogram.java, long, TimeLimit, numberOfWindows

2. Can a Java program have two different variables with the names aVariable and avariable?

3. Give the declaration for a variable called count of type int. The variable should be initialized to zero in the declaration.

4. Give the declaration for two variables of type double. The variables are to be named rate and time. Both variables should be initialized to zero in the declaration.

5. Write the declaration for two variables called miles and flowRate. Declare the variable miles to be of type int and initialize it to zero in the declaration. Declare the variable flowRate to be of type double and initialize it to 50.56 in the declaration.

6. What is the normal spelling convention for named constants?

7. Give a definition for a named constant for the number of hours in a day.

8. Write a Java assignment statement that will set the value of the variable `interest` to the value of the variable `balance` multiplied by 0.05.

9. Write a Java assignment statement that will set the value of the variable `interest` to the value of the variable `balance` multiplied by the value of the variable `rate`. The variables are of type `double`.

10. Write a Java assignment statement that will increase the value of the variable `count` by 3. The variable is of type `int`.

11. What is the output produced by the following lines of program code?

```
char a, b;
a = 'b';
System.out.println(a);
b = 'c';
System.out.println(b);
a = b;
System.out.println(a);
```

12. In the Programming Tip entitled "Type Casting a Character to an Integer," you saw that the following does not display the integer 7:

```
char symbol = '7';
System.out.println((int)symbol);
```

Thus, `(int)symbol` does not produce the number corresponding to the digit in `symbol`. Can you write an expression that will work to produce the integer that intuitively corresponds to the digit in `symbol`, assuming that `symbol` contains one of the ten digits 0 through 9? (*Hint*: The digits do correspond to consecutive integers, so if `(int)'7'` is 55, then `(int)'8'` is 56.)

Arithmetic Operators

In Java, you can perform arithmetic involving addition, subtraction, multiplication, and division by using the arithmetic operators +, −, *, and /, respectively. You indicate arithmetic in basically the same way that you do in ordinary arithmetic or algebra. You can combine variables or numbers—known collectively as **operands**—with these operators and parentheses to form an **arithmetic expression**. Java has a fifth arithmetic operator, %, that we will define shortly.

An arithmetic expression combines operands, operators, and parentheses

The meaning of an arithmetic expression is basically what you expect it to be, but there are some subtleties about the type of the result and, occasionally, even about the value of the result. All five of the arithmetic operators can be used with operands of any of the integer types, any of the floating-point types, and even with operands of differing types. The type of the value produced depends on the types of the operands being combined.

Let's start our discussion with simple expressions that combine only two operands, that is, two variables, two numbers, or a variable and a number. If both operands are of the same type, the result is of that type. If one of the operands is of a floating-point type and the other is of an integer type, the result is of the floating-point type.

Operands in an arithmetic expression can have mixed data types

For example, consider the expression

```
amount + adjustment
```

If the variables `amount` and `adjustment` are both of type `int`, the result—that is, the value returned by the operation—is of type `int`. If either `amount` or `adjustment`, or both, are of type `double`, the result is of type `double`. If you replace the addition operator, +, with any of the operators −, *, /, or %, the type of the result is determined in the same way.

Larger expressions using more than two operands can always be viewed as a series of steps, each of which involves only two operands. For example, to evaluate the expression

```
balance + (balance * rate)
```

you (or the computer) evaluate `balance * rate` and obtain a number, and then you form the sum of that number and `balance`. This means that the same rule we used to determine the type of an expression containing two operands can also be used for more complicated expressions: If all of the items being combined are of the same type, the result is of that type. If some of the items being combined are of integer types and some are of floating-point types, the result is of a floating-point type.

Knowing whether the value produced has an integer type or a floating-point type is typically all that you need to know. However, if you need to know the exact type of the value produced by an arithmetic expression, you can find out as follows: The type of the result produced is one of the types used in the expression. Of all the types used in the expression, it is the one that appears rightmost in the following list:

```
byte → short → int → long → float → double
```

Note that this is the same sequence as the one used to determine automatic type conversions.

The division operator (/) deserves special attention, because the type of the result can affect the value produced in a dramatic way. When you combine two operands with the division operator and at least one of the operands is of type `double`—or of some other floating-point type—the result is what you would normally expect of a division. For example, 9.0/2 has one operand of type `double`, namely, 9.0. Hence, the result is the type `double` number 4.5. However, when both operands are of an integer type, the result can be surprising. For example, 9/2 has two operands of type `int`, so it yields the type `int` result 4, not 4.5. The fraction after the decimal point is simply lost. Be sure to notice that when you divide two integers, the result *is not rounded;*

Integer division truncates the result

the part after the decimal point is discarded—that is, truncated—no matter how large it is. So 11/3 is 3, not 3.6666. . . . Even if the fractional portion after the decimal point is zero, that decimal point and zero are still lost. Surprisingly, this seemingly trivial difference can be of some significance. For example, 8.0/2 evaluates to the type double value 4.0, which is only an approximate quantity. However, 8/2 evaluates to the int value 4, which is an exact quantity. The approximate nature of 4.0 can affect the accuracy of any further calculation that is performed using this result.

Java's fifth arithmetic operator is the **remainder operator,** or **modulus operator,** denoted by %. When you divide one number by another, you get a result (which some call a quotient) and a remainder—that is, the amount left over. The % operator gives you the remainder. Typically, the % operator

The % operator gets the remainder after division

is used with operands of integer types to recover something equivalent to the fraction after the decimal point. For example, 14 divided by 4 yields 3 with a remainder of 2, that is, with 2 left over. The % operation gives the remainder after doing the division. So 14/4 evaluates to 3, and 14 % 4 evaluates to 2, because 14 divided by 4 is 3 with 2 left over.

The % operator has more applications than you might at first suspect. It allows your program to count by 2s, 3s, or any other number. For example, if you want to perform a certain action only on even integers, you need to know whether a given integer is even or odd. An integer n is even if n % 2 is equal to 0, and the integer is odd if n % 2 is equal to 1. Similarly, if you want your program to do something with every third integer, you can have it step through all the integers, using an int variable n to store each one. Your program would then perform the action only when n % 3 is equal to 0.

FAQ How does the % operator behave with floating-point numbers?

The remainder operator is usually used with integer operands, but Java does allow you to use it with floating-point operands. If *n* and *d* are floating-point numbers, *n* % *d* equals *n* − (*d* * *q*), where *q* is the integer portion of *n* / *d*. Note that the sign of *q* is the same as the sign of *n* / *d*. For example, 6.5 % 2.0 is 0.5, −6.5 % 2.0 is −0.5, and 6.5 % −2.0 is 0.5.

Finally, notice that sometimes we use + and − as the sign of a number, while at other times + and − indicate addition and subtraction. In fact, Java always treats + and − as operators. A **unary operator** is an operator that has only one operand (one thing that it applies to), such as the operator − in the assignment statement

```
bankBalance = -cost;
```

A **binary operator** has two operands, such as the operators + and * in

```
total = cost + (tax * discount);
```

Note that the same operator symbol can sometimes be used as both a unary operator and a binary operator. For example, the − and + symbols can serve as either binary or unary operators.

FAQ Do spaces matter in an arithmetic expression?

The spaces in *any* Java statement usually do not matter. The only exception is when spaces appear within a pair of double quotes or single quotes. However, adding spaces in other situations can make a Java statement easier to read. For example, you should add a space both before and after any binary operator, as we have done in our examples.

Parentheses and Precedence Rules

Parentheses can be used to group items in an arithmetic expression in the same way that you use parentheses in algebra and arithmetic. With the aid of parentheses, you can tell the computer which operations to perform first, second, and so forth. For example, consider the following two expressions that differ only in the positioning of their parentheses:

```
(cost + tax) * discount
cost + (tax * discount)
```

To evaluate the first expression, the computer first adds `cost` and `tax` and then multiplies the result by `discount`. To evaluate the second expression, it multiplies `tax` and `discount` and then adds the result to `cost`. If you evaluate these expressions, using some numbers for the values of the variables, you will see that they produce different results.

If you omit the parentheses, the computer will still evaluate the expression. For example, the following assignment statement

```
total = cost + tax * discount;
```

is equivalent to

```
total = cost + (tax * discount);
```

When parentheses are omitted, the computer performs multiplication before addition. More generally, when the order of operations is not determined by parentheses, the computer will perform the operations in an order specified by

FIGURE 2.2 Precedence Rules

> *Highest Precedence*
>
> First: the unary operators +, -, !, ++, and --
>
> Second: the binary arithmetic operators *, /, and %
>
> Third: the binary arithmetic operators + and -
>
> *Lowest Precedence*

Precedence rules and parentheses determine the order of operations

the **precedence rules** shown in Figure 2.2.[3] Operators that are higher on the list are said to have **higher precedence.** When the computer is deciding which of two operations to perform first and the order is not dictated by parentheses, it begins with the operation having higher precedence and then performs the one having lower precedence. Some operators have equal precedence, in which case the order of operations is determined by where the operators appear in the expression. Binary operators of equal precedence are performed in left-to-right order. Unary operators of equal precedence are performed in right-to-left order.

These precedence rules are similar to the rules used in algebra. Except for some very standard cases, it is best to include the parentheses, even if the intended order of operations is the one indicated by the precedence rules, because the parentheses can make the expression clearer to a person reading the program code. Too many unnecessary parentheses can have the opposite effect, however. One standard case in which it is normal to omit parentheses is a multiplication within an addition. Thus,

```
balance = balance + (interestRate * balance);
```

would usually be written

```
balance = balance + interestRate * balance;
```

VideoNote
**Writing arithmetic
expressions and statements**

Both forms are acceptable, and the two forms have the same meaning.

Figure 2.3 shows some examples of how to write arithmetic expressions in Java and indicates in color some of the parentheses that you can normally omit.

Specialized Assignment Operators

You can precede the simple assignment operator (=) with an arithmetic operator, such as +, to produce a kind of special-purpose assignment operator.

---

[3] Figure 2.2 shows all the operators we will use in this chapter. More precedence rules will be given in Chapter 3, and an even more complete list of precedence rules is given on an inside cover of the book.

FIGURE 2.3   Some Arithmetic Expressions in Java

Ordinary Math	Java (Preferred Form)	Java (Parenthesized)
$rate^2 + delta$	rate * rate + delta	(rate * rate) + delta
$2(salary + bonus)$	2 * (salary + bonus)	2 * (salary + bonus)
$\dfrac{1}{time + 3mass}$	1 / (time + 3 * mass)	1 / (time + (3 * mass))
$\dfrac{a-7}{t+9v}$	(a - 7) / (t + 9 * v)	(a - 7) / (t + (9 * v))

For example, the following will increase the value of the variable amount by 5:

```
amount += 5;
```

This statement is really just shorthand for

```
amount = amount + 5;
```

This is hardly a big deal, but it can sometimes be handy.

You can do the same thing with any of the other arithmetic operators, –, *, /, and %. For example, you could replace the line

> You can combine an arithmetic operator with = as a shorthand notation

```
amount = amount * 25;
```

with

```
amount *= 25;
```

Although you might not care to use these special assignment operators right now, many Java programmers do use them, so you are likely to encounter them in other programmers' code.

SELF-TEST QUESTIONS   myprogramming**lab**

13. What is the output produced by the following lines of program code?

```
int quotient = 7 / 3;
int remainder = 7 % 3;
System.out.println("quotient = " + quotient);
System.out.println("remainder = " + remainder);
```

14. What is the output produced by the following lines of program code?

```
double result = (1 / 2) * 2;
System.out.println("(1 / 2) * 2 equals " + result);
```

15. What is the output produced by the following code?

```
int result = 3 * 7 % 3 - 4 - 6;
System.out.println("result is " + result);
```

16. What is the output produced by the following code?

```
int result = 11;
result /= 2;
System.out.println("result is " + result);
```

CASE STUDY Vending Machine Change

Vending machines often have small computers to control their operation. In this case study, we will write a program that handles one of the tasks that such a computer would need to perform. The input and output will be performed via the keyboard and screen. To integrate this program into a vending machine computer, you would have to embed the code into a larger program that takes its data from someplace other than the keyboard and sends its results to someplace other than the screen, but that's another story. In this case study, the user enters an amount of change from 1 to 99 cents. The program responds by telling the user one combination of coins that equals that amount of change.

Specify the task

For example, if the user enters 55 for 55 cents, the program tells the user that 55 cents can be given as two quarters and one nickel—that is, two 25-cent coins and one 5-cent coin. Suppose we decide that the interaction between the user and the program should be like this:

```
Enter a whole number from 1 to 99.
I will find a combination of coins
that equals that amount of change.
87
87 cents in coins:
3 quarters
1 dime
0 nickels and
2 pennies
```

Write down a sample dialogue with the user

Actually writing a sample dialogue, as we did here, before coding the program will help us to solve our problem.

The program will need variables to store the amount of change and the number of each type of coin. So it will need at least the following variables:

```
int amount, quarters, dimes, nickels, pennies;
```

That takes care of some routine matters; now we are ready to tackle the heart of the problem.

Pseudocode (first try)

We need an algorithm to compute the number of each kind of coin. Suppose we come up with the following pseudocode:

Algorithm to compute the number of coins in amount cents:

1. Read the amount into the variable `amount`.

2. Set the variable `quarters` equal to the maximum number of quarters in `amount`.

3. Reset `amount` to the change left after giving out that many quarters.

4. Set the variable `dimes` equal to the maximum number of dimes in `amount`.

5. Reset `amount` to the change left after giving out that many dimes.

6. Set the variable `nickels` equal to the maximum number of nickels in `amount`.

7. Reset `amount` to the change left after giving out that many nickels.

8. `pennies = amount;`

9. Display the original amount and the numbers of each coin.

These steps look reasonable, but before we rush into code, let's try an example. If we have 87 cents, we set `amount` to 87. How many quarters are in 87? Three, so `quarters` becomes 3, and we have 87 – 3 * 25, or 12, cents left in `amount`. We extract one dime and are left with 2 cents in `amount`. Thus, `dimes` is 1, `nickels` is 0, and `pennies` is 2.

Let's display our results. How much did we have originally? We look in `amount` and find 2. What happened to our 87? The algorithm changes the value of `amount`, but we need the original amount at the end so that we can display it. To fix the algorithm, we could either display the original value in `amount` before we change it or copy the original value into one more variable—called `originalAmount`. If we choose the latter approach, we can modify our pseudocode as follows:

Pseudocode (revised)

Algorithm to compute the number of coins in amount cents:

1. Read the amount into the variable `amount`.

2. `originalAmount = amount;`

3. Set the variable `quarters` equal to the maximum number of quarters in `amount`.

4. Reset `amount` to the change left after giving out that many quarters.

5. Set the variable `dimes` equal to the maximum number of dimes in `amount`.

6. Reset `amount` to the change left after giving out that many dimes.

7. Set the variable `nickels` equal to the maximum number of nickels in `amount`.

8. Reset `amount` to the change left after giving out that many nickels.

9. `pennies = amount;`

10. Display `originalAmount` and the numbers of each coin.

We now need to produce Java code that does the same thing as our pseudocode. Much of it is routine. The first line of pseudocode simply calls for prompting the user and then reading input from the keyboard. The following Java code corresponds to this first line of pseudocode:

```java
System.out.println("Enter a whole number from 1 to 99.");
System.out.println("I will find a combination of coins");
System.out.println("that equals that amount of change.");

Scanner keyboard = new Scanner(System.in);
amount = keyboard.nextInt();
```

The next line of pseudocode, which sets the value of originalAmount, is already Java code, so you need not do any translating.

Thus far, the main part of our program reads as follows:

```java
public static void main(String[] args)
{
    int amount, originalAmount,
        quarters, dimes, nickels, pennies;

System.out.println("Enter a whole number from 1 to 99.");
System.out.println("I will find a combination of coins");
System.out.println("that equals that amount of change.");

Scanner keyboard = new Scanner(System.in);
amount = keyboard.nextInt();
originalAmount = amount;
```

Next, we need to translate the following to Java code:

3. Set the variable quarters equal to the maximum number of quarters in amount.

4. Reset amount to the change left after giving out that many quarters.

Let's think. In our earlier example, we had 87 cents. To get the number of quarters in 87 cents, we see how many times 25 goes into 87. That is, we divide 87 by 25 to get 3 with 12 left over. So quarters is 3. Since the remainder, 12, is less than 25, we don't have four quarters in 87 cents, only three. Ah! We realize that we can use the operators / and % for this kind of division. For example,

Use / and % with
integers to solve
our problem

87 / 25 is 3 (the maximum number of 25s in 87)
87 % 25 is 12 (the remainder)

Using amount instead of 87 gives us the following two statements:

```java
quarters = amount / 25;
amount = amount % 25;
```

We can treat dimes and nickels in a similar way, so we get the following code:

```java
dimes = amount / 10;
amount = amount % 10;
nickels = amount / 5;
amount = amount % 5;
```

The rest of the program coding is straightforward. Our final program is shown in Listing 2.3.

LISTING 2.3   A Change-Making Program

```java
import java.util.Scanner;

public class ChangeMaker
{
    public static void main(String[] args)
    {
        int amount, originalAmount,
            quarters, dimes, nickels, pennies;

        System.out.println("Enter a whole number from 1 to 99.");
        System.out.println("I will find a combination of coins");
        System.out.println("that equals that amount of change.");

        Scanner keyboard = new Scanner(System.in);
        amount = keyboard.nextInt();

        originalAmount = amount;
        quarters = amount / 25;
        amount = amount % 25;
        dimes = amount / 10;
        amount = amount % 10;
        nickels = amount / 5;
        amount = amount % 5;
        pennies = amount;

        System.out.println(originalAmount +
                           " cents in coins can be given as:");
        System.out.println(quarters + " quarters");
        System.out.println(dimes + " dimes");
        System.out.println(nickels + " nickels and");
        System.out.println(pennies + " pennies");
    }
}
```

25 goes into 87 three times with 12 left over.

87 / 25 *is 3.*
87 % 25 *is 12.*

87 cents is three quarters with 12 cents left over.

Sample Screen Output

```
Enter a whole number from 1 to 99.
I will find a combination of coins
that equals that amount of change.
87
87 cents in coins can be given as:
3 quarters
1 dimes
0 nickels and
2 pennies
```

Test your program using data that produces as many different kinds of results as you can think of

After writing a program, you need to test it on a number of different kinds of data. For our program, we should try data values that give zero for all possible coins, as well as other data, such as 25 and 26 cents, that produce results ranging from all quarters to quarters and another coin. For example, we could test our program on each of the following inputs: 0, 4, 5, 6, 10, 11, 25, 26, 35, 55, 65, 75, 76, and a number of other cases.

Although all our tests will be successful, the output does not exactly use correct grammar. For example, an input of 26 cents produces the output

```
26 cents in coins:
1 quarters
0 dimes
0 nickels and
1 pennies
```

The numbers are correct, but the labels would be better if they said `1 quarter` instead of `1 quarters` and `1 penny` instead of `1 pennies`. The techniques you need to produce this nicer-looking output will be presented in the next chapter. For now, let's end this project here. The output is correct and understandable.

■ PROGRAMMING TIP   The Basic Structure of a Program

Many application programs, including the one we just wrote in the previous case study, have a similar basic structure. Their fundamental steps are like the advice once given to public speakers by Dale Carnegie (1888–1955): "Tell the audience what you're going to say, say it; then tell them what you've said." Programs often take the following steps:

1. Prepare: Declare variables and explain the program to the user.
2. Input: Prompt for and get input from the user.
3. Process: Perform the task at hand.
4. Output: Display the results.

This structure, which we can abbreviate as PIPO, is particularly true of our initial programs. Keeping these steps in mind can help you to organize your thoughts as you design and code your programs.   ■

---

myprogramminglab   **SELF-TEST QUESTION**

17. Consider the following statement from the program in Listing 2.3:

```
System.out.println(originalAmount +
                " cents in coins can be given as:");
```

Suppose that you replaced the preceding line with the following:

```
System.out.println(amount +
                  "cents in coins can be given as:");
```

How would this change the sample output given in Listing 2.3?

Increment and Decrement Operators

Java has two special operators that are used to increase or decrease the value of a variable by 1. Since these operators are so specialized, both you and Java could easily get along without them. But they are sometimes handy, and they are of cultural significance because programmers use them. So to be "in the club," you should know how they work, even if you do not want to use them in your own programs.

The **increment operator** is written as two plus signs (++). For example, the following will increase the value of the variable count by 1:

Increment operator ++

```
count++;
```

This is a Java statement. If the variable count has the value 5 before this statement is executed, it will have the value 6 after the statement is executed. The statement is equivalent to

```
count = count + 1;
```

The **decrement operator** is similar, except that it subtracts 1 rather than adds 1 to the value of the variable. The decrement operator is written as two minus signs (--). For example, the following will decrease the value of the variable count by 1:

Decrement operator - -

```
count--;
```

If the variable count has the value 5 before this statement is executed, it will have the value 4 after the statement is executed. The statement is equivalent to

```
count = count - 1;
```

You can use the increment operator and the decrement operator with variables of any numeric type, but they are used most often with variables of integer types, such as the type int.

As you can see, the increment and decrement operators are really very specialized. Why does Java have such specialized operators? It inherited them from C++, and C++ inherited them from C. In fact, this increment operator is where the ++ came from in the name of the C++ programming language. Why was it added to the C and C++ languages? Because adding or subtracting 1 is a very common thing to do when programming.

More About the Increment and Decrement Operators

Although we do not recommend doing so, the increment and decrement operators can be used in expressions. When used in an expression, these operators both change the value of the variable they are applied to and **return,** or produce, a value.

Be careful if you use the operators ++ and -- in expressions

In expressions, you can place the ++ or -- either before or after the variable, but the meaning is different, depending on where the operator is placed. For example, consider the code

```
int n = 3;
int m = 4;
int result = n * (++m);
```

After this code is executed, the value of n is unchanged at 3, the value of m is 5, and the value of result is 15. Thus, ++m both changes the value of m and returns that changed value to be used in the arithmetic expression.

In the previous example, we placed the increment operator before the variable. If we place it after the variable m, something slightly different happens. Consider the code

```
int n = 3;
int m = 4;
int result = n * (m++);
```

In this case, after the code is executed, the value of n is 3 and the value of m is 5, just as in the previous case, but the value of result is 12, not 15. What is the story?

The two expressions n*(++m) and n*(m++) both increase the value of m by 1, but the first expression increases the value of m *before* it does the multiplication, whereas the second expression increases the value of m *after* it does the multiplication. Both ++m and m++ have the same effect on the final value of m, but when you use them as part of an arithmetic expression, they give a different value to the expression.

The -- operator works in the same way when it is used in an arithmetic expression. Both --m and m-- have the same effect on the final value of m, but when you use them as part of an arithmetic expression, they give a different value to the expression. For --m, the value of m is decreased *before* its value is used in the expression, but for m--, the value of m is decreased *after* its value is used in the expression.

When an increment or decrement operator is placed before a variable, we get what is called the **prefix form.** When it is placed after a variable, we get a **postfix form.** Note that the increment and decrement operators can be applied only to variables. They cannot be applied to constants or to more complicated arithmetic expressions.

SELF-TEST QUESTION

18. What output is produced by the following lines of program code?

```
int n = 2;
n++;
System.out.println("n is " + n);
n--;
System.out.println("n is " + n);
```

2.2 THE CLASS String

*string n. 1. A cord usually made of fiber, used for fastening, tying, or lacing.
. . . 4. A set of objects threaded together. . . . 6. Computer Science. A set of
consecutive characters.*

—THE AMERICAN HERITAGE DICTIONARY OF THE ENGLISH LANGUAGE, FOURTH EDITION*

Words, words, mere words, no matter from the heart.

—WILLIAM SHAKESPEARE, TROILUS AND CRESSIDA

Strings of characters, such as "Enter the amount:" are treated slightly differently than values of the primitive types. Java has no primitive type for strings. However, Java supplies a class called String that can be used to create and process strings of characters. In this section, we introduce you to the class String.

Classes are central to Java, and you will soon define and use your own classes. However, this discussion of the class String gives us an opportunity to review some of the notation and terminology used for classes that Chapter 1 introduced.

The class String comes with Java

String Constants and Variables

You have already been using constants of type String. The quoted string

```
"Enter a whole number from 1 to 99."
```

which appears in the following statement from the program in Listing 2.3, is a string constant:

```
System.out.println("Enter a whole number from 1 to 99.");
```

A value of type String is one of these quoted strings. That is, a value of type String is a sequence of characters treated as a single item. A variable of type String can name one of these string values.

The following declares greeting to be the name for a String variable:

```
String greeting;
```

---

*Full and partial dictionary entries from THE AMERICAN HERITAGE DICTIONARY OF THE ENGLISH LANGUAGE. Copyright © 2010 by Houghton Mifflin Harcourt Publishing Company. Adapted and reproduced by permission from THE AMERICAN HERITAGE DICTIONARY OF THE ENGLISH LANGUAGE, Fourth Edition.

The next statement sets the value of `greeting` to the `String` value `"Hello!"`:

```
greeting = "Hello!";
```

These two statements are often combined into one, as follows:

```
String greeting = "Hello!";
```

Once a `String` variable, such as `greeting`, has been given a value, you can display it on the screen as follows:

```
System.out.println(greeting);
```

This statement displays

```
Hello!
```

assuming that the value of `greeting` has been set as we just described.

A string can have any number of characters. For example, `"Hello"` has five characters. A string can even have zero characters. Such a string is called the **empty string** and is written as a pair of adjacent double quotes, like so:`""`. You will encounter the empty string more often than you might think. Note that the string `" "` is not empty: It consists of one blank character.

Concatenation of Strings

You can connect—or join or paste—two strings together to obtain a larger string. This operation is called **concatenation** and is performed by using the + operator. When this operator is used with strings, it is sometimes called the **concatenation operator.** For example, consider the following code:

```
String greeting, sentence;
greeting = "Hello";

sentence = greeting + "my friend";
System.out.println(sentence);
```

You can use
+ to join, or
concatenate,
strings together

This code sets the variable `sentence` to the string `"Hellomy friend"` and will write the following on the screen:

```
Hellomy friend
```

Notice that no spaces are added when you concatenate two strings by means of the + operator. If you wanted `sentence` set to `"Hello my friend"`, you could change the assignment statement to

```
sentence = greeting + "my friend";
```

Notice the space before the word *my*.

You can concatenate any number of `String` objects by using the + operator. You can even use + to connect a `String` object to any other type of object. The result is always a `String` object. Java will figure out some way to express any object as a string when you connect it to a string using the + operator. For simple things like numbers, Java does the obvious thing. For example,

```
String solution = "The answer is " + 42;
```

will set the String variable solution to the string "The answer is 42". This is so natural that it may seem as though nothing special is happening, but a conversion from one type to another does occur. The constant 42 is a number—not even an object—whereas "42" is a String object consisting of the character '4' followed by the character '2'. Java converts the number constant 42 to the string constant "42" and then concatenates the two strings "The answer is" and "42" to obtain the longer string "The answer is 42".

RECAP Using the + Symbol with Strings

You can concatenate two strings by connecting them with the + operator.

EXAMPLE

```
String name = "Chiana";
String greeting = "Hi " + name;
System.out.println(greeting);
```

This sets greeting to the string "Hi Chiana" and then displays the following on the screen:

```
Hi Chiana
```

Note that we added a space at the end of "Hi" to separate the words in the output.

String Methods

A String variable is not a simple variable, as a variable of type int is. A String variable is a variable of a class type that names a String object. Recall that an object has methods as well as data. For example, objects of the class String store data consisting of strings of characters, such as "Hello". The methods provided by the class String can be used to manipulate this data.

Most of the String methods return some value. For example, the method length returns the number of characters in a String object. So "Hello".length( ) returns the integer 5. That is, the value of "Hello".length( ) is 5, which we can store in an int variable as follows:

```
int n = "Hello".length( );
```

Call the method length to get the length of a string

As you have learned, you call, or invoke, a method into action by writing the name of the object, followed by a dot, followed by the method name, and ending with parentheses. Although the object can be a constant, such as "Hello", it is more common to use a variable that names the object, as illustrated by the following:

```
String greeting = "Hello";
int n = greeting.length( );
```

For some methods—such as length—no arguments are needed, so the parentheses are empty. For other methods, as you will see soon, some information must be provided inside the parentheses.

All objects of a class have the same methods, but each object can have different data. For example, the two String objects "Hello" and "Good-bye" have different data— that is, different strings of characters. However, they have the same methods. Thus, since we know that the String object "Hello" has the method length, we know that the String object "Good-bye" must also have the method length. All string objects have this method.

Spaces, special symbols, and repeated characters are all counted when computing the length of a string. For example, suppose we declare String variables as follows:

```
String command = "Sit Fido!";
String answer = "bow-wow";
```

Then command.length( ) returns 9 and answer.length( ) returns 7.

You can use a call to the method length anywhere that you can use a value of type int. For example, all of the following are legal Java statements:

Positions, or indices, in a string begin with 0

```
int count = command.length( );
System.out.println("Length is " + command.length( ));
count = command.length( ) + 3;
```

Many of the methods for the class String depend on counting **positions** in the string. Positions in a string begin with 0, not with 1. In the string "Hi Mom", 'H' is in position 0, 'i' is in position 1, the blank character is in position 2, and so forth. A position is usually referred to as an **index** in computer parlance. So it would be more normal to say that 'H' is at index 0, 'i' is at index 1, and so on. Figure 2.4 illustrates how index positions are numbered in a string. The 12 characters in the string "Java is fun." have indices 0 through 11. The index of each character is shown above it in the figure.

A **substring** is simply a portion of a string. For example, the string defined by

A substring is a portion of a string

```
String phrase = "Java is fun.";
```

has a substring "fun" that begins at index 8. The method indexOf returns the index of a substring given as its argument. The invocation phrase. indexOf("fun") will return 8 because the 'f' in "fun" is at index 8. If the

FIGURE 2.4 String Indices

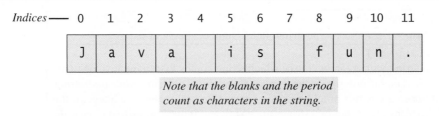

Note that the blanks and the period count as characters in the string.

substring occurs more than once in a string, indexOf returns the index of the first occurrence of its substring argument.

Figure 2.5 describes some of the methods for the class String. In the next chapter, you will learn how to make use of methods such as equals and compareTo that compare strings. Other methods listed in this figure may become more useful to you in subsequent chapters. You can learn about additional String methods by consulting the documentation for the Java Class Library on the Oracle Web site.

FAQ When calling a method, we write the name of an object and a dot before the method's name. What term do we use to refer to this object?

An object has methods. When you invoke one of these methods, the object receives the call and performs the actions of the method. Thus, the object is known as a **receiving object**, or **receiver**. Documentation, such as that in Figure 2.5, often describes the receiving object simply as **this object**.

FAQ What is whitespace?

Any characters that are not visible when displayed are collectively known as whitespace. Such characters include blanks, tabs, and new-line characters.

String Processing

Technically, objects of type String cannot be changed. Notice that none of the methods in Figure 2.5 changes the value of a String object. The class String has more methods than those shown in Figure 2.5, but none of them lets you write statements that do things like "Change the fifth character in this

FIGURE 2.5   Some Methods in the Class `String`

`charAt` (*Index*) Returns the character at *Index* in this string. Index numbers begin at 0.
`compareTo`(*A_String*) Compares this string with *A_String* to see which string comes first in the lexicographic ordering. (Lexicographic ordering is the same as alphabetical ordering when both strings are either all uppercase letters or all lowercase letters.) Returns a negative integer if this string is first, returns zero if the two strings are equal, and returns a positive integer if *A_String* is first.
`concat`(*A_String*) Returns a new string having the same characters as this string concatenated with the characters in *A_String*. You can use the + operator instead of `concat`.
`equals`(*Other_String*) Returns true if this string and *Other_String* are equal. Otherwise, returns false.
`equalsIgnoreCase`(*Other_String*) Behaves like the method `equals`, but considers uppercase and lowercase versions of a letter to be the same.
`indexOf`(*A_String*) Returns the index of the first occurrence of the substring *A_String* within this string. Returns -1 if *A_String* is not found. Index numbers begin at 0.
`lastIndexOf`(*A_String*) Returns the index of the last occurrence of the substring *A_String* within this string. Returns -1 if *A_String* is not found. Index numbers begin at 0.
`length`() Returns the length of this string.
`toLowerCase`() Returns a new string having the same characters as this string, but with any uppercase letters converted to lowercase.
`toUpperCase`() Returns a new string having the same characters as this string, but with any lowercase letters converted to uppercase.
`replace`(*OldChar*, *NewChar*) Returns a new string having the same characters as this string, but with each occurrence of *OldChar* replaced by *NewChar*.
`substring`(*Start*) Returns a new string having the same characters as the substring that begins at index *Start* of this string through to the end of the string. Index numbers begin at 0.
`substring`(*Start*, *End*) Returns a new string having the same characters as the substring that begins at index *Start* of this string through, but not including, index *End* of the string. Index numbers begin at 0.
`trim`() Returns a new string having the same characters as this string, but with leading and trailing whitespace removed.

string to 'z'". This was done intentionally to make the implementation of the String class more efficient—that is, to make the methods execute faster and use less computer memory. Java has another string class, StringBuilder, that has methods for altering its objects. But we will not discuss this class here because we do not need it.

Although you cannot change the value of a String object, such as "Hello", you can still write programs that change the value of a String *variable*, which is probably all you want to do anyway. To make the change, you simply use an assignment statement, as in the following example:

```
String name = "D'Aargo";
name = "Ka " + name;
```

The assignment statement in the second line changes the value of the name variable from "D' Aargo" to "Ka D'Aargo". Listing 2.4 shows a sample program that performs some simple string processing and changes the value of a String variable. The backslash that appears within the argument to the println method is explained in the next section.

VideoNote
Processing strings

LISTING 2.4   Using the String Class

```
public class StringDemo
{
    public static void main(String[] args)
    {
        String sentence = "Text processing is hard!";
        int position = sentence.indexOf("hard");
        System.out.println(sentence);
        System.out.println("012345678901234567890123");
        System.out.println("The word \"hard\" starts at index "
                          + position);
        sentence = sentence.substring(0, position) + "easy!";
        sentence = sentence.toUpperCase();
        System.out.println("The changed string is:");
        System.out.println(sentence);
    }
}
```

> The meaning of \" is discussed in the section entitled "Escape Characters."

Screen Output

```
Text processing is hard!
012345678901234567890123
The word "hard" starts at index 19
The changed string is:
TEXT PROCESSING IS EASY!
```

GOTCHA   String Index Out of Bounds

The first character in a string is at index 0, not 1. So if a string contains *n* characters, the last character is at index *n* – 1. Whenever you call a string method—such as charAt—that takes an index as an argument, the value of that index must be valid. That is, the index value must be greater than or equal to zero and less than the length of the string. An index value outside of this range is said to be **out of bounds** or simply **invalid**. Such an index will cause a run-time error. ∎

Escape Characters

Suppose you want to display a string that contains quotation marks. For example, suppose you want to display the following on the screen:

Quotes within quotes

```
The word "Java" names a language, not just a drink!
```

The following statement will not work:

```
System.out.println("The word "Java" names a language, " +
                   "not just a drink!");
```

This will produce a compiler error message. The problem is that the compiler sees

```
"The word "
```

as a perfectly valid quoted string. Then the compiler sees Java", which is not anything valid in the Java language (although the compiler might guess that it is a quoted string with one missing quote or guess that you forgot a + sign). The compiler has no way to know that you mean to include the quotation marks as part of the quoted string, unless you tell it that you mean to do so. You tell the compiler that you mean to include the quote in the string by placing a backslash (\) before the troublesome character, like so:

```
System.out.println("The word \"Java\" names a language, " +
                   "not just a drink!");
```

Figure 2.6 lists some other special characters that are indicated with a backslash. These are often called **escape sequences** or **escape characters,** because they escape from the usual meaning of a character, such as the usual meaning of the double quote.

It is important to note that each escape sequence represents one character, even though it is written as two symbols. So the string "\"Hi"\" contains four characters—a quote, H, i, and another quote—not six characters. This point is significant when you are dealing with index positions.

An escape character requires two symbols to represent it

Including a backslash in a quoted string is a little tricky. For example, the string "abc\def" is likely to produce the error message "Invalid escape character." To include a backslash in a string, you need to use two backslashes. The string "abc\\def", if displayed on the screen, would produce

```
abc\def
```

FIGURE 2.6   Escape Characters

\" Double quote.
\' Single quote.
\\ Backslash.
\n New line. Go to the beginning of the next line.
\r Carriage return. Go to the beginning of the current line.
\t Tab. Add whitespace up to the next tab stop.

The escape sequence \n indicates that the string starts a new line at the \n. For example, the statement

```
System.out.println("The motto is\nGo for it!");
```

will write the following two lines to the screen:

```
The motto is
Go for it!
```

Including a single quote inside a quoted string, such as "How's this", is perfectly valid. But if you want to define a single quote as a constant, you need to use the escape character \', as in

```
char singleQuote = '\'';
```

The Unicode Character Set

A **character set** is a list of characters, each associated with a standard number. The **ASCII** character set includes all the characters normally used on an English-language keyboard. (ASCII stands for American Standard Code for Information Interchange.) Each character in ASCII is represented as a 1-byte binary number. This encoding provides for up to 256 characters. Many programming languages other than Java use the ASCII character set.

The **Unicode** character set includes the entire ASCII character set, plus many of the characters used in languages other than English. A Unicode character occupies 2 bytes. This encoding provides more than 65,000 different characters.

Unicode includes ASCII as a subset

To appeal to international users, the developers of Java adopted the Unicode character set. As it turns out, this is not likely to be a big issue if you are using an English-language keyboard. Normally, you can just program as though Java were using the ASCII character set, because the ASCII character set is a subset of the Unicode character set. The advantage of the Unicode character set is that it makes it easy to handle languages other than English. The disadvantage is that it sometimes requires more computer memory to store each character than it would if Java used only the ASCII character set. You can see the subset of the Unicode character set that is synonymous with the ASCII character set in the appendix of this book.

SELF-TEST QUESTIONS

19. What output is produced by the following statements?

```
String greeting = "How do you do";
System.out.println(greeting + "Seven of Nine.");
```

20. What output is produced by the following statements?

```
String test = "abcdefg";
System.out.println(test.length());
System.out.println(test.charAt(1));
```

21. What output is produced by the following statements?

```
String test = "abcdefg";
System.out.println(test.substring(3));
```

22. What output is produced by the following statement?

```
System.out.println("abc\ndef");
```

23. What output is produced by the following statement?

```
System.out.println("abc\\ndef");
```

24. What output is produced by the following statements?

```
String test = "Hello John";
test = test.toUpperCase();
System.out.println(test);
```

25. What is the value of the expression s1.equals(s2) after the following statements execute?

```
String s1 = "Hello John";
String s2 = "hello john";
```

26. What is the value of the expression s1.equals(s2) after the following statements execute?

```
String s1 = "Hello John";
String s2 = "hello john";
s1 = s1.toUpperCase();
s2 = s2.toUpperCase();
```

2.3 KEYBOARD AND SCREEN I/O

Garbage in, garbage out.

—PROGRAMMER'S SAYING

Input and output of program data are usually referred to as **I/O**. A Java program can perform I/O in many different ways. This section presents some very simple ways to handle text as either input typed at the keyboard or output sent to the screen. In later chapters, we will discuss more elaborate ways to do I/O.

Screen Output

We have been using simple output statements since the beginning of this book. This section will summarize and explain what we have already been doing. In Listing 2.3, we used statements such as the following to send output to the display screen:

```
System.out.println("Enter a whole number from 1 to 99.");
        . . .
System.out.println(quarters + "quarters");
```

Earlier in this chapter, we noted that `System` is a standard class, `out` is a special object within that class, and `out` has `println` as one of its methods. Of course, you need not be aware of these details in order to use these output statements. You can simply consider `System.out.println` to be one peculiarly spelled statement. However, you may as well get used to this dot notation and the notion of methods and objects.

To use output statements of this form, simply follow the expression `System.out.println` with what you want to display, enclosed in parentheses, and then follow that with a semicolon. You can output strings of text in double quotes, like `"Enter a whole number from 1 to 99"` or `"quarters"`; variables, like `quarters`; numbers, like `5` or `7.3`; and almost any other object or value. If you want to display more than one thing, simply place a + between the things you want to display. For example,

```
System.out.println("Lucky number = " + 13 +
                "Secret number = " + number);
```

Use + to join the things you want to display

If the value of `number` is 7, the output will be

```
Lucky number = 13Secret number = 7
```

Notice that no spaces are added. If you want a space between the 13 and the word `Secret` in the preceding output—and you probably do—you should add a space at the beginning of the string

```
"Secret number = "
```

so that it becomes

```
"Secret number = "
```

Notice that you use double quotes, not single quotes, and that the left and right quotes are the same symbol. Finally, notice that you can place the statement on several lines if it is too long. However, you cannot break a line in the middle of a variable name or a quoted string. For readability, you should break the line before or after a + operator, and you should indent the continuation line.

You can also use the `println` method to display the value of a `String` variable, as illustrated by the following:

```
String greeting = "Hello Programmers!";
System.out.println(greeting);
```

This will cause the following to be written on the screen:

```
Hello Programmers!
```

Every invocation of `println` ends a line of output. For example, consider the following statements:

```
System.out.println("One, two, buckle my shoe.");
System.out.println("Three, four, shut the door.");
```

These two statements will cause the following output to appear on the screen:

```
One, two, buckle my shoe.
Three, four, shut the door.
```

If you want two or more output statements to place all of their output on a single line, use `print` instead of `println`. For example,

print versus
println

```
System.out.print("One, two,");
System.out.print(" buckle my shoe.");
System.out.print(" Three, four,");
System.out.println("shut the door.");
```

will produce the following output:

```
One, two, buckle my shoe. Three, four, shut the door.
```

Notice that a new line is not started until you use a `println` instead of a `print`. Notice also that the new line starts *after* the items specified in the `println` have been displayed. This is the only difference between `print` and `println`.

That is all you need to know in order to write programs with this sort of output, but we can still explain a bit more about what is happening. Consider the following statement:

```
System.out.println("The answer is " + 42);
```

The expression inside the parentheses should look familiar:

```
"The answer is " + 42
```

In our discussion of the class `String` in Section 2.2, we said that you could use the + operator to concatenate a string, such as `"The answer is"`, and another item, such as the number constant 42. The + operator within a `System.out.println` statement is the same + operator that performs string concatenation. In the preceding example, Java converts the number constant 42 to the string `"42"` and then uses the + operator to obtain the string `"The answer is 42"`. The `System.out.println` statement then displays this string. The `println` method always outputs strings. Technically speaking, it never outputs numbers, even though it looks as though it does.

RECAP `println`

You can display lines of text using the method `System.out.println`. The items of output can be quoted strings, variables, constants such as numbers, or almost any object you can define in Java.

SYNTAX

```
System.out.println (Output_1 + Output_2 + ... + Output_Last);
```

EXAMPLES

```
System.out.println("Hello out there!");
System.out.println("Area = " + theArea + " square inches");
```

RECAP `println` **Versus** `print`

`System.out.println` and `System.out.print` are almost the same method. The `println` method advances to a new line *after* it displays its output, whereas the `print` method does not. For example,

```
System.out.print("one");
System.out.print("two");
System.out.println("three");
System.out.print("four");
```

produces the following output:

```
one two three
four
```

The output would look the same whether the last statement involved `print` or `println`. However, since our last statement uses `print`, subsequent output will appear on the same line as `four`.

Keyboard Input

As we mentioned earlier in this chapter, you can use the class `Scanner` for handling keyboard input. This standard class is in the package `java.util`. To make `Scanner` available to your program, you write the following line near the beginning of the file containing your program:

```
import java.util.Scanner;
```

You use an object of the class `Scanner` to perform keyboard input. You create such an object by writing a statement in the following form:

```
Scanner Scanner_Object_Name = new Scanner(System.in);
```

where *Scanner_Object_Name* is any Java variable. For example, in Listing 2.3, we used the identifier keyboard for the *Scanner_Object_Name*, as follows:

```
Scanner keyboard = new Scanner(System.in);
```

We often use the identifier keyboard for our `Scanner` object because it suggests keyboard input. However, you may use other names instead. For example, you could use the variable scannerObject everywhere we use keyboard.

After you define a `Scanner` object, you can use methods of the class `Scanner` to read data typed at the keyboard. For example, the method invocation

nextInt reads an int value

```
keyboard.nextInt()
```

reads one `int` value typed at the keyboard and returns that `int` value. You can assign that value to a variable of type `int`, as follows:

```
int n1 = keyboard.nextInt();
```

nextDouble reads a double value

What if you want to read a number of some type other than `int`? The method nextDouble works in exactly the same way as nextInt, except that it reads a value of type `double`. `Scanner` has similar methods for reading values of other numeric types.

The method next reads a word, as illustrated by the following statements:

next reads a word

```
String s1 = keyboard.next();
String s2 = keyboard.next();
```

If the input line is

```
plastic spoons
```

the string `"plastic"` is assigned to s1 and the string `"spoons"` is assigned to s2. Note that any two input values entered at the keyboard must be separated by whitespace characters such as one or more blanks or one or more line breaks or some combination of blanks and line breaks. In this context, the separators are called **delimiters**. For the method next, a word is any string of nonwhitespace characters delimited by whitespace characters.

A delimiter is a separator in input data; by default, it is whitespace

If you want to read an entire line, you would use the method nextLine. For example,

```
String sentence = keyboard.nextLine();
```

reads in one line of input and places the resulting string into the variable sentence. The end of an input line is indicated by the escape character '\n'. When you press the Enter (Return) key at the keyboard, you enter the '\n' character. On the screen, however, you simply see one line end and another begin. When nextLine reads a line of text, it reads this '\n' character, but the '\n' does not become part of the string value returned. So in the previous example, the string named by the variable sentence does not end with the '\n' character.

nextLine reads an entire line

Listing 2.5 shows a program that demonstrates the Scanner methods that we just introduced.

LISTING 2.5 A Demonstration of Keyboard Input *(part 1 of 2)*

```java
import java.util.Scanner;          // Gets the Scanner class from the package (library) java.util

public class ScannerDemo
{
    public static void main(String[] args)
    {
        Scanner keyboard = new Scanner(System.in);   // Sets things up so the program can accept keyboard input

        System.out.println("Enter two whole numbers");
        System.out.println("separated by one or more spaces:");

        int n1, n2;
        n1 = keyboard.nextInt();     // Reads one int value from the keyboard
        n2 = keyboard.nextInt();
        System.out.println("You entered " + n1 + " and " + n2);

        System.out.println("Next enter two numbers.");
        System.out.println("A decimal point is OK.");

        double d1, d2;
        d1 = keyboard.nextDouble();   // Reads one double value from the keyboard
        d2 = keyboard.nextDouble();
        System.out.println("You entered " + d1 + " and " + d2);

        System.out.println("Next enter two words:");

        String s1, s2;
        s1 = keyboard.next();         // Reads one word from the keyboard
        s2 = keyboard.next();
        System.out.println("You entered \"" +
                             s1 + "\" and \"" + s2 + "\"");

        s1 = keyboard.nextLine(); //To get rid of '\n'    // This line is explained in the next Gotcha section.

        System.out.println("Next enter a line of text:");
        s1 = keyboard.nextLine();     // Reads an entire line
        System.out.println("You entered: \"" + s1 + "\"");
    }
}
```

(continued)

LISTING 2.5   A Demonstration of Keyboard Input *(part 2 of 2)*

Sample Screen Output

```
Enter two whole numbers
separated by one or more spaces:
  42    43
You entered 42 and 43
Next enter two numbers.
A decimal point is OK.
 9.99  21
You entered 9.99 and 21.0
Next enter two words:
plastic spoons
You entered "plastic" and "spoons"
Next enter a line of text:
May the hair on your toes grow long and curly.
You entered "May the hair on your toes grow long and curly."
```

RECAP **Keyboard Input Using the Class** Scanner

You can use an object of the class Scanner to read input from the keyboard. To set things up, you place the following statement at the beginning of your program file:

```
import java.util.Scanner;
```

You also need a statement in the following form before the first statement involving keyboard input:

```
Scanner Scanner_Object_Name = new Scanner(System.in);
```

where *Scanner_Object_Name* is any Java identifier that is not a keyword. For example,

```
Scanner scannerObject = new Scanner(System.in);
```

The methods nextInt, nextDouble, and next read and return, respectively, a value of type int, a value of type double, and a word as the value of a String object. The method nextLine reads and returns the remainder of the current input line as a string. The terminating '\n' is read but not included in the string value returned.

(continued)

SYNTAX

```
Int_Variable= Scanner_Object_Name.nextInt();
Double_Variable= Scanner_Object_Name.nextDouble();
String_Variable= Scanner_Object_Name.next();
String_Variable= Scanner_Object_Name.nextLine();
```

EXAMPLES

```
int count = scannerObject.nextInt();
double distance = scannerObject.nextDouble();
String word = scannerObject.next();
String wholeLine = scannerObject.nextLine();
```

Figure 2.7 lists some other methods in the class Scanner.

REMEMBER Prompt for Input

Your program should always display a **prompt** when it needs the user to enter some data as input, as in the following example:

```
System.out.println("Enter a whole number:");
```

GOTCHA   Problems with the Methods next and nextLine

VideoNote
Pitfalls involving
nextLine()

The methods next and nextLine of the class Scanner read text starting wherever the last keyboard reading left off. For example, suppose you create an object of the class Scanner as follows:

```
Scanner keyboard = new Scanner(System.in);
```

and suppose you continue with the following code:

```
int n = keyboard.nextInt();
String s1 = keyboard.nextLine();
String s2 = keyboard.nextLine();
```

Finally, assume that the corresponding input is typed at the keyboard, as follows:

```
42 is the answer
and don't you
forget it.
```

This will set the value of the variable n to 42, the variable s1 to "is the answer", and the variable s2 to "and don't you".

FIGURE 2.7 **Some Methods in the Class** Scanner

Scanner_Object_Name.next()
Returns the String value consisting of the next keyboard characters up to, but not including, the first delimiter character. The default delimiters are whitespace characters.

Scanner_Object_Name.nextLine()
Reads the rest of the current keyboard input line and returns the characters read as a value of type String. Note that the line terminator '\n' is read and discarded; it is not included in the string returned.

Scanner_Object_Name.nextInt()
Returns the next keyboard input as a value of type int.

Scanner_Object_Name.nextDouble()
Returns the next keyboard input as a value of type double.

Scanner_Object_Name.nextFloat()
Returns the next keyboard input as a value of type float.

Scanner_Object_Name.nextLong()
Returns the next keyboard input as a value of type long.

Scanner_Object_Name.nextByte()
Returns the next keyboard input as a value of type byte.

Scanner_Object_Name.nextShort()
Returns the next keyboard input as a value of type short.

Scanner_Object_Name.nextBoolean()
Returns the next keyboard input as a value of type boolean. The values of true and false are entered as the words *true* and *false*. Any combination of uppercase and lowercase letters is allowed in spelling *true* and *false*.

Scanner_Object_Name.useDelimiter(*Delimiter_Word*);
Makes the string *Delimiter_Word* the only delimiter used to separate input. Only the exact word will be a delimiter. In particular, blanks, line breaks, and other whitespace will no longer be delimiters unless they are a part of *Delimiter_Word*.

This is a simple case of the use of the useDelimiter method. There are many ways to set the delimiters to various combinations of characters and words, but we will not go into them in this book.

So far it may not seem as though there is any potential for problems, but suppose the input were instead

```
42
and don't you
forget it.
```

Under these circumstances, you might expect that n is set to 42, s1 to "and don't you", and s2 to "forget it". But that is not what happens.

Actually, the value of the variable n is set to 42, the variable s1 is set to the empty string, and the variable s2 is set to "and don't you". The method nextInt reads the 42 but does not read the end-of-line character '\n'. So the first nextLine invocation reads the rest of the line that contains the 42. There is nothing more on that line, except for '\n'. Thus, nextLine reads and discards the end-of-line character '\n' and then returns the empty string, which is assigned to s1. The next invocation of nextLine begins on the next line and reads "and don't you".

When combining methods that read numbers from the keyboard with methods that read strings, you sometimes have to include an extra invocation of nextLine to get rid of the end-of-line character '\n'. This problem is illustrated near the end of the program in Listing 2.5. ■

REMEMBER The Empty String

Recall that an empty string has zero characters and is written as "". If the nextLine method executes, and the user simply presses the Enter (Return) key, the nextLine method returns the empty string.

Other Input Delimiters (Optional)

When using the Scanner class for keyboard input, you can change the delimiters that separate keyboard input to almost any combination of characters and strings, but the details are a bit involved. In this book we will describe only one simple kind of delimiter change. We will tell you how to change the delimiters from whitespace to one specific delimiter string.

For example, suppose you create a Scanner object as follows:

```
Scanner keyboard2 = new Scanner(System.in);
```

You can change the delimiter for the object keyboard2 to "##" as follows:

```
keyboard2.useDelimiter("##");
```

After this invocation of the useDelimiter method, "##" will be the *only* input delimiter for the input object keyboard2. Note that whitespace will no longer be a delimiter for keyboard input involving keyboard2. So given the keyboard input

```
funny wo##rd   ##
```

the following code would read the two strings "funny wo" and "rd":

```
System.out.println("Enter two words as a line of text:");
String s1 = keyboard2.next();
String s2 = keyboard2.next();
```

Note that no whitespace characters, not even line breaks, serve as an input delimiter once this change is made to keyboard2. Also note that you can have two different objects of the class Scannerwith different delimiters in the same program. These points are illustrated by the program in Listing 2.6.

LISTING 2.6 **Changing Delimiters** *(Optional)*

```java
import java.util.Scanner;

public class DelimitersDemo
{
    public static void main(String[] args)
    {
        Scanner keyboard1 = new Scanner(System.in);
        Scanner keyboard2 = new Scanner(System.in);
        keyboard2.useDelimiter("##");
        //The delimiters for keyboard1 are the whitespace
        //characters.
        //The only delimiter for keyboard2 is ##.

        String s1, s2;

        System.out.println("Enter a line of text with two words:");
        s1 = keyboard1.next();
        s2 = keyboard1.next();
        System.out.println("The two words are \"" + s1 +
                           "\" and \"" + s2 + "\"");

        System.out.println("Enter a line of text with two words");
        System.out.println("delimited by ##:");
        s1 = keyboard2.next();
        s2 = keyboard2.next();
        System.out.println("The two words are \"" + s1 +
                           "\" and \"" + s2 + "\"");
    }
}
```

> keyboard1 *and* keyboard2 *have different delimiters.*

Sample Screen Output

```
Enter a line of text with two words:
funny wo##rd##
The two words are "funny" and "wor##rd##"
Enter a line of text with two words
delimited by ##:
funny wor##rd##
The two words are "funny wo" and "rd"
```

Formatted Output with `printf` (Optional)

Starting with version 5.0, Java includes a method named `printf` that can be used to give output in a specific format. It is used in the same manner as the `printf` function in the C programming language. The method works like the `print` method except it allows you to add formatting instructions that specify things such as the number of digits to include after a decimal point. For example, consider the following:

```java
double price = 19.5;
System.out.println("Price using println:" + price);
System.out.printf("Price using printf formatting:%6.2f",
                  price);
```

This code outputs the following lines:

```
Price using println:19.5
Price using printf formatting: 19.50
```

Using `println` the price is output as "19.5" immediately after the colon because we did not add an additional space. Using `printf` the string after the colon is " 19.50" with a blank preceding the 19.50. In this simple example, the first argument to `printf` is a string known as the **format specifier** and the second argument is the number or other value to be output in that format.

The format specifier `%6.2f` says to output a floating-point number in a **field** (number of spaces) of width six (room for six characters) and to show exactly two digits after the decimal point. So, 19.5 is expressed as "19.50" in a field of width six. Because "19.50" only has five characters, a blank character is added to obtain the six-character string " 19.50". Any extra blank space is added to the front of the value output. If the output requires more characters than specified in the field (e.g., if the field in this case was set to 1 via `%1.2f`), then the field is automatically expanded to the exact size of the output (five in our example). The `f` in `%6.2f` means the output is a floating-point number, that is, a number with a decimal point.

Figure 2.8 summarizes some of the common format specifiers.

We can combine multiple format specifiers into a single string. For example, given

```java
double price = 19.5;
int quantity = 2;
String item = "Widgets";
System.out.printf("%10s sold:%4d at $%5.2f. Total = $%1.2f",
                  item, quantity, price, quantity * price);
```

the output is: " Widgets sold:2 at $19.50. Total = $39.00". There are three blank spaces in front of "Widgets" to make a field of ten characters. Similarly, there are three blank spaces in front of the 2 to make a field of four characters. The 19.50 fits in exactly five characters and the last field for the total is expanded to five from one so it will fit the 39.00.

FIGURE 2.8   Selected Format Specifiers for `System.out.printf`

Format Specifier	Type of Output	Examples
%c	Character	A single character: %c
		A single character in a field of two spaces: %2c
%d	Decimal integer number	An integer: %d
		An integer in a field of 5 spaces: %5d
%f	Floating-point number	A floating-point number: %f
		A floating-point number with 2 digits after the decimal: %1.2f
		A floating-point number with 2 digits after the decimal in a field of 6 spaces: %6.2f
%e	Exponential floating-point number	A floating-point number in exponential format: %e
%s	String	A string formatted to a field of 10 spaces: %10s

SELF-TEST QUESTIONS

27. Write Java statements that will cause the following to be written to the screen:

    Once upon a time,
    there were three little programmers.

28. What is the difference between the methods `System.out.println` and `System.out.print`?

29. Write a complete Java program that reads a line of keyboard input containing two values of type int—separated by one or more spaces—and then displays the two numbers.

30. Write a complete Java program that reads one line of text containing exactly three words—separated by any kind or amount of whitespace—and then displays the line with spacing corrected as follows: The output has no space before the first word and exactly two spaces between each pair of adjacent words.

31. What output is produced by the following statements?

```
String s = "Hello" + "" + "Joe";
System.out.println(s);
```

2.4 DOCUMENTATION AND STYLE

"Don't stand there chattering to yourself like that," Humpty Dumpty said, looking at her for the first time, "but tell me your name and your business."

"My name is Alice, but—"

"It's a stupid name enough!" Humpty Dumpty interrupted impatiently. "What does it mean?"

"Must a name mean something?" Alice asked doubtfully.

"Of course it must," Humpty Dumpty said with a short laugh: "my name means the shape I am—and a good handsome shape it is too. With a name like yours, you might be any shape, almost."

—LEWIS CARROLL, THROUGHTHE LOOKING GLASS

A program that gives the correct output is not necessarily a good program. Obviously, you want your program to give the correct output, but that is not the whole story. Most programs are used many times and are changed at some point either to fix bugs or to accommodate new demands by the user. If the program is not easy to read and understand, it will not be easy to change, and it might even be impossible to change with any realistic effort. Even if the program will be used only once, you should pay some attention to readability. After all, you will have to read the program to debug it.

In this section, we discuss four aspects of a program that help to make it more readable: meaningful names, comments, indentation, and named constants.

Meaningful Variable Names

As we mentioned earlier in this chapter, the names x and y are almost never good variable names. The name you give to a variable should be suggestive of its intended use. If the variable holds a count of something, you might name it count. If the variable holds a tax rate, you might name it taxRate.

In addition to giving variables meaningful names and giving them names that the compiler will accept, you should choose names that follow the normal practice of programmers. That way, your code will be easier for others to read and to combine with their code, should you work on a project with more than one programmer. Typically, variable names are made up entirely of letters and digits. You start each name with a lowercase letter, as we have been doing so far. The practice of starting with a lowercase letter may look strange at first, but it is a convention that is commonly used, and you will quickly get used to it. We use names that start with an uppercase letter for something else, namely, for class names like String.

Name your variables to suggest their use

If the name consists of more than one word, "punctuate" it by using capital letters at the word boundaries, as in `taxRate`, `numberOfTries`, and `timeLeft`.

Comments

Write programs that are self-documenting

The documentation for a program tells what the program does and how it does it. The best programs are **self-documenting.** This means that, thanks to a very clean style and very well-chosen identifiers, what the program does and how it does it will be obvious to any programmer who reads the program. You should strive for such self-documenting programs, but your programs may also need a bit of additional explanation to make them completely clear. This explanation can be given in the form of comments.

Use comments to explain details

Comments are notes that you write into your program to help a person understand the program but that are ignored by the compiler. You can insert comments into a Java program in three ways. The first way is to use the two symbols // at the beginning of a comment. Everything after these symbols up to the end of the line is treated as a comment and is ignored by the compiler. This technique is handy for short comments, such as

// comment

```
String sentence; //Spanish version
```

If you want a comment of this form to span several lines, each line must contain the symbols // at the beginning of the comment.

The second kind of comment can more easily span multiple lines. Anything written between the matching symbol pairs /* and */ is a comment and is ignored by the compiler.

For example,

/* */ comment

```
/*
This program should only
be used on alternate Thursdays,
except during leap years, when it should
only be used on alternate Tuesdays.
*/
```

This is not a very likely comment, but it does illustrate the use of /* and */.

Many text editors automatically highlight comments by showing them in a special color. In this book, we will also write comments in a different color, as illustrated by the following comment

/** */ comment

```
/**
This program should only
be used on alternate Thursdays,
except during leap years, when it should
only be used on alternate Tuesdays.
*/
```

Notice that this comment uses two asterisks rather than one in the opening /**. This is not required to make it a comment, but it is needed when we use a program named javadoc that automatically extracts documentation from Java software. We will discuss how to use javadoc later in this book, but we will start using the double asterisks now.

It is difficult to explain just when you should and should not insert a comment. Too many comments can be as bad as too few comments. With too many comments, the really important information can be lost in a sea of comments that just state the obvious. As we show you more Java features, we will mention likely places for comments. For now, you should normally need them in only two situations.

First, every program file should have an explanatory comment at its beginning. This comment should give all the important information about the file: what the program does, the name of the author, how to contact the author, and the date the file was last changed, as well as other information particular to your situation, such as course assignment number. This comment should be similar to the one shown at the top of Listing 2.7.

Second, you should write comments that explain any nonobvious details. For example, look at the program in Listing 2.7. Note the two variables named radius and area. Obviously, these two variables will hold the values for the radius and area of a circle, respectively. You should *not* include comments like the following:

```
double radius; //the radius of a circle   ◄────── A poor comment
```

However, something is not obvious. What units are used for the radius? Inches? Feet? Meters? Centimeters? You should add a comment that explains the units used, as follows:

```
double radius; //in inches
double area; //in square inches
```

These two comments are also shown in Listing 2.7.

REMEMBER Write Self-Documenting Code

Self-documenting code uses well-chosen names and has a clear style. The program's purpose and workings should be obvious to any programmer who reads the program, even if the program has no comments. To the extent that it is possible, you should strive to make your programs self-documenting.

LISTING 2.7 Comments and Indentation

```java
import java.util.Scanner;
```
This `import` *can go after the big comment if you prefer.*

```java
/**
 Program to compute area of a circle.
 Author: Jane Q. Programmer.
 E-mail Address: janeq@somemachine.etc.etc.
 Programming Assignment 2.
 Last Changed: October 7, 2008.
*/
public class CircleCalculation
{
    public static void main(String[] args)
    {
        double radius; //in inches
        double area;   //in square inches
        Scanner keyboard = new Scanner(System.in);
        System.out.println("Enter the radius of a circle in inches:");
        radius = keyboard.nextDouble();
        area = 3.14159 * radius * radius;
        System.out.println("A circle of radius " + radius + " inches");
        System.out.println("has an area of " + area + " square inches.");
    }
}
```

The vertical lines indicate the indenting pattern.

Later in this chapter, we will give an improved version of this program.

Sample Screen Output

```
Enter the radius of a circle in inches:
2.5
A circle of radius 2.5 inches
has an area of 19.6349375 square inches.
```

RECAP Java Comments

There are three ways to add comments in Java:

- Everything after the two symbols // to the end of the line is a comment and is ignored by the compiler.

- Anything written between the symbol pairs /* and */ is a comment and is ignored by the compiler.

- Anything written between the symbol pairs /** and */ is a comment that is processed by the documentation program `javadoc` but is ignored by the compiler.

Indentation

A program has a lot of structure. There are smaller parts within larger parts. For example, one part starts with

```
public static void main(String[] args)
{
```

The body of this main method begins with an open brace { and ends with a closing brace }. Within these braces are Java statements, which we indent by a consistent number of spaces.

The program in Listing 2.7 has three levels of indentation—as indicated by the vertical lines—that clearly show its **nested structure.** The outermost structure, which defines the class CircleCalculation, is not indented at all. The next level of nested structure—the main method—is indented. The body of that method is indented yet again.

Use consistent indentation to show a program's structure

We prefer to indent by four spaces for each level of indenting. Indenting more than that leaves too little room on the line for the statement itself, whereas a smaller indent might not show up well. Indenting two or three spaces is not unreasonable, but we find four spaces to be the clearest. If you are in a course, follow the rules given by your instructor. On a programming project, you likely will have a style sheet that dictates the number of spaces you should indent. In any event, you should indent consistently within any one program.

If a statement does not fit on one line, you can write it on two or more lines. However, when you write a single statement on more than one line, indent the second and all subsequent continuation lines more than the first line.

Although the levels of nesting shown in Listing 2.7 are delimited by braces, {}, that is not always the case. Regardless of whether there are any braces, you should still indent each level of nesting.

Indent each level of nesting

Using Named Constants

Look again at the program in Listing 2.7. You probably recognize the number 3.14159 as the approximate value of pi, the number that is used in many calculations involving a circle and that is often written as. However, you might not be sure that 3.14159 is pi and not some other number. Somebody other than you might have no idea as to where the number 3.14159 came from. To avoid such confusion, you should always give a name to constants such as 3.14159 and use the name instead of writing out the number.

For example, you might give the number 3.14159 the name PI and define it as follows:

```
public static final double PI = 3.14159;
```

Then the assignment statement

```
area = 3.14159 * radius * radius;
```

could be written more clearly as

```
area = PI * radius * radius;
```

In Listing 2.8, we have rewritten the program from Listing 2.7 so that it uses the name PI as a defined name for the constant 3.14159. Note that the definition of PI is placed outside of the main method. Although named constants need not be defined near the beginning of a file, it is a good practice to place them there. That way, they will be handy if you need to correct their

LISTING 2.8   Naming a Constant

```java
import java.util.Scanner;

/**
 Program to compute area of a circle.
 Author: Jane Q. Programmer.
 E-mail Address: janeq@somemachine.etc.etc.
 Programming Assignment 2.
 Last Changed: October 7, 2008.
*/

public class CircleCalculation2
{
    public static final double PI = 3.14159;

    public static void main(String[] args)
    {
        double radius; //in inches
        double area; //in square inches
        Scanner keyboard = new Scanner(System.in);

        System.out.println("Enter the radius of a circle in inches:");
        radius = keyboard.nextDouble();
        area = PI * radius * radius;
        System.out.println("A circle of radius " + radius + " inches");
        System.out.println("has an area of " + area + " square inches.");
    }
}
```

Although it would not be as clear, it is legal to place the definition of PI here instead.

Sample Screen Output

```
Enter the radius of a circle in inches:
2.5
A circle of radius 2.5 inches
has an area of 19.6349375 square inches.
```

values. For example, suppose you have a banking program that contains the named constant

```
public static final double MORTGAGE_INTEREST_RATE = 6.99;
```

and suppose the interest rate changes to 8.5 percent. You can simply change the value of the named constant to

```
public static final double MORTGAGE_INTEREST_RATE = 8.5;
```

You would then need to recompile your program, but you need not change anything else in it.

Using a named constant, like MORTGAGE_INTEREST_RATE, can save you a lot of work. To change the mortgage interest rate from 6.99 percent to 8.5 percent, you change only one number. If the program did not use a named constant, you would have to change every occurrence of 6.99 to 8.5. Although a text editor makes this task easy, this change might not be right. If some occurrences of 6.99 represent the mortgage interest rate, while other occurrences of 6.99 represent something else, you would have to decide just what each 6.99 means. That would surely produce confusion and probably introduce errors.

> Name your constants to make your program clearer and easier to maintain

SELF-TEST QUESTIONS

myprogramminglab

32. What are the kinds of comments in Java?

33. What is the output produced by the following Java code:

```
/**
   Code for Question 33  .
*/
System.out.println("One");
//System.out.println("Two");
System.out.println("And hit it!");
```

34. Although it is kind of silly, state legislatures have been known to pass laws that "change" the value of pi. Suppose you live in a state where, by law, the value of pi is exactly 3.14. How must you change the program in Listing 2.8 to make it comply with the law?

2.5 GRAPHICS SUPPLEMENT

It ain't over till it's over.

—YOGI BERRA

This section begins with an applet from Chapter 1 redone following the style rules discussed in this chapter. However, the rest of the section is devoted to the classes JFrame and JOptionPane. These classes provide you with a way to use graphics in a Java application and windowing for I/O in your Java programs.

Chapter 3 also has a small amount of material on JOptionPane. All the material on JOptionPane in this chapter and in Chapter 3 is independent of the other material in this book. You may cover the material on JOptionPane whether you cover the other material in the other graphics supplements or not. You can also omit the material on JOptionPane and still cover the other material in the graphics supplements.

Style Rules Applied to a Graphics Applet

Listing 2.9 revises the applet program that appears in Listing 1.2 of Chapter 1, adding named constants for all the integer arguments as well as explanatory comments. At first glance it may seem that all these named constants simply complicate the code. However, they make writing and changing the code much easier.

Writing such constants helps you to plan and organize your drawing. The named constants enable you to clearly and explicitly specify constraints. For example, the statement

```
public static final int Y_LEFT_EYE = Y_RIGHT_EYE;
```

ensures that the two eyes appear at the same level.

A graphics program like this one often needs to be tuned by adjusting the various integer values. Finding the right value to change when you need to adjust, say, the mouth width is much easier when you use named constants.

■ PROGRAMMING TIP   Use Named Constants in a Graphics Applet

When designing a drawing, identify the components and their dimensions. Give names to these dimensions and define them as named constants. As much as possible and reasonable, make these constants interdependent. That is, since it is likely that certain dimensions are related to others, define one named constant in terms of another one. Fine-tuning the values of these constants is easier if you can describe the relationships among the various dimensions symbolically by using named constants.   ■

Creating a Java GUI Application with the JFrame Class

Use the class JFrame when creating a GUI for an application program

A **graphical user interface** or **GUI** is simply a windowing interface for a program. An applet is a kind of GUI that runs from a Web page. To obtain GUIs (windowing interfaces) that can be run as regular Java applications, you use the class JFrame rather than JApplet. An application built using the JFrame class is very similar to one using JApplet. In this chapter we will provide a template to turn an applet into an application, but a full explanation of how the code works is not covered until Chapter 8.

LISTING 2.9   Revision of Listing 1.2 Using Comments and Named Constants

```java
import javax.swing.JApplet;
import java.awt.Graphics;
```
These can go after the big comment if you prefer

```java
/**
 Applet that displays a happy face.
 Author: Jane Q. Programmer.
 Revision of Listing 1.2.
*/
public class HappyFace extends JApplet
{
    public static final int FACE_DIAMETER = 200;
    public static final int X_FACE = 100;
    public static final int Y_FACE = 50;

    public static final int EYE_WIDTH = 10;
    public static final int EYE_HEIGHT = 20;
    public static final int X_RIGHT_EYE = 155;
    public static final int Y_RIGHT_EYE = 100;
    public static final int X_LEFT_EYE = 230;
    public static final int Y_LEFT_EYE = Y_RIGHT_EYE;

    public static final int MOUTH_WIDTH = 100;
    public static final int MOUTH_HEIGHT = 50;
    public static final int X_MOUTH = 150;
    public static final int Y_MOUTH = 160;
    public static final int MOUTH_START_ANGLE = 180;
    public static final int MOUTH_EXTENT_ANGLE = 180;

    public void paint(Graphics canvas)
    {
        //Draw face outline:
          canvas.drawOval(X_FACE, Y_FACE, FACE_DIAMETER, FACE_DIAMETER);
        //Draw eyes:
          canvas.fillOval(X_RIGHT_EYE, Y_RIGHT_EYE, EYE_WIDTH, EYE_HEIGHT);
          canvas.fillOval(X_LEFT_EYE, Y_LEFT_EYE, EYE_WIDTH, EYE_HEIGHT);
        //Draw mouth:
          canvas.drawArc(X_MOUTH, Y_MOUTH, MOUTH_WIDTH, MOUTH_HEIGHT,
                         MOUTH_START_ANGLE, MOUTH_EXTENT_ANGLE);
    }
}
```

The applet drawing is the same as the one shown in Listing 1.2.

For the applets we've covered so far there are four changes to convert an applet to an application. Let's make an application out of the happy face applet in Listing 2.9. Note that the name of the class is HappyFace.

1. Replace the line

   ```
   import javax.swing.JApplet
   ```

   with

   ```
   import javax.swing.JFrame
   ```

2. Replace the text

   ```
   extends JApplet
   ```

   with

   ```
   extends JFrame
   ```

3. Add a constructor with the following code. If your class is not named HappyFace, then the actual class name should be substituted in place of HappyFace. Constructors are explained in Chapter 6.

   ```
   public HappyFace()
   {
       setSize(600,400);
       setDefaultCloseOperation(EXIT_ON_CLOSE);
   }
   ```

   The constructor is a place where we can place initialization code. The line setSize(600,400) creates a window that is 600 pixels wide and 400 pixels tall. You can change these numbers if you would like a different window size. The method setSize also works for applets, but it is more common to set the size of an applet as part of the code that displays the applet on a Web page. (You will see this detail in Chapter 14, which is on the Web.) An applet viewer sets the size of an applet to a default size, so while it is legal to use setSize with applets, there is little reason to do so. On the other hand, if you do not use setSize with a GUI derived from JFrame, the GUI may be unreasonably small. The second line, setDefaultCloseOperation(EXIT_ON_CLOSE) tells Java to exit the program if the window is closed.

   setSize sets the dimensions of a JFrame window

4. Add a main method that displays the window. Replace HappyFace with the name of your class. Once again, the nuances of what the code is doing will be explained in later chapters.

   ```
   public static void main(String[] args)
       {
           HappyFace guiWindow = new HappyFace();
           guiWindow.setVisible(true);
       }
   ```

A complete conversion of the applet from Listing 2.9 to an application is given in Listing 2.10. The name of the class has been changed to `HappyFaceJFrame` to distinguish it from the applet version and the changes from the applet version are highlighted.

The graphics supplements in the next several chapters focus on applets. While we haven't yet explained how all of the code for an application works, you can use the basic template described here to construct a GUI application rather than an applet if you wish.

RECAP **The `setSize` Method**

The method `setSize` resizes a `JFrame` window to the specified width and height.

SYNTAX

```
JFrame_Object.setSize(Width, Height);
```

EXAMPLE

```
this.setSize(400, 300);
```

The method `setSize` is used most often within a constructor of a class derived from `JFrame`. The `this` is typically omitted. So a more typical example looks like the following:

```
setSize(400, 300);
```

FAQ **What units are used for the width and height in `setSize`?**

When using `setSize`, the arguments for the width and height are given in pixels. Pixels are discussed in the graphics supplement of Chapter 1.

Introducing the Class `JOptionPane`

Listing 2.11 contains a very simple Java application program that has a windowing interface. The program produces three windows, one at a time. The first window to appear is labeled Dialog 1 in Listing 2.11. The user enters a number in the text field of this window and then clicks the OK button with the mouse. The first window then goes away and the second window appears. The user handles the second window in a similar way. When the user clicks the OK button in the second window, the second window goes away and the third window appears. Let's look at the details.

Any application program can use windows for I/O

LISTING 2.10   A Java GUI Application using the JFrame Class

```java
import javax.swing.JFrame;
import java.awt.Graphics;

public class HappyFaceJFrame extends JFrame
{
    public static finalint FACE_DIAMETER = 200;
    public static final int X_FACE = 100;
    public static final int Y_FACE = 50;

    public static final int EYE_WIDTH = 10;
    public static final int EYE_HEIGHT = 20;
    public static final int X_RIGHT_EYE = 155;
    public static final int Y_RIGHT_EYE = 100;
    public static final int X_LEFT_EYE = 230;
    public static final int Y_LEFT_EYE = Y_RIGHT_EYE;

    public static final int MOUTH_WIDTH = 100;
    public static final int MOUTH_HEIGHT = 50;
    public static final int X_MOUTH = 150;
    public static final int Y_MOUTH = 160;
    public static final int MOUTH_START_ANGLE = 180;
    public static final int MOUTH_DEGREES_SHOWN = 180;

    public void paint(Graphics canvas)
    {
        //Draw face outline:
          canvas.drawOval(X_FACE, Y_FACE, FACE_DIAMETER, FACE_DIAMETER);
        //Draw eyes:
          canvas.fillOval(X_RIGHT_EYE, Y_RIGHT_EYE, EYE_WIDTH, EYE_HEIGHT);
          canvas.fillOval(X_LEFT_EYE, Y_LEFT_EYE, EYE_WIDTH, EYE_HEIGHT);
        //Draw mouth:
          canvas.drawArc(X_MOUTH, Y_MOUTH, MOUTH_WIDTH, MOUTH_HEIGHT,
                        MOUTH_START_ANGLE, MOUTH_DEGREES_SHOWN);
    }

    public HappyFaceJFrame()
    {
        setSize(600,400);
        setDefaultCloseOperation(EXIT_ON_CLOSE);
    }
    public static void main(String[] args)
    {
        HappyFaceJFrame guiWindow = new HappyFaceJFrame();
        guiWindow.setVisible(true);
    }
}
```

This application draws the same Happy Face image as the applet in Listing 2.9

LISTING 2.11   Program Using `JOptionPane` **for I/O** *(part 1 of 2)*

```java
import javax.swing.JOptionPane;

public class JOptionPaneDemo
{
    public static void main(String[] args)
    {
        String appleString =
           JOptionPane.showInputDialog("Enter number of apples:");
        int appleCount = Integer.parseInt(appleString);

        String orangeString =
           JOptionPane.showInputDialog("Enter number of oranges:");
        int orangeCount = Integer.parseInt(orangeString);

        int totalFruitCount = appleCount + orangeCount;

        JOptionPane.showMessageDialog(null,
                "The total number of fruits = " + totalFruitCount);

        System.exit(0);
    }
}
```

Dialog 1

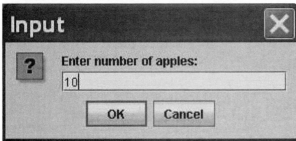

When the user clicks OK, the window goes away and the next window (if any) is displayed.

Dialog 2

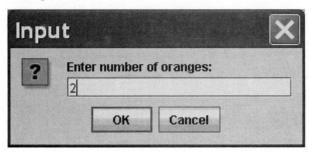

(continued)

LISTING 2.11 **Program Using** JOptionPane **for I/O** *(part 2 of 2)*

Dialog 3

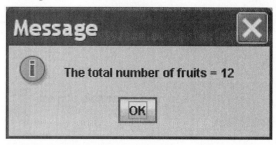

> **REMEMBER** **Running a** JOptionPane **Program**
>
> You run a program that uses JOptionPane, such as the one in Listing 2.11, in the same way you run any application program. You do not run it as if it were an applet.

This program uses the class JOptionPane to construct the windows that interact with the user. JOptionPane is a standard, predefined class that comes with every installation of Java. To make it available to your program, you write

Import JOptionPane from the Swing package

```
import javax.swing.JOptionPane;
```

This statement tells the computer where to find the definition of the JOptionPane class. You may recall that we mentioned a library called Swing, which is the library of classes that we will use for windowing interfaces. These libraries are called packages, and in a Java program the Swing package is denoted javax.swing, with a lowercase *s*. The class JOptionPane is in this package. The previous import statement indicates this fact. You put this statement at the start of any program file that uses the class JOptionPane.

The first program instruction for the computer is

```
String appleString =
    JOptionPane.showInputDialog("Enter number of apples:");
```

It declares appleString to be a variable of type String and then starts the windowing action. The two lines are a single statement, or instruction, and would normally be written on one line, except that doing so would make the line inconveniently long.

JOptionPane is a class used for producing special windows—called **dialog windows, dialog boxes,** or simply **dialogs**—that either obtain input or display output from your program. The method showInputDialog produces a dialog for obtaining input. The string argument, in this case "Enter number of apples:", is written in the window to tell the user what to enter. You the programmer choose this string, depending on what sort of input you want. This invocation of the method showInputDialog will produce the first dialog shown in Listing 2.11. The user clicks the mouse in the text field and then types in some input. The user can use the backspace key to back up and change the input if necessary. Once the user is happy with the input, the user clicks the OK button and the window goes away. As an alternative, the user can press the Enter (Return) key instead of clicking the OK button. That takes care of the responsibility of the user, but how does this input get to your program? Read on.

The method invocation

```
JOptionPane.showInputDialog("Enter number of apples:");
```

Defining a dialog for input

returns—that is, produces—the input that the user typed into the text field. This invocation is within an assignment statement that stores this input. Specifically, the string input is stored in the variable appleString. When you use JOptionPane to read user input, only string values are read. If you want numbers, your program must convert the input string to a number.

The next statement begins by declaring the variable appleCount as an int. The int says that the data stored in the variable appleCount must be an *integer*. The programmer who wrote this program wants the user to enter an integer into that first input window and wants the program to store this integer in the variable appleCount. Because JOptionPane reads only strings, this means converting the string to a value of type int. To see why this conversion is necessary, let's say that the user types 10 into the dialog box, indicating that there are 10 apples. What he or she has actually typed is the character '1' followed by the character '0' to produce the string "10". When using these input windows, you must be aware of the fact that all program input from the user—and all output to the user for that matter—consists of strings of characters. If you want your program to think of the input from an input window as a number, your program must convert the string, such as "10", into the corresponding number, in this case 10. To computers, "10" and 10 are very different things. (In real life they are also different, but we usually ignore that difference.) "10" is a string consisting of two characters, while 10 is a number that can, for example, be added to or subtracted from another number.

> **ASIDE   All Input and Output Are Strings**
>
> All program input from the user and all output to the user consist of strings of characters. When using the class JOptionPane to read numeric input, you must convert the string that is read to the desired numeric value, as you will see next. Even the class Scanner reads user input as a string. However, when you call a method like nextInt or nextDouble, for example, the conversion from string input to numeric input is done for you.

In Listing 2.11, the string typed in by the user is stored in the variable appleString. Since we expect the user to type the digits of an integer, our program needs to convert this string to an int. We store the resulting int value in the variable appleCount, as follows:

parseInt is a
method of the
class Integer

```
int appleCount = Integer.parseInt(appleString);
```

Integer is a class provided by Java, and parseInt is a method of the class Integer. The method invocation Integer.parseInt(appleString) converts the string stored in the variable appleString into the corresponding integer number. For example, if the string stored in appleString is "10", this method invocation will return the integer 10.

FAQ Why do you invoke some methods using a class name instead of an object name?

Normally, a method invocation uses an object name. For example, if greeting is a variable of type String, we write greeting.length() to invoke the method length. However, when we call the methods of the class JOptionPane, we use the class name JOptionPane in place of an object name. The same is true of the method parseInt in the class Integer. What is the story? Some special methods do not require an object to be invoked and, instead, are called using the class name. These methods are called static methods and are discussed in Chapter 6. Although static methods are only a very small fraction of all methods, they are used for certain fundamental tasks, such as I/O, and so we have encountered them early. You can tell whether a standard method in the Java Class Library is static by looking at the documentation for its class on the Oracle Web site.

GOTCHA   Inappropriate Input

A program is said to crash when it ends abnormally, usually because something went wrong. When a program uses the method JOptionPane. showInputDialog to get input—as in Listing 2.11—the user must enter the input in the correct format, or else the program is likely to crash. If your program expects an integer to be entered, and the user enters 2,000 instead of 2000, your program will crash, because integers in Java cannot contain a comma. Later you will learn how to write more robust windowing programs that do not require that the user be so knowledgeable and careful. Until then, you will have to simply tell the user to be very careful. ∎

A crash is an
abnormal end
to a program's
execution

The next few statements in Listing 2.11 are only a slight variation on what we have just discussed. A dialog box—the second one in Listing 2.11—is produced and gets an input string from the user. The string is converted to the corresponding integer and stored in the variable orangeCount.

The next line of the program contains nothing new to you:

```
int totalFruitCount = appleCount + orangeCount;
```

It declares `totalFruitCount` as a variable of type `int` and sets its value to the sum of the `int` values in the two variables `appleCount` and `orangeCount`.

The program now should display the number stored in the variable `totalFruitCount`. This output is accomplished by the following statement:

Defining a dialog for output

```
JOptionPane.showMessageDialog(null,
        "The total number of fruits = " + totalFruitCount);
```

This statement calls the method `showMessageDialog`, which is another method in the class `JOptionPane`. This method displays a dialog window that shows some output. The method has two arguments, which are separated by a comma. For now the first argument will always be written as `null`. You will have to wait for an explanation of what this `null` is. Until then, you will not go too far wrong in thinking of `null` as a place holder that is being used because we do not need any "real" first argument. The second argument is easy to explain; it is the string that is written in the output dialog. So the previous method invocation produces the third dialog shown in Listing 2.11. This dialog stays on the screen until the user clicks the OK button with the mouse or presses the Enter (Return) key, at which time the window disappears.

Note that you can give the method `showMessageDialog` its string argument using the plus symbol in the same way you do when you give a string as an argument to `System.out.println`. That is, you can append the integer value stored in `totalFruitCount` to a string literal. Moreover, Java will automatically convert the integer value stored in `totalFruitCount` to the corresponding string.

GOTCHA   Displaying Only a Number

In Listing 2.11 the final program output is sent to an output window by the following statement:

```
JOptionPane.showMessageDialog(null,
    "The total number of fruits = " + totalFruitCount);
```

It is good style to always label any output. So displaying the string

```
"The total number of fruits = "
```

is very important to the style and understandability of the program. Moreover, the invocation of the method `showMessageDialog` will not even compile unless you include a string in the output. For example, the following will not compile

```
JOptionPane.showMessageDialog(null, totalFruitCount);
    //Illegal
```

The method `showMessageDialog` will not accept an `int` value—or a value of any other primitive type—as its second argument. But if you connect the variable or number to a string by using the plus symbol, the number is converted to a string, and the argument will then be accepted. ∎

System.exit(0)
must end a
program that
uses dialogs

The last program statement in Listing 2.11,

```
System.exit(0);
```

simply says that the program should end. System is a predefined Java class that is automatically provided by Java, and exit is a method in the class System. The method exit ends the program as soon as it is invoked. In the programs that we will write, the integer argument 0 can be any integer, but by tradition we use 0 because it is used to indicate the normal ending of a program. The next chapter formally presents this method.

GOTCHA   Forgetting System.exit(0);

If you omit the last line

```
System.exit(0);
```

from the program in Listing 2.11, everything will work as we described. The user will enter input using the input windows, and the output window will show the output. However, when the user clicks the OK button in the output window, the output window will go away, but the program will not end. The "invisible" program will still be there, using up computer resources and possibly keeping you from doing other things. With windowing programs, *it ain't over till it's over*. System.exit(0) is what really ends the program, not running out of statements to execute. So do not forget to invoke System.exit(0) in all of your windowing programs.

What do you do if you forget to call System.exit(0) and the program does not end by itself? You can end a program that does not end by itself, but the way to do so depends on your particular operating system. On many systems (but not all), you can stop a program by typing control-C, which you type by holding down the control (Ctrl) key while pressing the C key.

When you write an application program that has a windowing interface—rather than an applet—you always need to end the program with the statement

```
System.exit(0);
```

If the program does not use a windowing interface, such as the programs in Sections 2.1 through 2.4, you do not need to invoke System.exit(0).   ■

FAQ Why do some programs need System.exit and some do not?

An application program that uses a windowing interface, such as the one in Listing 2.11, must end with the following method invocation:

```
System.exit(0);
```

(continued)

An applet or a program that uses simple text input and output—like the ones in previous sections of this chapter—does not require this call. What is the reason for this difference?

If a program uses simple text input and output, Java can easily tell when it should end; the program should end when all the statements have executed. An applet also has a built-in mechanism for ending its execution. The applet ends when the Web page displaying it goes away or when the applet viewer window is closed.

The situation is not so simple for application programs that have windowing interfaces. Java cannot easily tell when a windowing program should end. Many windowing programs end only when the user clicks a certain button or takes certain other actions. Those details are determined by the programmer, not by the Java language. The simple program in this section does happen to end when all its statements have executed. But for more complicated windowing programs, the end is not so easy to find, so you must tell Java when to end a program's execution by invoking `System.exit`.

RECAP `JOptionPane` **for Windowing Input/Output**

You can use the methods `showInputDialog` and `showMessageDialog` to produce input and output windows—called dialogs—for your Java programs. When using these methods, you include the following at the start of the file that contains your program:

```
import javax.swing.JOptionPane;
```

The syntax for input and output statements using these methods is given below:

SYNTAX FOR INPUT

```
String_Variable = JOptionPane.showInputDialog(String_
                    Expression);
```

The *String_Expression* is displayed in a dialog window that has both a text field in which the user can enter input and a button labeled OK. When the user types in a string and clicks the OK button in the window, the method returns the string. That string is stored in the *String_Variable*. As an alternative, pressing the Enter (Return) key is equivalent to clicking the OK button. Note that when input is done in this way, it is read as a string. If you want the user to enter, for example, integers, your program must convert the input string to the equivalent number.

(continued)

EXAMPLE

```
String orangeString =
    JOptionPane.showInputDialog("Enter number of oranges:");
```

SYNTAX FOR OUTPUT

```
JOptionPane.showMessageDialog(null, String_Expression);
```

The *String_Expression* is displayed in a dialog window that has a button labeled OK. When the user clicks the OK button with the mouse or presses the Enter (Return) key, the window disappears.

EXAMPLE

```
JOptionPane.showMessageDialog(null,
    "The total number of fruits = " + totalFruitCount);
```

SELF-TEST QUESTIONS

35. In the following two lines, one identifier names a class, one identifier names a method, and something is an argument. What is the class name? What is the method name? What is the argument?

```
appleString =
    JOptionPane.showInputDialog("Enter number of apples:");
```

36. Give a Java statement that will display a dialog window on the screen with the message

    I Love You.

37. Give a Java statement that, when executed, will end the program.

38. What would happen if you omitted System.exit(0) from the program in Listing 2.11? Would the program compile? Would it run without problems?

39. Write a complete Java program that produces a dialog window containing the message HelloWorld!. Your program does nothing else.

40. Write a complete Java program that behaves as follows. The program displays an input dialog window asking the user to enter a whole number. When the user enters a whole number and clicks the OK button, the

window goes away and an output dialog window appears. This window simply tells the user what number was entered. When the user clicks the OK button in the window, the program ends. (Hey, this is only Chapter 2. The programs will get complicated soon enough.)

Reading Input as Other Numeric Types

Since the method `JOptionPane.showInputDialog` reads a string from the user, we had to convert it to an `int` in our previous program by using the method `parseInt` from the class `Integer`. You can convert a number represented as a string to any of the other numeric types by using other methods. For example, the following code asks the user to enter a value of type `double` and stores it in the variable `decimalNumber` of type double:

```
String numberString = JOptionPane.showInputDialog(
                      "Enter a number with a decimal point:");
double decimalNumber = Double.parseDouble(numberString);
```

Figure 2.9 lists the correct conversion method for each numeric primitive type. To convert a value of type `String` to a value of the type given in the first column of the figure, you use the method given in the second column. Each of the methods in this second column returns a value of the type given in the first column. The *String_To_Convert* must be a correct string representation of a value of the type given in the first column. For example, to convert to an `int`, *String_To_Convert* must be a whole number written in the usual way without any decimal point and in the range of the type `int`. Chapter 6 will discuss these classes and methods in more detail.

FIGURE 2.9   Methods for Converting Strings to Numbers

Result Type	Method for Converting
byte	`Byte.parseByte`(*String_To_Convert*)
short	`Short.parseShort`(*String_To_Convert*)
int	`Integer.parseInt`(*String_To_Convert*)
long	`Long.parseLong`(*String_To_Convert*)
float	`Float.parseFloat`(*String_To_Convert*)
double	`Double.parseDouble`(*String_To_Convert*)

■ PROGRAMMING TIP   Multiline Output in a Dialog Window

If you want to display multiple lines by using JOptionPane's method showMessageDialog, you can insert the new-line character '\n'into the string used as the second argument. If the string becomes too long, which almost always happens with multiline output, you can write each line as a separate string ending with '\n'and connect them with plus symbols. If the lines are long or numerous, the window will expand as needed to hold all the output.

For example, consider

```
JOptionPane.showMessageDialog(null,
                "The number of apples\n"
                + "plus the number of oranges\n"
                + "is equal to " + totalFruit);
```

This invocation will produce the dialog shown in Figure 2.10, provided totalFruit is a variable of type int whose value is 12.

FIGURE 2.10   A Dialog Window Containing Multiline Output

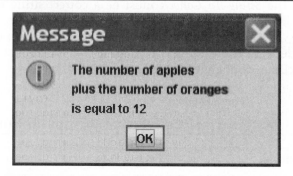

This invocation will produce the dialog shown in Figure 2.10, provided

PROGRAMMING EXAMPLE   Change-Making Program With Windowing I/O

The program in Listing 2.12 is the same as the one in Listing 2.3, but it has a windowing interface. Notice that both the input dialog and the output dialog display multiple lines of text. If any of the details about calculating the numbers of coins is unclear, look back at the explanation of Listing 2.3.

LISTING 2.12   A Change-Making Program with Windows for I/O *(part 1 of 2)*

```java
import javax.swing.JOptionPane;
public class ChangeMakerWindow
{
    public static void main(String[] args)
    {
        String amountString = JOptionPane.showInputDialog(
                "Enter a whole number from 1 to 99.\n" +
                "I will output a combination of coins\n" +
                "that equals that amount of change.");

        int amount, originalAmount,
        quarters, dimes, nickels, pennies;
        amount = Integer.parseInt(amountString);
        originalAmount = amount;

        quarters = amount / 25;
        amount = amount % 25;
        dimes = amount / 10;
        amount = amount % 10;
        nickels = amount / 5;
        amount = amount % 5;
        pennies = amount;

        JOptionPane.showMessageDialog(null, originalAmount +
                " cents in coins can be given as:\n" +
                quarters + " quarters\n" +
                dimes    + " dimes\n" +
                nickels  + " nickels and\n" +
                pennies  + " pennies");
        System.exit(0);
    }
}
```

Do not forget that you need `System.exit` *in a program with input or output windows.*

Input Dialog

(continued)

**LISTING 2.12   A Change-Making Program with
Windows for I/O** *(part 2 of 2)*

Output Dialog

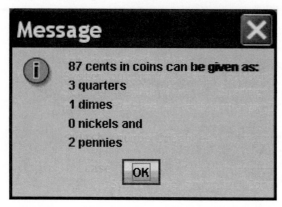

Note that we did not forget the `import` statement

```
import javax.swing.JOptionPane;
```

nor did we forget that an application program using `JOptionPane` must invoke the method `System.exit` to terminate execution. If you forget the `import` statement, the compiler will complain. However, if you omit the invocation of the method `System.exit`, the compiler will not complain, but your program will not end, even after all the statements are executed and all the windows have disappeared.

CHAPTER SUMMARY

- A variable can hold values, such as numbers. The type of the variable must match the type of the value stored in the variable.

- Variables and all other items in a program should be given names that indicate how they are used. These names are called identifiers in Java.

- All variables should be given an initial value before you use them in the program. You can do this using an assignment statement, optionally combined with the variable declaration.

- Parentheses in arithmetic expressions indicate the order in which the operations are performed.

- When you give a value to a variable by using an assignment statement, the data type of the variable must be compatible with the type of the value. Otherwise, a type cast is necessary.

- The methods in the class `Scanner` can be used to read keyboard input.

- Your program should display a message to prompt the user to enter data at the keyboard.

- The method `println` advances to a new line after it displays its output, whereas the method `print` does not.

- The method `printf` may be used for formatted output.

- You can have variables and constants of type `String`. `String` is a class type that behaves very much like a primitive type.

- You can use the plus symbol to indicate the concatenation of two strings.

- The class `String` has methods that you can use for string processing.

- You should define names for number constants in a program and use these names rather than writing out the numbers within your program.

- Programs should be self-documenting to the extent possible. However, you should also insert comments to explain any unclear points. Use `//` to begin a one-line comment, or use either of the pairs `/**` and `*/` or `/*` and `*/` to enclose multiline comments.

- The `JFrame` class can be used to make a GUI application in a manner similar to an applet.

- The method `setSize` resizes a `JFrame` window to the specified width and height.

- You can use the class `JOptionPane` to create a windowing interface for input and output.

Exercises

1. Write a program that demonstrates the approximate nature of floating-point values by performing the following tasks:

   - Use `Scanner` to read a floating-point value x.
   - Compute $1.0 / x$ and store the result in y.
   - Display x, y, and the product of x and y.
   - Subtract 1 from the product of x and y and display the result.

   Try your program with values of x that range from `2e-11` to `2e11`. What can you conclude?

2. Write a program that demonstrates type casting of `double` values by performing the following tasks:

   - Use Scanner to read a floating-point value x.
   - Type cast x to an int value and store the result in y.
   - Display x and y clearly labeled.
   - Type cast x to a byte value and store the result in z.
   - Display x and z clearly labeled.

   Try your program with positive and negative values of x that range in magnitude from `2e-11` to `2e11`. What can you conclude?

3. Write a program that demonstrates the operator % by performing the following tasks:

   - Use Scanner to read a floating-point value *x*.
   - Compute *x* % 2.0 and store the result in *y*.
   - Display *x* and *y* clearly labeled.
   - Type cast *x* to an int value and store the result in *z*.
   - Display *x*, *z*, and *z* % 2 clearly labeled.

   Try your program with positive and negative values of *x*. What implications do your results have for deciding whether a negative integer is odd?

4. If u = 2, v = 3, w = 5, x = 7, and y = 11, what is the value of each of the following expressions, assuming int variables?

   - u + v * w + x
   - u + y % v * w + x
   - u++ / v + u++ * w

5. What changes to the ChangeMaker program in Listing 2.3 are necessary if it also accepts coins for one dollar and half a dollar?

6. If the int variable x contains 10, what will the following Java statements display?

   ```
   System.out.println("Test 1" + x * 3 * 2.0);
   System.out.println("Test 2" + x * 3 + 2.0);
   ```

   Given these results, explain why the following Java statement will not compile:

   ```
   System.out.println("Test 3" + x * 3 - 2.0);
   ```

7. Write some Java statements that use the String methods indexOf and substring to find the first word in a string. We define *word* to be a string of characters that does not include whitespace. For example, the first word of the string

   ```
   "Hello, my good friend!"
   ```

   is the string "Hello," and the second word is the string "my".

8. Repeat the previous exercise, but find the second word in the string.

9. What does the following Java statement display?

   ```
   System.out.println("\"\tTest\\\\\rIt\'");
   ```

   Does replacing the r with an n make a difference in what is displayed?

10. Write a single Java statement that will display the words *one*, *two*, and *three*, each on its own line.

11. What does the Java code

    ```
    Scanner keyboard = new Scanner(System.in);
    System.out.println("Enter a string.");
    int n = keyboard.nextInt();
    String s = keyboard.next();
    System.out.println("n is" + n);
    System.out.println("s is" + s);
    ```

    display when the keyboard input is 2istheinput?

12. What does the Java code

    ```
    Scanner keyboard = new Scanner(System.in);
    keyboard.useDelimiter("y");
    System.out.println("Enter a string.");
    String a = keyboard.next();
    String b = keyboard.next();
    System.out.println("a is" + a);
    System.out.println("b is" + b);
    ```

    display when the keyboard input is

    ```
    By theprickingof my thumbs
    ```

13. Repeat the previous exercise, but change next to nextLine in the statement that assigns a value to b.

14. Many sports have constants embedded in their rules. For example, baseball has 9 innings, 3 outs per inning, 3 strikes in an out, and 4 balls per walk. We might encode the constants for a program involving baseball as follows:

    ```
    public static final int INNINGS = 9;
    public static final int OUTS_PER_INNING = 3;
    public static final int STRIKES_PER_OUT = 3;
    public static final int BALLS_PER_WALK = 4;
    ```

    For each of the following popular sports, give Java named constants that could be used in a program involving that sport:

    - Basketball
    - American football
    - Soccer
    - Cricket
    - Bowling

15. Repeat Exercise 18 in Chapter 1, but define and use named constants.   Graphics

16. Define named constants that you could use in Programming Project 8 in Chapter 1.

PROGRAMMING PROJECTS

Visit www.myprogramminglab.com to complete many of these Programming Projects online and get instant feedback.

1. Write a pr+ogram that reads three whole numbers and displays the average of the three numbers.

2. Write a program that uses Scannerto read two strings from the keyboard. Display each string, along with its length, on two separate lines. Then create a new string by joining the two strings, separated by a blank. Display the new string and its length on a third line.

3. Write a program that reads the amount of a monthly mortgage payment and the amount still owed—the outstanding balance—and then displays the amount of the payment that goes to interest and the amount that goes to principal (i.e., the amount that goes to reducing the debt). Assume that the annual interest rate is 7.49 percent. Use a named constant for the interest rate. Note that payments are made monthly, so the interest is only one twelfth of the annual interest of 7.49 percent.

4. Write a program that reads a four-digit integer, such as 1998, and then displays it, one digit per line, like so:

   1
   9
   9
   8

   Your prompt should tell the user to enter a four-digit integer. You can then assume that the user follows directions. (*Hint*: Use the division and remainder operators.)

5. Repeat the previous project, but read the four-digit integer as a string. Use String methods instead of the hint.

6. Write a program that converts degrees from Fahrenheit to Celsius, using the formula

   DegreesC = 5(DegreesF −32)/9

VideoNote
Solving a conversion problem

   Prompt the user to enter a temperature in degrees Fahrenheit as a whole number without a fractional part. Then have the program display the equivalent Celsius temperature, including the fractional part to at least one decimal point. A possible dialogue with the user might be

   ```
   Enter a temperature in degrees Fahrenheit: 72
   72 degrees Fahrenheit is 22.2 degrees Celsius.
   ```

7. Write a program that reads a line of text and then displays the line, but with the first occurrence of *hate* changed to *love*. For example, a possible sample dialogue might be

   ```
   Enter a line of text.
   I hate you.
   ```

I have rephrased that line to read:
I love you.

You can assume that the word *hate* occurs in the input. If the word *hate* occurs more than once in the line, your program will replace only its first occurrence.

8. Write a program that will read a line of text as input and then display the line with the first word moved to the end of the line. For example, a possible sample interaction with the user might be

Enter a line of text. No punctuation please.
Java is the language
I have rephrased that line to read:
Is the language Java

Assume that there is no space before the first word and that the end of the first word is indicated by a blank, not by a comma or other punctuation. Note that the new first word must begin with a capital letter.

9. Write a program that asks the user to enter a favorite color, a favorite food, a favorite animal, and the first name of a friend or relative. The program should then print the following two lines, with the user's input replacing the items in italics:

I had a dream that *Name* ate a *Color Animal*
and said it tasted like *Food*!

For example, if the user entered blue for the color, hamburger for the food, dog for the animal, and Jake for the person's name, the output would be

I had a dream that Jake ate a blue dog
and said it tasted like hamburger!

Don't forget to put the exclamation mark at the end.

10. Write a program that determines the change to be dispensed from a vending machine. An item in the machine can cost between 25 cents and a dollar, in 5-cent increments (25, 30, 35, . . . , 90, 95, or 100), and the machine accepts only a single dollar bill to pay for the item. For example, a possible dialogue with the user might be

Enter price of item
(from 25 cents to a dollar, in 5-cent increments): 45

You bought an item for 45 cents and gave me a dollar,
so your change is
2 quarters,
0 dimes, and
1 nickel.

11. Write a program that reads a 4-bit binary number from the keyboard as a string and then converts it into decimal. For example, if the input is 1100, the output should be 12. (*Hint:* Break the string into substrings and then

convert each substring to a value for a single bit. If the bits are b_0, b_1, b_2, and b_3, the decimal equivalent is $8b_0 + 4b_1 + 2b_2 + b_3$.)

12. Many private water wells produce only 1 or 2 gallons of water per minute. One way to avoid running out of water with these low-yield wells is to use a holding tank. A family of 4 will use about 250 gallons of water per day. However, there is a "natural" water holding tank in the casing (i.e., the hole) of the well itself. The deeper the well, the more water that will be stored that can be pumped out for household use. But how much water will be available?

    Write a program that allows the user to input the radius of the well casing in inches (a typical well will have a 3-inch radius) and the depth of the well in feet (assume water will fill this entire depth, although in practice that will not be true since the static water level will generally be 50 feet or more below the ground surface). The program should output the number of gallons stored in the well casing. For your reference:

    The volume of a cylinder is $\pi r^2 h$, where r is the radius and h is the height. 1 cubic foot = 7.48 gallons of water.

    For example, a 300-foot well full of water with a radius of 3 inches for the casing holds about 441 gallons of water—plenty for a family of 4 and no need to install a separate holding tank.

VideoNote
Solution to Project 13

13. The Harris-Benedict equation estimates the number of calories your body needs to maintain your weight if you do no exercise. This is called your basal metabolic rate, or BMR.

    The calories needed for a woman to maintain her weight is:

    BMR = 655 + (4.3 × weight in pounds) + (4.7 × height in inches) – (4.7× age in years)

    The calories needed for a man to maintain his weight is:

    BMR = 66 + (6.3 × weight in pounds) + (12.9 × height in inches) – (6.8 × age in years)

    A typical chocolate bar will contain around 230 calories. Write a program that allows the user to input their weight in pounds, height in inches, and age in years. The program should then output the number of chocolate bars that should be consumed to maintain one's weight for both a woman and a man of the input weight, height, and age.

Graphics

14. Repeat any of the previous programming projects using JOptionPane, which is described in the graphics supplement.

Graphics

15. Write a program that reads a string for a date in the format *month* / *day* / *year* and displays it in the format *day* . *month* . *year*, which is a typical format used in Europe. For example, if the input is 06 /17/11, the output should be 17.06.11. Your program should use JOptionPane for input and output.

Answers to Self-Test Questions

1. The following are all legal variable names:

   `rate1, TimeLimit, numberOfWindows`

   `TimeLimit`is a poor choice, however, since it violates the normal convention that variables should start with a lowercase letter. A better choice would be `timeLimit`. `1stPlayer` is illegal because it starts with a digit. `myprogram.java` is illegal because it contains an illegal character, the dot. Finally, `long`is illegal as a variable because it is a keyword.

2. Yes, a Java program can have two different variables with the names `aVariable` and `avariable`, since they use different capitalization and so are different identifiers in Java. However, it is not a good idea to use identifiers that differ only in the way they are capitalized.

3. `int count = 0;`

4. `double rate = 0.0, time = 0.0;`

   You could write this declaration as two statements, as follows:

   ```
   double rate = 0.0;
   double time = 0.0;
   ```

   It is also correct to replace 0.0 with 0, because Java will automatically convert the `int` value 0 to the `double` value 0.0:

5. ```
   int miles = 0;
   double flowRate = 50.56;
   ```

6. The normal practice of programmers is to spell named constants with all uppercase letters, using the underscore symbol to separate words.

7. `public static final int HOURS_PER_DAY = 24;`

8. `interest = 0.05 * balance;`

   The following is also correct:

   `interest = balance * 0.05;`

9. `interest = balance * rate;`

10. `count = count + 3;`

11. b
    c
    c

    The last output is c, because the last assignment (a = b) has no quotes. This last assignment sets the variable a equal to the value of the variable b, which is `'c'`.
   ```

12. `(int)symbol - (int)'0'`

    To see that this works, note that it works for `'0'`, and then see that it works for `'1'`, and then `'2'`, and so forth. You can use an actual number in place of `(int)'0'`, but `(int)'0'` is a bit easier to understand.

13. `quotient = 2`
    `remainder = 1`

14. `(1 / 2) * 2 is equal to 0.0`

    Because 1/2 is integer division, the part after the decimal point is discarded, producing 0 instead of 0.5.

15. `result is -10`

    The expression –3 * 7 % 3– 4– 6 is equivalent to (((–3 * 7) % 3) –4) – 6

16. `result is 5`

17. The output would change to the following:

    ```
    Enter a whole number from 1 to 99
    I will find a combination of coins
    that equals that amount of change.
    87
    2 cents in coins can be given as:
    3 quarters
    1 dimes
    0 nickels and
    2 pennies
    ```

18. `n is 3`
    `n is 2`

19. How do you doSeven of Nine.
    Note that there is no space in doSeven.

20. `7`
    `b`

21. `defg`

22. `abc`
    `def`

23. `abc\ndef`

24. `HELLO JOHN`

25. False, because the strings are not equal.

26. True, because the strings are equal.

27.
```
System.out.println("Once upon a time,");
System.out.println("there were three little programmers.");
```

Since we did not specify where the next output goes, the second of these statements could use print instead of println.

28. The method System.out.printlndisplays its output and then advances to the next line. Subsequent output would begin on this next line. In contrast, System.out.printdisplays its output but does not advance to the next line. Thus, subsequent output would begin on the same line.

29.
```
import java.util.Scanner;
public class Question29
{
    public static void main(String[] args)
    {
        Scanner keyboard = new Scanner(System.in);
        System.out.println("Enter two whole numbers:");
        int n1 = keyboard.nextInt( );
        int n2 = keyboard.nextInt( );
        System.out.println("You entered: " + n1 + " " + n2);
    }
}
```

30.
```
import java.util.Scanner;
public class Question30
{
    public static void main(String[] args)
    {
        Scanner keyboard = new Scanner(System.in);
        String word1, word2, word3;
        System.out.println("Type three words on one line:");
        word1 = keyboard.next( );
        word2 = keyboard.next( );
        word3 = keyboard.next( );
        System.out.println("You typed the words");
        System.out.println(word1 + " " + word2 +" " + word3);
    }
}
```

31. Since the empty string is the second of the three strings, the output is

```
HelloJoe
```

32. There are // comments, /* */ comments, and /** */ comments. Everything following a // on the same line is a comment. Everything between a /* and a matching */ is a comment. Everything between a /** and a matching */ is a comment that is recognized by the program javadoc.

33. One

```
And hit it
```

34. Change the line

    ```
    public static final double PI = 3.14159;
    ```

    to

    ```
    public static final double PI = 3.14;
    ```

    Since values of type double are stored with only a limited amount of accuracy, you could argue that this is not "exactly" 3.14, but any legislator who is stupid enough to legislate the value of pi is unlikely to be aware of this subtlety.

35. JOptionPane is a class, showInputDialog is a method, and "Enter number of apples:" is an argument.

36. JOptionPane.showMessageDialog(null, "I Love You.");

37. System.exit(0);

38. It would compile. It would run. It would even appear to run with no problems. However, even after all the windows have disappeared, the program would still be running. It would continue to run and consume resources, and nothing in the Java code would ever end the program. You would have to use the operating system to end the program.

39.
    ```
    import javax.swing.JOptionPane;
    public class Question39
    {
        public static void main(String[] args)
        {
            JOptionPane.showMessageDialog(null, "Hello World!");
            System.exit(0);
        }
    }
    ```

40. You might want to convert numberString to an int, but that will not affect anything the user sees when the program is run.

    ```
    import javax.swing.JOptionPane;
    public class Question40
    {
        public static void main(String[] args)
        {
            String numberString = JOptionPane.showInputDialog(
                            "Enter a whole number:");
            JOptionPane.showMessageDialog(null, "The number is "
                            + numberString);
            System.exit(0);
        }
    }
    ```

Flow of Control: Branching 3

3.1 THE if-else STATEMENT 138
The Basic if-else Statement 139
Boolean Expressions 145
Comparing Strings 150
Nested if-else Statements 155
Multibranch if-else Statements 157
Programming Example: Assigning Letter
   Grades 159
Case Study: Body Mass Index 162
The Conditional Operator (*Optional*) 165
The exit Method 165

3.2 THE TYPE boolean 166
Boolean Variables 167
Precedence Rules 168
Input and Output of Boolean Values 171

3.3 THE switch STATEMENT 173
Enumerations 179

3.4 GRAPHICS SUPPLEMENT 180
Specifying a Drawing Color 181
A Dialog Box for a Yes-or-No Question 184

Chapter Summary 187   **Programming Projects 190**   **Answers to Self-Test Questions 192**

"Would you tell me, please, which way I ought to go from here?"

"That depends a good deal on where you want to get to," said the Cat.

—LEWIS CARROLL, *Alice in Wonderland*

Flow of control is the order in which a program performs actions. Until this chapter, that order has been simple. Actions were taken in the order in which they were written down. In this chapter, we begin to show you how to write programs having a more complicated flow of control. Java, and most other programming languages, use two kinds of statements to regulate flow of control. A branching statement chooses one action from a list of two or more possible actions. A loop statement repeats an action again and again until some stopping condition is met. Both kinds of statements form **control structures** within a program. Because branching statements choose, or decide, among possible actions, they are also called decision structures. We talk about branching in this chapter and discuss loops in the next.

OBJECTIVES

After studying this chapter, you should be able to

- Use the Java branching statements—if-else and switch—in a program
- Compare values of a primitive type
- Compare objects such as strings
- Use the primitive data type boolean
- Use simple enumerations in a program
- Use color in a graphics program
- Use the class JOptionPane to create a dialog box for a yes-or-no question

PREREQUISITES

Before reading this chapter, you need to be familiar with all the material in Chapter 2.

3.1 THE if-else STATEMENT

When you have eliminated the impossible, that which remains, however improbable, must be the truth.

—SIR ARTHUR CONAN DOYLE

When you come to a fork in the road, take it.

—ATTRIBUTED TO YOGI BERRA

We begin our discussion of branching with a kind of Java statement that chooses between two alternative actions.

The Basic if-else Statement

In programs, as in everyday life, things can sometimes go in one of two different ways. If you have money in your checking account, some banks will pay you a little interest. On the other hand, if you have overdrawn your checking account, your account balance is negative, and you will be charged a penalty that will make your balance even more negative. This policy might be reflected in the bank's accounting program by the following Java statement, known as an if-else statement:

```java
if (balance >= 0)
    balance = balance + (INTEREST_RATE * balance) / 12;
else
    balance = balance - OVERDRAWN_PENALTY;
```

if-else offers a choice of two actions

The pair of symbols >= is used to mean *greater than or equal to* in Java, because the symbol ≥ is not on the keyboard.

The meaning of an if-else statement is really just the meaning it would have if read as an English sentence. When your program executes an if-else statement, it first checks the expression in parentheses after the keyword if. This expression must be something that is either true or false. If it is true, the statement before the else is executed. If the expression is false, the statement after the else is executed. In the preceding example, if balance is positive or zero, the following action is taken:

```java
balance = balance + (INTEREST_RATE * balance) / 12;
```

(Since we are adding interest for only one month, we have to divide the annual interest rate by 12.) On the other hand, if the value of balance is negative, the following is done instead:

```java
balance = balance - OVERDRAWN_PENALTY;
```

Figure 3.1 illustrates the action of this if-else statement, and Listing 3.1 shows it in a complete program.

The expression balance >= 0 is an example of a **boolean expression.** It is simply an expression that is either true or false. The name *boolean* is derived from George Boole, a 19th-century English logician and mathematician whose work was related to these kinds of expressions. We will investigate boolean expressions in the next section.

Notice that an if-else statement contains two smaller statements within it. For example, the if-else statement in Listing 3.1 contains within it the following two smaller statements:

```java
balance = balance + (INTEREST_RATE * balance) / 12;
balance = balance - OVERDRAWN_PENALTY;
```

FIGURE 3.1 **The Action of the `if-else` Statement in Listing 3.1**

```
if (balance >= 0)
    balance = balance + (INTEREST_RATE * balance) / 12;
else
    balance = balance - OVERDRAWN_PENALTY;
```

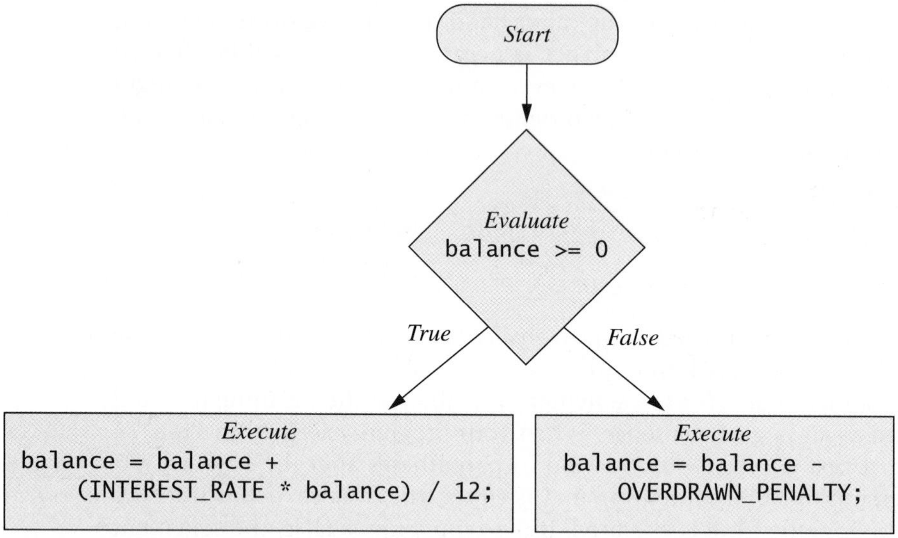

Note that these smaller statements are indented one more level than the `if` and the `else`.

■ PROGRAMMING TIP   Indentation

Indentation in
a program aids
readability

We talked about indentation in the previous chapter. It is a stylistic convention that you really should follow. Although the compiler ignores indentation, inconsistent use of this convention will confuse the people who read your program and likely will cause you to make mistakes.   ■

If you want to include more than one statement in each branch, simply enclose the statements in braces { }. Several statements enclosed within braces are considered to be one larger statement. So the following is one large statement that has two smaller statements inside it:

```
{
    System.out.println("Good for you. You earned interest.");
    balance = balance + (INTEREST_RATE * balance) / 12;
}
```

These statements formed by enclosing a list of statements within braces are called **compound statements**. They are seldom used by themselves but are

LISTING 3.1   A Program Using if-else

```java
import java.util.Scanner;
public class BankBalance
{
    public static final double OVERDRAWN_PENALTY = 8.00;
    public static final double INTEREST_RATE = 0.02; //2% annually

    public static void main(String[] args)
    {
        double balance;

        System.out.print("Enter your checking account
        balance: $");
        Scanner keyboard = new Scanner(System.in);
        balance = keyboard.nextDouble();
        System.out.println("Original balance $" + balance);

        if (balance >= 0)
            balance = balance + (INTEREST_RATE * balance)
            / 12;
        else
            balance = balance - OVERDRAWN_PENALTY;

        System.out.print("After adjusting for one month ");
        System.out.println("of interest and penalties,");
        System.out.println("your new balance is $" + balance);
    }
}
```

Sample Screen Output 1

```
Enter your checking account balance: $505.67
Original balance $505.67
After adjusting for one month of interest and penalties,
your new balance is $506.51278
```

Sample Screen Output 2

```
Enter your checking account balance: $-15.53
Original balance $ -15.53
After adjusting for one month of interest and penalties,
your new balance is $ -23.53
```

often used as substatements of larger statements, such as `if-else` statements. The preceding compound statement might occur in an `if-else` statement such as the following:

```
if (balance >= 0)
{
    System.out.println("Good for you. You earned interest.");
    balance = balance + (INTEREST_RATE * balance) / 12;
}
else
{
    System.out.println("You will be charged a penalty.");
    balance = balance - OVERDRAWN_PENALTY;
}
```

Braces group multiline actions to form a compound statement

Notice that compound statements can simplify our description of an `if-else` statement. Once we know about compound statements, we can say that every `if-else` statement is of the form

```
if(Boolean_Expression)
    Statement_1
else
    Statement_2
```

If you want one or both branches to contain several statements instead of just one, use a compound statement for *Statement_1* and/or *Statement_2*. Figure 3.2 summarizes the **semantics,** or meaning, of an `if-else` statement.

`else` is optional

FIGURE 3.2   **The Semantics of the `if-else` Statement**

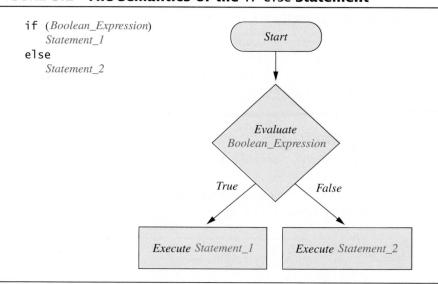

FIGURE 3.3   The Semantics of an if Statement Without an else

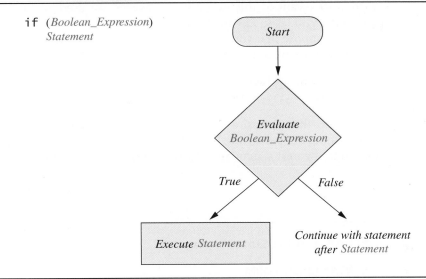

```
if (Boolean_Expression)
    Statement
```

If you omit the else part, the program simply skips *Statement* when the if statement's expression is false, as Figure 3.3 illustrates. For example, if your bank does not charge an overdraft penalty, the statement shown previously would be shortened to the following:

```
if (balance >= 0)
{
    System.out.println("Good for you. You earned interest.");
    balance = balance + (INTEREST_RATE * balance) / 12;
}
```

To see how this statement works, let's give it a little more context by adding some additional statements, as follows, where keyboard is a Scanner object of the usual sort:

```
System.out.print("Enter your balance $");
balance = keyboard.nextDouble();
if (balance >= 0)
{
    System.out.println("Good for you. You earned interest.");
    balance = balance + (INTEREST_RATE * balance) / 12;
}
System.out.println("Your new balance is $" + balance);
```

if without else
either performs
an action or does
not

Executing these statements when your checking account balance is $100 would produce the following interaction:

```
Enter your balance $100.00
Good for you. You earned interest.
Your new balance is $100.16
```

Since the expression balance >= 0 is true, you earn some interest. Exactly how much is irrelevant to this example. (However, we used an interest rate of 2 percent per year, as in Listing 3.1.)

Now suppose that your account is overdrawn and has a balance of minus $50. The output would then be as follows:

```
Enter your balance $ -50.00
Your new balance is $ -50.00
```

In this case, the expression balance >= 0 is false, but since there is no else part, nothing happens—the balance is not changed, and the program simply goes on to the next statement, which is an output statement.

RECAP `if-else` **Statements**

SYNTAX (BASIC FORM)

```
if (Boolean_Expression)
    Statement_1
else
    Statement_2
```

If the expression *Boolean_Expression* is true, *Statement_1* is executed; otherwise, *Statement_2* is executed.

EXAMPLE

```
if (time < limit)
    System.out.println("You made it.");
else
    System.out.println("You missed the deadline.");
```

SYNTAX (NO `else` PART)

```
if (Boolean_Expression)
    Statement
```

If the expression *Boolean_Expression* is true, *Statement* is executed; otherwise, *Statement* is ignored and the program goes on to the next statement.

EXAMPLE

```
if (weight > ideal)
    calorieAllotment = calorieAllotment - 500;
```

(continued)

COMPOUND STATEMENT ALTERNATIVES

Each of *Statement*, *Statement_1*, and *Statement_2* can be a compound statement. If you want to include several statements to be executed for a given branch of the expression, group them between braces, as in the following example:

```
if (balance >= 0)
{
    System.out.println("Good for you. You earned interest.");
    balance = balance + (INTEREST_RATE * balance) / 12;
}
else
{
    System.out.println("You will be charged a penalty.");
    balance = balance - OVERDRAWN_PENALTY;
}
```

Boolean Expressions

We have already been using simple boolean expressions in if-else statements. The simplest boolean expressions compare two smaller expressions, as in these examples:

```
balance >= 0
```

and

```
time < limit
```

Figure 3.4 shows the various Java **comparison operators** you can use to compare two expressions.

FIGURE 3.4   Java comparison operators

Math Notation	Name	Java Notation	Java Examples
=	Equal to	==	`balance == 0` `answer == 'y'`
≠	Not equal to	!=	`income != tax` `answer != 'y'`
>	Greater than	>	`expenses > income`
≥	Greater than or equal to	>=	`points >= 60`
<	Less than	<	`pressure < max`
≤	Less than or equal to	<=	`expenses <= income`

Note that a boolean expression need not begin and end with parentheses. However, a boolean expression does need to be enclosed in parentheses when it is used in an if-else statement.

GOTCHA   Using = Instead of = = to Test for Equality

The operator = is the assignment operator. Although this symbol means equality in mathematics, it does not have this meaning in Java. If you write if (x = y) instead of if (x == y) to test whether x and y are equal, you will get a syntax error message. ■

GOTCHA   Using = = or != to Compare Floating-Point Values

The previous chapter warned that floating-point numbers must be thought of as approximations. Numbers that have a fractional part can have an infinite number of digits. Since the computer can store only a limited number of digits in a fraction, floating-point numbers often are not exact. These approximations can get even less accurate after every operation in a calculation.

Thus, if you compute two floating-point values, they likely will not be exactly equal. Two values that are almost equal might be all you can hope for. Therefore, you should not use == to compare floating-point numbers. Using the != operator can cause the same problem.

Instead, to test two floating-point numbers for "equality," you see whether they differ by so little that it could only be due to their approximate nature. If so, you can conclude that they are "close enough" to be considered equal. ■

You can form more complicated boolean expressions from simpler ones by joining them with the **logical operator &&**, which is the Java version of *and*. For example, consider the following:

&& means and

```
if ((pressure > min) && (pressure < max))
    System.out.println("Pressure is OK.");
else
    System.out.println("Warning: Pressure is out of range.");
```

If the value of pressure is greater than min *and* the value of pressure is less than max, the output will be

```
Pressure is OK.
```

Otherwise, the output will be

```
Warning: Pressure is out of range.
```

Note that you cannot write

```
min < pressure < max          ◄──────────  Incorrect!
```

Instead, you must express each inequality separately and connect them with &&, as follows:

```
(pressure > min) && (pressure < max)
```

When you form a larger boolean expression by connecting two smaller expressions with &&, the entire larger expression is true only if both of the smaller expressions are true. If at least one of the smaller expressions is false, the larger expression is false. For example,

```
(pressure > min) && (pressure < max)
```

is true provided that both (pressure > min) and (pressure < max) are true; otherwise, the expression is false.

RECAP Use && for *and*

The symbol pair && means *and* in Java. You can use && to form a larger boolean expression out of two smaller boolean expressions.

SYNTAX

```
(Sub_Expression_1) && (Sub_Expression_2)
```

This expression is true if and only if both *Sub_Expression_1* and *Sub_Expression_2* are true.

EXAMPLE

```
if ((pressure > min) && (pressure < max))
    System.out.println("Pressure is OK.");
else
    System.out.println("Warning: Pressure is out of " +
                        "range.");
```

Instead of joining boolean expressions with *and*, you can join them with *or*. The Java way of expressing *or* is ||, which you create by typing two vertical lines. (The symbol | appears on some systems with a gap in the line.) The meaning of the operator || is essentially the same as the English word *or*. For example, consider

|| means *or*

```
if ((salary > expenses) || (savings > expenses))
    System.out.println("Solvent");
else
    System.out.println("Bankrupt");
```

If the value of salary is greater than the value of expenses *or* the value of savings is greater than the value of expenses *or both are true*, then the output will be Solvent; otherwise, the output will be Bankrupt.

RECAP Use || for *or*

The symbol pair || means *or* in Java. You can use || to form a larger boolean expression out of two smaller boolean expressions.

SYNTAX

(*Sub_Expression_1*) || (*Sub_Expression_2*)

This expression is true if either *Sub_Expression_1* or *Sub_Expression_2* is true or both are true.

EXAMPLE

```
if ((salary > expenses) || (savings > expenses))
    System.out.println("Solvent");
else
    System.out.println("Bankrupt");
```

As we noted earlier, the boolean expression in an if-else statement must be enclosed in parentheses. An if-else statement that uses the && operator is normally parenthesized as follows:

```
if ((pressure > min) && (pressure < max))
```

Parentheses clarify the meaning of a boolean expression

The parentheses in (pressure > min) and in (pressure < max) are not required, but we will normally include them to aid readability. Parentheses are used in expressions containing the operator || in the same way that they are used with &&.

In Java, you can negate a boolean expression by preceding it with !. For example,

```
if (!(number >= min))
    System.out.println("Too small");
else
    System.out.println("OK");
```

! means negate

If number is *not* greater than or equal to min, the output will be Too small; otherwise, the output will be OK.

You often can avoid using !, and you should do so when possible. For example, the previous if-else statement is equivalent to

FIGURE 3.5 Avoiding the Negation Operator

! (*A Op B*) Is Equivalent to (*A Op B*)	
<	>=
<=	>
>	<=
>=	<
==	!=
!=	==

```java
if (number < min)
    System.out.println("Too small");
else
    System.out.println("OK");
```

Figure 3.5 shows how to transform an expression of the form

```
!(A Comparison_Operator B)
```

to one without the negation operator.

If you can avoid using !, your programs should be easier to understand. However, we will encounter situations that use this operator naturally and clearly. In particular, we can use ! in the context of a loop—which we cover in the next chapter—to negate the value of a boolean variable, which we discuss later in this chapter.

RECAP Use ! for *not*

The symbol ! means *not* in Java. You can use ! to negate the value of a boolean expression. Doing so is more common when the expression is a boolean variable. Otherwise, you often can rewrite a boolean expression to avoid negating it.

SYNTAX

```
!Boolean_Expression
```

The value of this expression is the opposite of the value of the boolean expression: It is true if *Boolean_Expression* is false and false if *Boolean_Expression* is true.

(continued)

EXAMPLE

```java
if (!(number < 0))
    System.out.println("OK");
else
    System.out.println("Negative!");
```

VideoNote

Writing boolean expressions

Figure 3.6 summarizes the three logical operators. Java combines the values of true and false according to the rules given in the chart in Figure 3.7. For example, if boolean expression *A* is true, and boolean expression *B* is false, *A* && *B* evaluates to false.

Comparing Strings

To test whether two values of a primitive type—such as two numbers—are equal, you use the **equality operator** ==. But == has a different meaning when applied to objects. Recall that a string is an object of the class `String`, so == applied to two strings does not test whether the strings are equal. To see whether two strings have equal values, you must use the method `equals` rather than ==.

Use the `equals` method, not ==, to see whether two strings are equal

For example, the boolean expression `s1.equals(s2)` returns true if the strings `s1` and `s2` have equal values, and returns false otherwise. The program in Listing 3.2 illustrates the use of the method `equals`. Notice that the two expressions

```java
s1.equals(s2)
s2.equals(s1)
```

are equivalent.

Listing 3.2 also demonstrates the `String` method `equalsIgnoreCase`. This method behaves like `equals`, except that `equalsIgnoreCase` considers the uppercase and lowercase versions of the same letter to be the same. For example, "Hello" and "hello" are not equal because their first characters, 'H' and 'h', are different characters. But the method `equalsIgnoreCase` would consider them equal. For example, the following will display `Equal`:

```java
if ("Hello".equalsIgnoreCase("hello"))
    System.out.println("Equal");
```

FIGURE 3.6 Java Logical Operators

Name	Java Notation	Java Examples
Logical *and*	&&	(sum > min) && (sum < max)
Logical *or*	||	(answer == 'y') || (answer == 'Y')
Logical *not*	!	!(number < 0)

FIGURE 3.7 The Effect of the Boolean Operators && (*and*), || (*or*), and ! (*not*) on Boolean Values

Value of *A*	Value of *B*	Value of *A* && *B*	Value of *A* || *B*	Value of ! (*A*)
true	true	true	true	false
true	false	false	true	false
false	true	false	true	true
false	false	false	false	true

Notice that it is perfectly valid to use the quoted string "Hello" in the invocation of equalsIgnoreCase. A quoted string is an object of type String and has all the methods that any other object of type String has.

LISTING 3.2 Testing Strings for Equality (*part 1 of 2*)

```java
import java.util.Scanner;
public class StringEqualityDemo
{
    public static void main(String[] args)
    {
        String s1, s2;
        System.out.println("Enter two lines of text:");
        Scanner keyboard = new Scanner(System.in);
        s1 = keyboard.nextLine();
        s2 = keyboard.nextLine();

        if (s1.equals(s2))
            System.out.println("The two lines are equal.");
        else
            System.out.println("The two lines are not equal.");

        if (s2.equals(s1))
            System.out.println("The two lines are equal.");
        else
            System.out.println("The two lines are not equal.");

        if (s1.equalsIgnoreCase(s2))
            System.out.println(
                    "But the lines are equal, ignoring case.");
        else
            System.out.println(
                    "Lines are not equal, even ignoring case.");
    }
}
```

These two invocations of the method equals are equivalent.

(*continued*)

LISTING 3.2 **Testing Strings for Equality** *(part 2 of 2)*

Sample Screen Output

```
Enter two lines of text:
Java is not coffee.
Java is NOT COFFEE.
The two lines are not equal.
The two lines are not equal.
But the lines are equal, ignoring case.
```

GOTCHA   Using == with Strings

When applied to two strings (or any two objects), the operator == tests whether they are stored in the same memory location. We will discuss that concept in Chapter 5, but for now, we need only realize that == does not test whether two strings have the same values.

For the kinds of applications we consider in this chapter, using == to test for equality of strings can appear to give you the correct answer. However, doing so is a dangerous habit to acquire. You should always use the method equals rather than == to test strings. Analogous comments apply to the other comparison operators, such as <, and the method compareTo, as you will soon see. ■

RECAP The Methods equals and equalsIgnoreCase

When testing strings for equality, use either of the methods equals or equalsIgnoreCase.

SYNTAX

```
String.equals(Other_String)
String.equalsIgnoreCase(Other_String)
```

EXAMPLE

```
String s1 = keyboard.next(); //keyboard is a Scanner object
if (s1.equals("Hello"))
    System.out.println("The string is Hello.");
else
    System.out.println("The string is not Hello.");
```

Programs frequently need to compare two strings to see which is alphabetically before the other. Just as you should not use the == operator to test for equality of strings, you should not use operators such as < and > to test for alphabetic order. Instead you should use the `String` method `compareTo`, which we described in Figure 2.5 of Chapter 2.

Use the `compareTo` method to compare strings

The method `compareTo` tests two strings to determine their **lexicographic order.** Lexicographic order is similar to alphabetic order and is sometimes, but not always, the same as alphabetic order. In lexicographic ordering, the letters and other characters are ordered according to their Unicode sequence, which is shown in the appendix of this book.

If `s1` and `s2` are two variables of type `String` that have been given `String` values, the method call

```
s1.compareTo(s2)
```

compares the lexicographic ordering of the two strings and returns

- A negative number if `s1` comes before `s2`
- Zero if the two strings are equal
- A positive number if `s1` comes after `s2`

Thus, the boolean expression

```
s1.compareTo(s2) < 0
```

is true if `s1` comes before `s2` in lexicographic order and false otherwise. For example, the following will produce correct output:

```
if (s1.compareTo(s2) < 0)
    System.out.println(s1 + " precedes " + s2 "+"
                          "in lexicographic ordering");
else if (s1.compareTo(s2) > 0)
    System.out.println(s1 + " follows " + s2 "+"
                          "in lexicographic ordering");
else//s1.compareTo(s2) == 0
    System.out.println(s1 + " equals " + s2);
```

But suppose that we want to check for alphabetic ordering, not lexicographic ordering. If you look at a Unicode chart, you will see that *all* uppercase letters come before *all* lowercase letters in lexicographic order. For example, `'Z'` comes before `'a'` lexicographically. So when comparing two strings consisting of a mix of lowercase and uppercase letters, lexicographic order and alphabetic order are not the same. However, in Unicode, all the lowercase letters are in alphabetic order and all the uppercase letters are in alphabetic order. So for any two strings of all lowercase letters, lexicographic order is the same as ordinary alphabetic order. Similarly, for any two strings of all uppercase letters, lexicographic order is the same as ordinary alphabetic order. Thus, to compare two strings of letters for ordinary alphabetic order, you need only convert the two strings to either all uppercase letters or all lowercase letters and then compare them for lexicographic ordering. Let's look at the Java details.

Suppose we arbitrarily convert our two strings of letters, s1 and s2, to all uppercase. We then use compareTo to test the uppercase versions of s1 and s2 for lexicographic ordering. The following will produce correct output:

```java
String upperS1 = s1.toUpperCase();
String upperS2 = s2.toUpperCase();
if (upperS1.compareTo(upperS2) < 0)
    System.out.println(s1 + " precedes " + s2 "+"
                        "in ALPHABETIC ordering");
else if (upperS1.compareTo(upperS2) > 0)
    System.out.println(s1 + " follows " + s2 "+"
                        "in ALPHABETIC ordering");
else//s1.compareTo(s2) == 0
    System.out.println(s1 + " equals " + s2 + "
                        ignoring case");
```

■ **PROGRAMMING TIP**   Alphabetic Order

To see whether two strings of letters are in alphabetic order, you must ensure that all the letters have the same case before using the method compareTo to compare the strings. You can use either of the String methods toUpperCase or toLowerCase to accomplish this. If you were to omit this step, using compareTo would compare lexicographic order instead of alphabetic order.

■

SELF-TEST QUESTIONS

1. Suppose goals is a variable of type int. Write an if-else statement that displays the word Wow if the value of the variable goals is greater than 10 and displays the words Oh Well if the value of goals is at most 10.

2. Suppose goals and errors are variables of type int. Write an if-else statement that displays the word Wow if the value of the variable goals is greater than 10 and the value of errors is 0. Otherwise, the if-else statement should display the words Oh Well.

3. Suppose salary and deductions are variables of type double that have been given values. Write an if-else statement that displays OK and sets the variable net equal to salary minus deductions, provided that salary is at least as large as deductions. If, however, salary is less than deductions, the if-else statement should simply display the words No Way but not change the value of any variables.

4. Suppose `speed` and `visibility` are variables of type `int`. Write an `if` statement that sets the variable `speed` equal to 25 and displays the word `Caution`, provided the value of `speed` is greater than 25 and the value of `visibility` is under 20. There is no `else` part.

5. Suppose `salary` and `bonus` are variables of type `double`. Write an `if-else` statement that displays the word `OK` provided that either `salary` is greater than or equal to `MIN_SALARY` or `bonus` is greater than or equal to `MIN_BONUS`. Otherwise, it should display `Too low`. `MIN_SALARY` and `MIN_BONUS` are named constants.

6. Assume that `nextWord` is a `String` variable that has been given a value consisting entirely of letters. Write some Java code that displays the message `First half of the alphabet`, provided that `nextWord` precedes the letter *N* in alphabetic ordering. If `nextWord` does not precede *N* in alphabetic ordering, your code should display `Second half of the alphabet`. Be careful when you represent the letter *N*. You will need a `String` value, as opposed to a `char` value.

7. Suppose `x1` and `x2` are two variables that have been given values. How do you test whether the values are equal when the variables are of type `int`? How about when the variables are of type `String`?

Nested `if-else` Statements

An `if-else` statement can contain any sort of statements within it. In particular, you can **nest** one `if-else` statement within another `if-else` statement, as illustrated by the following:

```
if (balance >= 0)
if (INTEREST_RATE >= 0)
    balance = balance + (INTEREST_RATE * balance) / 12;
else
    System.out.println("Cannot have a negative interest.");
else
    balance = balance - OVERDRAWN_PENALTY;
```

Any action within an `if-else` statement can be another `if-else` statement

If the value of `balance` is greater than or equal to zero, the entire following `if-else` statement is executed:

```
if (INTEREST_RATE >= 0)
    balance = balance + (INTEREST_RATE * balance) / 12;
else
    System.out.println("Cannot have a negative interest.");
```

The nested statements can be made clearer by adding braces, as follows:

```
if (balance >= 0)
{
    if (INTEREST_RATE >= 0)
        balance = balance + (INTEREST_RATE * balance)/12;
    else
        System.out.println("Cannot have a negative interest.");
}
else
    balance = balance - OVERDRAWN_PENALTY;
```

In this case, the braces are an aid to clarity but are not, strictly speaking, needed.

In other cases, braces are needed. If we omit an `else`, for example, things get a bit trickier. The following two statements differ in appearance only in that one has a pair of braces, but they do *not* have the same meaning:

```
//First Version - Braces
if (balance >= 0)
{
    if (INTEREST_RATE >= 0)
        balance = balance + (INTEREST_RATE * balance)/12;
}
else
    balance = balance - OVERDRAWN_PENALTY;

//Second Version - No Braces
if (balance >= 0)
    if (INTEREST_RATE >= 0)
        balance = balance + (INTEREST_RATE * balance)/12;
else
    balance = balance - OVERDRAWN_PENALTY;
```

In an `if-else` statement, each `else` is paired with the nearest preceding unmatched `if`. The second version—without braces—pairs the `else` with the second `if`, despite the misleading indentation. Thus, the meaning is

```
//Equivalent to Second Version
if (balance >= 0)
{
    if (INTEREST_RATE >= 0)
        balance = balance + (INTEREST_RATE * balance)/12;
    else
        balance = balance  OVERDRAWN_PENALTY;
}
```

To clarify the difference a bit more, consider what happens when `balance` is greater than or equal to zero. In the first version, the following action occurs:

```
if (INTEREST_RATE >= 0)
    balance = balance + (INTEREST_RATE * balance)/12;
```

If `balance` is not greater than or equal to zero in the first version, the following action is taken instead:

```
balance = balance - OVERDRAWN_PENALTY;
```

In the second version, if `balance` is greater than or equal to zero, the following entire `if-else` statement is executed:

```
if (INTEREST_RATE >= 0)
    balance = balance + (INTEREST_RATE * balance)/12;
else
    balance = balance - OVERDRAWN_PENALTY;
```

If `balance` is not greater than or equal to zero in the second version, no action is taken.

■ **PROGRAMMING TIP**   Matching `else` and `if`

In an `if-else` statement, each `else` is paired with the nearest preceding unmatched `if`. Use indentation that is consistent with the meaning of the statement to clarify your intent. But remember that the compiler ignores indentation. When in doubt, use braces to make the statement's meaning explicit. ■

Multibranch `if-else` Statements

If you have the ability to branch two ways, you have the ability to branch four ways. Just branch two ways and have each of those two outcomes branch two ways. Using this trick, you can nest `if-else` statements to produce multiway branches that result in any number of possibilities. Programmers have a standard way of doing this. In fact, it has become so standard that it is treated as if it were a new kind of branching statement rather than just several nested `if-else` statements. Let's start with an example.

Suppose `balance` is a variable that holds your checking account balance, and you want to know whether your balance is positive, negative (overdrawn), or zero. To avoid any questions about accuracy, let's say `balance` is the number of dollars in your account, with the cents ignored. That is, let's assume that `balance` is of type `int`. To find out if your balance is positive, negative, or zero, you could use the following nested `if-else` statement:

```
if (balance > 0)
    System.out.println("Positive balance");
else
    if (balance < 0)
        System.out.println("Negative balance");
    else
        if (balance == 0)
            System.out.println("Zero balance");
```

A multibranch
if-else
statement offers
a choice among
several actions

An equivalent, clearer, and preferred way to write this statement is as follows:

```java
if (balance > 0)
    System.out.println("Positive balance");
else if (balance < 0)
    System.out.println("Negative balance");
else if (balance == 0)
    System.out.println("Zero balance");
```

We call this form a **multibranch** if-else statement. This statement is really an ordinary nested if-else statement, but the way we have indented it reflects the way we think about multibranch if-else statements.

When a multibranch if-else statement is executed, the computer tests the boolean expressions one after the other, starting from the top. When the first true boolean expression is found, the statement following that true boolean expression is executed. For example, if balance is greater than zero, the preceding code will display Positive balance. If balance is less than zero, then Negative balance is displayed. Finally, if balance is equal to zero, the code displays Zero balance. Exactly one of the three possible outputs will be produced, depending on the value of the variable balance.

In this first example, we had three possibilities, but you can have any number of possibilities; just add more else-if parts. Also, the possibilities in this example were **mutually exclusive.** That is, only one possibility is true at a given time. However, you can use any boolean expressions, even if they are not mutually exclusive. If more than one boolean expression is true, only the action associated with the first true boolean expression is executed. A multibranch if-else statement never performs more than one action.

Only one action
occurs

If none of the boolean expressions is true, nothing happens. However, it is a good practice to add an else clause—without any if—at the end that will be executed in case none of the boolean expressions is true. In fact, we can rewrite our original checking-account example in this way. We know that, if balance is neither positive nor negative, it must be zero. So we do not need the last test:

```java
if (balance == 0)
```

Thus, our previous multibranch if-else statement is equivalent to the following one:

Write a final
else clause

```java
if (balance > 0)
    System.out.println("Positive balance");
else if (balance < 0)
    System.out.println("Negative balance");
else
    System.out.println("Zero balance");
```

VideoNote
Using multibranch if-else statements

RECAP **Multibranch** if-else **Statement**

SYNTAX

```
if (Boolean_Expression_1)
    Action_1
else if (Boolean_Expression_2)
    Action_2
       .
       .
       .
else if (Boolean_Expression_n)
    Action_n
else
    Default_Action
```

The actions are Java statements. The boolean expressions are tested one after the other, starting from the top one. As soon as a boolean expression is found to be true, the action following that true boolean expression is executed, and subsequent tests and actions are ignored. The *Default_Action* is executed if none of the boolean expressions is true. Figure 3.8 illustrates the semantics of this form of if-else statement.

EXAMPLE

```
if (number < 10)
    System.out.println("number < 10");
else if (number < 50)
    System.out.println("number >= 10 and number < 50");
else if (number < 100)
    System.out.println("number >= 50 and number < 100");
else
    System.out.println("number >= 100.");
```

PROGRAMMING EXAMPLE   Assigning Letter Grades

Listing 3.3 contains a program that assigns letter grades according to the traditional rule that a score of 90 or above is an A, a score in the 80s is a B, and so forth.

Note that, as with any multibranch if-else statement, the boolean expressions are evaluated in order, and so the second boolean expression is not checked unless the first boolean expression is found to be false. Thus,

FIGURE 3.8 The Semantics of a Multibranch `if-else` Statement

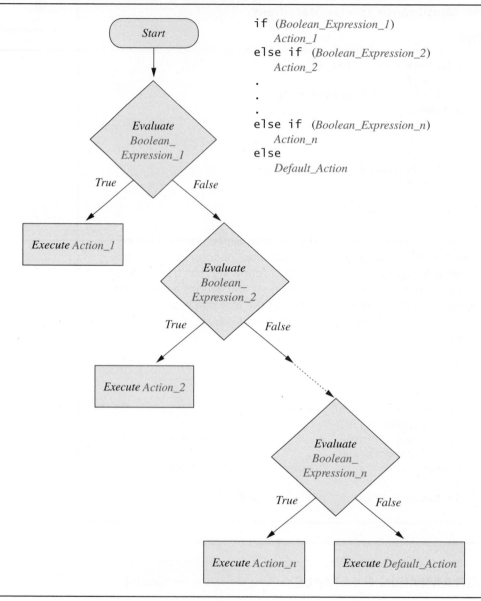

```
if (Boolean_Expression_1)
    Action_1
else if (Boolean_Expression_2)
    Action_2
    .
    .
    .
else if (Boolean_Expression_n)
    Action_n
else
    Default_Action
```

when and if the second boolean expression is checked, we know that the first boolean expression is false, and therefore we know that `score` is less than 90.

Thus, the multibranch `if-else` statement would have the same meaning if we replaced

(score >= 80)

with

```
((score >= 80) && (score < 90))
```

Using the same sort of reasoning on each boolean expression, we see that the multibranch if-else statement in Listing 3.3 is equivalent to the following:

```
if (score >= 90)
    grade = 'A';
else if ((score >= 80) && (score < 90))
    grade = 'B';
else if ((score >= 70) && (score < 80))
    grade = 'C';
else if ((score >= 60) && (score < 70))
    grade = 'D';
else
    grade = 'F';
```

Most programmers would use the version in Listing 3.3, because it is a bit more efficient and is more elegant, but either version is acceptable.

LISTING 3.3 Assigning Letter Grades Using a Multibranch if-else Statement *(part 1 of 2)*

```java
import java.util.Scanner;
public class Grader
{
    public static void main(String[] args)
    {
        int score;
        char grade;

        System.out.println("Enter your score: ");
        Scanner keyboard = new Scanner(System.in);
        score = keyboard.nextInt();

        if (score >= 90)
            grade = 'A';
        else if (score >= 80)
            grade = 'B';
        else if (score >= 70)
            grade = 'C';
        else if (score >= 60)
            grade = 'D';
        else
            grade = 'F';
        System.out.println("Score = " + score);
        System.out.println("Grade = " + grade);
    }
}
```

(continued)

LISTING 3.3   **Assigning Letter Grades Using a**
Multibranch `if-else` **Statement** *(part 2 of 2)*

Sample Screen Output

```
Enter your score:
85
Score = 85
Grade = B
```

CASE STUDY Body Mass Index

The body mass index (BMI) is used to estimate the risk of weight-related problems based on a subject's height and mass. It was designed by the mathematician Adolphe Quetelet in the 1800s and is sometimes referred to as the Quetelet index. The BMI is computed as

$$BMI = \frac{mass}{height^2}$$

In this formula, mass is in kilograms and height is in meters. The health risk associated with a BMI value is

- Underweight < 18.5
- Normal weight ≥ 18.5 and < 25
- Overweight ≥ 25 and < 30
- Obese ≥ 30

In this case study the users input their weight in pounds and height in feet and inches. The program then outputs the BMI and associated health risk. To do this we must first make our program convert from pounds to kilograms. One kilogram is 2.2 pounds. Additionally, the program must convert a height in feet and inches to meters. If we convert the height to all inches, then we can multiply by 0.0254 to convert inches into meters.

Algorithm to compute BMI

1. Read the weight in pounds into the variable pounds.

2. Read the height in feet into the variable feet.

3. Read the additional height in inches into the variable inches.

4. Set the variable heightMeters to the value ((feet * 12) + inches) * 0.0254.

5. Set the variable mass to the value pounds / 2.2.

6. Set the variable BMI to the value mass / (heightMeters * heightMeters).

7. Output BMI.

8. If BMI < 18.5 then output "Underweight."

9. Else if BMI ≥ 18.5 and BMI < 25 then output "Normal weight."

10. Else if BMI ≥ 25 and BMI < 30 then output "Overweight."

11. Otherwise, output "Obese."

This algorithm will work but it can be simplified a bit. If the BMI is less than 18.5, then the condition on line 8 will be true and the program will output "Underweight." Line 9 is only evaluated if line 8 is false. This means that if the program reaches line 9 we know that the BMI is not less than 18.5. In other words, the BMI is greater than or equal to 18.5. This makes the check on line 9 for the BMI greater than or equal to 18.5 redundant. The same condition applies to line 10. Consequently, we can change lines 9 and 10 of the algorithm to

9. Else if BMI < 25 then output "Normal weight."

10. Else if BMI < 30 then output "Overweight."

The algorithm translated to code is shown in Listing 3.4. The variables `heightMeters`, `mass`, and `BMI` are declared as `double` for additional precision after multiplying by the conversion factors.

LISTING 3.4   A Body Mass Index Calculation Program (*part 1 of 2*)

```java
import java.util.Scanner;
public class BMI
{
    public static void main(String[] args)
    {
        Scanner keyboard = new Scanner(System.in);
        int pounds, feet, inches;
        double heightMeters, mass, BMI;
        System.out.println("Enter your weight in pounds.");
        pounds = keyboard.nextInt();
        System.out.println("Enter your height in feet" +
            "followed by a space" +
            "then additional inches.");
        feet = keyboard.nextInt();
        inches = keyboard.nextInt();
        heightMeters = ((feet * 12) + inches) * 0.0254;
        mass = (pounds / 2.2);
        BMI = mass / (heightMeters * heightMeters);
        System.out.println("Your BMI is " + BMI);
        System.out.print("Your risk category is ");
        if (BMI < 18.5)
            System.out.println("Underweight.");
        else if (BMI < 25)
            System.out.println("Normal weight.");
```

(continued)

LISTING 3.4   A Body Mass Index Calculation Program *(part 2 of 2)*

```
        else if (BMI < 30)
            System.out.println("Overweight.");
        else
            System.out.println("Obese.");
    }
}
```

Sample Screen Output

```
Enter your weight in pounds.
150
Enter your height in feet followed
by a space then additional inches.
5 5
Your BMI is 25.013498117367398
Your risk category is Overweight.
```

SELF-TEST QUESTIONS

8. What output is produced by the following code?

```
int time = 2, tide = 3;
if (time + tide > 6)
    System.out.println("Time and tide wait for no one.");
else
    System.out.println("Time and tide wait for me.");
```

9. Suppose you change the code in the previous question so that the first line is the following:

```
int time = 4, tide = 3;
```

What output would be produced?

10. What output is produced by the following code?

```
int time = 2, tide = 3;
if (time + tide > 6)
    System.out.println("Time and tide wait for no one.");
else if (time + tide > 5)
    System.out.println("Time and tide wait for someone.");
else if (time + tide > 4)
    System.out.println("Time and tide wait for everyone.");
else
    System.out.println("Time and tide wait for me.");
```

11. Suppose number is a variable of type int that has been given a value. Write a multibranch if-else statement that displays the word High if number is greater than 10, Low if number is less than 5, and So-so if number is anything else.

The Conditional Operator (*Optional*)

To allow compatibility with older programming styles, Java includes an operator that is a notational variant on certain forms of the if-else statement. For example, the statement

```java
if (n1 > n2)
    max = n1;
else
    max = n2;
```

can be expressed as follows:

```java
max = (n1 > n2) ? n1 : n2;
```

Together, the ? and : on the right side of this assignment statement are known as the **conditional operator,** or **ternary operator.** The **conditional operator expression**

```java
(n1 > n2) ? n1 : n2;
```

starts with a boolean expression followed by a ? and then two expressions separated by a colon. If the boolean expression is true, the first of the two expressions is returned; otherwise, the second of the two expressions is returned.

As illustrated here, the most common use of the conditional operator is to set a variable to one of two different values, depending on a boolean condition. Be sure to note that a conditional expression always returns a value and so is equivalent to only certain special kinds of if-else statements.

Another example may help to illustrate the conditional operator. Suppose that an employee's weekly pay is the number of hours worked multiplied by the hourly wage. However, if the employee works more than 40 hours, the overtime is paid at 1.5 times the usual hourly rate. The following if-else statement performs this computation:

```java
if (hoursWork <= 40)
    pay = hoursWorked * payRate;
else
    pay = 40 * payRate + 1.5 * payRate * (hoursWorked - 40);
```

This statement can be expressed by using the conditional operator, as follows:

```java
pay = (hoursWorked <= 40) ? (hoursWorked * payRate) :
(40 * payRate + 1.5 * payRate * (hoursWorked - 40));
```

The exit Method

Sometimes your program can encounter a situation that makes continuing execution pointless. In such cases, you can end your program by calling the exit method, as follows:

```java
System.exit(0);
```

The preceding statement will end a Java program as soon as it is executed. For example, consider the following code:

```java
if (numberOfWinners == 0)
{
    System.out.println("Error: Dividing by zero.");
    System.exit(0);
}
else
{
    oneShare = payoff / numberOfWinners;
    System.out.println("Each winner will receive $" + oneShare);
}
```

This code will normally display the share that each winner should receive. However, if the number of winners is zero, a division by zero would be an invalid operation. To avoid this division by zero, the program checks the number of winners and, if it is zero, calls the `exit` method to end execution.

`System` is a class in the Java Class Library that is automatically available to your programs without requiring an `import` statement; `exit` is a method in the class `System`. The number 0 given as the argument to `System.exit` is returned to the operating system. Most operating systems use 0 to indicate a normal termination of the program and 1 to indicate an abnormal termination of the program (just the opposite of what most people would guess). Thus, if your `System.exit` statement ends the program normally, the argument should be 0. In this case, *normal* means that the program did not violate any system or other important constraints. It does not mean that the program did what you wanted it to do. So you would almost always use 0 as the argument.

RECAP **The `exit` Method**

An invocation of the `exit` method ends the program. The normal form for an invocation to `exit` is

    System.exit(0);

As mentioned in the previous chapter, any program that uses `JOptionPane` to create dialog boxes must call this method to end its execution. Other programs typically do not call `exit`, doing so only in unusual situations.

3.2 THE TYPE `boolean`

He who would distinguish the true from the false must have an adequate idea of what is true and false.

—BENEDICT SPINOZA, *ETHICS*

Truth is truth

To the end of reckoning.

—WILLIAM SHAKESPEARE, *MEASURE FOR MEASURE*

The type boolean is a primitive type, just like the types int, double, and char. As with these other types, you can have values of type boolean, constants of type boolean, variables of type boolean, and expressions of type boolean. However, the type boolean specifies only two values: true and false. You can use the two values true and false in a program, just as you use numeric constants, such as 2 and 3.45, and character constants, such as 'A'.

Boolean Variables

Boolean variables can be used, among other things, to make your program easier to read. For example, a program might contain the following statement, where systemsAreOK is a boolean variable that is true if, in fact, the launch systems are ready to go:

```
if (systemsAreOK)
    System.out.println("Initiate launch sequence.");
else
    System.out.println("Abort launch sequence.");
```

If you do not use a boolean variable, the preceding code is likely to read something like the following:

```
if ((temperature <= 100) && (thrust >= 12000) &&
    (cabinPressure > 30))
    System.out.println("Initiate launch sequence.");
else
    System.out.println("Abort launch sequence.");
```

Clearly, the boolean variable systemsAreOK makes the first version easier for a human being to understand. Of course, your program needs to set the value of this variable in some way. As you will see, that is easy to do.

A boolean expression such as number > 0 evaluates to one of the two values true or false. For example, if number > 0 is true, the following statement displays The number is positive:

```
if (number > 0)
    System.out.println("The number is positive");
else
    System.out.println("The number is negative or zero");
```

If, on the other hand, number > 0 is false, the output is The number is negative or zero. The meaning of a boolean expression like number > 0 is a bit easier to understand within a context, such as an if-else statement. However, when programming with boolean variables, you need to think about a boolean expression more or less without a context. A boolean expression can be evaluated and can produce a value of `true` or `false` without reference to any context such as an `if-else` statement.

A boolean variable can be given the value of a boolean expression by using an assignment statement, in the same way that you use an assignment statement to set the value of any other type of variable. For example, the following sets the value of the boolean variable `isPositive` to `false`:

```java
int number = -5;
boolean isPositive = (number > 0);
```

The parentheses are not needed, but they make the statement a bit easier to read.

Once a boolean variable has a value, you can use the variable just as you would use any other boolean expression. For example,

```java
boolean isPositive = (number > 0);
if (isPositive)
    System.out.println("The number is positive");
else
    System.out.println("The number is negative or zero");
```

is equivalent to our previous `if-else` statement.

Of course, this is just a toy example, but you might use something like it if the value of `number`, and therefore the value of the boolean expression, might change. Such is more likely to be the case in the context of a loop, which we will study in the next chapter.

More complicated boolean expressions can be used in the same way. For example, our opening example that checks whether we are ready for a launch would be preceded by a statement such as

```java
boolean systemsAreOK = (temperature <= 100) &&
(thrust >= 12000) && (cabinPressure > 30)
```

FAQ Why can I write if (b)... instead of if (b == true)... when b is a boolean variable?

The boolean variable b is a boolean expression. So is the expression b == true. If b is true, both of these expressions are true. If b is false, both expressions are false. Thus, you can use these two expressions interchangeably.

Precedence Rules

Java evaluates boolean expressions using the same strategy that it uses to evaluate arithmetic expressions. For example, if the integer variable `score` is 95 in the expression

```java
(score >= 80) && (score < 90)
```

the first subexpression (`score >= 80`) is true, but the second subexpression (`score < 90`) is false. So the entire expression is equivalent to

```
true && false
```

As you saw earlier in this chapter, Java combines the values of `true` and `false` according to the rules given in Figure 3.7. So the preceding expression evaluates to `false`.

Just as when writing arithmetic expressions, it is usually best to use parentheses to indicate the order of operations within boolean expressions. However, if you omit parentheses, Java performs the operations in the order specified by the precedence rules shown in Figure 3.9. This figure is an augmented version of Figure 2.2 and shows all the operators you are likely to use for some time. A more complete list of precedence rules is given inside the cover of this book. As we mentioned in Chapter 2, operators listed higher on the list have a higher precedence. When the order of two operations is not dictated by parentheses, Java considers their precedence and performs the operation with the higher precedence before performing the other one. Some operators have equal precedence, in which case they are performed in order of appearance: Binary operators of equal precedence are performed in left-to-right order. Unary operators of equal precedence are performed in right-to-left order. Recall that a unary operator has only one operand—one thing that it applies to. A binary operator has two operands.

Let's consider an example. The following is written in rather poor style because it lacks parentheses, but the computer has no problem with it:

```
score < min / 2 - 10 || score > 90
```

FIGURE 3.9 Operator Precedence

Highest Precedence

First: the unary operators $+$, $-$, $++$, $--$, and `!`

Second: the binary arithmetic operators $*$, $/$, $\%$

Third: the binary arithmetic operators $+$, $-$

Fourth: the boolean operators $<$, $>$, $<=$, $>=$

Fifth: the boolean operators $==$, $!=$

Sixth: the boolean operator $\&$

Seventh: the boolean operator $|$

Eighth: the boolean operator $\&\&$

Ninth: the boolean operator $||$

Lowest Precedence

Of all the operators in the expression, the division operator has the highest precedence, and so the division is performed first. We indicate that fact by adding parentheses, as follows:

Parentheses clarify operator precedence in a boolean expression

```
score <(min / 2) - 10 || score > 90
```

Of the remaining operators in the expression, the subtraction operator has the highest precedence, and so the subtraction is performed next:

```
score <(min / 2) - 10) || score > 90
```

Of the remaining operators in the expression, the comparison operators > and < have the highest precedence and so are performed next. Because > and < have equal precedence, they are performed in left-to-right order:

```
(score <((min / 2) - 10)) || (score > 90)
```

Finally, the results of the two comparisons are combined with the operator ||, since it has the lowest precedence.

We have produced a parenthesized version of the expression by using the precedence rules. To the computer, this version and the original unparenthesized version are equivalent. You should include most parentheses in order to make your arithmetic and boolean expressions easier to understand. However, you can safely omit parentheses when the expression contains a simple sequence of &&s or of ||s. For example, the following is good style even though a few parentheses are omitted:

```
(temperature > 95) || (rainFall > 20) || (humidity >= 60)
```

You might conclude that the three comparisons in the previous expression occur first and then are combined with the operator ||. But the rules are a bit more complicated than what you have seen so far. Suppose that the value of `temperature` is 99. In this case we know that the entire boolean expression is true no matter what the values of `rainFall` and `humidity` are. We know this because `true || true` is true and so is `true || false`. So regardless of whether `rainFall > 20` is true, the value of

```
(temperature > 95) || (rainFall > 20)
```

is bound to be true. By a similar reasoning, we conclude that

```
true || (humidity >= 60)
```

is true regardless of whether `humidity >= 60` is true.

Java uses short-circuit evaluation

Java evaluates the first subexpression, and if that is enough information to learn the value of the whole expression, it does not evaluate subsequent subexpressions. So in this example, Java never bothers to evaluate the subexpressions involving `rainFall` and `humidity`. This way of evaluating an expression is called **short-circuit evaluation,** or sometimes **lazy evaluation,** and is what Java does with expressions involving || or &&.

Now let's look at an expression containing &&. We'll give the boolean expression some context by placing it in an `if-else` statement:

```
if ( (assignmentsDone > 0) &&
    ((totalScore / assignmentsDone) > 60) )
    System.out.println("Good work.");
else
    System.out.println("Work harder.");
```

Suppose `assignmentsDone` has a value of zero. Then the first subexpression is `false`. Since both `false && true` and `false && false` are false, the entire boolean expression is false, regardless of whether the second expression is true or false. Therefore, Java does not bother to evaluate the second subexpression:

```
(totalScore / assignmentsDone) > 60
```

In this case, not evaluating the second subexpression makes a big difference, because the second subexpression includes a division by zero. If Java had tried to evaluate the second subexpression, it would have produced a run-time error. By using short-circuit evaluation, Java has prevented this error.

Java also allows you to ask for **complete evaluation.** In complete evaluation, when two expressions are joined by an *and* or an *or* operator, both subexpressions are *always evaluated*, and then the truth tables are used to obtain the value of the final expression. To obtain a complete evaluation in Java, you use & rather than && for *and* and use | in place of || for *or*.

Java also offers complete evaluation

In most situations, short-circuit evaluation and complete evaluation give the same result, but as you have just seen, there are times when short-circuit evaluation can avoid a run-time error. There are also some situations in which complete evaluation is preferred, but we will not use those techniques in this book. We will always use && and || and so will obtain short-circuit evaluation.

REMEMBER Short-Circuit Evaluation

For a boolean expression of the form *Expr_A* || *Expr_B*, if *Expr_A* is true, Java concludes that the entire expression is true without evaluating *Expr_B*. Likewise, for an expression of the form *Expr_A* && *Expr_B*, if *Expr_A* is false, Java concludes that the entire expression is false without evaluating *Expr_B*.

Input and Output of Boolean Values

The values `true` and `false` of the type `boolean` can be read as input or written as output in the same way as values of the other primitive types, such as `int` and `double`. For example, consider the following fragment from a Java program:

```
boolean booleanVar = false;
System.out.println(booleanVar);
System.out.println("Enter a boolean value:");
Scanner keyboard = new Scanner(System.in);
booleanVar = keyboard.nextBoolean();
System.out.println("You entered " + booleanVar);
```

This code could produce the following interaction with the user:

```
false
Enter a boolean value:
true
You entered true
```

As you can see from this example, the class Scanner has a method named next Boolean that will read a single boolean value. For this input method, you may spell true and false using either uppercase or lowercase letters or a combination of both. In a Java program, the constants true or false must be spelled with all lowercase letters, but the input method nextBoolean is more forgiving.

myprogramminglab

SELF-TEST QUESTIONS

12. What output is produced by the following statements?

```
int number = 7;
boolean isPositive = (number > 0);
if (number > 0);
    number = -100;
if (isPositive)
    System.out.println("Positive.");
else
    System.out.println("Not positive.");
    System.out.println(number);
```

13. What output is produced by the following statements?

```
System.out.println(false);
System.out.println(7 < 0);
System.out.println(7 > 0);
int n = 7;
System.out.println(n > 0);
```

14. What output is produced by the following statements?

```
System.out.println(true &&false);
System.out.println(true || false);
System.out.println(false && (x > 0));
System.out.println(true || (x > 0));
```

3.3 THE `switch` STATEMENT

Each decision we make, each action we take, is born out of an intention.

—SHARON SALZBERG

When a multiway `if-else` statement has many possible outcomes, it can be hard to read. If the choice is based on the value of an integer or character expression, the **switch statement** can make your code easier to understand.

The `switch` statement begins with the keyword `switch` followed by a **controlling expression** in parentheses:

```
switch (Controlling_Expression)
{
    . . .
}
```

The `switch`
statement offers
a choice of
actions according
to the value of
a controlling
expression

The body of the statement is always enclosed in a pair of braces. Listing 3.5 shows a sample `switch` statement, whose controlling expression is the variable `numberOfBabies`. Within the braces is a list of cases, each case consisting of the keyword `case` followed by a constant—called a **case label**—then a colon, and then a list of statements, which are the actions for that case:

```
case Case_Label:
    List_of_Statements
```

When the `switch` statement is executed, the controlling expression—`numberOfBabies` in this example—is evaluated. The list of alternatives is then searched until a case label that matches the value of the controlling expression is found, and the action associated with that label is executed. You cannot have duplicate case labels, since that would produce an ambiguous situation.

Notice that the action for each case in Listing 3.5 ends with a **break statement,** which consists of the word `break` followed by a semicolon. When execution reaches a `break` statement, the `switch` statement's execution ends. If no `break` statement is found within the statements for a particular case, execution continues on with the next case until either a `break` statement is encountered or the end of the `switch` statement is reached.

Sometimes you want a case without a `break` statement. You cannot have multiple labels in one case, but you can list cases one after the other so they all produce the same action. For example, in Listing 3.5, both case 4 and case 5 produce the same case action, because case 4 has no `break` statement; in fact, case 4 has no action statements at all.

If no case matches the value of the controlling expression, the **default case**—which begins with the keyword `default` and a colon—is executed. However, the default case is optional. If you omit the default case and no match is found to any of the cases, no action is taken. Although the default case is optional, you are encouraged to always use it. If you think your cases cover all the possibilities without a default case, you can insert an error message as the default case. You never know when you might have missed some obscure case.

A default case
is optional but
useful

LISTING 3.5 A `switch` Statement *(part 1 of 2)*

```java
import java.util.Scanner;
public class MultipleBirths
{
    public static void main(String[] args)
    {
        int numberOfBabies;
        System.out.print("Enter number of babies: ");
        Scanner keyboard = new Scanner(System.in);
        numberOfBabies = keyboard.nextInt();

        switch (numberOfBabies)          ◄———— Controlling expression
        {
          case 1:            ◄————————— Case label
              System.out.println("Congratulations.");
              break;
          case 2:
              System.out.println("Wow. Twins.");
              break;         ◄——————————— break statement
          case 3:
              System.out.println("Wow. Triplets.");
              break;
          case 4:            ◄——————————— Case with no break
          case 5:
              System.out.print("Unbelievable; ");
              System.out.println(numberOfBabies +
                                  " babies.");
              break;
          default:
              System.out.println("I don't believe you.");
              break;
        }
    }
}
```

Sample Screen Output 1

```
Enter number of babies: 1
Congratulations.
```

Sample Screen Output 2

```
Enter number of babies: 3
Wow. Triplets.
```

(continued)

LISTING 3.5 A switch Statement *(part 2 of 2)*

Sample Screen Output 3

```
Enter number of babies: 4
Unbelievable; 4 babies.
```

Sample Screen Output 4

```
Enter number of babies: 6
I don't believe you.
```

Here is another example of a switch statement, one that has a char variable as its controlling expression:

```java
switch (eggGrade)
{
    case 'A':
    case 'a':
        System.out.println("Grade A");
        break;
    case 'C':
    case 'c':
        System.out.println("Grade C");
        break;
    default:
        System.out.println("We only buy grade A and grade C.");
        break;
}
```

In this example, grade A and grade C eggs can be indicated by either uppercase or lowercase letters. Other values of eggGrade are handled by the default case.

Note that the case labels need not be consecutive or even ordered. You can have 'A' and 'C' and no 'B', as in the preceding example. Similarly, in a switch statement with integer case labels, you could have integers 1 and 3, but no 2. Case labels must be discrete values; one label cannot indicate a range. If, for example, you wanted to take the same action for the values 1 through 4, you would need to write a case for each value. For a large range, an if-else statement would be more practical than a switch statement.

The controlling expression in a switch statement can be more complicated than a single variable; for example, it can involve arithmetic operators. Prior to Java Development Kit (JDK) version 7, the controlling expression had to evaluate to a value of an integer type, such as the type int, or to a value of type char. Starting with JDK version 7, a controlling expression of type String is allowed. The following example will run on JDK version 7 or higher but will cause a compilation error on previous versions. Note that we invoke a method that returns the variable answer in lowercase as the controlling expression.

```java
System.out.println("Which US state has only one syllable in " +
                    "its name?");
Scanner keyboard = new Scanner(System.in);
String answer = keyboard.next();
switch (answer.toLowerCase())
{
    case "maine":
        System.out.println("Correct!");
        break;
    default:
        System.out.println("Incorrect, the answer is Maine.");
        break;
}
```

VideoNote
Using switch **statements**

RECAP The switch Statement

SYNTAX

```java
switch (Controlling_Expression)
    {
        case Case_Label:
            Statement;

            . . .

            Statement;
            break;
        case Case_Label:
            Statement;

            . . .

            Statement;
            break;
        default:
            Statement;

            . . .

            Statement;
            break;
    }
```

The Controlling_Expression must be of an integer type such as int, short, or byte, or of type char.

Each Case_Label is a constant of the same type as the Controlling_ Expression. Each case must have a different Case_Label.

A break may be omitted. Without a break, execution just continues to the next case.

Any number of cases is allowed.

A default case is optional. Without one, no action occurs in the event of a mismatch.

(continued)

EXAMPLE

```java
int seatLocationCode;

...

switch (seatLocationCode)
{
    case 1:
        System.out.println("Orchestra.");
        price = 40.00;
        break;
    case 2:
        System.out.println("Mezzanine.");
        price = 30.00;
        break;
    case 3:
        System.out.println("Balcony.");
        price = 15.00;
        break;
    default:
        System.out.println("Unknown ticket code.");
        break;
}
```

GOTCHA   Omitting a break Statement

If you test a program that contains a switch statement and it executes two cases when you expect it to execute only one case, you probably have forgotten to include a break statement where one is needed.   ∎

GOTCHA   Omitting the Default Case

If the cases of a switch statement assign values to a variable, omitting a default case can cause a syntax error. The compiler might think that the variable has an undefined value after the switch executes. To avoid this error, either provide a default case or initialize the variable before the switch statement executes.   ∎

SELF-TEST QUESTIONS

myprogramminglab

15. What output is produced by the following code?
```java
int code = 2;
switch (code)
```

```
    {
        case 1:
            System.out.println("Hello.");
        case 3:
            System.out.println("Good-bye.");
            break;
        default:
            System.out.println("Till we meet again.");
            break;
    }
```

16. Suppose you change the code in the previous question so that the first line is the following:

    ```
    int code = 1;
    ```

    What output would be produced?

17. What output is produced by the following code?

    ```
    char letter = 'B';
    switch (letter)
    {
        case'A':
        case'a':
            System.out.println("Some kind of A.");
        case'B':
        case'b':
            System.out.println("Some kind of B.");
            break;
        default:
            System.out.println("Something else.");
            break;
    }
    ```

18. What output is produced by the following code?

    ```
    int key = 1;
    switch (key + 1)
    {
        case 1:
            System.out.println("Cake");
        break;
        case 2:
            System.out.println("Pie");
            break;
        case 3:
            System.out.println("Ice cream");
        case 4:
            System.out.println("Cookies");
            break;
    ```

```
    default:
        System.out.println("Diet time");
}
```

19. Suppose you change the first line of the code in the previous question to

    `int key = 3;`

    What output would be produced?

20. Suppose you change the first line of the code in Self-Test Question 18 to

    `int key = 5;`

    What output would be produced?

Enumerations

Imagine a reviewer who rates movies as either excellent, average, or bad. If you wrote a Java program to organize these reviews, you could represent the ratings as, for example, the integers 3, 2, and 1 or the characters E, A, and B. If you define a variable whose data type is either `int` or `char` to contain the rating, it might end up with a value other than one of the three valid ratings. Instead, to restrict the contents of the variable to certain values, you could declare it as an **enumerated data type**, or **enumeration**. An enumeration lists the values that a variable can have.

For example, the following statement defines `MovieRating` as an enumeration:

`enum MovieRating {E, A, B}`

> An enumeration provides a way to restrict the values of a variable

Notice that no semicolon follows an enumeration's definition. Including one, however, will not cause a syntax error; the semicolon will simply be ignored. Also, notice that the values E, A, and B are not enclosed in single quotes, since they are not `char` values.

An enumeration acts as a class type, so we can use it to declare a variable `rating`, as follows:

`MovieRating rating;`

In the definition of `MovieRating`, the items listed between the braces are objects that we can assign to `rating` as values. For example, we could write

`rating = MovieRating.A;`

to assign A to `rating`. Note that we must preface the value A with the name of the enumeration and a dot. Assigning a value other than E, A, or B to `rating` will cause a syntax error.

Once we have assigned a value to a variable whose data type is an enumeration, we can use it within a switch statement to choose a course of action. For example, the following statement displays a message based upon the value of `rating`:

```
switch (rating)
{
case E: //Excellent
   System.out.println("You must see this movie!");
   break;
case A: //Average
   System.out.println("This movie is OK, but not great.");
   break;
case B: //Bad
   System.out.println("Skip it!");
   break;
default:
   System.out.println("Something is wrong.");
}
```

Since the data type of the expression in the `switch` statement is an enumeration, the case labels are assumed to belong to that enumeration without writing its name. In fact, writing `case MovieRating.E`, for example, is a syntax error. However, if you need to reference one of the enumerated values elsewhere within the `switch` statement, you must precede it with the enumeration's name. Although we wrote a default case, it is unnecessary here, because we know that `rating` cannot have values other than those in the enumeration.

The values of an enumeration behave much like named constants. For this reason, we will use the same naming convention for them as we do for named constants, that is, all letters will be uppercase. The names need not be single letters. We could, for example, define our previous enumeration as

```
enum MovieRating {EXCELLENT, AVERAGE, BAD}
```

and then write an assignment like

```
rating = MovieRating.AVERAGE;
```

or a case statement like

```
case EXCELLENT:
```

An enumeration is actually a class. You typically define it within another class, but always outside of method definitions. We will talk more about enumerations as classes in Chapter 6.

3.4 GRAPHICS SUPPLEMENT

One picture in color is worth a thousand black-and-white pictures.

—VARIATION ON A CHINESE PROVERB

The oldest, shortest words—'yes' and 'no'—are those which require the most thought.

—PYTHAGORAS

In this section, we continue our discussion of drawing that we began in Chapter 1 and our discussion of JOptionPane that we began in Chapter 2. First, we tell you how to add color to your applet drawings. In particular, we add color to our happy face applet. Next, we show you how to use one more kind of dialog window, namely one for asking yes-or-no questions. We did not present this window in Chapter 2, because you need the branching mechanisms introduced in this chapter to use this kind of window effectively. If you skipped the previous material about JOptionPane, you can skip the description of this dialog window. None of the JOptionPane material in this chapter or in Chapter 2 is used in future chapters.

Specifying a Drawing Color

When drawing shapes with methods such as drawOval inside the definition of an applet's paint method, you can think of your drawing as being done with a pen that can change colors. The method setColor, which is in the class Graphics, will change the color of your pen.

The setColor method sets the color of the pen

For example, the happy face that is drawn in Listing 3.6 is a yellow face with blue eyes and red lips. Aside from the color, the face is basically the same as the one shown in Listing 1.2, except that we have now added a nose. The code in Listing 3.6 is based on the code in Listing 2.9, which is simply a more stylistic version of the code in Listing 1.2.

LISTING 3.6 **Adding Color** *(part 1 of 2)*

```java
import javax.swing.JApplet;
import java.awt.Color;
import java.awt.Graphics;

public class YellowFace extends JApplet
{
    public static final int FACE_DIAMETER = 200;
    public static final int X_FACE = 100;
    public static final int Y_FACE = 50;
    public static final int EYE_WIDTH = 10;
    public static final int EYE_HEIGHT = 20;
    public static final int X_RIGHT_EYE = 155;
    public static final int Y_RIGHT_EYE = 100;
    public static final int X_LEFT_EYE = 230;
    public static final int Y_LEFT_EYE = Y_RIGHT_EYE;
    public static final int NOSE_DIAMETER = 10;
    public static final int X_NOSE = 195; //Center of nose will
                                          //be at 200
    public static final int Y_NOSE = 135;
    public static final int MOUTH_WIDTH = 100;
    public static final int MOUTH_HEIGHT = 50;
```

(continued)

LISTING 3.6   Adding Color *(part 2 of 2)*

```
public static final int X_MOUTH = 150;
public static final int Y_MOUTH = 160;
public static final int MOUTH_START_ANGLE = 180;
public static final int MOUTH_EXTENT_ANGLE = 180;
public void paint(Graphics canvas)
{
    //Draw face interior and outline:
    canvas.setColor(Color.YELLOW);
    canvas.fillOval(X_FACE, Y_FACE, FACE_DIAMETER,
    FACE_DIAMETER);
    canvas.setColor(Color.BLACK);
    canvas.drawOval(X_FACE, Y_FACE, FACE_DIAMETER,
    FACE_DIAMETER);
    //Draw eyes:
    canvas.setColor(Color.BLUE);
    canvas.fillOval(X_RIGHT_EYE, Y_RIGHT_EYE, EYE_WIDTH,
    EYE_HEIGHT);
    canvas.fillOval(X_LEFT_EYE, Y_LEFT_EYE, EYE_WIDTH,
    EYE_HEIGHT);
    //Draw nose:
    canvas.setColor(Color.BLACK);
    canvas.fillOval(X_NOSE, Y_NOSE, NOSE_DIAMETER,
    NOSE_DIAMETER);
    //Draw mouth:
    canvas.setColor(Color.RED);
    canvas.drawArc(X_MOUTH, Y_MOUTH, MOUTH_WIDTH, MOUTH_HEIGHT,
        MOUTH_START_ANGLE, MOUTH_EXTENT_ANGLE);
}
}
```

> *The filled yellow circle is drawn first so that the other drawings will be on top of the yellow.*

Use of the method setColor in Listing 3.6 is routine. For example, the statement

```
canvas.setColor(Color.YELLOW);
```

sets the color of the pen to yellow. So now the statement

```
canvas.fillOval(X_FACE, Y_FACE, FACE_DIAMETER, FACE_DIAMETER);
```

draws a circle for the face that is filled in with yellow.

We need to emphasize one point. The order in which you draw the components of the face affects the final outcome. Note that the solid yellow circle is drawn first, so that the other drawings, such as the eyes, will be on top of the yellow. As when using an actual pen or brush, the drawings are done one on top of the other in the order of the code in the paint method. If we had instead drawn the yellow circle last, it would be on top of the eyes, nose,

FIGURE 3.10   Predefined Colors for the setColor **Method**

Color.BLACK	Color.MAGENTA
Color.BLUE	Color.ORANGE
Color.CYAN	Color.PINK
Color.DARK_GRAY	Color.RED
Color.GRAY	Color.WHITE
Color.GREEN	Color.YELLOW
Color.LIGHT_GRAY	

and mouth, and only the yellow circle would be visible. Unlike drawing with an actual pen, however, placing one color over another does not blend the two colors. The newest drawing hides—actually, replaces—any earlier drawing made in the same spot. You are simply setting the state and color of pixels, replacing their earlier values.

The order in which you draw affects the outcome

Certain colors are already defined for you as public named constants in the class Color; these are given in Figure 3.10. You can define other colors as well, but we will not go into that here.

RECAP The setColor Method

When you draw using an object of the class Graphics, you can set the color of the drawing by invoking the method setColor. You can later change the color by invoking setColor again, so a single drawing can have multiple colors.

EXAMPLE

```
canvas.setColor(Color.RED);
```

SELF-TEST QUESTIONS

myprogramminglab

21. Suppose you change the order of the drawing commands in Listing 3.6 to the following. Will the applet picture change? If so, how will it change?

```
//Draw mouth:
canvas.setColor(Color.RED);
canvas.drawArc(X_MOUTH, Y_MOUTH, MOUTH_WIDTH,
    MOUTH_HEIGHT, MOUTH_START_ANGLE,
    MOUTH_EXTENT_ANGLE);
```

```
//Draw face interior and outline:
canvas.setColor(Color.YELLOW);
canvas.fillOval(X_FACE, Y_FACE,
    FACE_DIAMETER, FACE_DIAMETER);
canvas.setColor(Color.BLACK);
canvas.drawOval(X_FACE, Y_FACE,
    FACE_DIAMETER, FACE_DIAMETER);
//Draw eyes:
canvas.setColor(Color.BLUE);
canvas.fillOval(X_RIGHT_EYE, Y_RIGHT_EYE,
    EYE_WIDTH, EYE_HEIGHT);
canvas.fillOval(X_LEFT_EYE, Y_LEFT_EYE,
    EYE_WIDTH, EYE_HEIGHT);
//Draw nose:
canvas.setColor(Color.BLACK);
canvas.fillOval(X_NOSE, Y_NOSE,
    NOSE_DIAMETER, NOSE_DIAMETER);
```

22. Repeat the previous question, but use the following changes instead:

```
//Draw face interior:
canvas.setColor(Color.YELLOW);
canvas.fillOval(X_FACE, Y_FACE,
    FACE_DIAMETER, FACE_DIAMETER);
//Draw mouth:
canvas.setColor(Color.RED);
canvas.drawArc(X_MOUTH, Y_MOUTH, MOUTH_WIDTH,
    MOUTH_HEIGHT, MOUTH_START_ANGLE,
    MOUTH_EXTENT_ANGLE);
//Draw face outline:
canvas.setColor(Color.BLACK);
canvas.drawOval(X_FACE, Y_FACE,
    FACE_DIAMETER, FACE_DIAMETER);
//Draw nose:
canvas.setColor(Color.BLACK);
canvas.fillOval(X_NOSE, Y_NOSE,
    NOSE_DIAMETER, NOSE_DIAMETER);
//Draw eyes:
canvas.setColor(Color.BLUE);
canvas.fillOval(X_RIGHT_EYE, Y_RIGHT_EYE,
    EYE_WIDTH, EYE_HEIGHT);
canvas.fillOval(X_LEFT_EYE, Y_LEFT_EYE,
    EYE_WIDTH, EYE_HEIGHT);
```

A Dialog Box for a Yes-or-No Question

Chapter 2 showed how to use the class JOptionPane to produce two kinds of windows called dialogs. One kind asked the user to enter input data that the program could read. The other kind of dialog displayed a message to the user.

`JOptionPane` provides yet another dialog box for asking yes-or-no questions of the user. The dialog has a title and contains the question you specify along with two buttons labeled Yes and No. For example, the code

```
int answer =
    JOptionPane.showConfirmDialog(null, "End program?",
            "Click Yes or No:", JOptionPane.YES_NO_OPTION);
if (answer == JOptionPane.YES_OPTION)
    System.exit(0);
else if (answer == JOptionPane.NO_OPTION)
    System.out.println("One more time");
else
    System.out.println("This is impossible");
```

produces the dialog box shown in Figure 3.11.

Let's describe the list of arguments for the method `showConfirmDialog` by considering the argument list in our example:

```
(null, "End program?", "Click Yes or No:",
JOptionPane.YES_NO_OPTION)
```

The first argument has to do with where the dialog is placed on the screen, but we have not developed enough material to allow us to consider the possible options. So we will simply write `null` as the first argument, which gives us the default placement. We will explain the actual meaning of `null` in Chapter 6.

The second argument is a string that appears in the dialog containing the Yes and No buttons. Of course, the string should normally be a yes-or-no question. In our example, this argument is `"End program?"`.

The third argument is a string displayed as the title of the dialog. In our example, this argument is `"Click Yes or No:"`.

The last argument, `JOptionPane.YES_NO_OPTION`, indicates that we want a dialog containing Yes and No buttons. Other options are possible, but we will not discuss them here.

If the user clicks the Yes button, the method `showConfirmDialog` will return the `int` value `JOptionPane.YES_OPTION` and the window will disappear.

FIGURE 3.11   A Yes-or-No Dialog Box

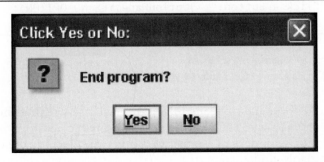

In our example, the multibranch if-else statement will then invoke System. exit(0) to end the program. If the user clicks the No button, the method showConfirmDialog will return the intvalue JOptionPane.NO_OPTION, and then the multibranch if-else statement will invoke System.out.println to display One more time.

The class JOptionPane defines several named constants, including the int constants YES_NO_OPTION, YES_OPTION, and NO_OPTION that we have used here. Note that to use these constants, you must precede each of their names with the name of the class and a dot. What int values are actually named by these constants? It does not matter. Think of the value that showConfirmDialog returns as the answer to a yes-or-no question.

Java code on the book's Web site

The code that we used in our example appears in the file JOptionPaneYesNo-Demo.java, which is available on the Web along with the other source code for this book.

RECAP Dialog Boxes for Yes-or-No Questions

The class JOptionPane in the package javax.swing defines the method show-ConfirmDialog. You can use this method to create a dialog box to ask a yes-or-no question and get the user's response.

SYNTAX

```
Integer_Response = JOptionPane.showConfirmDialog(null,
    Question_String, Title_String, Option);
```

The displayed dialog box is titled *Title_String* and contains the text *Question_String* and buttons as indicated by *Option*. When *Option* is JOptionPane.YES_NO_OPTION,two buttons labeled Yes and No are displayed. The method returns the int constant YES_OPTION if the user clicks the Yes button, or NO_OPTION if the user clicks the No button.

EXAMPLE

```
int answer = JOptionPane.showConfirmDialog(null, "Done?",
    "Click a Button:", JOptionPane.YES_NO_OPTION);
```

[myprogramminglab]

SELF-TEST QUESTION

23. Write code for a JOptionPane dialog that will ask whether the user is at least 18 years of age. Then set the boolean variable adult equal to either true, if the user is at least 18, or false otherwise. Include the declaration of the variable adult.

CHAPTER SUMMARY

- A branching statement chooses and then performs one of a number of actions. The `if-else` statement and `switch` statement are branching statements.

- A boolean expression combines variables and comparison operators such as < to produce a value that is either true or false.

- An `if-else` statement tests the value of a boolean expression and takes one of two actions according to whether the value is true or false.

- You can omit the `else` part to get an `if` statement that takes an action if a boolean expression is true but takes no action if the expression is false.

- A compound statement is a sequence of Java statements, all enclosed in a pair of braces.

- You can nest `if-else` statements. Either or both of the `if` part and the `else` part can have another `if-else` statement as its action. Using braces to form compound statements can clarify your intent. Without braces, remember that each `else` is paired with the nearest preceding and unpaired `if`.

- A special form of nested `if-else` statements forms a multibranch structure. In this form, you typically write the next `if` part immediately after an `else`. Thus, you write `if`, `else if`, `else if`,..., `else`. Although a final `else` is not mandatory, it usually is a good idea to include it.

- Boolean expressions can be combined with the logical operators &&, ||, and `!` to form a larger expression. Java uses short-circuit evaluation in these cases.

- Calling the `exit` method ends a program's execution. Although you must call `exit` to end a program that uses `JOptionPane`, you typically do not call it under ordinary circumstances.

- The value of a boolean expression can be stored in a variable of type `boolean`. This variable is itself a boolean expression, and so it can then be used to control an `if-else` statement. That is, a boolean variable can be used anyplace that a boolean expression is allowed.

- The `switch` statement provides another multibranch decision structure. It tests the value of an integer, character, or string expression and executes a case according to that value. Providing a default case is usually a good idea.

- You can define an enumeration to provide a data type whose values are like named constants.

- You can add color to an applet drawing by using the `Graphics` method `setColor` and the colors defined as named constants within the class `Color`.

- `JOptionPane` enables you to use a dialog box for yes-or-no questions.

Exercises

1. Write a fragment of code that will test whether an integer variable `score` contains a valid test score. Valid test scores are in the range 0 to 100.

2. Write a fragment of code that will change the integer value stored in x as follows. If x is even, divide x by 2. If x is odd, multiply x by 3 and subtract 1.

3. Suppose you are writing a program that asks the user to give a yes-or-no response. Assume that the program reads the user's response into the String variable response.

   a. If `response` is yes or y, set the boolean variable `accept` to true; otherwise, set it to false.
   b. How would you change the code so that it will also accept Yes and Y?

4. Consider the following fragment of code:

```
if (x > 5)
    System.out.println("A");
else if (x < 10)
    System.out.println("B");
else
    System.out.println("C");
```

   What is displayed if x is

   a. 4;   b. 5;   c. 6;   d. 9;   e. 10;   f. 11

5. Consider the following fragment of code:

```
if (x > 5)
{
    System.out.println("A");
    if (x < 10)
    System.out.println("B");
}
else
    System.out.println("C");
```

   What is displayed if x is

   a. 4;   b. 5;   c. 6;   d. 9;   e. 10;   f. 11

6. We would like to assess a service charge for cashing a check. The service charge depends on the amount of the check. If the check amount is less than $10, we will charge $1. If the amount is greater than $10 but less than $100, we will charge 10 percent of the amount. If the amount is greater than $100, but less than $1,000, we will charge $5 plus 5 percent of the amount. If the value is over $1,000, we will charge $40 plus 1 percent of

the amount. Use a multibranch if-else statement in a fragment of code to compute the service charge.

7. What is the value of each of the following boolean expressions if x is 5, y is 10, and z is 15?

   a. (x < 5 && y > x)
   b. (x < 5 || y > x)
   c. (x > 3 || y < 10 && z == 15)
   d. (! (x > 3) && x!= z || x + y == z)

8. The following code fragment will not compile. Why?

```
if !x > x + y
    x = 2 * x;
else
    x = x + 3;
```

9. Consider the boolean expression((x > 10) || (x < 100)). Why is this expression probably not what the programmer intended?

10. Consider the boolean expression((2 < 5) && (x < 100)). Why is this expression probably not what the programmer intended?

11. Write a switch statement to convert a letter grade into an equivalent numeric value on a four-point scale. Set the value of the variable gradeValue to 4.0 for an A, 3.0 for a B, 2.0 for a C, 1.0 for a D, and 0.0 for an F. For any other letter, set the value to 0.0 and display an error message.

12. Consider the previous question, but include + or – letter grades. A+ is 4.25, A– is 3.75, B+ is 3.25, B– is 2.75, and so on.

   a. Why can't we use one switch statement with no other conditionals to convert these additional letter grades?
   b. Write a fragment of code that will do the conversion using a multi-branch if-else statement.
   c. Write a fragment of code that will do the conversion using nested switch statements.

13. Imagine a program that displays a menu of five possible choices, lettered *a* through *e*. Suppose the user's selection is read into the character variable choice. Write a switch statement that reacts to this choice by displaying a message that indicates the choice. Display an error message if the user makes an invalid choice.

14. Repeat the previous exercise, but define an enumeration and use it within the switch statement.

15. Repeat Exercise 13, but use a multibranch if-else statement instead of a switch statement.

16. Given that the `int` variable `temp` contains a temperature that is not negative, write a Java statement that uses the conditional operator to set the `String` variable `label` to either "degree" or "degrees". We want to use `label` to produce grammatically correct output, such as 0 degrees, 1 degree, 2 degrees, and so on. If you have not studied the conditional operator, use an `if-else` statement instead.

17. Write Java statements that create a yes-or-no dialog box to answer the question, "Are you in college?"

PROGRAMMING PROJECTS

myprogramminglab *Visit www.myprogramminglab.com to complete many of these Programming Projects online and get instant feedback.*

1. A number *x* is **divisible** by *y* if the remainder after the division is zero. Write a program that tests whether one number is divisible by another number. Read both numbers from the keyboard.

VideoNote
Solution to Project 2

2. Write a program to read in three nonnegative integers from the keyboard. Display the integers in increasing order.

3. Write a program that reads three strings from the keyboard. Although the strings are in no particular order, display the string that would be second if they were arranged lexicographically.

VideoNote
Responding to user input

4. Write a program that reads a one-line sentence as input and then displays the following response: If the sentence ends with a question mark (?) and the input contains an even number of characters, display the word Yes. If the sentence ends with a question mark and the input contains an odd number of characters, display the word No. If the sentence ends with an exclamation point (!), display the word Wow. In all other cases, display the words You always say followed by the input string enclosed in quotes. Your output should all be on one line. Be sure to note that in the last case, your output must include quotation marks around the echoed input string. In all other cases, there are no quotes in the output. Your program does not have to check the input to see that the user has entered a legitimate sentence.

5. Write a program that allows the user to convert a temperature given in degrees from either Celsius to Fahrenheit or Fahrenheit to Celsius. Use the following formulas:

```
Degrees_C = 5(Degrees_F- 32)/9
Degrees_F = (9(Degrees_C)/5) + 32)
```

Prompt the user to enter a temperature and either a C or c for Celsius or an F or f for Fahrenheit. Convert the temperature to Fahrenheit if Celsius is entered, or to Celsius if Fahrenheit is entered. Display the result in a readable format. If anything other than C, c, F, or f is entered, print an error message and stop.

6. Repeat Programming Project 10 of Chapter 2, but include input checking. Display the change only if a valid price is entered (no less than 25 cents, no more than 100 cents, and an integer multiple of 5 cents). Otherwise, display separate error messages for any of the following invalid inputs: a cost under 25 cents, a cost that is not an integer multiple of 5, and a cost that is more than a dollar.

7. Repeat any of the previous programming projects using `JOptionPane`, which is described in the graphics supplement at the end of Chapter 2.   Graphics

8. Suppose that we are working for an online service that provides a bulletin board for its users. We would like to give our users the option of filtering out profanity. Suppose that we consider the words *cat*, *dog*, and *llama* to be profane. Write a program that reads a string from the keyboard and tests whether the string contains one of our profane words. Your program should find words like *cAt* that differ only in case. *Option*: As an extra challenge, have your program reject only lines that contain a profane word exactly. For example, *Dogmatic concatenation is a small category* should not be considered profane.

9. Write a program that reads a string from the keyboard and tests whether it contains a valid date. Display the date and a message that indicates whether it is valid. If it is not valid, also display a message explaining why it is not valid.

   The input date will have the format *mm/dd/yyyy*. A valid month value *mm* must be from 1 to 12 (January is 1). The day value *dd* must be from 1 to a value that is appropriate for the given month. September, April, June, and November each have 30 days. February has 28 days except for leap years when it has 29. The remaining months all have 31 days each. A leap year is any year that is divisible by 4 but not divisible by 100 unless it is also divisible by 400.

10. Repeat the calorie-counting program described in Programming Project 13 from Chapter 2. This time ask the user to input the string "M" if the user is a man and "W" if the user is a woman. Use only the male formula to calculate calories if "M" is entered and use only the female formula to calculate calories if "W" is entered. Output the number of chocolate bars to consume as before.

11. Repeat Programming Project 10 but in addition ask the user if he or she is

    a. Sedentary
    b. Somewhat active (exercise occasionally)
    c. Active (exercise 3–4 days per week)
    d. Highly active (exercise every day)

If the user answers "Sedentary," then increase the calculated BMR by 20 percent. If the user answers "Somewhat active," then increase the calculated BMR by 30 percent. If the user answers "Active," then increase the calculated BMR by 40 percent. Finally, if the user answers "Highly active," then increase the calculated BMR by 50 percent. Output the number of chocolate bars based on the new BMR value.

Graphics

12. Write a Java applet or application to draw the five interlocking rings that are the symbol of the Olympics. The color of the rings, from left to right, is blue, yellow, black, green, and red.

Graphics

13. Repeat Programming Project 8 in Chapter 1, but add yes-or-no dialogs to allow the user to make the following color changes:

- Change the color of the solid center circle from black to red.
- Change the color of the outer circle from black to blue.
- Change the color of the spines from black to green.

Answers to Self-Test Questions

1. ```java
if (goals > 10)

    System.out.println("Wow");
else
    System.out.println("Oh Well");
```

2. ```java
if ((goals > 10) && (errors == 0))

    System.out.println("Wow");
else
    System.out.println("Oh Well");
```

3. ```java
if (salary >= deductions)

{
    System.out.println("OK");
    net = salary - deductions;
}
else
{
    System.out.println("No Way");
}
```

It is also acceptable to omit the braces in the else part.

4. ```java
if ((speed > 25) && (visibility < 20))

{
    speed = 25;
    System.out.println("Caution");
}
```

5. `if((salary >= MIN_SALARY) || (bonus >= MIN_BONUS))`

```
    System.out.println("OK");
else
    System.out.println("Too low");
```

6. `String upperWord = nextWord.toUpperCase();`

```
if(upperWord.compareTo("N") < 0)
    System.out.println("First half of the alphabet");
else
    System.out.println("Second half of the alphabet");
```

7. If they are of type `int`, you use `x1 == x2`. If they are of type `String`, you use `x1.equals(x2)`.

8. Time and tide wait for me.

9. Time and tide wait for no one.

10. Time and tide wait for everyone.

11. `if(number > 10)`

```
    System.out.println("High");
else if (number < 5)
    System.out.println("Low");
else
    System.out.println("So-so");
```

12. Positive
    -100

13. The output produced is

```
false
false
true
true
```

14. The output produced is

```
false
true
false
true
```

Because of short-circuit evaluation, you do not need to know the value of x.

15. `Till we meet again.`

16. `Hello`
    `Good-bye`

17. Some kind of B.

18. Pie

19. Cookies

20. Diet time

21. The mouth will not be visible because it will be covered by the filled yellow circle. The rest of the face will be the same as that drawn by Listing 3.6.

22. The face drawn will be exactly the same as that drawn by Listing 3.6.

23. You are not required to give a complete program, but we have embedded the answer in a complete program.

```java
import javax.swing.JOptionPane;
public class Question23
{
    public static void main(String[] args)
    {
        boolean adult = false;
        //Initialized to keep the compiler happy.
        int answer = JOptionPane.showConfirmDialog(null,
            "Are you at least 18 years old?",
            "Age Check", JOptionPane.YES_NO_OPTION);
        if (answer == JOptionPane.YES_OPTION)
            adult = true;
        else if (answer == JOptionPane.NO_OPTION)
            adult = false;
        else
            System.out.println("Error");
        if (adult)
            JOptionPane.showMessageDialog
                      (null, "You are old enough.");
        else
            JOptionPane.showMessageDialog(null,
                      "Sorry. you must be 18.");
            System.exit(0);
    }
}
```

Flow of Control: Loops 4

4.1 JAVA LOOP STATEMENTS 196
The `while` Statement 197
The `do-while` Statement 200
Programming Example: Bug Infestation 205
Programming Example: Nested Loops 211
The `for` Statement 213
Declaring Variables Within a `for` Statement 219
Using a Comma in a `for` Statement (*Optional*) 220
The `for-each` Statement 222

4.2 PROGRAMMING WITH LOOPS 222
The Loop Body 223
Initializing Statements 224

Controlling the Number of Loop Iterations 225
Case Study: Using a Boolean Variable to End a
 Loop 227
Programming Example: Spending Spree 229
The `break` Statement and `continue` Statement in
 Loops (*Optional*) 232
Loop Bugs 235
Tracing Variables 237
Assertion Checks 239

4.3 GRAPHICS SUPPLEMENT 241
Programming Example: A Multiface Applet 241
The `drawString` Method 247

Chapter Summary 247   **Programming Projects** 251   **Answers to Self-Test Questions** 255

One more time

—COUNT BASIE, *recording of "April in Paris"*

Play it again, Sam

—*Reputed, incorrectly, to be in the movie* Casablanca, *which does contain similar phrases, such as "Play it, Sam."*

We now continue our discussion of flow of control that we began in the previous chapter. Although Java statements that choose among two or more paths through the logic of a program are extremely important, the real power of a computer is its ability to repeat a group of instructions numerous times. Java provides statements that enable us to make use of this ability.

OBJECTIVES

After studying this chapter, you should be able to

- Design a loop
- Use the Java statements while, do, and for in a program
- Use the for-each statement with enumerations
- Use assertion checks in a program
- Use repetition in a graphics program
- Use the method drawString to display text in a graphics program

PREREQUISITES

The examples in this chapter use the if-else statement, the switch statement, and enumerations, all of which were presented in Chapter 3.

4.1 JAVA LOOP STATEMENTS

And go round and round and round

—JONI MITCHELL, "THE CIRCLE GAME"

Programs often need to repeat some action. For example, a grading program would contain branching statements that assign a letter grade to a student on the basis of the student's scores on assignments and exams. To assign grades to the entire class, the program would repeat this action for each student in the class. A portion of a program that repeats a statement or group of statements is called a **loop.** The statement or group of statements to be repeated in a loop is called the **body** of the loop. Each repetition of the loop body is called an **iteration** of the loop.

A loop repeats a group of statements

When you design a loop, you need to determine what action the body of the loop will take. In addition, you need a mechanism for deciding when the repetition of the loop body should stop. Java has several loop statements that provide this mechanism. We examine these statements in this chapter.

Java has several statements for controlling loops

The while Statement

One way to construct a loop in Java is by using a **while statement,** also known as a **while loop.** A while statement repeats its action again and again as long as a controlling boolean expression is true. That is why it is called a while loop; the loop is repeated *while* the controlling boolean expression is true. When the expression is false, the repetition ends. For example, Listing 4.1 contains a toy example of a while statement. The statement starts with the keyword while followed by a boolean expression in parentheses. That is the controlling boolean expression. The loop's body is repeated while that controlling boolean expression is true. Often, the body is a compound statement enclosed in braces {}. The loop's body normally contains an action that can change the value of the controlling boolean expression from true to false and so end the loop. Let's step through the execution of the while loop in Listing 4.1.

A while loop repeats its body while a boolean expression is true

Consider the first sample run for the while statement in Listing 4.1. The user enters a 2, and so 2 becomes the value of the variable number. The controlling boolean expression is

```
count <= number
```

Since count is 1 and number is 2, this boolean expression is true, so the loop body, shown here, is executed:

```
{
    System.out.print(count + ", ");
    count++;
}
```

The loop body displays the value of count, which is 1, on the screen and then increases the value of count by 1 so it becomes 2.

After one iteration of the loop body, the controlling boolean expression is checked again. Since count is 2 and number is 2, the boolean expression is still true. So the loop body executes one more time. It again displays the value of count, which is 2, on the screen and again increases the value of count by 1 so it becomes 3.

After the second iteration of the loop body, the controlling boolean expression is checked again. The value of count is now 3 and the value of number is still 2, and so the controlling boolean expression count <= number is now false. As a result, when this expression is checked again, the while loop ends and the program goes on to execute the two System.out.println statements that follow the while loop. The first of these two statements ends the line of numbers displayed by the while loop, and the second one displays Buckle my shoe. Figure 4.1 summarizes the action of this loop.

LISTING 4.1 A while **Loop**

```java
import java.util.Scanner;
public class WhileDemo
{
    public static void main(String[] args)
    {
        int count, number;

        System.out.println("Enter a number");
        Scanner keyboard = new Scanner(System.in);
        number = keyboard.nextInt();

        count = 1;
        while (count <= number)
        {
            System.out.print(count + ", ");
            count++;
        }

        System.out.println();
        System.out.println("Buckle my shoe.");
    }
}
```

Sample Screen Output 1

```
Enter a number:
2
1, 2,
Buckle my shoe.
```

Sample Screen Output 2

```
Enter a number:
3
1, 2, 3,
Buckle my shoe.
```

Sample Screen Output 3

```
Enter a number:
0

Buckle my shoe.
```
The loop body is iterated zero times.

FIGURE 4.1 **The Action of the** while **Loop in Listing 4.1**

```java
while (count <= number)
{
    System.out.print(count + ", ");
    count++;
}
```

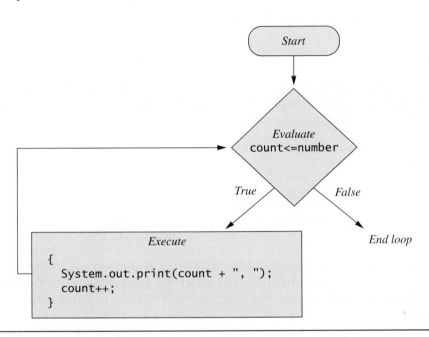

RECAP The while **Statement**

SYNTAX

```java
while (Boolean_Expression)
    Body
```

The *Body* may be either a simple statement or, more likely, a compound statement consisting of a list of statements enclosed in braces {}.

EXAMPLE

```java
//Get next positive integer entered as input data
int next = 0;
while (next <= 0)
    next = keyboard.nextInt(); //keyboard is a Scanner object
```
(continued)

EXAMPLE

```
//Sum positive integers read until one is not positive
int total = 0;
int next = keyboard.nextInt();
while (next > 0)
{
    total = total + next;
    next = keyboard.nextInt();
}
```

The body of a while loop often is a compound statement

All while statements are formed in a way similar to the sample shown in Listing 4.1. The body can be a simple statement, but it is more likely to be a compound statement, as in Listing 4.1. So the most common form of a while loop is

```
while (Boolean_Expression)
{
    First_Statement
    Second_Statement
      . . .
    Last_Statement
}
```

The semantics, or meaning, of a while loop is summarized in Figure 4.2. This semantics assume that no break statement is in the body of the loop. We discuss the possible use of the break statement within loops later in this chapter.

■ **PROGRAMMING TIP**   **A while Loop Can Perform Zero Iterations**

The body of a while loop can be executed zero times. When a while loop executes, the controlling boolean expression is immediately checked. If that boolean expression is false, the loop body is not executed, not even one time. This may seem strange. After all, why write a loop if the body is never executed? The answer is that you may want a loop whose body is executed zero times or more than zero times, depending on input from the user. Perhaps the loop adds up the sum of all your bills for the day. If you have no bills, you do not want the loop body to be executed at all. Sample Screen Output 3 in Listing 4.1 shows a toy example of a while loop that iterates its loop body zero times. ■

The do-while Statement

The do-while **statement,** or do-while **loop,** is very similar to the while statement. The main difference is that the body of a do-while loop is always executed at least once. As you will recall, the body of a while loop might not be executed at all.

FIGURE 4.2   The Semantics of the while Statement

while (*Boolean_Expression*)
　　　Body

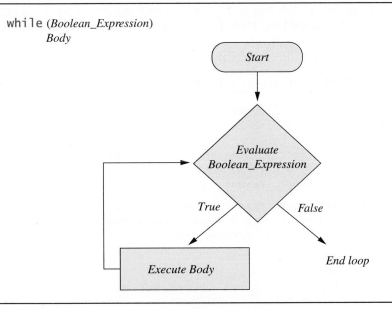

When a do-while loop is executed, the loop body executes first. After that, a do-while loop behaves in exactly the same way as a while loop. The boolean expression is checked. If the boolean expression is true, the loop body executes one more time. This is done again and again as long as the boolean expression is true. If the boolean expression is false, the loop ends.

A do-while loop also repeats its body while a boolean expression is true

The syntax for a do-while statement is as follows:

```
do
      Body
while (Boolean_Expression); ◄────── Note the semicolon!
```

The *Body* can be a simple statement, but it is more likely to be a compound statement. So the most common form of a do-while loop is

```
do
{
    First_Statement
    Second_Statement
      . . .
    Last_Statement
} while (Boolean_Expression);
```

The body of a do-while loop often is a compound statement

Notice the semicolon after the closing parenthesis that follows the *Boolean_Expression*. Also note that although we place the ending brace } and the while on the same line, some programmers prefer to place them on different lines. Either form is fine, but be consistent.

A do-while loop
repeats its body
at least once

Listing 4.2 contains a sample do-while loop that is similar to the while loop in Listing 4.1 but produces different output. Note in Sample Screen Output 3 that the loop body is executed even though the boolean expression starts out false. Again, the body of a do-while loop always executes at least once. Figure 4.3 summarizes the action of this loop.

LISTING 4.2 **A do-while Loop**

```java
import java.util.Scanner;
public class DoWhileDemo
{
    public static void main(String[] args)
    {
        int count, number;

        System.out.println("Enter a number");
        Scanner keyboard = new Scanner(System.in);
        number = keyboard.nextInt();

        count = 1;
        do
        {
            System.out.print(count + ", ");
            count++;
        } while (count <= number);

        System.out.println();
        System.out.println("Buckle my shoe.");
    }
}
```

Sample Screen Output 1

```
Enter a number:
2
1, 2,
Buckle my shoe.
```

Sample Screen Output 2

```
Enter a number:
3
1, 2, 3,
Buckle my shoe.
```

Sample Screen Output 3

```
Enter a number:
0
1, ◄─────────────────  The loop body always
Buckle my shoe.          executes at least once.
```

FIGURE 4.3   The Action of the do-while Loop in Listing 4.2

```java
do
{
    System.out.print(count + ", ");
    count++;
} while (count <= number);
```

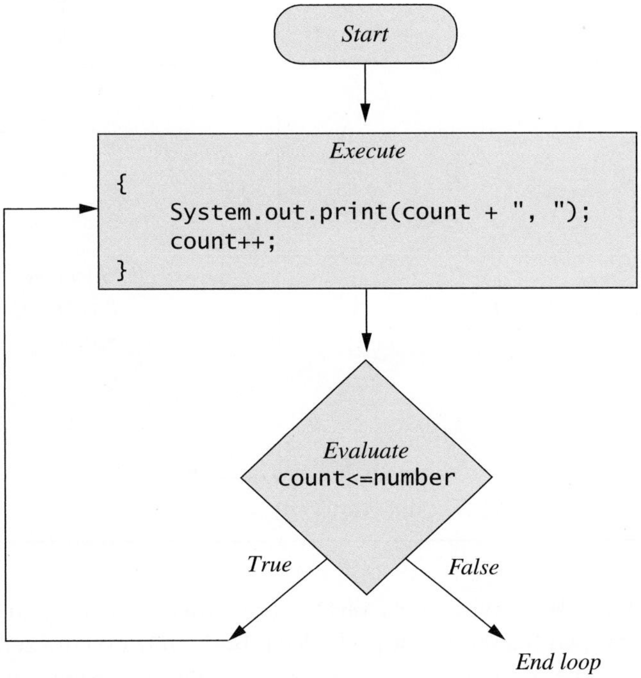

The do-while loop in Listing 4.2 can be rewritten as an equivalent while loop, as follows:

```java
    {
        System.out.print(count + ", ");
        count++;
    }
    while (count <= number)
    {
        System.out.print(count + ", ");
        count++;
    }
```

Although we do not recommend rewriting your do-while loops in this way, this example helps illustrate the difference between these two types of loop

FIGURE 4.4 The Semantics of the do-while Statement

```
do
      Body
while (Boolean_Expression)
```

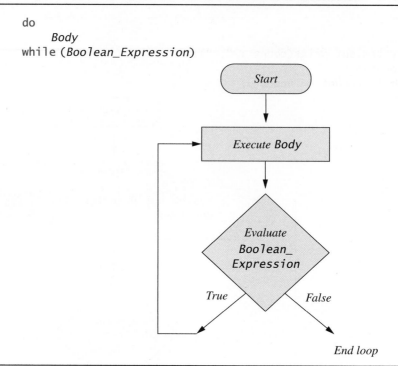

statements. With a do-while loop, the loop body always executes at least once; with a while loop, the loop body may execute zero times.

The semantics of a do-while loop is shown in Figure 4.4. Like the semantics of the while loop shown in Figure 4.2, this semantics assumes that the body of the loop contains no break statement.

RECAP The do-while Statement

SYNTAX

```
do
      Body
while (Boolean_Expression);
```

The *Body* may be either a simple statement or, more likely, a compound statement consisting of a list of statements enclosed in braces {}. The *Body* is always executed at least once. Be sure to notice the semicolon at the end of the entire statement.

(continued)

EXAMPLE

```
//Get the next positive integer entered as input data
int next;
do
    next = keyboard.nextInt();//keyboard is a Scanner object
while (next <= 0);
```

EXAMPLE

```
//Sum the positive integers read until one is not positive
int total = 0;
int next = 0;
do
{
    total = total + next;
    next = keyboard.nextInt();
} while (next > 0);
```

PROGRAMMING EXAMPLE Bug Infestation

This example involves real bugs, not programming bugs! Your hometown has been hit with an infestation of roaches. This is not the most pleasant topic, but fortunately a local company called Debugging Experts Inc. has a treatment that can eliminate roaches from a house. As the saying goes, "It's a dirty job, but somebody has to do it." The only problem is that the town's citizens are too complacent and might not exterminate the roaches before they get out of hand. So the company has installed a computer at the local shopping mall to let people know how bad the problem could be at their particular house. The program in this computer calculates the number of weeks that a population of roaches takes to completely fill a house from floor to ceiling.

The roach population grows relatively slowly—for roaches—but that is still pretty bad. Left unchecked, the population of roaches will almost double every week. If the population did double every week, the growth rate would be 100 percent per week, but fortunately it is only 95 percent per week. These roaches are also rather big. Expressed in terms of volume, their average size is 0.002 cubic foot, which is just a bit smaller than 0.3 cubic inch. The program does make some simplifying assumptions. It assumes that the house has no furniture and that the roaches fill the house with no space between them. The real situation would, of course, be far more complicated than the one portrayed by this program.

Let's think of the steps necessary to solve this problem. A first draft of an algorithm might look like this:

Algorithm for roach population program (rough draft)

Basic steps of our algorithm

1. Get volume of house.
2. Get initial number of roaches in house.
3. Compute number of weeks until the house is full of roaches.
4. Display results.

Since we know the growth rate of the roach population and their average size, we won't read these values but rather will define them as constants in the program.

Our algorithm seems simple enough, but let's not rush to call in the programmers. What about step 3? It's the heart of the solution but gives no hint as to how to perform the calculation. Let's think some more. We need to compute a number of weeks, so let's use a counter that begins at zero to count them. Since we know the volume of the average roach and the initial number of roaches, we can compute their total volume simply by multiplying these two values. This gives the volume of the roach population at week 0. Are we done? We are if the roaches have already filled the house! If they haven't, we now must add in the volume of the new roaches hatched during the first week. Once again we ask whether we are done. If not, we add in the volume of the new roaches hatched during the second week, and so on. Ahh! We need a loop.

What kind of loop should we use? In some situations, we might not be able to decide just yet, and that would be all right. But for this problem we have already observed that the initial infestation might fill the house. If that were the case, we would not need to calculate anything. That is, we would not want the body of our proposed loop to execute. Thus, we should use a `while` loop, not a `do-while` loop. But let's see how we might proceed if we hadn't already reached this conclusion.

Regardless of whether we know what loop to use, let's choose some constants and variables, as follows:

Begin a list of constants and variables

GROWTH_RATE—weekly growth rate of the roach population (a constant 0.95)
ONE_BUG_VOLUME—volume of an average roach (a constant 0.002)
houseVolume—volume of the house
startPopulation—initial number of roaches
countWeeks—week counter
population—current number of roaches
totalBugVolume—total volume of all the roaches
newBugs—number of roaches hatched this week
newBugVolume—volume of new roaches

You might not think of the variables you need all at once. As you refine your pseudocode, you can add other variables to the list as they come to mind. Maintaining a separate list of variables and their meanings can be an invaluable resource while designing and writing a program.

■ PROGRAMMING TIP Take Notes

Before you write your first Java statement, take time to design your program. Write pseudocode, draw pictures, and make a list of proposed variables and their meanings. That is, organize your thoughts and commit them to paper. Your resulting Java program is likely to be better organized and more correct than one that you begin to code too soon. ■

We can now replace step 3 of our algorithm with the following steps:

3a. `countWeeks = 0`
3b. Repeat until house is full of bugs

```
{
    newBugs = population * GROWTH_RATE
    newBugVolume = newBugs * ONE_BUG_VOLUME
    population = population + newBugs
    totalBugVolume = totalBugVolume + newBugVolume
    countWeeks = countWeeks + 1
}
```

Step 3: Compute number of weeks until the house is full of roaches

Looking at step 3b, we note that Java does not have a *repeat until* construct. We can reword *Repeat until house is full of bugs* as *Repeat while house is not full of bugs*, or *Repeat while volume of bugs is less than volume of house*. Thus, we use the construct

```
while (totalBugVolume < houseVolume)
```

Assembling the pieces gives us the following algorithm:

Algorithm for roach population program

1. Read `houseVolume`
2. Read `startPopulation`
3. `population = startPopulation`
4. `totalBugVolume = population * ONE_BUG_VOLUME`
5. `countWeeks = 0`
6. `while (totalBugVolume < houseVolume)`

```
{
    newBugs = population * GROWTH_RATE
    newBugVolume = newBugs * ONE_BUG_VOLUME
    population = population + newBugs
    totalBugVolume = totalBugVolume + newBugVolume
    countWeeks = countWeeks + 1
}
```

We use a while loop in case the house is already full of bugs

7. Display `startPopulation`, `houseVolume`, `countWeeks`, `population`, and `totalBugVolume`

Our loop simply updates the population of the roaches, the volume of roaches, and the week counter. Because the growth rate and the volume of one bug are both positive numbers, we know that the value of population, and hence the value of totalBugVolume, will increase with each loop iteration. So eventually, the value of totalBugVolume will exceed the value of houseVolume, and the controlling boolean expression

```
totalBugVolume < houseVolume
```

will become false and end the while loop.

The variable countWeeks starts out as zero and is increased by 1 on each loop iteration. Thus, when the loop ends, the value of countWeeks is the total number of weeks it takes for the volume of roaches to exceed the volume of the house.

Listing 4.3 shows our Java program and sample output.

LISTING 4.3   **Roach Population Program** *(part 1 of 2)*

```java
import java.util.Scanner;
/**
 Program to calculate how long it will take a population of
 roaches to completely fill a house from floor to ceiling.
*/
public class BugTrouble
{
    public static final double GROWTH_RATE = 0.95;    //95% per week
    public static final double ONE_BUG_VOLUME = 0.002; //cubic feet

    public static void main(String[] args)
    {
        System.out.println("Enter the total volume of your house");
        System.out.print("in cubic feet: ");
        Scanner keyboard = new Scanner(System.in);
        double houseVolume = keyboard.nextDouble();

        System.out.println("Enter the estimated number of");
        System.out.print("roaches in your house: ");
        int startPopulation = keyboard.nextInt();
        int countWeeks = 0;
        double population = startPopulation;
        double totalBugVolume = population * ONE_BUG_VOLUME;
        double newBugs, newBugVolume;

        while (totalBugVolume < houseVolume)
        {
            newBugs = population * GROWTH_RATE;
            newBugVolume = newBugs * ONE_BUG_VOLUME;
            population = population + newBugs;
            totalBugVolume = totalBugVolume + newBugVolume;
            countWeeks++;
        }
```

(continued)

LISTING 4.3   Roach Population Program *(part 2 of 2)*

```
        System.out.println("Starting with a roach population of " +
                           startPopulation);
        System.out.println("and a house with a volume of " + houseVolume +
                           " cubic feet,");
        System.out.println("after " + countWeeks + " weeks,");
        System.out.println("the house will be filled with " +
                           (int)population + " roaches.");
        System.out.println("They will fill a volume of " +
                           (int)totalBugVolume + " cubic feet.");
        System.out.println("Better call Debugging Experts Inc.");
    }
}
```

*(int) is a
type cast as
discussed in
Chapter 2.*

Sample Screen Output

```
Enter the total volume of your house
in cubic feet: 20000
Enter the estimated number of
roaches in your house: 100
Starting with a roach population of 100
and a house with a volume of 20000.0 cubic feet,
after 18 weeks,
the house will be filled with 16619693 roaches.
They will fill a volume of 33239 cubic feet.
Better call Debugging Experts Inc.
```

GOTCHA   Infinite Loops

A common program bug is a loop that does not end, but simply repeats its loop body again and again forever. (Well, conceptually forever.) A loop that iterates its body repeatedly without ever ending is called an **infinite loop**. Normally, some statement in the body of a `while` loop or `do-while` loop will change one or more variables so that the controlling boolean expression becomes false. However, if the variable or variables do not change in the right way, you could get an infinite loop.

An infinite loop executes repeatedly due to an error in logic

For example, let's consider a slight variation of the program in Listing 4.3. Suppose your town is hit by an infestation of roach-eating frogs. These frogs eat roaches so quickly that the roach population actually decreases. As a result, the roaches have a negative growth rate. To reflect this fact, you could change the definition of one named constant to the following and recompile the program:

```
public static final double GROWTH_RATE = -0.05;
//-5% per week
```

If you make this change and run the program, the `while` loop will be an infinite loop, provided the house starts out with a relatively small number of roaches. Because the total number of roaches, and so the volume of roaches, continually *decreases*, the controlling boolean expression, `totalBugVolume < houseVolume`, is always true. Therefore, the loop never ends.

Some infinite loops will not really run forever but will instead end your program when some system resource is exhausted. However, some infinite loops will run forever if left alone. To be able to end a program containing an infinite loop, you should learn how to force a program to stop running. The way to do this depends on your operating system. On many systems—but not all—you can stop program execution by typing control-C, which you do by holding down the control (Ctrl) key while pressing the C key.

Sometimes a programmer might intentionally write an infinite loop. For example, an ATM machine would typically be controlled by a program's infinite loop that handles deposits and withdrawals indefinitely. However, at this point in your programming, an infinite loop is likely to be an error. ■

Learn how to force a program to stop running

---

myprogramminglab

SELF-TEST QUESTIONS

1. What output is produced by the following code?

```
int count = 0;
while (count < 5)
{
    System.out.println(count);
    count++;
}
System.out.println("count after loop = " + count);
```

2. Can the body of a `while` loop execute zero times? Can the body of a do-while loop execute zero times?

3. What output is produced by the following code?

```
int count = 0;
do
{
    System.out.println(count);
    count++;
} while (count < 0);
System.out.println("count after loop = " + count);
```

4. Revise the following code so that it uses a `while` loop instead of a `do-while` loop:

```java
Scanner keyboard = new Scanner(System.in);
int number;
do
{
    System.out.println("Enter a whole number:");
    number = keyboard.nextInt();
    System.out.println("You entered " + number);
} while (number > 0);
System.out.println("number after loop = " + number);
```

5. What output is produced by the following code?

```java
int count = 0;
while (count < 5)
{
    System.out.println(count);
    count;
}
System.out.println("count after loop = " + count);
```

6. Imagine a program that reads the population of a city using the following statements:

```java
System.out.print("Enter the population of the city: ");
int population = keyboard.nextInt( );
```

Write a `while` loop after these statements that ensures that `population` is positive. If the user enters a population that is either negative or zero, ask the user to enter a nonnegative value.

PROGRAMMING EXAMPLE   Nested Loops

The body of a loop can contain any sort of statements. In particular, you can have a loop statement within the body of a larger loop statement. For example, the program in Listing 4.4 uses a `while` loop to compute the average of a list of nonnegative scores. The program asks the user to enter all the scores followed by a negative sentinel value to mark the end of the data. This `while` loop is placed inside a `do-while` loop so that the user can repeat the entire process for another exam, and another, until the user wishes to end the program.

The body of one loop can contain another loop

LISTING 4.4   Nested Loops *(part 1 of 2)*

```java
import java.util.Scanner;
/**
 Computes the average of a list of (nonnegative) exam scores.
 Repeats computation for more exams until the user says to stop.
*/
public class ExamAverager
{
    public static void main(String[] args)
    {
        System.out.println("This program computes the average of");
        System.out.println("a list of (nonnegative) exam scores.");
        double sum;
        int numberOfStudents;
        double next;
        String answer;
        Scanner keyboard = new Scanner(System.in);

        do
        {
            System.out.println();
            System.out.println("Enter all the scores to be averaged.");
            System.out.println("Enter a negative number after");
            System.out.println("you have entered all the scores.");
            sum = 0;
            numberOfStudents = 0;
            next = keyboard.nextDouble();
            while (next >= 0)
            {
                sum = sum + next;
                numberOfStudents++;
                next = keyboard.nextDouble();
            }
            if (numberOfStudents > 0)
                System.out.println("The average is " +
                                    (sum / numberOfStudents));
            else
                System.out.println("No scores to average.");

            System.out.println("Want to average another exam?");
            System.out.println("Enter yes or no.");
            answer = keyboard.next();
        } while (answer.equalsIgnoreCase("yes"));
    }
}
```

(continued)

LISTING 4.4   Nested Loops *(part 2 of 2)*

Sample Screen Output

```
This program computes the average of
a list of (nonnegative) exam scores.

Enter all the scores to be averaged.
Enter a negative number after
you have entered all the scores.
100
90
100
90
-1
The average is 95.0
Want to average another exam?
Enter yes or no.
yes

Enter all the scores to be averaged.
Enter a negative number after
you have entered all the scores.
90
70
80
-1
The average is 80.0
Want to average another exam?
Enter yes or no.
no
```

VideoNote
Using nested while loops

The for Statement

The **for statement,** or **for loop,** enables you to easily write a loop that is controlled by some sort of counter. For example, the following pseudocode defines a loop that iterates three times and is controlled by the counter count:

> Do the following for each value of count from 1 to 3:
>   Display count

This particular pseudocode can be expressed in Java as the following for statement:

```
for (count = 1; count <= 3; count++)
    System.out.println(count);
```

This for statement causes the output

```
1
2
3
```

After the for statement ends, any statement after the loop body executes.
In this first example of a for statement, the loop body is

```
System.out.println(count);
```

The iteration of the loop body is controlled by the line

```
for (count = 1; count <= 3; count++)
```

The first of the three expressions in parentheses, count = 1, tells what happens before the loop body is executed for the first time. The third expression, count++, is executed after each iteration of the loop body. The middle expression, count <= 3, is a boolean expression that determines when the loop will end, and it does so in the same way as the controlling boolean expression in a while loop. Thus, the loop body is executed while the value of count is less than or equal to 3. To rephrase what we just said, the for statement

```
for (count = 1; count <= 3; count++)
    Body
```

is equivalent to

```
count = 1;
while (count <= 3)
{
    Body
    count++;
}
```

The syntax of a for statement is as follows:

A for statement groups the major aspects of a loop

```
for (Initializing_Action; Boolean_Expression; Update_Action)
    Body
```

The *Body* can be a simple statement, as in our first example, but it more likely is a compound statement. Thus, the more common form of a for loop can be described as follows:

```
for (Initializing_Action; Boolean_Expression; Update_Action)
{
    Statements
       . . .
}
```

When it is executed, a for statement is equivalent to code involving a while loop. So a for statement of the preceding form is equivalent to the following:

A for loop is logically equivalent to a while loop

```
Initializing_Action;
while (Boolean_Expression)
{
    Statements
        . . .
    Update_Action;
}
```

Since a for statement is basically another notation for a kind of while loop, a for statement—just like a while statement—might not repeat its loop body at all.

Listing 4.5 provides an example of a for statement. Its action is summarized in Figure 4.5. Figure 4.6 describes the semantics of a for loop in general.

LISTING 4.5   **An Example of a for Statement**

```java
public class ForDemo
{
    public static void main(String[] args)
    {
        int countDown;
        for (countDown = 3; countDown >= 0; countDown--)
        {
            System.out.println(countDown);
            System.out.println("and counting.");
        }
        System.out.println("Blast off!");
    }
}
```

Screen Output

```
3
and counting.
2
and counting.
1
and counting.
0
and counting.
Blast off!
```

FIGURE 4.5   The Action of the for Loop in Listing 4.5

```
for (countDown = 3; countDown >= 0; countDown-)
{
    System.out.println(countDown);
    System.out.println("and counting.");
}
```

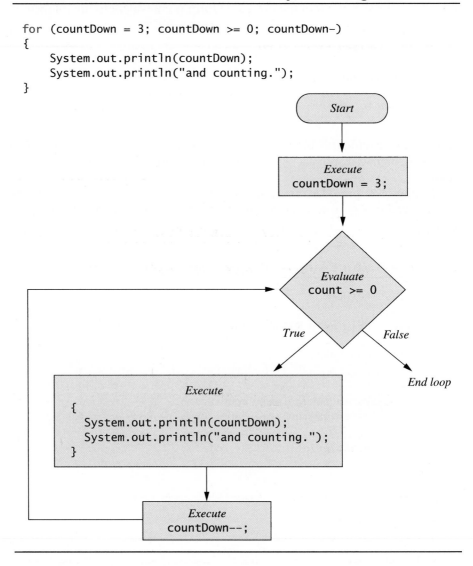

RECAP **The for Statement**

SYNTAX

```
for (Initializing_Action; Boolean_Expression; Update_Action)
    Body
```

(continued)

The *Body* may be either a simple statement or, more likely, a compound statement consisting of a list of statements enclosed in braces {}. Notice that the three items in parentheses are separated by two, not three, semicolons.

EXAMPLE

```java
for (next = 0; next <= 10; next = next + 2)
{
    sum = sum + next;
    System.out.println("sum now is " + sum);
}
```

FIGURE 4.6   The Semantics of the `for` Statement

```
for (Initializing_Action; Boolean_Expression; Update_Action)
    Body
```

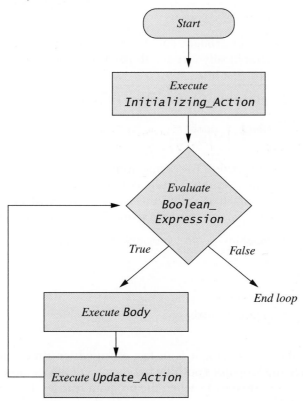

GOTCHA   Extra Semicolon in a Loop Statement

The following code looks quite ordinary. Moreover, it will compile and run with no error messages. It does, however, contain a mistake. See if you can find the mistake before reading on.

```java
int product = 1, number;
for (number = 1; number <= 10; number++);
{
    product = product * number;
}
System.out.println("Product of the numbers 1 through " +
                   "10 is " + product);
```

If you include this code in a program and run the program, the output will be

```
Product of the numbers 1 through 10 is 11
```

Now can you see what is wrong? Try to explain the problem before reading on.

If you were testing the program that produced this puzzling output, it could leave you bewildered. Clearly, something is wrong with the for loop, but what? The for loop is supposed to set the value of product equal to

$$1 \times 2 \times 3 \times 4 \times 5 \times 6 \times 7 \times 8 \times 9 \times 10$$

but instead, it sets the value of product equal to 11. How could that happen?

The problem is typographically very small. The for statement has an extra semicolon at the end of the first line:

Do not write a semicolon after the beginning of a for statement

```java
for (number = 1; number <= 10; number++)(;)
{
    product = product * number;
}
```

What does this for statement do? The semicolon at the end means that the body of the for statement is empty. A semicolon by itself is considered a statement that does nothing. It is called the **empty statement** or the **null statement.** This for statement with the extra semicolon is equivalent to

```java
for (number = 1; number <= 10; number++)
{
    //Do nothing.
}
{
    product = product * number;
}
```

Thus, the body of the for statement is in fact executed ten times; however, each time it executes, the loop does nothing but increment the variable number by 1. That leaves number equal to 11 when the program reaches the statement

```java
product = product * number;
```

(Remember, `number` starts out equal to 1 and is increased by 1 ten times, so the value becomes 11.) With `product` still 1 and `number` equal to 11, the assignment statement sets the value of `product` to 1 times 11, or 11, as the output says. To fix the problem, simply remove the extra semicolon at the end of the line that begins with `for`.

The same sort of problem can occur with a `while` loop. The following `while` loop has the same problem as our troublesome `for` loop, but the results are even worse:

```
int product = 1, number = 1;
while (number <= 10);
{
    product = product * number;
    number++;
}
System.out.println("Product of the numbers 1 through 10 is "
                   + product);
```

Do not write a semicolon after the beginning of a while statement

The extra semicolon ends the `while` loop, and so the body of the `while` loop is the empty statement. Because the body of the loop is the empty statement, nothing happens on each loop iteration. Therefore, the value of `number` never changes, and the condition

```
number <= 10
```

is always true. So the loop is an infinite loop that does nothing and does it forever! ■

Declaring Variables Within a for Statement

You can declare a variable within the initialization part of a `for` statement, as in the following example:

```
int sum = 0;
for (int n = 1; n <= 10; n++)
    sum = sum + n * n;
```

In this case, the variable `n` is **local** to the `for` loop, meaning that it cannot be used outside of the loop. For example, you would not be able to display `n` in a `println` statement after the loop completes:

```
for (int n = 1; n <= 10; n++)
    sum = sum + n * n;
System.out.println(n); //Invalid
```

The portion of a program in which a variable has meaning is known as the variable's **scope**. In the previous example, the scope of the variable `n` is the `for` statement, including its body. Thus, `n` has no meaning beyond the `for` statement.

A variable's scope is where it has meaning in a program

When a variable exists solely to control a for loop, you should declare it within the initialization portion instead of before the loop. If we had taken this advice in the example given in the previous Gotcha, we would have written the code as follows:

```
int product = 1;
for (int number = 1; number <= 10; number++)⊙
    product = product * number; //Invalid
```

Since number is now local to the for loop, and because the stray semicolon ends the loop, number is not defined after the loop. We would get a syntax error.

We will talk more about variable declarations and scope in the next chapter.

Using a Comma in a for Statement (*Optional*)

A for loop can perform more than one initialization. To use a list of initialization actions, simply separate the actions with commas, as in the following example:

```
for (n = 1, product = 1; n <= 10; n++)
    product = product * n;
```

This for loop initializes n to 1 and also initializes product to 1. Note that we use a comma, not a semicolon, to separate the initialization actions. Such a comma is called the **comma operator.**

A comma can separate multiple initializations in a for statement

Likewise, you can have multiple update actions by separating them with commas. This practice can sometimes result in a for statement that has an empty body but still does something useful. For example, the previous for statement can be rewritten as follows:

```
for (n = 1, product = 1; n <= 10; product = product * n, n++);
```

In effect, we have made the loop body part of the update action. However, your code will be more readable if you use the update action only for the variables that control the loop, as in the previous version of this for loop. We do not advocate using for loops with no body, but many programmers consider them "clever." As indicated in the previous Gotcha section, often a for loop without a body is the result of a programmer error.

You cannot have multiple boolean expressions to test for ending a for loop. However, you can string together multiple tests using the && or || operators to form one larger boolean expression.

Note that the comma operator can be used only in for statements. Be careful if you have programmed in other programming languages that allow a comma operator to be used elsewhere.

SELF-TEST QUESTIONS

7. What output is produced by the following code?

```java
for (int n = 1; n <= 4; n++)
    System.out.println(n);
```

8. What output is produced by the following code?

```java
int n;
for (n = 1; n > 4; n++)
    System.out.println(n);
```

9. What output is produced by the following code?

```java
for (int n = 4; n > 0; n--)
    System.out.println(n);
```

10. What output is produced by the following code?

```java
for (int n = 4; n > 0; n--);
    System.out.println(n);
```

(This is not the same as the previous question. Look carefully.)

11. What output is produced by the following code?

```java
for (double test = 0; test < 3; test = test + 0.5)
    System.out.println(test);
```

12. Write a for statement that displays the even numbers 2, 4, 6, 8, and 10. Each number should appear on a separate line. Declare all the variables you use.

13. What output is produced by the following code?

```java
for (int count = 0; count <= 3; count++)
    for (int count2 = 0; count2 < count; count2++)
        System.out.println(count2);
```

■ PROGRAMMING TIP   Choosing a Loop Statement

Suppose that your program needs a loop. How do you decide whether to use a while statement, a do-while statement, or a for statement? We can give you some general guidelines. You *cannot* use a do-while statement unless you are certain that, for all possible inputs to your program, the loop should be iterated at least one time. If you know that your loop should always be iterated at least one time, a do-while statement is likely to be a good choice. However, more often than you might think, a loop requires the possibility of iterating

VideoNote
Comparing loop statements

the body zero times. In those cases, you must use either a `while` statement or a `for` statement. If your computation changes some numeric quantity—such as a counter—by an equal amount on each iteration, consider a `for` statement. If the `for` statement does not seem clear, use a `while` statement. The `while` statement is always a safe choice, because you can use it to realize any sort of loop. This is not to say that you should use `while` loops exclusively; sometimes one of the other alternatives is clearer or easier to write. Many programmers use `for` statements to clarify the logic of their code. ■

The `for-each` Statement

When you want to restrict the value of a variable to a handful of values, you can define an enumeration, as you saw in the previous chapter. If you need to repeat some action for each item in an enumeration, you can use any of the loop statements that we have presented. But Java also provides another form of the `for` statement for use when you have a collection of data such as an enumeration. This form is called the **for-each statement.**

A `for-each` statement iterates for each item in a data collection

For example, in a program that plays a card game, you could define an enumeration for the four suits—clubs, diamonds, hearts, and spades—as follows:

```
enum Suit {CLUBS, DIAMONDS, HEARTS, SPADES}
```

To display these suits, you can write the following `for-each` loop:

```
for (Suit nextSuit : Suit.values())
    System.out.print(nextSuit + " ");
System.out.println();
```

The expression `Suit.values()` represents all the values in the enumeration. The variable `nextSuit` takes on each of these values one at a time as the iteration progresses. Thus, the output from this loop is

```
CLUBS DIAMONDS HEARTS SPADES
```

Chapters 7 and 12 will show you how to use the `for-each` statement for data collections other than enumerations.

4.2 PROGRAMMING WITH LOOPS

The cautious seldom err.

—CONFUCIUS

A loop typically involves three elements: the initializing statements that must precede any repetition, the loop body, and the mechanism for ending the loop. In this section we give you techniques for designing each of these loop components. Although the initializing statements come before the loop body, the loop body is naturally designed first, and so we will start our discussion there.

The Loop Body

One way to design a loop body is to write out the sequence of actions that you want your code to accomplish. For example, you might write the following actions:

Write down a sequence of actions when designing a loop

1. Display instructions to the user.
2. Initialize variables.
3. Read a number into the variable `next`.
4. `sum = sum + next`
5. Display the number and the sum so far.
6. Read another number into the variable `next`.
7. `sum = sum + next`
8. Display the number and the sum so far.
9. Read another number into the variable `next`.
10. `sum = sum + next`
11. Display the number and the sum so far.
12. Read another number into the variable `next`.
13. and so forth.

Now look for a repeated pattern in the list of actions. In this case, the repeated pattern is

Read another number into the variable `next`.
`sum = sum + next`
Display the number and the sum so far.

So the body of the loop, expressed in pseudocode, can be the preceding three actions. The entire pseudocode can be

1. Display instructions to the user.
2. Initialize variables.
3. Repeat the following for the appropriate number of times:

    {

        Read a number into the variable `next`.
        `sum = sum + next`
        Display the number and the sum so far.

    }

Note that the pattern need not start with the first action in the pseudocode. Some actions might need to occur before or after the loop is executed.

Initializing Statements

A loop depends
on correct initial
values

Consider the pseudocode we designed in the previous section. Notice that the variable sum is expected to have a value every time the instruction

```
sum = sum + next
```

is executed within the loop body. In particular, sum must have a value the first time the loop is iterated. So sum must be initialized to a value before the loop starts. When trying to decide on the correct initializing value for a variable, consider what you want to happen after one loop iteration. For our current loop, the value of sum should be set to the first value of next after one loop iteration. The only way that sum + next can evaluate to next is if sum is zero. This means that the value of sum must be initialized to zero. Thus, one of the initializations must be

```
sum = 0
```

The only other variable used in the loop is next. The first statement performed that involves next is

```
Read a number into the variable next.
```

This statement gives next a value, so next does not need to have a value before the loop is started. Thus, the only variable that needs to be initialized is sum. We can rewrite the pseudocode as follows:

1. Display instructions to the user.
2. sum = 0
3. Repeat the following for the appropriate number of times:

{

Read a number into the variable next.
sum = sum + next
Display the number and the sum so far.

}

Variables are not always initialized to zero. To see this, consider another example. Suppose your loop computes the product of *n* numbers as follows:

```
for (int count = 1; count <= n; count++)
{
    Read a number into the variable next.
    product = product * next;
}
```

In this case, let's say that all variables are of type int. If you initialize the variable product to 0, no matter how many numbers are read in and multiplied, the value of product will still be 0. So 0 clearly is not the correct initialization value for `product`. The correct initializing value for `product` is 1. To see that 1 is the correct initial value, notice that the first time through the loop, you want `product` to be set equal to the first number read in. Initializing `product` to 1 will make this happen. Thus, the loop, and its correct initialization statement, is

```
int product = 1;
for (int count = 1; count <= n; count++)
{
    Read a number into the variable next.
    product = product * next;
}
```

Controlling the Number of Loop Iterations

We now will discuss some standard techniques for ending a loop. If you are lucky, you will be able to specify exactly how many times the loop body must be repeated before the loop starts. For example, suppose that we want to know the average score on a given exam in a course. We need the number of students in the class, so we read that number into the integer variable `numberOfStudents`. In this simple case, we can use a `for` loop to repeat the loop body `numberOfStudents` times. The following will do nicely:

```
double next, average, sum = 0;
for (int count = 1; count <= numberOfStudents; count++)
{
    next = keyboard.nextDouble();
    sum = sum + next;
}
if (numberOfStudents > 0)
    average = sum/numberOfStudents;
else
    System.out.println("No scores to average.");
```

Notice that the `for` loop mechanism controls the repetition of the loop body by using the variable `count` to count from 1 to `numberOfStudents`. Loops such as this one that know the number of loop iterations before the loop starts are called **count-controlled loops.** In this particular example, `count` is not used within the loop body, but in other situations, a counter might be. Count-controlled loops do not need to be implemented as `for` loops, but that is the easiest way to do so. Notice that if no students are in the class, the loop body is iterated zero times and the `if-else` statement prevents a division by zero.

A counter can control a loop's repetition

Knowing the number of loop iterations ahead of time is not always possible. One straightforward way of ending a loop is simply to ask the user if it is time to end the loop. This technique is called **ask before iterating.** For

A loop's repetition can be controlled by asking the user whether to continue example, the following code helps a customer figure the cost of purchasing multiples of several items:

```
do
{
    System.out.println("Enter price $");
    price = keyboard.nextDouble();
    System.out.print("Enter number purchased:");
    number = keyboard.nextInt();
    System.out.println(number + " items at $" + price);
    System.out.println("Total cost $" + price * number);
    System.out.println("Want to make another purchase?");
    System.out.println("Enter yes or no.");
    answer = keyboard.next();
} while (answer.equalsIgnoreCase("yes"));
```

If you know that each user will make at least one purchase, this do-while loop will work fine. In other situations, a while loop would be best.

This code works well if each customer makes only a few purchases. The technique becomes tedious for the user, however, if the total number of loop iterations is not fairly small. For lengthy input lists, you can sometimes use a **sentinel value** to signal the end of the input. A sentinel value must be different from all possible actual data values. For example, suppose you want some code to compute the highest and lowest scores on an exam. If you know that at least one person completed the exam, and no one is ever given a negative score, you can ask the user to enter a negative number after entering the last score. The negative number is the sentinel value, not one of the exam scores. It is just an end marker.

A user can signal the end of repetition by entering a sentinel value

The code for computing the highest and lowest scores could be as follows:

```
System.out.println("Enter scores for all students.");
System.out.println("Enter a negative number after");
System.out.println("you have entered all the scores.");
Scanner keyboard = new Scanner(System.in);
double max = keyboard.nextDouble();
double min = max; //The max and min so far are the first score.
double next = keyboard.nextDouble();
while (next >= 0)
{
    if (next > max)
        max = next;
    else if (next < min)
        min = next;
    next = keyboard.nextDouble();
}
System.out.println("The highest score is " + max);
System.out.println("The lowest score is " + min);
```

If the user enters the scores

100
90

```
10
-1
```

the output will be

```
The highest score is 100
The lowest score is 10
```

The sentinel value here is –1; it is not used in the computation. That is, the lowest score is 10, not –1. The –1 is just an end marker.

The three previous techniques—using a counter, asking the user, and detecting a sentinel value—cover most situations you are likely to encounter. The next case study involves a sentinel value and uses a boolean variable to end the loop's iteration.

CASE STUDY   Using a Boolean Variable to End a Loop

In this case study, we will not solve a complete problem, but we will design a loop for a commonly occurring subtask and place it in a demonstration program. In doing so, you will become familiar with one of the most common uses of boolean variables.

Our loop will read a list of numbers and compute the sum of all the numbers on the list. The numbers will all be nonnegative. For example, they might be the number of hours worked by each person on a programming team. Because nobody works a negative number of hours, we know that the numbers are all nonnegative, and so we can use a negative number as a sentinel value to mark the end of the list. For this task, we will assume that the numbers will all be integers, but the same technique would work for other kinds of numbers and even for nonnumeric data.

Task specification

You will get a better grasp of the problem and possible solutions if we first design the loop in pseudocode. Let's begin with the following:

```
int sum = 0;
Do the following for each number on the list:
if (the number is negative)
    Make this the last loop iteration.
else
    sum = sum + the number
```

First-draft pseudocode

Because we know that a negative number marks the end of the list, we can refine the pseudocode as follows:

```
int next, sum = 0;
while (there are more numbers to read)
{
    next = keyboard.nextInt();
    if (next < 0)
        Make this the last loop iteration.
    else
        sum = sum + next;
}
```

We can finish converting this pseudocode to Java code in a number of different ways. One way is to use a boolean variable. A nice thing about using a boolean variable is that our code can read much like an English sentence. For example, let's use a boolean variable named `thereAreMoreNumbersToRead`. Simply declaring this boolean variable and substituting it for the phrase "there are more numbers to read" in our pseudocode yields the following:

```
int next, sum = 0;
boolean thereAreMoreNumbersToRead = initial value;
while (thereAreMoreNumbersToRead)
{
    next = keyboard.nextInt();
    if (next < 0)
        Make this the last loop iteration.
    else
        sum = sum + next;
}
```

Completing the conversion of this loop to working Java code is straightforward. We can translate the phrase *Make this the last loop iteration* by observing that the loop ends when the boolean variable `thereAreMoreNumbersToRead` is false. So the way to end the loop is to set `thereAreMoreNumbersToRead` equal to `false`. Thus, *Make this the last loop iteration* will translate into

```
thereAreMoreNumbersToRead = false;
```

Using a boolean
variable for loop
control

All that is left to do is to determine the initial value for `thereAreMoreNumbersToRead`. We know that even if the list of numbers is empty, we will have at least the sentinel value to read. Therefore, we know that the loop body must be iterated at least once. So to get the loop started, `thereAreMoreNumbersToRead` must be true, meaning that we must initialize it to `true`. Thus, we get the following code:

```
int next, sum = 0;
boolean thereAreMoreNumbersToRead = true;
while (thereAreMoreNumbersToRead)
{
    next = keyboard.nextInt();
    if (next < 0)
        thereAreMoreNumbersToRead = false;
    else
        sum = sum + next;
}
```

When the loop ends, the variable `sum` contains the sum of the numbers on the input list, not including the sentinel value.

The loop is ready to use in a program. Since the variable name `thereAreMoreNumbersToRead` is a bit long, we shorten it to `areMore` and produce the program shown in Listing 4.6.

LISTING 4.6   Using a Boolean Variable to End a Loop

```java
import java.util.Scanner;
/**
 Illustrates the use of a boolean variable to end loop iteration.
*/
public class BooleanDemo
{
    public static void main(String[] args)
    {
        System.out.println("Enter nonnegative numbers.");
        System.out.println("Place a negative number at the end");
        System.out.println("to serve as an end marker.");
        int sum = 0;
        boolean areMore = true;
        Scanner keyboard = new Scanner(System.in);
        while (areMore)
        {
            int next = keyboard.nextInt();
            if (next < 0)
                areMore = false;
            else
                sum = sum + next;
        }
        System.out.println("The sum of the numbers is " + sum);
    }
}
```

Sample Screen Output

```
Enter nonnegative numbers.
Place a negative number at the end
to serve as an end marker.
1 2 3 -1
The sum of the numbers is 6
```

PROGRAMMING EXAMPLE   Spending Spree

Imagine that you have won a $100 gift certificate in a contest. You must spend the money in a particular store, but you can buy at most only three items. The store's computer tracks the amount of money you have left to spend as well as the number of items you have bought. Each time you choose an item, the computer will tell you whether you can buy it. Although we have chosen small numbers for our example, we want to write a program for the computer so that both the dollar amount available and the number of items you can buy are easily changed.

Clearly, we have a repetitive process here. You will continue buying as long as you have enough money and have bought fewer than three items. Our loop control will be based on these two criteria. We can reflect this situation in the following pseudocode, which is likely not our first draft:

Algorithm for the store's computer program

```
1. amountRemaining = amount of gift certificate
2. totalSpent = 0
3. itemNumber = 1
4. while (we have money left to spend and (itemNumber <=max number
   of items))
   {
       Display amount of money left and number of items that can
       be bought.
       Read cost of proposed purchase.
       if (we can afford the purchase)
       {
           Display a message.
           totalSpent = totalSpent + cost of item
           Update amountRemaining
           if (amountRemaining > 0)
           {
               Display amount of money left.
               itemNumber++
           }

           else
           {
               Display a message (no more money).
               Make this the last loop iteration.
           }
       }

       else
           Display a message (item is too expensive).
   }
   Display amount of money spent and farewell message.
```

We want to focus on how we will implement the criteria for ending the loop. Just as in the previous case study, we will use a boolean variable to indicate whether we have money left to spend. We can name this variable haveMoney. Before the loop, we can make this variable true, and when we are ready to exit the loop, we can change the value of haveMoney to false.

Listing 4.7 shows our completed program and some sample output. Notice our use of named constants for both the amount of the gift certificate—our spending money—and the maximum number of items we can purchase. For simplicity, we assume that all our dollar amounts are integers.

The next section uses a break statement to exit this loop. Doing so is typically an inferior technique.

LISTING 4.7   **Spending Spree Program** *(part 1 of 2)*

```java
import java.util.Scanner;
public class SpendingSpree
{
    public static final int SPENDING_MONEY = 100;
    public static final int MAX_ITEMS = 3;
    public static void main(String[] args)
    {
        Scanner keyboard = new Scanner(System.in);
        boolean haveMoney = true;
        int leftToSpend = SPENDING_MONEY;
        int totalSpent = 0;
        int itemNumber = 1;
        while (haveMoney && (itemNumber <= MAX_ITEMS))
        {
            System.out.println("You may buy up to " +
                            (MAX_ITEMS - itemNumber + 1) +
                            " items");
            System.out.println("costing no more than $" +
                            leftToSpend + ".");
            System.out.print("Enter cost of item #" +
                            itemNumber + ": $");
            int itemCost = keyboard.nextInt();
            if (itemCost <= leftToSpend)
            {
                System.out.println("You may buy this item. ");
                totalSpent = totalSpent + itemCost;
                System.out.println("You spent $" + totalSpent +
                                " so far.");
                leftToSpend = SPENDING_MONEY - totalSpent;
                if (leftToSpend > 0)
                    itemNumber++;
                else
                {
                    System.out.println("You are out of money.");
                    haveMoney = false;
                }
            }
        }
```

(continued)

LISTING 4.7 Spending Spree Program *(part 2 of 2)*

```
                else
                    System.out.println("You cannot buy that item.");
            }
            System.out.println("You spent $" + totalSpent +
                                ", and are done shopping.");
        }
}
```

Sample Screen Output

```
You may buy up to 3 items
costing no more than $100.
Enter cost of item #1: $80
You may buy this item.
You spent $80 so far.
You may buy up to 2 items
costing no more than $20.
Enter cost of item #2: $20
You may buy this item.
You spent $100 so far.
You are out of money.
You spent $100, and are done shopping.
```

The break Statement and continue Statement in Loops (*Optional*)

As we have presented loops so far, the while, do-while, and for statements always exit when their controlling boolean expression—*Boolean_Expression*—becomes false. For the previous program in Listing 4.7, this controlling expression involves the boolean variable haveMoney. So when haveMoney becomes false, the controlling expression is false and the loop ends.

In addition, a loop can exit when it encounters a break statement. When a break statement executes, the immediately enclosing loop ends, and the remainder of the loop body does not execute. Java allows a break statement to be used within a while loop, a do-while loop, or a for loop. This is the same break statement that we used earlier in switch statements.

The boolean variable haveMoney occurs three times in the program in Listing 4.7. If we omitted its use in the first two occurrences and replaced the statement

```
haveMoney = false;
```

with

```
break;
```

the loop in the resulting program would have the form shown in Listing 4.8. When `leftToSpend` is no longer positive, the `println` method executes, followed by the `break` statement, which ends the iteration. The next statement to execute would be the one after the body of the `while` statement.

If the loop containing a `break` statement is within a larger loop, the `break` statement ends only the innermost loop. Similarly, if the `break` statement is within a `switch` statement that is inside a loop, the `break` statement ends the `switch` statement but not the loop. The `break` statement ends only the *innermost* loop or `switch` statement that contains the `break` statement.

A loop without a `break` statement has a simple, easy-to-understand structure. One boolean expression is tested to decide whether to end the loop. When you add a `break` statement, the loop might end because either the controlling boolean expression is false or a `break` statement executes. Thus, using a `break` statement within a loop can make the loop more difficult to understand.

For example, the loop in Listing 4.8 begins with

```
while (itemNumber <= MAX_ITEMS)
```

The loop appears to have only one condition that causes it to end. To realize that another condition exists, you need to study the body of the loop to discover the `break` statement. In contrast, the loop in Listing 4.7 begins with

```
while (haveMoney && (itemNumber <= MAX_ITEMS))
```

A break statement within a loop ends its iteration

LISTING 4.8   **Ending a Loop with a break Statement**

```
while (itemNumber <= MAX_ITEMS)
{
    . . .
    if (itemCost <= leftToSpend)
    {
        . . .
        if (leftToSpend > 0)
            itemNumber++;
        else
        {
            System.out.println("You are out of money.");
            break;
        }
    }
    else
        . . .
}
System.out.println( . . . );
```

You quickly can see that the loop ends when you either run out of money or exceed the maximum number of items.

A `continue`
statement within
a loop ends the
current iteration

A `continue` statement within the body of a loop ends its current iteration and begins the next one. Using a `continue` statement in this way has the same problems as using a `break` statement. The `continue` statement, like the `break` statement, can and should be avoided in a loop.

■ **PROGRAMMING TIP**   Avoid the `break` and `continue`
Statements in Loops

Because of the complications they introduce, `break` statements and `continue` statements within loops should be avoided. Any loop that includes either of these statements can be written without one.   ■

SELF-TEST QUESTIONS

14. Write a Java loop that will display the phrase One more time four times. Also give any declarations or initializing statements that are needed.

15. Write a Java loop that will set the variable result equal to 2^5. Initialize the value of result to 1 and then multiply it by 2 for each of five loop iterations. Also give any declarations or initializing statements that are needed.

16. Write a Java loop that will read a list of numbers of type double and then display their average. The numbers are all greater than or equal to 1.0. The input data ends with a sentinel value, which you must specify. Also give any declarations or initializing statements that are needed.

17. What output is produced by the following code?

```java
for (int n = 1; n <= 3; n++)
{
    switch (n)
    {
        case 1:
            System.out.println("One");
            break;
        case 2:
            System.out.println("Two");
            break;
        case 3:
            System.out.println("Three");
            break;
```

```
        default:
            System.out.println("Default case");
            break;
    }
}
System.out.println("After the loop");
```

18. What output is produced by the following code?

```
for (int n = 1; n <= 5; n++)
{
    if (n == 3)
        break;
    System.out.println("Hello");
}
System.out.println("After the loop");
```

19. What output is produced by the following code?

```
for (int n = 1; n <= 5; n++)
{
    if (n == 3)
        System.exit(0);
    System.out.println("Hello");
}
System.out.println("After the loop");
```

20. Revise the loop shown in Listing 4.6 to use a break statement instead of the boolean variable areMore. Comment on how your loop compares with the original one.

Loop Bugs

Programs containing loops are more likely to have mistakes than the simpler programs you saw before you started using loops. Fortunately, the kinds of mistakes you are most likely to make when writing a loop form a pattern, so we can tell you what to look for. Moreover, some standard techniques will help you locate and fix bugs in your loops.

The two most common kinds of loop errors are

Two common
loop bugs

- Unintended infinite loops
- Off-by-one errors

Let's consider them in order.

We have already discussed infinite loops, but we need to emphasize one subtlety about them. A loop might terminate for some input data values but repeat infinitely for other values. Let's consider an example. Suppose a friend's checking account is overdrawn. The bank charges a penalty each month that the balance is negative. Our friend wants a program that will tell him how long it will take to get a nonnegative account balance if he deposits a fixed amount each month. We design the following code:

```
count = 0;
while (balance < 0)
{
    balance = balance - penalty;
    balance = balance + deposit;
    count++;
}
System.out.println("You will have a nonnegative " +
                "balance in " + count + " months.");
```

Certain data can cause an infinite loop

We place this code in a complete program and test it using some reasonable data, like $15 for the penalty and $50 for the size of the deposit. The program runs fine. So we give it to our friend, who runs it and finds that it goes into an infinite loop. What happened? Our friend obviously does not have a head for numbers and has decided to make small deposits of only $10 per month. But the bank charges a penalty of $15 per month when an account balance is negative. So the account becomes more overdrawn every month, even though your friend makes deposits.

Code should try to guard against user error

This situation might seem impossible. Our friend would not make such a stupid mistake. Don't count on it! It can happen even if our friend is not stupid. People are sometimes careless and often unpredictable. One way to fix this bug is to add code that will test to see whether the loop is infinite. For example, we might change the code to the following:

```
if (deposit <= penalty)
    System.out.println("Deposit is too small.");
else
{
    count = 0;
    while (balance < 0)
    {
        balance = balance - penalty;
        balance = balance + deposit;
        count++;
    }
    System.out.println("You will have a nonnegative " +
                    "balance in " + count + " months.");
}
```

Off-by-one errors are caused by an incorrect boolean expression

The other common kind of loop bug is an **off-by-one error.** This error causes your loop to repeat its body either one too many times or one too few times. These sorts of errors can result from a careless design of a controlling boolean expression. For example, if we use < in the controlling boolean expression when we should use <=, our loop could easily repeat the body the wrong number of times.

Another common problem with the controlling boolean expression of a loop has to do with the use of == to test for equality. This equality operator works satisfactorily for integers and characters, but it is not reliable for floating-point numbers because they are approximate quantities; == tests for exact equality. The result of such a test is unpredictable. When comparing floating-point numbers, always use something involving less-than or greater-than, such as <=. Using == or != to compare floating-point numbers can produce an off-by-one error, an unintended infinite loop, or even some other type of error.

Do not compare floating-point values using == or !=

Off-by-one errors can easily go unnoticed. If a loop iterates one too many times—or one too few times—the results might still look reasonable but be off by enough to cause trouble later on. Always make a specific check for off-by-one errors by comparing your loop results to results you know to be true by some other means, such as a pencil-and-paper calculation of a simple case.

Off-by-one errors might be unnoticed.

■ **PROGRAMMING TIP**   **Always Retest**

Whenever you find a bug in a program and "fix" it, always retest the program. Yet another bug might be waiting, or your "fix" may have introduced a new bug. The process of retesting a modified program is called **regression testing**. ■

Tracing Variables

If your program misbehaves but you cannot see what is wrong, your best bet is to trace some key variables. **Tracing variables** means watching the variables change value while the program is running. A program typically does not display the value of a variable every time it changes, but seeing how the variables change can help you debug your program.

Trace variables as their values change during execution

Many systems have a built-in utility that lets you easily trace variables without making any changes to your program. These debugging systems vary from one installation to another. If you have such a debugging facility, learning how to use it is worthwhile. If you do not have such a debugging facility, you can trace variables simply by inserting some extra, temporary println statements in your program.

For example, suppose you want to trace the variables in the following code, which contains an error:

```
count = 0;
while (balance < 0)
{
    balance = balance + penalty;
    balance = balance - deposit;
    count++;
}
System.out.println("Nonnegative balance in " + count +
                " months.");
```

You can trace the variables by adding `println` statements, as follows:

```
count = 0;
System.out.println("count == " + count);                        //*
System.out.println("balance == " + balance);                    //*
System.out.println("penalty == " + penalty);                    //*
System.out.println("deposit == " + deposit);                    //*
while (balance < 0)
{
    balance = balance + penalty;
    System.out.println("balance + penalty == " + balance);//*
    balance = balance - deposit;
    System.out.println("balance - deposit == " + balance);//*
    count++;
    System.out.println("count == " + count);                    //*
}
System.out.println("Nonnegative balance in " + count +
                   " months.");
```

After you have discovered the error and fixed the bugs in the code, you can remove the trace statements. Tagging these statements with a distinctive comment, as we have done here, will facilitate locating them.

Inserting all the trace statements in the preceding example might seem like a lot of bother, but it is not so very much work. If you wish, you can first try tracing only some of the variables to see if that gives you enough information to find the problem. However, it is usually fastest to just trace all, or almost all, of the variables right from the start.

VideoNote
Debugging a loop

■ PROGRAMMING TIP   Use a DEBUG Flag When Tracing Variables

Sometimes while debugging a program, you want to temporarily skip any statements you have added to trace the values of certain variables. You can conveniently do this by defining a boolean constant DEBUG, as follows:

```
public static final boolean DEBUG = true;
. . .
if (DEBUG)
{
    <Statements that display the values of certain variables>
}
```

In this example, the statements within the body of the `if` statement will execute. Later, if you wish to skip them, you can change the value of DEBUG to false. ■

Assertion Checks

An **assertion** is a statement that says something about the state of your program. An assertion can be either true or false but should be true if there are no mistakes in your program. For example, all the comments in the following code are assertions:

An assertion states a truth if a program's logic is correct

```
//n == 1
while (n < limit)
{
    n = 2 * n;
}
//n >= limit
//n is the smallest power of 2 >= limit
```

Note that while each of these assertions can be either true or false, depending on the values of n and limit, they all should be true if the program is performing correctly. An assertion "asserts" that something is true about your program code when program execution reaches the location of the assertion. Although our example involves a loop, you can write assertions for other situations as well.

In Java, you can actually check to see whether an assertion is true and, if it is not true, you can stop the program and display an error message. An **assertion check** in Java has the following form:

```
assert Boolean_Expression;
```

An assert statement checks an assertion

If you run your program in a certain way, and if *Boolean_Expression* is false, the program ends after displaying an error message saying that an assertion failed. However, if *Boolean_Expression* is true, nothing special happens and execution continues.

For example, the previous code can be written as follows, with two of the comments replaced by assertion checks:

```
assert n == 1;
while (n < limit)
{
    n = 2 * n;
}
assert n >= limit;
//n is the smallest power of 2 >= limit.
```

Note that we translated only two of the three comments into assertion checks. Not all assertion comments lend themselves to becoming assertion checks. For example, the final comment is an assertion. It is either true or false, and if the program code is correct, it will be true. However, there is no simple way to convert this last comment into a boolean expression. Doing so would not be impossible, but you would need to use code that would itself be more complicated than what you would be checking. Your decision as to whether to translate a comment into an assertion check will depend on the details of the particular case.

Assertion
checking can be
on or off

You can turn assertion checking on and off. You can turn it on when debugging code so that a failed assertion will stop your program and display an error message. Once your code is debugged, you can turn assertion checking off so that the assertion checks are ignored, making your code run more efficiently. Thus, you can leave the assertion checks in your program but ignore them after your program is debugged.

The normal way of running a program has assertion checking turned off. To run your program with assertion checking turned on, use the following command:

```
java -enableassertions YourProgram
```

If you are using an integrated development environment (IDE), check its documentation for a way to set options for assertion checking.

RECAP Assertion Checking

SYNTAX

```
Assert Boolean_Expression;
```

You can place an assertion check anywhere in your code. If assertion checking is turned on and *Boolean_Expression* is false, your program will display a suitable error message and end execution. If assertion checking is not turned on, the assertion check is treated as a comment.

EXAMPLE

```
assert n >= limit;
```

SELF-TEST QUESTIONS

21. What is the bug in the code in the section "Tracing Variables"?

22. Add some suitable output statements to the following code, so that all variables are traced:

```
int sum = 0;
for (int n = 1; n < 10; n++)
    sum = sum + n;
System.out.println("1 + 2 + ... + 9 + 10 == " + sum);
```

23. What is the bug in the code in the previous question?

24. What is an assertion? Give some examples of assertions.

25. Suppose that you did not have assertion checking in Java. (Earlier versions of Java did not.) Write some code to simulate the following assertion check, where `balance` is a variable of type `double`:

```
assert balance > 0;
```

4.3 GRAPHICS SUPPLEMENT

Life is like an ever-shifting kaleidoscope—a slight change, and all patterns alter.

—SHARON SALZBERG

In this section we create an applet that uses a loop to produce its drawing. The applet will also use an `if` statement and the method `setColor`, both of which are described in the previous chapter. In addition, we introduce the method `drawString` and use it to write text in the applet's window.

PROGRAMMING EXAMPLE A Multiface Applet

Listing 4.9 contains an applet that displays a sequence of seven faces. The first five faces alternate in color between yellow and white, and each has a bit more of a smile than the one before. The sixth face is throwing a kiss to the user, and the seventh face is blushing (presumably because it is shy about kissing). Think of the seven faces as an animation or a sequence of time-lapse snapshots. (There is no reason for the faces to alternate between yellow and white, except to make the program more interesting.)

The first five faces are the same except for minor variations, and so they are drawn within a `for` loop whose loop control variable is `i`. The body of the `for` loop draws a face, with changes given in terms of `i`. For each value of `i`, a face is drawn at the point (X_FACE0 + 50 * i, Y_FACE0 + 30 * i). So, when `i` is zero, the first face is drawn at the point (X_FACE0, Y_FACE0). For each successive value of `i`, another face is drawn 50 pixels further to the right and 30 pixels lower on the screen. X_FACE0 and Y_FACE0 are named constants. Instead of computing 50 * i and 30 * i over and over, we compute them once and store them in the variables xOffset and yOffset, respectively.

LISTING 4.9 An Applet That Uses Looping and Branching *(part 1 of 4)*

```java
import javax.swing.JApplet;
import java.awt.Graphics;
import java.awt.Color;

public class MultipleFaces extends JApplet
{
    public static final int FACE_DIAMETER = 50;
    public static final int X_FACE0 = 10;
    public static final int Y_FACE0 = 5;

    public static final int EYE_WIDTH = 5;
    public static final int EYE_HEIGHT = 10;
    public static final int X_RIGHT_EYE0 = 20;
    public static final int Y_RIGHT_EYE0 = 15;
    public static final int X_LEFT_EYE0 = 45;
    public static final int Y_LEFT_EYE0 = Y_RIGHT_EYE0;

    public static final int NOSE_DIAMETER = 5;
    public static final int X_NOSE0 = 32;
    public static final int Y_NOSE0 = 25;

    public static final int MOUTH_WIDTH = 30;
    public static final int MOUTH_HEIGHT0 = 0;
    public static final int X_MOUTH0 = 20;
    public static final int Y_MOUTH0 = 35;
    public static final int MOUTH_START_ANGLE = 180;
    public static final int MOUTH_EXTENT_ANGLE = 180;

    public void paint(Graphics canvas)
    {
        int i, xOffset, yOffset; //Want i to exist after the loop ends
        for (i = 0; i <= 4; i++)
        {   //Draw one face:
            xOffset = 50 * i;
            yOffset = 30 * i;

            //Draw face circle:
            if (i % 2 == 0) //if i is even

            {   //Make face light gray
                canvas.setColor(Color.LIGHT_GRAY);
                canvas.fillOval(X_FACE0 + xOffset, Y_FACE0 + 30 * i,
                            FACE_DIAMETER, FACE_DIAMETER);
            }
            canvas.setColor(Color.BLACK);
            canvas.drawOval(X_FACE0 + xOffset, Y_FACE0 + yOffset,
                            FACE_DIAMETER, FACE_DIAMETER);
```

(continued)

LISTING 4.9   An Applet That Uses Looping and Branching *(part 2 of 4)*

```
        //Draw eyes:
        canvas.setColor(Color.BLUE);
        canvas.fillOval(X_RIGHT_EYE0 + xOffset, Y_RIGHT_EYE0 +
                        yOffset, EYE_WIDTH, EYE_HEIGHT);
        canvas.fillOval(X_LEFT_EYE0 + xOffset, Y_LEFT_EYE0 +
                        yOffset, EYE_WIDTH, EYE_HEIGHT);
        //Draw nose:
        canvas.setColor(Color.BLACK);
        canvas.fillOval(X_NOSE0 + xOffset, Y_NOSE0 + yOffset,
                        NOSE_DIAMETER, NOSE_DIAMETER);
        //Draw mouth:
        canvas.setColor(Color.RED);
        canvas.drawArc(X_MOUTH0 + xOffset, Y_MOUTH0 + yOffset,
                        MOUTH_WIDTH, MOUTH_HEIGHT0 + 3 * i,
                        MOUTH_START_ANGLE, MOUTH_EXTENT_ANGLE);
}
//i is 5 when the previous loop ends
xOffset = 50 * i;
yOffset = 30 * i;

//Draw kissing face:
//Draw face outline:
canvas.setColor(Color.BLACK);
canvas.drawOval(X_FACE0 + xOffset, Y_FACE0 + yOffset,
                FACE_DIAMETER, FACE_DIAMETER);
//Draw eyes:
canvas.setColor(Color.BLUE);
canvas.fillOval(X_RIGHT_EYE0 + xOffset, Y_RIGHT_EYE0 + yOffset,
                EYE_WIDTH, EYE_HEIGHT);
canvas.fillOval(X_LEFT_EYE0 + xOffset, Y_LEFT_EYE0 + yOffset,
                EYE_WIDTH, EYE_HEIGHT);
//Draw nose:
canvas.setColor(Color.BLACK);
canvas.fillOval(X_NOSE0 + xOffset, Y_NOSE0 + yOffset,
                NOSE_DIAMETER, NOSE_DIAMETER);
//Draw mouth in shape of a kiss:
canvas.setColor(Color.RED);
canvas.fillOval(X_MOUTH0 + xOffset + 10, Y_MOUTH0 + yOffset,
                MOUTH_WIDTH - 20, MOUTH_WIDTH - 20);
```

> After the last iteration of the loop body, the value of i is incremented one last time to become 5.

(continued)

LISTING 4.9 An Applet That Uses Looping and Branching *(part 3 of 4)*

```
//Add text:
canvas.drawString("Kiss, Kiss.",
       X_FACE0 + xOffset + FACE_DIAMETER, Y_FACE0 + yOffset);

//Draw blushing face:
i++;
xOffset = 50 * i;
yOffset = 30 * i;

//Draw face circle:
canvas.setColor(Color.GRAY);
canvas.fillOval(X_FACE0 + xOffset, Y_FACE0 + yOffset,
                FACE_DIAMETER, FACE_DIAMETER);
canvas.setColor(Color.BLACK);
canvas.drawOval(X_FACE0 + xOffset, Y_FACE0 + yOffset,
                FACE_DIAMETER, FACE_DIAMETER);

//Draw eyes:
canvas.setColor(Color.BLACK);
canvas.fillOval(X_RIGHT_EYE0 + xOffset, Y_RIGHT_EYE0 +
                yOffset, EYE_WIDTH, EYE_HEIGHT);
canvas.fillOval(X_LEFT_EYE0 + xOffset, Y_LEFT_EYE0 + yOffset,
                EYE_WIDTH, EYE_HEIGHT);

//Draw nose:
canvas.setColor(Color.BLACK);
canvas.fillOval(X_NOSE0 + xOffset, Y_NOSE0 + yOffset,
                NOSE_DIAMETER, NOSE_DIAMETER);

//Draw mouth:
canvas.setColor(Color.BLACK);
canvas.drawArc(X_MOUTH0 + xOffset, Y_MOUTH0 + yOffset,
               MOUTH_WIDTH, MOUTH_HEIGHT0 + 3 * (i - 2),
               MOUTH_START_ANGLE, MOUTH_EXTENT_ANGLE);

//Add text:
canvas.drawString("Tee Hee.",
       X_FACE0 + xOffset + FACE_DIAMETER, Y_FACE0 + yOffset);
    }
}
```

(continued)

LISTING 4.9   **An Applet That Uses Looping and Branching** *(part 4 of 4)*

Applet Output

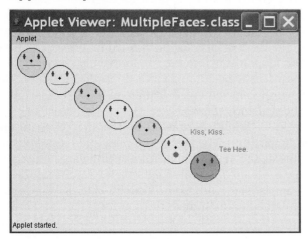

The following code adds the color yellow to the face whenever i is an even number:

```
if (i % 2 == 0) //if i is even
{   //Make face yellow
    canvas.setColor(Color.YELLOW);
    canvas.fillOval(X_FACE0 + xOffset, Y_FACE0 + yOffset,
                    FACE_DIAMETER, FACE_DIAMETER);
}
```

Draw a yellow face, then its black outline

After this, the black outline of the circle is drawn by the statements

```
canvas.setColor(Color.BLACK);
canvas.drawOval(X_FACE0 + xOffset, Y_FACE0 + yOffset,
                FACE_DIAMETER, FACE_DIAMETER);
```

Each yellow face has its interior drawn before the black outline of the circle so that the black outline shows on top of the filled circle.

The next few lines of the loop body draw the eyes and nose, which are the same for each face. The mouth is drawn by the following statements at the end of the loop body:

```
//Draw mouth:
canvas.setColor(Color.RED);
canvas.drawArc(X_MOUTH0 + xOffset, Y_MOUTH0 + yOffset,
               MOUTH_WIDTH, MOUTH_HEIGHT0 + 3 * i,
               MOUTH_START_ANGLE, MOUTH_EXTENT_ANGLE);
```

Each mouth is drawn in the same way but differs a little for each value of i. The height of each mouth increases by 3 pixels as i is increased by 1. The height of the first mouth, when i is zero, is MOUTH_HEIGHT0, which is a named constant set to zero. Thus, the first mouth is straight across with no curve. The second mouth, when i is 1, is 3 pixels in height, so its curve is more pronounced to look more like a smile. The smile continues to grow for the first five faces.

The last two faces are given by code that comes after the loop body. However, the code for each of these two faces is just a minor variation on the loop body. In particular, the last two faces are positioned in terms of i, like the faces produced by the for loop. Just before the for loop ends, the value of i is increased by 1, so the next face is positioned correctly in the sequence. Then, before the last face is drawn, i is incremented again, and so the last face is also correctly positioned in the sequence of faces.

The mouth of the next-to-last face is drawn as a red filled circle to make it appear to be in a kissing position. The last face is pink and has a full smile. The full smile is the same as the smile drawn for the fifth face, when i was equal to 4. Since i is now 6, we use a mouth height of i-2 for the last face.

The last two faces are labeled with some text by calls to the method drawString, which is explained in the next section.

The drawString Method

The method drawString is similar to the methods for drawing ovals, but drawString displays text rather than a drawing. For example, the following writes the word Hello starting at the point (10, 20):

```
canvas.drawString("Hello", 10, 20);
```

The invocation

```
//Add text:
canvas.drawString("Kiss, Kiss.",
        X_FACE0 + xOffset + FACE_DIAMETER, Y_FACE0 + yOffset);
```

from Listing 4.9 writes the phrase Kiss, Kiss starting at the point whose x- and y-coordinates are X_FACE0 + xOffset + FACE_DIAMETER and Y_FACE0 + yOffset, respectively.

RECAP The drawString Method

SYNTAX

```
canvas.drawString(String, X, Y);
```

The method drawString writes the text given by the argument *String* within the applet's window at the point (*X, Y*).

EXAMPLE

```
canvas.drawString("Hello", 10, 20);
```

SELF-TEST QUESTION

26. Write a loop that can be used in a Java applet to draw the following row of identical circles:

CHAPTER SUMMARY

- A loop is a programming construct that repeats an action some number of times. The part that is repeated is called the body of the loop. Every repetition of the loop body is called a loop iteration.

- Java has three kinds of loop statements: the `while` statement, the `do-while` statement, and the `for` statement.

- Both the `while` statement and the `do-while` statement repeat the body of the loop while a boolean expression is true. The `do-while` statement executes its body at least once, but the `while` statement might not execute its body at all.

- The logic of a `for` statement is identical to that of a `while` loop. Its initialization, test, and update steps are given together, rather than dispersed throughout the loop. The `for` statement often is used for loops controlled by a counter.

- The `for-each` statement is a variation of the `for` statement that iterates through all the elements in a collection of data such as an enumeration.

- One way to end an input loop is to place a sentinel value at the end of the data and have the loop check for the sentinel value.

- A variable of type `boolean` can be used to control a loop statement.

- The most common kinds of loop bugs are unintended infinite loops and off-by-one errors.

- Tracing a variable means to display its value at selected places in the program. Tracing can be done using special debugging utilities or by inserting temporary output statements.

- An assertion is a statement—made at a certain point within a method—of what should be true if the method is correct. Java provides an assertion check to test whether an assertion is actually true.

- You can display text in an applet drawing by using the method `drawString`.

Exercises

1. Write a fragment of code that will read words from the keyboard until the word done is entered. For each word except done, report whether its first character is equal to its last character. For the required loop, use a

   a. while statement
   b. do-while statement

2. Develop an algorithm for computing the month-by-month balance in your savings account. You can make one transaction—a deposit or a withdrawal—each month. Interest is added to the account at the beginning of each month. The monthly interest rate is the yearly percentage rate divided by 12.

3. Develop an algorithm for a simple game of guessing at a secret five-digit code. When the user enters a guess at the code, the program returns two values: the number of digits in the guess that are in the correct position and the sum of those digits. For example, if the secret code is 53840, and the user guesses 83241, the digits 3 and 4 are in the correct position. Thus, the program should respond with 2 and 7. Allow the user to guess a fixed number of times.

4. Write a fragment of code that will compute the sum of the first n positive odd integers. For example, if n is 5, you should compute $1 + 3 + 5 + 7 + 9$.

5. Convert the following code so that it uses nested while statements instead of for statements:

```
int s = 0;
int t = 1;
for (int i = 0; i < 10; i++)
{
    s = s + i;
    for (int j = i; j > 0; j--)
    {
        t = t * (j - i);
    }
    s = s * t;
    System.out.println("T is " + t);
}
System.out.println("S is " + s);
```

6. Write a for statement to compute the sum $1 + 2^2 + 3^2 + 4^2 + 5^2 + \ldots + n^2$.

7. (*Optional*) Repeat the previous question, but use the comma operator and omit the for statement's body.

8. Write a loop that will count the number of blank characters in a given string.

9. Write a loop that will create a new string that is the reverse of a given string.

10. Write a program that will compute statistics for eight coin tosses. The user will enter either an h for heads or a t for tails for the eight tosses. The program will then display the total number and percentages of heads and tails. Use the increment operator to count each h and t that is entered. For example, a possible sample dialogue between the program and the user might be

```
For each coin toss enter either h for heads or t for tails.
First toss: h
Second toss: t
Third toss: t
Fourth toss: h
Fifth toss: t
Sixth toss: h
Seventh toss: t
Eighth toss: t
Number of heads: 3
Number of tails: 5
Percent heads: 37.5
Percent tails: 62.5
```

11. Suppose we attend a party. To be sociable, we will shake hands with everyone else. Write a fragment of code using a for statement that will compute the total number of handshakes that occur. (*Hint*: Upon arrival, each person shakes hands with everyone that is already there. Use the loop to find the total number of handshakes as each person arrives.)

12. Define an enumeration for each of the months in the year. Use a for-each statement to display each month.

13. Write a fragment of code that computes the final score of a baseball game. Use a loop to read the number of runs scored by both teams during each of nine innings. Display the final score afterwards.

14. Suppose that you work for a beverage company. The company wants to know the optimal cost for a cylindrical container that holds a specified volume. Write a fragment of code that uses an ask-before-iterating loop. During each iteration of the loop, your code will ask the user to enter the volume and the radius of the cylinder. Compute and display the height and cost of the container. Use the following formulas, where V is the volume, r is the radius, h is the height, and C is the cost.

$$h = \frac{V}{\pi r^2}$$
$$C = 2\pi r(r + h)$$

15. Suppose that we want to compute the geometric mean of a list of positive values. To compute the geometric mean of k values, multiply them all together and then compute the kth root of the value. For example, the geometric mean of 2, 5, and 7 is $\sqrt[3]{2 \times 5 \times 7}$. Use a loop with a sentinel value to allow a user to enter an arbitrary number of values. Compute and display the geometric mean of all the values, excluding the sentinel. (*Hint:* `Math.pow(x, 1.0/k)` will compute the kth root of x.)

16. Imagine a program that compresses files by 80 percent and stores them on storage media. Before the compressed file is stored, it must be divided into blocks of 512 bytes each. Develop an algorithm for this program that first reads the number of blocks available on the storage media. Then, in a loop, read the uncompressed size of a file and determine whether the compressed file will fit in the space left on the storage media. If so, the program should compress and save the file. It continues until it encounters a file that will exceed the available space on the media.

    For example, suppose the media can hold 1000 blocks. A file of size 1100 bytes will compress to size 880 and require 2 blocks. The available space is now 998 blocks. A file of size 20,000 bytes will compress to size 16,000 and require 32 blocks. The available space is now 966.

Graphics

17. Create an applet that draws a pattern of circles whose centers are evenly spaced along a horizontal line. Use six constants to control the pattern: the number of circles to draw, the diameter of the first circle, the x- and y-coordinates of the center of the first circle, the distance between adjacent centers, and the change in the diameter of each subsequent circle.

18. What does the following fragment of code display? What do you think the programmer intended the code to do, and how would you fix it?

```
int product = 1;
int max = 20;
for (int i = 0; i <= max; i++)
    product = product * i;
System.out.println("The product is " + product);
```

19. What does the following fragment of code display? What do you think the programmer intended the code to do, and how would you fix it?

```
int sum = 0;
int product = 1;
int max = 20;
for (int i = 1; i <= max; i++)
    sum = sum + i;
    product = product * i;
System.out.println("The sum is " + sum +
                " and the product is " + product);
```

PROGRAMMING PROJECTS

Visit www.myprogramminglab.com to complete many of these Programming Projects `myprogramminglab`
online and get instant feedback.

1. Repeat Programming Project 4 of Chapter 3, but use a loop that reads and processes sentences until the user says to end the program.

2. Write a program that implements your algorithm from Exercise 2.

3. Repeat Programming Project 5 of Chapter 3, but use a loop so the user can convert other temperatures. If the user enters a letter other than *C* or *F*—in either uppercase or lowercase—after a temperature, print an error message and ask the user to reenter a valid selection. Do not ask the user to reenter the numeric portion of the temperature again, however. After each conversion, ask the user to type Q or q to quit or to press any other key to repeat the loop and perform another conversion.

4. Repeat the previous project, but use `JOptionPane` windows for input and output. Offer the user Yes and No buttons to end execution instead of asking for character input of Q or q. `JOptionPane` is described in the graphics supplements of Chapters 2 and 3.

Graphics

5. Write a program to read a list of nonnegative integers and to display the largest integer, the smallest integer, and the average of all the integers. The user indicates the end of the input by entering a negative sentinel value that is not used in finding the largest, smallest, and average values. The average should be a value of type `double` so that it is computed with a fractional part.

6. Write a program to read a list of exam scores given as integer percentages in the range 0 to 100. Display the total number of grades and the number of grades in each letter-grade category as follows: 90 to 100 is an A, 80 to 89 is a B, 70 to 79 is a C, 60 to 69 is a D, and 0 to 59 is an F. Use a negative score as a sentinel value to indicate the end of the input. (The negative value is used only to end the loop, so do not use it in the calculations.) For example, if the input is

```
98 87 86 85 85 78 73 72 72 72 70 66 63 50 -1
```

the output would be

```
Total number of grades = 14
Number of A's = 1
Number of B's = 4
Number of C's = 6
Number of D's = 2
Number of F's = 1
```

7. Combine the programs from Programming Projects 5 and 6 to read integer exam scores in the range 0 to 100 and to display the following statistics:

   Total number of scores
   Total number of each letter grade

Percentage of total for each letter grade
Range of scores: lowest and highest
Average score

As before, enter a negative score as a sentinel value to end the data input and display the statistics.

8. Write a program that implements your algorithm from Exercise 3.

VideoNote
Solution to Project 9

9. For all of the following words, if you move the first letter to the end of the word, and then spell the result backwards, you will get the original word:

banana dresser grammar potato revive uneven assess

Write a program that reads a word and determines whether it has this property. Continue reading and testing words until you encounter the word *quit*. Treat uppercase letters as lowercase letters.

10. Write a program that reads a bank account balance and an interest rate and displays the value of the account in ten years. The output should show the value of the account for three different methods of compounding interest: annually, monthly, and daily. When compounded annually, the interest is added once per year at the end of the year. When compounded monthly, the interest is added 12 times per year. When computed daily, the interest is added 365 times per year. You do not have to worry about leap years; assume that all years have 365 days. For annual interest, you can assume that the interest is posted exactly one year from the date of deposit. In other words, you do not have to worry about interest being posted on a specific day of the year, such as December 31. Similarly, you can assume that monthly interest is posted exactly one month after it is deposited. Since the account earns interest on the interest, it should have a higher balance when interest is posted more frequently. Be sure to adjust the interest rate for the time period of the interest. If the rate is 5 percent, you use 5/12 percent when posting monthly interest and 5/365 percent when posting daily interest. Perform this calculation using a loop that adds in the interest for each time period, that is, do not use some sort of algebraic formula. Your program should have an outer loop that allows the user to repeat this calculation for a new balance and interest rate. The calculation is repeated until the user asks to end the program.

11. Modify Programming Project 10 from Chapter 2 to check the validity of input data. Valid input is no less than 25 cents, no more than 100 cents, and an integer multiple of 5 cents. Compute the change only if a valid price is entered. Otherwise, print separate error messages for any of the following invalid inputs: a price under 25 cents, a price that is not an integer multiple of 5, and a price that is more than a dollar.

Graphics 12. Repeat either Programming Project 7 or 8 using JOptionPane, which is described in the graphics supplements of Chapters 2 and 3.

13. Write a program that asks the user to enter the size of a triangle (an integer from 1 to 50). Display the triangle by writing lines of asterisks. The first line will have one asterisk, the next two, and so on, with each line having one more asterisk than the previous line, up to the number entered by the user. On the next line write one fewer asterisk and continue by decreasing the number of asterisks by 1 for each successive line until only one asterisk is displayed. (*Hint*: Use nested for loops; the outside loop controls the number of lines to write, and the inside loop controls the number of asterisks to display on a line.) For example, if the user enters 3, the output would be

VideoNote
Nesting for statements

```
*
**
***
**
*
```

14. Write a program that simulates a bouncing ball by computing its height in feet at each second as time passes on a simulated clock. At time zero, the ball begins at height zero and has an initial velocity supplied by the user. (An initial velocity of at least 100 feet per second is a good choice.) After each second, change the height by adding the current velocity; then subtract 32 from the velocity. If the new height is less than zero, multiply both the height and the velocity by –0.5 to simulate the bounce. Stop at the fifth bounce. The output from your program should have the following form:

```
Enter the initial velocity of the ball: 100
Time: 0 Height: 0.0
Time: 1 Height: 100.0
Time: 2 Height: 168.0
Time: 3 Height: 204.0
Time: 4 Height: 208.0
Time: 5 Height: 180.0
Time: 6 Height: 120.0
Time: 7 Height: 28.0
Bounce!
Time: 8 Height: 48.0
. . .
```

15. You have three identical prizes to give away and a pool of ten finalists. The finalists are assigned numbers from 1 to 10. Write a program to randomly select the numbers of three finalists to receive a prize. Make sure not to pick the same number twice. For example, picking finalists 3, 6, 2 would be valid but picking 3, 3, 11 would be invalid because finalist number 3 is listed twice and 11 is not a valid finalist number. Random number generation is discussed in Chapter 6, but for this problem you can insert the following line of code to generate a random number between 1 and 10:

```
int num = (int) (Math.random() * 10) +1;
```

16. Suppose we can buy a chocolate bar from the vending machine for $1 each. Inside every chocolate bar is a coupon. We can redeem six coupons for one chocolate bar from the machine. This means that once you have started buying chocolate bars from the machine, you always have some coupons. We would like to know how many chocolate bars can be eaten if we start with *N* dollars and always redeem coupons if we have enough for an additional chocolate bar.

    For example, with 6 dollars we could consume 7 chocolate bars after purchasing 6 bars giving us 6 coupons and then redeeming the 6 coupons for one bar. This would leave us with one extra coupon. For 11 dollars, we could have consumed 13 chocolate bars and still have one coupon left. For 12 dollars, we could have consumed 14 chocolate bars and have two coupons left.

    Write a program that inputs a value for *N* and outputs how many chocolate bars we can eat and how many coupons we would have left over. Use a loop that continues to redeem coupons as long as there are enough to get at least one chocolate bar.

17. Repeat Programming Project 14, but write the program as an applet. Use a constant for the initial velocity of the ball. Draw a circle for the position of the ball at each second. The *y*-coordinate should be proportional to the height of the ball, and the *x*-coordinate should change by a small constant amount.

    Graphics

18. Write a Java applet or application that draws a bull's-eye pattern. The center should be a filled-in blue circle with a diameter of 100 pixels. The center circle should be surrounded by five rings that alternate in color from green to blue. Each ring should have a width of 30 pixels.

    Graphics

19. Create an applet or application that draws a pattern of evenly spaced circles. Use four constants to control the pattern: the number of circles to draw, the radius of the first circle, the change in the radius of each subsequent circle, and the change in the *x*-coordinate of the circle. Cycle the colors of the circles through red, green, and blue.

    Graphics

20. (*Challenge*) Repeat the previous project, but position the centers of the circles on a spiral. The center of each circle will depend on both an angle and a distance from the origin. A constant change in both the angle and the distance will result in a spiral pattern.

    Graphics

21. Write an applet or application that displays a series of pictures of a person with arms, legs, and of course a head. Use a happy face for the head. Use ovals for the body, arms, and legs. Draw a sequence of figures that appear one after the other, as in Listing 4.9. Make the figures assume a running position. Change the color of the person's face in each succeeding figure, going from white to pink to red to yellow to green. Have the smiling face gradually change its mouth shape from a smile on the first person to a frown on the last person. Use a `switch` statement to choose the color. Embed the `switch` statement in a loop.

    Graphics

Answers to Self-Test Questions

1. 0
   1
   2
   3
   4
   count after loop = 5

2. Yes, the body of a while loop can execute zero times. No, the body of a do-while loop must execute at least once.

3. 0
   count after loop = 1

4. ```
   Scanner keyboard = new Scanner(System.in);
   int number;
   System.out.println("Enter a whole number:");
   number = keyboard.nextInt();
   System.out.println("You entered " + number);

   while (number > 0)
   {
       System.out.println("Enter a whole number:");
       number = keyboard.nextInt();
       System.out.println("You entered " + number);
   }
   System.out.println("number after loop = " + number);
   ```

5. This is an infinite loop. The println statement after the loop will never be executed. The output begins

   0
   -1
   -2
   -3
   .
   .
   .

6. ```
   while (population <= 0)
   {
       System.out.println("Population must be positive.");
       System.out.print("Reenter population: ");
       population = keyboard.nextInt( );
   }
   ```

7. 1
   2
   3
   4

8. This loop produces no output. The boolean expression n > 4 is false the first time through the loop, so the loop ends without iterating its body.

9. 4
   3
   2
   1

10. The only output is

    0

    Be sure to notice the semicolon that was added at the end of the first line of the for loop.

11. 0.0
    0.5
    1.0
    1.5
    2.0
    2.5

12. ```
    for (int n = 1; n <= 5; n++)
        System.out.println(2 * n);
    ```

    or

    ```
    for (int n = 2; n <= 10; n = n + 2)
        System.out.println(n);
    ```

13. 0
    0
    1
    0
    1
    2

14. ```
    for (int time = 1; time < = 4; time++)
        System.out.println("One more time.");
    ```

15. ```
    int result = 1;
    for (int count = 1; count < = 5; count++)
        result = 2 * result;
    ```

16. You can use any number less than 1.0 as a sentinel value, but to avoid any problems with the approximate nature of double values, the number you choose should be significantly less than 1.0.

    ```
    System.out.println("Enter a list of numbers.");
    System.out.println("All the numbers must be 1.0 or larger.");
    ```
    ```

```
System.out.print("Enter 0 after the last number ");
System.out.println("on the list.");

double sum = 0;
int count = 0;
Scanner keyboard = new Scanner(System.in);
double next = keyboard.nextDouble();
while (next > 0.9)
//next >= 1.0 has a risk of inaccuracy.
{
    sum = sum + next;
    count++;
    next = keyboard.nextDouble();
}
if (count > 0)
    System.out.println("Average is " + (sum / count));
else
System.out.println("No numbers to average.");
```

17. One
    Two
    Three
    After the loop

    Note that the break statement ends the switch statement but does not end the for loop.

18. Hello
    Hello
    After the loop 1

19. Hello
    Hello

    Note that After the loop is not displayed because the program ends.

20. ```
    int sum = 0;
    Scanner keyboard = new Scanner(System.in);
    while (true)
    {
        int next = keyboard.nextInt();
        if (next < 0)
            break;
        else
            sum = sum + next;
    }
    ```

    This version of the loop hides its stopping criterion within its body. The original version that uses the boolean variable areMore is easier to understand.
    ```

21. The code contains

```
balance = balance + penalty;
balance = balance - deposit;
```

but it should contain

```
balance = balance - penalty;
balance = balance + deposit;
```

Even after it is fixed in this way, it still has the following problem: If `penalty` is greater than `deposit`, the loop is infinite.

22.
```
int sum = 0;
System.out.println("sum == " + sum); // *
for (int n = 1; n < 10; n++)
{
    sum = sum + n;
    System.out.println("n == " + n); // *
    System.out.println("sum == " + sum); // *
}
System.out.println("1 + 2 + . . . ) + 9 + 10 == " + sum);
```

23. The boolean expression should be `n <= 10`, not `n < 10`. This is an off-by-one error.

24. An assertion is a statement that says something about the state of your program at a particular point. An assertion should be true if there are no mistakes in the program. The following is an example of an assertion given two times, once as a comment and once as an assertion check:

```
// (timeLeft > 30) && (points < 10)
assert (timeLeft > 30) && (points < 10);
```

25.
```
if (balance <= 0) //if (balance > 0) is false.
{
    System.out.println("Assertion(balance > 0)failed.");
    System.out.println("Aborting program.");
    System.exit(0);
}
```

26. You are not required to give a complete applet, but we have embedded the answer in one.

```
import javax.swing.JApplet;
import java.awt.Graphics;
import java.awt.Color;

public class Question26 extends JApplet
{
    public static final int DIAMETER = 30;
```

```java
        public static final int X_CENTER = 100;
        public static final int Y_CENTER = 100;
        public static final int GAP = 10;

        public void paint(Graphics canvas)
        {
            int radius = DIAMETER / 2;
            int x = X_CENTER - radius; //upper left corner
            int y = Y_CENTER - radius;
            for (int i = 1; i <= 6; i++)
            {
                canvas.setColor(Color.BLUE);
                canvas.fillOval(x, y, DIAMETER, DIAMETER);

                canvas.setColor(Color.BLACK);
                canvas.drawOval(x, y, DIAMETER, DIAMETER);
                x = x + DIAMETER + GAP;
            }
        }
    }
```

Defining Classes and Methods 5

5.1 CLASS AND METHOD DEFINITIONS 263
Class Files and Separate Compilation 265
Programming Example: Implementing a **Dog**
  Class 265
Instance Variables 266
Methods 269
Defining **void** Methods 272
Defining Methods That Return a Value 273
Programming Example: First Try at Implementing a
  Species Class 278
The Keyword **this** 282
Local Variables 284
Blocks 286
Parameters of a Primitive Type 287

**5.2 INFORMATION HIDING
   AND ENCAPSULATION** 293
Information Hiding 294
Precondition and Postcondition Comments 294
The **public** and **private** Modifiers 296
Programming Example: A Demonstration of Why
  Instance Variables Should Be Private 299
Programming Example: Another Implementation of a
  Class of Rectangles 300

Accessor Methods and Mutator Methods 302
Programming Example: A Purchase Class 306
Methods Calling Methods 310
Encapsulation 316
Automatic Documentation with **javadoc** 319
UML Class Diagrams 320

5.3 OBJECTS AND REFERENCES 321
Variables of a Class Type 322
Defining an **equals** Method for a Class 327
Programming Example: A Species Class 331
Boolean-Valued Methods 334
Case Study: Unit Testing 336
Parameters of a Class Type 338
Programming Example: Class-Type Parameters
  Versus Primitive-Type Parameters 342

5.4 GRAPHICS SUPPLEMENT 346
The **Graphics** Class 346
Programming Example: Multiple Faces, But with a
  Helping Method 348
The **init** Method 352
Adding Labels to an Applet 352

Chapter Summary 356   **Programming Projects** 361   **Answers to Self-Test Questions** 367

class n. 1. A set, collection, group, or configuration containing members regarded as having certain attributes or traits in common; a kind or category....

—THE AMERICAN HERITAGE DICTIONARY OF THE ENGLISH LANGUAGE, *Fourth Edition** *

Recall that an object is named by a variable of a class type. Objects have data, but they also can take actions. These actions are defined by methods. You have already been using some objects and invoking their methods. For example, you have created and used objects of type `String`. If `name` is an object of type `String`, its method `length` will return its length. In particular, the length of the string object `name` is the value returned by the expression `name.length()`. The class `String` is already defined for you in the Java Class Library. In this chapter, we will show you how to define your own simple classes and how to use objects and methods of those classes.

OBJECTIVES

After studying this chapter, you should be able to

- Describe the concepts of a class and of an object of a class
- Create objects of a class
- Define a Java class and its methods
- Describe how parameters work in a method definition
- Use the modifiers `public` and `private`
- Define accessor methods and mutator methods for a class
- Write and use private methods within a class
- Describe information hiding and encapsulation
- Write preconditions and postconditions for a method
- Describe the purpose of `javadoc`
- Draw simple UML diagrams
- Describe references as well as variables of a class type and parameters of a class type
- Define an `equals` method and other boolean-valued methods
- Use methods of the class `Graphics`, and add labels and the method `init` to an applet

PREREQUISITES

You need to be familiar with the material in the first four chapters before reading this chapter. You might want to review the section in Chapter 1 entitled "Object-Oriented Programming."

---

*Full and partial dictionary entries from THE AMERICAN HERITAGE DICTIONARY OF THE ENGLISH LANGUAGE. Copyright © 2010 by Houghton Mifflin Harcourt Publishing Company. Adapted and reproduced by permission from THE AMERICAN HERITAGE DICTIONARY OF THE ENGLISH LANGUAGE, Fourth Edition.

5.1 CLASS AND METHOD DEFINITIONS

The greatest invention of the nineteenth century was the invention of the method of invention.

ALFRED NORTH WHITEHEAD, *SCIENCE AND THE MODERN WORLD*

A Java program consists of objects of various class types, interacting with one another. Before we go into the details of how you define your own classes and objects in Java, let's review and elaborate on what we already know about classes and objects.

Objects in a program can represent either objects in the real word—like automobiles, houses, and employee records—or abstractions like colors, shapes, and words. A class is the definition of a kind of object. It is like a plan or a blueprint for constructing specific objects. For example, Figure 5.1 describes a class called Automobile. The class is a general description of what an automobile is and what it can do.

> Objects in a program can represent real-world things or abstractions

FIGURE 5.1   A Class as a Blueprint

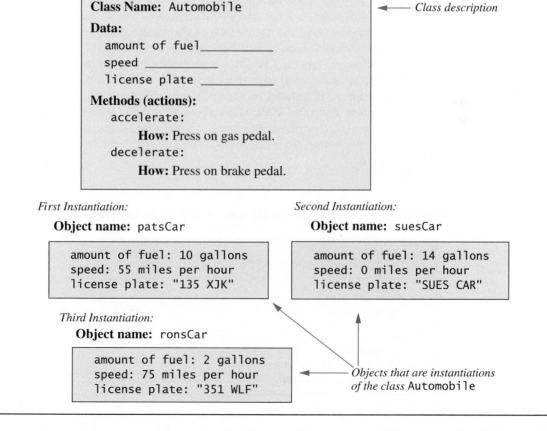

Objects of this class are particular automobiles. The figure shows three `Automobile` objects. Each of these objects satisfies the class definition of an `Automobile` object and is an **instance** of the `Automobile` class. Thus, we can create, or **instantiate,** several objects of the same class. The objects here are individual automobiles, while the `Automobile` class is a generic description of what an automobile is and does. This is, of course, a very simplified version of an automobile, but it illustrates the basic idea of what a class is. Let's look at some details.

An instance of a class is an object

A class specifies the attributes, or data, that objects of the class have. The `Automobile` class definition says that an `Automobile` object has three attributes or pieces of data: a number telling how many gallons of fuel are in the fuel tank, another number telling how fast the automobile is moving, and a string that shows what is written on the license plate. The class definition has no data—that is, no numbers and no string. The individual objects have the data, but the class specifies what kind of data they have.

A class is like a blueprint for creating objects

The class also specifies what actions the objects can take and how they accomplish those actions. The `Automobile` class specifies two actions: `accelerate` and `decelerate`. Thus, in a program that uses the class `Automobile`, the only actions an `Automobile` object can take are `accelerate` and `decelerate`. These actions are described within the class by methods. All objects of any one class have the same methods. In particular, all objects of the class `Automobile` have the same methods. As you can see in our sample `Automobile` class, the definitions of the methods are given in the class definition and describe how objects perform the actions.

A class specifies an object's attributes and defines its behaviors as methods

The notation in Figure 5.1 is a bit cumbersome, so programmers often use a simpler graphical notation to summarize some of the main properties of a class. This notation, illustrated in Figure 5.2, is called a **UML class diagram,** or simply a **class diagram. UML** is an abbreviation for **Universal Modeling Language.** The class described in Figure 5.2 is the same as the one described in Figure 5.1. Any annotations in Figure 5.2 that are new will be explained later in the chapter.

Use a UML class diagram to help design a class

FIGURE 5.2   A Class Outline as a UML Class Diagram

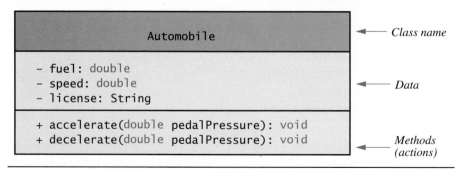

Notice a few more things about a class and the objects that instantiate the class. Each object has a name. In Figure 5.1, the names are patsCar, suesCar, and ronsCar. In a Java program, these object names would be variables of type Automobile. That is, the data type of the variables is the class type Automobile.

Before we get further into the nitty-gritty of defining a simple class, let's review some of the things we said in Chapter 1 about storing classes in files and compiling them.

Class Files and Separate Compilation

Whether you use a class taken from this book or one that you write yourself, you place each Java class definition in a file by itself. There are exceptions to this rule, but we will seldom encounter them, and we need not be concerned about them yet. The name of the file should begin with the name of the class and end in .java. So if you write a definition for a class called Automobile, it should be in a file named Automobile.java.

Each class is in a separate file

You can compile a Java class before you have a program in which to use it. The compiled bytecode for the class will be stored in a file of the same name, but ending in .class rather than .java. So compiling the file Automobile.java will create a file called Automobile.class. Later, you can compile a program file that uses the class Automobile, and you will not need to recompile the class definition for Automobile. This naming requirement applies to full programs as well as to classes. Notice that every program having a main method has a class name at the start of the file; this is the name you need to use for the file that holds the program. For example, the program you will see later in Listing 5.2 should be in a file named DogDemo.java. As long as all the classes you use in a program are in the same directory as the program file, you need not worry about directories. In Chapter 6, we will discuss how to use files from more than one directory.

| **PROGRAMMING EXAMPLE** | Implementing a Dog Class |

To introduce the way that Java classes are defined let's create a simple class to represent a dog. Thus, we name our class Dog in Listing 5.1. Although its simplicity makes this first example easier to explain, it violates several important design principles. As we progress through this chapter we will discuss the weaknesses of the example's design and show how to improve it.

Each object of the Dog class stores the name, breed, and age of a dog. Additionally, each object has two actions, defined by the methods writeOutput and getAgeInHumanYears. The writeOutput method outputs the data stored about the dog and the getAgeInHumanYears method approximates the dog's equivalent age as if it were a human. Both the data items and the methods are

Instance variables and methods are members of a class.

sometimes called **members** of the object because they belong to the object. We will call the data items **instance variables**. In the following subsections we will discuss the instance variables and then the methods.

LISTING 5.1 Definition of a Dog Class

```java
public class Dog
{
    public String name;
    public String breed;
    public int age;
    public void writeOutput()
    {
        System.out.println("Name: " + name);
        System.out.println("Breed: " + breed);
        System.out.println("Age in calendar years: " +
                           age);
        System.out.println("Age in human years: " +
                           getAgeInHumanYears());
        System.out.println();
    }
    public int getAgeInHumanYears()
    {
        int humanAge = 0;
        if (age <= 2)
        {
            humanAge = age * 11;
        }
        else
        {
            humanAge = 22 + ((age-2) * 5);
        }

            return humanAge;
    }
}
```

> Later in this chapter we will see that the modifier `public` for instance variables should be replaced with `private`.

Instance Variables

The following three lines from the start of the class definition in Listing 5.1 define three instance variables:

```java
public String name;
public String breed;
public int age;
```

The word `public` simply means that there are no restrictions on how these instance variables are used. You will soon see that using `public` here is a bad idea, but let's ignore that for now. Each of these lines declares one instance variable. Notice that each instance variable has a data type. For example, the instance variable name is of type String.

You can think of an object of the class as a complex item having instance variables inside of it. In this case, the instance variables are called name, breed, and age. Each object, or instance, of the class has its own copy of these three instance variables, which is why they are called instance variables. The program in Listing 5.2 demonstrates how to use the Dog class and handle these instance variables.

LISTING 5.2 Using the Dog Class and Its Methods

```java
public class DogDemo
{
    public static void main(String[] args)
    {
        Dog balto = new Dog();
        balto.name = "Balto";
        balto.age = 8;
        balto.breed = "Siberian Husky";
        balto.writeOutput();

        Dog scooby = new Dog();
        scooby.name = "Scooby";
        scooby.age = 42;
        scooby.breed = "Great Dane";
        System.out.println(scooby.name + " is a " +
                            scooby.breed + ".");
        System.out.print("He is " + scooby.age +
                        " years old, or ");
        int humanYears = scooby.getAgeInHumanYears();
        System.out.println(humanYears + " in human years.");
    }
}
```

Sample Screen Output

```
Name: Balto
Breed: Siberian Husky
Age in calendar years: 8
Age in human years: 52

Scooby is a Great Dane.
He is 42 years old, or 222 in human years.
```

The following line from Listing 5.2 creates an object of type Dog and attaches the name balto to the object:

```java
Dog balto = new Dog();
```

The variables `balto` and `scooby` reference distinct Dog objects, each with their own instance variables of `name`, `breed`, and `age`. You can refer to one of these instance variables by writing the object name followed by a dot and then the instance variable's name. For example,

```
balto.name
```

Since `name` is of type `String`, `balto.name` is a variable of type `String` and can be used anywhere that you can use a variable of type `String`. For example, all of the following are valid Java statements:

```
balto.name = "Balto";
System.out.println("The dog's name is " + balto.name);
String niceName = balto.name;
```

Since each object of type `Dog` has its own three instance variables, if your program also contained the statement

```
Dog scooby = new Dog();
```

Then `balto.name` and `scooby.name` would be two different instance variables that might have different string values. In Listing 5.2 they do have different values since `balto.name` is set to "Balto" and `scooby.name` is set to "Scooby".

FAQ Why do we need new?

In Java, new is a unary operator that we use to create objects of a class. When new is used in an expression such as

```
Dog scooby = new Dog();
```

it creates an object of the class Dog. The new operator then returns the memory address of the object. The preceding Java statement assigns this address to the variable scooby. An object can have variables inside of it, namely, the instance variables of the object. The new operator places these instance variables inside of the object when it creates the object.

FAQ If the program in Listing 5.2 is a class, why doesn't it have instance variables?

A program is simply a class that has a method named main. But a program can have other methods and can have instance variables, even though none of the programs we have written so far have instance variables or any methods other than main.

Methods

When you use a method, you are said to invoke or call it. You have already invoked methods. For example, your programs have invoked the method `nextInt` using objects of the class `Scanner`. You have also invoked the method `println` of the object `System.out`, as in the following statement:

You invoke, or call, a method

```
System.out.println("Hello out there!");
```

Java has two kinds of methods:

- Methods that return a single item
- Methods that perform some action other than returning an item

Two kinds of methods

The method `nextInt` is an example of a method that returns a single value, one of type `int`. The method `println` is an example of a method that performs some action other than returning a single value. Methods that perform some action other than returning a value are called **void methods.**

REMEMBER Two Kinds of Methods

Java has two kinds of methods: those that return a single value or object and those that perform some action other than returning an item. These two different kinds of methods are normally used in slightly different ways.

Let's review how you invoke a method. The method `nextInt` of the class `Scanner` is a method that returns a single value. Suppose the declaration

```
int theNextInteger;
```

is in a program. The following statement invokes the method `nextInt` using the object `keyboard`, which we assume is an object of the class `Scanner`:

```
theNextInteger = keyboard.nextInt();
```

Calling a method that returns a value

Let's look at this method invocation in more detail.

A method defined in a class is usually invoked using an object of that class. You write the receiving object name—such as `keyboard`—followed by a dot, and then the name of the method—such as `nextInt`—and finally a set of parentheses that can contain arguments for the method. If the method is one that returns a single quantity, such as the method `nextInt`, you can use this method invocation anywhere that you can use an item of the type returned by the method. The method `nextInt` returns a value of type `int`, and so you can use the expression

```
keyboard.nextInt()
```

anywhere that it is valid to use a value of type int. The expression behaves as if it were replaced by the value returned. For example, since the assignment statement

```
int data = 6;
```

is valid, so is the statement

```
int data = keyboard.nextInt();
```

Calling a void method

Methods that perform some action other than returning a single quantity are invoked in a similar way. But since they do not return a value, their invocations stand alone; they are not embedded in another Java statement. For example, the following statement includes an invocation of the method println:

```
System.out.println("Hello out there!");
```

This method call causes the sentence Hello out there! to be displayed on the screen.

Calling the method writeOutput for the class Dog, as in Listing 5.2 has a similar effect, except that you do not have to tell writeOutput what to write by including arguments inside the parentheses. Instead, the method writeOutput gets the information it needs from its receiving object.

For example, the latter part of the program in Listing 5.2 sets the values of the instance variables of the object balto using the following three assignment statements:

```
balto.name = "Balto";
balto.age = 8;
balto.breed = "Siberian Husky";
```

The program then uses the following statement to display these values:

```
balto.writeOutput();
```

The method writeOutput gets data from the object balto to produce the output

```
Name: Balto
Breed: Siberian Husky
Age in calendar years: 8
Age in human years: 52
```

At the end of Listing 5.2 we perform essentially the same task as the writeOutput method by accessing the instance variables directly from the scooby object. While this can be useful to generate a customized message, if we are happy with the writeOutput output then the last four lines of main can be simplified down to

```
scooby.writeOutput();
```

REMEMBER Invoking (Calling) a Method

You invoke a method by writing the name of the receiving object followed by a dot, the name of the method, and finally a set of parentheses that can contain arguments providing information for the method.

RECAP Calling a Method That Returns a Quantity

If a method returns a single quantity, you can invoke it anywhere that you can use a value of the type returned by the method. For example, the following statement includes an invocation of the method getAgeInHumanYears, and the value returned is assigned to the int variable humanYears:

```
humanYears = scooby.getAgeInHumanYears();
```

RECAP Calling a void Method

If a method performs some action other than returning a single quantity, you write its invocation followed by a semicolon. The resulting Java statement performs the action defined by the method. For example, the following is an invocation of the method writeOutput for the object balto:

```
balto.writeOutput();
```

This method invocation displays several lines of output on the screen.

FAQ What about main? If it is indeed a method, why don't I invoke it?

When you run a program, the system invokes the void method named main. Of course, this is a special kind of method invocation—one that you do not write—but it is a method invocation nonetheless.

Defining void Methods

A definition of a
void method

Let's look at the definition of the method writeOutput to see how method definitions are written. The definition is given in Listing 5.1 and is repeated here:

```
public void writeOutput()
    {
        System.out.println("Name: " + name);
        System.out.println("Breed: " + breed);
        System.out.println("Age in calendar years: " + age);
        System.out.println("Age in human years: " +
                            getAgeInHumanYears());
        System.out.println();
    }
```

All method definitions appear inside the definition of the class to which they belong. If you look at Listing 5.1, you will see that this method definition is inside the definition of the class Dog. This means that the method can be used only with objects of the class Dog.

For now, our method definitions begin with the keyword public. The word public indicates that there are no special restrictions on the use of the method. Later in this chapter, you will see that the word public can sometimes be replaced by other modifiers that restrict the use of the method.

For a method like writeOutput that does not return a value, you next write the keyword void. This keyword indicates that the method does not return a value and is the reason why this kind of method is called a void method. After the keyword void, you write the name of the method and a pair of parentheses. The parentheses enclose representations of any arguments that the method will need. In our example, no extra information is needed, and so there is nothing inside the parentheses. Later in the chapter, you will see examples of the sorts of things that might appear inside these parentheses for other method definitions. This first part of the method definition is called the **heading** for the method. The heading is normally written on a single line, but if it is too long for one line, it can be broken into two or more lines.

A method
definition has a
heading and a
body

After the heading comes the rest of the method definition, which is called the **body.** The statements in the body of the method definition are enclosed between braces {}. Any statement or declaration that you can place in a program can appear within the body. You can use instance variables within the body. Any other variables used in a method definition must be declared within that method definition. Such variables are called **local variables.**

Local variables
are those
declared within a
method's body

When a void method is invoked, it is as if the method invocation were replaced by the body of the method definition and its statements were then executed. There are some subtleties about this replacement process, but for the simple examples we will look at now, think of the body of the method definition as literally replacing the method invocation. Eventually, you'll want to think of the method definition as defining an action to be taken, rather than as a list of statements to substitute for the method invocation, but this substitution idea is correct and is a good way to start understanding method invocations.

For example, you can imagine replacing the method invocation

```
balto.writeOutput();
```

with the body of the method writeOutput. In this case, it is as if the preceding method invocation were replaced by the following statements:

```
System.out.println("Name: " + name);
System.out.println("Breed: " + breed);
System.out.println("Age in calendar years: " + age);
System.out.println("Age in human years: " +
                   getAgeInHumanYears());
System.out.println();
```

The names—name, breed, and age—refer to the instance variables of the receiving object balto. So, to be more precise, the method invocation is equivalent to the statements

```
System.out.println("Name: " + balto.name);
System.out.println("Breed: " + balto.breed);
System.out.println("Age in calendar years: " + balto.age);
System.out.println("Age in human years: " +
                   balto.getAgeInHumanYears());
System.out.println();
```

REMEMBER main **Is a** void **Method**

It is indeed true that main is a void method. For now, those extra words like static and String[]args in its heading will have to remain a mystery. Just put them in, and eventually we will explain them all. Only a class that is run as a program needs a main method, but any class can have one. If a class has a main method but the class is not run as a program, main is simply ignored.

Defining Methods That Return a Value

You define a method that returns a value in basically the same way that you define a void method, with one added concern—namely, specifying the value returned. Let's consider the method getAgeInHumanYears from the class Dog. This method estimates a dog's equivalent age in human years. We called this method as follows:

```
int humanYears = scooby.getAgeInHumanYears();
```

This statement sets the value of the variable humanYears equal to the value returned by the method invocation

```
scooby.getAgeInHumanYears()
```

The definition of the method getAgeInHumanYears tells the computer how to compute the value returned.

Let's look at that method definition in Listing 5.1. Like a void method definition, the definition of a method that returns a value can be divided into two parts: the method heading and the method body. Here is the heading for the method getAgeInHumanYears:

```
public int getAgeInHumanYears()
```

The heading for a method that returns a value is almost the same as the heading for a void method. The only difference is that a method that returns a value uses a type name instead of the keyword void. The heading begins with the keyword public, followed by a type name—which is the type of the value to be returned—followed by the name of the method and a pair of parentheses. As is true of void methods, the parentheses enclose representations of any arguments that the method will need. In this example, the parentheses are empty. As before, the keyword public indicates that there are no special restrictions on the use of the method.

The heading of a method that returns a value contains the return type

The body of a method that returns a value contains a return statement:

The body of a method definition that returns a value is just like the body of a void method definition, except that it must contain at least one return statement:

```
return Expression;
```

A return statement says that the value returned by the method is the value of *Expression*. *Expression* can be any expression that produces a value of the type specified in the heading of the method definition. For example, the definition of the method getAgeInHumanYears contains the statement

```
return 22 + ((age - 2) * 5);
```

When a method that returns a value is invoked, the statements in the body of the method definition are executed. For example, when the assignment statement

```
int humanYears = scooby.getAgeInHumanYears();
```

executes, the body of the method definition for getAgeInHumanYears is executed. The statements in that body are as follows:

```
int humanAge = 0;
if (age <= 2)
{
    humanAge = age * 11;
}
else
{
    humanAge = 22 + ((age - 2) * 5);
}
return humanAge;
```

The instance variable age refers to the instance variable of the receiving object, which in this case is scooby. The value of age in Listing 5.2 is set to 42. Using the formula that each dog year is approximately equivalent to 11 human years up to age 2, and then each dog year is approximately equivalent to 5 human years thereafter, we return the appropriate human age for the dog. The variable humanAge is set to the calculated value and returned at the end of the method.

Execution of a return statement ends a method's execution

When a return statement executes, not only does it provide the value returned by the method but it also ends the method's execution. If more statements follow the return statement, they are not executed.

A method that returns a value may perform some other action as well, such as reading a value from the keyboard, but it definitely must return a value.

REMEMBER Naming Methods

Java will let you use any valid identifier—but not a keyword—as the name for a method. However, you should choose clear, meaningful names to make your code easier to read. Since methods perform actions, you should use a verb or verb phrase as the name of a method. The normal convention is to begin all method names with a lowercase letter. Recall that, by convention, we begin class names with an uppercase letter.

■ **PROGRAMMING TIP**   Use One return Statement

Although you can use more than one return statement within the body of a method that returns a value, you typically should use only one. Placing that one return statement at or near the physical end of the method's body makes your method easier to read. ■

We used a single return statement in the definition of the method getAgeInHumanYears. Instead, we could have used multiple return statements, one for the case where age ≤ 2 and another when age > 2:

```
if (age <= 2)
{
    return age * 11;
}
else
{
    return 22 + ((age-2) * 5);
}
```

Some programmers find this to be clear, particularly since the return statements are at or near the end of the method definition. However, if the logic of the method were more complicated, and a return statement occurred far from the physical end of the method definition, understanding the logic would be more difficult. We prefer to use only one return statement in a method.

FAQ I've heard of functions. Does Java have functions?

No, Java does not have functions. In some other programming languages, methods that return a value are called *functions*, as they correspond to the mathematical notion of a function. However, in Java, regardless of whether a method returns a value or not, it is called a *method*, not a *function*.

FAQ Can a void method contain a return statement?

Since a void method returns no value, it typically does not have any return statement. However, you can write a return statement within a void method without an accompanying expression, as follows:

```
return;
```

This statement is just like the other return statements you have seen, except that you do not include any expression for the value returned. When executed, this return statement simply ends the execution of the void method.

Some programmers use this statement to end a method invocation early, such as when the method discovers some sort of problem. For example, you might add the following method to the definition of the class SpeciesFirstTry in Listing 5.3.

```
public void showLandPortion()
{
    if  (population == 0)
    {
        System.out.println("Population is zero.");
        return; //Ends here to avoid division by zero.
    }
    double fraction = 6.0 / population;
    System.out.println("If the population were spread ");
    System.out.println("over 6 continents, each " +
                        "individual");
    System.out.println("would have a fraction of its ");
    System.out.println("continent equal to " + fraction);
}
```

The method's execution would end at the return statement if the rest of the method would involve a division by zero.

(continued)

Sometimes, using a `return` statement within a `void` method is the clearest and easiest approach, but more often, a better solution is possible. Such is the case with our example. Adding an `else` portion to the `if` statement, as follows, clarifies the logic of the method:

```java
public void showLandPortion()
{
    if (population == 0)
        System.out.println("Population is zero.");
    else
    {
        double fraction = 6.0 / population;
        System.out.println("If the population were spread ");
        System.out.println("over 6 continents, each " +
                            "individual");
        System.out.println("would have a fraction of its ");
        System.out.println("continent equal to " +
                            fraction);
    }
}
```

RECAP Method Definitions

Every method belongs to some class and is available to objects created from that class. The definition of a method is given in the definition of the class to which it belongs. Each method either returns a single quantity or does not return any value. The latter kind of method is called a `void` method.

SYNTAX

```
public Return_Type Method_Name(Parameters)
{
    Statements
}
```

where *Return_Type* is either `void` or the data type of the quantity returned by the method. In the latter case, *Statements* must contain at least one `return` statement of the form

```
return Expression;
```

A `return` statement defines the value returned by the method and ends the method's execution. A `void` method does not need a `return` statement, but it can have one if you want to end the method invocation

(continued)

before the physical end of the code. If that is the case, the `return` statement omits *Expression*. Using a `return` statement in a void method is not typical.

So far, we have not discussed *Parameters*, but we will do so shortly. If there are no *Parameters*, the parentheses are empty.

EXAMPLES

```java
public void writeOutput()
{
    System.out.println("Name: " + name);
    System.out.println("Breed: " + breed);
    System.out.println("Age in calendar years: " + age);
}
public int halveThePopulation()
{
    return population / 2;
}
```

PROGRAMMING EXAMPLE First Try at Implementing a Species Class

The next example in Listing 5.3 is designed to hold records of endangered species. This class is slightly more complex than the Dog class but still violates several important design principles. Later we will improve on this example as we discuss these principles. Thus, we name our class `SpeciesFirstTry`.

LISTING 5.3 A Species Class Definition—First Attempt
(part 1 of 2)

We will give a better version of this class later in this chapter.

```java
import java.util.Scanner;
public class SpeciesFirstTry
{
    public String name;  ⟵
    public int population;
    public double growthRate;

    public void readInput()
    {
        Scanner keyboard = new Scanner(System.in);
        System.out.println("What is the species' name?");
        name = keyboard.nextLine();
        System.out.println("What is the population of the " +
                           "species?");
        population = keyboard.nextInt();
```

Later in this chapter you will see that the modifier `public` *for instance variables should be replaced with* `private`*.*

(continued)

LISTING 5.3 A Species Class Definition—First Attempt
(part 2 of 2)

```
        System.out.println("Enter growth rate " +
                            "(% increase per year):");
        growthRate = keyboard.nextDouble();
    }
    public void writeOutput()
    {
        System.out.println("Name = " + name);
        System.out.println("Population = " + population);
        System.out.println("Growth rate = " + growthRate + "%");
    }
    public int getPopulationIn10()
    {
        int result = 0;
        double populationAmount = population;
        int count = 10;
        while ((count > 0) && (populationAmount > 0))
        {
            populationAmount = populationAmount +
                                (growthRate / 100) *
                                populationAmount;
            count--;
        }
        if (populationAmount > 0)
                result = (int)populationAmount;
        return result;
    }
}
```

Each object of this class has three pieces of data: a name, a population size, and a growth rate. The data is contained in three instance variables, `name`, `population`, and `growthRate`. The objects have three actions, defined by the methods `readInput`, `writeOutput`, and `getPopulationIn10`.

The code in Listing 5.4 creates an object of type `SpeciesFirstTry` and attaches the name `speciesOfTheMonth` to this object. Based on the population and growth rate it outputs the expected population in ten years.

LISTING 5.4 Using the Species Class and Its Methods
(part 1 of 2)

```
public class SpeciesFirstTryDemo
{
    public static void main(String[] args)
    {
        SpeciesFirstTry speciesOfTheMonth = new SpeciesFirstTry();
        System.out.println("Enter data on the Species of "+
                            "the Month:");
```

(continued)

LISTING 5.4 **Using the Species Class and Its Methods**
(part 2 of 2)

```
        speciesOfTheMonth.readInput();
        speciesOfTheMonth.writeOutput();
        int futurePopulation =
            speciesOfTheMonth.getPopulationIn10();
        System.out.println("In ten years the population will be "
                            + futurePopulation);
        //Change the species to show how to change
        //the values of instance variables:
        speciesOfTheMonth.name = "Klingon ox";
        speciesOfTheMonth.population = 10;
        speciesOfTheMonth.growthRate = 15;
        System.out.println("The new Species of the Month:");
        speciesOfTheMonth.writeOutput();
        System.out.println("In ten years the population will "
                "be " + speciesOfTheMonth.getPopulationIn10());
    }
}
```

Sample Screen Output

```
Enter data on the Species of the Month:
What is the species' name?
Ferengie fur ball
What is the population of the species?
1000
Enter growth rate (% increase per year):
-20.5
Name = Ferengie fur ball
Population = 1000
Growth rate = 20.5%
In ten years the population will be 100
The new Species of the Month:
Name = Klingon ox
Population = 10
Growth rate = 15.0%
In ten years the population will be 40
```

Like all objects of type SpeciesFirstTry, the object speciesOfTheMonth
has three instance variables called name, population, and growthRate. Rather
than set the values of the instance variable from the main method as in

Listing 5.2, instead we invoke the readInput method to input values from the keyboard. The input values are stored with the instance variables associated with the speciesOfTheMonth object.

The statements in that body of the getPopulationIn10 are as follows:

```
int result = 0;
double populationAmount = population;
int count = 10;
while ((count > 0) && (populationAmount > 0))
{
    populationAmount = (populationAmount + (growthRate / 100)
                            * populationAmount);
    count--;
}
if (populationAmount > 0)
    result = (int)populationAmount;
return result;
```

The instance variable population refers to the instance variable of the receiving object, which in this case is speciesOfTheMonth. The value of population is copied into the variable populationAmount, and then the while loop is executed. Each iteration of the loop increases the value of populationAmount by the amount that the population will change in one year, and the loop is iterated ten times. When the while loop ends, the value of populationAmount is the projected size of the population in ten years. At that point, populationAmount has the value we want the method to return. For now, let's assume that populationAmount is positive—that is, the species is not extinct. Thus, the if statement will set result to the value (int) populationAmount. The (int) is a type cast that changes the double value to an int value so that you do not have a fraction of an animal. The value of result is returned by the method invocation via the statement:

```
return result;
```

The effect is like replacing the method invocation with (int)population Amount. In this case, the assignment statement

```
int futurePopulation = speciesOfTheMonth.getPopulationIn10();
```

sets the variable futurePopulation to the value of(int)populationAmount.

If populationAmount happens to be zero or negative, the statement leaves result unchanged from its initial value of zero. So the return statement, and hence the method invocation, returns zero. This is a minor detail that ensures that the projected population will not be negative. After all, in the real world, once a population reaches zero individuals, it just stays at zero.

The Keyword this

Look back at the class definition of the class SpeciesFirstTry in Listing 5.3, and then look at the program in Listing 5.4 that uses this class. Notice that instance variables are written differently, depending on whether they are within the class definition or someplace outside the class definition, such as in a program that uses the class. Outside the class definition, you name an instance variable by giving the name of an object of the class followed by a dot and the name of the instance variable, as in the following reference to the instance variable name that appears in Listing 5.4:

```
speciesOfTheMonth.name = "Klingon ox";
```

However, inside the definition of a method of that same class, you can simply use the instance variable name without any object name or dot. For example, the following line occurs inside the definition of the method readInput of the class SpeciesFirstTry in Listing 5.3:

```
name = keyboard.nextLine();
```

Within a class definition, this is a name for the receiving object

As you know, every instance variable, including name, is an instance variable of some object. In cases like this, the object is understood to be there, but its name usually is omitted. This understood object has the somewhat unusual name of this. Although this is frequently omitted—but understood to be there—you can include it if you want. For example, the preceding assignment of the instance variable name is equivalent to the following:

```
this.name = keyboard.nextLine();
```

As another example, the following method is equivalent to the version of writeOutput used in Listing 5.3:

```
public void writeOutput()
{
    System.out.println("Name = " + this.name);
    System.out.println("Population = " + this.population);
    System.out.println("Growth rate = " + this.growthRate + "%");
}
```

The keyword this stands for the receiving object. For example, in the invocation

```
speciesOfTheMonth.writeOutput();
```

the receiving object is speciesOfTheMonth. So this invocation of the method writeOutput is equivalent to

```
{
    System.out.println("Name = " + speciesOfTheMonth.name);
    System.out.println("Population = " +
        speciesOfTheMonth.population);
```

```
    System.out.println("Growth rate = " +
        speciesOfTheMonth.growthRate + "%");
}
```

which we got by replacing `this` with `speciesOfTheMonth`.

The keyword `this` is like a blank waiting to be filled in with the object that receives the method invocation. Because you would be using `this` so often if it were required, Java lets you omit it, along with the dot that follows it, but the `this` and the dot are understood to be there implicitly. Many programmers seldom use the keyword `this` when doing so is optional, but some situations do require it. On the other hand, some programmers always use the keyword `this` to make it clear that the object is being referenced.

RECAP The Keyword `this`

Within a method definition, you can use the keyword `this` as a name for the object receiving the method call.

SELF-TEST QUESTIONS

myprogramminglab

1. Consider the program in Listing 5.4. Suppose you wanted to add another species object called `speciesOfTheYear`, and suppose you wanted the user to provide its name, population, and growth rate. What code do you need to add to the program? (*Hint:* Only a few lines of code are needed.)

2. Suppose `Employee` is a class containing a `void` method named `readInput`, and `dilbert` is an object of the class `Employee` that was named and created by the following statement:

   ```
   Employee dilbert = new Employee();
   ```

   Write an invocation of the method `readInput` using `dilbert` as the receiving object. The method `readInput` needs no information in parentheses.

3. Let's say you want to assign a number as well as a name to each species in the world, perhaps to make it easier to catalog them. Modify the definition of the class `SpeciesFirstTry` in Listing 5.3 so that it allows for a number. The number is to be of type `int`. (*Hint:* You mostly just have to add stuff.)

4. Suppose every species in the world has a peculiar birthing pattern. After a female is born, a male is born, then a female, and so on. Give the

definition of a method, called `getFemalePopulation`, that you could add to the definition of the class `SpeciesFirstTry` in Listing 5.3 to return the number of females in the population. Also, give the definition of a method called `getMalePopulation` that similarly returns the number of males in the population. If the population is an odd number, you have one species member left over after pairing males and females. Assume that species member is a female. For example, if the population is 7, there are 3 males and 4 females. But if the population is 8, there are 4 males and 4 females. (*Hint:* The definitions are very short.)

5. Revise the definition of the method `writeOutput` in Listing 5.3, using the keyword `this`. Do not change the meaning of the definition at all. You will just write it slightly differently. (*Hint:* All you need to do is add `this` and dots in certain places.)

6. Revise the definition of the method `readInput` in Listing 5.3, using the keyword `this`.

7. Revise the definition of the method `getPopulationIn10` in Listing 5.3, using the keyword `this`.

8. What is the meaning of `(int)` that appears in the definition of the method `getPopulationIn10` in Listing 5.3, and why is it needed?

Local Variables

The meaning of a local variable is confined to the method containing its declaration

Notice the definition of the method `getPopulationIn10` given in Listing 5.3. That method definition includes the declaration of variables called `populationAmount` and `count`. As we mentioned earlier in this chapter, a variable declared within a method is called a local variable. We say the variable is local because its meaning is local to—that is, confined to—the method definition.

Suppose you have two methods defined within the same class. If each method declares a variable of the same name—`result`, for example—we would have two different variables that just happened to have the same name. Any change made to the value of `result` within one method would not affect the variable named `result` in the other method. It would be as if the two methods were executed on different computers, or as if the computer changed the name of `result` in one of the two methods to `result2`.

All variables declared in a program's `main` method are local to `main`. If one happens to have the same name as a variable declared in some other method, they are two different variables that just happen to have the same name. For example, look at the class definition and program in Listing 5.5. First consider the program, which is shown in the lower half of the listing. The method `main` in the program includes the declaration of a variable named `newAmount`. Now look at the class definition in the upper half of the listing. The method

LISTING 5.5   Local Variables

This class definition is in a file named `BankAccount.java`.

```
/**
This class is used in the program LocalVariablesDemoProgram.
*/
public class BankAccount
{
    public double amount;
    public double rate;
    public void showNewBalance()
    {
        double newAmount = amount + (rate / 100.0) *
                                    amount;
        System.out.println("With interest added, the new amount
                            is $" + newAmount);
    }
}
```

This does not change the value of the variable `newAmount` *in* `main`.

Two different variables named `newAmount`

This program is in a file named `LocalVariableDemoProgram.java`.

```
/**
A toy program to illustrate how local variables behave.
*/
public class LocalVariablesDemoProgram
{
    public static void main(String[] args)
    {
        BankAccount myAccount = new BankAccount();
        myAccount.amount = 100.00;
        myAccount.rate = 5;

        double newAmount = 800.00;
        myAccount.showNewBalance();
        System.out.println("I wish my new amount were $" +
                            newAmount);
    }
}
```

Screen Output   *Chapter 6 will fix the appearance of dollar amounts.*

```
With interest added, the new amount is $105.0
I wish my new amount were $800.0
```

showNewBalance in the class also declares a variable named newAmount. These two variables are different. In main, newAmount is set equal to 800.00 and then the method showNewBalance is called:

```
myAccount.showNewBalance();
```

If you look at the definition of this method and do a little arithmetic, you will see that showNewBalance sets newAmount to 105.00. Yet this assignment has no effect on the other variable named newAmount within main. Displaying newAmount in main after the method invocation shows that its value is still 800.00. Changing the value of newAmount in the method showNewBalance had no effect on the variable named newAmount in main. In this case, the two methods that each use a local variable named newAmount are in different classes in two different files. However, the situation would be the same if the two methods were in the same class definition and thus in the same file.

RECAP Local Variables

A variable declared within a method definition is called a local variable. One method's local variables have no meaning within another method. Moreover, if two methods each have a local variable with the same name, they are considered two different variables.

FAQ I've heard about global variables. What are they?

Thus far, we have discussed two kinds of variables: instance variables, whose meaning is confined to an object of a class, and local variables, whose meaning is confined to a method definition. Some programming languages have another kind of variable, called a **global variable**, whose meaning is confined only to the program, that is, it's not confined at all. Java does not have these global variables. However, as you will see in the next chapter, Java does have a kind of variable—the static variable—that in a sense can take the place of global variables.

Java has no global variables

Blocks

A block is a compound statement that declares a local variable

In Chapter 3, you saw that a compound statement is a group of Java statements enclosed in braces { }. The term **block** really means the same thing. However, the two terms tend to be used in different contexts. When you declare a variable within a compound statement, the compound statement is usually called a block.

If you declare a variable within a block—that is, within a compound statement—the variable is local to the block. Recall from the previous chapter that the portion of a program in which a variable has meaning is known as the variable's scope. So the scope of a local variable extends from its declaration to the end of the block containing the declaration. This means that when the block ends, all variables declared within the block disappear. You can even use that variable's name to name some other variable outside of the block. If you declare a variable outside a block, you can use it both inside and outside the block, and it will have the same meaning throughout.

RECAP **Blocks**

A block is the same as a compound statement, that is, a list of statements enclosed in braces. However, we tend to use the term *block* when a variable declaration occurs within the braces. The variables declared in a block are local to the block, and so these variables disappear when the execution of the block ends.

GOTCHA   Variables Declared in a Block

When you declare a variable within a block, you cannot use the variable outside the block. Declaring the variable outside the block will let you use the variable both outside and inside the block. ■

Parameters of a Primitive Type

Consider the method `getPopulationIn10` for the class `SpeciesFirstTry` defined in Listing 5.3. It returns the projected population of a species ten years in the future. But what if you want the projection for five years in the future or fifty years in the future? The method would be much more useful if it projected the population for any given number of years into the future. To do this, we need some way of leaving a blank in a method so that each call of the method can fill in the blank with a different value for the number of years. The things that serve as blanks in methods are called **formal parameters,** or simply **parameters.** They are a bit more complicated than simple blanks, but you will not go too far wrong if you think of them as blanks or place holders to be filled in with some value when the method is invoked.

A formal parameter in a method definition represents the actual argument

Let's revise the class `SpeciesFirstTry` to use this new idea. The class `SpeciesSecondTry` defined in Listing 5.6 includes a method called `predictPopulation` that has one formal parameter called years. When you invoke this method, you give it the value that you want to have substituted for the parameter years. For example, if `speciesOfTheMonth` is declared to be of type `SpeciesSecondTry`, you can use the method `predictPopulation` to calculate the population in 12 years as follows:

```
int futurePopulation = speciesOfTheMonth.predictPopulation(12);
```

The program in Listing 5.7 is like the program in Listing 5.4, but instead it uses the class `SpeciesSecondTry` and its method `predictPopulation`. With this version of the class, we could project a population any number of years into the future. We could even use a variable for the number of years, as follows:

```
System.out.println("Enter the projected number of years:");
int projectedYears = keyboard.nextInt();
int futurePopulation = speciesOfTheMonth.
                               predictPopulation(projectedYears);
System.out.println("In " + projectedYears + " years, the");
System.out.println("population will be "+ futurePopulation);
```

Let's look at the definition of the method predictPopulation in more detail. The heading, shown below, has something new:

```
public int predictPopulation(int years)
```

The word years is a formal parameter. It is a stand-in for a value that will be plugged in when the method is called. The item that is plugged in is called an argument, as you know from earlier chapters. In some other books, arguments are called **actual parameters.** For example, in the following call, the value 10 is an argument:

```
int futurePopulation =
    speciesOfTheMonth.predictPopulation(10);
```

The argument 10 is plugged in for the formal parameter years everywhere that years occurs in the definition of the method predictPopulation in Listing 5.6. After that, the method invocation proceeds as in all previous method invocations you have seen.

Notice that only the *value* of the argument is used in this substitution process. If the argument in a method invocation is a variable, only the value of the variable is plugged in, not the variable name. For example, consider the following, which might occur in some program that uses the class SpeciesSecondTry:

```
SpeciesSecondTry mySpecies = new SpeciesSecondTry();
int yearCount = 12;
int futurePopulation =
    mySpecies.predictPopulation(yearCount);
```

Java passes
arguments to a
method using
call-by-value

In this case, it is the value 12, *not* the variable yearCount, that is plugged in for the formal parameter years in the definition of the method predictPopulation. Because only the value of the argument is used, this way of plugging in arguments for formal parameters is known as the **call-by-value** mechanism. In Java, this is the only mechanism used for parameters of a primitive type, such as int, double, and char. As you will eventually see, parameters of a class type involve a somewhat different substitution mechanism, but for now, we are concerned only with parameters and arguments of primitive types.

The exact details of this parameter substitution are a bit more complicated than what we have described so far. Usually, you need not be concerned with these extra details, but occasionally, you will need to know how the substitution mechanism actually works. So here are the exact technical details: The formal parameter that occurs in the method definition is a *local variable* that is initialized to the value of the argument given in the method invocation. For example, the parameter `years` of the method `predictPopulation` in Listing 5.6 is a local variable of that method, and `int years` is its declaration. Given the method call,

Parameters are local variables

```
int futurePopulation =
    mySpecies.predictPopulation(yearCount);
```

the local variable `years` is set equal to the value of the argument `yearCount`. The effect is the same as if the method definition began as follows:

```
public int predictPopulation(int years)
{
    years = yearCount;          ←——    This is the effect of plugging in the
    int result = 0;                    argument yearCount
    double populationAmount = population;
    int count = years;
    . . .
```

LISTING 5.6 A Method That Has a Parameter

```
import java.util.Scanner;                We will give an even better version of
public class SpeciesSecondTry           the class later in the chapter.
{
    <The declarations of the instance variables name, population,
    and growthRate are the same as in Listing 5.3.>
    <The definitions of the methods readInput and writeOutput
    are the same as in Listing 5.3.>
    /**
    Returns the projected population of the receiving object
    after the specified number of years.
    */
    public int predictPopulation(int years)
    {
        int result = 0;
        double populationAmount = population;
        int count = years;
        while ((count > 0) && (populationAmount > 0))
        {
            populationAmount = (populationAmount +
            (growthRate / 100) * populationAmount);
            count--;
        }
        if (populationAmount > 0)
            result = (int)populationAmount;
        return result;
    }
}
```

> **RECAP Parameter Names Are Local to the Method**
>
> In Java, you can choose the name of a method's formal parameter without any concern that this name will be the same as an identifier used in some other method. Formal parameters are really local variables, and so their meanings are confined to their respective method definitions.

Parameters have a type

The data type of a formal parameter in a method heading is written before the parameter. In our example, the data type of the parameter `years` is `int`. Every formal parameter has a data type, and the argument that is plugged in for the parameter in a method invocation must match the type of the parameter. Thus, for the method `predictPopulation`, the argument we give in parentheses when we invoke the method must be of type `int`.

This rule is not as strict in practice as we have just implied. In many cases, Java will perform an automatic type conversion—a type cast—if you use an argument in a method call that does not match the type of the formal parameter exactly. For example, if the type of the argument in a method call is `int` and the type of the parameter is `double`, Java will convert the value of type `int` to the corresponding value of type `double`. The following list shows the type conversions that will be performed for you automatically. An argument in a method invocation that is of any of these types will automatically be converted to any of the types that appear to its right if that is needed to match a formal parameter:[1]

Automatic type casting

`byte`→`short`→`int`→`long`→`float`→`double`

Note that this list is exactly the same as the one used for automatic type casting for variables, which we discussed in Chapter 2. Thus, we can express the automatic type casting for both arguments and variables as one rule: You can use a value of any of the listed types anywhere that Java expects a value of a type further down on the list.

So far, our discussion of parameters has involved methods that return a value, but everything we have said about formal parameters and arguments applies to `void`

> **RECAP Parameters of a Primitive Type**
>
> In a method definition, a formal parameter is given in the heading, within the parentheses right after the method name. A formal
>
> *(continued)*

---

[1] An argument of type `char` will also be converted to a matching number type if the formal parameter is of type `int` or any type to the right of `int` in our list of types. However, we do not advocate using this feature.

> parameter of a primitive type—such as `int`, `double`, or `char`—is a local variable.
>
> When a method is invoked, each parameter is initialized to the value of the corresponding argument in the method invocation. This type of substitution is known as the call-by-value parameter mechanism. The argument in a method invocation can be a literal constant, such as 2 or `'A'`; a variable; or any expression that yields a value of the appropriate type.
>
> Note that if you use a variable of a primitive type as an argument in a method invocation, the method invocation cannot change the value of this argument variable.

methods as well: `void` methods can have formal parameters, which are handled in exactly the same way as we just described for methods that return a value.

It is possible, even common, to have more than one formal parameter in a method definition. In that case, each formal parameter is listed in the method heading, and each parameter is preceded by a data type. For example, the following might be the heading of a method definition:

Several parameters are possible in a method

```
public void doStuff(int n1, int n2, double cost, char code)
```

Even if more than one parameter has the same type, each parameter must be preceded by a type name.

The number of arguments given in a method invocation must be exactly the same as the number of formal parameters in the heading of the method definition. For example, the following might be an invocation of our hypothetical method `doStuff`:

```
anObject.doStuff(42, 100, 9.99, Z);
```

As suggested by this example, the correspondence is one of order and type. The first argument in the method call is plugged in for the first parameter in the method definition heading, the second argument in the method call is plugged in for the second parameter in the heading of the method definition, and so forth. Each argument must match its corresponding parameter in data type, except for the automatic type conversions that we discussed earlier.

One word of warning: Parameters of a class type behave differently from parameters of a primitive type. We will discuss parameters of a class type later in this chapter.

Arguments must match parameters in number, order, and type

> **ASIDE** **Use of the Terms *Parameter* and *Argument***
>
> Our use of the terms *parameter* and *argument* is consistent with common usage. We use *parameter* to describe the definition of the data type and variable inside the header of a method and *argument* to describe items passed into a method when it is invoked. However, people often use these terms interchangeably. Some people use the term *parameter* both for what we call a *formal parameter* and for what we call an *argument*. Other people use the term *argument* both for what we call a *formal parameter* and for what we call an *argument*. When you see the term *parameter* or *argument* in other books, you must figure out its exact meaning from the context.

VideoNote
Writing and invoking methods

RECAP **Correspondence Between Formal Parameters and Arguments**

Within a method definition, formal parameters are given within the parentheses after the method name. In a method invocation, arguments are given within the parentheses after the method name. Arguments must match the formal parameters in the method heading with respect to their number, their order, and their data types.

The arguments are plugged in for their corresponding formal parameters. The first argument in the method invocation is plugged in for the first parameter in the method definition, the second argument in the method invocation is plugged in for the second parameter in the method definition, and so forth. Arguments should be of the same types as their corresponding formal parameters, although in some cases, Java will perform an automatic type conversion when the types do not match exactly.

RECAP **Class Definitions**

SYNTAX

```
public class Class_Name
{
    Instance_Variable_Declarations
    ...
    Method_Definitions
}
```

Although this is the form we will use most often, you are also allowed to intermix the method definitions and the instance variable declarations.

RECAP **Method Headings**

SYNTAX

The method headings we have seen thus far are all of the form

```
public Type_Name_Or_void  Method_Name(Parameter_List)
```

The *Parameter_List* is a list of formal parameter names, each preceded by a data type. If the list has more than one entry, the entries are separated by commas. A method might have no parameters at all, in which case nothing is inside the parentheses.

(continued)

EXAMPLES

```
public double getTotal(double price, double tax)
public void setValue(int count, char rating)
public void readInput()
public int predictPopulation(int years)
```

The syntax for a complete method definition is given on page 277.

SELF-TEST QUESTIONS

myprogramminglab

9. What is the difference between the unqualified term *parameter* and the term *formal parameter*?

10. Define a method called getDensity that could be added to the definition of the class SpeciesSecondTry in Listing 5.6. This method has one parameter of type double that is named area. The parameter area gives the area occupied by the species, expressed in square miles. The method getDensity returns a value of type double that is equal to the number of individuals per square mile of the species. You can assume that the area is always greater than zero. (*Hint:* The definition is very short.)

11. Define a method called changePopulation that could be added to the definition of the class SpeciesSecondTry in Listing 5.6. This method has one parameter of type double that is named area. The parameter area gives the area occupied by the species, expressed in square miles. The method changePopulation changes the value of the instance variable population so that there will be two individuals per square mile.

12. Define a method called changePopulation that could be added to the definition of the class SpeciesSecondTry in Listing 5.6. This method has two parameters. One parameter, named area, is of type double and gives the area occupied by the species in square miles. The other parameter, named numberPerMile, is of type int and gives the desired number of individuals per square mile. The method changePopulation changes the value of the instance variable population so that the number of individuals per square mile is (approximately) equal to numberPerMile.

5.2 INFORMATION HIDING AND ENCAPSULATION

The cause is hidden, but the result is well known.

—OVID, *METAMORPHOSE*

Never tell people how to do things. Tell them what to do and they will surprise you with their ingenuity.

—GEORGE S. PATTON

Information hiding sounds as though it could be a bad thing to do. What advantage could hiding information have? As it turns out, in computer science hiding certain kinds of information is considered a good programming technique, one that makes the programmer's job simpler and the programmer's code easier to understand. It is basically a way to avoid "information overload."

Information Hiding

A programmer who is using a method that you have defined does not need to know the details of the code in the body of the method definition to be able to use the method. If a method—or other piece of software—is well written, a programmer who uses the method need only know *what* the method accomplishes and not *how* the method accomplishes its task. For example, you can use the Scanner method nextInt without even looking at the definition of that method. It is not that the code contains some secret that is forbidden to you. The point is that viewing the code will not help you use the method, but it will give you more things to keep track of, which could distract you from your programming tasks.

Designing a method so that it can be used without any need to understand the fine detail of the code is called **information hiding.** The term emphasizes the fact that the programmer acts as though the body of the method were hidden from view. If the term *information hiding* sounds too negative to you, you can use the term **abstraction.** The two terms mean the same thing in this context. This use of the term *abstraction* should not be surprising. When you abstract something, you lose some of the details. For example, an abstract of a paper or a book is a brief description of the paper or book, as opposed to the entire document.

Separate the what *from the* how

■ **PROGRAMMING TIP** When You Design a Method, Separate What from How

Methods should be self-contained units that are designed separately from the incidental details of other methods and separately from any program that uses the method. A programmer who uses a method should need only know what the method does, not how it does it. ■

Precondition and Postcondition Comments

An efficient and standard way to describe what a method does is by means of specific kinds of comments known as preconditions and postconditions. A method's **precondition** comment states the conditions that must be true before the method is invoked. The method should not be used, and cannot be expected to perform correctly, unless the precondition is satisfied.

A precondition states a method's requirements

The **postcondition** comment describes all the effects produced by a method invocation. The postcondition tells what will be true after the method is executed in a situation in which the precondition holds. For a method that returns a value, the postcondition will include a description of the value returned by the method.

A postcondition states a method's effect

For example, the following shows some suitable precondition and postcondition comments for the method `writeOutput` shown in Listing 5.3:

```
/**
    Precondition: The instance variables of the calling
    object have values.
    Postcondition: The data stored in (the instance variables
    of) the receiving object have been written to the screen.
*/
public void writeOutput()
```

The comments for the method `predictPopulation` in Listing 5.6 can be expressed as follows:

```
/**
    Precondition: years is a nonnegative number.
    Postcondition: Returns the projected population of the
    receiving object
    after the specified number of years.
*/
public int predictPopulation(int years)
```

If the only postcondition is a description of the value returned, programmers usually omit the word *postcondition*. The previous comment would typically be written in the following alternative way:

```
/**
    Precondition: years is a nonnegative number.
    Returns the projected population of the receiving object
    after the specified number of years.
*/
public int predictPopulation(int years)
```

Some design specifications may require preconditions and postconditions for all methods. Others omit explicit preconditions and postconditions from certain methods whose names make their action obvious. Names such as `readInput`, `writeOutput`, and `set` are often considered self-explanatory. However, the sound rule to follow is to adhere to whatever guidelines your instructor or supervisor gives you, and when in doubt, add preconditions and postconditions.

Some programmers prefer not to use the words *precondition* and *postcondition* in their comments. However, you should always think in terms of preconditions and postconditions when writing method comments. The really important thing is not the words *precondition* and *postcondition*, but the concepts they name. Note that precondition and postcondition comments are examples of assertions.

The public and private Modifiers

Any class can use a public class, method, or instance variable

As you know, the modifier public, when applied to a class, method, or instance variable, means that any other class can directly use or access the class, method, or instance variable by name. For example, the program in Listing 5.7 contains the following three lines, which set the values of the public instance variables for the object speciesOfTheMonth:

```
speciesOfTheMonth.name = "Klingon ox";
speciesOfTheMonth.population = 10;
speciesOfTheMonth.growthRate = 15;
```

LISTING 5.7   Using a Method That Has a Parameter

```java
/**
Demonstrates the use of a parameter
with the method predictPopulation.
*/
public class SpeciesSecondTryDemo
{
    public static void main(String[] args)
    {
        SpeciesSecondTry speciesOfTheMonth = new
                            SpeciesSecondTry();
        System.out.println("Enter data on the Species of the " +
                            "Month:");
        speciesOfTheMonth.readInput();
        speciesOfTheMonth.writeOutput();
        int futurePopulation =
            speciesOfTheMonth.predictPopulation(10);
        System.out.println("In ten years the population will be " +
                            futurePopulation);
        //Change the species to show how to change
        //the values of instance variables:
        speciesOfTheMonth.name = "Klingon ox";
        speciesOfTheMonth.population = 10;
        speciesOfTheMonth.growthRate = 15;
        System.out.println("The new Species of the Month:");
        speciesOfTheMonth.writeOutput();
        System.out.println("In ten years the population will be " +
                            speciesOfTheMonth.predictPopulation(10));
    }
}
```

Sample Screen Output

The output is exactly the same as in Listing 5.4.

The object `speciesOfTheMonth` is an object of the class `SpeciesSecondTry`, whose definition appears in Listing 5.6. As you can see by looking at that class definition, the instance variables `name`, `population`, and `growthRate` all have the modifier `public`, and so the preceding three statements are perfectly valid.

While it is normal to have public classes and methods, it is *not* a good programming practice to make the instance variables of a class public. Typically, all instance variables should be private. You make an instance variable private by using the modifier `private` instead of the modifier `public`. The keywords `public` and `private` are examples of **access modifiers**.

Instance variables should be private

Suppose that we change the modifier that is before the instance variable `name` in the definition of the class `SpeciesSecondTry` in Listing 5.6 from `public` to `private` so that the class definition begins as follows:

```
public class SpeciesSecondTry
{
    private String name; //Private!
    public int population;
    public double growthRate;
```

With this change, the following Java statement in Listing 5.7 is invalid:

```
speciesOfTheMonth.name = "Klingon ox"; //Invalid when private.
```

The following two statements remain valid, because we left the modifiers of `population` and `growthRate` as `public`:

```
speciesOfTheMonth.population = 10;
speciesOfTheMonth.growthRate = 15;
```

When an instance variable is private, its *name* is not accessible *outside* of the class definition. Even so, you can still use its name in any way you wish within any method *inside* the class definition. In particular, you can directly change the value of the instance variable. Outside of the class definition, however, you cannot make any direct reference to the instance variable's name.

Private instance variables are accessible by name only within their own class

For example, let's make the three instance variables in the class `SpeciesSecondTry` private, but leave the method definitions unchanged. The result is shown in Listing 5.8 as the class `SpeciesThirdTry`. Because the instance variables are all private, the last three of the following statements would be invalid within any class other than the class `SpeciesThirdTry`:

```
SpeciesThirdTry secretSpecies = new SpeciesThirdTry();
//Valid
secretSpecies.readInput(); //Valid
secretSpecies.name = "Aardvark"; //Invalid
System.out.println(secretSpecies.population); //Invalid
System.out.println(secretSpecies.growthRate); //Invalid
```

LISTING 5.8 A Class with Private Instance Variables

```
import java.util.Scanner;
public class SpeciesThirdTry
{
    private String name;
    private int population;
    private double growthRate;
    <The definitions of the methods readInput, writeOutput, and
    predictPopulation are the same as in Listing 5.3 and
    Listing 5.6.>
}
```

We will give an even better version of this class later in the chapter.

Notice, however, that the invocation of the method `readInput` is valid. So there is still a way to set the instance variables of an object, even though those instance variables are private. Within the definition of the method `readInput` (shown in Listing 5.3) are assignment statements such as

```
name = keyboard.nextLine();
```

and

```
population = keyboard.nextInt();
```

that set the value of instance variables. Thus, making an instance variable private does not mean that you cannot change it. It means only that you cannot use the instance variable's *name* to refer directly to the variable anywhere outside of the class definition.

Private methods are called only within their own class.

Methods can also be private. If a method is marked `private`, it cannot be invoked outside of the class definition. However, a private method can still be invoked within the definition of any other method in that same class. Most methods are public, but if you have a method that will be used only within the definition of other methods of that class, it makes sense to make this "helping" method private. Using private methods is another way of hiding implementation details within the class.

Classes themselves can be private as well, but we will not discuss that until Chapter 12.

RECAP The `public` and `private` Modifiers

Within a class definition, each instance variable declaration and each method definition, as well as the class itself, can be preceded by either `public` or `private`. These access modifiers specify where a class, instance variable, or method can be used. If an instance variable is private, its name cannot be used to access it outside of the class definition. However, it can be used within the definitions of methods in its class. If an instance variable is public, there are no restrictions on where you can use its name.

(continued)

If a method definition is private, the method cannot be invoked outside of the class definition. However, it can be invoked within the definitions of methods in its class. If the method is public, you can invoke it anywhere without restriction.

Normally, all instance variables are private and most methods are public.

■ PROGRAMMING TIP   Instance Variables Should Be Private

You should make all the instance variables in a class private. By doing so, you force the programmer who uses the class—whether that person is you or someone else—to access the instance variables only via the class's methods. This allows the class to control how a programmer looks at or changes the instance variables. The next programming example illustrates why making instance variables private is important.   ■

PROGRAMMING EXAMPLE   A Demonstration of Why Instance Variables Should Be Private

Listing 5.9 shows a simple class of rectangles. It has three private instance variables to represent a rectangle's width, height, and area. The method setDimensions sets the width and height, and the method getArea returns the rectangle's area.

LISTING 5.9   **A Class of Rectangles**

```java
/**
 Class that represents a rectangle.
*/
public class Rectangle
{
    private int width;
    private int height;
    private int area;

    public void setDimensions(int newWidth, int newHeight)
    {
        width = newWidth;
        height = newHeight;
        area = width * height;
    }
    public int getArea()
    {
        return area;
    }
}
```

You might use the class `Rectangle` in the following way:

```
Rectangle box = new Rectangle( );
box.setDimensions(10, 5);
System.out.println("The area of our rectangle is " +
box.getArea());
```

The output from these statements would be

```
The area of our rectangle is 50
```

Public instance variables can lead to the corruption of an object's data

What would happen if the three instance variables in `Rectangle` were public instead of private? After creating a 10-by-5 rectangle box, you would be able to change the value of any or all of the instance variables. So while `area` is 50, you could change `width`, for example, to 6 by writing

```
box.width = 6; //You could do this if width were public.
```

Private instance variables enable the class to restrict how they are accessed or changed

If you then called `getArea`, you would still get 50 as the area, instead of the new area, 30. By making the instance variables in `Rectangle` public, we create the possibility that the instance variable `area` will be unequal to `width * height`. Making the instance variables private enables you to restrict how they are accessed or changed.

GOTCHA   Public Instance Variables Can Lead to the Corruption of a Class's Data

VideoNote
Investigating public and private access

The previous programming example shows how the ability to change an instance variable directly by name can cause inconsistent data within an object. Since public instance variables provide this ability, always make instance variables private. ■

PROGRAMMING EXAMPLE   Another Implementation of a Class of Rectangles

Let's look at another class, `Rectangle2` in Listing 5.10, that has exactly the same methods as the previous class `Rectangle`, but implements them in a slightly different way. Our new class computes the area of the rectangle only when the method `getArea` is called. Additionally, the area is not saved in an instance variable.

Notice that you would use the class `Rectangle2` in the same way that you would use `Rectangle`. The only change you would make to the three statements that we wrote in the previous programming example to demonstrate `Rectangle` would be to replace `Rectangle` with `Rectangle2`:

```
Rectangle2 box = new Rectangle2( );
box.setDimensons(10, 5);
System.out.println("The area of our rectangle is " +
box.getArea());
```

That is, you invoke the methods in the same way, and they have the same behavior, regardless of their class.

> **REMEMBER Implementation Should Not Affect Behavior**
>
> Two classes can have the same behavior but different implementations.

We have two classes—Rectangle and Rectangle2—that behave in the same way. That is, *what* they do is the same, but *how* they perform their tasks differs. In Rectangle2, the method getArea, computes and then returns the area without saving it. Rectangle, however, has an instance variable—area—for the rectangle's area. The method setDimensions in Rectangle computes the area and stores it in area. The method getArea then simply returns the value in the instance variable area.

Is one of these two classes "better" than the other? The answer depends on what we mean by "better" and how we use the class. We can make the following observations:

Classes can define the same behaviors but have different implementations

- Rectangle uses more memory than Rectangle2 because it has an additional instance variable.
- Rectangle always computes the area, even if it is not needed.

LISTING 5.10 **Another Class of Rectangles**

```java
/**
Another class that represents a rectangle.
*/
public class Rectangle2
{
    private int width;
    private int height;
    public void setDimensions(int newWidth, int newHeight)
    {
        width = newWidth;
        height = newHeight;
    }
    public int getArea()
    {
        return width * height;
    }
}
```

The implication of our second observation is that using `Rectangle` could require more computer time than using `Rectangle2`. To appreciate this, you need to imagine that both classes have several more methods, so that not invoking `getArea` is a real possibility. If you rarely ask for the area of a particular rectangle, using `Rectangle2` saves you both execution time and memory. However, if you repeatedly invoke `getArea` for a particular rectangle, using `Rectangle` will save you execution time because it computes the area only once.

> **REMEMBER Implementation Can Affect Efficiency**
>
> The way you implement a class can affect its execution time and memory requirements.

Accessor Methods and Mutator Methods

An accessor method retrieves data in an object

Making all instance variables private does control access to them, but what if you have a legitimate reason to access an instance variable? For these cases, you should provide accessor methods. An **accessor method** or **get method,** or **getter,** is simply a method that allows you to look at data contained in an instance variable. In Listing 5.11, we have rewritten the class for a species yet another time. This version has accessor methods for obtaining the value of each instance variable. The names of these methods start with the word `get`, as in `getName`.

A mutator method changes data in an object

Accessor methods allow you to look at the data in a private instance variable. Other methods, known as **mutator methods**, or **set methods**, or **setters,** allow you to change the data stored in private instance variables. Our class definition has a mutator method, called `setSpecies`, for setting the instance variables to new values. The program in Listing 5.12 illustrates the use of the mutator method `setSpecies`. That program is similar to the one in Listing 5.7, but because this version of our species class has private instance variables, we must use the mutator method `setSpecies` to reset the values of the instance variables.

Defining accessor methods and mutator methods might appear to defeat the purpose of making instance variables private, but that is not true. A mutator method can check that any change is appropriate and warn the user of a problem. For example, the mutator method `setSpecies` checks to see whether the program inadvertently tries to set `population` equal to a negative number.

LISTING 5.11   A Class with Accessor and Mutator Methods

```java
import java.util.Scanner;
public class SpeciesFourthTry
{
    private String name;
    private int population;
    private double growthRate;
```

Yes, we will define an even better version of this class later.

<The definitions of the methods readInput, writeOutput, and
 predictPopulation go here. They are the same as in Listing
 5.3 and Listing 5.6.>

```java
    public void setSpecies(String newName, int newPopulation,
                           double newGrowthRate)
    {
        name = newName;
        if (newPopulation >= 0)
            population = newPopulation;
        else
        {
            System.out.println(
                    "ERROR: using a negative population.");
            System.exit(0);
        }
        growthRate = newGrowthRate;
    }
    public String getName()
    {
        return name;
    }
    public int getPopulation()
    {
        return population;
    }
    public double getGrowthRate()
    {
        return growthRate;
    }
}
```

A mutator method can check to make sure that instance variables are set to proper values.

The names of these methods need not involve get and set; you can use any method name that is convenient. For example, you might prefer to give them names such as retrieveValue, reset, or giveNewValues. However, it is traditional to begin the names of accessor methods with get and mutator methods with set.

LISTING 5.12   Using a Mutator Method *(part 1 of 2)*

```java
import java.util.Scanner;
/**
 Demonstrates the use of the mutator method setSpecies.
*/
public class SpeciesFourthTryDemo
{
    public static void main(String[] args)
    {
        SpeciesFourthTry speciesOfTheMonth =
                                new SpeciesFourthTry();
        System.out.println("Enter number of years to project:");
        Scanner keyboard = new Scanner(System.in);
        int numberOfYears = keyboard.nextInt();

        System.out.println(
                    "Enter data on the Species of the Month:");
        speciesOfTheMonth.readInput();
        speciesOfTheMonth.writeOutput();

        int futurePopulation =
        speciesOfTheMonth.predictPopulation(numberOfYears);
        System.out.println("In " + numberOfYears +
                        " years the population will be " +
                        futurePopulation);
        //Change the species to show how to change
        //the values of instance variables:
        speciesOfTheMonth.setSpecies("Klingon ox", 10, 15);
        System.out.println("The new Species of the Month:");
        speciesOfTheMonth.writeOutput();

        futurePopulation =
            speciesOfTheMonth.predictPopulation(numberOfYears);
        System.out.println("In " + numberOfYears +
                        " years the population will be " +
                        futurePopulation);
    }
}
```

Sample Screen Output

```
Enter number of years to project:
10
Enter data on the Species of the Month:
What is the species' name?
Ferengie fur ball
```

(continued)

LISTING 5.12   Using a Mutator Method *(part 2 of 2)*

```
What is the population of the species?
1000
Enter growth rate (% increase per year):
-20.5
Name = Ferengie fur ball
Population = 1000
Growth rate = -20.5%
In 10 years the population will be 100
The new Species of the Month:
Name = Klingon ox
Population = 10
Growth rate = 15.0%
In 10 years the population will be 40
```

RECAP Accessor and Mutator Methods

A public method that returns data from a private instance variable is called an accessor method, a get method, or a getter. The names of accessor methods typically begin with get. A public method that changes the data stored in one or more private instance variables is called a mutator method, a set method, or a setter. The names of mutator methods typically begin with set.

SELF-TEST QUESTIONS

myprogramminglab

13. In Listing 5.12, we set the data for the object `speciesOfTheMonth` as follows:

    ```
    speciesOfTheMonth.setSpecies("Klingon ox", 10, 15);
    ```

    Could we have used the following code instead?

    ```
    speciesOfTheMonth.name = "Klingon ox";
    speciesOfTheMonth.population = 10;
    speciesOfTheMonth.growthRate = 15;
    ```

    If we could have used this alternative code, why didn't we? If we could not have used this alternative code, explain why we could not use it.

14. Give preconditions and postconditions for the following method, assuming that it is in the class `SpeciesFourthTry` in Listing 5.11:

```
public void updatePopulation()
{
    population = (int)(population + (growthRate / 100) *
            population);
}
```

15. What is an accessor method? What is a mutator method?

16. Give the complete definition of a class called `Person` that has two instance variables, one for the person's name and the other for the person's age. Include accessor methods and mutator methods for each instance variable. Also, include a method that sets both the name and age of a person. There are no other methods.

PROGRAMMING EXAMPLE   A Purchase Class

Listing 5.13 contains a class for a single purchase of multiple identical items, such as 12 apples or 2 quarts of milk. It is designed to be part of a program used at the checkout stand of a supermarket. Recall that supermarkets often give prices for a group of items, such as 5 for $1.25 or 3 for $1.00, instead of the price for one item. They hope that if they price apples at 5 for $1.25, you will buy 5 apples instead of 2. But 5 for $1.25 is really $0.25 each, and if you buy 2 apples, they charge you only $0.50.

The instance variables are as follows:

```
private String name;
private int groupCount; //Part of a price, like the 2
                        // in 2 for $1.99.
private double groupPrice;//Part of a price, like the $1.99
                          //in 2 for $1.99.
private int numberBought;//Number of items bought.
```

Let's explain the meaning of these instance variables by giving an example. If you buy 12 apples at 5 for $1.25, name has the value "apples", groupCount has the value 5, groupPrice has the value 1.25, and numberBought has the value 12. Note that the price of 5 for $1.25 is stored in the two instance variables groupCount—for the 5—and groupPrice—for the $1.25.

Consider the method getTotalCost, for example. The total cost of the purchase is calculated as

```
(groupPrice / groupCount) * numberBought
```

LISTING 5.13   The Purchase Class *(part 1 of 3)*

```java
import java.util.Scanner;
/**
Class for the purchase of one kind of item, such as 3 oranges.
Prices are set supermarket style, such as 5 for $1.25.
*/
public class Purchase
{
    private String name;
    private int groupCount;       //Part of a price, like the 2 in
                                  //2 for $1.99.
    private double groupPrice;    //Part of a price, like the $1.99
                                  // in 2 for $1.99.
    private int numberBought;     //Number of items bought.
    public void setName(String newName)
    {
        name = newName;
    }
    /**
    Sets price to count pieces for $costForCount.
    For example, 2 for $1.99.
    */
    public void setPrice(int count, double costForCount)
    {
        if ((count <= 0) || (costForCount <= 0))
        {
            System.out.println("Error: Bad parameter in " +
                                "setPrice.");
            System.exit(0);
        }
        else
        {
            groupCount = count;
            groupPrice = costForCount;
        }
    }
    public void setNumberBought(int number)
    {
        if (number <= 0)
        {
            System.out.println("Error: Bad parameter in " +
                                "setNumberBought.");
            System.exit(0);
        }
        else
            numberBought = number;
    }
```

(continued)

LISTING 5.13   The Purchase Class *(part 2 of 3)*

```java
/**
 Reads from keyboard the price and number of a purchase.
*/
public void readInput()
{
    Scanner keyboard = new Scanner(System.in);
    System.out.println("Enter name of item you are purchasing:");
    name = keyboard.nextLine();
    System.out.println("Enter price of item as two numbers.");
    System.out.println("For example, 3 for $2.99 is entered as");
    System.out.println("3 2.99");
    System.out.println("Enter price of item as two numbers, " +
                        "now:");
    groupCount = keyboard.nextInt();
    groupPrice = keyboard.nextDouble();

    while ((groupCount <= 0) || (groupPrice <= 0))
    { //Try again:
        System.out.println("Both numbers must " +
                            "be positive. Try again.");
        System.out.println("Enter price of " +
                            "item as two numbers.");
        System.out.println("For example, 3 for " +
                            "$2.99 is entered as");
        System.out.println("3 2.99");
        System.out.println(
                        "Enter price of item as two numbers, now:");
        groupCount = keyboard.nextInt();
        groupPrice = keyboard.nextDouble();
    }
    System.out.println("Enter number of items purchased:");
    numberBought = keyboard.nextInt();

    while (numberBought <= 0)
    { //Try again:
        System.out.println("Number must be positive. " +
                            "Try again.");
        System.out.println("Enter number of items purchased:");
        numberBought = keyboard.nextInt();
    }
}
```

(continued)

LISTING 5.13 **The** Purchase **Class** *(part 3 of 3)*

```java
/**
 Displays price and number being purchased.
*/
public void writeOutput()
{
    System.out.println(numberBought + " " + name);
    System.out.println("at " + groupCount +
                        " for $" + groupPrice);
}
public String getName()
{
    return name;
}
public double getTotalCost()
{
    return (groupPrice / groupCount) * numberBought;
}
public double getUnitCost()
{
    return groupPrice / groupCount;
}
public int getNumberBought()
{
    return numberBought;
}
}
```

If this purchase is 12 apples at 5 for $1.25, the total cost is

(1.25 / 5) * 12

Also notice the methods `readInput`, `setPrice`, and `setNumberBought`. All of these methods check for negative numbers when it does not make sense to have a negative number, such as when the user enters the number purchased. A simple demonstration program that uses this class is given in Listing 5.14.

LISTING 5.14 **Use of the** Purchase **Class** *(part 1 of 2)*

```java
public class PurchaseDemo
{
    public static void main(String[] args)
    {
        Purchase oneSale = new Purchase();
        oneSale.readInput();
```

(continued)

LISTING 5.14 Use of the Purchase **Class** *(part 2 of 2)*

```
        oneSale.writeOutput();
        System.out.println("Cost each $" + oneSale.getUnitCost());
        System.out.println("Total cost $" +
                oneSale.getTotalCost());
    }
}
```

Sample Screen Output

```
Enter name of item you are purchasing:
pink grapefruit
Enter price of item as two numbers.
For example, 3 for $2.99 is entered as
3 2.99
Enter price of item as two numbers, now:
4 5.00
Enter number of items purchased:
0
Number must be positive. Try again.
Enter number of items purchased:
3
3 pink grapefruit
at 4 for $5.0
Cost each $1.25
Total cost $3.75
```

Methods Calling Methods

A method body can contain an invocation of another method. The situation for this sort of method call is exactly the same as it would be if the method call had occurred in the main method of a program. However, if the called method is in the same class, it is typically invoked without writing any receiving object. This is true regardless of whether the called method is public or private.

Listing 5.15 contains the definition of a class called Oracle. The method chat of this class conducts a dialogue with the user that answers a series of one-line questions that the user asks. Notice that the definition of the method chat contains a call to the method answer, which is also a method in the class Oracle. If you look at the definition of the method answer, you will see that it in turn includes calls to two other methods, seekAdvice and update, both of which are also in the class Oracle.

LISTING 5.15   **Methods Calling Other Methods**

```java
import java.util.Scanner;
public class Oracle
{
    private String oldAnswer = "The answer is in your heart.";
    private String newAnswer;
    private String question;

    public void chat()
    {
        System.out.print("I am the oracle. ");
        System.out.println("I will answer any one-line question.");
        Scanner keyboard = new Scanner(System.in);
        String response;
        do
        {
            answer();
            System.out.println("Do you wish to ask " +
                "another question?");
            response = keyboard.next();
        } while (response.equalsIgnoreCase("yes"));
        System.out.println("The oracle will now rest.");
    }

    private void answer()
    {
        System.out.println("What is your question?");
        Scanner keyboard = new Scanner(System.in);
        question = keyboard.nextLine();
        seekAdvice();
        System.out.println("You asked the question:");
        System.out.println(" " + question);
        System.out.println("Now, here is my answer:");
        System.out.println(" " + oldAnswer);
        update();
    }
    private void seekAdvice()
    {
        System.out.println("Hmm, I need some help on that.");
        System.out.println("Please give me one line of advice.");
        Scanner keyboard = new Scanner(System.in);
        newAnswer = keyboard.nextLine();
        System.out.println("Thank you. That helped a lot.");
    }
    private void update()
    {
        oldAnswer = newAnswer;
    }
}
```

Let's first consider the invocation of the method answer within the definition of the method chat. Note that the method named answer is not preceded by an object and a dot. The receiving object is understood to be the receiving object of the method chat. The demonstration program in Listing 5.16 creates an object named delphi of the class Oracle and then uses this object to invoke the method chat, as follows:

```
delphi.chat();
```

So when chat calls answer, the invocation

```
answer();
```

in the definition of is understood to mean

```
delphi.answer();
```

LISTING 5.16 **Oracle Demonstration Program** *(part 1 of 2)*

```java
public class OracleDemo
{
    public static void main(String[] args)
    {
        Oracle delphi = new Oracle();
        delphi.chat();
    }
}
```

Sample Screen Output

```
I am the oracle. I will answer any one-line question.
What is your question?
What time is it?
Hmm, I need some help on that.
Please give me one line of advice.
Seek and ye shall find the answer.
Thank you. That helped a lot.
You asked the question:
    What time is it?
Now, here is my answer:
    The answer is in your heart.
Do you wish to ask another question?
yes
What is your question?
What is the meaning of life?
Hmm, I need some help on that.
```

(continued)

LISTING 5.16   Oracle Demonstration Program *(part 2 of 2)*

```
Please give me one line of advice.
Ask the car guys.
Thank you. That helped a lot.
You asked the question:
    What is the meaning of life?
Now, here is my answer:
    Seek and ye shall find the answer.
Do you wish to ask another question?
no
The oracle will now rest.
```

When you write the definition of a method like `chat`, you do not know what the name of the receiving object will be. It could be different at different times. Because you do not—in fact, cannot—know the name of the receiving object, you omit it. Therefore, in the definition of the class `Oracle` in Listing 5.15, when you write

```
answer();
```

within the definition of the method, it means

> *Receiving_Object.* `answer()`;

Because the keyword `this` means the receiving object, you can also write the call as

> `this.answer();`

You typically omit `this` when calling a method from another method in the same class

Omitting the keyword `this` and a dot when you invoke a method in the same class is not really new. We have already been doing this with instance variables. But it works only with methods in the same class. If you call a method of one class within the definition of a method of another class, you must include an object and a dot.[2] Note also that omitting the receiving object is possible only if the receiving object can be expressed as `this`. If the receiving object is some object that is declared and created within a method definition, you must include the object name and dot within that method definition.

Let's continue with our discussion of method definitions in the class `Oracle`. You can have methods that call other methods that in turn call yet

___

[2] This rule about calling a method of one class within the definition of another class does not apply to static methods, which we discuss in the next chapter. However, the rule does apply to all the kinds of methods we have discussed thus far.

other methods. In the class `Oracle`, the definition of the method `answer` includes calls to the two methods `seekAdvice` and `update`, both of which are also in the class `Oracle`. As we just discussed, these calls are not preceded by an object and a dot.

Let's consider the following invocation from the program in Listing 5.16:

```
delphi.chat();
```

The definition of includes the invocation

```
answer();
```

which is equivalent to

```
this.answer();
```

Because the receiving object is `delphi`, this statement is also equivalent to the invocation

```
delphi.answer();
```

The definition of answer includes the invocations

```
seekAdvice();
```

and

```
update();
```

which are equivalent to

```
this.seekAdvice();
```

and

```
this.update();
```

Because the receiving object again is `delphi`, these are also equivalent to

```
delphi.seekAdvice();
```

and

```
delphi.update();
```

You can have methods calling methods calling methods for any number of method calls. The details are always handled just as we've described here.

REMEMBER Omitting the Receiving Object

When the receiving object in a method invocation is represented as the keyword `this`, you can omit the `this` and the dot. For example, the method

(continued)

```
    public void answer()
    {
        ...
        this.seekAdvice();
        ...
        this.update();
    }
```
is equivalent to
```
    public void answer()
    {
        ...
        seekAdvice();
        ...
        update();
    }
```

■ PROGRAMMING TIP   Make Helping Methods Private

Look again at Listing 5.15. The methods answer, seekAdvice, and update are labeled private rather than public. Recall that if a method is labeled private, it can be called only from within the definitions of other methods of the same class. Thus, in some other class or program, the following invocation of the private method answer would be invalid and would produce a compiler error message:

```
Oracle myOracle = new Oracle();
myOracle.answer(); //Invalid: answer is private.
```

where as the following call to the public method would be perfectly valid:

```
myOracle.chat(); //Valid.
```

We made the methods answer, seekAdvice, and update private because they are just helping methods. A programmer using the class Oracle is not expected to invoke these methods. They are used only within the definition of the method chat. This means that the methods answer, seekAdvice, and update are part of the class's implementation and should not be available to a user of the class. As we emphasize in the next section, entitled "Encapsulation," it is good programming practice to keep the implementation portion of a class private.   ■

SELF-TEST QUESTIONS   myprogramminglab

17. Can you invoke a method inside the definition of another method in the same class?

18. In the definition of the method in Listing 5.15, what is the effect of changing the statement

```
seekAdvice();
```

to

```
this.seekAdvice();
```

Encapsulation

Encapsulation
groups instance
variables and
methods into a
class

In Chapter 1, we said that encapsulation involves hiding the details of how a piece of software works. Now that you have more knowledge of Java and information hiding, we can expand upon this basic definition, to say that encapsulation is the process of hiding all the details of a class definition that are not necessary to understanding how objects of the class are used. Let's look at an example.

Suppose you want to drive an automobile. Given this task, what is the most useful way to describe an automobile? It clearly is not to list the number of cylinders and explain how they go through a cycle of taking in air and gasoline, igniting the gasoline–air mixture, and expelling exhaust. Such details won't help you learn how to drive.

To a person who wants to learn to drive an automobile, the most useful description consists of information such as the following:

- If you press your foot on the accelerator pedal, the automobile will move faster.
- If you press your foot on the brake pedal, the automobile will slow down and eventually stop.
- If you turn the steering wheel to the left or right, the automobile will turn in the same direction.

Although we can describe other details, these are perhaps the main ones and are enough to illustrate the concept of encapsulation.

Encapsulation
hides
implementation
details

The principle of encapsulation says that, when describing an automobile to somebody who wants to learn to drive, you should provide something like the previous list. In the context of programming, encapsulation means the same thing. To use a piece of software, a programmer does not need all the details of its definition. In particular, if your piece of software is ten pages long, the description given to another programmer who will use the software should be much shorter than ten pages, perhaps only a half page. Of course, that is possible only if you write your software in such a way that it lends itself to this sort of short description.

Another analogy that may help is that an automobile has certain things that are visible, such as the pedals and steering wheel, while other things are hidden under the hood. The automobile is encapsulated: Only the controls needed to drive the automobile are visible, and the details are hidden.

Similarly, a piece of software should be encapsulated so that only the necessary controls are visible and its details are hidden. The programmer who uses the software is thus spared the bother of worrying about its internal details. Encapsulation is important because it simplifies the job of the programmer who uses the encapsulated software to write more software.

We have already discussed some of the techniques of encapsulation earlier in this chapter, under the topic of information hiding. Encapsulation is a form of information hiding. For encapsulation to be useful, a class definition must be given in such a way that a programmer can use the class without seeing the hidden details. Encapsulation, when done correctly, neatly divides a class definition into two parts, which we will call the interface3 and the implementation. The **class interface** tells programmers all they need to know to use the class in their programs. The class interface consists of the headings for the public methods and public named constants of the class, along with comments that tell a programmer how to use these public methods and constants.

A class interface describes the class's public view

The **implementation** of a class consists of all of the private elements of the class definition, principally the private instance variables of the class, along with the definitions of both the public methods and private methods. Note that the class interface and the implementation of a class definition are not separate in your Java code, but are mixed together. For example, the class interface for the class Purchase in Listing 5.13 is highlighted. Although you need a class's implementation when you run a program that uses the class, you should not need to know anything about the implementation to write the program itself.

A class's implementation is hidden from public view

When defining a class using the principle of encapsulation, you must neatly separate the class interface from the implementation conceptually so that the interface is a simplified and safe description of the class. One way to think of this separation is to imagine a wall between the implementation and the interface, with well-regulated communication across the wall. This wall is illustrated graphically in Figure 5.3. When you use encapsulation to define a class in this way, we say that the class is **well encapsulated.**

Here are some of the most important guidelines for defining a well-encapsulated class:

- Place a comment before the class definition that describes how the programmer should think about the class data and methods. If the class describes an amount of money, for example, the programmer should think in terms of dollars and cents and not in terms of how the class represents money. The comment in this case should be written to help the programmer think in this way.

---

[3] The word *interface* also has a technical meaning in the Java language, as you will see in Chapter 8. We are using the word somewhat differently when we say *class interface*, although in spirit, the two uses of the word *interface* are the same.

FIGURE 5.3 A Well-Encapsulated Class Definition

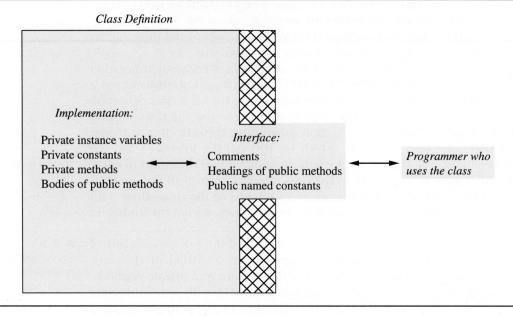

Class Definition

Implementation:

Private instance variables
Private constants
Private methods
Bodies of public methods

Interface:

Comments
Headings of public methods
Public named constants

Programmer who uses the class

- Declare all the instance variables in the class as private.
- Provide public accessor methods to retrieve the data in an object. Also provide public methods for any other basic needs that a programmer will have for manipulating the data in the class. Such methods could include public mutator methods.
- Place a comment before each public method heading that fully specifies how to use the method.
- Make any helping methods private.
- Write comments within the class definition to describe implementation details.

Encapsulation guidelines

The comments in a class definition that describe how to use both the class and each public method are part of the class interface. As we indicated, these comments are usually placed before the class definition and before each method definition. Other comments clarify the implementation. A good rule to follow is to use the /** */ style for class-interface comments and the // style for implementation comments.

When you use encapsulation to define your class, you should be able to go back and change the implementation details of the class definition without requiring changes in any program that uses the class. This is a good way to test whether you have written a well-encapsulated class definition. Often, you will have very good reasons for changing the implementation details of a class definition. For example, you may come up with a more efficient way to implement a method so that the method invocations run faster. You might even decide to change some details of what the implementation does without changing the way the methods are invoked and the basic things they do. For example, if you have a class for bank account objects, you might change the rules for charging a penalty to an overdrawn account.

FAQ Is a class interface related to an application programming interface?

We encountered the term *API*, or application programming interface, in Chapter 1 when we introduced the Java API. The API for a class is essentially the same thing as the class interface for the class. You will often see the term *API* when reading the documentation for class libraries.

FAQ What is an ADT?

The term **ADT** is short for **abstract data type.** It is a specification for a set of data and the operations on that data. These specifications describe what the operations do but do not indicate how to store the data or how to implement the operations. Thus, an ADT uses good information-hiding techniques.

RECAP Encapsulation

Encapsulation is a term often heard when describing modern programming techniques. Encapsulation is the process of hiding (encapsulating) all the details of how a piece of software works and describing only enough about the software to enable a programmer to use it. Encapsulation means that data and actions are combined into a single item—in our case, a class object—that hides the details of the implementation. Thus, the terms *information hiding*, *ADT*, and *encapsulation* all involve the same general idea. In very operational terms, the idea is to spare the programmer who uses your class from having to know the details of how your class is implemented.

Automatic Documentation with javadoc

Java systems—including the one from Sun Microsystems—usually provide a program named javadoc that will automatically generate documentation for the class interfaces of your classes. This documentation tells other programmers what they need to know to use your class. To get a more useful javadoc document, you must write your comments in a particular way. The classes in this book are commented for use with javadoc, although because of space constraints, the comments are sparser than would be ideal. If you comment your class definition correctly, javadoc will take it as input and produce a nicely formatted display of its class interface. For example, if javadoc is run on the class definition in Listing 5.13, the output will consist only of the /***/ comments and the headings of public methods, after adjusting line breaks, spacing, and such. To read the documents produced by javadoc, you must use a Web browser or other HTML viewer.

javadoc comments result in neat HTML documentation

You do not need to use javadoc to understand this book. Nor do you do need to use javadoc to be able to write Java programs. However, you are likely to find javadoc both easy to use and very useful. Appendix 5 will get you started in using javadoc and shows an example of its output.

UML Class Diagrams

We gave an example of a class diagram in Figure 5.2 at the start of the chapter. You now know enough to understand all the notation in that diagram. However, rather than looking at that class diagram, let's look at a new one. Figure 5.4 contains a UML class diagram for the class Purchase from Listing 5.13. The

FIGURE 5.4   A UML Class Diagram for the Class Purchase
(Listing 5.13)

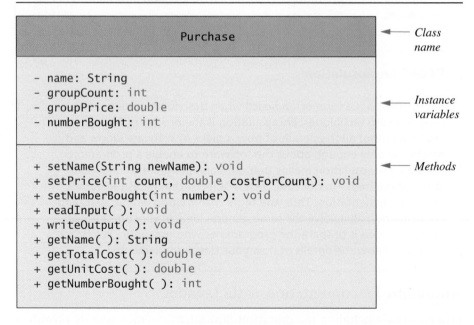

A minus sign (–) means the member is private.
A plus sign (+) means the member is public.

details are pretty much self-explanatory, except for the plus and minus signs. A plus sign (+) before an instance variable or method means the variable or method is public. A minus sign (–), on the other hand, means it is private.

Notice that the class diagram contains more than the interface for the class and less than a full implementation. Often, you write a class diagram well before you define the class in Java. A class diagram is an outline of both the class interface and the implementation. It is primarily for the programmer defining the class. A class interface is for the programmer who will use the class when producing additional software.

UML is useful for designing and building a class

 SELF-TEST QUESTIONS

myprogramminglab

19. What is a well-encapsulated class definition?

20. When should an instance variable in a class definition be private, and when should it be public?

21. Under what circumstances would you define a private method?

22. In a class definition, is anything private ever part of the class interface?

23. In a class definition, is the body of any method definition ever part of the class interface?

5.3 OBJECTS AND REFERENCES

"You are sad," the Knight said in an anxious tone: "let me sing you a song to comfort you."

"Is it very long" Alice asked, for she had heard a good deal of poetry that day.

"It's long," said the Knight, "but it's very, very beautiful. Everybody that hears me sing it—either it brings the tears into their eyes, or else—"

"Or else what?" said Alice, for the Knight had made a sudden pause.

"Or else it doesn't, you know. The name of the song is called 'Haddocks' Eyes.' "

"Oh, that's the name of the song, is it?" Alice asked, trying to feel interested.

"No, you don't understand," the Knight said, looking a little vexed. "That's what the name is called.

The name really is 'The Aged Aged Man.' "

"Then I ought to have said 'That's what the song is called'?" Alice corrected herself.

"No, you oughtn't: that's quite another thing! The song is called 'Ways and Means': but that's only what it's called, you know!"

"Well, what is the song, then?" said Alice, who was by this time completely bewildered.

"I was coming to that," the Knight said. "The song really is 'A-sitting on a Gate': and the tune's my own invention."

—LEWIS CARROLL, *Through the Looking-Glass*

Variables of a class type, such as the variable `oneSale` in Listing 5.14, behave very differently from variables of a primitive type. Variables of a class type are names for objects of their class, but the objects are not the values of the variables in the same way that, say, the number 6 can be the value of a variable of type `int`. A variable of a class type can name an object, but the naming process is a bit subtle. In this section, we discuss how a variable of a class type names objects, and we also discuss the related topic of how method parameters of a class type behave in Java.

Variables of a Class Type

Variables of a class type name objects in a way that is different from how variables of a primitive type store their values. Every variable, whether of a primitive type or a class type, is implemented as a memory location. If the variable has a primitive type, a data value is stored in the memory location assigned to the variable. However, a variable of a class type contains the memory address of the object named by the variable. The object itself is not stored in the variable, but rather in some other location in memory. The address of this other memory location is called a **reference** to the object. For this reason, class types are often called reference types. A **reference type** is just a type whose variables hold references—that is, memory addresses—as opposed to actual values of objects.

Class types are reference types

There is a reason why variables of a primitive type and variables of a class type name behave in different ways. Every value of a given primitive type, such as the type `int`, always requires the same amount of memory. Java has a maximum value of type `int`, and so values of type `int` cannot exceed a certain size in memory. However, an object, such as an object of the class `String`, might be any size, making it difficult for the system to set aside a fixed amount of space for variables that name objects. On the other hand, it can easily store the address of any string in a variable, since a computer's memory, and thus the size of a memory address, is finite.

Since variables of a class type contain references and behave very differently from variables of a primitive type, we can get some surprising results. Consider the following lines of code that might begin the main part of a program:

```
SpeciesFourthTry klingonSpecies = new SpeciesFourthTry();
SpeciesFourthTry earthSpecies = new SpeciesFourthTry();
int n = 42;
int m = n;
```

We have two variables of type int: n and m. Both have a value of 42, but if you change one, the other still has a value of 42. For example, if the program continues with

```
n = 99;
System.out.println(n + " and " + m);
```

the output produced will be

```
99 and 42
```

Assignments to variables of a class type

No surprises so far, but let's suppose the program continues as follows:

```
klingonSpecies.setSpecies("Klingon ox", 10, 15);
earthSpecies.setSpecies("Black rhino", 11, 2);
earthSpecies = klingonSpecies;
earthSpecies.setSpecies("Elephant", 100, 12);
System.out.println("earthSpecies:");
earthSpecies.writeOutput();
System.out.println("klingonSpecies:");
klingonSpecies.writeOutput();
```

You might think that the klingonSpecies is the Klingon ox and the earthSpecies is the elephant, but that is not so, as the following output indicates:

```
earthSpecies:
Name = Elephant
Population = 100
Growth rate = 12%
klingonSpecies:
Name = Elephant
Population = 100
Growth rate = 12%
```

What has happened? You have two variables, klingonSpecies and earthSpecies. At first, the two variables reference different objects. Each object is stored in the computer's memory in some location, and that location has an address. Because variables of a class type store memory addresses for objects, not the objects themselves, the assignment statement

```
earthSpecies = klingonSpecies;
```

copies the memory address in klingonSpecies into the variable earthSpecies so that both variables contain the same memory address and therefore both variables name the same object. Regardless of which variable you use to invoke setSpecies, the same object actually receives the method call, and so the same object is changed. What happens to the second object we had before? It is no longer accessible to the program. Figure 5.5 illustrates this behavior.

FIGURE 5.5 **Behavior of Class Variables**

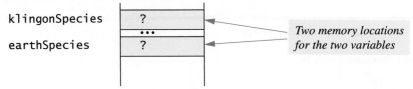

```
SpeciesFourthTry klingonSpecies, earthSpecies;
```

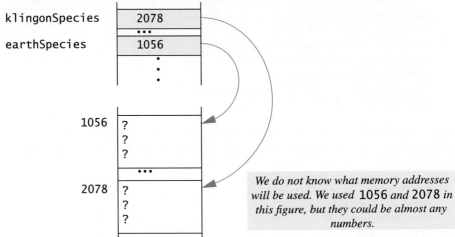

```
klingonSpecies = new SpeciesFourthTry();
earthSpecies = new SpeciesFourthTry();
```

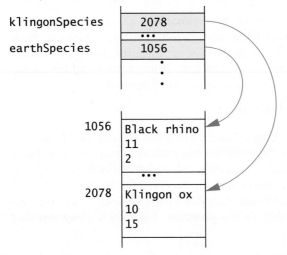

```
klingonSpecies.setSpecies("Klingon ox", 10, 15);
earthSpecies.setSpecies("Black rhino", 11, 2);
```

FIGURE 5.5 **Behavior of Class Variables** *(Continued)*

`earthSpecies = klingonSpecies;`

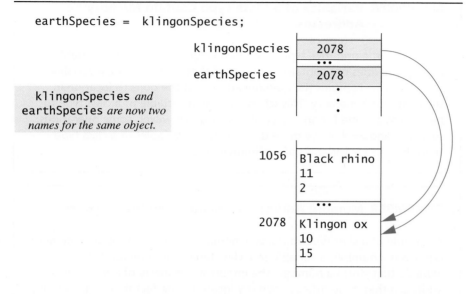

`klingonSpecies` *and*
`earthSpecies` *are now two names for the same object.*

`earthSpecies.setSpecies("Elephant", 100, 12);`

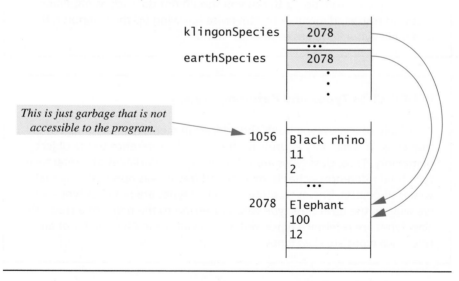

This is just garbage that is not accessible to the program.

One word of warning about memory addresses: A memory address is a number, but it is not the same kind of number as an `int` value. So do not try to treat it as an ordinary integer.

REMEMBER Variables of a Class Type Contain Memory Addresses

A variable of a primitive type contains a value of that type. A variable of a class type does not contain an object of that class. Instead, a variable of a class type contains the memory address of the object's location in the computer's memory. This scheme allows a variable of a class type to be used as a name for an object of that class. However, some operations, such as = and ==, behave quite differently for variables of a class type than they do for variables of a primitive type.

REMEMBER Memory Addresses Are and Are Not Numbers

A variable of a class type contains a memory address. Although a memory address is a number, a variable of a class type cannot be used like a variable that stores a number. The important property of a memory address is that it identifies a memory location. The fact that addresses are numbers, rather than letters or colors or something else, is an accidental property. Java prevents you from using this accidental property. It does so to keep you from doing things you should not do, such as obtaining access to restricted memory or otherwise screwing up the computer. It also makes your code easier to understand.

VideoNote
Objects and References

RECAP Class Types and Reference Types

A variable of a class type holds the address in memory of an object of that class. This memory address is often called a reference to the object in memory. Thus, class types are reference types. Variables of a reference type hold references—that is, memory addresses—as opposed to actual values of objects. However, some reference types are not class types, so we will use the term *class type* when referring to the name of a class. All class types are reference types, but as you will see in Chapter 7, not all reference types are class types.

GOTCHA Use of == with Variables of a Class Type

In the previous section, you saw some of the surprises you can get when using the assignment operator with variables of a class type. The test for equality also behaves in a way that may seem peculiar. Suppose the class

SpeciesFourthTry is defined as shown in Listing 5.11, and suppose you have the following in a program:

```
SpeciesFourthTry klingonSpecies = new SpeciesFourthTry();
SpeciesFourthTry earthSpecies = new SpeciesFourthTry();
klingonSpecies.setSpecies("Klingon ox", 10, 15);
earthSpecies.setSpecies("Klingon ox", 10, 15);
if (klingonSpecies == earthSpecies)
    System.out.println("They are EQUAL.");
else
    System.out.println("They are NOT equal.");
```

This will produce the output.

```
They are NOT equal.
```

Figure 5.6 illustrates the execution of this code.

Two objects of type SpeciesFourthTry are in memory. Both of them represent the same species in the real world, but they have different memory addresses. The problem is that, although the two objects are equal in an intuitive sense, a variable of a class type really contains only a memory address. The == operator checks only to see whether the memory addresses are equal. It tests for a kind of equality, but not the kind of equality you usually care about. When defining a class, you should normally define a method for the class that is called equals and that tests objects to see whether they are equal. The next section will show you how. ∎

Defining an equals Method for a Class

When you compare two objects using the == operator, you are checking to see whether they have the same address in memory. You are not testing for what you would intuitively call equality. To test for your intuitive notion of equality, you should define a method called equals. In Listing 5.17, we have revised our definition of a class for a species one last time to include an equals method.

You use the equals method of any class in exactly the same way that we used String's method equals with objects of type String. The program in Listing 5.18 demonstrates the use of the method equals defined in our revised class Species.

Test objects for equality by using an equals method

Our definition of the method equals in the class Species considers two Species objects equal if they have the same name—ignoring any differences in case—the same population, and the same growth rate. To compare the names, we use the method equalsIgnoreCase of the class String. It compares two strings, treating uppercase letters as equal to their lowercase counterparts. As we pointed out in Chapter 2, this method is automatically provided as part of the Java language. We use the == operator to compare the populations and growth rates, since they are primitive values.

FIGURE 5.6 The Dangers of Using == with Objects

```
klingonSpecies = new SpeciesFourthTry();
earthSpecies = new SpeciesFourthTry();
```

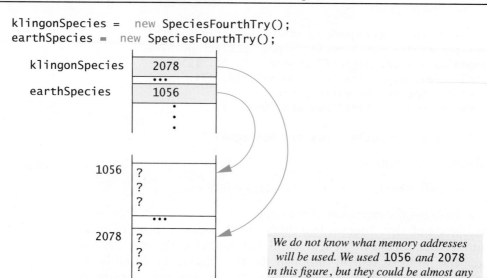

We do not know what memory addresses will be used. We used 1056 and 2078 in this figure, but they could be almost any numbers.

```
klingonSpecies.setSpecies("Klingon ox", 10, 15);
earthSpecies.setSpecies("Klingon ox", 10, 15);
```

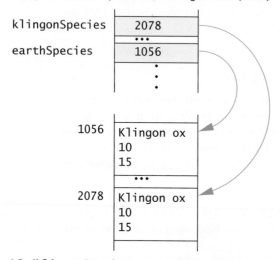

```
if (klingonSpecies == earthSpecies)
    System.out.println("They are EQUAL.");
else
    System.out.println("They are NOT equal.");
```

The output is They are Not equal, *because 2078 is not equal to 1056.*

LISTING 5.17   **Defining an** equals **Method**

```java
import java.util.Scanner;
public class Species
{
    private String name;
    private int population;
    private double growthRate;
```

<The definition of the methods readInput, writeOutput, and predictPopulation go here. They are the same as in Listing 5.3 and Listing 5.6.>

<The definition of the methods setSpecies, getName, getPopulation, and getGrowthRate go here. They are the same as in Listing 5.11.>

```java
    public boolean equals(Species otherObject)
    {
        return (this.name.equalsIgnoreCase(otherObject.name)) &&
               (this.population == otherObject.population) &&
               (this.growthRate == otherObject.growthRate);
    }
}
```

equalsIgnoreCase *is a method of the class* String.

Notice that the method equals in Listing 5.17 always returns a true or false value, and so the method's return type is boolean. The return statement may seem a bit strange, but it is nothing other than a boolean expression of the kind you might use in an if-else statement. It may help you to understand this method if you note that the definition of equals in Listing 5.17 can be expressed by the following pseudocode:

A method can return a boolean *value*

```java
if ((this.name.equalsIgnoreCase(otherObject.name)) &&
    (this.population == otherObject.population) &&
    (this.growthRate == otherObject.growthRate))
then return true
otherwise return false
```

This change would make the following statement from the program in Listing 5.18:

```java
if (s1.equals(s2))
    System.out.println("Match with the method equals.");
else
    System.out.println("Do Not match with the method " +
                       "equals.");
```

equivalent to

```
if ((s1.name.equalsIgnoreCase(s2.name)) &&
    (s1.population == s2.population) &&
    (s1.growthRate == s2.growthRate))
    System.out.println("Match with the method equals.");
else
    System.out.println("Do Not match with the method " +
                       "equals. ");
```

We will say more about methods that return a value of type boolean in the section "Boolean-Valued Methods" a little later in this chapter.

There is no unique definition of equals that has been handed down by the gods for all time. The definition of equals that you write will depend on how you intend to use the class. The definition in Listing 5.17 says that two objects of the class Species are equal if they represent the same species name, the same population size, and the same growth rate. In some other context, you might want to define equality to mean that two objects have the same species name but possibly different populations or different growth rates. This would correspond to considering two objects to be equal if they are records for the same species but reflect data taken at different times.

LISTING 5.18 Demonstrating an equals Method *(part 1 of 2)*

```
public class SpeciesEqualsDemo
{
    public static void main(String[] args)
    {
        Species s1 = new Species(), s2 = new Species();

        s1.setSpecies("Klingon ox", 10, 15);
        s2.setSpecies("Klingon ox", 10, 15);

        if (s1 == s2)
            System.out.println("Match with ==.");
        else
            System.out.println("Do Not match with ==.");
        if (s1.equals(s2))
            System.out.println("Match with the method " +
                               "equals.");
        else
            System.out.println("Do Not match with the method " +
                               "equals.");
        System.out.println("Now change one Klingon ox to " +
                           "lowercase.");
```

(continued)

LISTING 5.18 Demonstrating an equals Method *(part 2 of 2)*

```
        s2.setSpecies("klingon ox", 10, 15); //Use lowercase
        if (s1.equals(s2))
            System.out.println("Match with the method equals.");
        else
            System.out.println("Do Not match with the method " +
                                "equals.");
    }
}
```

Screen Output

```
Do Not match with ==.
Match with the method equals.
Now change one Klingon ox to lowercase.
Match with the method equals.
```

You should always use the identifier equals for the name of any method you create to test whether two objects are equal. Do not use some other identifier, such as same; do not even use equal without an s. Certain software that is part of Java depends on your using the exact name equals to test for equality of objects. This software invokes a method named equals, so your method had better have that name.

If you do not define an equals method for your class, Java will automatically create a default definition of equals, but it is unlikely to behave the way you want it to. Thus, it is best to define your own equals method.

PROGRAMMING EXAMPLE   A Species Class

The final version of our class for species objects, as given in Listing 5.17, is repeated in Listing 5.19, but this time we have included all of the details so that you can see a complete example. We have also written the definition of the method equals without using the keyword this, since that is the form most programmers use. The definition of equals in Listing 5.19 is completely equivalent to the definition in Listing 5.17. Figure 5.7 contains the class diagram for this class Species.

LISTING 5.19   The Complete Species **Class** *(part 1 of 2)*

```java
import java.util.Scanner;
/**
Class for data on endangered species.
*/
public class Species
{
    private String name;
    private int population;
    private double growthRate;

    public void readInput()
    {
        Scanner keyboard = new Scanner(System.in);
        System.out.println("What is the species' name?");
        name = keyboard.nextLine();

        System.out.println(
                     "What is the population of the species?");
        population = keyboard.nextInt();
        while (population < 0)
        {
            System.out.println("Population cannot be negative.");
            System.out.println("Reenter population:");
            population = keyboard.nextInt();
        }
        System.out.println(
                     "Enter growth rate (% increase per year):");
        growthRate = keyboard.nextDouble();
    }
    public void writeOutput()
    {
        System.out.println("Name = " + name);
        System.out.println("Population = " + population);
        System.out.println("Growth rate = " + growthRate + "%");
    }
    /**
    Precondition: years is a nonnegative number.
    Returns the projected population of the receiving object
    after the specified number of years.
    */
    public int predictPopulation(int years)
    {
        int result = 0;
        double populationAmount = population;
```

> This is the same class definition as in Listing 5.17, but with all the details shown.

(continued)

LISTING 5.19 **The Complete** Species **Class** *(part 2 of 2)*

```
        int count = years;
        while ((count > 0) && (populationAmount > 0))
        {
            populationAmount = (populationAmount +
                                (growthRate / 100) *
                                  populationAmount);
            count--;
        }
        if (populationAmount > 0)
            result = (int)populationAmount;
        return result;
    }
    public void setSpecies(String newName, int newPopulation,
                            double newGrowthRate)
    {
        name = newName;
        if (newPopulation >= 0)
            population = newPopulation;
        else
        {
            System.out.println("ERROR: using a negative " +
                                "population.");
            System.exit(0);
        }
        growthRate = newGrowthRate;
    }
    public String getName()
    {
        return name;
    }
    public int getPopulation()
    {
        return population;
    }

    public double getGrowthRate()
    {
        return growthRate;
    }
    public boolean equals(Species otherObject)
    {
        return (name.equalsIgnoreCase(otherObject.name)) &&
               (population == otherObject.population) &&
               (growthRate == otherObject.growthRate);
    }
}
```

This version of equals *is equivalent to the version in Listing 5.17. Here, the keyword* this *is understood to be there implicitly.*

FIGURE 5.7 **Class Diagram for the Class Species in Listing 5.19**

Species
- name: String - population: int - growthRate: double
+ readInput(): void + writeOutput(): void + predictPopulation(int years): int + setSpecies(String newName, int newPopulation,   double newGrowthRate): void + getName(): String + getPopulation(): int + getGrowthRate(): double + equals(Species otherObject): boolean

Boolean-Valued Methods

Methods can return a value of type boolean. There is really nothing new about this: You just specify a return type of boolean and use a boolean expression in the return statement. You have already seen one such method, namely the equals method for the class Species in Listing 5.19. This method simply evaluates the boolean expression in the return statement, yielding a value of true or false. The method then returns this value.

As you have already seen, you can use an invocation of the method equals in an if statement, a while statement, or another statement that requires a boolean expression. You can also store the value returned by the method equals, or any other boolean-valued method, in a variable of type boolean. For example,

```
Species s1 = new Species(), s2 = new Species();
<Some code to set the values of s1 and s2.>
boolean areEqual = s1.equals(s2);
<Some more code.>
if (areEqual)
    System.out.println("They are equal.");
else
    System.out.println("They are not equal.");
```

As another example of a boolean-valued method, the following is a method you might add to the definition of the class Species in Listing 5.19:

```
/**
    Precondition: This object and the argument otherSpecies
both have values for their population. Returns true if the
population of this object is greater than the population of
otherSpecies; otherwise, returns false.
*/
public boolean isPopulationLargerThan(Species otherSpecies)
{
    return population > otherSpecies.population;
}
```

A boolean-valued method

You can then use the method isPopulationLargerThan in the same sorts of ways that you use the method equals. For example, the following might appear in a program:

```
Species s1 = new Species(), s2 = new Species();
<Some code to set the values of s1 and s2.>
String nameOfLarger = s1.getName();
if (s2.isPopulationLargerThan(s1))
    nameOfLarger = s2.getName();
System.out.println(nameOfLarger + " has the larger population.");
```

The following method is another you might add to the definition of the class Species in Listing 5.19:

```
/**
    Precondition: This object has a value for its population.
    Returns true if the population of this object is zero;
    otherwise, returns false.
*/
public Boolean isExtinct()
{
    return population == 0;
}
```

The following sample code might then appear in a program:

```
Species s1 = new Species();
<Some code to set the value of s1.>
if (s1.isExtinct())
    System.out.println(s1.getName() + " is extinct.");
else
    System.out.println(s1.getName() + " is still with us.")
```

■ PROGRAMMING TIP   Naming Boolean-Valued Methods

When our boolean-valued method isExtinct is invoked within an if statement, we can understand its meaning simply by reading the statement in English. For example,

```
if (s1.isExtinct())
```

means "if s1 is extinct." Beginning the name of a boolean-valued method with a word such as *is* or *has* clarifies the meaning of your program. Not only will others benefit from this naming convention, you likely will make fewer errors while writing the program. ■

SELF-TEST QUESTIONS

24. What is a reference type? Are class types reference types? Are primitive types, such as `int`, reference types?

25. When comparing two quantities of a class type to see whether they are "equal," should you use `==` or the method `equals`?

26. When comparing two quantities of type `int` to see whether they are "equal," should you use `==` or the method `equals` ?

27. Write a method definition for a method called `isGrowthRateLargerThan` that could be added to the class `Species` in Listing 5.19. This method has one argument of type `Species`. The method returns true if the receiving object has a larger growth rate than the growth rate of the argument; otherwise, it returns false.

CASE STUDY Unit Testing

Unit testing verifies if individual units of code are working correctly

So far we've tested our programs by running them, typing in some input, and visually checking the results to see if the output is what we expected. This is fine for small programs but is generally insufficient for large programs. In a large program there are usually so many combinations of interacting inputs that it would take too much time to manually verify the correct result for all inputs. Additionally, it is possible that code changes result in unintended side effects. For example, a fix for one error might introduce a different error. One way to attack this problem is to write **unit tests**. Unit testing is a methodology in which the programmer tests the correctness of individual units of code. A unit is often a method but it could be a class or other group of code.

The collection of unit tests becomes the **test suite**. Each test is generally automated so that human input is not required. Automation is important because it is desirable to have tests that run often and quickly. This makes it possible to run the tests repeatedly, perhaps once a day or every time code is changed, to make sure that everything is still working. The process of running tests repeatedly is called **regression testing**.

Let's start with a simple test case for the `Species` class in Listing 5.19. Our first test might be to verify that the name, initial population, and growth rate is correctly set in the `setSpecies` method. We can accomplish this by creating an object of type Species, invoking setSpecies, and verifying if all the values match.

```
Species testSpecies = new Species();
// Test the setSpecies method
testSpecies.setSpecies("Tribbles", 100, 50);
if (testSpecies.getName().equals("Tribbles") &&
    (testSpecies.getPopulation() == 100) &&
    (testSpecies.getGrowthRate() >= 49.99) &&

    (testSpecies.getGrowthRate() <= 50.01))
{
    System.out.println("Pass: setSpecies test.");
}
else
{
    System.out.println("FAIL: setSpecies test.");
}
```

Since **getGrowthRate** *returns a* **double** *we should not attempt* **testSpecies. getGrowthRate() ==50**

In this simple example we came up with inputs for the test case, invoked the code, and checked to see if the results matched our expectations. If there was an error, such as forgetting to copy the growth rate into an instance variable in the setSpecies method, then the test case would find the problem.

Often the design of the test case is more complicated. Consider testing the predictPopulation method. Once again we must determine appropriate inputs and see if the unit to be tested produces the expected outputs. One type of test we might try is a **negative test.** This is a test to confirm that the system doesn't crash when given unexpected inputs. For example, if the number of years passed to predictPopulation is negative, then we might expect the method to return the initial population. In addition, we might test the method with inputs of 1 and 5 years into the future. Such a test case using the testSpecies object is shown in Listing 5.20.

A common practice is to write tests using the assert statement. For example, instead of the if-else statement we could write:

```
assert (testSpecies.getPopulation() == 100);
```

Don't be fooled into thinking that the program is guaranteed to work if all tests pass. It is possible that there is an untested combination of input values that will cause the program to fail. There may also be bugs at the level where working units are integrated. However, a successful test run gives us some confidence that basic functionality is working.

Ideally, the test cases should be kept separate from the implementation of the class. In our simple example we created a separate class with a main method to test the Species class. For larger projects you might consider a test framework such as JUnit that is designed to help organize and run test suites.

LISTING 5.20 Sample Tests for the Species Class

```java
public class SpeciesTest
{
    public static void main(String[] args)
    {
        Species testSpecies = new Species();

        // Test the setSpecies method
        testSpecies.setSpecies("Tribbles", 100, 50);
        if (testSpecies.getName().equals("Tribbles") &&
            (testSpecies.getPopulation() == 100) &&
            (testSpecies.getGrowthRate() >= 49.99) &&
            (testSpecies.getGrowthRate() <= 50.01))
        {
            System.out.println("Pass: setSpecies test.");
        }
        else
        {
            System.out.println("FAIL: setSpecies test.");
        }

        // Test the predictPopulation method
        if ((testSpecies.predictPopulation(-1) == 100) &&
            (testSpecies.predictPopulation(1) == 150) &&
            (testSpecies.predictPopulation(5) == 759))

        {
            System.out.println("Pass: predictPopulation test.");
        }
        else
        {
            System.out.println("FAIL: predictPopulation test.");
        }
    }
}
```

Sample Screen Output

```
Pass: setSpecies test.
Pass: predictPopulation test.
```

Parameters of a Class Type

Parameters of a class type

A method's parameters of a class type are treated differently than its parameters of a primitive type. We touched upon this difference when we discussed using the assignment operator with objects. The following two points from that discussion will help us describe how parameters of a class type work:

- First, recall how the assignment operator works with objects. Suppose that Species is the class defined in Listing 5.19, and consider the following code:

```
Species species1 = new Species();
species1.readInput();
Species species2 = species1;
```

When you use an assignment operator with objects of a class type, you are actually copying a memory address. Thus, as we discussed in the previous section, species1 and species2 are now two names for the same object.

- Now recall how parameters of a primitive type work. For example, the definition of the method predictPopulation in Listing 5.19 begins as follows:

Parameters of a primitive type

```
public int predictPopulation(int years)
{
    int result = 0;
    double populationAmount = population;
    int count = years;
    . . .
```

We said previously that the formal parameter years is actually a local variable. When we invoke the method predictPopulation, this local variable years is initialized to the value of the argument given in the method call. So, for example, when we use the following call in Listing 5.12:

```
int futurePopulation =
        speciesOfTheMonth.predictPopulation(numberOfYears);
```

the parameter years is initialized to numberOfYears. The effect is like temporarily inserting the assignment statement

```
years = numberOfYears;
```

into the method definition. In other words, it is as if the definition of the method predictPopulation were, for the duration of this method invocation, changed as follows:

```
public int predictPopulation(int years)
{
    years = numberOfYears;//You cannot do this, but Java
            //acts as if you could and did do this.
    int result = 0;
    double populationAmount = population;
    int count = years;
    . . .
```

Wow—that's a long preamble, but if you understand these two points, it will be very easy to understand how parameters of a class type work. Parameters of a class type work like parameters of a primitive type, but because the assignment operator means something different for variables of a class type, the effect is very different!

Let's go through that explanation again with slightly different words, but with the same message. Consider the following call to the method equals that was used in Listing 5.18:

```
if (s1.equals(s2))
    System.out.println("Match with the method equals.");
else
    System.out.println("Do Not match with the method " +
                        "equals.");
```

In this call, s2 is an argument of the class type Species defined in Listing 5.19. We reproduce here the definition for the method equals given in Listing 5.19:

```
public boolean equals(Species otherObject)
{
    return (name.equalsIgnoreCase(otherObject.name)) &&
            (population == otherObject.population) &&
            (growthRate == otherObject.growthRate);
}
```

When the method equals is called in s1.equals(s2), it is as if the following assignment statement were temporarily inserted at the start of the method definition:

```
otherObject = s2;
```

In other words, the method definition, for the duration of this call to equals, is equivalent to

```
public boolean equals(Species otherObject)
{
    otherObject = s2; //You cannot do this, but Java acts
            //as if you could and did do this.
    return (name.equalsIgnoreCase(otherObject.name)) &&
            (population == otherObject.population) &&
            (growthRate == otherObject.growthRate);
}
```

Recall, however, that this assignment statement merely copies the memory address of s2 into the variable otherObject, so otherObject becomes just another name for the object named by s2. Thus, anything done with the object named otherObject will in fact be done with the object named s2. It is as if the method performed the following action:

```
return (name.equalsIgnoreCase(s2.name)) &&
    (population == s2.population) &&
    (growthRate == s2.growthRate);
```

Notice that any action taken with a formal parameter of a class type—in this example, otherObject—is actually taken with the argument used in the method call—in this case, s2. So the argument used in the method call is actually acted upon and can be changed by the method call.

In the case of the method equals, the effect of this parameter-passing mechanism for parameters of a class type is not so different from what happens with parameters of a primitive type. With some other methods, however, the difference is more striking. The next section gives a more dramatic example of how parameters of a class type differ from parameters of a primitive type.

ASIDE Call by Reference

Some programmers refer to the parameter mechanism for parameters of a class type as call-by-reference parameter passing. Others say that this terminology is incorrect. The problem is that there is more than one commonly used definition of call by reference. In addition, parameters of a class type in Java behave a bit differently than call-by-reference parameters in other languages. Therefore, we will not use the term *call by reference* here. The important thing is to understand how parameters of a class type work, regardless of what you call them.

RECAP Parameters of a Class Type

Formal parameters are given in parentheses after the method name at the beginning of a method definition. A formal parameter of a class type is a local variable that holds the memory address of an object of that class type. When the method is invoked, the parameter is initialized to the address of the corresponding argument in the method invocation. In less technical terms, this means that the formal parameter will serve as an alternative name for the object given as the corresponding argument in a method invocation.

**REMEMBER A Method Can Change an Object Passed
as an Argument**

An object that is an argument in a method invocation is actually acted upon and can be altered by the method call. However, the object cannot be replaced by another object. The next programming example will demonstrate these points.

PROGRAMMING EXAMPLE	**Class-Type Parameters Versus Primitive-Type Parameters**

A method cannot change the value of an argument of a primitive type

Suppose we add three methods to the class Species to form a new class called DemoSpecies, as shown in Listing 5.21. This class is only for our demonstration, so do not worry about the rest of the class definition. Let's play with this toy class.

LISTING 5.21   A Demonstration Class *(part 1 of 2)*

```
import java.util.Scanner;
/**
This version of the class Species is only a toy example designed
to demonstrate the difference between parameters of a class type
and parameters of a primitive type.
*/
public class DemoSpecies
{
    private String name;
    private int population;
    private double growthRate;
    /**
    Tries to set intVariable equal to the population of this
    object. But arguments of a primitive type cannot be
    changed.
    */
    public void tryToChange(int intVariable)
    {
        intVariable = this.population;
    }
    /**
    Tries to make otherObject reference this object.
    But arguments of a class type cannot be replaced.
    */
    public void tryToReplace(DemoSpecies otherObject)
    {
        otherObject = this;
    }
    /**
    Changes the data in otherObject to the data in this object,
    which is unchanged.
    */
```

(continued)

LISTING 5.21   A Demonstration Class *(part 2 of 2)*

```
    public void change(DemoSpecies otherObject)
    {
        otherObject.name = this.name;
        otherObject.population = this.population;
        otherObject.growthRate = this.growthRate;
    }
    <The rest of the class definition is the same as that of the class
    Species in Listing 5.19.>
}
```

Look at the method `tryToChange` within our new class `DemoSpecies`. This method has a formal parameter of the primitive type `int`. Within the method's body is an assignment to that parameter. The program in Listing 5.21 calls `tryToChange`, passing it the argument `aPopulation` of type `int`. However, the assignment performed in the method body has no effect on the argument `aPopulation`. Since variables of a primitive type hold actual values, not memory addresses, Java's call-by-value parameter mechanism copies the value of the argument to the parameter, which really is a local variable. Thus, any changes the method makes to the parameter are made to this local variable and not to the argument.

The method `tryToReplace` has a parameter whose type is `DemoSpecies`, so it is of a class type. Once again, Java's call-by-value parameter mechanism copies the value of the argument to the parameter. But since both the argument and the parameter are of a class type, the memory address of the object argument is copied to the parameter. The assignment statement within the body of the method then assigns a new value to the parameter. (In fact, this new value is the address of the receiving object—indicated by the keyword `this`—but the value is irrelevant.) Just as in the previous method `tryToChange`, this assignment to the parameter does not affect the argument. Thus, `s2`, an object of `DemoSpecies` that the program in Listing 5.22 passes to `tryToReplace`, is unaffected.

> A method cannot replace an argument object with another object

Finally, the data type of the parameter of the method `change` is the class type `DemoSpecies`. The program in Listing 5.22 calls `change`, passing it the argument `s2`. The assignment statements within the body of the method actually change the values of the instance variables of the object argument `s2`. A method can change the state of an argument of a class type.

> A method can change the state of an argument object

As you can see, parameters of a class type are more versatile than parameters of a primitive type. Parameters of a primitive type pass values to a method, but a method cannot change the value of any primitive-type variable

LISTING 5.22 Parameters of a Class Type Versus Parameters of a Primitive Type

```java
public class ParametersDemo
{
    public static void main(String[] args)
    {
        DemoSpecies s1 = new DemoSpecies(),
                    s2 = new DemoSpecies();
        s1.setSpecies("Klingon ox", 10, 15);
        int aPopulation = 42;
        System.out.println("aPopulation BEFORE calling " +
                           "tryToChange: " + aPopulation);
        s1.tryToChange(aPopulation);
        System.out.println("aPopulation AFTER calling " +
                           "tryToChange: aPopulation);
        s2.setSpecies("Ferengie Fur Ball", 90, 56);
        System.out.println("s2 BEFORE calling tryToReplace: ");
        s2.writeOutput();
        s1.tryToReplace(s2);
        System.out.println("s2 AFTER calling tryToReplace: ");
        s2.writeOutput();
        s1.change(s2);
        System.out.println("s2 AFTER calling change: ");
        s2.writeOutput();
    }
}
```

Screen Output

```
aPopulation BEFORE calling tryToChange: 42      An argument of a primitive
aPopulation AFTER calling tryToChange: 42       type cannot change in value.
s2 BEFORE calling tryToReplace:
Name = Ferengie Fur Ball
Population = 90
Growth Rate = 56.0%
s2 AFTER calling tryToReplace:                  An argument of a class
Name = Ferengie Fur Ball                        type cannot be replaced.
Population = 90
Growth Rate = 56.0%
s2 AFTER calling change:
Name = Klingon ox
Population = 10                                  An argument of a class
Growth Rate = 15.0%                             type can change in state.
```

that is given to it as an argument. On the other hand, not only can parameters of a class type be used to give information to a method, but the method can also change the state of the object named by an argument of a class type. The method, however, cannot replace the object passed to it as an argument with another object.

> **REMEMBER Differences Between Primitive-Type and Class-Type Parameters**
>
> A method cannot change the value of an argument of a primitive type that is passed to it. In addition, a method cannot replace an object passed to it as an argument with another object. On the other hand, a method can change the values of the instance variables of an argument of a class type.

VideoNote
Exploring parameters of class types

SELF-TEST QUESTIONS

myprogramminglab

28. Given the class Species as defined in Listing 5.19, why does the following program cause an error message?

```
public class SpeciesEqualsDemo
{
public static void main(String[] args)
{
    Species s1, s2; s1.
    setSpecies("Klingon ox", 10, 15);
    s2.setSpecies("Klingon ox", 10, 15);
    if (s1 == s2)
        System.out.println("Match with ==.");
    else
        System.out.println("Do Not match with ==.")
}
}
```

29. After correcting the program in the previous question, what output does the program produce?

30. What is the biggest difference between a parameter of a primitive type and a parameter of a class type?

31. Given the class Species, as defined in Listing 5.19, and the class

```
public class ExerciseClass
{
    public void mystery(Species s, int m)
    {
        s.setSpecies("Klingon ox", 10, 15);
        m = 42;
    }
}
```

what output is produced by the following program?

```
public class ExerciseProgram
{
    public static void main(String[] args)
    {
        Species s1 = new Species();
        ExerciseClass mysteryMaker = new ExerciseClass();
        int n = 0;
        s1.setSpecies("Hobbit", 100, 2);
        mysteryMaker.mystery(s1, n);
        s1.writeOutput();
        System.out.println("n = " + n);
    }
}
```

32. Write an `equals` method for the class `Person` described in Self-Test Question 16.

5.4 GRAPHICS SUPPLEMENT

The whole is more than the sum of its parts.

—PROVERB

Now that we have explained methods and parameters more completely, we will revisit material from the previous graphics supplements to give more detailed explanations. We will

- Explain the `Graphics` class more completely.
- Use methods to rewrite one of our previous graphics applets in a cleaner way.
- Introduce some additional drawing methods.
- Introduce the method `init`, which is another applet method similar to `paint` but used for different purposes.

The Graphics Class

An object of the class `Graphics` represents an area of the screen, but it is more than that. Such an object has methods that allow it to draw figures and

FIGURE 5.8 **Some Methods in the Class** Graphics

Graphics_Object.drawOval(*X*, *Y*, *Width*, *Height*) Draws the outline of an oval having the specified width and height at the point (*X*, *Y*).
Graphics_Object.fillOval(*X*, *Y*, *Width*, *Height*) Same as drawOval, but the oval is filled in.
Graphics_Object.drawArc(*X*, *Y*, *Width*, *Height*, *Start_Angle*, *ArcAngle*) Draws an arc—that is, draws part of an oval. See the graphics supplement section of Chapter 1 for details.
Graphics_Object.fillArc(*X*, *Y*, *Width*, *Height*, *Start_Angle*, *ArcAngle*) Same as drawArc, but the visible portion of the oval is filled in.
Graphics_Object.drawRect(*X*, *Y*, *Width*, *Height*) Draws the outline of a rectangle of the specified width and height at the point (*X*, *Y*).
Graphics_Object.fillRect(*X*, *Y*, *Width*, *Height*) Same as drawRect, but the rectangle is filled in.
Graphics_Object.drawLine(*X1*, *Y1*, *X2*, *Y2*) Draws a line between points (*X1*, *Y1*) and (*X2*, *Y2*).
Graphics_Object.drawString(*A_String*, *X*, *Y*) Writes the specified string starting at the point (*X*, *Y*).
Graphics_Object.setColor(*Color_Object*) Sets the color for subsequent drawings and text. The color stays in effect until it is changed by another invocation of setColor.

write text in the area of the screen it represents. A summary of some of these methods is given in Figure 5.8. You have already seen most of these methods used within previous applet examples. But at least two obvious questions arise from this brief explanation:

- How does a Graphics object represent an area of the screen?
- What Graphics object is plugged in for the parameter in an applet's paint method? (We usually named this parameter canvas in our applet examples.)

A Graphics object has instance variables that specify the area of the screen it represents. In our examples, the Graphics object has always represented the area corresponding to the inside of our applets. The exact details of this representation need not concern us. All we need to know is that the relevant Graphics object for an applet somehow represents the area inside the applet.

The question still remains: Where does this Graphics object for an applet come from? The answer is that when you run an applet, a suitable Graphics

Running an applet creates a Graphics object and invokes the paint method

object is created automatically, and this object is used as an argument to the applet's paint method when the method is (automatically) invoked. That's a lot to have happening automatically. You would otherwise need to generate the Graphics object and invoke the paint method yourself each time you wrote an applet. Instead, the code in the applet library does all this for you. How do you add this library code to your applet definition? The words extends JApplet do that, but we will have to postpone any more details until Chapter 8, when we discuss something known as inheritance.

RECAP The Graphics Class

Objects of the class Graphics represent an area of the screen and have methods for drawing figures and writing text in that area. The method paint of an applet has a parameter of type Graphics. When the applet is run, a Graphics object representing the area inside the applet is generated automatically and passed to the method paint, which is automatically invoked, as its argument.

SELF-TEST QUESTIONS

33. Suppose we replace the identifier canvas with g throughout the method paint in Listing 3.5 of Chapter 3. What effect will this revision have on the applet in Listing 3.5?

34. Our applets—such as those in Listing 2.9 and Listing 3.5—that contain a definition of the method paint contain no invocations of the method paint. Why does the method paint have any effect on the drawings in the applet? After all, if a method is not invoked, its actions are not taken.

PROGRAMMING EXAMPLE   Multiple Faces, But with a Helping Method

In Listing 5.23 we have revised the applet shown in Listing 4.9. In this new version, we have extracted the code for drawing all of a face except the mouth and skin color and placed it into the body of a method named drawFaceSansMouth. In our older version of this applet (Listing 4.9), the code for the face was repeated three times: once in the body of the for loop and twice after the for loop. In Listing 5.23, this code is written only once—in the body of the method drawFaceSansMouth. This saves some typing, but more importantly, it makes the code easier to read and to maintain. The method drawFaceSansMouth packages the complex task of drawing most of the face. Instead of writing several lines of code each time you want to draw a face, you write one method call to drawFaceSansMouth. It is much easier to understand.

A helping method simplifies code

```
drawFaceSansMouth(canvas, i);
```

than it is to understand

```
g.setColor(Color.BLACK);
g.drawOval(X_FACE0 + 50 * i, Y_FACE0 + 30 * i,
    FACE_DIAMETER, FACE_DIAMETER);
//Draw eyes:
g.setColor(Color.BLUE);
g.fillOval(X_RIGHT_EYE0 + 50 * i, Y_RIGHT_EYE0
    + 30 * i, EYE_WIDTH, EYE_HEIGHT);
g.fillOval(X_LEFT_EYE0 + 50 * i, Y_LEFT_EYE0
    + 30 * i, EYE_WIDTH, EYE_HEIGHT);
//Draw nose:
g.setColor(Color.BLACK);
g.fillOval(X_NOSE0 + 50 * i, Y_NOSE0 + 30 * i,
    NOSE_DIAMETER, NOSE_DIAMETER);
```

LISTING 5.23 Using a Method for a Recurrent Subtask
(part 1 of 3)

```
import javax.swing.JApplet;
import java.awt.Graphics;
import java.awt.Color;

public class MultipleFaces extends JApplet
{
    public static final int FACE_DIAMETER = 50;
    public static final int X_FACE0 = 10;
    public static final int Y_FACE0 = 5;

    public static final int EYE_WIDTH = 5;
    public static final int EYE_HEIGHT = 10;
    public static final int X_RIGHT_EYE0 = 20;
    public static final int Y_RIGHT_EYE0 = 15;
    public static final int X_LEFT_EYE0 = 45;
    public static final int Y_LEFT_EYE0 = Y_RIGHT_EYE0;

    public static final int NOSE_DIAMETER = 5;
    public static final int X_NOSE0 = 32;
    public static final int Y_NOSE0 = 25;

    public static final int MOUTH_WIDTH = 30;
    public static final int MOUTH_HEIGHT0 = 0;
```

(continued)

LISTING 5.23 Using a Method for a Recurrent Subtask
(part 2 of 3)

```java
public static final int X_MOUTH0 = 20;
public static final int Y_MOUTH0 = 35;
public static final int MOUTH_START_ANGLE = 180;
public static final int MOUTH_EXTENT_ANGLE = 180;
/**
 g is the drawing area. pos indicates the position of the
 face. As pos increases, the face is drawn lower and further
 to the right.
*/
private void drawFaceSansMouth(Graphics g, int pos)
{
    g.setColor(Color.BLACK);
    g.drawOval(X_FACE0 + 50 * pos, Y_FACE0 + 30 * pos,
               FACE_DIAMETER, FACE_DIAMETER);
    //Draw eyes:
    g.setColor(Color.BLUE);
    g.fillOval(X_RIGHT_EYE0 + 50 * pos, Y_RIGHT_EYE0 + 30 * pos,
               EYE_WIDTH, EYE_HEIGHT);
    g.fillOval(X_LEFT_EYE0 + 50 * pos, Y_LEFT_EYE0 + 30 * pos,
               EYE_WIDTH, EYE_HEIGHT);
    //Draw nose:
    g.setColor(Color.BLACK);
    g.fillOval(X_NOSE0 + 50 * pos, Y_NOSE0 + 30 * pos,
               NOSE_DIAMETER, NOSE_DIAMETER);
}
public void paint(Graphics canvas)
{
    int i;
    for (i = 0; i < 5; i++)
    {//Draw one face:
    if (i % 2 == 0)//If i is even,
        { //make face yellow
            canvas.setColor(Color.YELLOW);
            canvas.fillOval(X_FACE0 + 50 * i,
                   Y_FACE0 + 30 * i,
                   FACE_DIAMETER, FACE_DIAMETER);
    }
    drawFaceSansMouth(canvas, i);
    //Draw mouth:
    canvas.setColor(Color.RED);
    canvas.drawArc(X_MOUTH0 + 50 * i, Y_MOUTH0 + 30 * i,
               MOUTH_WIDTH, MOUTH_HEIGHT0 + 3 * i,
               MOUTH_START_ANGLE, MOUTH_EXTENT_ANGLE);
    }
    //i == 5
```

(continued)

LISTING 5.23 **Using a Method for a Recurrent Subtask**
(part 3 of 3)

```
            //Draw kissing face:
            drawFaceSansMouth(canvas, i);
            //Draw mouth in shape of a kiss:
            canvas.setColor(Color.RED);
            canvas.fillOval(X_MOUTH0 + 50 * i + 10, Y_MOUTH0 + 30 * i,
                        MOUTH_WIDTH - 20, MOUTH_WIDTH - 20);
            //Add text:
            canvas.setColor(Color.BLACK);
            canvas.drawString("Kiss, Kiss.",
                X_FACE0 + 50 * i + FACE_DIAMETER, Y_FACE0 + 30 * i);
            //Draw blushing face:
            i++;
            //Draw face circle:
            canvas.setColor(Color.PINK);
            canvas.fillOval(X_FACE0 + 50 * i, Y_FACE0 + 30 * i,
                             FACE_DIAMETER, FACE_DIAMETER);
            drawFaceSansMouth(canvas, i);
            //Draw mouth:
            canvas.setColor(Color.RED);
            canvas.drawArc(X_MOUTH0 + 50 * i, Y_MOUTH0 + 30 * i,
                        MOUTH_WIDTH, MOUTH_HEIGHT0 + 3 * (i - 2),
                        MOUTH_START_ANGLE, MOUTH_EXTENT_ANGLE);
            //Add text:
            canvas.setColor(Color.BLACK);
            canvas.drawString("Tee Hee.",
                X_FACE0 + 50 * i + FACE_DIAMETER, Y_FACE0 + 30 * i);
    }
}
```
Applet Output

> The drawing produced is identical to the one shown in Listing 4.9 except for some of the colors used to draw the faces.

Of course, you must still understand how to design and write the helping method, but you do not have to write it three times, as you did in the older version in Listing 4.9.

Notice that since the method drawFaceSansMouth is only a helping method for the method paint, we have made drawFaceSansMouth a private method.

SELF-TEST QUESTION

`myprogramminglab`

35. Rewrite the method drawFaceSansMouth in Listing 5.23 so that it colors the skin according to the color specified by one additional parameter.

The `init` Method

So far, whenever we have defined an applet, we have defined the method paint. You also can define another method named `init` anytime you write an applet. Like paint, the method `init` is called automatically when you run the applet. In some sense, however, the `init` method is more fundamental to the applet than the paint method. The paint method is used only for drawing, that is, for invoking methods of the class Graphics. All other actions in an applet go, or at least start, in the `init` method. The `init` method for applets serves a purpose similar to the main method in an application program. Whenever you define an applet class, you normally should define the `init` method. We give an example of an applet containing an `init` method in the next section.

An applet class may contain definitions for both an `init` method and a paint method, although we have not yet seen any examples of such a class. It may also contain any other method definitions you want, such as the method drawFaceSansMouth in Listing 5.23. However, the methods `init` and paint are special because they are called automatically when the applet is run.

Like paint, the method `init` is called automatically

Use `init` to initialize and begin actions; use paint for drawing

---

FAQ What is the difference between the methods paint and init?

Both the paint and init methods are called automatically when you run an applet, but you can do different things in the two methods. You use the method paint to draw figures and to call drawString to write text. You use the method init to add such things as labels and buttons to an applet. An applet can have a paint method or an init method or both a paint method and an init method. Although you could omit both methods from an applet, doing so would be extremely unusual. Getting an applet to do much without at least one of these two methods is difficult.

Adding Labels to an Applet

A label adds text to an applet

A **label** in an applet is little more than a quoted string, but it is handled in the same way that many other applet components, such as buttons, are handled. Thus, labels provide another way to add text to an applet. We add labels to an applet in the same way that we will eventually add other items.

Listing 5.24 contains an applet that displays the text Hello out there!, but this applet does not use drawString to create the displayed text; it uses labels instead. When we add a component such as a label to an applet, we use the method init rather than the method paint. In this section we add only labels, but in the next chapter we will add buttons to applets.

Before going into the major details of the code in Listing 5.24, let's look at a couple of simple but new things that are used in that applet. First note the following statement:

```
Container contentPane = getContentPane();
```

The method getContentPane returns something called the **content pane** of the applet. You can think of the content pane as the inside of the applet. When you add components to an applet, you add them to the content pane of

LISTING 5.24   Adding Labels to an Applet

```java
import javax.swing.JApplet;
import javax.swing.JLabel;
import java.awt.Color;
import java.awt.Container;
import java.awt.FlowLayout;

/**
 An applet that uses a label to display text.
*/
public class LabelDemo extends JApplet
{
    public void init()
    {
        Container contentPane = getContentPane();
        contentPane.setBackground(Color.WHITE);
        //Create labels:
        JLabel label1 = new JLabel("Hello ");
        JLabel label2 = new JLabel("out there!");
        //Add labels:
        contentPane.setLayout(new FlowLayout());
        contentPane.add(label1);
        contentPane.add(label2);
    }
}
```

Applet Output

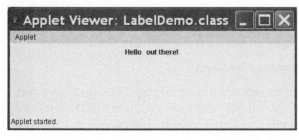

the applet. The content pane is an object of type `Container`, which is a class defined for you in the Java Class Library. Our main use of `Container` is to declare variables to name the content pane of an applet.

An applet's content pane is its inside area

The identifier `contentPane` is a variable of type `Container`. If you wish, you may use any other identifier—except for keywords—in place of `contentPane`. The method `getContentPane` retrieves the applet's content pane. By giving the content pane a name, we can use this name instead of using `getContentPane` every time we want to do something with the content pane of the applet.

For example, the following statement from Listing 5.24 sets the color of the content pane to white:

setBackground sets the color of the content pane

```
contentPane.setBackground(Color.WHITE);
```

The content pane of an applet, as well as most of the other components we will discuss, can be given a color by calling the method `setBackground`. If you do not call this method, the content pane or other component is given a default color.

RECAP The Method `setBackground`

The method sets the color of the content pane of an applet and of most of the other components we will discuss.

SYNTAX

```
Container Content_Pane = getContentPane();
Content_Pane.setBackground(Color_Object);
```

EXAMPLE

```
Container contentPaneOfApplet = getContentPane();
contentPaneOfApplet.setBackground(Color.PINK);
```

In Listing 5.24 we add two labels to our applet. We could have added only one label containing all the text and had the same result, but we wanted an example of adding more than one component to an applet. Typically, you will add multiple items to an applet. When you do so, you need to specify how the components should be arranged. In Listing 5.24 we did this as follows:

```
contentPane.setLayout(new FlowLayout());
```

This statement says that the components will be arranged in left-to-right order as we add them to `contentPane`. We will eventually explain this line in detail, but for now, just notice that our two labels appear side by side in the output shown in Listing 5.24.

Labels are created and added to the content pane of an applet in two separate steps. You create a label as an object of the class JLabel, as illustrated by the following line from Listing 5.24:

```
JLabel label1 = new JLabel("Hello ");
```

You add a label to the content pane of an applet by calling the method add, as we did in Listing 5.24:

```
contentPane.add(label1);
```

FAQ Why bother with labels? Why not just use drawString?

Using labels in an applet seems like a lot of work when you could get the same result simply by calling the method drawString within the paint method. So far, that is true, but you will soon see that we can do some special things with labels. Moreover, you will see that once you learn how to include labels, you can easily include lots of other kinds of components, such as buttons, because they are added to an applet in the same way that you add labels. You will start to see all this in the graphics supplement in the next chapter.

RECAP: Adding Labels to an Applet

You add a label to an applet's content pane by calling the method within the method of the init applet.

SYNTAX

```
Container Content_Pane = getContentPane();
JLabel Label_Name = new JLabel(A_String);
Content_Pane.setLayout(new FlowLayout());
Content_Pane.add(Label_Name);
```

EXAMPLE

See Listing 5.24.

 SELF-TEST QUESTIONS   myprogramminglab

36. In Listing 5.24, what is the effect of replacing the identifier contentPane in the init method with inside?

37. In Listing 5.24, what is the effect—other than stylistic—of replacing the line

```
contentPane.add(label1);
```

in the method with

```
getContentPane().add(label1);
```

CHAPTER SUMMARY

- Classes have instance variables to store data and method definitions that perform actions.

- Each class, instance variable, and method definition can be either public or private. Those that are public can be used or accessed anywhere. A private instance variable cannot be accessed by name outside of its class definition. However, it can be used within the definitions of methods in its class. A private method definition cannot be invoked outside of its class definition. However, it can be invoked within the definitions of methods in its class.

- Instance variables should be private, even though as a result, they cannot be referenced by name except within the definition of a method of the same class.

- Accessor methods return the value of an instance variable. Mutator methods set the value of one or more instance variables.

- Every method belongs to some class and is available to objects created from that class.

- There are two kinds of methods: methods that return a value and void methods, which do not return a value.

- You can use the invocation of a method that returns a single quantity anyplace that you can use a value of the method's return type.

- You follow the invocation of a void method with a semicolon to form a statement that performs an action.

- The keyword this, when used within a method definition, represents the object that receives the invocation of the method.

- A local variable is a variable declared within a method definition. The variable does not exist outside of its method.

- Arguments in a method invocation must match the formal parameters in the method heading with respect to their number, their order, and their data types.

- The formal parameters of a method behave like local variables. Each is initialized to the value of the corresponding argument when the method is called. This mechanism of substituting arguments for formal parameters is known as the call-by-value mechanism.

■ Methods can have parameters of a primitive type and/or parameters of a class type, but the two types of parameters behave differently. A parameter of a primitive type is initialized to the primitive value of its corresponding argument. A parameter of a class type is initialized to the memory address, or reference, of the corresponding argument object.

■ Any change made to a parameter of a primitive type is *not* made to the corresponding argument.

■ A parameter of a class type becomes another name for the corresponding argument in a method invocation. Thus, any change that is made to the state of the parameter will be made to the corresponding argument. However, if a parameter is replaced by another object within the method definition, the original argument is not affected.

■ A method definition can include a call to another method that is in either the same class or a different class.

■ A block is a compound statement that declares a local variable.

■ Encapsulation means that data and actions are combined into a single item—a class object—and that the details of the implementation are hidden. Making all instance variables private is part of the encapsulation process.

■ A method's precondition comment states the conditions that must be true before the method is invoked. Its postcondition comment tells what will be true after the method is executed. That is, the postcondition describes all the effects produced by an invocation of the method if the precondition holds. Preconditions and postconditions are kinds of assertions.

■ The utility program javadoc creates documentation from a class's comments that are written in a certain form.

■ Class designers use a notation called UML to represent classes.

■ Unit testing is a methodology in which the programmer writes a suite of tests to determine if individual units of code are operating properly.

■ The operators = and ==, when used on objects of a class, do not behave the same as they do when used on primitive types.

■ You usually want to provide an equals method for the classes you define.

■ Graphics drawn in an applet are normally performed from within the paint method. Most other applet instructions should go in the init method.

■ The parameter to the paint method in an applet is of type Graphics. The applet drawing methods we have used are methods in the class Graphics.

■ The method `setBackground` sets the color of the content pane of an applet and most other components we will discuss.

■ You add a label to an applet's content pane by calling the method from within the method `init` of the applet.

Exercises

1. Design a class to represent a credit card. Think about the attributes of a credit card; that is, what data is on the card? What behaviors might be reasonable for a credit card? Use the answers to these questions to write a UML class diagram for a credit card class. Then give three examples of instances of this class.

2. Repeat Exercise 1 for a credit card account instead of a credit card. An account represents the charges and payments made using a credit card.

3. Repeat Exercise 1 for a coin instead of a credit card.

4. Repeat Exercise 1 for a collection of coins instead of a credit card.

5. Consider a Java class that you could use to get an acceptable integer value from the user. An object of this class will have the attributes

   • Minimum accepted value
   • Maximum accepted value
   • Prompt string

   and the following method:

   • `getValue` displays the prompt and reads a value using the class `Scanner`. If the value read is not within the allowed range, the method should display an error message and ask the user for a new value, repeating these actions until an acceptable value is entered. The method then returns the value read.

   a. Write preconditions and postconditions for the method getValue.
   b. Implement the class in Java.
   c. Write some Java statements that test the class.

6. Consider a class that keeps track of the sales of an item. An object of this class will have the attributes

   • Number sold
   • Total sales
   • Total discounts
   • Cost per item
   • Bulk quantity
   • Bulk discount percentage

   and the following methods:

- `registerSale(n)` records the sale of *n* items. If *n* is larger than the bulk quantity, the cost per item will be reduced by the bulk discount.
- `displaySales` displays the number sold, the total sales, and total discount.

   a. Implement the class in Java.
   b. Write some Java statements that test the class.

7. Consider a class `MotorBoat` that represents motorboats. A motorboat has attributes for

   - The capacity of the fuel tank
   - The amount of fuel in the tank
   - The maximum speed of the boat
   - The current speed of the boat
   - The efficiency of the boat's motor
   - The distance traveled

   The class has methods to

   - Change the speed of the boat
   - Operate the boat for an amount of time at the current speed
   - Refuel the boat with some amount of fuel
   - Return the amount of fuel in the tank
   - Return the distance traveled so far

   If the boat has efficiency *e*, the amount of fuel used when traveling at a speed *s* for time *t* is $e \times s^2 \times t$. The distance traveled in that time is $s \times t$.

   a. Write a method heading for each method.
   b. Write preconditions and postconditions for each method.
   c. Write some Java statements that test the class.
   d. Implement the class.

8. Consider a class `PersonAddress` that represents an entry in an address book. Its attributes are

   - The first name of the person
   - The last name of the person
   - The e-mail address of the person
   - The telephone number of the person

   It will have methods to

   - Access each attribute
   - Change the e-mail address
   - Change the telephone number
   - Test whether two instances are equal based solely on name

    a. Write a method heading for each method.
    b. Write preconditions and postconditions for each method.
    c. Write some Java statements that test the class.
    d. Implement the class.

9. Consider a class `RatingScore` that represents a numeric rating for something such as a movie. Its attributes are

   - A description of what is being rated
   - The maximum possible rating
   - The rating

   It will have methods to

   - Get the rating from a user
   - Return the maximum rating possible
   - Return the rating
   - Return a string showing the rating in a format suitable for display

   a. Write a method heading for each method.
   b. Write preconditions and postconditions for each method.
   c. Write some Java statements that test the class.
   d. Implement the class.

10. Consider a class `ScienceFairProjectRating` that will be used to help judge a science fair project. It will use the class `RatingScore` described in the previous exercise. The attributes for the new class are

    - The name of the project
    - A unique identification string for the project
    - The name of the person
    - A rating for the creative ability (max. 30)
    - A rating for the scientific thought (max. 30)
    - A rating for thoroughness (max. 15)
    - A rating for technical skills (max. 15)
    - A rating for clarity (max. 10)

    It will have methods to

    - Get the number of judges
    - Get all the ratings for a particular project
    - Return the total of the ratings for a particular project
    - Return the maximum total rating possible
    - Return a string showing a project's rating in a format suitable for display

    a. Write a method heading for each method.
    b. Write preconditions and postconditions for each method.
    c. Write some Java statements that test the class.
    d. Implement the class.

PROGRAMMING PROJECTS

Visit www.myprogramminglab.com to complete many of these Programming Projects online and get instant feedback.

myprogramminglab

1. Write a program to answer questions like the following: Suppose the species Klingon ox has a population of 100 and a growth rate of 15 percent, and the species elephant has a population of 10 and a growth rate of 35 percent. How many years will it take for the elephant population to exceed the Klingon ox population? Use the class Species in Listing 5.19. Your program will ask for the data on both species and will respond by telling you how many years it will take for the species that starts with the lower population to outnumber the species that starts with the higher population. The two species may be entered in any order. It is possible that the species with the smaller population will never outnumber the other species. In this case, your program should display a suitable message stating this fact.

2. Define a class called Counter. An object of this class is used to count things, so it records a count that is a nonnegative whole number. Include methods to set the counter to 0, to increase the count by 1, and to decrease the count by 1. Be sure that no method allows the value of the counter to become negative. Also include an accessor method that returns the current count value, as well as a method that displays the count on the screen. Do not define an input method. The only method that can set the counter is the one that sets it to zero. Write a program to test your class definition. (*Hint:* You need only one instance variable.)

3. Write a grading program for an instructor whose course has the following policies:

   - Two quizzes, each graded on the basis of 10 points, are given.
   - One midterm exam and one final exam, each graded on the basis of 100 points, are given.
   - The final exam counts for 50 percent of the grade, the midterm counts for 25 percent, and the two quizzes together count for a total of 25 percent. (Do not forget to normalize the quiz scores. They should be converted to percentages before they are averaged in.)

   Any grade of 90 percent or more is an A, any grade between 80 and 89 percent is a B, any grade between 70 and 79 percent is a C, any grade between 60 and 69 percent is a D, and any grade below 60 percent is an F.

   The program should read in the student's scores and display the student's record, which consists of two quiz scores, two exam scores, the student's total score for the entire course, and the final letter grade. The total score is a number in the range 0 to 100, which represents the weighted average of the student's work.

Define and use a class for the student record. The class should have instance variables for the quizzes, midterm, final, total score for the course, and final letter grade. The class should have input and output methods. The input method should not ask for the final numeric grade, nor should it ask for the final letter grade. The class should have methods to compute the overall numeric grade and the final letter grade. These last two methods will be void methods that set the appropriate instance variables. Remember, one method can call another method. If you prefer, you can define a single method that sets both the overall numeric score and the final letter grade, but if you do this, use a helping method. Your program should use all the methods described here. Your class should have a reasonable set of accessor and mutator methods, whether or not your program uses them. You may add other methods if you wish.

4. Add methods to the Person class from Self-Test Question 16 to perform the following tasks:

   • Set the name attribute of a Person object.
   • Set the age attribute of a Person object.
   • Test whether two Person objects are equal (have the same name and age).
   • Test whether two Person objects have the same name.
   • Test whether two Person objects are the same age.
   • Test whether one Person object is older than another.
   • Test whether one Person object is younger than another.

   Write a driver (test) program that demonstrates each method, with at least one true and one false case for each of the methods tested.

5. Create a class that represents a grade distribution for a given course. Write methods to perform the following tasks:

   • Set the number of each of the letter grades A, B, C, D, and F.
   • Read the number of each of the letter grades A, B, C, D, and F.
   • Return the total number of grades.
   • Return the percentage of each letter grade as a whole number between 0 and 100, inclusive.
   • Draw a bar graph of the grade distribution.

   The graph will have five bars, one per grade. Each bar can be a horizontal row of asterisks, such that the number of asterisks in a row is proportionate to the percentage of grades in each category. Let one asterisk represent 2 percent, so 50 asterisks correspond to 100 percent. Mark the horizontal axis at 10 percent increments from 0 to 100 percent, and label each line with its letter grade.

For example, if the grades are 1 A, 4 Bs, 6 Cs, 2 Ds, and 1 F, the total number of grades is 14, the percentage of As is 7, the percentage of Bs is 29, the percentage of Cs is 43, the percentage of Ds is 14, and the percentage of Fs is 7. The A row would contain 4 asterisks (7 percent of 50 rounded to the nearest integer), the B row 14, the C row 21, the D row 7, and the F row 4. The graph would look like this:

```
0    10   20   30   40   50   60   70   80   90  100%
|    |    |    |    |    |    |    |    |    |    |
***************************************************
**** A
************** B
********************* C
******* D
**** F
```

6. Write a program that uses the `Purchase` class in Listing 5.13 to set the following prices:

   Oranges: 10 for $2.99
   Eggs: 12 for $1.69
   Apples: 3 for $1.00
   Watermelons: $4.39 each
   Bagels: 6 for $3.50

   Then calculate the cost of each of the following five items and the total bill:

   2 dozen oranges
   3 dozen eggs
   20 apples
   2 watermelons
   1 dozen bagels

7. Write a program to answer questions like the following: Suppose the species Klingon ox has a population of 100 and a growth rate of 15 percent, and it lives in an area of 1500 square miles. How long would it take for the population density to exceed 1 per square mile? Use the class `Species` in Listing 5.19 with the addition of the `getDensity` method from Self-Test Question 10.

8. Consider a class that could be used to play a game of hangman. The class has the following attributes:

   VideoNote
   Developing a solution to Project 8

   • The secret word.
   • The disguised word, in which each unknown letter in the secret word is replaced with a question mark (?). For example, if the secret word is *abracadabra* and the letters *a, b,* and *e* have been guessed, the disguised word would be *ab?a?a?ab?a*.

- The number of guesses made.
- The number of incorrect guesses.

It will have the following methods:

- makeGuess(c) guesses that character c is in the word.
- getDisguisedWord returns a string containing correctly guessed letters in their correct positions and unknown letters replaced with ?.
- getSecretWord returns the secret word.
- getGuessCount returns the number of guesses made.
- isFound returns true if the hidden word has been discovered.

a. Write a method heading for each method.
b. Write preconditions and postconditions for each method.
c. Write some Java statements that test the class.
d. Implement the class.
e. List any additional methods and attributes needed in the implementation that were not listed in the original design. List any other changes made to the original design.
f. Write a program that implements the game of hangman using the class you wrote for Part *d*.

9. Consider a class BasketballGame that represents the state of a basketball game. Its attributes are

- The name of the first team
- The name of the second team
- The score of the first team
- The score of the second team
- The status of the game (finished or in progress)

BasketballGame has methods to

- Record one point scored for a team
- Record two points scored for a team
- Record three points scored for a team
- Change the status of the game to finished
- Return the score of a team
- Return the name of the team that is currently winning

a. Write a method heading for each method.
b. Write preconditions and postconditions for each method.
c. Write some Java statements that test the class.
d. Implement the class.
e. List any additional methods and attributes needed in the implementation that were not listed in the original design. List any other changes made to the original design.

f. Write a program that uses the class `BasketballGame` to keep track of the score of a basketball game. Use a loop that reads input each time a basket is scored. (You will need to indicate the scoring team and the number of points scored for each basket: 1, 2, or 3.) After each input is read, display the current score of the game. For example, a portion of the interaction with the program might be as follows:

```
Enter a score:
a 1
Cats 1, Dogs 0; Cats are winning.
Enter a score:
a 2
Cats 3, Dogs 0; Cats are winning.
Enter a score:
b 2
Cats 3, Dogs 2; Cats are winning.
Enter a score:
b 3
Cats 3, Dogs 5; Dogs are winning.
```

10. Consider a class `ConcertPromoter` that records the tickets sold for a performance. Before the day of the concert, tickets are sold only over the phone. Sales on the day of the performance are made only in person at the concert venue. The class has the following attributes:

   • The name of the band
   • The capacity of the venue
   • The number of tickets sold
   • The price of a ticket sold by phone
   • The price of a ticket sold at the concert venue
   • The total sales amount

   It has methods to

   • Record the sale of one or more tickets
   • Change from phone sales to sales at the concert venue
   • Return the number of tickets sold
   • Return the number of tickets remaining
   • Return the total sales for the concert

   a. Write a method heading for each method.

   b. Write preconditions and postconditions for each method.

   c. Write some Java statements that test the class.

   d. Implement the class.

   e. List any additional methods and attributes needed in the implementation that were not listed in the original design. List any other changes made to the original design.

   f. Write a program using the class you wrote for Part *d* that will be used to record sales for a concert. Your program should record phone sales, then sales at the venue. As tickets are sold, the number of seats remaining should be displayed. At the end of the program, display the number of tickets sold and the total sales amount for the concert.

11. Rewrite the Dog class given in Listing 5.1 by utilizing the information and encapsulation principles described in Section 5.2. The new version should include accessor and mutator methods. Also define an equals method for the class that returns true if the dog's name, age, and breed match the same variables for the other object that is being compared. Include a main method to test the functionality of the new Dog class.

12. Consider a class Movie that contains information about a movie. The class has the following attributes:

   • The movie name
   • The MPAA rating (e.g., G, PG, PG-13, R)
   • The number of people that have rated this movie as a 1 (Terrible)
   • The number of people that have rated this movie as a 2 (Bad)
   • The number of people that have rated this movie as a 3 (OK)
   • The number of people that have rated this movie as a 4 (Good)
   • The number of people that have rated this movie as a 5 (Great)

   Implement the class with accessors and mutators for the movie name and MPAA rating. Write a method addRating that takes an integer as an input parameter. The method should verify that the parameter is a number between 1 and 5, and if so, increment by one the number of people rating the movie that matches the input parameter. For example, if 3 is the input parameter, then the number of people that rated the movie as a 3 should be incremented by one. Write another method, getAverage, that returns the average value for all of the movie ratings.

   Test the class by writing a main method that creates at least two movie objects, adds at least five ratings for each movie, and outputs the movie name, MPAA rating, and average rating for each movie object.

Graphics

13. Repeat Programming Project 18 from Chapter 4, but use a method that displays a circular disk as a subtask.

14. Create an applet or Java application that displays something like the following picture. You should have methods for drawing a monkey face and a hand.

Hear no evil   See no evil   Speak no evil

Answers to Self-Test Questions

1. ```java
   SpeciesFirstTry speciesOfTheYear = new SpeciesFirstTry();
   System.out.println("Enter data for Species of the Year:");
   speciesOfTheYear.readInput();
   ```

2. ```java
   dilbert.readInput();
   ```

3. ```java
   import java.util.Scanner;
   public class SpeciesFirstTry
   {
       public String name;
       public int number;
       public int population;
       public double growthRate;
       public void readInput()
       {
           Scanner keyboard = new Scanner(System.in);
           System.out.println("What is the species name?");
           name = keyboard.nextLine();
           System.out.println("What is the species number?");
           number = keyboard.nextInt();
           System.out.println("What is the population of the " +
                               "species?");
           population = keyboard.nextInt();
           System.out.println("Enter growth rate (% increase " +
                               "per year):");
           growthRate = keyboard.nextDouble();
       }
       public void writeOutput()
       {
           System.out.println("Name = " + name);
           System.out.println("Number = " + number);
           System.out.println("Population = " + population);
           System.out.println("Growth rate = " + growthRate + "%");
   ```
   ```

```java
    }
    public int getPopulationIn10()
    <This method does not change.>
    }
```

4.
```java
   public int getFemalePopulation()
   {
       return population / 2 + population % 2;
   }
   public int getMalePopulation()
   {
       return population / 2;
   }
```

5.
```java
   public void writeOutput()
   {
       System.out.println("Name = " + this.name);
       System.out.println("Population = " + this.population);
       System.out.println("Growth rate = " + this.growthRate + "%");
   }
```

6.
```java
   public void readInput()
   {
       Scanner keyboard = new Scanner(System.in); System.out.
       println("What is the species name?");
       this.name = keyboard.nextLine();
       System.out.println(
           "What is the population of the species?");
       this.population =   keyboard.nextInt();
       System.out.println(
           "Enter growth rate (% increase per year):");
       this.growthRate = keyboard.nextDouble();
   }
```

7.
```java
   public int getPopulationIn10()
   {
       int result = 0;
       double populationAmount = this.population;
       int count = 10;
       while ((count > 0) && (populationAmount > 0))
       {
           populationAmount = (populationAmount +
               (this.growthRate / 100) * populationAmount);
           count----;
       }
       if (populationAmount > 0)
           result = (int)populationAmount;
       return result;
   }
```

8. The expression (int)is a type cast. It is needed because the method heading specifies that the type of the returned value is int, and so the value of populationAmount must be changed from double to int before it is returned.

9. In this book the terms *parameter* and *formal parameter* mean exactly the same thing.

10.
```
public double getDensity(double area)
{
    return population / area;
}
```

11.
```
public void changePopulation(double area)
{
    population = (int)(2 * area);
}
```

12.
```
public void changePopulation(double area, int numberPerMile)
{
    population = (int)(numberPerMile * area);
}
```

13. We cannot use the alternative code, because the instance variables are labeled private in the class definition and so cannot be accessed by name except within a method definition of the class SpeciesFourthTry.

14.
```
/**
 Precondition: This objects population and growth rate have
 been given values.
 Postcondition: This object population was updated to reflect
 one year's change. Other data values are unchanged.
*/
```

15. An accessor method is a public method that returns the data from a private instance variable. The name of an accessor method typically begins with get. A mutator method is a public method that changes the data stored in one or more private instance variables. The name of a mutator method typically begins with set.

16.
```
import java.util.Scanner;
public class Person
{
    private String name;
    private int age;
    public void setName(String newName)
    {
        name = newName;
    }
```

```
        public void setAge(int newAge)
        {
                if (newAge >= 0)
                        age = newAge;
                else
                {
                        System.out.println("ERROR: Age is " +
                          "negative.");
                        System.exit(0);
                }
        }
        public void setPerson(String newName, int newAge)
        {
                setName(newName);
                setAge(newAge)
        }
        public String getName()
        {
                return name;
        }
        public int getAge()
        {
                return age;
        }
}
```

17. Yes. See Listing 5.15 for an example.

18. No effect at all. The two statements are equivalent in this context.

19. A well-encapsulated class definition logically separates into class interface and implementation. A programmer should be able to use the class knowing only the information given in the class interface and should need to know nothing about the implementation.

20. Instance variables should always be private.

21. If a method is a helping method that is used only within the definitions of other methods, it should be private.

22. No, it is part of the implementation.

23. No, it is part of the implementation.

24. A reference type is a type whose variables hold references—that is, memory addresses—as opposed to actual values of objects. Class types are reference types. Not all reference types are class types, but we will not see any examples of this until later in the book. Primitive types are not reference types.

25. Normally, you use the method `equals` when testing two objects to see whether they are "equal." The only time you would use = = is if you wanted to see whether the objects were in the same place in memory, that is, were identical.

26. You use == when comparing two quantities of a primitive type (like `int`) to see whether they are "equal." Primitive types have no `equals` method.

27. ```
/**
 Precondition: This object and the argument otherSpecies both
 have values for their growth rates.
 Returns true if the growth rate of this object is greater than
 the growth rate of otherSpecies; otherwise, returns false.
*/
public boolean isGrowthRateLargerThan(Species otherSpecies)
{
    return growthRate > otherSpecies.growthRate;
}
```

28. The variables `s1` and `s2` are names for objects of type `Species`, but this program does not create any objects for them to name. They are just names, not yet objects. The program should begin as follows:

```
public class SpeciesEqualsDemo
{
    public static void main(String[] args)
    {
        Species s1 = new Species(), s2 = new Species();
        <The rest of the code is OK.>
```

29. `Do Not match with ==.`

30. The biggest difference is in how a method handles arguments that correspond to the different kinds of parameters. A method cannot change the value of a variable of a primitive type that is an argument to the method, nor can it replace an argument of a class type with another object. On the other hand, a method can change the values of the instance variables of an object of a class type whose name is an argument to the method.

31. ```
Name = Klingon ox
Population = 10
Growth rate = 15.0%
n = 0
```

32. Here are two possible definitions of `equals`. The first definition considers two `Person` objects equal if they have the same name, regardless of their ages. The second one considers two `Person` objects equal if they have both the same name and the same age.

```
public boolean equals(Person otherObject)
{
    return this.name.equalsIgnoreCase(otherObject.name);
}
public boolean equals(Person otherObject)
{
    return this.name.equalsIgnoreCase(otherObject.name) &&
            (this.age == otherObject.age);
}
```

You can omit all the occurrences of this and the dot that follows.

33. It would have no effect. The applet would behave in exactly the same way. Since canvas is only a parameter, you may use any other (nonkeyword) identifier in place of canvas.

34. The method paint is invoked automatically when the applet is run.

35.
```
private void drawFaceSansMouth(Graphics g, int pos, Color skinColor)
{
    g.setColor(skinColor);
    g.fillOval(X_FACE0 + 50 * pos, Y_FACE0 + 30 * pos,
                        FACE_DIAMETER, FACE_DIAMETER);
    g.setColor(Color.BLACK);
    g.drawOval(X_FACE0 + 50 * pos, Y_FACE0 + 30 * pos,
                        FACE_DIAMETER, FACE_DIAMETER);
    //Draw eyes:
    g.setColor(Color.BLUE);
    g.fillOval(X_RIGHT_EYE0 + 50 * pos,
    Y_RIGHT_EYE0 + 30 * pos,
    EYE_WIDTH, EYE_HEIGHT);
    g.fillOval(X_LEFT_EYE0 + 50 * pos,
    Y_LEFT_EYE0 + 30 * pos,
    EYE_WIDTH, EYE_HEIGHT);
    //Draw nose:
    g.setColor(Color.BLACK);
    g.fillOval(X_NOSE0 + 50 * pos, Y_NOSE0 + 30 * pos,
                NOSE_DIAMETER, NOSE_DIAMETER);
}
```

36. The change would have no effect, as long as you also replace contentPane with inside wherever else it occurs in the method init.

37. The change would have no effect.

More About Objects and Methods

6.1 CONSTRUCTORS 375
Defining Constructors 375
Calling Methods from Constructors 384
Calling a Constructor from Other Constructors
 (Optional) 387

**6.2 STATIC VARIABLES AND STATIC
 METHODS** 389
Static Variables 389
Static Methods 390
Dividing the Task of a `main` Method into
 Subtasks 397
Adding a `main` Method to a Class 398
The `Math` Class 400
Wrapper Classes 403

6.3 WRITING METHODS 409
Case Study: Formatting Output 409
Decomposition 415
Addressing Compiler Concerns 416
Testing Methods 418

6.4 OVERLOADING 420
Overloading Basics 420
Overloading and Automatic Type Conversion 423

Overloading and the Return Type 426
Programming Example: A Class for **Money** 428

6.5 INFORMATION HIDING REVISITED 435
Privacy Leaks 435

6.6 ENUMERATION AS A CLASS 439

6.7 PACKAGES 441
Packages and Importing 441
Package Names and Directories 443
Name Clashes 446

6.8 GRAPHICS SUPPLEMENT 447
Adding Buttons 447
Event-Driven Programming 449
Programming Buttons 449
Programming Example: A Complete Applet with
 Buttons 453
Adding Icons 456
Changing Visibility 458
Programming Example: An Example of Changing
 Visibility 458

Chapter Summary 462   **Programming Projects** 466   **Answers to Self-Test Questions** 471

A tourist stopped an elderly gentleman on the streets of New York City and asked him, "Please sir, could you tell me how I can get to Carnegie Hall?" "Practice, practice, practice," the old gentleman replied.

—A VERY OLD JOKE

In this chapter, we continue our discussion of how to define and use classes and their methods. As part of that discussion, we introduce constructors, which are methods used to create a new object. You have already used a constructor when you used the operator new. Java supplied that constructor, but we will show you how to write your own constructors.

In addition, we examine static methods. The method main is static, so our discussion will help you understand it. But you can also write other static methods that can be invoked using the class name, rather than an object name.

You will also learn about overloading, which allows you to give two or more methods the same name within the same class. We also discuss packages, which are libraries of classes that you can use in other class definitions. Again, you have used packages when you used classes in the Java Class Library. Along the way, we cover a number of program design techniques that will help you write better method definitions.

Finally, in the graphics supplement, you will see how to add buttons and icons—which are small pictures—to your applets. We also discuss an important programming technique—event-driven programming—that is often used for applets and other graphics programs.

OBJECTIVES

After studying this chapter, you should be able to

- Define and use a class's constructors
- Write and use static variables and static methods
- Use methods in the predefined Math class
- Use the predefined wrapper classes
- Use stubs, drivers, and other techniques to test your classes and programs
- Write and use overloaded methods
- Define and use enumeration methods
- Define and use packages and import statements
- Add buttons and icons to your applets
- Use basic event-driven programming in an applet

PREREQUISITES

You must cover the material in Chapter 5 before reading this chapter. As we describe next, certain sections of this chapter can be postponed until after you've read some of the subsequent chapters.

Section 6.5 discusses some subtle points about using instance variables of a class type. Strictly speaking, this section is not required for the rest of the material in this book and so can be postponed. However, Section 6.5 does discuss fundamental issues that you should read at some point.

The material on writing packages in Section 6.7 requires a knowledge of folders (directories) and path variables. Folders and path variables are not Java topics; they are operating system topics, and the details depend on what operating system you are using. Section 6.7 is not required for any other material in this book, so you need not cover this section until you are ready to do so.

6.1 CONSTRUCTORS

First things first.

—COMMON SAYING

When you create an object of a class using the new operator, you invoke a special kind of method called a constructor. At that time, you often want certain initializing actions to occur, such as giving specific values to the instance variables. A constructor will perform such initializations. In this section, we tell you how to define and use constructors.

> Constructors create and initialize new objects

Defining Constructors

A **constructor** is a special method that is called when you use the new operator to create a new object. Until now, Java has supplied a constructor for us. For example, given the class Species in Listing 5.19 of the previous chapter, we can create a new Species object by writing

> Using new calls a constructor

```
Species earthSpecies = new Species();
```

The first part of this statement, Species earthSpecies, declares the variable earthSpecies to be a name for an object of the class Species. The second part, newSpecies(), creates and initializes a new object, whose address is then assigned to earthSpecies. Here Species() is a call to the constructor that Java provided for the class. The parentheses are empty because this particular constructor takes no arguments.

For the classes you've seen thus far, the constructors create objects and give their instance variables default initial values. These values might not be what you want, however. Instead, you may wish to have some or all instance variables initialized to your specifications at the time an object is created. You can do this by writing your own constructors.

> A constructor supplied by Java uses default initial values

A constructor can perform any action you write into its definition, but a constructor is meant to perform initializing actions, such as initializing the values of instance variables. Constructors serve essentially the same purpose as set methods. But unlike set methods, constructors create an object as well as initializing it. Like set methods, constructors can have parameters.

Let's consider a simple class to represent our pets. Suppose that we describe a pet by its name, its age, and its weight. We could give basic behaviors to a pet object that simply set or get these three attributes. Now imagine that we draw a class diagram like the one in Figure 6.1 for a class named `Pet`. Notice the four methods that set different instance variables. One sets all three of the instance variables `name`, `age`, and `weight`. The other three methods set only one instance variable each. This class diagram does not include constructors, as is typical.

One property of constructors that may seem strange at first is that each constructor has the same name as its class. So if the class is named `Species`, its constructors are named `Species`. If the class is named `Pet`, the constructors are named `Pet`.

Constructors often have multiple definitions, each with different numbers or types of parameters, and they sometimes parallel a class's set methods. As an example, Listing 6.1 contains a definition of our class `Pet` that includes several constructors. Note that the headings of these constructors do not have the word `void`. When you define a constructor, you do not specify any return type, not even `void`. These constructors look very much like our set methods, which *are* void methods. In fact, we have grouped each constructor with its similar set method, just for this example. Unlike some of the set methods, however, the constructors give values to *all* the instance variables, even though they might not have a parameter for each instance variable. If you do not initialize a particular instance variable, Java will do so by giving it a default value. However, it is normal programming practice to explicitly give values to all the instance variables when defining a constructor.

A class diagram does not include constructors

Instance variables that you do not initialize are given default initial values by Java

FIGURE 6.1 **Class Diagram for a Class** `Pet`

```
┌─────────────────────────────────────────────────────────────┐
│                            Pet                               │
├─────────────────────────────────────────────────────────────┤
│   - name: String                                             │
│   - age: int                                                 │
│   - weight: double                                           │
├─────────────────────────────────────────────────────────────┤
│   + writeOutput(): void                                      │
│   + setPet(String newName, int newAge, double newWeight): void│
│   + setName(String newName): void                            │
│   + setAge(int newAge): void                                 │
│   + setWeight(double newWeight): void                        │
│   + getName(): String                                        │
│   + getAge(): int                                            │
│   + getWeight(): double                                      │
└─────────────────────────────────────────────────────────────┘
```

LISTING 6.1   The Class Pet: An Example of Constructors and Set Methods *(part 1 of 3)*

```java
/**
 Class for basic pet data: name, age, and weight.
*/
public class Pet
{
    private String name;
    private int age;       //in years
    private double weight;//in pounds

    public Pet() ← ─────── Default constructor
    {
        name = "No name yet.";
        age = 0;
        weight = 0;
    }
    public Pet(String initialName, int initialAge,
                double initialWeight)
    {
        name = initialName;
        if ((initialAge < 0) || (initialWeight < 0))
        {
            System.out.println("Error: Negative age or weight.");
            System.exit(0);
        }
        else
        {
            age = initialAge;
            weight = initialWeight;
        }
    }
    public void setPet(String newName, int newAge,
                    double newWeight)
    {
        name = newName;
        if ((newAge < 0) || (newWeight < 0))
        {
            System.out.println("Error: Negative age or weight.");
            System.exit(0);
        }
        else
        {
            age = newAge;
            weight = newWeight;
        }
    }
```

(continued)

LISTING 6.1 **The Class Pet: An Example of Constructors and Set Methods** *(part 2 of 3)*

```java
public Pet(String initialName)
{
    name = initialName;
    age = 0;
    weight = 0;
}

public void setName(String newName)
{
    name = newName; //age and weight are unchanged.
}
```

```java
public Pet(int initialAge)
{
    name = "No name yet.";
    weight = 0;
    if (initialAge < 0)
    {
        System.out.println("Error: Negative age.");
        System.exit(0);
    }
    else
        age = initialAge;
}

public void setAge(int newAge)
{
    if (newAge < 0)
    {
        System.out.println("Error: Negative age.");
        System.exit(0);
    }
    else
        age = newAge;
    //name and weight are unchanged.
}
```

```java
public Pet(double initialWeight)
{
    name = "No name yet";
    age = 0;
    if (initialWeight < 0)
    {
        System.out.println("Error: Negative weight.");
        System.exit(0);
    }
```

(continued)

LISTING 6.1   The Class Pet: **An Example of Constructors and Set Methods** *(part 3 of 3)*

```
        else
            weight = initialWeight;
    }
    public void setWeight(double newWeight)
    {
        if (newWeight < 0)
        {
            System.out.println("Error: Negative weight.");
            System.exit(0);
        }
        else
            weight = newWeight; //name and age are unchanged.
    }
    public String getName()
    {
        return name;
    }

    public int getAge()
    {
        return age;
    }

    public double getWeight()
    {
        return weight;
    }

    public void writeOutput()
    {
        System.out.println("Name: " + name);
        System.out.println("Age: " + age + " years");
        System.out.println("Weight: " + weight + " pounds");
    }
}
```

REMEMBER Constructors and Set Methods Are Used in Related but Different Ways

Constructors are called only when you create an object. To change the state of an existing object, you need one or more set methods.

A default
constructor has
no parameters

Listing 6.1 includes a constructor named `Pet` that has no parameters. Such a constructor is called a **default constructor.** Typically, whenever you define at least one constructor, you should also include a constructor without parameters. If you look at the definition of the class `Species` in the previous chapter, you will not find any constructor definitions at all.

Java defines a
constructor if you
do not

Whenever a class definition does not have a constructor definition, Java automatically defines a default constructor, that is, one without parameters. This automatically defined constructor creates an object of the class and initializes the instance variables to default values. If, however, you define at least one constructor in a class, no constructors are created for you automatically. Thus, for the class `Pet` in Listing 6.1, since we defined constructors, we were careful to include a constructor without parameters, that is, a default constructor.

Constructors
can require
arguments

When you create a new object by using the operator `new`, you must always include a call to a constructor. As with any method invocation, you list any arguments in parentheses after the constructor's name—which, remember, is the same as the class name. For example suppose you want to use `new` to create a new object of our class `Pet`. You might do so as follows:

```
Pet fish = new Pet("Wanda", 2, 0.25);
```

The part `Pet("Wanda", 2, 0.25)` is a call to the constructor in `Pet` that takes three arguments: one of type `String`, one of type `int`, and the last of type `double`. This statement creates a new object to represent a pet named Wanda who is 2 years old and weighs 0.25 pound.

You can think of a constructor invocation as returning a reference to— that is, the memory address of—an object of the class `Pet`. The previous example assigns this reference to the variable `fish`. Figure 6.2 illustrates how this works.

Let's look at another example. The statement

```
Pet myPet = new Pet();
```

creates a new object of the class `Pet` by calling the default constructor—that is, the constructor without parameters. If you look at the definition of the class `Pet` in Listing 6.1, you will see that the default constructor gives the object the name `No name yet` and sets the instance variables age and weight to zero. (A newborn pet does not weigh zero, of course. The value of zero is just a place holder until the actual weight can be determined.)

You cannot
use an existing
object to call a
constructor

You cannot use an existing object to call a constructor, so the following invocation involving the object `myPet` of the class `Pet` is invalid:

```
myPet.Pet("Fang", 1, 150.0); //Invalid!
```

You need some other way to change the values of the instance variables of an object, once it has been created. That way involves calling one or more set

FIGURE 6.2 A Constructor Returning a Reference

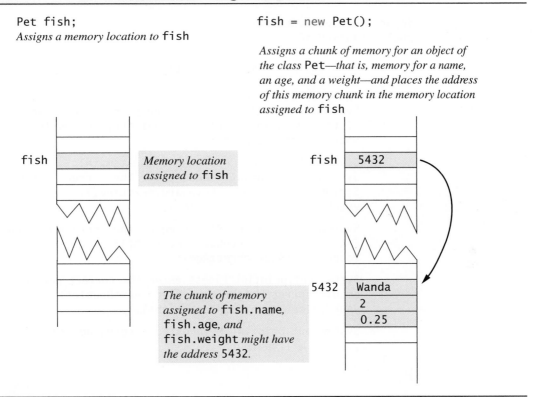

```
Pet fish;
```
Assigns a memory location to `fish`

```
fish = new Pet();
```
Assigns a chunk of memory for an object of the class `Pet`—*that is, memory for a name, an age, and a weight—and places the address of this memory chunk in the memory location assigned to* `fish`

`fish`   *Memory location assigned to* `fish`

`fish`   5432

The chunk of memory assigned to `fish.name`, `fish.age`, *and* `fish.weight` *might have the address 5432.*

5432   Wanda
2
0.25

---

methods. Thus, given the class defined in Listing 6.1, instead of the preceding invalid invocation of the constructor `Pet`, we could call `setPet` as follows:

A set method can change the state of an existing object

```
myPet.setPet("Fang", 1, 150.0);
```

A sample program illustrating the use of a constructor and several set methods is given in Listing 6.2.

■ PROGRAMMING TIP   Group the Constructor Definitions

In Listing 6.1, we have written an analogous set method after each constructor definition. We did this to emphasize the similarities and differences between these two kinds of methods. However, programmers usually group the definitions of constructors, often placing them before all the other methods in the class.   ■

LISTING 6.2 Using a Constructor and Set Methods

```java
import java.util.Scanner;
public class PetDemo
{
    public static void main(String[] args)
    {
        Pet yourPet = new Pet("Jane Doe");
        System.out.println("My records on your pet are inaccurate.");
        System.out.println("Here is what they currently say:");
        yourPet.writeOutput();

        Scanner keyboard = new Scanner(System.in);
        System.out.println("Please enter the correct pet name:");
        String correctName = keyboard.nextLine();
        yourPet.setName(correctName);

        System.out.println("Please enter the correct pet age:");
        int correctAge = keyboard.nextInt();
        yourPet.setAge(correctAge);

        System.out.println("Please enter the correct pet weight:");
        double correctWeight = keyboard.nextDouble();
        yourPet.setWeight(correctWeight);

        System.out.println("My updated records now say:");
        yourPet.writeOutput();
    }
}
```

Sample Screen Output

```
My records on your pet are inaccurate.
Here is what they currently say:
Name: Jane Doe
Age: 0
Weight: 0.0 pounds
Please enter the correct pet name:
Moon Child
Please enter the correct pet age:
5
Please enter the correct pet weight:
24.5
My updated records now say:
Name: Moon Child
Age: 5
Weight: 24.5 pounds
```

method that both `setPet` and the constructor can call, as the following code demonstrates:

```java
public Pet(String initialName, int initialAge,
            double initialWeight)
{
    set(initialName, initialAge, initialWeight);
}
public void setPet(String newName, int newAge,
        double newWeight)
{
    set(newName, newAge, newWeight);
}
private void set(String newName, int newAge, double newWeight)
{
    name = newName;
    if ((newAge < 0) || (newWeight < 0))
    {
        System.out.println("Error: Negative age or weight.");
        System.exit(0);
    }
    else
    {
        age = newAge;
        weight = newWeight;
    }
}
```

The other constructors and set methods in `Pet` can also be revised to invoke the private method set, as Listing 6.3 shows.

LISTING 6.3 Constructors and Set Methods That Call a Private Method *(part 1 of 3)*

```java
/**
 Revised class for basic pet data: name, age, and weight.
*/
public class Pet2
{
    private String name;
    private int age;       //in years
    private double weight;//in pounds

    public Pet2(String initialName, int initialAge,
                double initialWeight)
    {
        set(initialName, initialAge, initialWeight);
    }
```

(continued)

LISTING 6.3 **Constructors and Set Methods That Call a Private Method** *(part 2 of 3)*

```java
public Pet2(String initialName)
{
    set(initialName, 0, 0);
}
public Pet2(int initialAge)
{
    set("No name yet.", initialAge, 0);
}

public Pet2(double initialWeight)
{
    set("No name yet.", 0, initialWeight);
}

public Pet2( )
{
    set("No name yet.", 0, 0);
}

public void setPet(String newName, int newAge,
                   double newWeight)
{
    set(newName, newAge, newWeight);
}
public void setName(String newName)
{
    set(newName, age, weight);//age and weight unchanged
}
public void setAge(int newAge)
{
    set(name, newAge, weight);//name and weight unchanged
}
public void setWeight(double newWeight)
{
    set(name, age, newWeight);//name and age unchanged
}
private void set(String newName, int newAge,
                 double newWeight)
{
    name = newName;
    if ((newAge < 0) || (newWeight < 0))
    {
        System.out.println("Error: Negative age or weight.");
        System.exit(0);
    }
```

(continued)

LISTING 6.3   Constructors and Set Methods That Call a Private Method *(part 3 of 3)*

```
        else
        {
            age = newAge;
            weight = newWeight;
        }
    }
    <The methods getName, getAge, getWeight, and writeOutput
    are the same as in Listing 6.1.>
}
```

VideoNote
Writing constructors

SELF-TEST QUESTIONS

myprogramminglab

1. If a class is named Student, what name can you use for a constructor for this class?

2. When defining a constructor, what do you specify for the type of the value returned? A primitive type? A class type? void?

3. What is a default constructor?

4. Does every class in Java automatically have a default constructor? If not, when is a default constructor provided automatically by Java and when is it not provided?

5. In the program PetDemo shown in Listing 6.2, you can replace the calls to the three set methods with one call to setPet. Write this invocation.

Calling a Constructor from Other Constructors (*Optional*)

Let's again consider Pet2 in Listing 6.3. Once we have defined the first constructor—the one having three parameters—and the private method set, we could make the other constructors invoke this first constructor. To do so, we use the keyword this as if it were the name of a method in an invocation. For example, the statement

A constructor can call another constructor by using the keyword this

```
    this(initialName, 0, 0);
```

would invoke the three-parameter constructor from within the body of another constructor in our class. The invocation must be the first action taken within the body of the constructor. Listing 6.4 shows how we could revise the constructors in Listing 6.3 in this way. Note that the set methods do not use this statement; they invoke the private method set, as they did in Pet2. Using the keyword this to invoke a constructor can occur only within the body of another constructor within the same class.

LISTING 6.4 Constructors That Call Another Constructor

```java
/**
 Revised class for basic pet data: name, age, and weight.
*/
public class Pet3
{
    private String name;
    private int age;      //in years
    private double weight;//in pounds

    public Pet3(String initialName, int initialAge,
                double initialWeight)
    {
        set(initialName, initialAge, initialWeight);
    }

    public Pet3(String initialName)
    {
        this(initialName, 0, 0);
    }

    public Pet3(int initialAge)
    {
        this("No name yet.", initialAge, 0);
    }

    public Pet3(double initialWeight)
    {
        this("No name yet.", 0, initialWeight);
    }

    public Pet3( )
    {
        this("No name yet.", 0, 0);
    }
    <The rest of the class is like Pet2 in Listing 6.3.>
}
```

RECAP Constructors Calling Other Constructors in the Same Class

When defining a constructor for a class, you can use this as a name for another constructor in the same class. Any call to this must be the first action taken by the constructor.

(continued)

EXAMPLE

```java
public Pet3(String initialName)
{
    this(initialName, 0, 0);
}
```

■ **PROGRAMMING TIP**   Write Interdependent Constructors

When writing multiple constructors for a class, identify one that the others can call by using `this`. Writing constructors in this way places the actual initialization in one place, making the class easier to maintain and less prone to error. Chapter 8 will talk more about this way of writing constructors.   ■

6.2 STATIC VARIABLES AND STATIC METHODS

> . . .there's no there there.
>
> —GERTRUDE STEIN

A class can have variables that are static as well as methods that are static. Static variables and static methods belong to a class as a whole and not to an individual object. In this section, we show you how to define static variables and static methods.

Static Variables

We have already used **static variables** in one special case, namely, in the definition of named constant values such as the following:

Static variables are shared by all objects of a class

```java
public static final double FEET_PER_YARD = 3;
```

Only one copy of `FEET_PER_YARD` exists. It belongs to the class, so individual objects of the class that contains this definition do not have their own versions of this constant. Instead, they have access to and share this one constant.

This particular static variable cannot change in value—it is a constant—because its definition includes the keyword `final`. However, we can have static variables that can change in value. They are declared like instance variables, but with the keyword `static`. For example, the following static variable can change in value:

```java
private static int numberOfInvocations;
```

A static variable can be public or private; however, like instance variables, static variables that are not constants should normally be private and should be accessed or changed only via accessor and mutator methods.

Static variables that are not constants should be private

Chapter 2 mentioned that out is an object of the class System. But it is actually a static constant that has the following declaration:

```
public static final
    PrintStream out;
```

Since out is public, we can access it by name outside of the class System. However, when we do so we must precede its name with System and a dot, as in System.out. The statement just shown creates out as an object of the class PrintStream, which is in the Java Class Library. The methods print and println are methods in this class. To invoke these methods, you write the name of an object of PrintStream, a dot, and the name of the method. So when we write System.out.println(), for example, we are invoking the method println of the object out.

There is only one variable named numberOfInvocations, and it can be accessed by every object of its class. This means that the static variable could allow objects to communicate with one another or perform some joint action. For example, each method in its class could increment numberOfInvocations and so track how many method calls are made by all objects of the class. The next section gives an example of a static variable in use. You can initialize a static variable in the same way that you initialize a named constant, except that you omit the keyword final:

```
private static int
    numberOfInvocations = 0;
```

Static variables are also called **class variables**. Do not confuse the term *class variable*—which simply means a static variable within a class—with the notion of a variable of a class type—which means a variable whose type is a class, that is, a variable that is used to name objects of a class. Both static variables and instance variables are sometimes called **fields** or **data members**.

RECAP Static, or Class, Variables

The declaration of a static variable contains the keyword static. A static variable is shared by all the objects of its class.

REMEMBER Three Kinds of Variables

Java has three kinds of variables: local variables, instance variables, and static (class) variables.

Static Methods

Sometimes you need a method that has no relation to an object of any kind. For example, you might need a method to compute the maximum of two integers, or a method to compute the square root of a number, or a method to convert a letter character from lowercase to uppercase. None of these methods

LISTING 6.5   Static Methods

```
/**
 Class of static methods to perform dimension conversions.
 */
public class DimensionConverter
{
    public static final int INCHES_PER_FOOT = 12;

    public static double convertFeetToInches(double feet)
    {
        return feet * INCHES_PER_FOOT;
    }

    public static double convertInchesToFeet(double inches)
    {
        return inches / INCHES_PER_FOOT;
    }
}
```

A static constant; it could be private here.

has any obvious object to which it should belong. In these cases, you can define the method as static. When you define a **static method**, the method is still a member of a class, since you define it in a class, but the method can be invoked without using any object. You normally invoke a static method by using the class name instead of an object name.

Invoke a static method using the class name, not an object name

For example, Listing 6.5 contains a class named `DimensionConverter`, which defines two static methods for converting between measurements in feet and measurements in inches. You define a static method in the same way that you would define any other method, but you add the keyword `static` to the method's heading.

The following examples show how these methods are called:

```
double feet = DimensionConverter.convertInchesToFeet(53.7);
double inches = DimensionConverter.convertFeetToInches(2.6);
```

Calling a static method

When you call a static method, you write the class name instead of an object name. Listing 6.6 shows these methods in use in a complete program. Although you could create an object of the class `DimensionConverter` and use it to invoke either static method in the class, doing so can be confusing to programmers reading your code.

REMEMBER A Class of Static Methods

You can create a collection of static methods to perform computations that are somehow related and group them within a single class.

LISTING 6.6   Using Static Methods

```java
import java.util.Scanner;
/**
 Demonstration of using the class DimensionConverter.
*/
public class DimensionConverterDemo
{
    public static void main(String[] args)
    {
        Scanner keyboard = new Scanner(System.in);
        System.out.println("Enter a measurement in inches: ");
        double inches = keyboard.nextDouble();
        double feet =
                DimensionConverter.convertInchesToFeet(inches);
        System.out.println(inches + " inches = " +
                                feet + " feet.");

        System.out.print("Enter a measurement in feet: ");
        feet = keyboard.nextDouble();
        inches = DimensionConverter.convertFeetToInches(feet);
        System.out.println(feet + " feet = " +
                                inches + " inches.");
    }
}
```

Sample Screen Output

```
Enter a measurement in inches: 18
18.0 inches = 1.5 feet.
Enter a measurement in feet: 1.5
1.5 feet = 18.0 inches.
```

In the class DimensionConverter in Listing 6.5, both the named constant and the two methods are static and public. (We could have declared the named constant INCHES_PER_FOOT as private if we did not want it to be accessible outside of this class.) Although this class declares no instance variables, a class can have instance variables, static variables, static constants, static methods, and non-static methods. While such a combination is possible, you do need to be a bit careful.

Let's study the interaction among various static and non-static members of a class by examining the class SavingsAccount in Listing 6.7. This class maintains the balance of individual savings accounts, and so it declares an instance variable balance. All accounts can earn the same rate of interest, so the class has a static variable interestRate. The class also counts the number of accounts opened by using the static variable numberOfAccounts.

LISTING 6.7   Mixing Static and Non-static Members in a Class *(part 1 of 2)*

```java
import java.util.Scanner;
/**
 Class with static and nonstatic members.
*/
public class SavingsAccount
{
    private double balance;              ← An instance variable (nonstatic)
    public static double interestRate = 0;   ← Static variables
    public static int numberOfAccounts = 0;
    public SavingsAccount()
    {
        balance = 0;
        numberOfAccounts++;              ← A nonstatic method can reference a static variable.
    }

    public static void setInterestRate(double newRate)
    {
        interestRate = newRate;          ← A static method can reference a static variable but not an instance variable.
    }

    public static double getInterestRate()
    {
        return interestRate;
    }

    public static int getNumberOfAccounts()
    {
        return numberOfAccounts;
    }

    public void deposit(double amount)
    {
        balance = balance + amount;
    }

    public double withdraw(double amount)
    {
        if (balance >= amount)
            balance = balance - amount;
        else
            amount = 0;
        return amount;
    }
```

(continued)

LISTING 6.7 Mixing Static and Non-static Members in a Class *(part 2 of 2)*

```
public void addInterest()
{
    double interest = balance * interestRate;
    // you can replace interestRate with getInterestRate()
    balance = balance + interest;
}

public double getBalance()
{
    return balance;
}

public static void showBalance(SavingsAccount account)
{
    System.out.print(account.getBalance());
}
}
```

A nonstatic method can reference a static variable or call a static method.

A static method cannot call a nonstatic method unless it has an object to do so.

The class has static set and get methods for the interest rate, a static get method for the number of accounts, and non-static methods for making deposits, making withdrawals, adding interest, and getting an account balance. Lastly, the class has a static method that displays the balance of any given savings account.

A static method cannot reference an instance variable

Within the definition of a static method, you cannot reference an instance variable. Because a static method can be invoked without using any object name, there is no instance variable to refer to. For example, the static method `setInterestRate` can reference the static variable `interestRate` but not the instance variable `balance`, which is not static.

A static method can call only a static method

main is a static method

A static method—and remember that `main` is a static method—cannot call a non-static without having an instance of a class to use in the invocation. For example, the static method `showBalance` has an object of `SavingsAccount` as its parameter. It uses this object to invoke the non-static method `getBalance`. The only way `showBalance` can get data for the balance of an account is from an object that represents that account.

A non-static method can reference any variable or call any method within its class

The non-static `addInterest` can reference the static variable `interestRate` or call the static method `getInterestRate`. Preceding the method name in the invocation of `getInterestRate` with the name of the class and a dot is optional, since the methods are all within `SavingsAccount`. Notice that the constructor also is not static. It increments the static variable `numberOfAccounts` to count the number of times it is called, thus counting the number of new account objects.

Listing 6.8 shows a sample program that demonstrates the class `SavingsAccount`. Because we use a `double` variable to represent an account's balance, one of the dollar amounts shown in the screen output isn't as neat as it could be. Somewhat later in this chapter, we will present one remedy for this situation.

LISTING 6.8 Using Static and Non-static Methods

```java
public class SavingsAccountDemo
{
    public static void main(String[] args)
    {
        SavingsAccount.setInterestRate(0.01);
        SavingsAccount mySavings = new SavingsAccount( );
        SavingsAccount yourSavings = new SavingsAccount( );
        System.out.println("I deposited $10.75.");
        mySavings.deposit(10.75);
        System.out.println("You deposited $75.");
        yourSavings.deposit(75.00);
        System.out.println("You deposited $55.");
        yourSavings.deposit(55.00);
        double cash = yourSavings.withdraw(15.75);
        System.out.println("You withdrew $" + cash + ".");
        if (yourSavings.getBalance() > 100.00)
        {
            System.out.println("You received interest.");
            yourSavings.addInterest();
        }
        System.out.println("Your savings is $" +
                            yourSavings.getBalance());
        System.out.print("My savings is $");
        SavingsAccount.showBalance(mySavings);
        System.out.println();
        int count = SavingsAccount.getNumberOfAccounts();
        System.out.println("We opened " + count +
                            " savings accounts today.");
    }
}
```

Screen Output

```
I deposited $10.75.
You deposited $75.
You deposited $55.
You withdrew $15.75.
You received interest.
Your savings is $115.3925
My savings is $10.75
We opened 2 savings accounts today.
```

GOTCHA Invoking a Non-static Method from Within a Static Method

You will often hear people say, "You cannot invoke a non-static method within the definition of a static method." This is not quite true, however. A more precise, and correct, statement is, "You cannot invoke a non-static method within a static method *unless you have an object to use in the call of the non-static method.*" Put another way, in the definition of a static method—such as main—you cannot use an instance variable or method that has an implicit or explicit this as its calling object. Since a static method can be invoked without any calling object, it can be invoked when there is no meaning for this. To paraphrase Gertrude Stein, in a static method, "there is no this there." ■

RECAP Static Methods

If you place the keyword static in the heading of the definition of a method, the method can be invoked using the class name in place of an object name. Since it does not need an object in its invocation, a static method cannot reference an instance variable of the class. It also cannot invoke a non-static method of the class, unless it has an object of the class and uses this object in the invocation. In other words, the definition of a static method cannot use an instance variable or a non-static method that has an implicit or explicit this as its calling object.

VideoNote
Using static and non-static methods

SELF-TEST QUESTIONS

6. What is the difference between a static variable and an instance variable?

7. Can a class contain both instance variables and static methods?

8. Can you reference a static variable by name within the definition of a static method without using a class name and a dot?

9. Can you reference an instance variable by name within the definition of a static method without using a class name or an object name and a dot?

10. Can you reference a static variable by name within the definition of a non-static method without using a class name and a dot?

11. Can you reference an instance variable by name within the definition of a non-static method without using a class name or an object name and a dot?

12. Is the following valid, given the class `DimensionConverter` in Listing 6.5?

    ```
    DimensionConverter dc = new DimensionConverter();
    double inches = dc.convertFeetToInches(2.5);
    ```

13. Can a class contain both static and non-static methods?

14. Can you invoke a non-static method within a static method?

15. Can you invoke a static method within a non-static method?

16. Is the following valid, given the class `SavingsAccount` in Listing 6.7?

    ```
    SavingsAccount.addInterest();
    ```

Dividing the Task of a `main` Method into Subtasks

When a program's logic is involved or its code is repetitive, you can create static methods to accomplish various subtasks and invoke these methods from your `main` method. Recall from the previous chapter the program in Listing 5.18 that we used to test the `equals` methods in the class `Species`. Listing 6.9 reproduces that program here. We have highlighted two sections of code that are identical. Rather than repeat this code, we could place it into a static method and invoke it twice within the `main` method. We have made this revision in Listing 6.10 and have also created an additional method from the code within the unfilled colored rectangle in Listing 6.9. Our two new helping methods are static as well as private.

The method `main` can invoke other static methods

■ PROGRAMMING TIP   Helping Methods for a `main` Method

Simplify the logic of a `main` method within an application program by having it call helping methods. These methods should be static, since `main` is static. As helping methods, they likely should be private as well.   ■

REMEMBER `main` Is a Static Method

Since the method `main` is static, you must adhere to the points made in the previous section about static methods. Generally, a static method can invoke only static methods and reference only static variables. It cannot invoke a non-static method of the same class unless you have an object of the class to use in the invocation.

LISTING 6.9   A `main` **Method with Repetitive Code**

```
public class SpeciesEqualsDemo
{
    public static void main(String[] args)
    {
        Species s1 = new Species(), s2 = new Species();

        s1.setSpecies("Klingon Ox", 10, 15);
        s2.setSpecies("Klingon Ox", 10, 15);

        if (s1 == s2)
            System.out.println("Match with ==.");
        else
            System.out.println("Do Not match with ==.");

        if (s1.equals(s2))
            System.out.println("Match with the method equals.");
        else
            System.out.println("Do Not match with the method "+
                                "equals.");

        System.out.println("Now change one Klingon Ox to "+
                            "lowercase.");
        s2.setSpecies("klingon ox", 10, 15); //Use lowercase

        if (s1.equals(s2))
            System.out.println("Match with the method equals.");
        else
            System.out.println("Do Not match with the method "+
                                "equals.");
    }
}
```

Adding a `main` Method to a Class

So far, whenever we have written a `main` method, it was by itself in its own class definition within a separate file. However, sometimes it makes sense to have a `main` method within a class definition. The class can then be used for two purposes: It can be used to create objects in other classes, or it can be run as a program. For example, you can write a `main` method inside the definition of the class `Species`, which is given in Listing 5.19 of the previous chapter. The result is shown in Listing 6.11.

After redefining the class `Species` in this way, running it as a program causes the `main` method to be invoked. When `Species` is used as an ordinary class to create objects, the `main` method is ignored.

Since a `main` method is static, it cannot contain an invocation of a non-static method of the same class unless it has an object of the class and uses it in the invocation of the non-static method. The `main` method in Listing 6.11

Any class can have a main method

LISTING 6.10   A `main` **Method That Uses Helping Methods**

```
public class SpeciesEqualsDemo
{
    public static void main(String[] args)
    {
        Species s1 = new Species(), s2 = new Species();

        s1.setSpecies("Klingon Ox", 10, 15);
        s2.setSpecies("Klingon Ox", 10, 15);
        testEqualsOperator(s1, s2);
        testEqualsMethod(s1, s2);

        System.out.println("Now change one Klingon Ox to "+
                           "lowercase.");
        s2.setSpecies("klingon ox", 10, 15); //Use lowercase

        testEqualsMethod(s1, s2);
    }

    private static void testEqualsOperator(Species s1, Species s2)
    {
        if (s1 == s2)
            System.out.println("Match with ==.");
        else
            System.out.println("Do Not match with ==.");
    }

    private static void testEqualsMethod(Species s1, Species s2)
    {
        if (s1.equals(s2))
            System.out.println("Match with the method equals.");
        else
            System.out.println("Do Not match with the method "+
                               "equals.");
    }
}
```

On the Web, this class is `SpeciesEqualsDemo2`.

invokes the methods of the class `Species` by first creating an object of the class `Species` and then using it to invoke other methods. Doing so is necessary even though the `main` method is inside the definition of the class `Species`.

■ PROGRAMMING TIP   Add a `main` Method to a Class to Test It

You should not place just any `main` method in a class definition that is to be used as a regular class to create objects. However, placing a small diagnostic `main` method inside of your class definition provides a handy way to test it. Doing so also alerts other programmers about the tests you have done. We talk more about testing later in this chapter.   ■

LISTING 6.11   Placing a `main` Method in a Class Definition

```java
import java.util.Scanner;
public class Species
{
    private String name;
    private int population;
    private double growthRate;
```

<The methods readInput, writeOutput, predictPopulation, set-Species, getName, getPopulation, getGrowthRate, and equals go here. They are the same as in Listing 5.19.>

```java
    public static void main(String[] args)
    {
        Species speciesToday = new Species( );
        System.out.println("Enter data on today's species:");
        speciesToday.readInput( );
        speciesToday.writeOutput( );

        System.out.println("Enter number of years to project:");
        Scanner keyboard = new Scanner(System.in);
        int numberOfYears = keyboard.nextInt( );
        int futurePopulation =
                    speciesToday.predictPopulation(numberOfYears);
        System.out.println("In " + numberOfYears +
                            " years the population will be " +
                            futurePopulation);
        speciesToday.setSpecies("Klingon ox", 10, 15);
        System.out.println("The new species is:");
        speciesToday.writeOutput( );
    }
}
```

The Math Class

The class Math contains a collection of mathematical methods and constants

The predefined class Math provides you with a number of standard mathematical methods. This class is automatically provided when you use the Java language; no import statement is needed. Some of the methods in the class Math are described in Figure 6.3. All of these methods are static, which means that you do not need—and in fact have no real use for—an object of the class Math. You normally call these methods by using the class name, Math, in place of an object name. For example, the following displays the maximum of the two numbers 2 and 3.

```java
int ans = Math.max(2, 3);
System.out.println(ans);
```

You could also omit the variable ans and simply write

```
System.out.println(Math.max(2, 3));
```

The class Math also defines two named constants, PI and E. The constant PI—often written as π in mathematical formulas—is used in calculations involving circles, spheres, and other geometric figures based on circles. PI is approximately 3.14159. The constant E is the base of the natural logarithm system—often written e in mathematical formulas. E is approximately 2.71828. The constants PI and E are static, so you reference them as Math.PI and Math.E. For example, the following computes the area of a circle, given its radius:

```
area = Math.PI * radius * radius;
```

You should use the constants Math.PI and Math.E in the definition of your classes instead of defining your own versions.

If you look at the methods in the table in Figure 6.3, you will find three similar, but not identical, methods named round, floor, and ceil. Some of these return a value of type double, but they all return a value that is intuitively a whole number that is close to the value of their arguments. The method round rounds a number to the nearest whole number. If the argument is a double, the method returns a value of type long. If you want that whole number as a value of type int, you must use a type cast, as in the following:[1]

```
double start = 3.56;
int answer = (int)Math.round(start);
```

Here, answer is assigned the value 4.

The methods floor and ceil are similar to round, with slight differences. They both return a whole number as a value of type double, not of type int or long, that is close to their argument. The method floor returns the nearest whole number that is less than or equal to its argument. This action is called **rounding down.** So Math.floor(3.9) returns 3.0, not 4.0. Math.floor(3.3) also returns 3.0.

The method ceil—short for *ceiling*—returns the nearest whole number that is greater than or equal to its argument. This action is called **rounding up.** So Math.ceil(3.1) returns 4.0, not 3.0. Of course, Math.ceil(3.9) also returns 4.0.

If you want to store the value returned by either floor or ceil in a variable of type int, you must use a type cast, as in the following example:

```
double start = 3.56;
int lowAnswer = (int)Math.floor(start)
int highAnswer = (int)Math.ceil(start);
```

In this example, Math.floor(start) returns the double value 3.0, and the variable lowAnswer receives the int value 3. Math.ceil(start) returns the double value 4.0, and the variable highAnswer receives the int value 4.

---

[1] You cannot store a long value in a variable of type int, even if it is a small value like 4 that would fit in an int variable.

FIGURE 6.3   Static Methods in the Class Math

Name	Description	Argument Type	Return Type	Example	Value Returned
pow	Power	double	double	Math.pow(2.0,3.0)	8.0
abs	Absolute value	int, long, float, or double	Same as the type of the argument	Math.abs(-7) Math.abs(7) Math.abs(-3.5)	7 7 3.5
max	Maximum	int, long, float, or double	Same as the type of the arguments	Math.max(5, 6) Math.max(5.5, 5.3)	6 5.5
min	Minimum	int, long, float, or double	Same as the type of the arguments	Math.min(5, 6) Math.min(5.5, 5.3)	5 5.3
random	Random number	none	double	Math.random()	Random number in the range ≥ 0 and < 1
round	Rounding	float or double	int or long, respectively	Math.round(6.2) Math.round(6.8)	6 7
ceil	Ceiling	double	double	Math.ceil(3.2) Math.ceil(3.9)	4.0 4.0
floor	Floor	double	double	Math.floor(3.2) Math.floor(3.9)	3.0 3.0
sqrt	Square root	double	double	Math.sqrt(4.0)	2.0

Finally, the method random returns a random double that is ≥ 0 and < 1. Often a number between 0 and 1 is not what is desired, in which case the random number can be scaled to the desired range by multiplication and addition. If an integer is desired, then type casting is necessary. For example, to simulate rolling a six-sided die, we could use the following:

```
int die = (int)(6.0 * Math.random()) + 1;
```

Multiplying the random number by 6.0 gives us a value in the range ≥ 0 and < 6.0. Type casting this to an `int` truncates the result, which is an integer that is 0, 1, 2, 3, 4, or 5. Adding 1 results in a random integer that is in the range 1–6.

SELF-TEST QUESTIONS

17. What values are returned by each of the following?

    a. `Math.round(2.3)`
    b. `Math.round(2.7)`
    c. `Math.floor(2.3)`
    d. `Math.floor(2.7)`
    e. `Math.ceil(2.3)`
    f. `Math.ceil(2.7)`
    g. `(int) (Math.random() * 10.0) + 10;`

18. Suppose that `speed` is a variable of type `double` and you want to assign `Math.round(speed)` to the variable `approxSpeed`, which is of type `int`. How do you write the assignment statement?

19. Repeat the previous question, but instead assign `Math.round(speed)` to the variable `longSpeed`, which is of type `long`.

20. Suppose that `n1` is of type `int` and `n2` is of type `long`. What is the type of the value returned by `Math.min(n1, n2)`?

21. Define a class `CircleCalculator` that has only two methods, `getArea` and `getCircumference`. These methods return the area and circumference, respectively, of a circle, given its radius. Both methods are static. Do not define your own value for pi.

Wrapper Classes

Java makes a distinction between the primitive types, such as `int`, `double`, and `char`, and the class types, such as the class `String` and the programmer-defined classes. For example, you saw in Chapter 5 that an argument to a method is treated differently, depending on whether the argument is of a primitive type or a class type. If a method needs an argument of a class type, but we have a value of a primitive type, we need to convert the primitive value—such as the `int` value 42—to an "equivalent" value of some class type that corresponds to the primitive type `int`. To make this conversion, Java provides a **wrapper class** for each of the primitive types. Such classes define methods that can act on values of a primitive type.

For example, the wrapper class for the primitive type `int` is the predefined class `Integer`. If you want to convert an `int` value, such as 42, to an object of type `Integer`, you can do so as follows:

Integer is a wrapper class for the primitive type int

```
Integer n = new Integer(42);
```

After the preceding executes, `n` names an object of the class `Integer` that corresponds to the `int` value 42. In fact, the object `n` has an instance variable containing the `int` value 42. Conversely, the following statement converts an object of type `Integer` to an `int` value:

```
int i = n.intValue();//n names an object of the class Integer.
```

The method `intValue` recovers the equivalent `int` value from an object of type `Integer`.

Other wrapper classes

The wrapper classes for the primitive types `long`, `float`, `double`, and `char` are `Long`, `Float`, `Double`, and `Character`, respectively. And, of course, rather than the method `intValue`, the classes `Long`, `Float`, `Double`, and `Character` use the methods `longValue`, `floatValue`, `doubleValue`, and `charValue`, respectively.

The conversion from a primitive type, such as `int`, to its corresponding wrapper class, such as `Integer`, is done automatically in Java. This type casting is called **boxing**. You can think of the object as a "box" into which you place the value of the primitive type as the value of a private instance variable. So the statements

Boxing converts from a primitive type to a wrapper class

```
Integer n = new Integer(42);
Double d = new Double(9.99);
Character c = new Character('Z');
```

can be written in the simpler form:

Boxing examples

```
Integer n = 42;
Double d = 9.99;
Character c = 'Z';
```

These simple-looking assignments are really just abbreviations for the longer versions that include the `new` operator. The situation is analogous to what happens when a value of type `int` is assigned to a variable of type `double`; a type cast is made automatically.

The reverse conversion from an object of a wrapper class to a value of its associated primitive type is called **unboxing**. Unboxing is also done automatically. So if `n` is an object of the class `Integer`, for example, the statement

Unboxing converts from a wrapper class to a primitive type

```
int i = n.intValue();//n names an object of the class Integer.
```

can be written in the abbreviated form

```
int i = n;//n names an object of the class Integer.
```

The following are also examples of automatic unboxing:

```
int i = new Integer(42);
double f = new Double(9.99);
char s = new Character('Z');
```

Unboxing
examples

What really takes place is that Java automatically applies the appropriate accessor method—intValue, doubleValue, or charValue in these examples— to obtain the value of the primitive type that is assigned to the variable.

Automatic boxing and unboxing applies to parameters as well as to the simple assignment statements we just discussed. You can plug in a value of a primitive type, such as a value of type int, for a parameter of the associated wrapper class, such as Integer. Similarly, you can plug in a wrapper class argument, such as an argument of type Integer, for a parameter of the associated primitive type, such as int.

At this point, the main importance of these wrapper classes is that they contain a number of useful constants and static methods. For example, you can use the associated wrapper class to find the largest and smallest values of any of the primitive number types. The largest and smallest values of type int are

Constants in
wrapper classes

```
Integer.MAX_VALUE and Integer.MIN_VALUE
```

Largest and
smallest values

The largest and smallest values of type double are

```
Double.MAX_VALUE and Double.MIN_VALUE
```

MAX_VALUE and MIN_VALUE are defined as static named constants in each of the wrapper classes Integer, Long, Float, Double, and Character. For example, the class Integer defines MAX_VALUE as

```
public static final int MAX_VALUE = 2147483647;
```

Static methods in the wrapper classes can be used to convert a string to the corresponding number of type int, double, long, or float. For example, the static method parse Double of the wrapper class Double will convert a string to a value of type double. So

```
Double.parseDouble("199.98")
```

Methods in
wrapper classes

returns the double value 199.98. Of course, you knew this by simply looking at the statement, and so it hardly seems worth all this effort. But the same technique can be used to change the value of a string variable. For example, suppose theString is a variable of type String whose value is the string representation of a number of type double. The following will return the double value corresponding to the string value of theString:

```
Double.parseDouble(theString)
```

If there is any possibility that the string named by `theString` has extra leading or trailing blanks, you should instead use

```
Double.parseDouble(theString.trim())
```

The method `trim` is in the class `String` and trims off leading and trailing whitespace, such as blanks. It is always safest to use `trim` when invoking a method like `parseDouble`. You never know when leading or trailing blanks might appear. If the string is not a correctly formed number, the invocation of `Double.parseDouble` will cause your program to end. The use of `trim` helps avoid this problem.

This conversion of a string to a number can be done with any of the wrapper classes `Integer`, `Long`, and `Float`, as well as with the wrapper class `Double`. Just use one of the static methods `Integer.parseInt`, `Long.parseLong`, or `Float.parseFloat` instead of `Double.parseDouble`.

Each of the numeric wrapper classes also has a static method called `toString` that will convert in the other direction—that is, it converts from a numeric value to a string representation of the numeric value. For example,

```
Integer.toString(42)
```

returns the string value `"42"`. And

```
Double.toString(199.98)
```

returns the string value `"199.98"`.

Character is the wrapper class for the type char

`Character` is the wrapper class for the primitive type `char`. The following piece of code illustrates some of the basic methods for this class:

```
Character c1 = new Character('a');
Character c2 = new Character('A');
if (c1.equals(c2))
    System.out.println(c1.charValue() + " is the same as " +
                                    c2.charValue());
else
    System.out.println(c1.charValue() + "is not the same as" +
                                    c2.charValue());
```

This code displays

```
a is not the same as A
```

The `equals` method checks for equality of characters, so uppercase and lowercase letters are considered different.

The class `Character` also has other useful static methods. Some of these methods, which convert between uppercase and lowercase letters or test whether a character is a letter or a digit, are listed in Figure 6.4.

We will not use the wrapper class Boolean

Java also has a wrapper class `Boolean`. It has names for the two constants of type `boolean`: `Boolean.TRUE` and `Boolean.FALSE`. However, the Java keywords `true` and `false` are much easier to use.

FIGURE 6.4 **Static Methods in the Class** Character

Name	Description	Argument Type	Return Type	Examples	Return Value
toUpperCase	Convert to uppercase	char	char	Character.toUpperCase('a') Character.toUpperCase('A')	'A' 'A'
toLowerCase	Convert to lowercase	char	char	Character.toLowerCase('a') Character.toLowerCase('A')	'a' 'a'
isUpperCase	Test for uppercase	char	boolean	Character.isUpperCase('A') Character.isUpperCase('a')	true false
isLowerCase	Test for lowercase	char	boolean	Character.isLowerCase('A') Character.isLowerCase('a')	true false
isLetter	Test for a letter	char	boolean	Character.isLetter('A') Character.isLetter('%')	true false
isDigit	Test for a digit	char	boolean	Character.isDigit('5') Character.isDigit('A')	true false
isWhitespace	Test for whitespace	char	boolean	Character.isWhitespace(' ') Character.isWhitespace('A')	true false

Whitespace characters are those that print as white space, such as the blank, the tab character ('\t'), and the line-break character ('\n').

RECAP **Wrapper Classes**

Every primitive type has a wrapper class. Wrapper classes allow you to have a class object that corresponds to a value of a primitive type. Wrapper classes also contain a number of useful predefined constants and methods. Thus, each wrapper class has two related but distinct uses.

For example, you can create objects of the wrapper class Integer that correspond to values of type int, as in

```
Integer n = new Integer(42);
```

The wrapper class Integer also serves as a library of useful static methods, such as the method parseInt, as in

(continued)

```
String numeralString;
  ...
int number = Integer.parseInt(numeralString);
```

Any one program can use both personalities of a wrapper class.

GOTCHA   Wrapper Classes Have No Default Constructor

The wrapper classes Boolean, Byte, Character, Double, Float, Integer, Long, and Short have no default constructors. Thus, a statement such as

```
Integer n = new Integer();//Invalid!
```

is incorrect. When you create a new object of one of these classes, you must provide an initializing value as an argument to the constructor, as in the following example:

```
Character myMark = new Character('Z');
```

Wrapper classes do not have set methods, so you cannot change the value of existing objects of these classes. The designers, therefore, decided not to allow the creation of objects that have default values, and so they did not define default constructors. ■

SELF-TEST QUESTIONS

22. Which of the following statements are legal?

```
Integer n = new Integer(77);
int m = 77;
n = m;
m = n;
```

   If any are illegal, tell how to write a valid Java statement that does what the illegal statement is trying to do.

23. Write a Java expression to convert the number in the double variable x to a string.

24. Consider the variable s of type String that contains a string, such as "123", that is the normal way of writing some integer. Write a Java expression to convert the string in s to the corresponding value of type int.

25. Repeat the previous question, but accommodate a string that might contain leading or trailing blanks, such as "123".

26. Write Java code to display the largest and smallest values of type double that you can have in Java.

6.3 WRITING METHODS

It is common sense to take a method and try it. If it fails, admit it frankly and try another. But above all, try something.

—FRANKLIN DELANO ROOSEVELT, ADDRESS AT OGLETHORPE UNIVERSITY
(MAY 22, 1932)

In this section we discuss some basic techniques that will help you to design, code, and test methods. We start with a case study.

CASE STUDY Formatting Output

If you have a variable of type `double` that stores some amount of money, your programs should display the amount in a nice format. However, you are likely to get output that looks like this:

```
Your cost, including tax, is $19.98123576432
```

Instead, we would like the output to look like this:

```
Your cost, including tax, is $19.98
```

In this case study, we will define a class called `DollarFormat` containing two static methods named `write` and `writeln` that can be used to produce this kind of nicely formatted output.[2] For example, if the amount of money is in a variable of type `double` named `amount`, we could write the following to get such output:

Task specification

```
System.out.print("Your cost, including tax, is ");
DollarFormat.writeln(amount);
```

Note that `write` and `writeln` should add the dollar sign for you and should always display exactly two digits after the decimal point. So these methods would display $2.10, not $2.1.

When the amount has more than two digits after the decimal point, we must decide what to do with the extra digits. Suppose we decide to round the number. Then if the amount is 9.128, for example, we would get an output of $9.13.

The difference between `write` and `writeln` will be the same as the difference between `print` and `println`. After writing its output, `write` does not advance to the next line, but `writeln` does. So the method `writeln` can simply call `write` and then use `println` to go the next line.

---

[2] In addition to the `printf` method, Java has other classes that allow you to output numbers in any format that you wish. However, using these classes can get quite involved. It will be instructive, and perhaps even easier, to program the details ourselves. If you want to know more about such formatting classes, look at Appendix 4, which has a brief discussion of the class `DecimalFormat`.

Pseudocode
for the write
method

Now that we know what we want these methods to do, how do we implement them? To display an amount like 9.87, we have little choice but to break it into the pieces 9 and 87 and then display each piece separately. The following pseudocode outlines what the method write must do:

Algorithm to display a *double* amount as dollars and cents
(The variable amount contains the amount to be displayed.)

1. dollars = the number of whole dollars in amount.

2. cents = the number of cents in amount. Round if there are more than two digits after the decimal point.

3. Display a dollar sign, dollars, and a decimal point.

4. Display cents as a two-digit integer.

We now need to convert our pseudocode to Java code. Let's assume that the variable amount already contains a double value. To obtain the number of whole dollars and the number of cents as two int values, we need to somehow get rid of the decimal point. One way to do this is to convert the amount to all cents. For example, to convert 10.95 dollars to all cents, we multiply by 100 to obtain 1095.0. If there is a fraction of a penny, such as when converting 10.9567 dollars to 1095.67 cents, we can use the round method: Math.round(1095.67) returns 1096 as a value of type long.

Note that we will want to store the result of this rounding in an int variable for holding the total amount expressed as all cents. However, Math.round returns a value of type long, and you cannot store a value of type long in a variable of type int, even if it is a small integer. So you need to perform a type cast to convert this long value to an int value as follows:

    (int)(Math.round(1095.67))

This returns 1096 as an int value. Thus, our code will begin with something like

    int allCents = (int)(Math.round(amount * 100));

Now we need to convert allCents to a dollar amount and a cents amount. For example, since 1096 cents is $10.96, we need to convert 1096 to the integers 10 and 96. Since a dollar is 100 cents, we can use integer division to obtain the number of dollars:

    int dollars = allCents / 100;

The amount left over after this division is the number of cents, so we can use the % operator to obtain it:

    int cents = allCents % 100;

Thus, we have translated the first two steps of our pseudocode into the following Java code:

```java
int allCents = (int)(Math.round(amount * 100));
int dollars = allCents / 100;
int cents = allCents % 100;
```

The third step in our pseudocode, when expressed in Java, is simply

```java
System.out.print('$');
System.out.print(dollars);
System.out.print(.);
```

All that is left to do is to translate the last pseudocode instruction,

```
Display cents as a two-digit integer.
```

into Java code. This looks easy. Suppose we try the following:

```java
System.out.println(cents);
```

Testing our code with amount equal to 10.9567 would result in the output   Early testing

```
$10.96
```

which looks pretty good. (By the way, a simple assignment statement to initialize amount provides a quick way to test our initial code.) When we try some more examples, however, we run into a problem. For example, if amount is 7.05, we get

```
$7.5
```

instead of

```
$7.05
```

This quick test makes us realize that we need to display a zero before the number of cents whenever it is less than 10. The following statement will fix the problem:

```java
if (cents < 10)
{
    System.out.print(0);
    System.out.print(cents);
}
else
    System.out.print(cents);
```

Listing 6.12 shows our class. Now that we have a complete definition of the class, it is time for some serious testing. Listing 6.13 shows a program that tests the method write. These sorts of programs are often called **driver programs,** or simply **drivers,** because they do nothing but exercise, or "drive," the method. Any method can be tested in a program like this.   Use a driver program to test a class

LISTING 6.12 The Class DollarFormatFirstTry

```java
public class DollarFormatFirstTry
{
    /**
     Displays amount in dollars and cents notation.
     Rounds after two decimal places.
     Does not advance to the next line after output.
    */
    public static void write(double amount)
    {
        int allCents = (int)(Math.round(amount * 100));
        int dollars = allCents / 100;
        int cents = allCents % 100;

        System.out.print('$');
        System.out.print(dollars);
        System.out.print('.');

        if (cents < 10)
        {
            System.out.print('0');
            System.out.print(cents);
        }
        else
            System.out.print(cents);
    }
    /**
     Displays amount in dollars and cents notation.
     Rounds after two decimal places.
     Advances to the next line after output.
    */
    public static void writeln(double amount)
    {
        write(amount);
        System.out.println();
    }
}
```

The testing goes quite well until we decide to try a negative number. After all, a negative amount of money is feasible; it's called a debt. But the amount −1.20 produces the output $−1.0 − 20. Something is wrong with the way our method handles negative amounts.

Examining our calculation when amount is negative indicates that both dollars and cents will contain negative numbers. A negative value in dollars is correct, and we display $−1 for our test case. But now we need to display 20, not −20. We could fix this mistake in a number of ways, but here is a clean and simple one. Since our code works correctly for nonnegative

LISTING 6.13 **A Driver That Tests** `DollarFormatFirstTry`

```java
import java.util.Scanner;
public class DollarFormatFirstTryDriver
{
    public static void main(String[] args)
    {
        double amount;
        String response;
        Scanner keyboard = new Scanner(System.in);

        System.out.println(
                    "Testing DollarFormatFirstTry.write:");
        do
        {
            System.out.println("Enter a value of type double:")
            amount = keyboard.nextDouble();
            DollarFormatFirstTry.write(amount);
            System.out.println();
            System.out.println("Test again?");
            response = keyboard.next();
        } while (response.equalsIgnoreCase("yes"));
        System.out.println("End of test.");
    }
}
```

This kind of testing program is often called a driver program.

Sample Screen Output

```
Testing DollarFormatFirstTry.write:
Enter a value of type double:
1.2345
$1.23
Test again?
yes
Enter a value of type double:
1.235
$1.24
Test again?
yes
Enter a value of type double:
9.02
$9.02
Test again?
yes
Enter a value of type double:
-1.20
$-1.0-20          ◄——————  Oops. There's
Test again?                 a problem here.
no
```

numbers, we can convert any negative number to a positive number. We then display the minus sign followed by the positive number.

The revised version of our class is shown in Listing 6.14. Notice that the new method `writePositive` is almost the same as the old method `write`. The only difference is that `writePositive` does not display the dollar sign; a new version of the method `write` does that.

LISTING 6.14 **The Corrected Class** DollarFormat *(part 1 of 2)*

```java
public class DollarFormat
{
    /**
     Displays amount in dollars and cents notation.
     Rounds after two decimal places.
     Does not advance to the next line after output.
    */
    public static void write(double amount)
    {
        if (amount >= 0)
        {
            System.out.print('$');
            writePositive(amount);
        }
        else
        {
            double positiveAmount = amount;          The case for negative
            System.out.print('$');                   amounts of money
            System.out.print('-');
            writePositive(positiveAmount);
        }
    }

    //Precondition: amount >= 0;
    //Displays amount in dollars and cents notation. Rounds
    //after two decimal places. Omits the dollar sign.
    private static void writePositive(double amount)
    {
        int allCents = (int)(Math.round(amount * 100));
        int dollars = allCents / 100;
        int cents = allCents % 100;

        System.out.print(dollars);
        System.out.print('.');

        if (cents < 10)                              We have simplified this logic,
            System.out.print('0');                   but it is equivalent to that used
        System.out.print(cents);                     in Listing 6.12.
    }
```

(continued)

LISTING 6.14   **The Corrected Class** `DollarFormat` *(part 2 of 2)*

```java
    /**
     Displays amount in dollars and cents notation.
     Rounds after two decimal places.
     Advances to the next line after output.
    */
    public static void writeln(double amount)
    {
        write(amount);
        System.out.println();
    }
}
```

DollarFormatDriver.java *in the source code on the Web is a testing and demonstration program for this class.*

Testing the class `DollarFormat` with a program similar to the one we used to test `DollarFormatFirstTry` is successful. Such a driver program is in the file `DollarFormatDriver.java` included with the source code for this book that is available on the Web.

Extra code on the Web

■ PROGRAMMING TIP   Retest

Every time you change the definition of a class or method, you should test it.

■

Decomposition

In the previous case study, we used the following pseudocode for our first attempt to design a method that displays a `double` number that represents a monetary value:

1. `dollars` = the number of whole dollars in `amount`.
2. `cents` = the number of cents in `amount`. Round if there are more than two digits after the decimal point.
3. Display a dollar sign, `dollars`, and a decimal point.
4. Display `cents` as a two-digit integer.

What we have done with this pseudocode is to **decompose** the task for displaying an amount of money into a number of subtasks. For example, the first step of our pseudocode is shorthand for the task

Decompose a task into subtasks

```
Calculate the number of whole dollars in amount and store it
in an int variable called dollars.
```

We then solved each of these subtasks separately and produced code for each subtask. After that, all we had to do to produce the final definition of the method was to combine the code for the subtasks.

As it turned out, we ended up using the code derived from the preceding pseudocode for the method `writePositive` rather than for the method `write`. But this was just a further illustration of using subtasks. The method `writePositive` solved a subtask that we used in the final definition of the method `write`.

Often, though not always, the solutions to subtasks are implemented as private helping methods. If a subtask is large, you divide it into smaller sub-subtasks and solve the sub-subtasks separately. These sub-subtasks may be further decomposed into even smaller tasks, but eventually the tasks become small enough to be easy to design and code.

Addressing Compiler Concerns

The compiler has a reason for giving an error message

The compiler checks to make sure you have done certain necessary things, such as initializing variables or including a `return` statement in the definition of a method that returns a value. Sometimes you may find that the compiler is asking you to do one of these things, yet you are certain either that you have done it or that you do not need to do it. In such cases, it does no good to argue with the compiler. It most likely is correct. If you cannot find a mistake in your code, change it anyway, so that it is more obvious that you have done what the compiler is asking for.

For example, suppose that you have a method that returns a value of type `int` and the method definition ends as follows:

```
if (something > somethingElse)
    return something;
else if (something < somethingElse)
    return somethingElse;
```

Note that this statement does not address the possibility that `something` could be equal to `somethingElse`, and the compiler will complain that you need a `return` statement. Even if you think that you are correct, because you know that `something` will never equal `somethingElse`, you will have to change this last `if-else` statement to either

```
if (something > somethingElse)
    return something;
else if (something < somethingElse)
    return somethingElse;
else
    return 0;
```

or the equivalent

```
int answer = 0;
if (something > somethingElse)
    answer = something;
else if (something < somethingElse)
    answer = somethingElse;
return answer;
```

In the previous chapter, we suggested that a method should contain no more than one `return` statement. If you adhere to that advice, the compiler is less likely to complain.

As another example, suppose that you declare a variable like this:

```
String line;
```

If the compiler insists that you must initialize the variable, you could change the declaration to

```
String line = null;
```

The constant value `null` is a special predefined constant that you can use to give a value to any variable of any class type. Because `null` is like an address, you use = = and != rather than the method `equals` when you test to see whether a variable contains `null`.

null is a predefined constant

Note that `null` is not an object but a sort of place holder for an object's address. Use `null` to initialize a variable of a class type only when you know that, before the variable is used in the invocation of some method, your code will assign an object to the class variable. This means that you should use `null` to initialize a variable of a class type only when it is conceptually necessary. However, the compiler will sometimes insist on an initialization even when it is not needed.

GOTCHA Null Pointer Exception

Since `null` is not an object, you cannot use it to invoke a method. If you try, you will get an error message that says "Null Pointer Exception." For example, the statements

```
Pet myDog = null;
myDog.setPet("Spot", 2, 35.4);
```

will produce this error message no matter how the class `Pet` is defined. The way to correct the problem is to use `new` to create an object of type `Pet`, as follows:

```
Pet myDog = new Pet();
myDog.setPet("Spot", 2, 35.4);
```

As you do more programming, you will probably encounter other situations that produce a "Null Pointer Exception" message. In these cases, look for an uninitialized variable of a class type. ■

■ PROGRAMMING TIP The Compiler Is Always Right

Well, we hope it is. If you approach debugging with the thought that you didn't make a mistake, you are less likely to find the error that caused the compiler to complain. ■

Testing Methods

Use a driver program to test a method

When you test a method, you can use a driver program like the one in Listing 6.13. These driver programs are just for your use, and so they can be quite simple. They need not have any fancy output or anything else very elaborate. All they have to do is give the method some arguments and invoke the method.

Every method you write for a class should be tested. Moreover, it should be tested in a program in which it is the only method that has not yet been fully tested. In that way, if you discover that something is wrong, you know which method contains the mistake. If you test more than one method in the same program, you can easily be fooled into thinking that the mistake is in one method when in fact it is in some other method.

■ PROGRAMMING TIP   Test Methods Separately

Test each method in a program in which it is the only untested method.   ■

Test methods one at a time

One way to test each method separately is called **bottom-up testing.** If method A calls method B, bottom-up testing asks that method B be fully tested before you test method A. Bottom-up testing is a good and safe technique, but it can become tedious. Other ways of testing can find bugs faster and less painfully. And sometimes you want to test a method before all the methods it uses are tested. For example, you might want to test your general approach to the problem before even writing all the methods. However, you should still test each method in a program in which it is the only untested method. This presents a problem. If method A calls method B and method B is not yet tested, how can you test method A in a program in which it is the only untested method? The answer is to use a stub for method B.

A stub is a temporary definition of a method used in testing

A **stub** is a simplified version of a method that is not good enough for the final class definition but is good enough for testing and is simple enough for you to be sure—or as sure as possible—that it is correct. For example, suppose you are testing the class DollarFormat in Listing 6.14 and you want to test the method writeln before you test the method write. You can use a stub for the method write, as follows:

```
public static void write(double amount)
{
    System.out.print("$99.12"); //STUB
}
```

This is certainly not a correct definition of the method write. It always displays 99.12 no matter what it gets as an argument. However, it is good enough to use in testing the method writeln. If you test the method writeln using this stub for the method write, and writeln displays $99.12 in the correct way, then writeln is almost certain to be correct. Note that using this stub for write will let you test the method writeln before you complete either of the methods write or writePositive.

SELF-TEST QUESTIONS

27. Given the class `DollarFormat` in Listing 6.14, what is displayed by the invocation `DollarFormat.writeln(7.0)`?

28. Consider the variable `allCents` in the method `writePositive` in Listing 6.14. It holds an amount of money as if it were all cents. So for the amount $12.95, the `int` variable `allCents` would be set to 1295. Using an `int` variable is somewhat limiting. The largest value of type `int` is 2147483647, meaning that the largest amount the method can handle is $21,474,836.47. That is more than $21 million, a nice large sum, but we often need to consider larger amounts, such as the national budget or even the salary for the CEO of a large company. How can you easily change the definitions of the methods in the class `DollarFormat` so that they handle larger amounts of money?

29. What is wrong with a program that starts as follows? (The class `Species` is defined in Listing 5.19 in Chapter 5.)

```
public class SpeciesDemo
{
    public static void main(String[] args)
{
    Species s1 = null;
    Species s2 = null;
    s1.setSpecies("Klingon Ox", 10, 15);
    s2.setSpecies("Naked Mole Rat", 10000, 25);
```

30. Design a class to display values of type `double` that are not necessarily for money amounts. Call the class `OutputFormat`. It should have two static methods, `write` and `writeln`, each of which takes two arguments. The first argument gives a `double` value to be written to the screen. The second argument is an `int` value telling how many digits to show after the decimal point. Have your methods round any extra digits. These methods are similar to the methods `write` and `writeln` in the class `DollarFormat`. Although you can use the class `DollarFormat` as a model, the methods in these two classes have some differences. As you would expect, any output occurring after `write` executes will be on the same line, and output occurring after `writeln` executes will be on the following line; otherwise, `write` and `writeln` do the same thing.

    For example, the statements

```
OutputFormat.writeln(9.1234667, 4);
OutputFormat.writeln(9.9999, 2);
OutputFormat.writeln(7.01234, 4);
```

should produce the following output:

```
9.1235
10.00
7.0123
```

Do not forget to test your methods with numbers that have zeros after the decimal point, like 1.023 and 1.0023. (*Hint*: You may find the static method `Math.pow` (Figure 6.3) helpful as part of an expression to move a decimal point.) This is a fairly difficult exercise, so allow yourself some time to complete it. If you do not succeed in writing this class, be sure that you at least understand the answer given at the end of the chapter. This is a very useful class.

31. In your definition of the class `OutputFormat` in the previous question, would it be valid to use the names `print` and `println`, rather than `write` and `writeln`, or would this produce a name conflict with `System.out.println`?

6.4 OVERLOADING

A good name is better than precious ointment . . .

—ECCLESIASTES 7:1

You have seen that two or more different classes can define methods having the same name. For example, many classes have a method named `readInput`. This is not so surprising. The type of the calling object allows Java to decide which definition of the method `readInput` to use. You may be more surprised to hear that you can also have two or more methods *in the same class* that have the same method name. How is this possible? Read on.

Overloading Basics

Overloading a method name means giving the same name to more than one method within a class

When you give two or more methods the same name *within the same class*, you are **overloading** the method name. To do this, you must ensure that the different method definitions have something different about their parameter lists.

For example, Listing 6.15 contains a very simple example of overloading. The class `Overload` in this listing defines three different static methods, all named `getAverage`. When `Overload.getAverage` is invoked, how does Java know which definition of `getAverage` to use? If all the arguments are of type `double`, Java can tell which definition of `getAverage` to use by the number of arguments: If there are two arguments of type `double`, it uses the first definition of `getAverage`. If there are three arguments, it uses the second definition.

LISTING 6.15   Overloading

```java
/**
 This class illustrates overloading.
*/
public class Overload
{
    public static void main(String[] args)
    {
        double average1 = Overload.getAverage(40.0, 50.0);
        double average2 = Overload.getAverage(1.0, 2.0, 3.0);
        char average3 = Overload.getAverage('a', 'c');

        System.out.println("average1 = " + average1);
        System.out.println("average2 = " + average2);
        System.out.println("average3 = " + average3);
    }
    public static double getAverage(double first, double second)
    {
        return (first + second) / 2.0;
    }

    public static double getAverage(double first, double second,
                                        double third)
    {
        return (first + second + third) / 3.0;
    }

    public static char getAverage(char first, char second)
    {
        return (char)(((int)first + (int)second) / 2);
    }
}
```

Sample Screen Output

```
average1 = 45.0
average2 = 2.0
average3 = b
```

Now suppose that an invocation of the method getAverage has two arguments of type char. Java knows that it should use the third definition of getAverage because of the types of the arguments. Only one of the definitions has two arguments of type char. (For now, don't worry about how this method averages two characters. That's a side issue that we will come back to shortly.)

If you overload a method name—that is, if you give the same name to more than one method definition within the same class—Java distinguishes them according to the number of parameters and the types of the parameters. If an invocation of a method matches a definition of a method in name, and if the first argument has the same type as the first parameter, the second argument has the same type as the second parameter, and so forth—then that method definition is used. If there is no such match, Java will try some simple type conversions of the kinds we discussed earlier in this book, such as casting an `int` to a `double`, to see whether that produces a match. If this fails, you will get an error message.

A method's name and the number and types of its parameters are called the method's **signature.** So another way to describe the rule about overloading is to say that the methods in a class must have different signatures. Alternatively, a class cannot define two or more methods with the same signature.

Methods in a class need unique signatures

Note that you have already been using overloading, even though you may not have known the term before. The method names `print` and `println` are overloaded in the class `PrintStream` of the Java Class Library. Each method has one parameter, but in one version, the parameter type is `String`, in another it is `int`, or `double`, and so on. In addition, many of the methods of the class `Math`, which we discussed earlier in this chapter, use overloading. For example, `Math` has several versions of the method `max`, all having the same name and each with two parameters. Their invocations also are distinguished according to the type of the arguments. If its two arguments are of type `int`, `max` returns a value of type `int`. If its two arguments are of type `double`, it returns a value of type `double`.

Overloading can be applied to any kind of method. It can be applied to `void` methods, to methods that return a value, to static methods, to non-static methods, or to any combination of these. You can also overload constructors. The constructors in the class `Pet` in Listing 6.1 all have the same name and so are overloaded. They provide an explicit example that we can analyze.

Let's recall the headings of the constructors defined in Listing 6.1:

- `public Pet()`
- `public Pet(String initialName, int initialAge,`
        `double initialWeight)`
- `public Pet(String initialName)`
- `public Pet(int initialAge)`
- `public Pet(double initialWeight)`

Notice that each constructor has either a different number of parameters or a parameter whose type is different from those in the other constructors. Thus, each invocation of a constructor involves a different definition.

For example, each of the following `Pet` objects is created by a call to a different constructor:

Calling various constructors of the class Pet

```
Pet aPet     = new Pet();
Pet myCat    = new Pet("Fluffy", 2, 4.5);
Pet myDog    = new Pet("Spot");
Pet myTurtle = new Pet(20);
Pet myHorse  = new Pet(750.5);
```

The first statement calls the default constructor, since no arguments are provided. In the second statement, the object assigned to myCat is the result of calling the constructor that takes three arguments. Each of the remaining three statements calls a constructor that requires only one argument. Which constructor is chosen? The one whose parameter matches in type the argument in the invocation. Thus, Pet("Spot") calls the constructor whose parameter is a String, Pet(20) calls the constructor whose parameter is an int, and Pet(750.5) calls the constructor whose parameter is a double.

RECAP Overloading

Within one class, you can have two or more definitions of a method that have the same name but either have different numbers of parameters or have corresponding parameters with differing types. That is, the methods must have different signatures. This is called overloading the method name.

Overloading and Automatic Type Conversion

In some situations, two friends are not better than one. Two good things can sometimes interact in a bad way. Overloading is a friend, or at least a helpful feature of the Java language. Automatic type conversion of arguments—whereby an int like 2 is converted to a double like 2.0 when a method wants a double as an argument—is also a helpful feature of the Java language. But these two nice features can sometimes get in the way of each other.

Overloading and automatic type conversion can conflict

For example, the statement

```
Pet myHorse = new Pet(750.0);
```

creates a Pet object weighing 750 pounds. Suppose, however, that we forget the decimal point and the zero, and write the following instead:

```
Pet myHorse = new Pet(750);
```

Instead of creating a Pet object whose weight is 750, we create one whose age is 750. Because the argument 750 is of type int, it matches the constructor that has one parameter of type int. That constructor sets the instance variable age, not the instance variable weight, to the value of the argument. If Java can find a definition of a method whose parameters match the number and types of arguments, it will not do any type conversions, such as from int to double.

In the case we just looked at, we needed a type conversion, but we did not get one. There are also cases in which you do not want a type conversion but

Let's take a short side trip to explain how we average two characters. For our previous example, it does not matter whether we use a crazy way of averaging two characters, but, in fact, the technique we use in Listing 6.15 for the third version of getAverage is a very sensible way to average characters, or at least to average two letters. If the two letters are both lowercase, the average computed will be the lowercase letter halfway between them in alphabetical order, or as close to halfway as possible. Similarly, if the two letters are both uppercase, the average computed will be the uppercase letter halfway between them in alphabetical order. This approach works because Unicode assigns sequential numbers to the letters when arranged in alphabetical order. The number assigned to 'b' is one more than the number assigned to 'a', the number assigned to 'c' is one more than the number assigned to 'b', and so forth. So if you convert two letters to numbers, average the numbers, and then convert them back to letters, you get the letter halfway in between.

you do get one. For example, suppose my dog is named Cha Cha, weighs 2 pounds, and is 3 years old. We might try the following:

```
Pet myDog = new Pet("Cha Cha", 2, 3);
```

This will set myDog's age to 2, not 3, and its weight to 3.0, not 2.0. The real problem, of course, is that we have reversed the second and third arguments, but let's look at it as Java does. Given the preceding invocation, Java looks for a constructor whose heading has the following form:

```
public Pet(String Parm_1, int Parm_2, int
                Parm_3)
```

Pet has no such constructor, so there is no exact match for the invocation. Java then tries to convert an int to a double to get a match. It notices that if it converts the 3 to 3.0, it will have a match to

```
public Pet(String newName, int newAge,
                double newWeight)
```

and so it does the type conversion.

What went wrong—besides reversing two arguments? We should have given the weight as 2.0, not 2. If we had used 2.0, or if Java had not done any automatic type conversions for us, we would have received an error message. In this case, Java tried to help, but the help just got in the way.

GOTCHA   Overloading and Automatic Type Conversion

Sometimes a method invocation can be resolved in two different ways, depending on how overloading and type conversion interact. Such ambiguous method invocations are not allowed in Java and will produce a run-time error message or sometimes even a compiler error message. For example, you can overload the method name problemMethod in SampleClass as follows:

```
public class SampleClass
{
    public static void problemMethod(double n1, int n2)
    . . .
    public static void problemMethod(int n1, double n2)
    . . .
```

The class will compile with no problem. However, an invocation such as

```
SampleClass.problemMethod(5, 10);
```

will produce an error message, because Java cannot decide which overloaded definition of problemMethod to use: Should it convert the int value 5 to a double value and use the first definition of problemMethod, or should it convert the int value 10 to a double value and use the second definition? In this situation, Java issues an error message indicating that the method invocation is ambiguous.

Although the following two method invocations are allowed:

```
SampleClass.problemMethod(5.0, 10);
SampleClass.problemMethod(5, 10.0);
```

such situations, while valid, are confusing and should be avoided. ■

REMEMBER Overloading Before Automatic Type Conversion

Java always tries to use overloading before it tries to use automatic type conversion. If Java can find a definition of a method that matches the types of the arguments, it will use that definition. Java will not do an automatic type conversion of a method's argument until after it has tried and failed to find a definition of the method name with parameter types that exactly match the arguments in the method invocation.

■ **PROGRAMMING TIP**   Choose Descriptive Names to Avoid Overloading

Had we given the four set methods of the class Pet in Listing 6.1 the same name—set, for instance—these methods would have demonstrated the same issues we just raised about overloading and automatic type conversion. Instead of overloading their names, we avoided these difficulties by choosing distinct names. Instead of calling each of them set, we used the more descriptive names setName, setAge, setWeight, and setPet. Use overloading when you have a good reason to do so, but don't use it when a distinct method name is more descriptive. You cannot follow this advice for constructors, since they must be named after the class. Even so, multiple, overloaded constructors are common. ■

Overloading and the Return Type

You cannot overload a method name by giving two definitions whose headings differ only in the type of the value returned. For example, you might have wanted to add another method called `getWeight` to the class `Pet` in Listing 6.1. Imagine that this new method returns a character telling you whether the pet is overweight or underweight—say, '+' for overweight, '-' for underweight, and '*' for just right. The return type would be `char`. So suppose we had two methods with the following headings:

```
/**
 Returns the weight of the pet.
*/
public double getWeight()

/**
Returns '+' if overweight, '-' if
underweight, and *if weight is OK.
*/
public char getWeight()
```

> You CANNOT have both of these methods within a single class.

> A method's signature does not include its return type

Unfortunately, this is invalid. In any class definition, two definitions of the same method name must have either different numbers of parameters or at least one pair of corresponding parameters of differing types. You cannot overload on the basis of the type returned. Recall that the definition of a method's signature does not include its return type. Thus, the signatures of the two `getWeight` methods are the same, which is illegal.

If you think about it, it is not even possible to write a compiler that overloads on the basis of the type returned. For example, suppose we have

```
Pet myPet = new Pet();
 . . .
double value = myPet.getWeight();
```

Now suppose that, contrary to actual fact, we were able to include both versions of the `getWeight` method. Consider the job of the poor compiler in this situation. Although we have not made an issue of it, you can store a value of type `char` in a variable of type `double`. Java will perform an automatic type cast to change the `char` to a `double`. Thus, in this hypothetical scenario, the variable `value` is happy with either a `double` or a `char`.

So the compiler has no way to judge which version of `getWeight` the programmer wanted. The compiler would have to ask the programmer for advice, and compilers are not allowed to ask the programmer questions.

GOTCHA   You Cannot Overload on the Basis of the Return Type

A class cannot have several methods that have the same name and the same parameters but different return types. Such methods would have the same signature, and that is illegal in Java.   ∎

32. Would the following constructor invocation be valid to include in the program in Listing 6.2?

    ```
    Pet myDog = Pet("Fido", 2, 7);
    ```

33. Can a class possibly contain both of the following method definitions?

    ```
    /**
     Postcondition: Returns the number of people in
     numberOfCouples couples.
    */
    public static int countPeople(int numberOfCouples)
    {
        return 2 * numberOfCouples;
    }
    /**
     Postcondition: Returns the number of children,
     assuming that each couple has 2.3 children.
    */
    public static double countPeople(int numberOfCouples)
    {
        return 2.3 * numberOfCouples;
    }
    ```

34. Can a class possibly contain both of the following method definitions?

    ```
    /**
     Postcondition: Returns the integer portion of a
     positive number or zero if the number is negative.
    */
    public static int convertValue(double number)
    {
        int result = 0;
        if (number > 0.0)
            result = (int)number;
        return result;
    }
    /**
     Postcondition: Returns the integer portion of a
     positive number or zero if the number is negative.
    */
    public static double convertValue(int number)
    {
        double result = 0;
        if (number > 0.0)
            result = (double)number;
        return result;
    }
    ```

35. Consider the class Species in Listing 5.19 of Chapter 5. It has a method called setSpecies that sets the name, population, and growth rate of a species. Could this class have another method setSpecies that has only one parameter for the name of the species and that sets both the population and the growth rate to zero? If so, give the definition of this other method named setSpecies.

36. Repeat the previous question for a method setSpecies that sets only the name of the species, not any other instance variables.

37. Still considering the class Species in Listing 5.19 of Chapter 5, could both of the methods named setSpecies defined in Self-Test Questions 35 and 36 of this chapter be added to the class Species?

PROGRAMMING EXAMPLE   A Class for Money

Listing 6.16 contains a class, named Money, whose objects represent amounts of U.S. money, such as $9.99, $500.00, $0.50, and so forth. You might be inclined to think of money amounts as values of type double, but to the programmer who uses the class Money, or to the end user of any software product using Money, the data values are not thought of as having the type double or int or any other Java predefined type.[3] The data values are of type Money. To the "person on the street," $9.99 is not a value of type double. And it shouldn't be to you. Sometimes you can get away with using values of type double to represent amounts of money, but doing so has a potential problem. A value of type double is, practically speaking, an approximate quantity, and for an accounting program in particular, approximate quantities are usually not good enough. If a bank has account balances that are off by a few dollars or even a few cents, customers will be dissatisfied and legal action would be likely.

Of course, to implement the class Money, we must choose some sort of data representation. We want to represent money amounts as exact quantities, so we will use an integer type. However, the type int cannot represent very large numbers, and so we will use the type long. An amount of money, such as $3500.36, can be represented as two integers—in this case, 3500 and 36—

---

[3] In Listing 6.14 we defined a class named DollarFormat that is concerned with displaying amounts of money given as values of type double. In this programming example, we do not use values of type double to represent amounts of money, and so we do not use the class DollarFormat.

LISTING 6.16   The Money **Class** *(part 1 of 3)*

```java
import java.util.Scanner;
/**
 Class representing nonnegative amounts of money,
 such as $100, $41.99, $0.05.
*/
public class Money
{
    private long dollars;
    private long cents;

    public void set(long newDollars)
    {
        if (newDollars < 0)
        {
            System.out.println(
                "Error: Negative amounts of money are not allowed.");
            System.exit(0);
        }
        else
        {
            dollars = newDollars;
            cents = 0;
        }
    }
    public void set(double newAmount)
    {
        if (newAmount < 0)
        {
            System.out.println(
                "Error: Negative amounts of money are not allowed.");
            System.exit(0);
        }
        else
        {
            long allCents = Math.round(newAmount * 100);
            dollars = allCents / 100;
            cents = allCents % 100;
        }
    }
    public void set(Money moneyObject)
    {
        this.dollars = moneyObject.dollars;
        this.cents = moneyObject.cents;
    }
```

(continued)

LISTING 6.16 **The Money Class** *(part 2 of 3)*

```java
/**
 Precondition: The argument is an ordinary representation
 of an amount of money, with or without a dollar sign.
 Fractions of a cent are not allowed.
*/
public void set(String amountString)
{
    String dollarsString;
    String centsString;

    //Delete '$' if any:
    if (amountString.charAt(0) == '$')
        amountString = amountString.substring(1);
    amountString = amountString.trim();

    //Locate decimal point:
    int pointLocation = amountString.indexOf(".");

    if (pointLocation < 0) //If no decimal point
    {
        cents = 0;
        dollars = Long.parseLong(amountString);
    }
    else //String has a decimal point.
    {
        dollarsString =
            amountString.substring(0, pointLocation);
        centsString =
            amountString.substring(pointLocation + 1);

        //one digit in cents means tenths of a dollar
        if (centsString.length() <= 1)
            centsString = centsString + "0";

        // convert to numeric
        dollars = Long.parseLong(dollarsString);
        cents = Long.parseLong(centsString);
        if ((dollars < 0) || (cents < 0) || (cents > 99))
        {
            System.out.println(
                "Error: Illegal representation of money.");
            System.exit(0);
        }
    }
}
```

(continued)

LISTING 6.16   **The** Money **Class** *(part 3 of 3)*

```java
public void readInput()
{
    System.out.println("Enter amount on a line by itself:");
    Scanner keyboard = new Scanner(System.in);
    String amount = keyboard.nextLine();
    set(amount.trim());
}

/**
 Does not go to the next line after displaying money.
*/
public void writeOutput()
{
    System.out.print("$" + dollars);
    if (cents < 10)
        System.out.print(".0" + cents);
    else
        System.out.print("." + cents);
}
/**
 Returns n times the calling object.
*/
public Money times(int n)
{
    Money product = new Money();
    product.cents = n * cents;
    long carryDollars = product.cents / 100;
    product.cents = product.cents % 100;
    product.dollars = n * dollars + carryDollars;
    return product;
}
/**
 Returns the sum of the calling object and the argument.
*/
public Money add(Money otherAmount)
{
    Money sum = new Money();
    sum.cents = this.cents + otherAmount.cents;
    long carryDollars = sum.cents / 100;
    sum.cents = sum.cents % 100;
    sum.dollars = this.dollars
                    + otherAmount.dollars + carryDollars;
    return sum;
}
```

We used nextLine instead of next because there may be a space between the dollar sign and the number.

stored in instance variables of type `long`. Negative amounts of money certainly make sense—and a final professional-strength `Money` class would allow for negative amounts of money—but we will limit ourselves to nonnegative amounts since we want a fairly simple example for learning purposes.

Four methods
named `set`

Notice the overloaded method name `set`. The four methods named `set` allow a programmer to set an amount of money in any way that is convenient. The programmer can use a single integer value for an amount of dollars without any cents, a single value of type `double`, another object of type `Money`, or a string, such as `"$9.98"` or `"9.98"`. The programmer does not, and should not, worry about what instance variables are used inside the class `Money`. Instead, the programmer should think only in terms of money amounts.

Let's look at some details in the definitions of the `set` methods. The `set` method having one parameter of type `long` is straightforward. It sets the whole number of dollars. The `set` method having one parameter of type `double` works by converting the `double` value to a value that represents the amount of money as the number of pennies in the amount. This is done as follows:

```
long allCents = Math.round(newAmount * 100);
```

The method `Math.round` eliminates any fractional part of a penny. It returns a value of type `long` when its argument is of type `double`, as it is here. The integer division operators / and % are then used to convert the pennies to dollars and cents.

The `set` method whose parameter is of type `Money` is also straightforward, but you should notice one important point. The instance variables of the parameter `moneyObject` are accessible by name inside the definition of the class `Money`. In this case, they are `moneyObject.dollars` and `moneyObject.cents`. Within the definition of any class, you can directly access the instance variables of any object of the class.

The `set` method whose parameter is of type `String` changes a string, such as `"$12.75"`or `"12.75"`, into two integers, such as 12 and 75. First, it checks whether the first character in the string is a dollar sign, as follows:

```
if (amountString.charAt(0) == '$')
    amountString = amountString.substring(1);
```

Use `String`
methods to
process the input

The first character in the string `amountString` is returned by an invocation of the `String` method `charAt`. If this character is a dollar sign, the string—which has index positions 0 through some last index—is replaced by the substring at indices 1 through the end of the string, effectively removing the first character. The `String` method `substring` does this for us. You may want to review the descriptions of the `substring` methods given in Figure 2.5 of Chapter 2.

One or more blanks might be between the $ symbol and the dollar amount. Blanks are trimmed off with an invocation of the `String` method `trim`, as follows:

```
amountString = amountString.trim();
```

The string is then broken into two substrings—one for dollars and one for cents—by locating the decimal point and breaking the string at the decimal point. The decimal point position is stored in the variable `pointLocation` as follows:

```
int pointLocation = amountString.indexOf(".");
```

The dollars and cents substrings are recovered as follows:

```
dollarsString = amountString.substring(0, pointLocation);
centsString = amountString.substring(pointLocation + 1);
```

Finally, the dollars and cents substrings are converted to values of type `long` by calling the static method `parseLong` in the wrapper class `Long`, which we introduced earlier in this chapter:

```
dollars = Long.parseLong(dollarsString);
cents = Long.parseLong(centsString);
```

Our method `times` is used to multiply an amount of money by an integer. The method `add` is used to add two objects of type `Money`. For example, if `m1` and `m2` are objects of type `Money` that both represent the amount $2.00, then `m1.times(3)` returns an object of the class `Money` that represents $6.00, and `m1.add(m2)` returns an object of the class `Money` that represents $4.00.

Methods that perform arithmetic on Money objects

To understand the definition of the methods `times` and `add`, remember that one dollar is 100 cents. So if `product.cents` has a value of 100 or more, the following will set the variable `carryDollars` equal to the number of whole dollars in that many cents.

```
long carryDollars = product.cents / 100;
```

The number of cents left over after removing that many dollars is given by

```
product.cents % 100
```

VideoNote
Writing and invoking overloaded methods

A demonstration program for the class Money is given in Listing 6.17.

LISTING 6.17 Using the Money Class *(part 1 of 2)*

```
public class MoneyDemo
{
    public static void main(String[] args)
    {
        Money start = new Money();
        Money goal = new Money();

        System.out.println("Enter your current savings:");
        start.readInput();
```

(continued)

LISTING 6.17   Using the Money Class *(part 2 of 2)*

```
        goal = start.times(2);
        System.out.print(
            "If you double that, you will have ");
        goal.writeOutput();

        System.out.println(", or better yet:");
        goal = start.add(goal);
        System.out.println(
            "If you triple that original amount, you will have:");
        goal.writeOutput();
        System.out.println();          End the line, because writeOutput
                                       does not end the line.
        System.out.println("Remember: A penny saved");
        System.out.println("is a penny earned.");
    }
}
```

Sample Screen Output

```
Enter your current savings:
Enter amount on a line by itself:
$500.99
If you double that, you will have $1001.98, or better yet:
If you triple that original amount, you will have
$1502.97
Remember: A penny saved
is a penny earned.
```

 SELF-TEST QUESTIONS

38. Rewrite the method add in Listing 6.16 so that it does not use the this parameter.

39. In Listing 6.16, the set method that has a String parameter does not allow extra leading and trailing blanks in the string. Rewrite it so that it ignores leading and trailing whitespace. For example, it should allow "$5.43" as an argument.

6.5 INFORMATION HIDING REVISITED

I don't like to meddle in my private affairs.

—KARL KRAUS (1874–1936)

The material in this section is not needed to understand most of the rest of this book. If you prefer, you can safely postpone reading this material until you are more comfortable with classes. This section discusses a subtle problem that can arise when defining certain kinds of classes. The problem does not apply to any class you define whose instance variables are either of a primitive type—such as int, double, char, and boolean—or of the type String. So you can define lots of classes without being concerned with this problem.

Privacy Leaks

A class can have instance variables of any type, including any class type. These often can be natural and useful things to have. However, using instance variables of a class type can introduce a problem that requires special care. The problem occurs because variables of a class type contain the memory address of the location where an object is stored in memory. For example, suppose that goodGuy and badGuy are both variables of the class type Pet, which we defined in Listing 6.1. Now suppose that goodGuy names some object and your program executes the following assignment statement:

```
badGuy = goodGuy;
```

After this assignment statement is executed, badGuy and goodGuy are two names for the same object. So if you change badGuy, you will also change goodGuy. (There must be a moral lesson there.)

Let's give this assignment statement a bit more context to see its implications:

```
Pet goodGuy = new Pet();
goodGuy.set("Faithful Guard Dog", 5, 75);
Pet badGuy = goodGuy;
badGuy.set("Dominion Spy", 1200, 500);
goodGuy.writeOutput();
```

Because badGuy and goodGuy name the same object, this code will produce the following output:

```
Name: Dominion Spy
Age: 1200 years
Weight: 500.0 pounds
```

The change to badGuy also changed goodGuy because goodGuy and badGuy name the same object. The same thing can happen with instance variables and can cause some subtle problems. Let's look at an example.

Listing 6.18 contains the definition of a class called PetPair, which represents a pair of Pet objects. The class has two private instance variables of type Pet. The programmer who wrote this class mistakenly thinks that the data named by the instance variables first and second cannot be changed by any program using the class PetPair. This is an easy mistake for a programmer to make. After all, the instance variables are private, so they cannot be accessed by name outside of the class. And just to be super safe, the programmer did not include any mutator methods that change the private instance variables. But anybody can look at the objects in a pair by using the public accessor methods getFirst and getSecond. Sound good? Unfortunately, the programmer is in for a rude awakening.

The program in Listing 6.19 creates an object of PetPair and then changes the state of that object's private instance variable first! How could that be? The problem is that a variable of a class type contains a memory address, and as you saw at the beginning of this section, you can use the assignment operator to produce two names for the same object. That is what our hacker

LISTING 6.18   An Insecure Class

```java
/**
Class whose privacy can be breached.
*/
public class PetPair
{
    private Pet first, second;
    public PetPair(Pet firstPet, Pet secondPet)
    {
        first = firstPet;
        second = secondPet;
    }
    public Pet getFirst()
    {
        return first;
    }
    public Pet getSecond()
    {
        return second;
    }
    public void writeOutput()
    {
        System.out.println("First pet in the pair:");
        first.writeOutput();
        System.out.println("\nSecond pet in the pair:");
        second.writeOutput();
    }
}
```

LISTING 6.19   Changing a Private Object in a Class
(part 1 of 2)

```
/**
Toy program to demonstrate how a programmer can access and
change private data in an object of the class PetPair.
*/
public class Hacker
{
    public static void main(String[] args)
    {
        Pet goodDog = new Pet("Faithful Guard Dog", 5, 75.0);
        Pet buddy = new Pet("Loyal Companion", 4, 60.5);

        PetPair pair = new PetPair(goodDog, buddy);
        System.out.println("Our pair:");
        pair.writeOutput( );

        Pet badGuy = pair.getFirst();
        badGuy.setPet("Dominion Spy", 1200, 500);

        System.out.println("\nOur pair now:");
        pair.writeOutput( );
        System.out.println("The pet wasn't so private!");
        System.out.println("Looks like a security breach.");
    }
}
```

Screen Output

```
Our pair:
First pet in the pair:
Name: Faithful Guard Dog
Age: 5 years
Weight: 75.0 pounds
Second pet in the pair:
Name: Loyal Companion
Age: 4 years
Weight: 60.5 pounds
Our pair now:
First pet in the pair:
Name: Dominion Spy ◄──────  This program has changed an
Age: 1200 years              object named by a private instance
Weight: 500.0 pounds         variable of the object pair.
Second pet in the pair:
Name: Loyal Companion
Age: 4 years
```

(continued)

LISTING 6.19   Changing a Private Object in a Class
(part 2 of 2)

```
Weight: 60.5 pounds
The pet wasn't so private!
Looks like a security breach.
```

A private instance variable having a class type could be changed outside of the class

programmer who wrote the program in Listing 6.19 did. By invoking the accessor method getFirst, one can get the address of the private instance variable first. That memory address is stored in the variable badGuy. So badGuy is another name for first. Our hacker cannot use the private name first but can use the equivalent name badGuy. All that our hacker needed to do was to use the name badGuy to invoke the method setPet of the class Pet, and because badGuy is another name for the object named by first, our hacker has changed the object named by the private instance variable first. This phenomenon is called a **privacy leak.**

Ways to avoid a privacy leak

How can you write your class definitions to avoid this problem? It might seem impossible to have a private instance variable of a class type that is truly secure. A hacker can always find a way to get at it, or so it would seem. There are, however, ways around this problem: Some are easier than others.

One easy way around this problem is to use only instance variables of a primitive type. This, of course, is a severe restriction. We can also use instance variables of a class type that has no mutator methods. String is such a class. Once a String object is created, its data cannot be changed, and so our hacker's trick will not work on these variables. Primitive types are not class types, and so the hacker's trick will not work on them either. This easy solution is the one we will take in this book.

Another easy way is to define accessor methods that return individual attributes of an object named by an instance variable of a class type instead of the object itself. Of course, any attribute that is itself another object might be a source of a similar problem. So, for example, instead of defining an accessor method in PetPair like getFirst, we could define three methods: getNameOfFirst, getAgeOfFirst, and getWeightOfFirst.

A clone is an exact duplicate

A more difficult solution also exists, but it is beyond the scope of this book. However, we can give you a hint of it. We could write a method to produce an exact duplicate of an object. These exact duplicates are called **clones.** Instead of returning an object named by a private instance variable of a class type that could be insecure, we return a clone of the object. That way a hacker can damage the clone, but the private data will not be affected. A brief introduction to cloning is given in Appendix 9 (on the book's Web site). After you become comfortable with classes, you may wish to look at that appendix.

Instance variables of a class type are natural and useful

Do not get the impression that instance variables of a class type are a bad idea. They are very natural and very useful. However, dealing with them effectively requires some care. We will talk more about such instance variables later in this book.

GOTCHA   **Privacy Leaks**

A private instance variable of a class type names an object that, for certain classes, can be modified outside of the class containing the instance variable. To avoid this problem, you can do any of the following:

- Declare the instance variable's type to be of a class that has no set methods, such as the class String.
- Omit accessor methods that return an object named by an instance variable of a class type. Instead, define methods that return individual attributes of such an object.
- Make accessor methods return a clone of any object named by an instance variable of a class type, instead of the object itself.   ■

SELF-TEST QUESTION   myprogramminglab

40. Give the definitions of three accessor methods that you can use instead of the single accessor method getFirst within the definition of the class PetPair in Listing 6.18. One method will return the pet's name, one will return the pet's age, and one will return the pet's weight. These new accessor methods will not produce the problem described in this section. They will return all of the data in an object of the class PetPair, but will not return any object whose mutator methods can change its state.

6.6 ENUMERATION AS A CLASS

You don't understand. I coulda had class.

—BUDD SCHULBERG, *ON THE WATERFRONT* (1954)

Chapter 3 introduced enumerations and mentioned that the compiler creates a class when it encounters an enumeration. This section talks about that class. Although you should consider using enumerations in your programs, the ideas in this section are not central to the presentation in the rest of the book.

Let's define a simple enumeration for the suits of playing cards, as follows:

```
enum Suit {CLUBS, DIAMONDS, HEARTS, SPADES}
```

The compiler creates a class Suit. The enumerated values are names of public static objects whose type is Suit. As you know, you reference each of these values by prefacing its name with Suit and a dot, as in the following assignment statement:

Some enumeration methods

```
Suit s = Suit.DIAMONDS;
```

The class Suit has several methods, among which are equals, compareTo, ordinal, toString, and valueOf. The following examples show how we can use these methods, assuming that the variable s references Suit.DIAMONDS:

- s.equals(Suit.HEARTS) tests whether s equals HEARTS. In this case, equals returns false, since DIAMONDS is not equal to HEARTS.
- s.compareTo(Suit.HEARTS) tests whether s is before, at, or after HEARTS in the definition of Suit. Like the method compareTo in the class String—which Chapter 3 describes—compareTo here returns an integer that is negative, zero, or positive, according to the outcome of the comparison. In this case, compareTo return a negative integer, since DIAMONDS appears before HEARTS in the enumeration.
- s.ordinal() returns the position, or **ordinal value**, of DIAMONDS in the enumeration. The objects within an enumeration are numbered beginning with 0. So in this example, s.ordinal() returns 1.
- s.toString() returns the string "DIAMONDS". That is, toString returns the name of its invoking object as a string.
- Suit.valueOf("HEARTS") returns the object Suit.HEARTS. The match between the string argument and the name of an enumeration object must be exact. Any whitespace within the string is *not* ignored. The method valueOf is a static method, so its name in an invocation is preceded by Suit and a dot.

You can define private instance variables and additional public methods—including constructors—for any enumeration. By defining an instance variable, you can assign values to the objects in the enumeration. Adding a get method will provide a way to access these values. We have done all of these things in the new definition of the enumeration Suit shown in Listing 6.20.

LISTING 6.20 **An Enhanced Enumeration** Suit

```java
/** An enumeration of card suits. */
enum Suit
{
    CLUBS("black"), DIAMONDS("red"), HEARTS("red"),
    SPADES("black");

    private final String color;

    private Suit(String suitColor)
    {
        color = suitColor;
    }
    public String getColor()
    {
        return color;
    }
}
```

We chose strings as the values for the enumerated objects, so we have added the instance variable color as a String object, as well as a constructor that sets its value. Notation such as CLUBS("black") invokes this constructor and sets the value of CLUBS's private instance variable color to the string "black". Note that color's value cannot change, since it is declared as final. Also observe that the constructor is private, so you cannot invoke it directly. It is called only within the definition of Suit. The method getColor provides public access to the value of color.

color is an instance variable; it is not static

Enumerations can have an access modifier such as public or private. If you omit the access modifier, the enumeration is private by default. You can define a public enumeration within its own file, just as you would define any other public class.

SELF-TEST QUESTION

41. If cardSuit is an instance of Suit and is assigned the value Suit.SPADES, what is returned by each of the following expressions?

    a. cardSuit.ordinal()
    b. cardSuit.equals(Suit.CLUBS)
    c. cardSuit.compareTo(Suit.CLUBS)
    d. Suit.valueOf("CLUBS")
    e. Suit.valueOf(cardSuit.toString())
    f. cardSuit.getColor()
    g. cardSuit.toString()

6.7 PACKAGES

From mine own library with volumes that I prize above my dukedom.

—WILLIAM SHAKESPEARE, *THE TEMPEST*

A package is a named collection of related classes that can serve as a library of classes for use in any program. With packages, you do not need to place all those classes in the same directory as your program. Although this is an important and useful topic, the rest of the material in this book does not use the discussion of packages presented here. Therefore, you may cover this section at any time during your reading of this book.

To understand this material, you need to know about folders, or directories; path names for folders; and how your operating system uses a path (environment) variable. If you do not know about these things, you may wish to skip this section until you have had some experience with them. These are not Java topics. They are part of your operating system, and the details depend on your particular system. If you can find out how to set the path variable, you will know enough about path variables to understand this section.

Packages and Importing

A package is a collection of classes

A package is simply a collection of classes that have been grouped together into a folder. The name of the folder is the name of the package. The classes in the package are each placed in a separate file, and the file name begins with the name of the class, just as we have been doing all along. The only difference is that each file in a package has the following line at the start of the file:

```
package Package_Name;
```

Each class in a package needs a package statement

Blank lines or comments can appear before this line, but nothing else may come before it. The *Package_Name* typically consists of all lowercase letters, often punctuated with the dot symbol. For example, if `general.utilities` is the name of the package, each of the files in the package would have the following statement at the start of the file:

```
package general.utilities;
```

Any program or class definition can use all of the classes in the package by placing a suitable `import` statement at the start of the file containing the program or class definition. This is true even if the program or class definition is not in the same directory as the classes in the package. For example, if you want to use the class `HelpfulClass` that is in the package `general.utilities`, you would place the following at the start of the file you are writing:

Using one class in a package

```
import general.utilities.HelpfulClass;
```

Notice that you write the class name, `HelpfulClass`, not the name of the class's file, `HelpfulClass.java`.

RECAP The package Statement

A package is a collection of classes grouped together into a folder and given a package name. Each class is in a separate file named after the class. Each file in the package must begin with a package statement, ignoring blank lines and comments.

SYNTAX FOR A CLASS IN A PACKAGE

```
<Blank lines or comments.>
package Package_Name;
<A class definition.>
```

EXAMPLES

```
package general.utilities;
package java.io;
```

RECAP The `import` **Statement**

You can use all the classes that are in a package within any program or class definition by placing an `import` statement that names the package at the start of the file containing the program or class definition. The program or class need not be in the same folder as the classes in the package.

SYNTAX

```
import Package_Name.Class_Name_Or_Asterisk;
```

Writing a class name imports just a single class from the package; writing an * imports all the classes in the package.

EXAMPLES

```
import java.util.Scanner;
import java.io.*;
```

To import all the classes in the package `general.utilities`, you would use the following `import` statement:

Using an entire package

```
import general.utilities.*;
```

The asterisk indicates that you want to import all of the files in the package. Although you might see this statement used, we prefer to import specific classes.

Package Names and Directories

A package name is not an arbitrary identifier. It tells the compiler where to find the classes in the package. In effect, the package name tells the compiler the path name for the directory containing the classes in the package. To find the directory for a package, Java needs two things: the name of the package and the directories listed in the value of your class path variable.

The value of your **class path variable** tells Java where to begin its search for a package, so we will discuss it first. The class path variable is not a Java variable. It is a variable that is part of your operating system and that contains the path names of a list of directories. When Java is looking for a package, it begins its search in these directories. Let us call these directories the **class path base directories.** We will tell you how Java uses these class path base directories and how packages are named, and then we will give you some information on how to set the class path variable.

A search for a package begins in the class path base directory

The name of a package specifies the relative path name for the directory that contains the package classes. It is a relative path name because it assumes that you start in a class path base directory and follow the path of

FIGURE 6.5 A Package Name

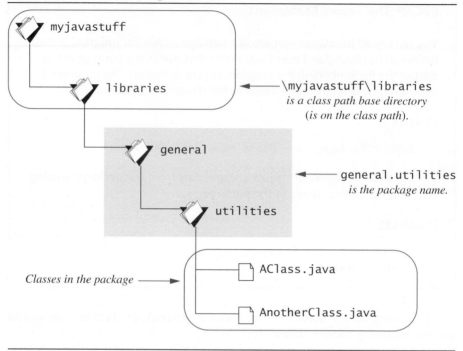

`\myjavastuff\libraries`
*is a class path base directory
(is on the class path).*

`general.utilities`
is the package name.

Classes in the package

subdirectories given by the package name. For example, suppose the following is a class path base directory (your operating system might use / instead of \):

    \myjavastuff\libraries

and suppose your package classes are in the directory

    \myjavastuff\libraries\general\utilities

In this case, the package *must* be named

    general.utilities

Notice that a package name is not arbitrary, but must be a list of directories leading from a class path base directory to the package classes. Thus, the package name tells Java what subdirectories to go through—starting from the base class directory—to find the package classes. This organization is depicted in Figure 6.5. The dot in the package name means essentially the same thing as the \ or /, whichever symbol your operating system uses for directory paths.

Setting the class path variable

You specify the class path base directories by setting the class path (environment) variable. The way you set the class path variable depends on your operating system. If you are on a UNIX system, you are likely to be able to set the class path with some command similar to the following:

    export CLASSPATH=/myjavastuff/libraries:/home/username/
    javaclasses;.

RECAP Package Names

A package name must be a path name for the directory that contains the classes in the package, but the package name uses dots in place of \ or / (whichever your operating system uses). When naming the package, you use a relative path name that starts from any directory named in the class path (environment) variable.

EXAMPLES

```
general.utilities
java.io
```

If you are using a Windows machine, you can set the class path variable by using the Control Panel to set or create an environment variable named CLASSPATH.

You can list more than one base directory in a class path variable, typically by separating them with semicolons. For example, the following might be a class path:

```
c:\myjavastuff\libraries;f:\yourjavastuff
```

This means that you can create package directories as either subdirectories of

```
c:\myjavastuff\libraries
```

or subdirectories of

```
f:\yourjavastuff
```

When looking for package directories, Java will first look in subdirectories of

```
c:\myjavastuff\libraries
```

If it does not find the package there, it will then look in subdirectories of

```
f:\yourjavastuff
```

Whenever you set or change the class path variable, be sure to include the current directory as one of the alternatives. The **current directory** is the directory in which your program (or other class) is located. On most systems, the current directory is indicated by a dot. So you would use the following for your class path variable:

> The current directory contains your program

```
c:\myjavastuff\libraries;f:\yourjavastuff;.
```

with the dot—the current directory—added to the end. Then if the package is not found in either of the previous two base directories, Java will look in the subdirectories of the current directory—that is, in subdirectories of your program (or whatever class you are compiling). If you want Java to check the current directory before it checks the other directories on the class path, list the current directory (the dot) first.

GOTCHA   Not Including the Current Directory in Your Class Path

Omitting the current directory from the class path variable not only will limit the locations you can use for your packages, but can interfere with programs that do not use packages. If you do not create packages, but instead place all classes in the same directory—as we do in the rest of this book—Java will not be able to find the classes unless the current directory is on the class path. (This problem will not occur if you have no class path variable at all; it arises only if you decide to set the class path variable.) ■

Name Clashes

Packages are a convenient way to group and use libraries of classes, but there is also another reason for using packages. They can help in dealing with name clashes; that is, they can help in handling situations in which two classes have the same name. If different programmers writing different packages have used the same name for a class, the ambiguity can be resolved by using the package name.

Avoid name clashes

For example, suppose a package named `mystuff` contains a class called `CoolClass`, and another package named `yourstuff` contains a different class named `CoolClass`. You can use both of these classes in the same program by using the more complete names `mystuff.CoolClass` and `yourstuff.CoolClass`, as the following statements demonstrate:

```
mystuff.CoolClass object1 = new mystuff.CoolClass();
yourstuff.CoolClass object2 = new yourstuff.CoolClass();
```

If you list the package name along with the class name like this, you do not need to import the package, since this longer class name includes the package name.

SELF-TEST QUESTIONS

42. Suppose you want to use classes in the package `mypackages.library1` in a program you write. What do you need to put near the start of the file containing your program?

43. Suppose you want to add a class to a package named `mypackages.library1`. What do you need to put in the file containing the class definition? Where does this statement go in the file?

44. Can a package have any name you might want, or are there restrictions on what you can use for a package name? Explain any restrictions.

45. On your system, place the class `Pet` (Listing 6.1) into a package so that you can use the class in any Java program by including a suitable `import` statement without moving `Pet` to the same directory (folder) as your program.

6.8 GRAPHICS SUPPLEMENT

Now you see it; now you don't.

—COMMON MAGICIAN'S SAYING

In this section we show you how to add buttons and icons to an applet or GUI application and how to make components, such as labels, icons, and buttons, change from visible to invisible and back. A **button** is an object in your applet or application that has a button-like appearance and that does something when you click it with your mouse. An **icon** is a small picture.

■ PROGRAMMING TIP   Code the Appearance and Actions Separately

When designing and coding an applet or GUI application, one good technique is to first program what the program will look like. For example, how many buttons will it display, and what is written on each button? After you have the applet looking the way you want, you can then go on to program the action(s) that it will perform, such as what will happen when the user clicks a button. In this way, one large task is broken down into two smaller and more manageable tasks. We will use this technique to introduce buttons. We will first show you how to add buttons to an applet. These buttons will not do anything when clicked. After you learn how to add buttons to an applet, we will go on to show you how to program actions to respond to button clicks. ■

Adding Buttons

You create a button object in the same way that you create a label object, but you use the class JButton instead of the class JLabel. For example, the applet in Listing 6.21 creates a button as follows:

```
JButton sunnyButton = new JButton("Sunny");
```

The argument to the constructor for the class JButton, in this case "Sunny", is a string that will appear on the button when the button is displayed. If you look at the applet's output in Listing 6.21, you will see that the two buttons are labeled Sunny and Cloudy.

After you create a button, you add it to the content pane of an applet in the same way that you add a label. For example, sunnyButton is added to the content pane of the applet in Listing 6.21 as follows:

Add buttons to the content pane

```
Container contentPane = getContentPane();
    ...

contentPane.add(sunnyButton);
```

Unlike labels, you can associate an action with a button so that when the user clicks the button with a mouse, the applet performs some action. If you click either of the buttons in the applet in Listing 6.21, nothing happens, because we haven't yet programmed actions for them. To do this, we use a different kind of programming technique known as **event-driven programming.** We will briefly introduce this technique before we show you how to program button actions.

LISTING 6.21 Adding Buttons to an Applet

```java
import javax.swing.JApplet;
import javax.swing.JButton;
import java.awt.Color;
import java.awt.Container;
import java.awt.FlowLayout;
import java.awt.Graphics;
/**
 Simple demonstration of adding buttons to an applet.
 These buttons do not do anything. That comes in a later version.
*/
public class PreliminaryButtonDemo extends JApplet
{
    public void init()
    {
        Container contentPane = getContentPene();
        contentPane.setBackground(Color.WHITE);

        contentPane.setLayout(new FlowLayout());

        JButton sunnyButton = new JButton("Sunny");
        contentPane.add(sunnyButton);

        JButton cloudyButton = new JButton("Cloudy");
        contentPane.add(cloudyButton);
    }
}
```

Applet Output

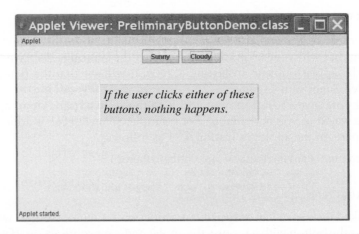

Event-Driven Programming

Applets and GUI applications use events and event handlers. An **event** is an object that represents some user action that elicits a response, such as clicking a button with the mouse. When an object generates an event, it is said to **fire** the event. For example, when the user clicks a button, the button fires an event. In an applet or application, every object that can fire events can have one or more **listener objects** that receive events automatically. A listener object has methods that specify what will happen when the listener receives events of various kinds. These methods are called **event handlers.**

Fire an event

Listeners handle events

You the programmer specify what objects are the listener objects for any given object that might fire an event. You also define the event-handler methods. The relationship between an event-firing object, such as a button, and its event-handling listener is illustrated in Figure 6.6.

Event-driven programming is very different from the kind of programming you've seen before now. In event-driven programming, you create objects that can fire events, and you create listener objects to react to the events. For the most part, your program does not determine the order in which things happen. The events determine that order. When an event-driven program is running, the next thing that happens depends on the next event.

Programming Buttons

To review, clicking a button using your mouse creates an object known as an event and sends the event to one or more other objects known as the listeners. This is called firing the event. The listener then performs some action.

When we say that the event is "sent" to the listener object, what we really mean is that some method in the listener object is invoked and given the event object as the argument. This invocation happens automatically. Your applet class definition will not normally contain an invocation of this method. However, your applet class definition does need to do two things:

FIGURE 6.6 **Event Firing and an Event Listener**

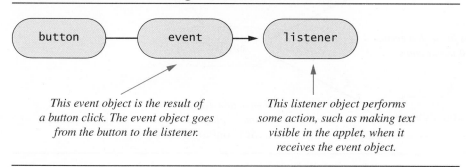

This event object is the result of a button click. The event object goes from the button to the listener.

This listener object performs some action, such as making text visible in the applet, when it receives the event object.

- For each button, it needs to specify what objects are listeners that will respond to events fired by that button; this is called **registering** the listener.
- It must define the method(s) that will be invoked when the event is sent to the listener.

Register the listener by calling addAction Listener

Recall that within the definition of a class, an object of that class is called `this`. The following statement registers `this` as a listener to receive events from the button named `sunnyButton`:

```
sunnyButton.addActionListener(this);
```

A similar statement also registers `this` as a listener to receive events from the button named `cloudyButton`. Because the argument is `this`, the statements mean that the class itself is the listener class for the buttons inside of it. To be a bit more precise, if `ButtonDemo` is our applet class, each applet object of `ButtonDemo` is the listener for the buttons in that object. This is diagrammed in Figure 6.7.

Next we explain how to make a class, such as `ButtonDemo`, into a listener class for events fired by buttons. Different kinds of components require different kinds of listener classes to handle the events they fire. A button fires **Steps to register a** events known as **action events**, which are handled by listeners known as **listener** **action listeners.**

An action listener is an object of type `ActionListener`. `ActionListener` is not a class but is a property that you can give to any class you define. Properties such as `ActionListener` are known as **interfaces** and are discussed in more detail in Chapter 8. To make a class into an action listener, we need to do two things:

- Add the phrase `implementsActionListener` to the beginning of the class definition, normally at the end of the first line.
- Define a method named `actionPerformed`.

FIGURE 6.7   **Buttons and an Action Listener**

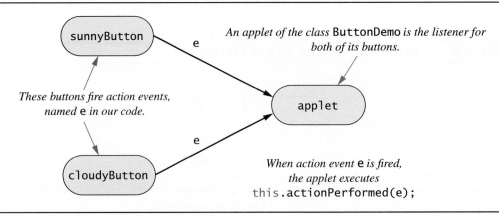

Here is an outline of the definition of the class `ButtonDemo`:

```
public class ButtonDemo extends JApplet implements
ActionListener
{
    . . .
    public void actionPerformed(ActionEvent e)
    {
    . . .
    }
    . . .
}
```

Although we could have defined a separate class that did nothing but handle button events, we instead made the applet class `ButtonDemo` into the action listener that will handle button events, because button events are supposed to change the applet, and the easiest way to change an applet is by using a method within the applet itself.

If the user clicks one of the buttons inside the applet, using the mouse, an action event is sent to the action listener for that button. Because the applet itself is the action listener for the buttons, the action event goes to the applet object. When an action listener receives an action event, the event is automatically passed to the method `actionPerformed`. The method `actionPerformed` typically contains a branching statement that asks what kind of action event was fired and then performs some appropriate action.

The method `actionPerformed` for our applet class `ButtonDemo` is

```
public void actionPerformed(ActionEvent e)
{
    Container contentPane = getContentPane();
    if (e.getActionCommand().equals("Sunny"))
        contentPane.setBackground(Color.BLUE);
    else if (e.getActionCommand().equals("Cloudy"))
        contentPane.setBackground(Color.GRAY);
    else
        System.out.println("Error in button interface.");
}
```

In this case, the method `actionPerformed` needs to know whether the action event came from the button labeled Sunny or the button labeled Cloudy. If `e` is an action event that was fired by clicking a button, `e.getActionCommand()` returns the string written on the button; in this case it returns either `"Sunny"` or `"Cloudy"`. This string is known as the **action command.** (You can specify a different action command, but we postpone that detail until Chapter 13, which is available on the book's Web site.)

All the method `actionPerformed` needs to do is see whether the action command returned by `e.getActionCommand()` is the string `"Sunny"` or

getAction Command returns an action command

the string "Cloudy" and perform the appropriate action for that button. Since e.getActionCommand() returns an object of the class String, we use String's method equals to make this test, using a method invocation of the following form:

```
e.getActionCommand().equals(String_Argument)
```

Using this invocation in an if statement allows us to change the color of the content pane accordingly by using a statement like

```
contentPane.setBackground(Color.BLUE);
```

Defining an action listener class requires the following additional import statements:

```
import java.awt.event.ActionEvent;
import java.awt.event.ActionListener;
```

RECAP Action Events and Action Listeners

Buttons and certain other components fire events as objects of the class ActionEvent. These events are action events and are handled by one or more action listeners. Any class—including an applet class—can become an action listener by taking the following steps:

- Add the phrase implements ActionListener to the end of the heading of the class definition.
- Make the button or other component that will fire the action event register the action listener by invoking the method addActionListener and passing it an object of the ActionListener class as an argument.
- Add a definition for a method named actionPerformed to the class.

An action listener may serve some other purpose in addition to being an action listener.

EXAMPLE

See Listing 6.22.

RECAP The Method actionPerformed

To be an action listener, a class must—among other things—have a method named actionPerformed that has one parameter of type ActionEvent. This is the only method required by the ActionListener interface.

(continued)

SYNTAX

```
public void actionPerformed(ActionEvent e)
{
    Code_for_Actions_Performed
}
```

The *Code_for_Actions_Performed* is typically a branching statement that depends on some property of the argument e. Often the branching depends on the invocation e.getActionCommand(), which returns an action command. If e is an event fired by clicking a button, the action command returned is the string written on the button.

EXAMPLE

See Listing 6.22.

PROGRAMMING EXAMPLE   A Complete Applet with Buttons

Listing 6.22 contains an applet that starts out looking just like the applet in Listing 6.21, but in this version the buttons "work." If you click the button labeled Sunny, the background turns blue. If you click the button labeled Cloudy, the background turns gray. Note that the final else clause should never execute. We wrote it to provide a warning if we made some unnoticed mistake in the code.

LISTING 6.22   Adding Actions to the Buttons *(part 1 of 3)*

```
import javax.swing.JApplet;
import javax.swing.JButton;
import java.awt.Color;
import java.awt.Container;
import java.awt.FlowLayout;
import java.awt.Graphics;
import java.awt.event.ActionEvent;
import java.awt.event.ActionListener;
/**
Simple demonstration of adding buttons to an applet.
These buttons do something when clicked.
*/
```

The code for this applet adds the highlighted text to Listing 6.21

Use of ActionEvent *and* ActionListener *requires these* import *statements.*

(continued)

LISTING 6.22 Adding Actions to the Buttons *(part 2 of 3)*

```java
public class ButtonDemo extends JApplet implements ActionListener
{
    public void init()
    {
        Container contentPane = getContentPane();
        contentPane.setBackground(Color.WHITE);

        contentPane.setLayout(new FlowLayout());

        JButton sunnyButton = new JButton("Sunny");
        contentPane.add(sunnyButton);
        sunnyButton.addActionListener(this);
        JButton cloudyButton = new JButton("Cloudy");
        contentPane.add(cloudyButton);
        cloudyButton.addActionListener(this);
    }
    public void actionPerformed(ActionEvent e)
    {
        Container contentPane = getContentPane();
        if (e.getActionCommand().equals("Sunny"))
            contentPane.setBackground(Color.BLUE);
        else if (e.getActionCommand().equals("Cloudy"))
            contentPane.setBackground(Color.GRAY);
        else
            System.out.println("Error in button interface.");
    }
}
```

Applet Output Initially

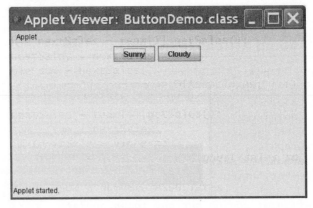

(continued)

LISTING 6.22 **Adding Actions to the Buttons** *(part 3 of 3)*

Applet Output After Clicking Sunny

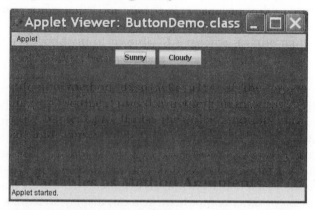

Applet Output After Clicking Cloudy

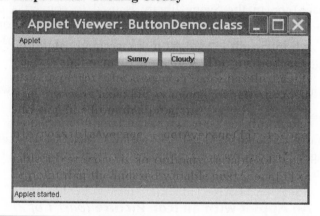

 PROGRAMMING TIP Applets Do Not Use Constructors

Applets are atypical classes in that they normally have no constructors. The initialization actions that you might expect to put in an applet's constructor are instead placed in the special method init. ∎

SELF-TEST QUESTIONS

myprogramminglab

46. The method actionPeformed in Listing 6.22 contains the following line:

```
Container contentPane = getContentPane();
```

Does the content pane have to be named contentPane, or could it be named something else, as in the following:

```
Container insideOfApplet = getContentPane();
```

47. What does it mean when we say that an event is "sent" to a listener object?

48. In Listing 6.22, suppose we replaced the parameter e in the method `actionPerformed` with the identifier `buttonEvent`. What effect would this change have on the program?

Adding Icons

As we mentioned at the beginning of this section, an icon is simply a picture. The picture usually is small, although it is not actually required to be. The picture you use can be of anything. Pictures are produced in a number of formats—such as GIF and JPEG—that can be displayed on a computer screen. You can use a picture in almost any standard format as the basis for an icon. You store the picture files in the same folder (directory) as your program.

Swing converts a digital picture file into an icon, and you can then add the icon to a label, button, or other component. You can display an icon, a string, or both an icon and a string on any label or button.

Use `ImageIcon` to convert a picture file to an icon

The class `ImageIcon` in the Swing library is used to convert a digital picture file into a Swing icon. For example, the following statement converts the digital picture file named duke_waving.gif to an icon named dukeIcon:

```
ImageIcon dukeIcon = new ImageIcon("duke_waving.gif");
```

Add an icon to a label

You can add this icon to a label by using the method `setIcon`, as follows:

```
niceLabel.setIcon(dukeIcon);
```

Listing 6.23 contains a simple example of these steps. The label `niceLabel` also has the string `"Java is fun!"`, so in this case the label displays both a string and an icon.

LISTING 6.23   An Applet with an Icon Picture *(part 1 of 2)*

```java
import javax.swing.ImageIcon;
import javax.swing.JApplet;
import javax.swing.JLabel;

public class IconDemo extends JApplet
{
    public void init()
    {
        JLabel niceLabel = new JLabel("Java Is fun!");
        ImageIcon dukeIcon = new ImageIcon("duke_waving.gif");
        niceLabel.setIcon(dukeIcon);
        getContentPane().add(niceLabel);
    }
}
```

(continued)

LISTING 6.23   An Applet with an Icon Picture *(part 2 of 2)*

Applet Output[4]

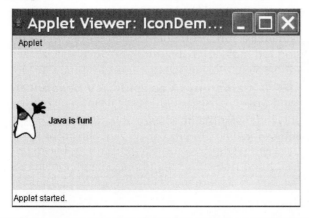

To omit the string from the label, you could change the definition of niceLabel in Listing 6.23 to the following:

```
JLabel niceLabel = new JLabel();//No argument, so no string.
```

As a result, the sentence Java is fun! would not appear in the applet.

You can also use the method setIcon to add an icon to a button. For example, if you add the highlighted statements in the following code to Listing 6.22, the button with the text Sunny will also display the picture in the file smiley.gif:

Add an icon to a button

```
JButton sunnyButton = new JButton("Sunny");
ImageIcon smileyFaceIcon = new ImageIcon("smiley.gif");
sunnyButton.setIcon(smileyFaceIcon);
contentPane.add(sunnyButton);
sunnyButton.addActionListener(this);
```

The screen output would appear as shown in Figure 6.8. The complete applet code is in the file ButtonIconDemo.java included with the source code for this book that is available on the Web.

Extra code on the Web

SELF-TEST QUESTION

myprogramminglab

49. The previous section showed you how to change the code in the applet in Listing 6.22 so that the button labeled Sunny contained the picture smiley.gif as well as text, as shown in Figure 6.8. Make additional

---

[4] Java, Duke, and all Java-based trademarks and logos are trademarks or registered trademarks of Oracle, Inc. in the United States and other countries. (Duke is the figure waving.)

FIGURE 6.8 A Button Containing an Icon

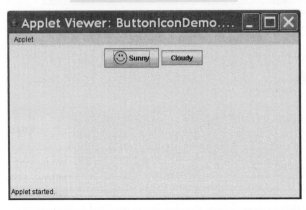

The code for this applet is in the file `ButtonIconDemo.java` *in the source code on the Web.*

changes to the code so that the button labeled `Cloudy` contains the picture `nasty.gif` as well as text. (The file `nasty.gif` is included with the source code provided on the Web.)

Changing Visibility

Every label and just about every button and other component we will introduce later has a method named `setVisible`. This method can change a component from visible to invisible or from invisible to visible according to the boolean value passed to it as an argument.

If a label or other component invokes the method `setVisible` and gives it an argument of `true`, the component will become visible. On the other hand, an argument of `false` makes the component invisible. If `setVisible` is not invoked at all, the component will be visible by default. When a component, such as a button, is invisible, you cannot click it with your mouse to get an action. An "invisible" component is not just invisible; it is not there at all. The next programming example demonstrates the use of the `setVisible` method.

An invisible button is inoperable

PROGRAMMING EXAMPLE An Example of Changing Visibility

The applet in Listing 6.24 defines a label that is initially invisible. When the user clicks the button in the applet, the label becomes visible. The label is named `response` and is made invisible by the following invocation of `setVisible` within the method `init`:

```
response.setVisible(false);
```

LISTING 6.24 **An Applet with a Label That Changes Visibility** *(part 1 of 2)*

```java
import javax.swing.ImageIcon;
import javax.swing.JApplet;
import javax.swing.JButton;
import javax.swing.JLabel;
import java.awt.Color;
import java.awt.Container;
import java.awt.FlowLayout;
import java.awt.Graphics;
import java.awt.event.ActionEvent;
import java.awt.event.ActionListener;

/**
 Simple demonstration of changing visibility in an applet.
*/
public class VisibilityDemo extends JApplet implements
ActionListener
{
    private JLabel response;
    private Container contentPane;
    public void init()
    {
        contentPane = getContentPane();
        contentPane.setBackground(Color.WHITE);

        //Create button:
        JButton aButton = new JButton("Push me!");
        aButton.addActionListener(this);

        //Create label:
        response = new JLabel("Thanks. That felt good!");
        ImageIcon smileyFaceIcon = new ImageIcon("smiley.gif");
        response.setIcon(smileyFaceIcon);
        response.setVisible(false);//Invisible until button is
                                   //clicked

        //Add button:
        contentPane.setLayout(new FlowLayout());
        contentPane.add(aButton);

        //Add label
        contentPane.add(response);
    }
    public void actionPerformed(ActionEvent e)
    {
        contentPane.setBackground(Color.PINK);
        response.setVisible(true);//Show label
    }
}
```

> The label **response** and the variable **contentPane** *are instance variables, so they can be used in both of the methods* **init** *and* **actionPerformed**.

(continued)

LISTING 6.24 An Applet with a Label That Changes Visibility *(part 2 of 2)*

Applet Output Initially

Applet Output After Clicking Button

When the user clicks the button, the method `actionPerformed` is invoked. This method executes the statement

```
response.setVisible(true);
```

making the label, which says `Thanks. That felt good!`, visible.

The label `response` and the variable `contentPane` are private instance variables in the applet, so they can be used in both of the methods `init` and `actionPerformed`. The variable `contentPane` is initialized to the content pane of the applet by an invocation of `getContentPane` in the method `init`. This initialization of the variable `contentPane` is an example of the method `init` behaving like a constructor.

RECAP The Method `setVisible`

Labels, buttons, and other applet components have a `setVisible` method. This method takes one argument of type `boolean`. If a `Component` is one of these components, the statement

    aComponent.setVisible(true);

will make aComponent visible. The call

    aComponent.setVisible(false);

will hide aComponent, that is, will make it invisible.

GOTCHA   The Meaning of "Invisible"

The term *invisible* as used with `setVisible` may need a bit of clarification. Suppose aButton is a button. After

    aButton.setVisible(false);

executes, the button is "invisible." But invisible here means more than the traditional meaning of the word. It really means the button is not there. Some programmers mistakenly think that this sort of "invisible" button is there, although it cannot be seen; so if they click the portion of the screen that formerly held the button, they expect to get the same effect as clicking the button. They are wrong. You cannot click an invisible button, unless you first make it visible. ∎

SELF-TEST QUESTIONS

myprogramminglab

50. In Listing 6.24 the parameter e in the method `actionPerformed` is never used. Is this OK?

51. Why is there no branching statement in the method `actionPerformed` in Listing 6.24?

52. Revise the applet in Listing 6.24 so that the button disappears after it is clicked.

CHAPTER SUMMARY

- A constructor is a method that creates and initializes an object of the class when you invoke it using the operator new. A constructor must have the same name as the class.

- A constructor without parameters is called a default constructor. A class that does not define a constructor will be given a default constructor automatically. A class that defines one or more constructors, none of which is a default constructor, will have no default constructor.

- When defining a constructor for a class, you can use this as a name for another constructor in the same class. Any call to this must be the first action taken by the constructor.

- The declaration of a static variable contains the keyword static. A static variable is shared by all the objects of its class.

- The heading of a static method contains the keyword static. A static method is typically invoked using the class name instead of an object name. A static method cannot reference an instance variable of the class, nor can it invoke a non-static method of the class without using an object of the class.

- Each primitive type has a wrapper class that serves as a class version of that primitive type. Wrapper classes also contain a number of useful predefined constants and methods.

- Java performs an automatic type cast from a value of a primitive type to an object of its corresponding wrapper class—and vice versa—whenever it is needed.

- When writing a method definition, divide the task to be accomplished into subtasks.

- Every method should be tested in a program in which it is the only untested method.

- Two or more methods within the same class can have the same name if they have different numbers of parameters or some parameters of differing types. That is, the methods must have different signatures. This is called overloading the method name.

- An enumeration is actually a class. Thus, you can define instance variables, constructors, and methods within an enumeration.

- You can form a package of class definitions you use frequently. Each such class must be in its own file within the same folder (directory) and contain a package statement at its beginning.

- You can use the classes in a package within any program without needing to move them to the same folder (directory) by simply including an import statement at the beginning of your program.

■ You can add buttons and icons to applets.

■ In event-driven programming, certain actions—like clicking a button—fire events. The events are received by listeners that perform actions, the details of which depend on the event fired.

■ An action listener is a class that has the phrase `implements ActionListener` at the end of its heading and defines a method `actionPerformed`. The method has one parameter of type `ActionEvent`.

■ You can use the method `setVisible` to make components, such as labels and buttons, visible or invisible.

Exercises

1. Create a class that will bundle together several static methods for tax computations. This class should not have a constructor. Its attributes are

   - `basicRate`—the basic tax rate as a static `double` variable that starts at 4 percent
   - `luxuryRate`—the luxury tax rate as a static `double` variable that starts at 10 percent

   Its methods are

   - `computeCostBasic(price)`—a static method that returns the given price plus the basic tax, rounded to the nearest penny.
   - `computeCostLuxury(price)`—a static method that returns the given price plus the luxury tax, rounded to the nearest penny.
   - `changeBasicRateTo(newRate)`—a static method that changes the basic tax rate.
   - `changeLuxuryRateTo(newRate)`—a static method that changes the luxury tax rate.
   - `roundToNearestPenny(price)`—a private static method that returns the given price rounded to the nearest penny. For example, if the price is 12.567, the method will return 12.57.

2. Consider a class `Time` that represents a time of day. It has attributes for the hour and minute. The hour value ranges from 0 to 23, where the range 0 to 11 represents a time before noon. The minute value ranges from 0 to 59.

   a. Write a default constructor that initializes the time to 0 hours, 0 minutes.
   b. Write a private method `isValid(hour, minute)` that returns true if the given hour and minute values are in the appropriate range.
   c. Write a method `setTime(hour, minute)` that sets the time if the given values are valid.

d. Write another method setTime(hour, minute, isAM) that sets the time if the given values are valid. The given hour should be in the range 1 to 12. The parameter isAm is true if the time is an a.m. time and false otherwise.

3. Write a default constructor and a second constructor for the class Rating-Score, as described in Exercise 9 of the previous chapter.

4. Write a constructor for the class ScienceFairProjectRating, as described in Exercise 10 of the previous chapter. Give this constructor three parameters corresponding to the first three attributes that the exercise describes. The constructor should give default values to the other attributes.

5. Consider a class Characteristic that will be used in an online dating service to assess how compatible two people are. Its attributes are

- description—a string that identifies the characteristic
- rating—an integer between 1 and 10 that indicates a person's desire for this characteristic in another person

  a. Write a constructor that sets the description of the characteristic to a given string and sets the rating to zero to indicate that it has not yet been determined.
  b. Write a private method isValid(aRating) that returns true if the given rating is valid, that is, is between 1 and 10.
  c. Write a method setRating(aRating) that sets the rating to aRating if it is valid.
  d. Write a method setRating that reads a rating from the keyboard, insisting that the rating supplied by the user be valid.

6. Create a class RoomOccupancy that can be used to record the number of people in the rooms of a building. The class has the attributes

- numberInRoom—the number of people in a room
- totalNumber—the total number of people in all rooms as a static variable

The class has the following methods:

- addOneToRoom—adds a person to the room and increases the value of totalNumber
- removeOneFromRoom—removes a person from the room, ensuring that numberInRoom does not go below zero, and decreases the value of totalNumber as needed
- getNumber—returns the number of people in the room
- getTotal—a static method that returns the total number of people

7. Write a program that tests the class RoomOccupancy described in the previous exercise.

8. Sometimes we would like a class that has just a single unique instance. Create a class Merlin that has one attribute, theWizard, which is static and of type Merlin. The class has only one constructor and two methods, as follows:

   - Merlin—a private constructor. Only this class can invoke this constructor; no other class or program can create an instance of Merlin.
   - summon—a static method that returns theWizard if it is not null; if theWizard is null, this method creates an instance of Merlin using the private constructor and assigns it to theWizard before returning it.
   - consult—a non-static method that returns the string "Pull the sword from the stone"

9. Create a program that tests the class Merlin described in the previous exercise. Use the toString method to verify that a unique instance has been created.

10. In the previous chapter, Self-Test Question 16 described a class Person to represent a person. The class has instance variables for a person's name, which is a string, and an integer age. These variables are name and age, respectively.

    a. Write a default constructor for Person that sets name to the string "No name yet" and age to zero.
    b. Write a second constructor for Person that sets name to a given string and age to a given age.
    c. Write a static method createAdult for Person that returns a special instance of this class. The instance represents a generic adult and has the name "An adult" and the age 21.

11. Create a class Android whose objects have unique data. The class has the following attributes:

    - tag—a static integer that begins at 1 and changes each time an instance is created
    - name—a string that is unique for each instance of this class

    Android has the following methods:

    - Android—a default constructor that sets the name to "Bob" concatenated with the value of tag. After setting the name, this constructor changes the value of tag by calling the private method changeTag.
    - getName—returns the name portion of the invoking object.
    - isPrime(n)—a private static method that returns true if n is prime—that is, if it is not divisible by any number from 2 to n – 1.
    - changeTag—a private static method that replaces tag with the next prime number larger than the current value of tag.

12. Create a program that tests the class Android described in the previous exercise.

PROGRAMMING PROJECTS

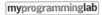

Visit www.myprogramminglab.com to complete many of these Programming Projects online and get instant feedback.

1. Define a utility class for displaying values of type `double`. Call the class `DoubleOut`. Include all the methods from the class `DollarFormat` in Listing 6.14, all the methods from the class `OutputFormat` of Self-Test Question 30, and a method called `scienceWrite` that displays a value of type `double` using e notation, such as `2.13e-12`. (This e notation is also called scientific notation, which explains the method name.) When displayed in e notation, the number should appear with exactly one nonzero digit before the decimal point—unless the number is exactly zero. The method `scienceWrite` will not advance to the next line. Also add a method called `scienceWriteln` that is the same as `scienceWrite` except that it does advance to the next line. All but the last two method definitions can simply be copied from the text (or more easily from the source code for this book that is available on the Web.). Note that you will be overloading the method names `write` and `writeln`.

   Write a driver program to test your method `scienceWriteln`. This driver program should use a stub for the method `scienceWrite`. (Note that this means you can write and test `scienceWriteln` before you even write `scienceWrite`.) Then write a driver program to test the method `scienceWrite`. Finally, write a program that is a sort of super driver program that takes a `double` value as input and then displays it using the two `writeln` methods and the `scienceWriteln` method. Use the number 5 for the number of digits after the decimal point when you need to specify such a number. This super driver program should allow the user to repeat this testing with additional numbers of type `double` until the user is ready to end the program.

2. Modify the definition of the class `Species` in Listing 5.19 of Chapter 5 by removing the method `setSpecies` and adding the following methods:

   - Five constructors: one for each instance variable, one with three parameters for the three instance variables, and a default constructor. Be sure that each constructor sets all of the instance variables.
   - Four methods named `set` that can reset values: one is the same as the method `setSpecies` in Listing 5.16, and the other three each reset one of the instance variables.

   Then write a test program to test all the methods you have added. Finally, repeat Programming Project 1 in Chapter 5, but be sure to use some constructor other than the default constructor when you define new objects of the class `Species`.

3. Repeat Programming Project 4 in Chapter 5. This time, add the following four constructor methods: one for each instance variable, one with two

parameters for the two instance variables, and a default constructor. Be sure that each constructor sets all of the instance variables. Write a driver program to test each of the methods, including each of the four constructors and at least one true and one false case for each of the test methods.

4. Write a new class `TruncatedDollarFormat` that is the same as the class `DollarFormat` from Listing 6.14, except that it truncates rather than rounds to obtain two digits after the decimal point. When truncating, all digits after the first two are discarded, so 1.229 becomes 1.22, not 1.23. Repeat Programming Project 10 in Chapter 4 using this new class.

5. Using the class `Pet` from Listing 6.1, write a program to read data for five pets and display the following data: name of smallest pet, name of largest pet, name of oldest pet, name of youngest pet, average weight of the five pets, and average age of the five pets.

6. Complete and fully test the class `Time` that Exercise 2 describes. Add two more constructors that are analogous to the `setTime` methods described in Parts *c* and *d* of Exercise 2. Also include the following methods:

   - `getTime24` returns a string that gives the time in 24-hour notation *hhmm*. For example, if the hour value is 7 and the minute value is 25, return `"0725"`. If the hour value is 0 and the minute value is 5, return `"0005"`. If the hour value is 15 and the minute value is 30, return `"1530"`.
   - `getTime12` returns a string that gives the time in 12-hour notation *h:mm xx*. For example, if the hour value is 7 and the minute value is 25, return `"7:25 am"`. If the hour value is 0 and the minute value is 5, return `"12:05 am"`. If the hour value is 15 and the minute value is 30, return `"3:30 pm"`.

7. Complete and fully test the class `Characteristic` that Exercise 5 describes. Include the following methods:

   - `getDescription`—returns the description of this characteristic.
   - `getRating`—returns the rating of this characteristic.
   - `getCompatability(Characteristic otherRating)`—returns the compatibility measure of two matching characteristics, or zero if the descriptions do not match.
   - `getCompatibilityMeasure(Characteristic otherRating)`—a private method that returns a compatibility measure as a `double` value using the formula.

$$\left[m = 1 - \frac{(r_1 - r_2)^2}{81} \right]$$

   when both ratings are nonzero; *m* is zero if either rating is zero. (Recall from Exercise 5 that the constructor sets the rating to zero, indicating that it has not yet been determined.)

- `isMatch(Characteristic otherRating)`—a private method that returns true if the descriptions match.

8. Write a Java enumeration `LetterGrade` that represents letter grades A through F, including plus and minus grades. Define a private instance variable to hold a boolean value that is true if the grade is passing. Also, define a constructor that initializes this instance variable, an accessor method `isPassing` to return its value, and a method `toString` that returns the grade as a string. Finally, write a program to demonstrate the enumeration.

9. Complete and fully test the class `Person` that Exercise 10 describes. Include the following additional methods:

   - `getName`—returns the name of the person as a string.
   - `getAge`—returns the age of the person.
   - `setName(first, last)`—sets the name of the person, given a first and last name as strings.
   - `setName(name)`—sets the name of the person, given the entire name as one string.
   - `setAge(age)`—sets the age of the person.
   - `createToddler`—a static method that returns a special instance of the class to represent a toddler. The instance has the name "A toddler" and the age 2.
   - `createPreschooler`—a static method that returns a special instance of the class to represent a preschooler. The instance has the name "A preschooler" and the age 5.
   - `createAdolescent`—a static method that returns a special instance of the class to represent an adolescent. The instance has the name "An adolescent" and the age 9.
   - `createTeenager`—a static method that returns a special instance of the class to represent a teenager. The instance has the name "A teenager" and the age 15.

VideoNote
Solving a similar problem

10. Write a `Temperature` class that represents temperatures in degrees in both Celsius and Fahrenheit. Use a floating-point number for the temperature and a character for the scale: either `'C'` for Celsius or `'F'` for Fahrenheit. The class should have

    - Four constructors: one for the number of degrees, one for the scale, one for both the degrees and the scale, and a default constructor. For each of these constructors, assume zero degrees if no value is specified and Celsius if no scale is given.
    - Two accessor methods: one to return the temperature in degrees Celsius, the other to return it in degrees Fahrenheit. Use the formulas from Programming Project 5 of Chapter 3 and round to the nearest tenth of a degree.

- Three set methods: one to set the number of degrees, one to set the scale, and one to set both.
- Three comparison methods: one to test whether two temperatures are equal, one to test whether one temperature is greater than another, and one to test whether one temperature is less than another.

Write a driver program that tests all the methods. Be sure to invoke each of the constructors, to include at least one true and one false case for each comparison method, and to test at least the following three temperature pairs for equality: 0.0 degrees C and 32.0 degrees F, –40.0 degrees C and –40.0 degrees F, and 100.0 degrees C and 212.0 degrees F.

11. Repeat Programming Project 10 of the previous chapter, but include constructors.

12. Write and fully test a class that represents rational numbers. A rational number can be represented as the ratio of two integer values, a and b, where b is not zero. The class has attributes for the numerator and denominator of this ratio. The ratio should always be stored in its simplest form. That is, any common factor of a and b should be removed. For example, the rational number 40/12 should be stored as 10/3.

VideoNote
Solution to Project 12

The class has the following constructors and methods:

- A default constructor that sets the rational number to 0/1.
- A constructor that has parameters for the numerator and denominator and converts the resulting ratio to simplified form.
- `simplify`—a private method that converts the rational number to simplified form.
- `getGCD(x, y)`—a private static method that returns the largest common factor of the two positive integers x and y, that is, their greatest common divisor. For example, the greatest common divisor of 40 and 12 is 4.
- `getValue`—returns the rational number as a `double` value.
- `toString`—returns the rational number as a string in the form a/b.

13. Write a program that will record the votes for one of two candidates by using the class `VoteRecorder`, which you will design and create. `Vote Recorder` will have static variables to keep track of the total votes for candidates and instance variables to keep track of the votes made by a single person. It will have the following attributes:

- `nameCandidatePresident1`—a static string that holds the name of the first candidate for president
- `nameCandidatePresident2`—a static string that holds the name of the second candidate for president
- `nameCandidateVicePresident1`—a static string that holds the name of the first candidate for vice president

- `nameCandidateVicePresident2`—a static string that holds the name of the second candidate for vice president
- `votesCandidatePresident1`—a static integer that holds the number of votes for the first candidate for president
- `votesCandidatePresident2`—a static integer that holds the number of votes for the second candidate for president
- `votesCandidateVicePresident1`—a static integer that holds the number of votes for the first candidate for vice president
- `votesCandidateVicePresident2`—a static integer that holds the number of votes for the second candidate for vice president
- `myVoteForPresident`—an integer that holds the vote of a single individual for president (0 for no choice, 1 for the first candidate, and 2 for the second candidate)
- `myVoteForVicePresident`—an integer that holds the vote of a single individual for vice president (0 for no choice, 1 for the first candidate, and 2 for the second candidate)

In addition to appropriate constructors, `VoteRecorder` has the following methods:

- `setCandidatesPresident(String name1, String name2)`—a static method that sets the names of the two candidates for president
- `setCandidatesVicePresident(String name1, String name2)`—a static method that sets the names of the two candidates for vice president
- `resetVotes`—a static method that resets the vote counts to zero
- `getCurrentVotePresident`—a static method that returns a string with the current total number of votes for both presidential candidates
- `getCurrentVoteVicePresident`—a static method that returns a string with the current total number of votes for both vice presidential candidates
- `getAndConfirmVotes`—a non-static method that gets an individual's votes, confirms them, and then records them
- `getAVote(String name1, String name2)`—a private method that returns a vote choice for a single race from an individual (0 for no choice, 1 for the first candidate, and 2 for the second candidate)
- `getVotes`—a private method that returns a vote choice for president and vice president from an individual
- `confirmVotes`—a private method that displays a person's vote for president and vice president, asks whether the voter is happy with these choices, and returns true or false according to a yes-or-no response
- `recordVotes`—a private method that will add an individual's votes to the appropriate static variables

Create a program that will conduct an election. The candidates for president are Annie and Bob. The candidates for vice president are John and

Susan. Use a loop to record the votes of many voters. Create a new Vote Recorder object for each voter. After all the voters are done, present the results.

14. Repeat Programming Project 12 from Chapter 5, but include constructors.

15. Change the applet in Listing 6.24 so that after the button is clicked, the button disappears. The label and the icon should remain visible just as in Listing 6.24. (*Hint:* This is not a big change.) Graphics

16. Write the code for an applet or GUI application that has three buttons labeled Red, White, and Blue. When a button is clicked, the background of the applet changes to the color named on the button. Graphics

17. Create an applet or GUI application Light that simulates a simple light. Create one button labeled On/Off. As you click this button, the background color will change between DARK_GRAY and YELLOW. Graphics

18. Create an applet or GUI application that plays a simple guessing game. Give it two buttons labeled Odd and Even. The user must guess whether a secret number is odd or even by clicking one of these buttons. After a guess is made, the applet should display either Congratulations, you are correct! or Sorry, you are wrong. In either case, also display The secret number was: followed by the secret number. Use labels for these three messages. Graphics

    The program will have a private instance variable secretNumber of type long that holds the secret number. You will need to set it in the init method using the following line of code:

    ```
    secretNumber =
       java.util.Calendar.getInstance().getTimeInMillis() % 100;
    ```

    In the actionPerformed method, check which button was pressed and make the appropriate response label visible. After that, make the two buttons invisible (only one guess is allowed) and the label containing the secret number visible.

Answers to Self-Test Questions

1. If a class is named Student, every constructor for this class must also be named Student.

2. You specify no return type for a constructor, not even void.

3. A default constructor is a constructor without parameters.

4. Classes do not always have a default constructor. If you give no constructor definition for a class, Java will automatically provide a default constructor. However, if you provide one or more constructors of any sort, Java does not provide any constructors for you. So if none of your constructors is a default constructor, the class has no default constructor.

5. `yourPet.setPet(correctName, correctAge, correctWeight);`

6. The declaration of an instance variable within a class definition has no keyword `static`, but the declaration of a static variable does use `static`. Every object of the class has its own instance variables. A class has only one of each static variable, and all objects share that static variable.

7. Yes.

8. Yes. An example is the static variable `interestRate` in the method `setInterestRate` in Listing 6.7.

9. No, you cannot reference an instance variable within the definition of a static method, because a static method can be invoked without an object, and so there are no instance variables.

10. Yes.

11. Yes. Note that this means you can reference both static variables and instance variables within a non-static method.

12. It is valid, but a more normal way of doing the same thing is

    `double inches = imensionConverter.convertFeetToInches(2.5);`

13. Yes.

14. Yes, you can invoke a non-static method within the definition of a static method, but only if you have an object of the class and use that object in the invocation of the non-static method.

15. Yes. Invoking a static method within the definition of a non-static method requires nothing special.

16. No, because `addInterest` is not a static method.

17. a. 2; b. 3; c. 2.0; d. 2.0; e. 3.0; f. 3.0; g. A random integer ≥ 10 and ≤ 19. Note that the first two values are of type `long`, while the last four values are of type `double`.

18. `approxSpeed = (int)Math.round(speed);`

    Because `Math.round` returns a value of type `long`, and you want a value of type `int`, you must use a type cast.

19. `longSpeed = Math.round(speed);`

    Because `Math.round` returns a value of type `long`, no type cast is necessary.

20. `long`. Since one argument is of type `long`, the result is of type `long`.

21. The following class and a demonstration program are included in the code that is on the Web.

```java
public class CircleCalculator
{
    public static double getArea(double radius)
    {
        return Math.PI * radius * radius;
    }
    public static double getCircumference(double radius)
    {
        return Math.PI * (radius + radius);
    }
}
```

22. They are all legal.

23. `Double.toString(x)`

24. `Integer.parseInt(s)`

25. `Integer.parseInt(s.trim())`

26. `System.out.println("Largest double is " + Double.MAX_VALUE);`

    `System.out.println("Smallest double is " + Double.MIN_VALUE);`

27. $7.00

28. Use variables of type `long`, rather than variables of type `int`. Note that, because the method `Math.round` returns a value of type `long`, you will not need a type cast in the method `writePositive`. For example,

    `int allCents = (int)(Math.round(amount * 100));`

    would become

    `long allCents = Math.round(amount * 100);`

    The variables `dollars` and `cents` should also be changed to type `long`.

29. This will produce a "Null Pointer Exception" error message. The variables `s1` and `s2` do not name any objects. The lines

    ```java
    Species s1 = null;
    Species s2 = null;
    ```

should be changed to

```
Species s1 = new Species();
Species s2 = new Species();
```

30. The class OutputFormat is in the file OutputFormat.java included with the source code provided on the Web. We also list it here:

```java
public class OutputFormat
{
/**
    Displays a number with digitsAfterPoint digits after the
    decimal point. Rounds any extra digits.
    Does not advance to the next line after output.
*/
public static void write(double number, int digitsAfterPoint)
{
    if (number >= 0)
        writePositive(number, digitsAfterPoint);
    else
    {
        double positiveNumber = -number;
        System.out.print('-');
        writePositive(positiveNumber, digitsAfterPoint);
    }
}
//Precondition: number >= 0
//Displays a number with digitsAfterPoint digits after
//the decimal point. Rounds any extra digits.
private static void writePositive(double number,
int digitsAfterPoint)
{
    int mover = (int)(Math.pow(10, digitsAfterPoint));
        //1 followed by digitsAfterPoint zeros
    int allWhole; //number with the decimal point
        //moved digitsAfterPoint places
    allWhole = (int)(Math.round(number * mover));
    int beforePoint = allWhole / mover;
    int afterPoint = allWhole % mover;
    System.out.print(beforePoint);
    System.out.print('.');
    writeFraction(afterPoint, digitsAfterPoint);
}
//Displays the integer afterPoint with enough zeros
//in front to make it digitsAfterPoint digits long.
private static void writeFraction(int afterPoint,
int digitsAfterPoint)
{
    int n = 1;
    while (n < digitsAfterPoint)
```

```
        {
            if (afterPoint < Math.pow(10, n))
                System.out.print('0');
            n = n + 1;
        }
        System.out.print(afterPoint);
    }
    /**
    Displays a number with digitsAfterPoint digits after the deci-
    mal point. Rounds any extra digits.
    Advances to the next line after output.
    */
    public static void writeln(double number,
    int digitsAfterPoint)
    {
        write(number, digitsAfterPoint);
        System.out.println();
    }
}
```

31. Yes, you could use the names print and println, rather than write and writeln, in the class OutputFormat. Java would have no name confusion with System.out.println, because when you invoke a method in Out-putFormat, you specify the class name before the dot. (If you invoke the method with an object instead of the class name, Java still knows the class name because it knows the type of the object.) However, the methods in OutputFormat behave a little differently from the method System.out. println, so using a different name would be clearer to people.

32. Yes, the 7 would be converted to 7.0 by Java so that the types would match the heading of the constructor having three parameters.

33. No, you cannot overload a method name on the basis of return type. These two methods have the same signatures.

34. Yes, they differ in the type of their parameter, so this is a valid overloading of the method name convertValue. The fact that the methods return values of different types does not affect whether or not both definitions can be used. Only the types of the parameters matter in making overloading valid in this case.

35. Yes, it would be valid because no other method named setSpecies has the same number and types of parameters. The definition follows:

```
public void setSpecies(String newName)
{
    name = newName;
    population = 0;
    growthRate = 0;
}
```

36. Yes, it would be valid because no other method named `setSpecies` has the same number and types of parameters. The definition follows:

```
public void setSpecies(String newName)
{
    name = newName;
}
```

37. No; if you add both of these new methods `setSpecies`, the class will have two definitions of this method that have the same number and types of parameters. That is, both methods have the same signature.

38. Simply delete all occurrences of `this.` from the definition.

39. Add an invocation of the method `trim`. The rewritten version follows

```
public void set(String amountString)
{
    String dollarsString;
    String centsString;
    amountString = amountString.trim();
<The rest of the method definition is the same as in Listing
6.16.>
```

40.
```
public String getNameOfFirst()
{
    return first.getName();
}
public int getAgeOfFirst()
{
    return first.getAge();
}
public double getWeightOrFirst()
{
    return first.getWeight();
}
```

41. a. 3
    b. false
    c. A positive integer
    d. `Suit.CLUBS`
    e. `Suit.SPADES`
    f. `"black"`
    g. `"spades"`

42. `import mypackages.library1.*;`

43. You must make the following the first instruction line in the file, ignoring blank lines and comments:
    `package mypackages.library1;`

44. A package name must be a path name for the directory that contains the classes in the package, but the package name uses dots in place of slashes. When naming the package, you use a relative path name that starts from any directory named in the setting of the class path (environment) variable.

45. The way to do this depends a little on your operating system and on your personal preferences. Here is an outline of what you should do: Choose a package name and insert the following at the start of the file Pet.java:

```
package Package_Name;
```

Compile the modified file Pet.java. Place both of the files Pet.java and Pet.class into the directory corresponding to Package_Name.

46. You may name the content pane anything you wish, other than a keyword. So the following is perfectly legal:

```
Container insideOfApplet = getContentPane();
```

Of course, if you make this change, you must replace contentPane with insideOfApplet wherever else it occurs in the method actionPerformed.

47. When we say that an event is "sent" to a listener object, what we really mean is that some method in the listener object is invoked and given the event object as the argument. This invocation happens automatically. Your applet class definition will not normally contain an invocation of this method.

48. It would have no effect on the program, as long as you also replace e with buttonEvent wherever else e occurs in the method actionPerformed. The e is a parameter for the method, and we can use any non-keyword identifier as the parameter.

49. Change the code

```
JButton cloudyButton = new JButton("Cloudy");
contentPane.add(cloudyButton);
cloudyButton.addActionListener(this);
```

to the following:

```
JButton cloudyButton = new JButton("Cloudy");
ImageIcon nastyFaceIcon = new ImageIcon("nasty.gif");
cloudyButton.setIcon(nastyFaceIcon);
contentPane.add(cloudyButton);
cloudyButton.addActionListener(this);
```

The complete applet code is in the file ButtonIconDemo2.java included with the source code for this book that is available on the Web.

50. Yes it is OK. The parameter e must be included in the method heading but need not be used in the method body.

51. The listener, which is the applet itself, is listening to only one button, so it need not decide which button was clicked. There is only one button and hence only one action.

52. Take the following three steps:

- Add the statement

```
aButton.setVisible(false);
```

as the last one in the definition of the method `actionPerformed`.

- Make `aButton` a private instance variable by adding the statement

```
private JButton aButton;
```

- Delete `JButton` from the statement that creates `aButton`.

Arrays 7

7.1 ARRAY BASICS 481
Creating and Accessing Arrays 482
Array Details 485
The Instance Variable `length` 488
More About Array Indices 491
Initializing Arrays 494

7.2 ARRAYS IN CLASSES AND METHODS 495
Case Study: Sales Report 495
Indexed Variables as Method Arguments 503
Entire Arrays as Arguments to a Method 505
Arguments for the Method `main` 507
Array Assignment and Equality 508
Methods That Return Arrays 511

7.3 PROGRAMMING WITH ARRAYS AND CLASSES 515
Programming Example: A Specialized List Class 515
Partially Filled Arrays 523

7.4 SORTING AND SEARCHING ARRAYS 525
Selection Sort 525
Other Sorting Algorithms 529
Searching an Array 531

7.5 MULTIDIMENSIONAL ARRAYS 532
Multidimensional-Array Basics 533
Multidimensional-Array Parameters and Returned Values 536
Java's Representation of Multidimensional Arrays 539
Ragged Arrays (*Optional*) 540
Programming Example: Employee Time Records 542

7.6 GRAPHICS SUPPLEMENT 548
Text Areas and Text Fields 548
Programming Example: A Question-and-Answer Applet 548
The Classes *JTextArea* and *JTextField* 551
Drawing Polygons 553

Chapter Summary 556   Programming Projects 562   Answers to Self-Test Questions 568

They stood at attention in a neat row, all with the same uniform, yet each with his own values.

—WARREN PEACE, *The Lieutenant's Array*

An array is a special kind of object used to store a collection of data. An array differs from the other objects you have seen in two ways:

- All the data stored in an array must be of the same type. For example, you might use an array to store a list of values of type double that record rainfall readings in centimeters. Or you might use an array to store a list of objects of some class called Species that contain the records for various endangered species.
- An array object has only a small number of predefined methods. Because arrays were used by programmers for many years before classes were invented, they use a special notation of their own to invoke those few predefined methods, and most people do not even think of them as methods.

In this chapter, we introduce you to arrays and show you how to use them in Java.

OBJECTIVES

After studying this chapter, you should be able to

- Describe the nature and purpose of an array
- Use arrays in simple Java programs
- Define methods that have an array as a parameter
- Define methods that return an array
- Use an array as an instance variable in a class
- Use an array that is not filled completely
- Order, or sort, the elements in an array
- Search an array for a particular item
- Define and use multidimensional arrays
- Insert text fields and text areas into your applets
- Draw arbitrary polygons in your applets

PREREQUISITES

This is the first point in this book where you have a significant choice as to what to read next. If you prefer, instead of reading this chapter now, you can go on in the book and return to this discussion of arrays at a later time. You can read Chapters 8.1 through 8.2, 8.5, 9, and 10, except for Section 10.5, as you wish before you read this chapter. Sections 8.3 and 8.4 include references to arrays for some of the examples.

Section 7.1 depends only on Chapters 1 through 4. However, you should be familiar with the material in all of the previous chapters before reading the remaining sections of this chapter.

If you are reading the graphics supplement sections in each chapter, you can—and are encouraged to—read the first part of this chapter's graphic supplement, whether you read the rest of the chapter or not.

7.1 ARRAY BASICS

And in such indexes, although small pricks
To their subsequent volumes, there is seen
The baby figure of the giant mass
Of things to come.

—WILLIAM SHAKESPEARE, *TROILUS AND CRESSIDA*

Suppose you want to compute the average temperature for the seven days in a week. You might use the following code:

```
Scanner keyboard = new Scanner(System.in);
System.out.println("Enter 7 temperatures:");
double sum = 0;
for (int count = 0; count < 7; count++)
{
    double next = keyboard.nextDouble();
    sum = sum + next;
}
double average = sum / 7;
```

This works fine if all you want to know is the average. But let's say you also want to know which temperatures are above and which are below the average. Now you have a problem. In order to compute the average, you must read the seven temperatures, and you must compute the average before comparing each temperature to it. Thus, to be able to compare each temperature to the average, you must remember the seven temperatures. How can you do this? The obvious answer is to use seven variables of type `double`. This is a bit awkward, because seven is a lot of variables to declare, and in other situations, the problem can be even worse. Imagine doing the same thing for each day of the year instead of just each day of the week. Writing 365 variable declarations would be absurd. Arrays provide us with an elegant way to declare a collection of related variables. An **array** is a collection of items of the same type. It is something like a list of variables, but it handles the naming of the variables in a nice, compact way.

Items in an array have the same data type

Creating and Accessing Arrays

In Java, an array is a special kind of object, but it is often more useful to think of an array as a collection of variables of the same type. For example, an array consisting of a collection of seven variables of type `double` can be created as follows:

```
double[] temperature = new double[7];
```

This is like declaring the following seven strangely named variables to have the type `double`:

```
temperature[0], temperature[1], temperature[2], temperature[3],
temperature[4], temperature[5], temperature[6]
```

An index is an integer expression that indicates an array element

Variables like `temperature[0]` and `temperature[1]` that have an integer expression in square brackets are called **indexed variables, subscripted variable, array elements,** or simply **elements.** The integer expression within the square brackets is called an **index** or a **subscript.** Note that the numbering starts with 0, not 1.

REMEMBER Array Indices Begin at 0

In Java, the indices of an array always start with 0. They never start with 1 or any number other than 0.

Each of these seven variables can be used just like any other variable of type `double`. For example, all of the following statements are allowed in Java:

```
temperature[3] = 32;
temperature[6] = temperature[3] + 5;
System.out.println(temperature[6]);
```

When we think of these indexed variables as being grouped together into one collective item, we will call them an array. So we can refer to the array named `temperature` without using any square brackets. Figure 7.1 illustrates the array `temperature`.

But these seven variables are more than just seven plain old variables of type `double`. The number in square brackets is part of the name of each of these variables, and it does not have to be an integer constant. Instead, you can use any expression that evaluates to an integer that is at least 0 and—for this example—at most 6. So the following code, for instance, is allowed:

```
Scanner keyboard = new Scanner(System.in);
System.out.println("Enter day number (0 - 6):");
int index = keyboard.nextInt();
System.out.println("Enter temperature for day " + index);
temperature[index] = keyboard.nextDouble();
```

FIGURE 7.1   A Common Way to Visualize an Array

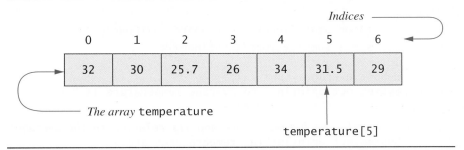

The array temperature

temperature[5]

Since an index can be an expression, we can write a loop to read values into the array temperature, as follows:

```
System.out.println("Enter 7 temperatures:");
for (int index = 0;index < 7; index++)
    temperature[index] = keyboard.nextDouble();
```

The user could type the seven values on separate lines or all on one line, separated by spaces. After the array values are read in, we can display them as follows:

```
System.out.println("The 7 temperatures are:");
for (int index = 0; index < 7; index++)
    System.out.print(temperature[index] + " ");
System.out.println( );
```

The program in Listing 7.1 shows an example that uses our sample array temperature as seven indexed variables, all of type double. Note that the program uses for loops similar to the ones we just considered.

LISTING 7.1   An Array of Temperatures *(part 1 of 2)*

```
/**
Reads 7 temperatures from the user and shows which are above
and which are below the average of the 7 temperatures.
*/
import java.util.Scanner;

public class ArrayOfTemperatures
{
    public static void main(String[] args)
    {
        double[] temperature = new double[7];

        // Read temperatures and compute their average:
        Scanner keyboard = new Scanner(System.in);
        System.out.println("Enter 7 temperatures:");
        double sum = 0;
        for (int index = 0; index < 7; index++)
```

(continued)

LISTING 7.1 An Array of Temperatures *(part 2 of 2)*

```java
    {
        temperature[index] = keyboard.nextDouble();
        sum = sum + temperature[index];
    }
    double average = sum / 7;
    System.out.println("The average temperature is " +
                        average);

    // Display each temperature and its relation to the average:
    System.out.println("The temperatures are");
    for (int index = 0; index < 7; index++)
    {
        if (temperature[index] < average)
            System.out.println(temperature[index] +
                                " below average");
        else if (temperature[index] > average)
            System.out.println(temperature[index] +
                                " above average");
        else //temperature[index] == average
            System.out.println(temperature[index] +
                                " the average");
    }

    System.out.println("Have a nice week.");
    }
}
```

Sample Screen Output

```
Enter 7 temperatures:
32
30
25.7
26
34
31.5
29
The average temperature is 29.7428
The temperatures are
32.0 above average
30.0 above average
25.7 below average
26.0 below average
34.0 above average
31.5 above average
29.0 below average
Have a nice week.
```

Array Details

You create an array in the same way that you would create an object of a class type using the operation new, but the notation is slightly different. When creating an array of elements of type *Base_Type*, the syntax is as follows:

```
Base_Type[] Array_Name = new Base_Type[Length];
```

For example, the following creates an array named pressure that is equivalent to 100 variables of type int:

```
int[] pressure = new int[100];
```

Alternatively, the preceding can be broken down into two steps:

```
int[] pressure;
pressure = new int[100];
```

The first step declares as an array of integers. The second step allocates enough memory for the array to hold up to 100 integers.

The type for the array elements is called the **base type** of the array. In this example, the base type is int. The number of elements in an array is called the **length, size,** or **capacity** of the array.

ASIDE **Alternative Syntax for Declaring an Array**

Although we do not encourage its use, there is an alternative syntax for array declarations that you may encounter. You can write the square brackets after the variable instead of after the base type, as in the following example:

```
char alphabet[];
```

So this sample array pressure has length 100, which means it has indexed variables pressure[0]through pressure[99]. Note that because the indices start at 0, an array of length 100, such as pressure, will have *no* indexed variable pressure[100].

The number of elements in an array is its length

The base type of an array can be any data type. In particular, it can be a class type. The following statement creates an array named entry whose elements are Species objects, where Species is a class:

The type of the array elements is the array's base type

```
Species[] entry = new Species[3];
```

This array is a collection of the three variables entry[0], entry[1], and entry[2], all of type Species.

RECAP **Declaring and Creating an Array**

You declare and create an array in almost the same way that you declare and create objects of classes. There is only a slight difference in the syntax.

(continued)

SYNTAX

```
Base_Type[] Array_Name  = new Base_Type[Length];
```

EXAMPLES

```
char[] symbol = new char[80];
double[] reading = new double[100];
Species[] specimen = new Species[80]; //Species is a class
```

REMEMBER How to Use Square Brackets with Arrays

There are three different ways to use square brackets [] with an array name. They can be used

- With a data type when declaring an array. For example,

    ```
    int[] pressure;
    ```

    declares—but does not allocate memory for—**pressure** as an array of integers.

- To enclose an integer expression when creating a new array. For example,

    ```
    pressure = new int[100];
    ```

    allocates memory for the array **pressure** of 100 integers.

- To name an indexed variable of the array. For example, **pressure[3]** in the following two lines is an indexed variable:

    ```
    pressure[3] = keyboard.nextInt();
    System.out.println("You entered" + pressure[3]);
    ```

As we mentioned previously, the value inside the square brackets can be any expression that evaluates to an integer. When creating an array, instead of using an integer literal, you can—and should—use a named constant. For example, you should use a constant such as NUMBER_OF_READINGS instead of 100 when you create the array pressure:

Use a named constant when defining an array

```
public static final int NUMBER_OF_READINGS = 100;
int[] pressure = new int[NUMBER_OF_READINGS];
```

Java allocates memory for an array, as well as for any other object, at execution time. So if you do not know how large to make an array when you write a program, you can read the array's length from the keyboard, as follows:

FIGURE 7.2   Array Terminology

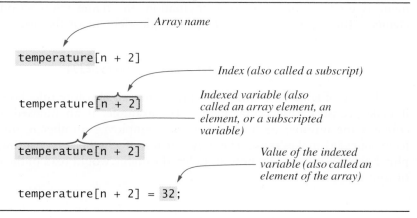

```
System.out.println("How many temperatures do you have?");
int size = keyboard.nextInt();
double[] temperature = new double[size];
```

Reading an array length

You can also use any expression that evaluates to an appropriate integer when naming an indexed variable of an array, as in the following examples:

```
int point = 2;
temperature[point + 3] = 32;
System.out.println("Temperature is " + temperature[point + 3]);
```

Note that `temperature[point + 3]`in the preceding code is the same indexed variable as `temperature[5]`, because `point + 3` evaluates to 5.

Figure 7.2 illustrates some of the most common terms used when referring to arrays. Notice that the word *element* has two meanings. It can be used to refer to an indexed variable as well as to the value of an indexed variable.

■ PROGRAMMING TIP   In General, Use Singular Names for Arrays

If you want an array to hold entries, each of which is an object of a class called `Species`, you might be tempted to use something like the following:

```
Species[] entries = new Species[20]; //Valid but not nice.
```

Using a plural, like `entries`, seems to make sense, since the array holds more than one element. However, programmers find that their programs often read better if they use a singular form for an array name, like the following:

```
Species[] entry = new Species[20]; //Nicer.
```

The reason that the singular form works better here is that, when the array name is used in some sort of computation, the name refers to only one element. The expression `entry[2]` is a single element of the array, as in a statement such as

```
System.out.println("The entry is " + entry[2]);
```

The use of singular names for arrays is not an absolute rule. Sometimes it makes sense to use plural names. For example, if an indexed variable contains the number of hours worked by employee number n, the plural form `hours[n]` makes sense. The only sure test of whether to use a singular or plural name is to consider how an indexed variable would read in the context of your Java code. ∎

The Instance Variable `length`

An array is a kind of object, and like other objects, it might have instance variables. As it turns out, an array has only one public instance variable, namely the variable `length`, which is equal to the length of the array. For example, if you create an array by writing

The array e has a length of e.length

```
Species[] entry = new Species[20];
```

`entry.length` has a value of 20. By using the instance variable `length` instead of a literal like 20, you can make your program clearer and more general. A name like `entry.length` means more to a reader of your program than a number whose meaning may not always be obvious. In addition, if you later decide to change the size of the array, you have no need to change occurrences of `entry.length`. Note that `length` is final, so its value cannot be changed.

GOTCHA   Assigning a Value to the Instance Variable `length`

Your program cannot assign a value to the instance variable `length`, as it is a final variable. For example, the following attempt to change the size of an array is invalid:

```
entry.length = 10; //Illegal!
```
∎

In Listing 7.2 we have rewritten the program in Listing 7.1 using the instance variable `length`. We have also read the size of the array `temperature` from the user into the variable `size`. In this example, we could use `size` instead of `temperature.length`. However, since `size` is not final, its value can change and so might not always equal the value of `temperature.length`.

LISTING 7.2   An Array of Temperatures—Revised *(part 1 of 2)*

```java
/**
 Reads temperatures from the user and shows which are above
 and which are below the average of all the temperatures.
*/
import java.util.Scanner;

public class ArrayOfTemperatures2
{
    public static void main(String[] args)
    {
        Scanner keyboard = new Scanner(System.in);
        System.out.println("How many temperatures do you have?");
        int size = keyboard.nextInt( );
        double[] temperature = new double[size];

        // Read temperatures and compute their average:
        System.out.println("Enter " + temperature.length +
                           " temperatures:");
        double sum = 0;
        for (int index = 0; index < temperature.length; index++)
        {
            temperature[index] = keyboard.nextDouble();
            sum = sum + temperature[index];
        }
        double average = sum / temperature.length;
        System.out.println("The average temperature is " +
                           average);

        // Display each temperature and its relation to the
        // average:
        System.out.println("The temperatures are");
        for (int index = 0; index < temperature.length; index++)
        {
            if (temperature[index] < average)
                System.out.println(temperature[index] +
                                   " below average");
            else if (temperature[index] > average)
                System.out.println(temperature[index] +
                                   " above average");
            else //temperature[index] == average
                System.out.println(temperature[index] +
                                   " the average");
        }

        System.out.println("Have a nice week.");
    }
}
```

(continued)

LISTING 7.2   An Array of Temperatures—Revised *(part 2 of 2)*

Sample Screen Output

```
How many temperatures do you have?
3
Enter 3 temperatures:
32
26.5
27
The average temperature is 28.5
The temperatures are
32.0 above average
26.5 below average
27.0 below average
Have a nice week.
```

■ **PROGRAMMING TIP**   Use a for Loop to Step Through an Array

The for statement is the perfect mechanism for stepping through the elements of an array. For example, the following for loop from Listing 7.2 illustrates one way to step through an array:

```java
for (int index = 0; index <temperature.length; index++)
{
    temperature[index] = keyboard.nextDouble();
    sum = sum + temperature[index];
}
```

Another way to step through an entire array—after its elements have been given values—uses the for-each statement that we introduced in Chapter 4. For example, the last loop in Listing 7.2 that displays the values in the array temperature can be revised as follows:

```java
for (int value : temperature)
{
    if (value < average)
        System.out.println(value + " below average.");
    else if (value > average)
        System.out.println(value + " above average.");
    else //value == average
        System.out.println(value + " the average.");
}
```

More About Array Indices

You know that the index of the first element in any Java array is 0. The last valid index of an array whose length is n is $n - 1$. In particular, the last valid index of the array temperature is temperature.length - 1.

An easy mistake to make when programming with arrays is to use an indexed expression that evaluates to an invalid array index. For example, consider the following array declaration:

```
double[] entry = new double[5];
```

Every index value for the array entry must be one of the five integers 0, 1, 2, 3, or 4. For example, if your program contains the indexed variable entry[n + 2], the value of the index n + 2 must be one of these five integers. If an index expression evaluates to some integer other than 0 through one less than the length of the array, the index is said to be **out of bounds** or **invalid**. If your code uses an index expression that is out of bounds, your code will compile without any error message, but you will get one when you run your program.

Beware of invalid indices

REMEMBER Array Indices Must Be Within Bounds to Be Valid

Since the index of the first element in a Java array is always 0, the last index number is not the length of the array, but is one less than the length of the array. Be sure that your indices stay within this range.

One common way that array indices go out of bounds is when an array-processing loop is iterated one too many times. For example, let's consider a loop that fills an array. Suppose we want to read a sequence of nonnegative numbers from the keyboard, using a negative number as a sentinel value at the end of the data. We might use the following code:

```java
System.out.println("Enter a list of nonnegative integers.");
System.out.println("Place a negative integer at the end.");
int[] list = new int[10];
Scanner keyboard = new Scanner(System.in);
int number = keyboard.nextInt();
int i = 0;
while (number >= 0)
{
    list[i] = number;
    i++;
    number = keyboard.nextInt();
}
```

If the user enters more numbers than can fit in the array, this code produces an array index that is out of bounds.

A better version of the preceding `while` loop is the following:

```
while ( (i <list.length) && (number >= 0) )
{
    list[i] = number;
    i++;
    number = keyboard.nextInt();
}
if (number >= 0)
{
    System.out.println("Could not read in all the numbers.");
    System.out.println("Only able to read" + list.length +
                        " numbers.");
}
```

This `while` loop will end if the array becomes full, because we ensure that the index `i` is less than `list.length`.

GOTCHA   Array Index Out of Bounds

An array index that is less than 0 or greater than or equal to the size of the array will cause an error message during program execution. ■

Suppose that you want to number the data stored in an array starting with 1. Perhaps your company's employees are numbered starting with 1. But Java always begins an array at index 0. One way to handle this situation is to have your code reconcile the array indices with the existing numbering scheme. For example, you might use code such as the following in a payroll program:

Adjusting code to deal with 0 indices

```
public static final int NUMBER_OF_EMPLOYEES = 100;
. . .
int[] hours = new int[NUMBER_OF_EMPLOYEES];
Scanner keyboard = new Scanner(System.in);
System.out.println("Enter hours worked for each employee:");
for (int index = 0; index < hours.length; index++);
{
    System.out.println("Enter hours for employee " +
                        (index + 1));
    hours[index] = keyboard.nextInt();
}
```

With this code, the employees are numbered 1 through 100, but their hours worked are stored in elements `hours[0]` through `hours[99]`.

Situations like this one might confuse you, however, leading to mistakes in your program. Overall, the code will be easier to understand if the two numbering schemes match. You can achieve this by rewriting the previous code to increase the size of the array by 1 and ignore the element at index 0, as follows:

```
int[] hours = new int[NUMBER_OF_EMPLOYEES + 1];
Scanner keyboard = new Scanner(System.in);
System.out.println("Enter hours worked for each employee:");
for (int index = 1; index <hours.length; index++);
{
    System.out.println("Enter hours for employee" + index);
    hours[index] = keyboard.nextInt();
}
```

Ignoring the element at index 0

With this revised code, the employees are still numbered 1 through 100, but their hours worked are stored in the elements hours[1] through hours[100]. We do not use hours[0], and since the size of the array is 101 instead of 100, hours[100] is valid.

Note that the last valid value of index is hours.length - 1, as it was in our first version of this code. However, hours.length here is one larger than it was earlier. Replacing

```
index < hours.length
```

in the for statement with

```
index <= NUMBER_OF_EMPLOYEES
```

is likely to be clearer to most people. However, if other programmers are going to be looking at your code, they may be expecting a value to be stored at index 0. The bottom line is that all programmers collaborating on a project should use the same coding practices or confusion and errors may result.

■ **PROGRAMMING TIP** **Don't Be Afraid to Waste an Element in an Array**

In our previous example, we never use hours[0]. Yes, we "wasted" an array element, but we also made our code easier to write and to understand. As a result, we likely will make fewer mistakes. However, other programmers who may be working with your code should be aware of your coding practice. In Java, the amount of memory we wasted is not significant. Even if we create an array of large objects, Java stores only the addresses of the objects in the array. This might not be the case for other programming languages. For example, C++ would store the object itself, not its address, in the array. Wasting a location in a C++ array might be more significant than doing so in a Java program. ■

■ **PROGRAMMING TIP** **Get Used to Index Values That Are 0**

The index of the first element in an array is 0. Java programmers know this. Unless your application gives you a good reason to adjust your code so that you can ignore this index, don't. The previous example showed an adjustment that aligns two numbering systems, reducing confusion and making errors less likely. However, adjusting your code to avoid using a 0 index should *not* be a routine practice. ■

Initializing Arrays

An array can be initialized at the time that it is declared. To do this, you enclose the values for the individual indexed variables in braces and place them after the assignment operator, as in the following example:

```
double[] reading = {3.3, 15.8, 9.7};
```

The size of the array—that is, its length—is set to the minimum that will hold the given values. So this initializing declaration is equivalent to the following statements:

```
double[] reading = new double[3];
reading[0] = 3.3;
reading[1] = 15.8;
reading[2] = 9.7;
```

If you do not initialize the elements of an array, they might automatically be initialized to a default value for the base type. For example, if you do not initialize an array of integers, each element of the array will be initialized to 0. However, it is usually clearer to do your own explicit initialization. You can initialize an array either by using the braces, as we just described, by reading values directly into array elements, or by assigning values, as we do in the following for loop:

Explicit initialization is safer than default initialization

```
int[] count = new int[100];
for (int i = 0; i < 100; i++)
    count[i] = 0;
```

SELF-TEST QUESTIONS

1. What output will be produced by the following code?

```
int[] anArray = new int[10];
for (int i = 0; i <anArray.length; i++)
    anArray[i] = 2 * i;
for (int element : anArray)
    System.out.print(element + " ");
System.out.println();
```

2. What output will be produced by the following code?

```
char[] vowel = {'a', 'e', 'i', 'o', 'u'};
for (int index = 0; index <vowel.length; index++)
    System.out.println(vowel[index]);
```

3. What output will be produced by the following code?

```java
double tide[] = {12.2, -7.3, 14.2, 11.3};
System.out.println("Tide 1 is " + tide[1]);
System.out.println("Tide 2 is " + tide[2]);
```

4. Consider the following array:

```java
int[] a = new int[10];
```

What is the last index of a? What is the value of a.length?

5. What is wrong with the following code to initialize an array b?

```java
int[] b = new int[10];
for (int i = 1; i <= b.length; i++)
    b[i] = 5 * i;
```

6. Write a complete Java program that reads 20 values of type double from the keyboard into an array. Display the last (20th) number read. Then display the numbers in the array and how much each number differs from the 20th number read. For example, if the last value typed by the user is 5.0, the difference between the array element 2.0 and 5.0 is –3.0. If an array element is 7.0, the difference is 2.0. Assume that the user enters 20 numbers, one per line, at the keyboard. You need not give elaborate instructions to the user.

7.2 ARRAYS IN CLASSES AND METHODS

A little more than kin, and less than kind.

—WILLIAM SHAKESPEARE, *HAMLET*

Arrays can be used as instance variables in classes. Methods can have an indexed variable or an entire array as an argument and can return an array. In short, arrays can be used with classes and methods just as other objects can. We begin with a case study that uses an array as an instance variable in a class.

CASE STUDY   Sales Report

In this case study, we will write a program to generate sales reports for a company's team of sales associates. The company wants to easily see which associate or associates have the highest sales and to know how the sales of each associate compare to the average.

The task's specification

Since we need to record a name and the sales figures for each associate, we can design a class for a single sales associate that holds these two data items. Our class can perform input and output and have a reasonable complement of accessor and mutator methods. This class definition is rather routine and is shown in Listing 7.3.

LISTING 7.3 Sales Associate Class

```java
import java.util.Scanner;
/**
 Class for sales associate records.
*/
public class SalesAssociate
{
    private String name;
    private double sales;
    public SalesAssociate()
    {
        name = "No record";
        sales = 0;
    }

    public SalesAssociate(String initialName, double initialSales)
    {
        set(initialName, initialSales);
    }

    public void set(String newName, double newSales)
    {
        name = newName;
        sales = newSales;
    }

    public void readInput()
    {
        System.out.print("Enter name of sales associate: ");
        Scanner keyboard = new Scanner(System.in);
        name = keyboard.nextLine();

        System.out.print("Enter associate's sales: $");
        sales = keyboard.nextDouble();
    }

    public void writeOutput()
    {
        System.out.println("Name: " + name);
        System.out.println("Sales: $" + sales);
    }

    public String getName()
    {
        return name;
    }

    public double getSales()
    {
        return sales;
    }
}
```

Our program will need an array to keep track of the data for all sales associates. It will also need to record the highest sales and the average sales. Therefore, we will need to design another class. We can give our new class the following instance variables to record the desired data:

```
private double highestSales;
private double averageSales;
private SalesAssociate[] team;
```

The instance
variables

We need to know the number of associates. This number will be the same as team.length, but having a separate well-named variable for the number of associates is a good idea. So let's include the following instance variable:

```
private int numberOfAssociates; //Same as team.length
```

The job of our program breaks down into these main subtasks:

The program's
subtasks

1. Get ready.

2. Obtain the data.

3. Compute some statistics (update the instance variables).

4. Display the results.

We should name our new class and its methods. To organize our thoughts, we can draw the class diagram shown in Figure 7.3. Thus, we know that our class will look like this:

```
public class SalesReporter
{
    private double highestSales;
    private double averageSales;
    private SalesAssociate[] team;
    private int numberOfAssociates; //Same as team.length

    public static void main(String[ ] args)
    {
        SalesReporter clerk = new SalesReporter();
        clerk.getData();
        clerk.computeStats();
        clerk.displayResults();
    }
    <More stuff needs to be added here.>
}
```

All that remains is to write the three methods, getData, computeStats, and displayResults and to test and debug the program. We will tackle the three methods in order.

FIGURE 7.3 **Class Diagram for the Class** Sales Reporter

```
┌────────────────────────────────────────────────────────┐
│                      SalesReporter                     │
├────────────────────────────────────────────────────────┤
│  - highestSales: double                                │
│  - averageSales: double                                │
│  - team: SalesAssociate[]                              │
│  - numberOfAssociates: int                             │
├────────────────────────────────────────────────────────┤
│  + getData(): void                                     │
│  + computeStats(): void                                │
│  + displayResults(): void                              │
└────────────────────────────────────────────────────────┘
```

The loop in getData

The input method getData is relatively straightforward, especially since we have an input method for objects of the class SalesAssociate. After we read the number of associates, we can write the following basic input loop:

```
for (int i = 1; i <= numberOfAssociates; i++)
{
    System.out.println("Enter data for associate number" + i);
    team[i].readInput();
}
```

Associate i is in team[i]

Although the array indices begin at 0, and the associates are numbered starting with 1, we have used team[i] for associate i. That is, we decided to ignore team[0]. Thus, we need to allocate an extra location in the array, as follows:

```
team = new SalesAssociate[numberOfAssociates + 1];
```

Since we read numberOfAssociates in getData, we will place this statement in that method as well.

But another problem remains. When we test the previous loop, we will get an error message saying something about a "null pointer." This problem arises because the base type of the array team is a class type. To see the problem, consider another situation first. Suppose we had the following code:

```
SalesAssociate s;
s.readInput();
```

This code would produce the same error message regarding a "null pointer." The problem is that the variable s is just a name; it does not yet reference any object of the class SalesAssociate. The preceding code omitted the usual use of new. The code should be

```
SalesAssociate s = new SalesAssociate();
s.readInput();
```

The indexed variable team[i] is also a variable of a class type, and so it is also just a name. You need to assign a SalesAssociate object to team[i] before executing

```
team[i].readInput();
```

Thus, we need to add the following statement to our loop:

```
team[i] = new SalesAssociate();
```

The complete definition of the method getData with this line inserted is shown in Listing 7.4.

LISTING 7.4   **A Sales Report Program** *(part 1 of 3)*

```java
import java.util.Scanner;
/**
 Program to generate sales report.
*/
public class SalesReporter
{
    private double highestSales;
    private double averageSales;
    private SalesAssociate[] team;  //The array object is
                                    //created in getData.
    private int numberOfAssociates; //Same as team.length
    /**
     Reads the number of sales associates and data for each one.
    */
    public void getData()
    {
        Scanner keyboard = new Scanner(System.in);
        System.out.println("Enter number of sales associates:");
        numberOfAssociates = keyboard.nextInt();
        team = new SalesAssociate[numberOfAssociates + 1];

        for (int i = 1; i <= numberOfAssociates; i++)
        {
            team[i] = new SalesAssociate();
            System.out.println("Enter data for associate " + i);
            team[i].readInput();
            System.out.println();
        }
    }
```

The main *method is at the end of the class.*

Array object created here.

SalesAssociate *objects created here.*

(continued)

LISTING 7.4   A Sales Report Program *(part 2 of 3)*

```java
/**
 Computes the average and highest sales figures.
 Precondition: There is at least one salesAssociate.
*/
public void computeStats()
{
    double nextSales = team[1].getSales();
    highestSales = nextSales;
    double sum = nextSales;
    for (int i = 2; i <= numberOfAssociates; i++)
    {
        nextSales = team[i].getSales();
        sum = sum + nextSales;
        if (nextSales > highestSales)
            highestSales = nextSales; //highest sales so far.
    }
    averageSales = sum / numberOfAssociates;
}
/**
 Displays sales report on the screen.
*/
public void displayResults()
{
    System.out.println("Average sales per associate is $" +
                        averageSales);
    System.out.println("The highest sales figure is $" +
                        highestSales);
    System.out.println();
    System.out.println("The following had the highest sales:");
    for (int i = 1; i <= numberOfAssociates; i++)
    {
        double nextSales = team[i].getSales();
        if (nextSales == highestSales)
        {
            team[i].writeOutput();
            System.out.println("$" + (nextSales - averageSales)
                            + " above the average.");
            System.out.println();
        }
    }

    System.out.println("The rest performed as follows:");
    for (int i = 1; i <= numberOfAssociates; i++)
    {
        double nextSales = team[i].getSales();
        if (team[i].getSales() != highestSales)
        {
```

Already processed **team[1]**, *so the loop starts with* **team[2]**.

(continued)

LISTING 7.4   A Sales Report Program *(part 3 of 3)*

```
                team[i].writeOutput();
                if (nextSales >= averageSales)
                    System.out.println("$" + (nextSales -
                            averageSales) + " above the average.");
                else
                    System.out.println("$" + (averageSales -
                            nextSales) + " below the average.");
                System.out.println();
            }
        }
    }
    public static void main(String[] args)
    {
        SalesReporter clerk = new SalesReporter();
        clerk.getData();
        clerk.computeStats();
        clerk.displayResults();
    }
}
```

Sample Screen Output

```
Enter number of sales associates:
3
Enter data for associate number 1
Enter name of sales associate: Dusty Rhodes
Enter associate's sales: $36000
Enter data for associate number 2
Enter name of sales associate: Natalie Dressed
Enter associate's sales: $50000
Enter data for associate number 3
Enter name of sales associate: Sandy Hair
Enter associate's sales: $10000
Average sales per associate is $32000.0
The highest sales figure is $50000.0
The following had the highest sales:
Name: Natalie Dressed
Sales: $50000.0
$18000.0 above the average.
The rest performed as follows:
Name: Dusty Rhodes
Sales: $36000.0
$4000.0 above the average.
Name: Sandy Hair
Sales: $10000.0
$22000.0 below the average.
```

Next we turn our attention to the method computeStats and come up with the following code:

A draft of
the loop in
computeStats

```
for (int i = 1; i <= numberOfAssociates; i++)
{
    sum = sum + team[i].getSales();
    if (team[i].getSales() > highest)
        highestSales = team[i].getSales();//highest sales
}                                        //so far.
average = sum / numberOfAssociates;
```

This loop is basically OK, but the variables sum and highest must be initialized before the loop begins. We can initialize sum to 0, but what value do we use to initialize highest? Perhaps a negative number, since sales cannot be negative. Or can they? If a customer returns goods that is considered a negative sale, so sales can indeed be negative. However, we know that the company always has at least one sales associate, and so we can initialize both sum and highest to the sales for the first associate. This takes one case outside the loop and places it before the loop, as follows:

```
highestSales = team[1].getSales();
double sum = team[1].getSales();
for (int i = 2; i <= numberOfAssociates; i++)
{
    sum = sum + team[1].getSales();
    if (team[i].getSales() > highest)
        highestSales = team[i].getSales();//highest sales
                                          //so far.

}
average = sum / numberOfAssociates;
```

The preceding loop will work, but notice the repeated calculation. We have three identical method invocations of team[i].getSales(). To avoid this duplication, we can store the result of one such invocation in a variable as follows:

```
double nextSales = team[1].getSales();
highestSales = nextSales;
double sum = nextSales;
for (int i = 2; i <= numberOfAssociates; i++)
{
    nextSales = team[i].getSales();
    sum = sum + nextSales;
    if (nextSales> highest)
        highest = nextSales; //highest sales so far.
}
average = sum / numberOfAssociates;
```

The complete definition of the method computeStats is given in Listing 7.4.

The design of the last method, displayResults, uses only techniques that you have already seen, and so we will not go over the details. Its definition is shown in Listing 7.4.

> ### SELF-TEST QUESTIONS
>
> myprogramminglab

7. Write some Java code that will declare an array named entry that has length 3, has SalesAssociate (Listing 7.3) as its base type, and is filled with three identical records. The records use the name "Jane Doe" and sales of $5000. Use a for loop.

8. Rewrite the method displayResults of the program SalesReporter (Listing 7.4) so that it uses the methods in the class DollarFormat (Listing 6.14 of Chapter 6) to display the dollar amounts in the correct format for dollars and cents.

Indexed Variables as Method Arguments

An indexed variable for an array a, such as a[i], can be used anywhere that you can use any other variable of the base type of the array. So an indexed variable can be an argument to a method in exactly the same way that any other variable of the array's base type can be an argument.

For example, the program in Listing 7.5 illustrates the use of an indexed variable as an argument to a method. The method getAverage takes two arguments of type int. The array nextScore has the base type int, and so the program can use nextScore[i] as an argument to the method getAverage, as in the following line from that program:

```java
double possibleAverage = getAverage(firstScore,nextScore[i]);
```

An indexed variable can be an argument

The variable firstScore is an ordinary variable of type int. To help drive home the point that the indexed variable nextScore[i] can be used just like any other variable of type int, note that getAverage would behave in exactly the same way if we interchanged its two arguments, as follows:

```java
double possibleAverage = getAverage(nextScore[i],firstScore);
```

The definition of the method getAverage contains no indication that its arguments can be indexed variables for an array of int. The method accepts arguments of type int, and neither parameter knows nor cares whether those ints came from an indexed variable, a regular int variable, or a constant value.

There is one subtlety that applies to indexed variables when used as method arguments. For example, consider either of the previous method calls. If the value of i is 2, the argument is nextScore[2]. On the other hand, if the value of i is 0, the argument is nextScore[0]. The expression used as an index is evaluated to determine exactly which indexed variable is the argument.

The value of the index affects the value of the argument

Be sure to note that an indexed variable of an array a, such as a[i], is a variable of the base type of the array. When a[i] is used as an argument to a method, it is handled in exactly the same way as any other variable of the base type of the array a. In particular, if the base type of the array is a primitive type,

LISTING 7.5   Indexed Variables as Arguments

```java
import java.util.Scanner;

/**
 A demonstration of using indexed variables as arguments.
*/
public class ArgumentDemo
{
    public static void main(String[] args)
    {
        Scanner keyboard = new Scanner(System.in);
        System.out.println("Enter your score on exam 1:");
        int firstScore = keyboard.nextInt();
        int[] nextScore = new int[3];

        for (int i = 0; i < nextScore.length; i++)
            nextScore[i] = firstScore + 5 * i;

        for (int i = 0; i < nextScore.length; i++)
        {
            double possibleAverage =
                          getAverage(firstScore, nextScore[i]);
            System.out.println("If your score on exam 2 is " +
                               nextScore[i]);
            System.out.println("your average will be " +
                               possibleAverage);
        }
    }

    public static double getAverage(int n1, int n2)
    {
        return (n1 + n2) / 2.0;
    }
}
```

Sample Screen Output

```
Enter your score on exam 1:
80
If your score on exam 2 is 80
your average will be 80.0
If your score on exam 2 is 85
your average will be 82.5
If your score on exam 2 is 90
your average will be 85.0
```

such as int, double, or char, the method cannot change the value of a[i]. On the other hand, if the base type of the array is a class type, the method can change the *state* of the object named by a[i]. This is nothing new. Just remember that an indexed variable, such as a[i], is a variable of the base type of the array and is handled just like any other variable of that data type.

RECAP Indexed Variables as Arguments

An indexed variable can be used as an argument anywhere that a variable of the array's base type can be used. For example, suppose you have

```
double[] a = new double[10];
```

Indexed variables such as a[3] and a[index] can then be used as arguments to any method that accepts a value as an argument.

FAQ When can a method change an argument that is an indexed variable?

Suppose a[i] is an indexed variable of the array a and a[i] is used as an argument in a method invocation such as

```
doStuff(a[i]);
```

Whether the method doStuff can change the array element a[i] depends on the base type of the array a. If the base type of the array a is a primitive type, such as int, double or char, the method doStuff receives the *value* of a[i], and so cannot change a[i] itself, However, if the base type of the array a is a class, the method dostuff receives a reference to a[i]. Thus, the method can change the *state* of the object named by a[i], but cannot replace the object with another one. (To review the details on method arguments, see Chapter 5.)

Entire Arrays as Arguments to a Method

You have already seen that an indexed variable of an array can be used as an argument to a method. An entire array can also be used as an argument to a method. The way you specify an array parameter in a method definition is similar to the way you declare an array. For example, the following method incrementArrayBy2 will accept as its one argument any array whose base type is double:

```
public class SampleClass
{
    public static void incrementArrayBy2(double[] anArray)
    {
        for (int i = 0; i <anArray.length; i++)
            anArray[i] = anArray[i] + 2;
    }
    <The rest of the class definition goes here.>
}
```

A parameter can represent an entire array

When you specify an array parameter, you give the base type of the array, but you do not fix the length of the array.

To illustrate the use of this sample class, suppose you have the statements

```
double[] a = new double[10];
double[] b = new double[30];
```

within some method definition, and suppose that the elements of the arrays a and b have been given values. Both of the following method invocations are then valid:

```
SampleClass.incrementArrayBy2(a);
SampleClass.incrementArrayBy2(b);
```

A method can change the values of the elements in its array argument

The method incrementArrayBy2 can take an array of any length as its argument and can change the values of the elements in the array. Following the previous invocations of the method, the elements in the arrays a and b have each been increased by 2.

RECAP Array Parameters

An argument to a method may be an entire array. You use the following syntax for the method's heading:

SYNTAX

```
public static Return_Type Method_Name(Base_Type[] Param_Name)
```

You can use other modifiers instead of public and static.

(continued)

EXAMPLES

```java
public static int getOneElement(char[] anArray, int index)
public void readArray(int[] anotherArray)
```

REMEMBER Array Parameters Do Not Specify the Array Length

An array parameter in a method's heading specifies the base type of the array, but not the length of the array. For example, the following method heading specifies an array of characters as a parameter:

```java
public static void showArray(char[] a)
```

REMEMBER Characteristics of Array Arguments

- No square brackets are written when you pass an entire array as an argument to a method.

- An array of any length can be the argument corresponding to an array parameter.

- A method can change the values in an array argument.

Each of these points is demonstrated by the preceding method incrementArrayBy2.

Arguments for the Method main

The heading for the main method of a program is as follows:

```java
public static void main(String[] args)
```

The parameter declaration String[] args indicates that args is an array whose base type is String. That is, the method main takes an array of String values as an argument. But we never have given main an argument when we ran any of our programs. In fact, we have never invoked main! What's the story?

As you know, an invocation of main is a very special sort of invocation that we do not make. When you run your program, main is invoked automatically and given a default array of strings as a default argument. But you can, if you like, provide additional strings when you run a program, and those strings will automatically be made elements of the array args that is provided to `main` as an argument. Normally, you do this by running the program from the command line of the operating system, like so:

```
java TestProgram Sally Smith
```

This command sets `args[0]` to `"Sally"` and `args[1]` to `"Smith"`. These two indexed variables can then be used within the method `main`.

For example, consider the following sample program:

```
public class TestProgram
{
    public static void main(String[] args)
    {
        System.out.println("Hello" + args[0] + " " + args[1]);
    }
}
```

After running `TestProgram` using the one-line command

```
java TestProgram Josephine Student
```

You can pass an array of strings to `main` as an argument

the output produced by the program will be

```
Hello Josephine Student
```

Be sure to note that the argument to `main` is an array of *strings*. If you want numbers, you must convert the string representations of the numbers to values of one or more number types. For example, to convert the first argument to an integer, you could use `Integer.parseInt(args[0])`. Since the identifier `args` is a parameter, you can use any other valid identifier in place of `args`, as long as you change any occurrences of `args` that also occur in the body of `main`. However, it is traditional to use the identifier `args` for this parameter.

Array Assignment and Equality

Arrays are objects, and so the assignment operator `=` and the equality operator `==` behave (and misbehave) in the same way with arrays as they do with the kinds of objects we saw before discussing arrays. To understand how this applies to arrays, you need to know a little bit about how arrays are stored in the computer's main memory. The important point for this discussion is that the entire array contents—that is, the contents of all of the indexed variables—are stored together in one, possibly large, section of memory. In this way, the location of the entire array contents can be specified by one memory address.

Recall that a variable for an object really contains the memory address of the object. The assignment operator copies this memory address. For example, consider the following code:

```
int[] a = new int[3];
int[] b = new int[3];
for (int i = 0; i <a.length; i++)
    a[i] = i;
```

```
b = a;
System.out.println("a[2] = " + a[2] + ", b[2] = " + b[2]);
a[2] = 2001;
System.out.println("a[2] = " + a[2] + ", b[2] = " + b[2]);
```

This will produce the following output:

```
a[2] = 2, b[2] = 2
a[2] = 2001, b[2] = 2001
```

The assignment b = a in the preceding code gives the array variable b the same memory address as the array variable a. So a and b are two different names for the same array. Thus, when we change the value of a[2], we are also changing the value of b[2]. For this reason, it is best simply not to use the assignment operator = with arrays. If you want the arrays a and b in the preceding code to be different arrays having the same values, you must write something like the following:

```
for (int i = 0; i < a.length; i++)
    b[i] = a[i];
```

Assigning one array to another results in one array having two names

instead of the assignment statement

```
b = a;
```

Note that the preceding loop assumes that the arrays a and b have the same length.

The equality operator = = tests whether two arrays are stored in the same place in the computer's memory. For example, the code

```
int[] a = new int[3];
int[] b = new int[3];
for (int i = 0; i < a.length; i++)
    a[i] = i;
for (int i = 0; i < b.length; i++)
    b[i] = i;
if (b == a)
    System.out.println("Equal by ==");
else
    System.out.println("Not equal by ==");
```

produces the output

```
Not equal by ==
```

The operator == tests whether two arrays are at the same place in memory

Even though the arrays and contain the same integers in the same order, the arrays are stored in different places in memory. So b == a is false, since == tests for equal memory addresses.

If you want to test whether two arrays contain the same elements, you must test whether each element in one array equals the corresponding element in the other array. Listing 7.6 contains a small demonstration class that shows one possible way to do this.

LISTING 7.6 **Two Kinds of Equality** *(part 1 of 2)*

```java
/**
 A demonstration program to test two arrays for equality.
*/
public class TestEquals
{
    public static void main(String[] args)
    {
        int[] a = new int[3];
        int[] b = new int[3];
        setArray(a);
        setArray(b);

        if (b == a)
            System.out.println("Equal by ==.");
        else
            System.out.println("Not equal by ==.");

        if (equals(b, a))
            System.out.println("Equal by the equals method.");
        else
            System.out.println("Not equal by the equals method.");
    }

    public static boolean equals(int[] a, int[] b)
    {
        boolean elementsMatch = true;//tentatively
        if (a.length != b.length)
            elementsMatch = false;
        else
        {
            int i = 0;
            while (elementsMatch && (i < a.length))
            {
                if (a[i] != b[i])
                    elementsMatch = false;
                i++;
            }
        }
        return elementsMatch;
    }

    public static void setArray(int[] array)
    {
        for (int i = 0; i < array.length; i++)
            array[i] = i;
    }
}
```

> The arrays **a** and **b** contain the same integers in the same order.

(continued)

LISTING 7.6   Two Kinds of Equality *(part 2 of 2)*

Screen Output

```
Not equal by ==.
Equal by the equals method.
```

GOTCHA   Using the Operators = and == with Arrays

You can use the assignment operator = to give an array more than one name. You cannot use it to copy the contents of one array to another, different array. Likewise, the equality operator == tests whether two array names reference the same memory address. It does not test whether two different arrays contain the same values. ∎

REMEMBER Array Types Are Reference Types

A variable of an array type holds only the address where the array is stored in memory. This memory address is called a reference to the array object in memory. For this reason, array types are often called reference types. Recall from Chapter 5 that a reference type is any type whose variables hold references—that is, memory addresses—as opposed to the actual item named by the variable. Array types and class types are both reference types. Primitive types are not reference types.

FAQ Are arrays really objects?

Arrays do not belong to any class. Some other features of class objects—such as inheritance, which we will discuss in Chapter 8—do not apply to arrays. So whether arrays should be considered objects is not 100 percent clear. However, that is primarily an academic debate. In Java, arrays are officially objects. Whenever Java documentation says that something applies to all objects, it also applies to arrays.

Methods That Return Arrays

A Java method may return an array. To have it do so, you specify the method's return type in the same way that you specify the type of an array parameter. For example, Listing 7.7 contains a revised version of the program in Listing 7.5. Both programs perform pretty much the same computations, but this new version computes the various possible average scores within a method named

LISTING 7.7 A Method That Returns an Array

```java
import java.util.Scanner;
/**
 A demonstration of a method that returns an array.
*/
public class ReturnArrayDemo
{
    public static void main(String[] args)
    {
        Scanner keyboard = new Scanner(System.in);
        System.out.println("Enter your score on exam 1:");
        int firstScore = keyboard.nextInt();
        int[] nextScore = new int[3];

        for (int i = 0; i < nextScore.length; i++)
            nextScore[i] = firstScore + 5 * i;

        double[] averageScore =
                getArrayOfAverages(firstScore, nextScore);
        for (int i = 0; i < nextScore.length; i++)
        {
            System.out.println("If your score on exam 2 is " +
                                nextScore[i]);
            System.out.println("your average will be " +
                                averageScore[i]);
        }
    }

    public static double[] getArrayOfAverages(int firstScore,
                                              int[] nextScore)
    {
        double[] temp = new double[nextScore.length];
        for (int i = 0; i < temp.length; i++)
            temp[i] = getAverage(firstScore, nextScore[i]);

        return temp;
    }

    public static double getAverage(int n1, int n2)
    {
        return (n1 + n2) / 2.0;
    }
}
```

The sample screen output is the same as in Listing 7.5.

getArrayofAverages. This new method returns these average scores as an array. The method does so by creating a new array and then returning it, using the following steps:

A method can return an entire array

```java
double temp = new double[nextScore.length];
<Fill the array temp.>
return temp;
```

RECAP **Returning an Array**

A method can return an array in basically the same way that it returns a value of another type.

SYNTAX

```
public static Base_Type[] Method_Name(Parameter_List)
{
    Base_Type[] temp = new Base_Type[Array_Size];
    Statements_To_Fill_Array
    return temp;
}
```

The method need not be static and need not be public. The following are some of the other acceptable method headings:

```
public Base_Type[] Method_Name(Parameter_List)
private static Base_Type[] Method_Name(Parameter_List)
private Base_Type[] Method_Name(Parameter_List)
```

EXAMPLE

```
public static char[] getVowels()
{
    char[] newArray = {'a', 'e', 'i', 'o', 'u'};
    return newArray;
}
```

RECAP **The Name of an Array's Data Type**

The data-type name for an array is always of the form

```
Base_Type[]
```

This is true when declaring an array variable, specifying the type of an array parameter, or specifying that a method returns an array.

EXAMPLES

```
int[] counter = new int[10];
Species[] ghost = new Species[20];
public static double[] halfAll(int[] arrayToBeHalved);
{
  ...
```

VideoNote
Using arrays within methods

GOTCHA   Privacy Leaks with Arrays

A private instance variable that has an array type can be modified outside of its class, if a public method in the class returns the array. This is the same problem we discussed in the previous chapter, and it has analogous solutions.   ■

SELF-TEST QUESTIONS

9. What output will be produced by the following code?

```java
char[] a = new char[3];
for (int i = 0; i <a.length; i++)
    a[i] = a;
char[] b = a;
System.out.println("a[1] = " + a[1] + ", b[1] = " + b[1]);
System.out.println("a[2] = " + a[2] + ", b[2] = " + b[2]);
b[2] = b;
System.out.println("a[1] = " + a[1] + ", b[1] = " + b[1]);
System.out.println("a[2] = " + a[2] + ", b[2] = " + b[2]);
```

10. Give the definition of a static method called showArray that has an array of base type char as a single parameter and that writes one line of text to the screen consisting of the characters in the array argument written in order.

11. Give the definition of a static method called getArrayOfHalves that has an array of base type double as a single parameter and that returns another array whose base type and length are the same as those of the parameter, but whose elements have each been divided by 2.0.

12. The following method compiles and executes but does not work as you might hope. What is wrong with it?

```java
/** Copies an array. */
public static int[] copyArray(int[] anArray)
{
    int[] temp = new int[anArray.length];
    temp = anArray;
    return temp;
}
```

13. The following method compiles and executes but does not work as you might hope. What is wrong with it?

```java
/** Doubles the size of an array. */
public static void doubleSize(int[] a)
{
    a = new int[a.length * 2];
}
```

14. Suppose that we add the following method to the class `SalesReporter` in Listing 7.4 so that a program using this class can access the sales associates:

```
/** Returns an array of SalesAssociate objects. */
public SalesAssociate[] getSalesTeam()
{
    return team;
}
```

Will this method compile and execute as indicated? Is adding this method to the class `SalesReporter` a good idea?

7.3 PROGRAMMING WITH ARRAYS AND CLASSES

The Moving Finger writes; and, having writ,
Moves on; nor all your Piety and Wit.
Shall lure it back to cancel half a line.
Nor all your Tears wash out a Word of it.

—OMAR KHAYYAM, *THE RUBA'IYAT* (FITZGERALD TRANSLATION)

In this section, we present some additional techniques for working with arrays. In particular, we discuss using an array variable as an instance variable in a class. We begin with a programming example that illustrates some basic techniques.

| PROGRAMMING EXAMPLE | A Specialized List Class |

One way to use an array for a special purpose is to make the array an instance variable of a class. The array is accessed only through the class methods, and so you can add any checks and automatic processing that you want. This allows you to define classes whose objects are something like special-purpose arrays. In this programming example, we present an example of one such class.

We will define a class whose objects can be used for keeping lists of items, such as a grocery list or a list of things to do. The class will have the rather long name OneWayNoRepeatsList.[1]

---

[1] Long names are traditional in Java, but we did not choose a long name just to be traditional. All the short names, like *Collection* and *List*, already have a meaning in Java, and it could be confusing to use these short names for something other than their usual meaning.

A class of lists of
strings

The class `OneWayNoRepeatsList` will have a method for adding items to the list. An item on the list is a string, which in an application would say whatever you want the item to say, such as "Buy milk." This class has no method to change a single item or delete an item from the list. It does, however, have a method that lets you erase the entire list and start over again with a blank list. Each object of the class `OneWayNoRepeatsList` has a maximum number of items it can hold. At any time, the list might contain anywhere from zero to the maximum number of items.

An array of
strings as an
instance variable

An object of the class `OneWayNoRepeatsList` has an array of strings as an instance variable. This array holds the items on the list. However, you do not access the array directly. Instead, you use accessor and mutator methods. You can use `int` variables to hold numbers that indicate positions in the list. One of these `int` variables is the same thing as an index, but the positions are numbered starting with 1 rather than 0. For example, a method named `getEntryAt` lets you recover the item at a given position. If `toDoList` is an object of the class `OneWayNoRepeatsList`, the following statement sets the string variable `next` to the entry at the second position:

```
String next = toDoList.getEntryAt(2);
```

Access to the
strings in a list is
only via methods

Other methods add an entry to the end of the list or erase the entire list. These are the only ways that the list can be changed. You cannot change or delete a particular entry on the list, and you cannot add an entry anywhere other than at the end of the list.

In Chapter 5 we discussed encapsulation. The class `OneWayNoRepeatsList` is a good example of a well-encapsulated class, since it hides its details from the programmer who uses it. But clearly, the programmer needs to know how to use the class. So it makes sense to tell you how to use this class before we give the definition.

Listing 7.8 contains a program that demonstrates how to use some of the methods for the class `OneWayNoRepeatsList`. Notice that the constructor takes an integer argument. This integer specifies the maximum number of entries that can be placed on the list. The number is small for our demonstration.

The method `addItem` adds a string to the end of the list. For example, the following adds the string named by the variable `next` to the end of the list `toDoList`:

```
toDoList.addItem(next);
```

If you look at the sample output in Listing 7.8, you will see that `Buy milk` is added to the list twice, but that it appears on the list only once. If the item being added is already on the list, the method `addItem` has no effect. That way the list has no repeats.

You can use an `int` variable to step through the list from beginning to end. The technique is illustrated at the end of Listing 7.8. You begin by initializing an `int` variable to the first position on the list, as follows:

Stepping through
a list

```
int position = toDoList.START_POSITION;
```

LISTING 7.8 **Using the Class** OneWayNoRepeatsList *(part 1 of 2)*

```java
import java.util.Scanner;

public class ListDemo
{
    public static final int MAX_SIZE = 3; //Assumed > 0

    public static void main(String[] args)
    {
        OneWayNoRepeatsList toDoList =
                        new OneWayNoRepeatsList(MAX_SIZE);
        System.out.println(
                "Enter items for the list, when prompted.");
        boolean moreEntries = true;
        String next = null;
        Scanner keyboard = new Scanner(System.in);

        while (moreEntries && !toDoList.isFull())
        {
            System.out.println("Enter an item:");
            next = keyboard.nextLine();
            toDoList.addItem(next);

            if (toDoList.isFull())
            {
                System.out.println("List is now full.");
            }
            else
            {
                System.out.print("More items for the list? ");
                String ans = keyboard.nextLine();
                if (ans.trim().equalsIgnoreCase("no"))
                    moreEntries = false; //User says no more
            }
        }

        System.out.println("The list contains:");
        int position = toDoList.START_POSITION;
        next = toDoList.getEntryAt(position);
        while (next != null) //null indicates end of list
        {
            System.out.println(next);
            position++;
            next = toDoList.getEntryAt(position);
        }
    }
}
```

(continued)

LISTING 7.8 **Using the Class** OneWayNoRepeatsList *(part 2 of 2)*

Sample Screen Output

```
Enter items for the list, when prompted.
Enter an item:
Buy milk
More items for the list? yes
Enter an item:
Walk dog
More items for the list? yes
Enter an item:
Buy milk
More items for the list? yes
Enter an item:
Write program
The list is now full.
The list contains:
Buy milk
Walk dog
Write program
```

The named constant toDoList.START_POSITION is simply another name for 1, but we use it because we are thinking of this as the start of the list, not as the number 1. You can invoke the method getEntryAt to retrieve the item at a given position in the list. For example, the following sets the string variable next equal to the string at the position given by the variable position:

```
next = toDoList.getEntryAt(position);
```

To obtain the next item on the list, the program simply increments the value of position. The following code, taken from Listing 7.8, illustrates stepping through the list:

```
int position = toDoList.START_POSITION;
next = toDoList.getEntryAt(position);
while (next != null)
{
    System.out.println(next);
    position++;
    next = toDoList.getEntryAt(position);
}
```

null signals the list's end

Once the value of position is incremented beyond the last position in the list, no entry will be at position. So we need some way to conveniently indicate that the end of the list has been reached. Otherwise, we might access some "garbage" value in the unused portion of the array. To take care of this problem, we will make `getEntryAt` return the value `null` when there is no entry at the given position. Note that `null` is different from any real string, and so it will not appear on any list. Thus, your program can test for the end of the list by checking for the value `null`. Recall that to test for equality or inequality with `null`, you use `==` or `!=`; you do not use an `equals` method.

The complete definition of the class `OneWayNoRepeatsList` is given in Listing 7.9. The entries on a list are kept in the instance variable `entry`, which is an array of base type `String`. Thus, the maximum number of entries that the list can hold is `entry.length`. However, the list normally will not be full, and so will contain fewer than `entry.length` entries. To keep track of how much of the array `entry` is currently used, the class has an instance variable called `countOfEntries`. The entries themselves are kept in the indexed variables `entry[0]`, `entry[1]`, `entry[2]`, and so on through `entry[countOfEntries - 1]`. The values of the elements whose indices are `countOfEntries` or higher are just garbage values and do not represent entries on the list. Thus, when you want to step through the items on the list, you stop after `entry[countOfEntries - 1]`.

Garbage values occur after the last entry in the list

For example, the definition of the method `isOnList` has a `while` loop that steps through the array, checking to see whether the argument is equal to any of the entries on the list:

```
while ((!found) && (i <countOfEntries))
{
    if (item.equalsIgnoreCase(entry[i]))
        found = true;
    else
        i++;
}
```

The loop in the method `isOnList`

The code checks only array elements whose indices are less than `countOfEntries`. It does not check the rest of the array, because those array entries are not on the list.

The complete class `OneWayNoRepeatsList` has a few more methods than those we used in the demonstration program in Listing 7.8. These extra methods make the class more useful for a wider variety of applications.

Note that although the array `entry` has indices starting with 0, if we use an `int` variable as a position marker—such as the variable position in Listing 7.9—the numbering starts at 1, not 0. The class methods automatically adjust the indices, so when you want the item at location `position`, you get `entry[position - 1]`. We could, of course, have compensated for the difference between array indices and list positions by allocating an extra element in the array `entry` and ignoring `entry[0]`, as we suggested earlier near the end of the section entitled "More About Array Indices." Exercise 14 at the end of the previous section asks you to do just that.

Positions of entries on a list begin at 1, but in an array, they begin at 0

LISTING 7.9   An Array Wrapped in a Class to Represent a List *(part 1 of 3)*

```
/**
 An object of this class is a special kind of list of strings.
 You can write the list only from beginning to end. You can add
 only to the end of the list. You cannot change individual en-
 tries, but you can erase the entire list and start over. No
 entry may appear more than once on the list. You can use int
 variables as position markers into the list. Position markers
 are similar to array indices, but are numbered starting with 1.
*/
public class OneWayNoRepeatsList
{
    public static int START_POSITION = 1;
    public static int DEFAULT_SIZE = 50;

    //entry.length is the total number of items you have room
    //for on the list (its capacity); countOfEntries is the number of
    //items currently on the list.
    private int countOfEntries; //can be less than entry.length.
    private String[] entry;

    /**
     Creates an empty list with a given capacity.
    */
    public OneWayNoRepeatsList(int maximumNumberOfEntries)
    {
        entry = new String[maximumNumberOfEntries];
        countOfEntries = 0;
    }

    /**
     Creates an empty list with a capacity of DEFAULT_SIZE.
    */
    public OneWayNoRepeatsList()
    {
        entry = new String[DEFAULT_SIZE];
        countOfEntries = 0;
// or replace these two statements with this(DEFAULT_SIZE);
    }

    public boolean isFull()
    {
        return countOfEntries == entry.length;
    }

    public boolean isEmpty()
    {
        return countOfEntries == 0;
    }
```

(continued)

LISTING 7.9   An Array Wrapped in a Class to Represent a List *(part 2 of 3)*

```java
/**
 Precondition: List is not full.
 Postcondition: If item was not on the list,
 it has been added to the list.
*/
public void addItem(String item)
{
    if (!isOnList(item))
    {
        if (countOfEntries == entry.length)
        {
            System.out.println("Adding to a full list!");
            System.exit(0);
        }
        else
        {
            entry[countOfEntries] = item;
            countOfEntries++;
        }
    } //else do nothing. Item is already on the list.
}

/**
 If the argument indicates a position on the list,
 the entry at that specified position is returned;
 otherwise, null is returned.
*/
public String getEntryAt(int position)
{
    String result = null;
    if ((1 <= position) && (position <= countOfEntries))
        result = entry[position - 1];

    return result;
}

/**
 Returns true if position indicates the last item
 on the list; otherwise, returns false.
*/
public boolean atLastEntry(int position)
{
    return position == countOfEntries;
}
```

(continued)

LISTING 7.9 An Array Wrapped in a Class to Represent a List *(part 3 of 3)*

```java
/**
 Returns true if item is on the list;
 otherwise, returns false. Does not differentiate
 between uppercase and lowercase letters.
*/
public boolean isOnList(String item)
{
    boolean found = false;
    int i = 0;
    while (!found && (i < countOfEntries))
    {
        if (item.equalsIgnoreCase(entry[i]))
            found = true;
        else
            i++;
    }

    return found;
}

public int getMaximumNumberOfEntries()
{
    return entry.length;
}

public int getNumberOfEntries()
{
    return countOfEntries;
}

public void eraseList()
{
    countOfEntries = 0;
}
}
```

Note that the class OneWayNoRepeatsList provides three ways to detect the end of a list, assuming you use an int variable position to access entries in the list:

Ways to detect the end of a list

- If position equals getNumberOfEntries(), position is at the last entry.
- If atLastEntry(position) returns true, position is at the last entry.
- If getEntryAt(position) returns null, position is beyond the last entry.

We end this programming example with a mention that the Java Class Library contains the class ArrayList that you can use to create lists that are more general and flexible than the list we used here. Like our class, `ArrayList` uses an array to represent the list. Chapter 12 will introduce you to this class, but if you like, you can skip ahead and read about it now. ∎

SELF-TEST QUESTIONS

15. Replace the last loop in Listing 7.8 with a `for` loop that uses the number of entries in the list.

16. Replace the last loop in Listing 7.8 with a loop that uses the method `atLastEntry`.

Partially Filled Arrays

The array entry in the class `OneWayNoRepeatsList` in Listing 7.9 contains the entries on a list. When the list is not yet full, entry is a **partially filled array**. In some situations, such as this one, we need some but not all of the indexed variables in an array. In these cases, we must keep track of how much of the array has been used so that we know how much of it is available. Normally, we can use an int variable to count the items in the array. For example, the class `OneWayNoRepeatsList` in Listing 7.9 uses the instance variable `countOfEntries` for this purpose. In particular, `countOfEntries` implies that the list contains the array elements whose indices are 0 through `countOfEntries` − 1, as Figure 7.4 illustrates. It is very important to keep track of how much of the array is currently being used, because the other array entries contain irrelevant values. When accessing a partially filled array, you want to access only those elements in the array that contain meaningful values. You want to ignore the rest of the array. Of course, as you add or delete entries from a partially filled array, the borderline between meaningful values and

An array can have fewer meaningful entries than its capacity

FIGURE 7.4 A Partially Filled Array

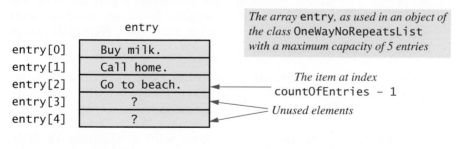

entry.length *has a value of 5.*
countOfEntries *has a value of 3.*

irrelevant values can move, and this movement must be recorded by changing the value of a suitable `int` variable, such as `countOfEntries`.

Typically, the meaningful part of an array begins at the beginning of the array, but this is not an absolute requirement. When you want to consider a portion of an array that does not begin at the index 0, you can define two `int` variables—such as `first` and `last`—to record the indices of the first and last elements, respectively, of the range of elements that you want to consider. These variables might be either instance variables or parameters to a method. For example, we could define a static method having the following heading:

```
/** Precondition: 0 <= first <= last < anArray.length */
public static void processArray(double[] anArray,
                                 int first, int last)
```

REMEMBER The Number of Entries in an Array vs. the Array's Length

Distinguish between the number of entries that you use in an array and the array's capacity. The capacity of an array a is a.length. This is the number of array elements that are created for you when you define the array. You might not use all of these elements. In this case, you need to keep track of how many you have used. Typically, you will have two integers: One is the capacity of the array, and one is the number of elements you have used.

---

myprogramminglab

SELF-TEST QUESTIONS

17. Suppose a is an array of values of type `double`. Write some code to display all the elements in a on the screen, one element per line.

18. Suppose a is an array of values of type `double` that is partially filled. The array contains meaningful values in only the first `numberUsed` elements, where `numberUsed` is a variable of type `int`. Write some code to display all the meaningful values in the array a.

19. If the array a in the previous question has room for ten elements but contains only three elements, what indexed variables will contain the three elements? What is the value of `numberUsed`?

20. Consider the partially filled array a from Self-Test Question 18. Write some code that will place the number 42 right after the last number currently in a. You can assume that the array a is not full. (*Hint:* You must update `numberUsed`.)

21. Repeat the previous question, but this time assume that you do not know whether the array a is full. If the array a is full, your code should display an appropriate message to the screen.

22. Write an accessor method `getEntryArray` for the class `OneWayNoRepeatsList` that returns a copy of the array `entry`. Since `entry` is an array of strings, you need not copy the strings themselves.

7.4 SORTING AND SEARCHING ARRAYS

A place for everything and everything in its place.

—ISABELLA MARY BEETON, *THE BOOK OF HOUSEHOLD MANAGEMENT* (1861)

Suppose you have an array of values. You might want the array values to be ordered in some way. For example, you might want to order an array of numbers from lowest to highest or from highest to lowest, or you might want to arrange an array of strings into alphabetical order. Arranging a collection of items into a particular order is called **sorting.** Typically, we sort arrays into ascending or descending order.

> Sorting arranges array elements into a particular order, such as ascending or descending

In this section, we will discuss and implement a simple sorting algorithm. We will present this algorithm as a way to sort an array of integers. However, with only minor changes, it can be adapted to sort arrays of values of any type that can be ordered. For example, we could sort an array of employee records according to identification numbers.

We also will consider searching a given array for a particular entry. We can search an array whose entries are sorted or one whose entries are completely unorganized. Both sorting and searching are quite important tasks, and efficient algorithms are important. We will, however, just introduce you to these topics.

Selection Sort

Imagine an array of integers that we want to sort into ascending order. That is, we will rearrange the values in the indexed variables of the array so that

```
a[0] ≤ a[1] ≤ a[2] ≤ ... ≤ a[a.length - 1]
```

We will discuss one of the easiest of the sorting algorithms to understand, the **selection sort.** This algorithm follows from the specification of what we want the algorithm to do. That is, we want the algorithm to rearrange the values of the array a so that a[0] is the smallest, a[1] is the next smallest, and so forth. That desire leads to the following pseudocode:

```
for (index = 0; index <a.length; index++)
    Place the (index + 1)ᵗʰ smallest element in a[index]
```

Interchange sorts swap values in an array

We want this algorithm to use only the one array a. Thus, the only way we can move an array element without losing any of the other elements is to make it swap places with another element of the array. Any sorting algorithm that swaps, or interchanges, values is called an **interchange sorting algorithm.** Thus, our selection sort algorithm is an interchange sorting algorithm.

Let's start with an example to see how the array elements are interchanged. Figure 7.5 shows how an array is sorted by interchanging values. Beginning

FIGURE 7.5 Selection Sort

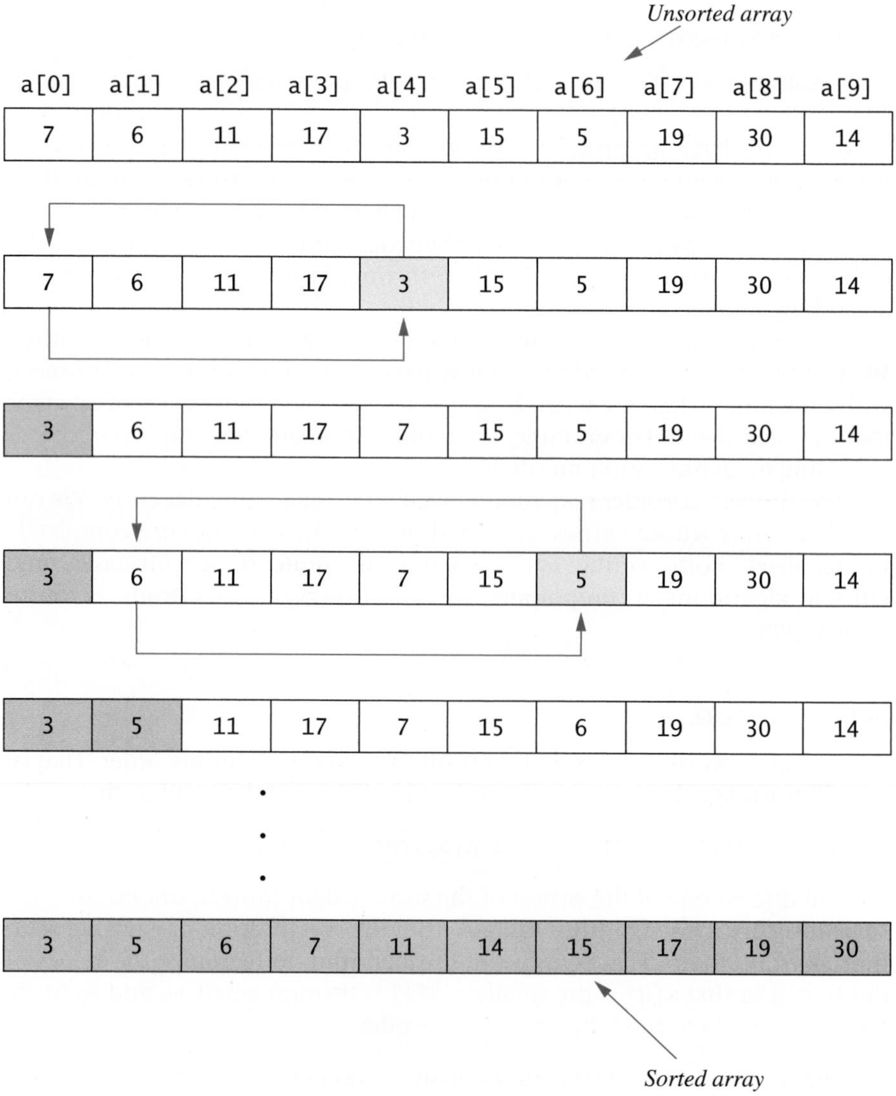

with an array of unsorted values, we locate the smallest value in the array. In our example, this value is the 3 in a[4]. Since we want this smallest value to be first in the array, we interchange the value in a[4] with the value in a[0]. After that interchange, the smallest value is in a[0] where it belongs.

The next smallest value in the array is the 5 in a[6]. It needs to be second in the array, so we interchange the value in a[6] with the value in a[1]. After that swap, the values in a[0] and a[1] are the smallest and next smallest values, which is what they should be in the final sorted array. The algorithm then interchanges the next smallest element with a[2] and so forth until the entire array is sorted.

Finding the smallest value in an array is analogous to finding the largest value, and we did that in the method computeStats in Listing 7.4. But how do we find the second smallest value, the third smallest, and so on? After finding the smallest value among a[0], a[1], . . . , a[n] and placing it into a[0], the second smallest value in the array a is the smallest value among a[1], . . . , a[n]. After placing it into a[2], the third smallest value in a is the smallest value among a[2], . . . , a[n], and so on.

The following pseudocode describes the selection sort algorithm:

Pseudocode for a
selection sort

Algorithm for a selection sort of an array

```
for (index = 0; index <a.length - 1; index++)
{   // Place the correct value in a[index]:
    indexOfNextSmallest = the index of the smallest value among
                          a[index], a[index+1],...,
                          a[a.length - 1]
    Interchange the values of a[index] and
                          a[indexOfNextSmallest].
    //Assertion: a[0] <= a[1] <= ... <= a[index] and these
    //are the smallest of the original array elements.
    //The remaining positions contain the rest of the
    //original array elements.
}
```

Notice that we effectively have two regions of the array: One region is sorted, and the other is not. The assertion in our algorithm implies that the sorted region encompasses the elements a[0] through a[index]. Notice that this assertion is true after each iteration of the loop. We repeatedly find the smallest value in the unsorted region and move it to the end of the sorted region by swapping elements. Thus, the sorted region grows by one element at each repetition of the loop, while the unsorted region shrinks by one element. In Figure 7.5, the sorted region is shaded blue.

Note that the for loop ends after correctly filling the element a[a.length – 2], even though the index of the last array element is a.length – 1. After the algorithm gets all but one element sorted, the correct value for the last element a[a.length – 1] is already in a[a.length – 1].

Listing 7.10 contains a class defining a static method named selectionSort that implements this selection sort algorithm. The method uses two private helping methods named getIndexOfSmallest and interchange. Once you

understand these private methods, you will see that the definition of the
method selectionSort is a direct translation of our pseudocode into Java code.
So let's discuss these two private methods.

LISTING 7.10   Implementation of the Selection Sort *(part 1 of 2)*

```
/**
 Class for sorting an array of base type int from smallest to largest.
*/
public class ArraySorter
{
    /**
     Precondition: Every element in anArray has a value.
     Action: Sorts the array into ascending order.
    */
    public static void selectionSort(int[] anArray)
    {
        for (int index = 0; index < anArray.length - 1; index++)
        {   // Place the correct value in anArray[index]
            int indexOfNextSmallest = getIndexOfSmallest(index, anArray);
            interchange(index, indexOfNextSmallest, anArray);
            //Assertion:anArray[0] <= anArray[1] <=...<= anArray[index]
            //and these are the smallest of the original array elements.
            //The remaining positions contain the rest of the original
            //array elements.
        }
    }
    /**
     Returns the index of the smallest value in the portion of the
     array that begins at the element whose index is startIndex and
     ends at the last element.
    */
    private static int getIndexOfSmallest(int startIndex, int[] a)
    {
        int min = a[startIndex];
        int indexOfMin = startIndex;
        for (int index = startIndex + 1; index < a.length; index++)
        {
            if (a[index] < min)
            {
                min = a[index];
                indexOfMin = index;
                //min is smallest of a[startIndex] through a[index]
            }
        }
        return indexOfMin;
    }
```

(continued)

LISTING 7.10 **Implementation of the Selection Sort** *(part 2 of 2)*

```
    /**
     Precondition: i and j are valid indices for the array a.
     Postcondition: Values of a[i] and a[j] have been interchanged.
    */
    private static void interchange(int i, int j, int[] a)
    {
        int temp = a[i];
        a[i] = a[j];
        a[j] = temp; //original value of a[i]
    }
}
```

The method getIndexOfSmallest searches the array elements

```
    a[startIndex], a[startIndex + 1],..., a[a.length - 1]
```

and returns the index of the smallest one. It does this using the two local variables min and indexOfMin. At any point in its search, min is equal to the smallest array value found so far, and indexOfMin is the index of that value. Thus, a[indexOfMin] has the value min. Initially, min is set to a[startIndex], which is the first value considered for min, and indexOfMin is set to startIndex. Then each array element is considered in turn to see whether it is a new minimum. If it is, the values of min and indexOfMin are updated. After checking all of the candidate array elements, the method returns the value of indexOfMin.

Find the next smallest entry in the array

The method named interchange interchanges the values of a[i] and a[j]. There is one subtle point about this method. If you execute the code

```
    a[i] = a[j];
```

you will lose the value originally held in a[i]. So before this statement is executed, we must save the value of a[i] in the local variable temp.

Place the next entry in its correct position by swapping

Listing 7.11 contains a demonstration program that shows the selection sort method in action.

Other Sorting Algorithms

Although the selection sort algorithm will suffice as an introduction to the general topic of sorting, it is not the most efficient sorting algorithm. In fact, it is significantly less efficient than a number of well-known sorting algorithms. The selection sort is, however, much simpler than these other algorithms. A simpler algorithm is less likely to have errors creep in when you code it. So if you need to code a sorting algorithm in a hurry, it is safer to use either a selection sort or some other simple algorithm.

Selection sort is simple, but not the fastest way to sort

LISTING 7.11   Demonstration of the Method selectionSort

```java
public class SelectionSortDemo
{
    public static void main(String[] args)
    {
        int[] b = {7, 5, 11, 2, 16, 4, 18, 14, 12, 30};

        display(b, "before");
        ArraySorter.selectionSort(b);
        display(b, "after");
    }

    public static void display(int[] array, String when)
    {
        System.out.println("Array values " + when + " sorting:");
        for (int i = 0; i < array.length; i++)
            System.out.print(array[i] + " ");
        System.out.println( );
    }
}
```

Screen Output

```
Array values before sorting:
7 5 11 2 16 4 18 14 12 30
Array values after sorting:
2 4 5 7 11 12 14 16 18 30
```

On the other hand, if efficiency is a major issue, you may wish to use a more complicated and more efficient algorithm. But be aware that the more complicated algorithm will take longer to code, test, and debug. Efficiency can be a subtle topic. Remember, getting the wrong result is always inefficient, no matter how quickly your program can come up with the result.

Fortunately, the Java Class Library provides for efficient sorting. The class Arrays, in the package java.util, defines the static method sort. If anArray is an array of either primitive values or objects, the statement

```java
Arrays.sort(anArray);
```

sorts the elements in the entire array into ascending order. To sort only the portion of the array beginning with the index first and ending with the index last, you would write

```java
Arrays.sort(anArray, first, last);
```

The class Arrays defines several versions of the method—that is, the name sort is overloaded—to accommodate arrays of class types as well as all the primitive types.

Programming Projects 4 and 5 at the end of this chapter describe two other sorting algorithms. A more efficient sorting algorithm—one similar to the algorithm that `Arrays.sort` uses—is described in Chapter 11 when we talk about recursion.

SELF-TEST QUESTIONS

myprogramminglab

23. Trace the steps that a selection sort takes as it sorts the following array into ascending order: 7 5 1 3 6.

24. Write the invocation of the method `selectionSort` to sort an array `myArray` of integers into ascending order.

25. How would you need to change the method `selectionSort` so that it can sort an array of values of type `double` instead of type `int`?

26. How would you need to change the method `selectionSort` so that it can sort an array of values of type `int` into decreasing order, instead of increasing order?

27. Consider an array `b` of `int` values in which a value occurs twice. For example, suppose 7 occurs in both `b[0]` and `b[5]`. If you sort the array using the method `selectionSort`, will the sorted array contain one or two copies of the repeated value?

Searching an Array

The method `isOnList` of the class `OneWayNoRepeatsList` in Listing 7.9 searches the array `entry` to see whether it contains the value represented by the parameter `item`. This is an example of a **sequential search** of an array. The sequential search algorithm is very simple and straightforward: It looks at the array elements from first to last to see whether the sought-after item is equal to any of the array elements. The search ends when either the desired item is found in the array or the end of the array is reached without finding the item. In the latter case, of course, the search is unsuccessful. If the array is partially filled, the search considers only the portion of the array that contains meaningful values.

A sequential search can search an unsorted array, which is an advantage of this simple algorithm. If, however, the array is sorted, we can improve the sequential search in situations in which the desired item does not exist within the array. Exercise 19 asks you to write this improved sequential search. An even faster algorithm, the binary search, is possible for sorted arrays. We will study this algorithm in Chapter 11.

A sequential search looks for an array element from beginning to end

7.5 MULTIDIMENSIONAL ARRAYS

Never trust to general impressions, my boy, but concentrate yourself upon details.

—SIR ARTHUR CONAN DOYLE, *A CASE OF IDENTITY* (SHERLOCK HOLMES)

An array having more than one index is sometimes useful. For example, suppose you wanted to store the dollar amounts shown in Figure 7.6 in some sort of array. The highlighted part of the table contains 60 such entries. If you use an array that has one index, the length of the array would be 60. Keeping track of which entry goes with which index number would be difficult. On the other hand, if you allow yourself two indices, you can use one index for the row of this table and one index for the column. Such an array is illustrated in Figure 7.7.

Two-dimensional arrays use two indices

Arrays that have exactly two indices can be displayed on paper as a two-dimensional table and are called **two-dimensional arrays**. By convention, we think of the first index as denoting the row of the table and the second index as denoting the column. Note that, as was true for the simple arrays we have already seen, we begin numbering indices with 0 rather than 1. The Java notation for an element of a two-dimensional array is

Array_Name[*Row_Index*][*Column_Index*]

For example, if the array is named `table` and it has two indices, `table[3][2]` is the entry whose row index is 3 and column index is 2. Because indices begin

FIGURE 7.6   A Table of Values

Savings Account Balances for Various Interest Rates Compounded Annually (Rounded to Whole Dollar Amounts)						
Year	**5.00%**	**5.50%**	**6.00%**	**6.50%**	**7.00%**	**7.50%**
1	$1050	$1055	$1060	$1065	$1070	$1075
2	$1103	$1113	$1124	$1134	$1145	$1156
3	$1158	$1174	$1191	$1208	$1225	$1242
4	$1216	$1239	$1262	$1286	$1311	$1335
5	$1276	$1307	$1338	$1370	$1403	$1436
6	$1340	$1379	$1419	$1459	$1501	$1543
7	$1407	$1455	$1504	$1554	$1606	$1659
8	$1477	$1535	$1594	$1655	$1718	$1783
9	$1551	$1619	$1689	$1763	$1838	$1917
10	$1629	$1708	$1791	$1877	$1967	$2061

FIGURE 7.7   Row and Column Indices for an Array Named table

Row index 3   Column index 2

Indices	0	1	2	3	4	5
0	$1050	$1055	$1060	$1065	$1070	$1075
1	$1103	$1113	$1124	$1134	$1145	$1156
2	$1158	$1174	$1191	$1208	$1225	$1242
3	$1216	$1239	($1262)	$1286	$1311	$1335
4	$1276	$1307	$1338	$1370	$1403	$1436
5	$1340	$1379	$1419	$1459	$1501	$1543
6	$1407	$1455	$1504	$1554	$1606	$1659
7	$1477	$1535	$1594	$1655	$1718	$1783
8	$1551	$1619	$1689	$1763	$1838	$1917
9	$1629	$1708	$1791	$1877	$1967	$2061

table[3][2] *has a value of* 1262

at 0, this entry is in the fourth row and third column of table, as Figure 7.7 illustrates. Trying to relate array indices to actual row and column numbers gets confusing and is likely to be unnecessary.

Arrays having more than one index are generally called **multidimensional arrays**. More specifically, an array that has n indices is said to be an **n-dimensional array**. Thus, an ordinary one-index array is a **one-dimensional array**. Although arrays having more than two dimensions are rare, they can be useful for some applications.

n-dimensional array

Multidimensional-Array Basics

Arrays having multiple indices are handled in much the same way as one-dimensional arrays. To illustrate the details, we will take you through an example Java program that displays an array like the one in Figure 7.7. The program is shown in Listing 7.12. The array is called table. The following statement declares the name table and creates the array:

Declaring and creating a two-dimensional array

```java
int[][] table = new int[10][6];
```

LISTING 7.12   Using a Two-Dimensional Array *(part 1 of 2)*

```
/**
 Displays a two-dimensional table showing how
 interest rates affect bank balances.
*/
public class InterestTable
{
    public static void main(String[] args)
    {
        int[][] table = new int[10][6];
        for (int row = 0; row < 10; row++)
            for (int column = 0; column < 6; column++)
                table[row][column] =
                    getBalance(1000.00, row + 1, (5 + 0.5 *
                                                column));
        System.out.println("Balances for Various Interest Rates " +
                        "Compounded Annually");
        System.out.println("(Rounded to Whole Dollar Amounts)");
        System.out.println();
        System.out.println("Years 5.00% 5.50% 6.00% 6.50% " +
                        "7.00% 7.50%");

        for (int row = 0; row < 10; row++)
        {
            System.out.print((row + 1) + " ");
            for (int column = 0; column < 6; column++)
                System.out.print("$" + table[row][column] + " ");
            System.out.println();
        }
    }
    /**
     Returns the balance in an account after a given number of years
     and interest rate with an initial balance of startBalance.
     Interest is compounded annually. The balance is rounded
     to a whole number.
    */
    public static int getBalance(double startBalance, int years,
                                double rate)
    {
        double runningBalance = startBalance;
        for (int count = 1; count <= years; count++)
            runningBalance = runningBalance * (1 + rate / 100);
        return (int)(Math.round(runningBalance));
    }
}
```

A real application would do something more with the array **table**. *This is just a demonstration program.*

(continued)

LISTING 7.12   **Using a Two-Dimensional Array** *(part 2 of 2)*

Sample Screen Output

```
Balances for Various Interest Rates Compounded Annually
(Rounded to Whole Dollar Amounts)
```

Years	5.00%	5.50%	6.00%	6.50%	7.00%	7.50%
1	$1050	$1055	$1060	$1065	$1070	$1075
2	$1103	$1113	$1124	$1134	$1145	$1156
3	$1158	$1174	$1191	$1208	$1225	$1242
4	$1216	$1239	$1262	$1286	$1311	$1335
5	$1276	$1307	$1338	$1370	$1403	$1436
6	$1340	$1379	$1419	$1459	$1501	$1543
7	$1407	$1455	$1504	$1554	$1606	$1659
8	$1477	$1535	$1594	$1655	$1718	$1783
9	$1551	$1619	$1689	$1763	$1838	$1917
10	$1629	$1708	$1791	$1877	$1967	$2061

The last line is out of alignment because 10 has two digits. This is easy to fix, but that would clutter the discussion of arrays with extraneous concerns.

This is equivalent to the following two statements:

```
int[][] table;
table = new int[10][6];
```

Note that this syntax is almost identical to the syntax we used for the one-dimensional case. The only difference is that we added a second pair of square brackets in two places, and we gave a number specifying the size of the second dimension, that is, the number of columns. You can have arrays with any number of indices. To get more indices, you just use more square brackets in the declaration.

Indexed variables for multidimensional arrays are just like indexed variables for one-dimensional arrays, except that they have multiple indices, each enclosed in a pair of square brackets. This is illustrated by the following `for` loop from Listing 7.12:

```
for (int row = 0; row < 10; row++)
    for (int column = 0; column < 6; column++)
        table[row][column] = getBalance(1000.00, row + 1,
                                (5 + 0.5 * column));
```

Using nested loops to process a two-dimensional array

Note that we used two for loops, one nested within the other, which is a common way of stepping through all the indexed variables in a two-dimensional array. If we had three indices, we would use three nested for loops, and so forth for higher numbers of indices. The illustration in Figure 7.7 may help you understand the meaning of the indices in table[row][column] and the meaning of the nested for loops.

Like indexed variables for one-dimensional arrays, indexed variables for multidimensional arrays are variables of the base type and can be used anywhere that a variable of the base type is allowed. For example, the indexed variable table[3][2] in the array in Listing 7.12 is a variable of type int and can be used anywhere that an ordinary int variable can be used.

RECAP Declaring and Creating a Multidimensional Array

You declare a name for a multidimensional array and then create the array in basically the same way that you declare and create a one-dimensional array. You simply use as many square brackets as there are indices.

SYNTAX

```
Base_Type[]...[]Array_Name = new Base_Type[Length_1]...
                                           [Length_n];
```

EXAMPLES

```
        char[][] page = new char[100][80];
        int[][] table = new int[10][6];
        double[][][]threeDPicture = new double[10][20][30];
        SomeClass[][]entry = new SomeClass[100][80];
SomeClass is a class.
```

Multidimensional-Array Parameters and Returned Values

Array parameters and return values can be multidimensional

Methods can have parameters and return values that are multidimensional arrays. The situation is similar to that of a one-dimensional array, except that you use more square brackets. For example, the program in Listing 7.13 is like the one in Listing 7.12, but it has a method to display the two-dimensional array passed to it as an argument. Note that the type for the array parameter is int[][]. We have also used named constants instead of literals to define the number of rows and columns.

LISTING 7.13   A Multidimensional-Array Parameter

```java
/**
 Displays a two-dimensional table showing how interest
 rates affect bank balances.
*/
public class InterestTable2
{
    public static final int ROWS = 10;
    public static final int COLUMNS = 6;

    public static void main(String[] args)
    {
        int[][] table = new int[ROWS][COLUMNS];
        for (int row = 0; row < ROWS; row++)
            for (int column = 0; column < COLUMNS; column++)
              table[row][column] =
                  getBalance(1000.00, row + 1, (5 + 0.5 * column));

        System.out.println("Balances for Various Interest Rates " +
                           "Compounded Annually");
        System.out.println("(Rounded to Whole Dollar Amounts)");
        System.out.println();
        System.out.println("Years 5.00% 5.50% 6.00% 6.50% 7.00% 7.50%");

        showTable(table);
    }

    /**
     Precondition: The array anArray has ROWS rows and COLUMNS columns.
     Postcondition: The array contents are displayed with dollar signs.
    */
    public static void showTable(int[][] anArray)
    {
        for (int row = 0; row < ROWS; row++)
        {
            System.out.print((row + 1) + " ");
            for (int column = 0; column < COLUMNS; column++)
                System.out.print("$" + anArray[row][column] + " ");
            System.out.println();
        }
    }

    public static int getBalance(double startBalance, int years, double rate)
    <The rest of the definition of getBalance is the same as in Listing 7.12.>
}
```

A better definition of **showTable** *is possible, as you will see.*

The output is the same as in Listing 7.12.

If you want to return a multidimensional array, you use the same sort of type specification as you use for a multidimensional-array parameter. For example, the following method returns a two-dimensional array whose base type is double:

```java
/**
 Precondition: Each dimension of startArray is the value
 of size.
 Postcondition: The array returned is a copy of the array
 startArray.
*/
public static double[][] copy(double[][] startArray, int size)
{
    double[][] temp = new double[size][size];
    for (int row = 0; row < size; row++)
        for (int column = 0; column < size; column++)
            temp[row][column] = startArray[row][column];
    return temp;
}
```

RECAP Multidimensional-Array Parameters and Return Types

A parameter or return type of a method can be an entire multidimensional array. The syntax for the method's heading is like that for one-dimensional-array parameters or return types, but you use more square brackets []:

SYNTAX

```java
public static Return_Type Method_Name(Base_Type[]...[]
                                    Parameter_Name)
```

or

```java
public static Base_Type[]...[] Method_Name(Parameter_List)
```

You can use other modifiers instead of public and static.

EXAMPLES

```java
public static int getOneElement(char[][] a, int row,
                                int column)
public void readArray (int[][] anArray)
public static char[][] copy(char[][] array)
public int[][] getArray()
```

Java's Representation of Multidimensional Arrays

The Java compiler represents a multidimensional array as several one-dimensional arrays. For example, consider the two-dimensional array

```java
int[][] table = new int[10][6];
```

The array `table` is in fact a one-dimensional array of length 10, and its base type is the type `int[]`. In other words, multidimensional arrays are arrays of arrays. Normally, you do not need to be concerned with this detail, since it is handled automatically by the compiler. However, a knowledge of how Java stores multidimensional arrays can come in handy.

For example, suppose you want to fill a two-dimensional array with values by writing a `for` loop. The program in Listing 7.13 uses the named constants `ROWS` and `COLUMNS` to control the `for` loops. A more general way would use the `length` instance variable to control the loops. But when using `length` with a multidimensional array, you need to think in terms of arrays of arrays.

The following is a revision of the nested `for` loop that appears in the `main` method in Listing 7.13:

```java
for (int row = 0; row <table.length; row++)
    for (int column = 0;column< table[row].length; column++)
        table[row][column]=
            getBalance(1000.00,row + 1,(5 + 0.5 * column));
```

Since the array `table` is actually a one-dimensional array of length 10, the first `for` loop can use `table.length` instead of `ROWS`, which is 10. Additionally, each of the 10 indexed variables `table[0]` through `table[9]` is a one-dimensional array whose length is 6 (`COLUMNS`). Thus, since `table[row]` is a one-dimensional array whose length is 6, the second `for` loop can use `table[row].length` instead of `COLUMNS`.

REMEMBER The Instance Variable `length` for a Two-Dimensional Array

For a two-dimensional array b, the value of b.length is the number of rows, that is, the integer in the first pair of brackets in the array's declaration. The value of b[i].length is the number of columns, that is, the integer in the second pair of brackets in the array's declaration. For the two-dimensional array table in Listing 7.13, the value of table.length is the number of rows—in this case, 10—and the value of table[row].length is the number of columns—in this case, 6.

You can use the fact that multidimensional arrays are arrays of arrays to rewrite the method `showTable` in Listing 7.13. Notice that in Listing 7.13, the method `showTable` assumes that its array argument has `ROWS` (10) rows and

VideoNote
Coding with two-dimensional arrays

COLUMNS (6) columns. That is fine for this particular program, but a better definition of showTable would work for an array of any two dimensions. We leave such a revision for you as an exercise (Self-Test Question 29).

myprogramminglab

SELF-TEST QUESTIONS

28. What output is produced by the following code?

```java
int[][] testArray = new int[3][4];
for (int row = 0; row < testArray.length; row++)
    for (int col = 0;
            col < testArray[row].length; col++)
            testArray[row][col] = col;
for (int row = 0; row < testArray.length; row++)
{
    for (int col = 0;
            col < testArray[row].length; col++)
            System.out.print(testArray[row][col] + " ");
    System.out.println();
}
```

29. Revise the method showTable in Listing 7.13 so that it will work for any two-dimensional array of integers.

30. Write code that will fill the following array a with numbers typed at the keyboard:

```java
int[][] a = new int[4][5];
```

Although the user will enter five numbers per line on four lines, your solution need not depend on how the input numbers are divided into lines.

31. Write a void method called display such that the invocation display(a) will display the contents of the array a in Self-Test Question 30 as four lines of five numbers per line. Your method definition should also work for two-dimensional arrays that have sizes other than 4 by 5. Write your method as a static method that can be added to a class.

Ragged Arrays (*Optional*)

In our previous examples of two-dimensional arrays, all rows have the same number of entries. For example, consider the two-dimensional array created as follows:

```java
int[][] a = new int[3][5];
```

This statement is equivalent to the following statements:

```java
int[][] a;
a = new int[3][];
```

```
a[0] = new int[5];
a[1] = new int[5];
a[2] = new int[5];
```

The line

```
a = new int[3][];
```

declares a as the name of an array of length 3 whose entries each name an array that can be of any length. The next three lines each create an array of integers of length 5 to be named by a[0], a[1], and a[2]. The net result is a two-dimensional array of base type int with three rows and five columns.

The statements

```
a[0] = new int[5];
a[1] = new int[5];
a[2] = new int[5];
```

invite the question "Do all the lengths need to be 5?" The answer is "No!" Because a two-dimensional array in Java is an array of arrays, its rows can have varying numbers of entries. That is, different rows can have different numbers of columns. Such an array is called a **ragged array.** The following statements define a ragged array b in which each row has a different length:

Rows in a two-dimensional array can have different lengths

```
int[][] b;
b = new int[3][];
b[0] = new int[5]; //First row,  5 elements
b[1] = new int[7]; //Second row, 7 elements
b[2] = new int[4]; //Third row,  4 elements
```

It is worth noting that after you fill the preceding array b with values, you could not display b using the method showTable as defined in Listing 7.13. However, we can revise that method, as Self-Test Question 29 asked you to do, as follows:

```
/**
 anArray can be any two-dimensional array.
*/
public static void showTable(int[][] anArray)
{
    for (int row = 0; row <anArray.length; row++)
    {
        System.out.print((row + 1) + " ");
        for (int column = 0; column < anArray[row].length;
                column++)
            System.out.print("$" +
                anArray[row][column] + " ");
        System.out.println();
    }
}
```

A revision of the method showTable from Listing 7.13

This revised method works for any two-dimensional array, even if it is ragged.

You can profitably use ragged arrays in some situations, but most applications do not require them. However, if you understand ragged arrays, you will have a better understanding of how all multidimensional arrays work in Java.

In this programming example, a two-dimensional array named hours is used to store the number of hours worked by each employee of a company for each of the five days Monday through Friday. The first array index is used to designate a day of the week, and the second array index is used to designate an employee. The two-dimensional array is a private instance variable in the class named TimeBook given in Listing 7.14. The class includes a method main that demonstrates the class for a small company having only three employees. The employees are numbered 1, 2, and 3 but are stored at array index positions 0, 1, and 2, since the array indices are numbered starting with 0. Thus, an adjustment of minus 1 is sometimes needed when specifying an employee's array index. We can number days as 0 for Monday, 1 for Tuesday, and so forth to avoid adjustments between day numbers and day indices.

For example, the hours worked by employee number 3 on Tuesday are recorded in hours[1][2]. The first index denotes the second workday of the week—Tuesday—and the second index denotes the third employee.

FAQ This is confusing. Why don't we avoid 0 indices, as we did earlier for one-dimensional arrays?

For a one-dimensional array a, we suggested that you could ignore a[0] if you defined one extra array element. Wasting one memory location that contains an address is not really a big deal. But with a two-dimensional array, if we ignore elements whose indices include 0, we would waste either an entire row, an entire column, or both a row and a column. In general, doing so is not a good idea. We will not avoid 0 indices in this example.

FAQ Can we use an enumeration somehow?

Yes, we could define an enumeration for the days of the workweek, as follows:

```
enum Days {MON, TUE, WED, THU, FRI}
```

Recall that the ordinal value of MON is 0, the ordinal value of TUE is 1, and so on. Using an enumeration can make our program easier to understand.

Instead of using an enumeration for the workdays, we will simply define five named constants, as follows, and use them as indices:

```
private static final int MON = 0;
private static final int TUE = 1;
...
private static final int FRI = 4;
```

The class TimeBook shown in Listing 7.14 is not yet complete. It needs more methods to be a really useful class, but it has enough methods for the demonstration program in main. You can think of the definition in Listing 7.14 as a first pass at writing the class definition. It even has a stub for the definition of the method setHours. Recall that a stub is a method whose definition can be used for testing but is not yet the final definition. At this stage, however, setHours is complete enough to illustrate the use of the two-dimensional array hours, which is an instance variable of the class.

setHours is a stub

In addition to the two-dimensional array hours, the class TimeBook uses two one-dimensional arrays as instance variables: The array weekHours records the total hours each employee works in a week. That is, weekHours[0] is the total number of hours worked by employee 1 in the week, weekHours[1] is the total number of hours worked by employee 2 in the week, and so forth. The array dayHours records the total number of hours worked by all the employees on each day of the week. That is, dayHours[MON] is the total number of hours worked on Monday by all of the employees combined, dayHours[TUE] is the total number of hours worked on Tuesday by all of the employees, and so on.

LISTING 7.14   **A Timekeeping Program** *(part 1 of 4)*

```
/**
 Class that records the time worked by each of a
 company's employees during one five-day week.
 A sample application is in the main method.
*/
public class TimeBook
{
    private int numberOfEmployees;
    private int[][] hours;      //hours[i][j] has the hours for
                                //employee j on day i.
    private int[] weekHours;    //weekHours[i] has the week's
                                //hours worked for employee i + 1.
    private int[] dayHours;     //dayHours[i] has the total hours
                                //worked by all employees on day i.
    private static final int NUMBER_OF_WORKDAYS = 5;
    private static final int MON = 0;
    private static final int TUE = 1;
    private static final int WED = 2;
    private static final int THU = 3;
    private static final int FRI = 4;
```

(continued)

LISTING 7.14   A Timekeeping Program *(part 2 of 4)*

```
/**
 Reads hours worked for each employee on each day of the
 work week into the two-dimensional array hours. (The method
 for input is just a stub in this preliminary version.)
 Computes the total weekly hours for each employee and
 the total daily hours for all employees combined.
*/

public static void main(String[] args)
{
    private static final int NUMBER_OF_EMPLOYEES = 3;
    TimeBook book = new TimeBook(NUMBER_OF_EMPLOYEES);
    book.setHours();
    book.update();
    book.showTable();
}
```

A class generally has more methods. We have defined only the methods used in **main**.

```
public TimeBook(int theNumberOfEmployees)
{
    numberOfEmployees = theNumberOfEmployees;
    hours = new int[NUMBER_OF_WORKDAYS][numberOfEmployees];
    weekHours = new int[numberOfEmployees];
    dayHours = new int[NUMBER_OF_WORKDAYS];
}
```

The **final** program would replace the stub **setHours** with a complete method to obtain the employee data from the user.

```
public void setHours() //This is a stub.
{
    hours[0][0] = 8; hours[0][1] = 0; hours[0][2] = 9;
    hours[1][0] = 8; hours[1][1] = 0; hours[1][2] = 9;
    hours[2][0] = 8; hours[2][1] = 8; hours[2][2] = 8;
    hours[3][0] = 8; hours[3][1] = 8; hours[3][2] = 4;
    hours[4][0] = 8; hours[4][1] = 8; hours[4][2] = 8;
}

public void update()
{
    computeWeekHours();
    computeDayHours();
}

private void computeWeekHours()
{
    for (employeeNumber = 1; employeeNumber <=
        numberOfEmployees; employeeNumber++)
```

(continued)

LISTING 7.14   A Timekeeping Program *(part 3 of 4)*

```java
    {//Process one employee:
        int sum = 0;
        for (int day = MON; day <= FRI; day++)
            sum = sum + hours[day][employeeNumber - 1];
            //sum contains the sum of all the hours worked in
            //one
            //week by the employee with number employeeNumber.
        weekHours[employeeNumber - 1] = sum;
    }
}

private void computeDayHours()
{
    for (int day = MON; day <= FRI; day++)
    {//Process one day (for all employees):
        int sum = 0;
        for (int employeeNumber = 1;
                employeeNumber <= numberOfEmployees;
                employeeNumber++)
            sum = sum + hours[day][employeeNumber - 1];
            //sum contains the sum of all hours worked by all
            //employees on one day.
        dayHours[day] = sum;
    }
}

public void showTable()
{
    // heading
    System.out.print("Employee ");
    for (int employeeNumber = 1;
            employeeNumber <= numberOfEmployees;
            employeeNumber++)
        System.out.print(employeeNumber + " ");
    System.out.println("Totals");
    System.out.println( );

    // row entries
    for (int day = MON; day <= FRI; day++)
    {
        System.out.print(getDayName(day) + " ");
        for (int column = 0; column < hours[day].length;
                column++)
            System.out.print(hours[day][column] + " ");
        System.out.println(dayHours[day]);
    }
```

> The method **showTable** *can and should be made more robust. See Programming Project 6.*

(continued)

LISTING 7.14   A Timekeeping Program *(part 4 of 4)*

```java
            System.out.println( );

            System.out.print("Total = ");
            for (int column = 0; column < numberOfEmployees; column++)
                System.out.print(weekHours[column] + " ");
            System.out.println( );
    }

    //Converts 0 to "Monday", 1 to "Tuesday", etc.
    //Blanks are inserted to make all strings the same length.
    private String getDayName(int day)
    {
        String dayName = null;
        switch (day)
        {
            case MON:
                dayName = "Monday ";
                break;
            case TUE:
                dayName = "Tuesday ";
                break;
            case WED:
                dayName = "Wednesday";
                break;
            case THU:
                dayName = "Thursday ";
                break;
            case FRI:
                dayName = "Friday ";
                break;
            default:
                System.out.println("Fatal Error.");
                System.exit(0);
                break;
        }
        return dayName;
    }
}
```

Sample Screen Output

```
Employee    1    2    3    Totals
Monday      8    0    9    17
Tuesday     8    0    9    17
Wednesday   8    8    8    24
Thursday    8    8    4    20
Friday      8    8    8    24
Total   =   40   24   38
```

FIGURE 7.8 **Arrays for the Class** TimeBook

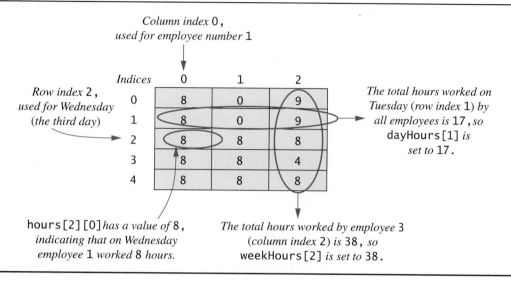

Column index 0 ,
used for employee number 1

Row index 2 ,
used for Wednesday
(the third day)

Indices

The total hours worked on
Tuesday (row index 1) *by*
all employees is 17 , *so*
dayHours[1] *is*
set to 17 .

hours[2][0] *has a value of* 8 ,
indicating that on Wednesday
employee 1 *worked* 8 *hours.*

The total hours worked by employee 3
(column index 2) *is* 38 , *so*
weekHours[2] *is set to* 38 .

The methods computeWeekHours and computeDayHours compute the values for weekHours and dayHours, respectively, from the values in the two-dimensional array hours. Figure 7.8 shows some sample data for the array hours and illustrates the relationship between hours and each of the arrays weekHours and dayHours.

Be sure to notice how the method computeWeekHours uses the array indices of the two-dimensional array hours. A for loop is nested inside of a for loop. The outer for loop cycles through all employees, and the inner for loop is executed once for each day of the week. The inner for loop—together with an assignment statement before and after—is reproduced here:

```
int sum = 0;
for (int day = MON; day <= FRI; day++)
    sum = sum + hours[day][employeeNumber - 1];
    //sum contains the sum of all the hours worked in
    //one week by the employee with number employeeNumber.
weekHours[employeeNumber - 1] = sum;
```

Using named constants to make the loop clearer

Note that when computing the sum of the hours for one employee, the second index, which represents the particular employee, is held constant.

The method computeDayHours works in a similar way to compute the total number of hours worked by all employees on each day of the week. However, in this case, the inner for loop cycles through the second index while the first index is held constant. Or, to phrase it another way, the roles of the employee index and the day of the week index are interchanged.

Although our class TimeBook is correct as written, it is not yet a finished piece of software ready to be saved and reused again and again. The method setHours

TimeBook needs to be completed

is just a stub and needs to be replaced by a more generally applicable method that obtains hours from the user at the keyboard. The method `showTable` will not always produce output that is as neat as the output shown in Listing 7.14, unless all the hours have the same number of digits. Thus, the method `showTable` needs to be made more robust so that it will neatly display any combination of hours worked. Finally, the class `TimeBook` should have more methods so that it will be useful in a wide range of situations. Programming Project 6 asks you to complete the definition of the class `TimeBook` in all of these ways.

7.6 GRAPHICS SUPPLEMENT

Write your answer in the space provided.

—WEB PAGE INSTRUCTION.

polygon n. A closed plane figure bounded by three or more line segments.

—*THE AMERICAN HERITAGE DICTIONARY OF THE ENGLISH LANGUAGE*, FOURTH EDITION

The first part of this section covers text areas and text fields, which are components that can be used for text input and output in your applets. It does not require any material from earlier in this chapter and so may be read even if you do not read the main body of this chapter. The remainder of this section shows you how to draw a very general kind of figure known as a *polygon*. It does require the basic material on arrays covered earlier in this chapter.

Text Areas and Text Fields

A **text area** is a window-like area in an applet or application that can be used for text input and text output. A text area can have room for any number of lines and any number of characters per line. A **text field** is similar but has room for only one line of text. For example, the user can ask a question in the text area of an applet. The applet can then display an answer to the question in the same text area. We will write such an applet in the next programming example. We will first discuss what happens when this applet is run and then describe the details of using text areas and text fields in general.

Text I/O can appear in a text area or a text field

| PROGRAMMING EXAMPLE | A Question-and-Answer Applet |

The applet in Listing 7.15 answers a question, any kind of question whatsoever. The user highlights the text in the text area, using a mouse, and then types in any question. At that point the text area contains the question and nothing else. To get an answer, the user clicks the Get Answer button. However, clicking this button does not produce an answer right away. Instead, other text appears in the text area, asking for advice in finding the answer. The user then enters some advice into the text field and clicks the Send Advice button. Finally, the applet gives an answer in the text field. After reading the answer, the user clicks the Reset button, which makes the applet look the same as when it was first run. The user is then supposed to leave the applet running so that another user can ask another question. This can proceed for any number of users asking questions, giving advice, and getting answers.

LISTING 7.15 An Applet with a Text Area *(part 1 of 2)*

```java
import javax.swing.JApplet;
import javax.swing.JButton;
import javax.swing.JLabel;
import javax.swing.JTextArea;
import java.awt.Container;
import java.awt.FlowLayout;
import java.awt.event.ActionEvent;
import java.awt.event.ActionListener;
public class Oracle extends JApplet implements ActionListener
{
    public static int LINES = 5;
    public static int CHAR_PER_LINE = 40;

    private JTextArea theText;
    private String question;
    private String answer;
    private String advice;

    public void int()
    {
        Container contentPane = getContentPane();
        contentPane.setLayout(new FlowLayout());

        JLabel instructions=
            new JLabel("I will answer any question, " +
                        "but may need some advice from you.");
        contentPane.add(instructions);

        JButton getAnswerButton = new JButton("Get Answer");
        getAnswerButton.addActionListener(this);
        contentPane.add(getAnswerButton);

        JButton sendAdviceButton = new JButton("Send Advice");
        sendAdviceButton.addActionListener(this);
        contentPane.add(sendAdviceButton);

        JButton resetButton = new JButton("Reset");
        resetButton.addActionListener(this);
        contentPane.add(resetButton);
```

(continued)

LISTING 7.15 An Applet with a Text Area *(part 2 of 2)*

```java
        theText = new JTextArea(LINES, CHAR_PER_LINE);
        theText.setText("Questions and advice go here.");
        contentPane.add(theText);
        answer = "The answer is: Look around."; //first answer
    }
    public void actionPerformed(ActionEvent e)
    {
        String actionCommand = e.getActionCommand();
        if (actionCommand.equals("Get Answer"))
        {
            question = theText.getText();
            theText.setText("That is a difficult question.\n" +
                            "Please give me some advice\n" +
                            "and click the Send Advice button.");
        }
        else if (actionCommand.equals("Send Advice"))
        {
            advice = theText.getText();
            theText.setText("That advice helped.\n" +
                            "You asked the question: " + question +
                            "\n" + answer +
                            "\nClick the Reset button and" +
                            "\nleave the program on for others.");
            answer = "The answer is: " + advice;
        }
        else if (actionCommand.equals("Reset"))
        {
            theText.setText("Questions and advice go here.");
        }
        else
            theText.setText("Error");
    }
}
```

Applet Output

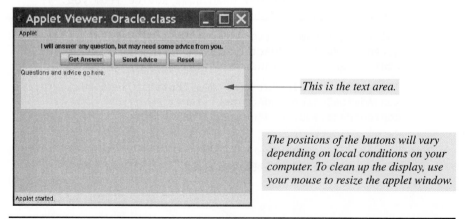

This is the text area.

The positions of the buttons will vary depending on local conditions on your computer. To clean up the display, use your mouse to resize the applet window.

Suppose there are a number of users who want to ask questions. If you are allowed only one question, after which you must go to the back of the line of users waiting to ask questions, the applet seems pretty smart. However, if you stand aside and watch the users, you quickly realize that the advice given by one user is used as the answer for the next user. Not a very fancy trick, but a good example of using a text area for input and output. The details about the text area in Listing 7.15 and about text areas and fields in general are given in the next section.

The Classes `JTextArea` and `JTextField`

A text area is an object of the class `JTextArea` and is displayed as a place for the user to enter several lines of text. The applet in Listing 7.15 uses the following code to create a text area named `theText` in which the user asks a question and receives an answer:

```
private JTextAreatheText;
...
theText = new JTextArea(LINES, CHAR_PER_LINE);
```

The object `theText` is a private instance variable, and the invocation of `JTextArea`'s constructor takes place inside the `init` method of the applet. The arguments `LINES` and `CHAR_PER_LINE` are named constants that, respectively, indicate the minimum number of lines and the minimum number of characters per line desired in the text area. For this applet, the text area will have room for at least 5 lines and at least 40 characters per line. The user can type more than 5 lines of text or lines longer than 40 characters in the text area, but the additional text might not be visible.

An applet can both read text from the text area and display text in the text area. The method `getText` returns the text entered in the text area by the user. For example, the following statement from Listing 7.15 sets a `String` variable named `question` to whatever string is in the text area `theText` at the time that the `getText` method is invoked:

```
question = theText.getText();
```

getText gets input from a text area

The method `setText` displays a new text string in a text field. For example, the following statement, also from Listing 7.15, will cause the text area `theText` to change the text it displays:

```
theText.setText("That is a difficult question.\n" +
                "Please give me some advice\n" +
                "and click the Send Advice button.");
```

setText writes text into a text area

The text displayed in the text area will be changed to the given string. Notice that the string has two line-break characters and so will be displayed as three lines of text.

Text fields are like
text areas, but
smaller

A text field is an object of the class JTextField. The details for creating and using a text field are the same as those for a text area, except that a text field has room for only one line of text containing a specified number of characters, and you use the class JTextField instead of JTextArea.

RECAP **The Classes** JTextArea **and** JTextField

The classes JTextArea and JTextField can be used to add areas for changeable text to an applet or application. An object of the class JTextArea has room for a specified number of lines and a specified number of characters per line. An object of the class JTextField has room for only one line that contains some specified number of characters. More text can be typed into a text area or text field than is specified in its size, but the extra text might not be visible.

EXAMPLES

```
//10 lines of 30 characters each
JTextAreasomeText = new JTextArea(10, 30);
getContentPane().add(someText);

//One line of 30 characters
JTextField name = new JTextField(30);
getContentPane().add(name);
```

RECAP **The Methods** getText **and** setText

Each of the classes JTextArea and JTextField define methods called getText and setText. The method getText retrieves the text written in the text area or text field. The method setText changes the text written in the text area or text field.

EXAMPLE

```
//theText is an object of either JTextArea or JTextField
String question = theText.getText();
theText.setText("The answer is 42.");
```

SELF-TEST QUESTION

32. Suppose theText is an instance of JTextArea. Write some code that will take the text currently in theText and replace it with that text written two times.

Drawing Polygons

You can draw a rectangle in an applet using the Graphics method drawRect. However, a rectangle has four sides and 90-degree (right-angle) corners, and sometimes you want a figure with different angles and more or fewer sides. A **polygon** is any closed figure made up of line segments that do not cross. A rectangle is a special case of a four-sided polygon, but polygons may have any number of sides, and the angles between sides need not be 90 degrees.

A polygon is a closed figure composed of straight lines

You can specify a polygon by giving the locations of the corners. The polygon consists of the figure obtained by drawing lines between successive corner points. A **polyline** is similar to a polygon, but it is not closed. Figure 7.9 illustrates the difference between a polygon and a polyline. The figure shows five points labeled p1 through p5 and five lines connecting these points to form a polygon. The polyline has no line from the last point back to the first point.

A polyline connects points with straight lines, but is not closed

The Graphics method drawPolygon enables you to draw any polygon. The method requires three arguments: The first is an array of ints specifying the *x*-coordinates of the points, the second is another array of ints specifying the corresponding *y*-coordinates of the points, and the third argument is the number of points. The two arrays contain the same number of values and can be partially filled, which is why the third argument is necessary.

drawPolygon, fillPolygon, and drawPolyline are in the class Graphics

The Graphics method fillPolygon is just like drawPolygon, but it fills the inside of the polygon with color. Likewise, the method drawPolyline is like drawPolygon but does not connect the last two points in the arrays with a line.

FIGURE 7.9 A Polygon and a Polyline

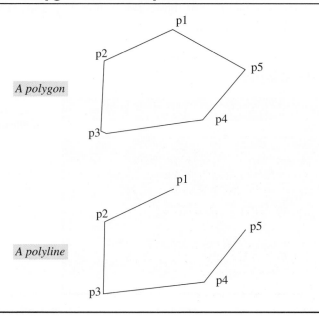

Listing 7.16 shows an applet that displays a simple picture of a house. The house itself is a filled polygon drawn using fillPolygon, the window is a polygon drawn using drawPolygon, and the door is a polyline drawn using drawPolyline. Finally, drawString labels the drawing.

LISTING 7.16   An Applet with Polygons and a Polyline

```java
import javax.swing.JApplet;
import java.awt.Color;
import java.awt.Graphics;

public class House extends JApplet
{
    private int[] xHouse = {150, 150, 200, 250, 250};
    private int[] yHouse = {100, 40, 20, 40, 100};
    private int[] xDoor = {175, 175, 200, 200};
    private int[] yDoor = {100, 60, 60, 100};
    private int[] xWindow = {220, 220, 240, 240};
    private int[] yWindow = {60, 80, 80, 60};

    public void paint(Graphics canvas)
    {
        this.setBackground(Color.LIGT_GRAY);
        canvas.setColor(Color.GREEN);
        canvas.fillPolygon(xHouse, yHouse, xHouse.length);
        canvas.setColor(Color.BLACK);
        canvas.drawPolyline(xDoor, yDoor, xDoor.length);
        canvas.drawPolygon(xWindow, yWindow, xWindow.length);
        canvas.drawString("Home sweet home!", 150, 120);
    }
}
```

Applet Output

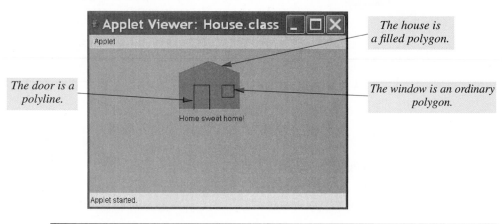

The house is a filled polygon.

The door is a polyline.

The window is an ordinary polygon.

Home sweet home!

RECAP **The Methods drawPolygon, fillPolygon, and drawPolyline**

The methods drawPolygon, fillPolygon, and drawPolyline are methods in the class Graphics.

SYNTAX

```
canvas.drawPolygon(Array_Of_Xs, Array_Of_Ys, Number_Of_
Points);
```

Draws a polygon by connecting the points (*Array_Of_Xs*[i], *Array_Of_Ys*[i]), for values of i ranging from 0 to *Number_Of_Points*, with line segments.

EXAMPLES

```
private int[] xCoord = {150, 150, 200, 250, 250};
private int[] yCoord = {100, 40, 20, 40, 100};
        ...
canvas.drawPolygon(xCoord, yCoord, xCoord.length);
```

SYNTAX

```
canvas.drawPolygon(Array_Of_Xs, Array_Of_Ys, Number_Of_
Points);
```

Draws the same polygon as drawPolygon, but the inside of the polygon is filled in.

EXAMPLE

```
canvas.fillPolygon(xCoord, yCoord, xCoord.length);
```

SYNTAX

```
canvas.fillPolygon(Array_Of_Xs, Array_Of_Ys,
                Number_Of_Points);
```

Draws a polyline using the same points as specified for drawPolygon, but no line segment is drawn from the last point to the first point, so the figure is normally not closed.

EXAMPLE

```
canvas.drawPolyline(xCoord, yCoord, xCoord.length);
```

SELF-TEST QUESTION

33. You can draw a rectangle using the method drawRect, but you could also use drawPolygon. With canvas as a calling object, write an invocation of drawPolygon that will draw a rectangle 10 pixels high and 20 pixels wide, whose upper left corner is at the point (7, 8).

CHAPTER SUMMARY

■ An array can be thought of as a collection of variables all of the same type.

■ Arrays are objects that are created using the operator new, although the syntax is slightly different from that used when creating objects of a class.

■ Array elements are numbered starting with 0 and ending with 1 less than the length of the array. If a is an array, a[i] is an indexed variable of the array. The index i must have a value greater than or equal to 0 and strictly less than a.length, the array's length. If i has any other value when you run your program, an array index out-of-bounds error will occur, causing an error message.

■ When an indexed variable is used as an argument to a method, it is treated just like any other argument whose data type is the same as the array's base type. In particular, if the base type is a primitive type, the method cannot change the value of the indexed variable, but if the base type is a class, the method can change the state of the object at the indexed variable.

■ You can pass an entire array to a method. The method can change the values of an array of primitive values or the states of objects in the array.

■ A method's return value can be an array.

■ When you use only part of an array, you normally store values in an initial segment of the array and set an int variable to the number of these values. In this case, you have a partially filled array.

■ An accessor method that returns an array corresponding to a private instance variable of an array type should be careful to return a copy of the array, as returning the private instance variable itself causes a privacy leak.

■ The selection sort algorithm orders an array of values, such as numbers, into either increasing or decreasing order.

■ Arrays can have more than one index, and so are called multidimensional. Multidimensional arrays are implemented in Java as arrays of arrays.

■ A two-dimensional array can be thought of as a two-dimensional table of rows and columns. An indexed variable of such an array is an element whose row and column are indicated by its indices, where the first index designates the row, and the second index designates the column.

- You can insert text fields and text areas into an applet or application to provide it with text input and output.

- You can draw arbitrary polygons and polylines in an applet or application.

Exercises

1. Write a program in a class `NumberAboveAverage` that counts the number of days that the temperature is above average. Read ten temperatures from the keyboard and place them in an array. Compute the average temperature and then count and display the number of days on which the temperature was above average.

2. Write a program in a class `CountFamiles` that counts the number of families whose income is below a certain value. Read an integer k from the keyboard and then create an array of `double` values of size k. Read k values representing family income from the keyboard and place them into the array. Find the maximum income among these values. Then count the families that make less than 10 percent of this maximum income. Display this count and the incomes of these families.

3. Write a program in a class `CountPoor` that counts the number of families that are considered poor. Write and use a class `Family` that has the attributes

   - `income`—a `double` value that is the income for the family
   - `size`—the number of people in the family

   and the following methods:

   - `Family(income, size)`—a constructor that sets the attributes
   - `isPoor(housingCost, foodCost)`—a method that returns true if `housingCost + foodCost * size` is greater than half the family income (`foodCost` is the average food cost for an individual, while `housingCost` is for the family)
   - `toString`—a method that returns a string containing the information about the family

   The program should read an integer k from the keyboard and then create an array of size k whose base type is `Family`. It should then create k objects of type `Family` and put them in the array, reading the income and size for each family from the keyboard. After reading an average housing cost and average food cost from the keyboard, it should display the families that are poor.

4. Write a program in a class `FlowerCounter` that computes the cost of flowers sold at a flower stand. Five kinds of flowers—petunia, pansy, rose, violet, and carnation—are stocked and cost, respectively, 50¢, 75¢, $1.50, 50¢,

and 80¢ per flower. Create an array of strings that holds the names of these flowers. Create another array that holds the cost of each corresponding flower. Your program should read the name of a flower and the quantity desired by a customer. Locate the flower in the name array and use that index to find the cost per stem in the cost array. Compute and print the total cost of the sale.

5. Write a program in a class `CharacterFrequency` that counts the number of times a digit appears in a telephone number. Your program should create an array of size 10 that will hold the count for each digit from 0 to 9. Read a telephone number from the keyboard as a string. Examine each character in the phone number and increment the appropriate count in the array. Display the contents of the array.

6. Create a class `Ledger` that will record the sales for a store. It will have the attributes

   * `sale`—an array of `double` values that are the amounts of all sales
   * `salesMade`—the number of sales so far
   * `maxSales`—the maximum number of sales that can be recorded

   and the following methods:

   * `Ledger(max)`—a constructor that sets the maximum number of sales to `max`
   * `addSale(d)`—adds a sale whose value is d
   * `getNumberOfSales`—returns the number of sales made
   * `getTotalSales`—returns the total value of the sales

7. Define the following methods for the class `Ledger`, as described in the previous exercise:

   * `getAverageSale()`—returns the average value of all the sales
   * `getCountAbove(v)`—returns the number of sales that exceeded v in value

8. Write a static method `isStrictlyIncreasing(double[] in)` that returns true if each value in the given array is greater than the value before it, or false otherwise.

9. Write a static method `removeDuplicates(Character[] in)` that returns a new array of the characters in the given array, but without any duplicate characters. Always keep the first copy of the character and remove subsequent ones. For example, if in contains b, d, a, b, f, a, g, a, a, and f, the method will return an array containing b, d a, f, and g. (*Hint*: One way to solve this problem is to create a boolean array of the same size as the given array `in` and use it to keep track of which characters to keep. The values in the new boolean array will determine the size of the array to return.)

10. Write a static method `remove(int v, int[] in)` that will return a new array of the integers in the given array, but with the value v removed. For example, if v is 3 and in contains 0, 1, 3, 2, 3, 0, 3, and 1, the method will return an array containing 0, 1, 2, 0, and 1.

11. Suppose that we are selling boxes of candy for a fund-raiser. We have five kinds of candy to sell: Mints, Chocolates with Nuts, Chewy Chocolates, Dark Chocolate Creams, and Sugar-Free Suckers. We will record a customer's order as an array of five integers, representing the number of boxes of each kind of candy. Write a static method `combineOrder` that takes two orders as its arguments and returns an array that represents the combined orders. For example, if `order1` contains 0, 0, 3, 4, and 7, and `order2` contains 0, 4, 0, 1, and 2, the method should return an array containing 0, 4, 3, 5, and 9.

12. Create a class `Polynomial` that is used to evaluate a **polynomial** function of x:

$$P(x) = a_0 + a_1 x + a_2 x + \cdots + a_{n-1} x^{n-1} + a_n x^n$$

The **coefficients** a_i are floating-point numbers, the exponents of x are integers, and the largest exponent n—called the **degree** of the polynomial—is greater than or equal to 0. The class has the attributes

- degree—the value of the largest exponent n
- coefficients—an array of the coefficients a_i

and the following methods:

- `Polynomial(max)`—a constructor that creates a polynomial of degree max whose coefficients are all 0
- `setConstant(i, value)`—sets the coefficient a_i to value
- `evaluate(x)`—returns the value of the polynomial for the given value x

For example, the polynomial

$$P(x) = 3 + 5x + 2x^3$$

is of degree 3 and has coefficients $a_0 = 3$, $a_1 = 5$, $a_2 = 0$, and $a_3 = 2$. The invocation `evaluate(7)` computes $3 + 5 \times 7 + 0 \times 7 + 2 \times 7^3$, which is $3 + 35 + 0 + 686$, and returns the result 724.

13. Write a method `beyondLastEntry(position)` for the class `OneWayNoRepeatsList`, as given in Listing 7.9, that returns true when `position` is beyond the last entry on the list.

14. Revise the class `OneWayNoRepeatsList`, as given in Listing 7.9, so that it allocates an extra element in the array entry and ignores `entry[0]`, as suggested earlier near the end of the section entitled "More About Array Indices."

15. Write a static method for selection sort that will sort an array of characters.

16. Overload the method `selectionSort` in Listing 7.10 so that it sorts an array whose indices range from `first` to `last`, where $0 \leq first \leq last$, and `last` is less than the length of the array.

17. Revise the method `selectionSort` that appears in Listing 7.10 so that it calls the method described in the previous exercise.

18. Revise the class `TimeBook` in Listing 7.14 to use an enumeration for the days of the week instead of named constants.

19. Write a sequential search of an array of integers, assuming that the array is sorted into ascending order. (*Hint*: Consider an array that contains the four integers 2, 4, 6, and 8. How can you tell that 5 is not in the array without comparing 5 to every integer in the array?)

20. Write a static method `findFigure(picture,threshold)`, where `picture` is a two-dimensional array of `double` values. The method should return a new two-dimensional array whose elements are either 0.0 or 1.0. Each 1.0 in this new array indicates that the corresponding value in `picture` exceeds `threshold` times the average of all values in `picture`. Other elements in the new array are 0.0.

    For example, if the values in `picture` are

1.2	1.3	4.5	6.0	2.7
1.7	3.3	4.4	10.5	17.0
1.1	4.5	2.1	25.3	9.2
1.0	9.5	8.3	2.9	2.1

the average value is 5.55. The resulting array for a threshold of 1.4 would be

0.0	0.0	0.0	0.0	0.0
0.0	0.0	0.0	1.0	1.0
0.0	0.0	0.0	1.0	1.0
0.0	1.0	0.0	0.0	0.0

and the resulting array for a threshold of 0.6 would be

0.0	0.0	1.0	1.0	0.0
0.0	0.0	1.0	1.0	1.0
0.0	1.0	0.0	1.0	1.0
0.0	1.0	1.0	0.0	0.0

21. Write a static method `blur(double[][]picture)` that you could use on a part of a picture file to obscure a detail such as a person's face or a license plate number. This method computes the weighted averages of the values in `picture` and returns them in a new two-dimensional array. To find a weighted average of a group of numbers, you count some of them more than others. Thus, you multiply each item by its weight, add these products together, and divide the result by the sum of the weights.

For each element in `picture`, compute the weighted average of the element and its immediate neighbors. Store the result in a new two-dimensional array in the same position that the element occupies in `picture`. This new array is the one the method returns.

The neighbors of an element in `picture` can be above, below, to the left of, and to the right of it, either vertically, horizontally, or diagonally. So each weighted average in the new array will be a combination of up to nine values from the array `picture`. A corner value will use only four values: itself and three neighbors. An edge value will use only six values: itself and five neighbors. But an interior value will use nine values: itself and eight neighbors. So you will need to treat the corners and edges separately from the other cells.

The weights to use are:

```
1   2   1
2   4   2
1   2   1
```

The element itself has the highest weight of 4, the horizontal and vertical neighbors have a weight of 2, and the diagonal neighbors have a weight of 1.

For example, suppose the values in `picture` are

1.2	1.3	4.5	6.0	2.7
1.7	3.3	4.4	10.5	17.0
1.1	4.5	2.1	25.3	9.2
1.0	9.5	8.3	2.9	2.1

and the new array is called `result`. In assigning weights, we will arbitrarily start with an element and consider neighbors in a clockwise direction. Thus, the interior value in `result[1][1]` is equal to

$$\frac{4(3.3) + 2(4.4) + 1(2.1) + 2(4.5) + 1(1.1) + 2(1.7) + 1(1.2) + 2(1.3) + 1(4.5)}{4 + 2 + 1 + 2 + 1 + 2 + 1 + 2 + 1}$$

To arrive at this equation, we started with the element at `picture[1][1]` and then, beginning with the neighbor to the right, we considered neighbors in a clockwise direction. The corner value in `result[0][0]` is equal to

$$\frac{4(1.2) + 2(1.3) + 1(3.3) + 2(1.7)}{4 + 2 + 1 + 2}$$

Note that `picture[0][0]` has fewer neighbors than an interior value such as `picture[1][1]`. The same is true for an edge value such as `picture[0][1]`. Thus, the edge value in `result[0][1]`is equal to

$$\frac{4(1.3) + 2(4.5) + 1(4.4) + 2(3.3) + 1(1.7) + 2(1.2)}{4 + 2 + 1 + 2 + 1 + 2}$$

The final array, `result`, would be

1.57	2.44	4.60	6.73	7.48
1.98	2.87	5.97	10.37	12.01
2.63	4.09	7.48	11.40	11.58
3.30	5.73	7.67	7.86	6.43

PROGRAMMING PROJECTS

myprogramminglab *Visit www.myprogramminglab.com to complete many of these Programming Projects online and get instant feedback.*

1. Write a program that reads integers, one per line, and displays their sum. Also, display all the numbers read, each with an annotation giving its percentage contribution to the sum. Use a method that takes the entire array as one argument and returns the sum of the numbers in the array. (*Hint*: Ask the user for the number of integers to be entered, create an array of that length, and then fill the array with the integers read. A possible dialogue between the program and the user follows:

```
How many numbers will you enter?
4
Enter 4 integers, one per line:
2
1
1
2
The sum is 6.
The numbers are:
2, which is 33.3333% of the sum.
1, which is 16.6666% of the sum.
1, which is 16.6666% of the sum.
2, which is 33.3333% of the sum.)
```

2. Write a program that will read a line of text that ends with a period, which serves as a sentinel value. Display all the letters that occur in the text, one per line and in alphabetical order, along with the number of times each letter occurs in the text. Use an array of base type `int` of length 26, so that the element at index 0 contains the number of *a*'s, the element at index 1 contains the number of *b*'s, and so forth. Allow both uppercase and lowercase letters

as input, but treat uppercase and lowercase versions of the same letter as being equal. (*Hints*: Use one of the methods toUpperCase or toLowerCase in the wrapper class Character, described in Chapter 6. You will find it helpful to define a method that takes a character as an argument and returns an int value that is the correct index for that character. For example, the argument 'a' results in 0 as the return value, the argument 'b' gives 1 as the return value, and so on. Note that you can use a type cast, such as (int) letter, to change a char to an int. Of course, this will not get the number you want, but if you subtract (int)'a', you will then get the right index.) Allow the user to repeat this task until the user says she or he is through.

3. A **palindrome** is a word or phrase that reads the same forward and backward, ignoring blanks and considering uppercase and lowercase versions of the same letter to be equal. For example, the following are palindromes:

- warts n straw
- radar
- Able was I ere I saw Elba
- xyzczyx

Write a program that will accept a sequence of characters terminated by a period and will decide whether the string—without the period—is a palindrome. You may assume that the input contains only letters and blanks and is at most 80 characters long. Include a loop that allows the user to check additional strings until she or he requests that the program end. (*Hint*: Define a static method called isPalindrome that begins as follows:

```
/**
 Precondition: The array a contains letters and blanks in
 positions a[0] through a[used - 1]. Returns true if the
 string is a palindrome and false otherwise.
*/
public static boolean isPalindrome(char[] a, int used)
```

Your program should read the input characters into an array whose base type is char and then call the preceding method. The int variable used keeps track of how much of the array is used, as described in the section entitled "Partially Filled Arrays."

4. Add a method bubbleSort to the class ArraySorter, as given in Listing 7.10, that performs a **bubble sort** of an array. The bubble sort algorithm examines all adjacent pairs of elements in the array from the beginning to the end and interchanges any two elements that are out of order. Each interchange makes the array more sorted than it was, until it is entirely sorted. The algorithm in pseudocode follows:

Bubble sort algorithm to sort an array a

Repeat the following until the array a is sorted:
```
for (index = 0; index <a.length - 1; index++)
    if (a[index] > a[index + 1])
        Interchange the values of a[index] and a[index + 1].
```

The bubble sort algorithm usually requires more time than other sorting methods.

VideoNote
Inserting into a sorted array

5. Add a method `insertionSort` to the class `ArraySorter`, as given in Listing 7.10, that performs an **insertion sort** of an array. To simplify this project, our insertion sort algorithm will use an additional array. It copies elements from the original given array to this other array, inserting each element into its correct position in the second array. This will usually require moving a number of elements in the array receiving the new elements. The algorithm in pseudocode is as follows:

Insertion sort algorithm to sort an array a

```
for (index = 0; index <a.length; index++)
        Insert the value of a[index] into its correct position in the array
            temp, so that all the elements copied into the array temp so far
            are sorted.
Copy all the elements from temp back to a.
```

The array `temp` is partially filled and is a local variable in the method `sort`.

6. The class `TimeBook` in Listing 7.14 is not really finished. Complete the definition of this class in the way described in the text. In particular, be sure to add a default constructor, as well as set and get methods that change or retrieve each of the instance variables and each indexed variable of each array instance variable. Be sure you replace the stub `setHours` with a method that obtains values from the keyboard. You should also define a private method having two `int` parameters that displays the first parameter in the number of spaces given by a second parameter. The extra spaces not filled by the first parameter are to be filled with blanks. This will let you write each array element in exactly four spaces, for example, and so will allow you to display a neat rectangular arrangement of array elements. Be sure that the `main` method in Listing 7.14 works correctly with these new methods. Also, write a separate test program to test all the new methods. (*Hint*: To display an `int` value *n* in a fixed number of spaces, use `Integer.toString(n)` to convert the number to a string value, and then work with the string value. This method is discussed in Chapter 6 in the section "Wrapper Classes.")

7. Define a class called `TicTacToe`. An object of type `TicTacToe` is a single game of tic-tac-toe. Store the game board as a single two-dimensional array of base type `char` that has three rows and three columns. Include methods

to add a move, to display the board, to tell whose turn it is (X or O), to tell whether there is a winner, to say who the winner is, and to reinitialize the game to the beginning. Write a `main` method for the class that will allow two players to enter their moves in turn at the same keyboard.

8. Repeat Programming Project 12 from Chapter 5 but use an array to store the movie ratings instead of separate variables. All changes should be internal to the class, so the `main` method to test the class should run identically with either the old `Movie` class or the new `Movie` class using arrays.

VideoNote
Solution to Project 8

9. Traditional password entry schemes are susceptible to "shoulder surfing" in which an attacker watches an unsuspecting user enter their password or PIN number and uses it later to gain access to the account. One way to combat this problem is with a randomized challenge-response system. In these systems the user enters different information every time based on a secret in response to a randomly generated challenge. Consider the following scheme in which the password consists of a five-digit PIN number (00000 to 99999). Each digit is assigned a random number that is 1, 2, or 3. The user enters the random numbers that correspond to their PIN instead of their actual PIN numbers.

   For example, consider an actual PIN number of 12345. To authenticate the user would be presented with a screen such as:

   ```
   PIN: 0 1 2 3 4 5 6 7 8 9
   NUM: 3 2 3 1 1 3 2 2 1 3
   ```

   The user would enter 23113 instead of 12345. This doesn't divulge the password even if an attacker intercepts the entry because 23113 could correspond to other PIN numbers, such as 69440 or 70439. The next time the user logs in, a different sequence of random numbers would be generated, such as:

   ```
   PIN: 0 1 2 3 4 5 6 7 8 9
   NUM: 1 1 2 3 1 2 2 3 3 3
   ```

   Write a program to simulate the authentication process. Store an actual PIN number in your program. The program should use an array to assign random numbers to the digits from 0 to 9. Output the random digits to the screen, input the response from the user, and output whether or not the user's response correctly matches the PIN number.

10. Write an applet or GUI application that displays a picture of a pine tree formed by drawing a triangle on top of a small rectangle that makes up the visible trunk. The tree should be green and have a gray trunk.

    Graphics

11. ELIZA was a program written in 1966 that parodied a psychotherapist session. The user typed sentences and the program used those words to compose a question.

    Graphics

Create a simple applet or GUI application based on this idea. The program will use a label to hold the program's question, a text field into which the user can type an answer, a button for the user to signal that the answer is complete, and a quit button.

The initial text for the question label should read: "What would you like to talk about?" When the user presses a button, get the text from the text field. Now extract the words from the text one at a time and find the largest word of length 4 or more. Let's call this largest word X for now. In response, create a question based on the length of the word. If the word is length 4, the new question is: "Tell me more about X." If the word is length 5, the new question is: "Why do you think X is important?" If the word is length 6 or more, the new question is: "Now we are getting somewhere. How does X affect you the most?" If there is no word of length 4, the new question is: "Maybe we should move on. Is there something else you would like to talk about?" (*Hint*: You can use the class Scanner to extract the words from a string, assuming blanks separate the words. For example, the following statements

```
String text = " one potato two potato ";
Scanner parser = new Scanner(text);
System.out.println(parser.next());
System.out.println(parser.next());
```

display one and potato on separate lines.)

12. Sudoku is a popular logic puzzle that uses a 9 by 9 array of squares that are organized into 3 by 3 subarrays. The puzzle solver must fill in the squares with the digits 1 to 9 such that no digit is repeated in any row, any column, or any of the nine 3 by 3 subgroups of squares. Initially, some squares are filled in already and cannot be changed. For example, the following might be a starting configuration for a Sudoku puzzle:

1	2	3	4	9	7	8	6	5
4	5	9						
6	7	8						
3			1					
2								
9				5				
8								
7								
5		9						

Create a class SudokuPuzzle that has the attributes

- board—a 9 by 9 array of integers that represents the current state of the puzzle, where 0 indicates a blank square
- start—a 9 by 9 array of boolean values that indicates which squares in board are given values that cannot be changed

and the following methods:

- SudokuPuzzle—a constructor that creates an empty puzzle
- toString—returns a string representation of the puzzle that can be printed
- addInitial(row, col, value)—sets the given square to the given value as an initial value that cannot be changed by the puzzle solver
- addGuess(row, col, value)—sets the given square to the given value; the value can be changed later by another call to addGuess
- checkPuzzle—returns true if the values in the puzzle do not violate the restrictions
- getValueIn(row, col)—returns the value in the given square
- getAllowedValues(row, col)—returns a one-dimensional array of nine booleans, each of which corresponds to a digit and is true if the digit can be placed in the given square without violating the restrictions
- isFull—returns true if every square has a value
- reset—changes all of the nonpermanent squares back to blanks (0s)

Write a main method in the class Sudoku that creates a SudokuPuzzle object and sets its initial configuration. Then use a loop to allow someone to play Sudoku. Display the current configuration and ask for a row, column, and value. Update the game board and display it again. If the configuration does not satisfy the restrictions, let the user know. Indicate when the puzzle has been solved correctly. In that case, both checkPuzzle and isFull would return true. You should also allow options for resetting the puzzle and displaying the values that can be placed in a given square.

13. Create an applet or GUI application that draws the following picture of a magic wand, using polygons and polylines: Graphics

Answers to Self-Test Questions

1. 0 2 4 6 8 10 12 14 16 18

2. a
   e
   i
   o
   u

3. Tide 1 is -7.3|
   Tide 2 is 14.2

4. The last index of a is 9. The value of a.length is 10.

5. The for loop references elements b[1] through b[10], but there is no element indexed by 10. The array elements are b[0] through b[9]. If included in a complete class or program, the code would compile without any error messages, but when it is run, you would get an error message saying that an array index is out of bounds.

6.
```java
import java.util.Scanner;
public class Question6
{
    public static void main(String[] args)
    {
        double[] array = new double[20];

        Scanner keyboard = new Scanner(System.in);
        System.out.println("Enter 20 numbers:");
        for (int index = 0; index <array.length; index++)
        array[index] = keyboard.nextDouble();

        double lastNumber = array[array.length - 1];
        System.out.println("The last number read is " +
                        lastNumber + ".");
        System.out.println("The numbers read and their " +
                        "differences from last number are:");
        for (int index = 0; index <array.length; index++)
        System.out.println(array[index] +
        " differs from the last number by " +
                        (array[index] - lastNumber));
    }
}
```

7.
```java
SalesAssociate[] entry = new SalesAssociate[3];
for (int i = 0; i <entry.length; i++)
    entry[i] = new SalesAssociate("Jane Doe", 5000);
```

8. The lines that are changed are shown in highlight in the following code. Note that you should also change the definition of the method writeOutput in the class SalesAssociate. We have also shown this method in the following code. Remember that you must make the class DollarFormat available, either by placing it in the same directory or by putting it in a package and importing the package.

```java
/**
 Displays sales report on the screen.
*/
public void displayResults()
{
    System.out.print("Average sales per associate is ");
    DollarFormat.writeln(averageSales);
    System.out.print("The highest sales figure is ");
    DollarFormat.writeln(highest);
    System.out.println();
    System.out.println("The following had the highest sales:");
    for (int i = 1; i <= numberOfAssociates; i++)
    {
        double nextSales = team[i].getSales();
        if (nextSales == highest)
        {
            team[i].writeOutput();
            DollarFormat.write(nextSales - averageSales);
            System.out.println(" above the average.");
            System.out.println();
        }
    }

    System.out.println("The rest performed as follows:");
    for (i = 1; i <= numberOfAssociates; i++)
    {
        double nextSales = team[i].getSales();
        if (team[i].getSales() != highest)
        {
            team[i].writeOutput();
            if (nextSales >= averageSales)
            {
                DollarFormat.write(nextSales - averageSales);
                System.out.println(" above the average.");
            }
            else
            {
                DollarFormat.write(averageSales - nextSales);
                System.out.println(" below the average.");
            }
            System.out.println();
        }
    }
}
```

The following is the rewritten version of the method `writeOutput` of the class `SalesAssociate`, with the changes shown in highlight:

```java
public void writeOutput()
{
    System.out.println("Sales associates: " + name);
    System.out.print("Sales: ");
    DollarFormat.writeln(sales);
}
```

9. `a[1] = a, b[1] = a`
   `a[2] = a, b[2] = a`
   `a[1] = a, b[1] = a`
   `a[2] = b, b[2] = b`

10. Here are two possible answers:

```java
public static void showArray(char[] a)
{
    for (int i = 0; i <a.length; i++)
        System.out.print(a[i]);
    System.out.println();
}
```

```java
public static void showArray(char[] line)
{
    for (char character : line)
        System.out.print(character);
    System.out.println();
}
```

11.
```java
public static double[] getArrayOfHalves(double[] a)
{
    double[] temp = new double[a.length];
    for (int i = 0; i < a.length; i++)
        temp[i] = a[i] / 2.0;
    return temp;
}
```

12. The method does not return an array distinct from the given argument array. Rather, it returns a reference to the array it is given. To make a duplicate array, you would replace the statement

```java
temp = anArray;
```

with

```java
for (int i = 0; i <anArray.length; i++)
    temp[i] = anArray[i];
```

13. If b is an array of length 10, the invocation

```java
doubleSize(b);
```

will run with no error messages, but the length of b will not change. In fact, nothing about b will change. The parameter a is a local variable that is initialized with a reference to b. The local variable a is changed so that it contains a reference to an array that is twice the size of b, but that reference goes away as soon as the invocation ends.

14. The method compiles and executes correctly. It returns a reference to the instance variable `team`, which is an array of `SalesAssociate` objects. However, this method causes a privacy leak. Once you have a reference to the array `team`, you could change the data in the array. For example, you could change your competitor's sales to zero by using the `SalesAssociate` method set.

15.
```
int count = toDoList.getNumberOfEntries();
for (int pos = toDoList.START_POSITION;
     pos <= count; pos++)
    System.out.println(toDoList.getEntryAt(position));
```

16.
```
if (!toDoList.isEmpty())
{
    int position = toDoList.START_POSITION;
    while (!toDoList.atLastEntry(position))
    {
        System.out.println(toDoList.getEntryAt(position));
        position++;
    }
    System.out.println(toDoList.getEntryAt(position));
}
```

17. One answer is

```
for (int i = 0; i <a.length; i++)
    System.out.println(a[i]);
```

Another answer is

```
for (double element : a)
    System.out.println(element);
```

18.
```
for (int i = 0; i <numberUsed; i++)
    System.out.println(a[i]);
```

A for-each loop is not possible here.

19. `a[0]`, `a[1]`, and `a[2]`.
    `numberUsed` is 3.

20.
```
a[numberUsed] = 42;
numberUsed++;
```

21.
```
if (numberUsed == a.length)
System.out.println("Array is full.
    Cannot add to it.");
```

```
    else
    {
        a[numberUsed] = 42;
        numberUsed++;
    }
```

22. ```
public String[] getEntryArray()
{
    String[] temp = new String[entry.length];
    for (int i = 0; i <countOfEntries; i++)
        temp[i] = entry[i];
    return temp;
}
```

23. 7 5 1 3 6
    1 5 7 3 6
    1 3 7 5 6
    1 3 5 7 6
    1 3 5 6 7

24. `ArraySorter.selectionSort(myArray);`

25. Change the base type of the array from `int` to `double`. You can simply replace all occurrences of `int` with `double`, except for those occurrences of `int` that give the type of an index. For example, you would replace

    `private static void interchange(int i, int j, int[] a)`

    with

    `private static void interchange(int i, int j, double[] a)`

    Note that i and j are indices, and so they are still of type `int`.

26. Replace the < with > in the following line of the definition of getIndexOfSmallest:

    `if (a[index] < min)`

    However, to make your code more readable, you should rename the method to something like `getIndexOfLargest`, rename the variable `min` to something like `max`, and rename the variable `indexOfMin` to something like `indexOfMax`. You should also rewrite some of the comments.

27. Two.

28. 0 1 2 3
    0 1 2 3
    0 1 2 3
```

29.
```java
/**
The array anArray can have any values for its dimensions.
Postcondition: The array contents are displayed with $s.
*/
public static void showTable(int[][] anArray)
{
    for (int row = 0; row <anArray.length; row++)
    {
        System.out.print((row + 1) + " ");
        for (int column = 0; column <anArray[row].length;
            column++)
            System.out.print("$"+anArray[row][column]
                             + " ");
        System.out.println();
    }
}
```

This method can be seen within the class InterestTable3 in the code available on the Web.

30.
```java
int[][] a = new int [4][5];
System.out.println("Enter numbers:");
Scanner keyboard = new Scanner(System.in);
    for (int row = 0; row < 4; row++)
    for (int column = 0; column < 5; column++)
        a[row][column] = keyboard.nextInt();
```

Alternatively, you could begin the for statements as

```java
for (int row = 0; row < a.length; row++)
    for (int column = 0; column < a[row].length;
        column++)
```

31.
```java
public static void display(int[][] anArray)
{
    for (int row = 0; row < anArray.length; row++)
    {
        for (int column = 0; column <
            anArray[row].length; column++)
        System.out.print(anArray[row][column] +" ");
        System.out.println();
    }
}
```

32.
```java
String text = theText.getText();
theText.setText(text + text);
```

33.
```java
private int[] xCoord = {7, 27, 27, 7};
private int[] yCoord = {8, 8, 18, 18};
...
canvas.drawPolygon(xCoord, yCoord, xCoord.length);
```

Inheritance, Polymorphism, and Interfaces 8

8.1 INHERITANCE BASICS 576

Derived Classes 578
Overriding Method Definitions 582
Overriding Versus Overloading 583
The `final` Modifier 583
Private Instance Variables and Private Methods of a Base Class 584
UML Inheritance Diagrams 586

8.2 PROGRAMMING WITH INHERITANCE 589

Constructors in Derived Classes 589
The `this` Method—Again 591
Calling an Overridden Method 591
Programming Example: A Derived Class of a Derived Class 592
Another Way to Define the `equals` Method in `Undergraduate` 597
Type Compatibility 597
The Class `Object` 602
A Better `equals` Method 604

8.3 POLYMORPHISM 606

Dynamic Binding and Inheritance 606
Dynamic Binding with `toString` 609

8.4 INTERFACES AND ABSTRACT CLASSES 611

Class Interfaces 611
Java Interfaces 612
Implementing an Interface 613
An Interface as a Type 615
Extending an Interface 618
Case Study: Character Graphics 619
Case Study: The `Comparable` Interface 632
Abstract Classes 636

8.5 GRAPHICS SUPPLEMENT 638

The Class `JApplet` 639
The Class `JFrame` 639
Window Events and Window Listeners 642
The `ActionListener` Interface 644
What to Do Next 644

Chapter Summary 644   Programming Projects 648   Answers to Self-Test Questions 651

To understand a name you must be acquainted with the particular of which it is a name.

—BERTRAND RUSSELL

Like mother, like daughter

—COMMON SAYING

This chapter covers inheritance, polymorphism, and interfaces, three key concepts in object-oriented programming. These concepts are also needed in order to use many of the libraries that come with the Java programming language. Polymorphism makes objects behave as you expect them to and allows you to focus on the specifications of those behaviors. Inheritance will enable you to use an existing class to define new classes, making it easier to reuse software. Finally, interfaces allow you to specify the methods that a class must implement.

OBJECTIVES

After studying this chapter, you should be able to

- Describe polymorphism and inheritance in general
- Define interfaces to specify methods
- Describe dynamic binding
- Define and use derived classes in Java
- Understand the role of inheritance to produce windowing interfaces within Java application programs

PREREQUISITES

You need to have read the material in Chapters 1 through 6 before you can understand the material in this chapter. Chapter 7 is needed to understand some of the examples presented in Sections 8.3 and 8.4.

8.1 INHERITANCE BASICS

Socrates is a person.

All people are mortal.

Therefore Socrates is mortal.

—TYPICAL SYLLOGISM

Suppose we define a class for vehicles that has instance variables to record the vehicle's number of wheels and maximum number of occupants. The class also has accessor and mutator methods. Imagine that we then define a class for automobiles that has instance variables and methods just like the ones in the class of vehicles. In addition, our automobile class would have added instance variables for such things as the amount of fuel in the fuel tank and the license plate number and would also have some added methods. Instead of repeating the definitions of the instance variables and methods of the class of vehicles within the class of automobiles, we could use Java's inheritance mechanism, and let the automobile class inherit all the instance variables and methods of the class for vehicles.

Inheritance allows you to define a very general class and then later define more specialized classes that add some new details to the existing general class definition. This saves work, because the more specialized class *inherits* all the properties of the general class and you, the programmer, need only program the new features.

Inheritance lets you define specialized classes from a general one

Before we construct an example of inheritance within Java, we first need to set the stage. We'll do so by defining a simple class called Person. This class—shown in Listing 8.1—is so simple that the only attribute it gives a

LISTING 8.1 **The Class** Person

```java
public class Person
{
    private String name;
    public Person()
    {
        name = "No name yet";
    }
    public Person(String initialName)
    {
        name = initialName;
    }
    public void setName(String newName)
    {
        name = newName;
    }
    public String getName()
    {
        return name;
    }
    public void writeOutput()
    {
        System.out.println("Name: " + name);
    }
    public boolean hasSameName(Person otherPerson)
    {
        return this.name.equalsIgnoreCase(otherPerson.name);
    }
}
```

person is a name. We will not have much use for the class `Person` by itself, but we will use it when defining other classes.

Most of the methods for the class `Person` are straightforward. For example, the method `hasSameName` is similar to the `equals` methods we've seen, but note that it considers uppercase and lowercase versions of a letter to be the same when comparing names.

Derived Classes

Suppose we are designing a college record-keeping program that has records for students, faculty, and other staff. There is a natural hierarchy for grouping these record types: They are all records of people. Students are one subclass of people. Another subclass is employees, which includes both faculty and staff. Students divide into two smaller subclasses: undergraduate students and graduate students. These subclasses may further subdivide into still smaller subclasses.

Figure 8.1 depicts a part of this hierarchical arrangement. Although your program may not need any class corresponding to people or employees, thinking in terms of such classes can be useful. For example, all people have names, and the methods of initializing, displaying, and changing a name will be the same for student, staff, and faculty records. In Java, you can define a class called `Person` that includes instance variables for the properties that belong to all subclasses of people. The class definition can also contain all the

FIGURE 8.1   A Class Hierarchy

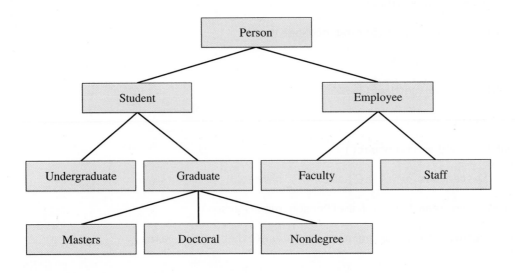

methods that manipulate the instance variables for the class Person. In fact, we have already defined such a Person class in Listing 8.1.

Listing 8.2 contains the definition of a class for students. A student is a person, so we define the class Student to be a **derived class**, or **subclass**, of the class Person. A derived class is a class defined by adding instance variables and methods to an existing class. We say that the derived class **extends** the existing class. The existing class that the derived class is built upon is called the **base class**, or **superclass**. In our example, Person is the base class and Student is the derived class. We indicated this in the definition of Student in Listing 8.2 by including the phrase extends Person on the first line of the class definition, so that the class definition of Student begins

> A derived class extends a base class and inherits the base class's public members

```
public class Student extends Person
```

LISTING 8.2 A Derived Class *(part 1 of 2)*

```
public class Student extends Person
{
    private int studentNumber;
    public Student()
    {
        super();
        studentNumber = 0;//Indicating no number yet
    }
    public Student(String initialName, int initialStudentNumber)
    {
        super(initialName);
        studentNumber = initialNumber;
    }
    public void reset(String newName, int newStudentNumber)
    {
        setName(newName);
        studentNumber = newStudentNumber;
    }
    public int getStudentNumber()
    {
        return studentNumber;
    }
    public void setStudentNumber(int newStudentNumber)
    {
        studentNumber = newStudentNumber;
    }
    public void writeOutput()
    {
        System.out.println("Name: " + getName());
        System.out.println("Student Number: " + studentNumber);
    }
```

super is explained in a later section. Do not worry about it until you reach the discussion of it in the text.

(continued)

LISTING 8.2 A Derived Class *(part 2 of 2)*

```
    public boolean equals(Student otherStudent)
    {
        return this.hasSameName(otherStudent) &&
            (this.studentNumber == otherStudent.studentNumber);
    }
}
```

The class Student—like any other derived class—is said to **inherit** the public instance variables and public methods of the base class that it extends. When you define a derived class, you give only the added instance variables and the added methods. Even though the class Student has all the public instance variables and all the public methods of the class Person, we do not declare or define them in the definition of Student. For example, every object of the class Student has the method getName, but we do not define getName in the definition of the class Student.

A derived class, such as Student, can also add some instance variables or methods to those it inherits from its base class. For example, Student defines the instance variable studentNumber and the methods reset, getStudentNumber, setStudentNumber, writeOutput, and equals, as well as some constructors. (We will postpone the discussion of constructors until we finish explaining the other parts of these class definitions.)

Notice that although Student does not inherit the private instance variable name from Person, it does inherit the method setName and all the other public methods of the base class. Thus, Student has indirect access to name and so has no need to define its own version. If s is a new object of the class Student, defined as

```
    Student s = new Student();
```

we could write

```
    s.setName("Warren Peace");
```

Because name is a private instance variable of Person, however, you cannot write s.name outside of the definition of the class Person, not even within the definition of Student. The instance variable exists, however, and it can be accessed and changed using methods defined within Person. Listing 8.3 contains a very small demonstration program to illustrate inheritance.

Inheritance should define a natural is-a relationship between two classes

An object of Student has all of the methods of Person in addition to all of the methods of Student. Earlier, we noted that a student is a person. The classes Student and Person model this real-world relationship in that Student has all the behaviors of Person. We call this relationship an **is-a relationship.** You should use inheritance only if an is-a relationship exists between a class and a proposed derived class.

LISTING 8.3   A Demonstration of Inheritance Using Student

```java
public class InheritanceDemo
{
    public static void main(String[] args)
    {
        Student s = new Student();
        s.setName("Warren Peace")
        s.setStudentNumber(1234);
        s.writeOutput();
    }
}
```

setName *is inherited from the class* Person.

Screen Output

```
Name: Warren Peace
Student Number: 1234
```

■ PROGRAMMING TIP   Use Inheritance Only to Model Is-a Relationships

If an is-a relationship does not exist between two proposed classes, do not use inheritance to derive one class from the other. Instead, consider defining an object of one class as an instance variable within the other class. That relationship is called has-a. The programming tip titled "Is-a and Has-a Relationships" talks more about these two relationships.   ■

When discussing derived classes, it is common to use terminology derived from family relationships. A base class is often called a **parent class** A derived class is then called a **child class**. This makes the language of inheritance very smooth. For example, we can say that a child class inherits public instance variables and public methods from its parent class.

This analogy is often carried one step further. A class that is a parent of a parent of a parent of another class (or some other number of "parent of" iterations) is often called an **ancestor class**. If class A is an ancestor of class B, then class B is often called a **descendant** of class A.

A base class is also called a superclass, a parent class, and an ancestor class

RECAP   Derived Class

You define a derived class, or subclass, by starting with another already defined class and adding (or changing) methods and instance variables. The class you start with is called the base class, or superclass. The derived

(continued)

class inherits all of the public methods and public instance variables from the base class and can add more instance variables and methods.

SYNTAX

```
public class Derived_Class_Name extends Base_Class_Name
{
    Declarations_of_Added_Instance_Variables
    Definitions_of_Added__And_Changed_Methods
}
```

EXAMPLE:

A derived class is also called a subclass, a child class, and a descendant class

See Listing 8.2.

As you will see in the next section, changed methods are said to be overridden.

Overriding Method Definitions

Overriding a method redefines it in a descendant class

The class Student in Listing 8.2 defines a method named writeOutput that has no parameters. But the class Person also has a method by the same name that has no parameters. If the class Student were to inherit the method writeOutput from the base class Person, Student would contain two methods with the name writeOutput, both of which have no parameters. Java has a rule to avoid this problem. If a derived class defines a method with the same name, the same number and types of parameters, and the same return type as a method in the base class, the definition in the derived class is said to **override** the definition in the base class. In other words, the definition in the derived class is the one that is used for objects of the derived class. For example, the invocation

```
s.writeOutput();
```

in Listing 8.3 will use the definition of writeOutput in the class Student, not the definition in the class Person, since s is an object of the class Student.

When overriding a method, you can change the body of the method definition to anything you wish, but you cannot make any changes in the method's heading, including its return type.

A method overrides another if both have the same name, return type, and parameter list

> ### RECAP Overriding Method Definitions
>
> In a derived class, if you include a method definition that has the same name, the *exact* same number and types of parameters, and the same return type as a method already in the base class, this new definition
>
> *(continued)*

replaces the old definition of the method when objects of the derived class receive a call to the method.

When overriding a method definition, you cannot change the return type of the method. Since the signature of a method does not include the return type, you can say that when one method overrides another, both methods must have the same signature and return type.

Overriding Versus Overloading

Do not confuse *overriding* a method with *overloading* a method. When you override a method definition, the new method definition given in the derived class has the same name, the same return type, and the exact same number and types of parameters. On the other hand, if the method in the derived class were to have the same name and the same return type but a different number of parameters or a parameter of a different type from the method in the base class, the method names would be overloaded. In such cases, the derived class would have both methods.

> A method overloads another if both have the same name and return type but different parameter lists

For example, suppose we added the following method to the definition of the class `Student` in Listing 8.2:

```java
public String getName(String title)
{
    return title + getName();
}
```

In this case, the class `Student` would have two methods named `getName`: It would inherit the method `getName`, with no parameters, from the base class `Person` (Listing 8.1), and it would also have the method named `getName`, with one parameter, that we just defined. This is because the two `getName` methods have different numbers of parameters, and thus the methods use overloading.

If you get overloading and overriding confused, remember this: Overloading places an additional "load" on a method name by using it for another method, whereas overriding replaces a method's definition.

The `final` Modifier

If you want to specify that a method definition cannot be overridden by a new definition within a derived class, you can add the `final` modifier to the method heading, as in the following sample heading:

> A final method cannot be overridden

```java
public final void specialMethod()
```

When a method is declared as final, the compiler knows more about how it will be used, and so the compiler can generate more efficient code for the method.

A final class
cannot be a base
class

An entire class can be declared final, in which case you cannot use it as a base class to derive any other class. You are not very likely to need the final modifier right now, but you will see it in the specifications of some methods in the standard Java libraries.

■ PROGRAMMING TIP   Constructors That Call Methods

If a constructor calls a public method, a derived class could override that method, thereby affecting the behavior of the constructor. To prevent that from happening, declare such public methods as final.   ■

Private Instance Variables and Private Methods of a Base Class

An object of the derived class Student (Listing 8.2) does not inherit the instance variable name from the base class Person (Listing 8.1), but it can access or change name's value via the public methods of Person. For example, the following statements create a Student object and set the values of the instance variables name and studentNumber:

```java
Student joe = new Student();
joe.reset("Joesy", 9892);
```

Since the instance variable name is a private instance variable in the definition of the class Person, it cannot be directly accessed by name within the definition of the class Student. Thus, the definition of the method reset in the class Student is

```java
public void reset(String newName, int newStudentNumber)
{
    setName(newName);                      Valid definition
    studentNumber = newStudentNumber;
}
```

Private instance
variables in a
base class are
not inherited by
a derived class;
they cannot
be referenced
directly by name
within a derived
class

It cannot be as follows:

```java
public void reset(String newName, int newStudentNumber)
{
    name = newName;//ILLEGAL!               Illegal definition
    studentNumber = newStudentNumber;
}
```

As the comment indicates, this assignment will not work, because a derived class does not inherit private instance variables from its base class. Thus, the definition of reset in the class Student uses the method setName to set the name instance variable.

GOTCHA Private Instance Variables Are Not Directly Accessible from Derived Classes

A derived class cannot access the private instance variables of its base class directly by name. It knows only about the public behavior of the base class. The derived class is not supposed to know—or care—how its base class stores data. However, an inherited public method may contain a reference to a private instance variable. ■

The fact that a private instance variable of a base class cannot be accessed by name within the definition of a method of a derived class often seems wrong to people. After all, students should be able to change their own names, rather than being told "Sorry, name is a private instance variable of the class Person." If you are a student, you are also a person. In Java, this is also true; an object of the class Student is also an object of the class Person. However, the rules regarding the use of private instance variables must be as we've described, or else the private designation would be pointless. If private instance variables of a class were accessible in method definitions of a derived class, whenever you wanted to access a private instance variable, you could simply create a derived class and access it in a method of that class. This would mean that all private instance variables would be accessible to anybody who wanted to put in a little extra effort.

Similarly, private methods in a base class are not directly accessible by name within any other class, not even a derived class. The private methods still exist, however. If a derived class calls an inherited *public* method that contains an invocation of a private method, that invocation still works. However, a derived class cannot define a method that invokes a private method of the base class. This should not be a problem. Private methods should serve only as helping methods, and so their use should be limited to the class in which they are defined. If you want a method to serve as a helping method in a number of derived classes, it is more than just a helping method, and you should make the method public.

Private methods in a base class are not inherited by a derived class; they cannot be called directly by name from a derived class

GOTCHA Private Methods Are Not Directly Accessible from Derived Classes

A derived class cannot call a private method defined within the base class. However, the derived class can call a public method that in turn calls a private method when both methods are in the base class. ■

PROGRAMMING TIP Assume That Your Coworkers Are Malicious

The reason private instance variables cannot be accessed by name in a derived class is that otherwise a malicious programmer could access them by using a trick. You may argue that your coworkers are not malicious. In fact, in a beginning course you may sometimes be the only programmer on an assignment, and you certainly are not trying to sabotage your own work. Those are good points. However, your coworkers—or even you yourself—might inadvertently do something that, although not intended to be malicious, still creates a problem. We think in terms of a malicious programmer not because we think our coworkers are malicious, but because that is the best way to protect against honest mistakes by well-meaning programmers—including you! ■

UML Inheritance Diagrams

An arrow points up from a derived class to a base class in a UML diagram

Figure 8.2 shows a portion of the class hierarchy given in Figure 8.1, but uses UML notation. Note that the class diagrams are incomplete. You normally show only as much of the class diagram as you need for the design task at

FIGURE 8.2 A Class Hierarchy in UML Notation

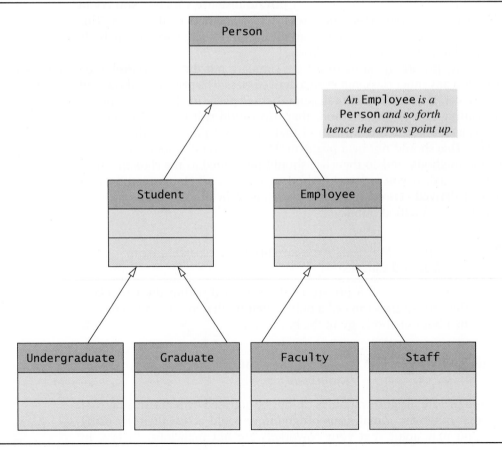

An Employee *is a* Person *and so forth hence the arrows point up.*

hand. The only significant difference between the notation in Figure 8.2 and that in Figure 8.1 is that the lines indicating inheritance in Figure 8.2 have unfilled arrowheads. Note that the arrowheads point up from the derived class to the base class. These arrows show the is-a relationship. For example, a Student is a Person. In Java terms, an object of type Student is also of type Person.

The arrows also help in locating method definitions. If you are looking for a method definition for some class, the arrows show the path you (or the computer) should follow. If you are looking for the definition of a method used by an object of the class Undergraduate, you first look in the definition of the class Undergraduate; if it is not there, you look in the definition of Student; if it is not there, you look in the definition of the class Person.

Figure 8.3 shows more details of the inheritance hierarchy for two classes: Person and one of its derived classes, Student. Suppose s references an object

FIGURE 8.3   Some Details of the UML Class Hierarchy Shown in Figure 8.2

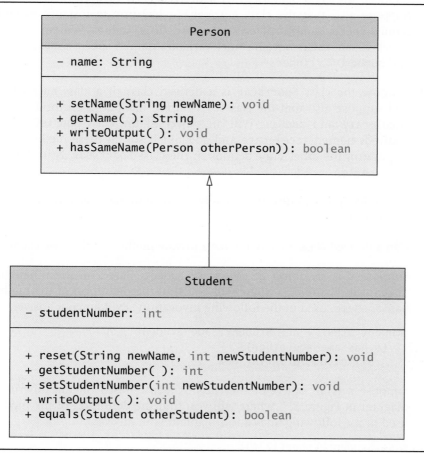

of the class `Student`. The diagram in Figure 8.3 tells you that definition of the method `getStudentNumber` in the call

```
int num = s.getStudentNumber();
```

is found within the class `Student`, but that the definition of `setName` in

```
s.setName("Joe Student");
```

is in the class `Person`.

SELF-TEST QUESTIONS

1. What is the difference between overriding a method and overloading a method name?

2. Suppose the class `SportsCar` is a derived class of a class `Automobile`. Suppose also that the class `Automobile` has private instance variables named `speed`, `manufacturer`, and `numberOfCylinders`. Will an object of the class `SportsCar` have instance variables named `speed`, `manufacturer`, and `numberOfCylinders`?

3. Suppose the class `SportsCar` is a derived class of a class `Automobile`, and suppose also that the class `Automobile` has public methods named `accelerate` and `addGas`. Will an object of the class `SportsCar` have methods named `accelerate` and `addGas`? If so, do these methods have to perform the exact same actions in the class `SportsCar` as in the class `Automobile`?

4. Can a derived class directly access by name a private instance variable of the base class?

5. Can a derived class directly invoke a private method of the base class?

6. Suppose `s` is an object of the class `Student`. Based on the inheritance diagram in Figure 8.3, where will you find the definition of the method `hasSameName`, used in the following invocation? Explain your answer.

```
Student other = new Student("Joe Student", 777);
if (s.hasSameName(other))
    System.out.println("Wow!");
```

7. Suppose `s` is an object of the class `Student`. Based on the inheritance diagram in Figure 8.3, where will you find the definition of the method used in the following invocation? Explain your answer.

```
s.setStudentNumber(1234);
```

8.2 PROGRAMMING WITH INHERITANCE

You do not have to die in order to pass along your inheritance.

—AD FOR AN ESTATE PLANNING SEMINAR

This section presents some basic programming techniques you need when defining or using derived classes.

Constructors in Derived Classes

A derived class, such as the class Student in Listing 8.2, has its own constructors. It does not inherit any constructors from the base class. A base class, such as Person, also has its own constructors. In the definition of a constructor for the derived class, the typical first action is to call a constructor of the base class. For example, consider defining a constructor for the class Student. One thing that needs to be initialized is the student's name. Since the instance variable name is defined in the definition of Person, it is normally initialized by the constructors for the base class Person.

> A derived class does not inherit constructors from its base class

Consider the following constructor definition in the derived class Student (Listing 8.2):

```java
public Student(String initialName, int initialStudentNumber)
{
    super(initialName);
    studentNumber = initialStudentNumber;
}
```

> Constructors in a derived class invoke constructors from the base class

This constructor uses the reserved word super as a method name to call a constructor of the base class. Although the base class Person defines two constructors, the invocation

```java
super(initialName);
```

is a call to the constructor in that class that has one parameter, a string. Notice that you use the keyword super, not the name of the constructor. That is, you do *not* use

```java
Person(initialName); //ILLEGAL
```

> Use super within a derived class as the name of a constructor in the base class (superclass)

FAQ How can I remember that super invokes a constructor in the base class instead of in a derived class?

Recall that another name for a base class is superclass. So super invokes the constructor in a class's superclass.

The use of super involves some details: It must always be the first action taken in a constructor definition. You cannot use super later in the definition.

Any call to
super must be
first within a
constructor

If you do not include an explicit call to the base-class constructor in any constructor for a derived class, Java will automatically include a call to the base class's default constructor. For example, the definition of the default constructor for the class Student given in Listing 8.2,

```java
public Student()
{
    super();
    studentNumber = 0;//Indicating no number yet
}
```

Without super,
a constructor
invokes
the default
constructor in the
base class

is completely equivalent to the following definition:

```java
public Student()
{
    studentNumber = 0;//Indicating no number yet
}
```

RECAP Calling a Base-Class Constructor

When defining a constructor for a derived class, you can use super as a name for the constructor of the base class. Any call to super must be the first action taken by the constructor.

EXAMPLE

```java
public Student(String initialName, int initialStudentNumber)
{
    super(initialName);
    studentNumber = initialStudentNumber;
}
```

GOTCHA Omitting a Call to super in a Constructor

When you omit a call to the base-class constructor in any derived-class constructor, the default constructor of the base class is called as the first action in the new constructor. This default constructor—the one without parameters—might not be the one that should be called. Thus, including your own call to the base-class constructor is often a good idea.

For example, omitting super(initialName) from the second constructor in the class Student would cause Person's default constructor to be invoked. This action would set the student's name to "No name yet" instead of to the string initialName.

The this Method—Again

Another common action when defining a constructor is to call another constructor in the same class. Chapter 6 introduced you to this idea, using the keyword this. Now that you know about super, it's clear that you can use this and super in similar ways.

You can use both this and super to call a constructor

We can revise the default constructor in the class Person (Listing 8.1) to call another constructor in that class by using this, as follows:

```
public Person()
{
    this("No name yet");
}
```

In this way, the default constructor calls the constructor

```
public Person(String initialName)
{
    name = initialName;
}
```

thereby setting the instance variable name to the string "No name yet".

As with super, any use of this must be the first action in a constructor definition. Thus, a constructor definition cannot contain both a call using super and a call using this. What if you want to include both calls? In that case, use this to call a constructor that has super as its first action.

REMEMBER this and super Within a Constructor

When used in a constructor, this calls a constructor of the same class, but super invokes a constructor of the base class.

Calling an Overridden Method

We just saw how a constructor of a derived class can use super as a name for a constructor of the base class. A method of a derived class that overrides (redefines) a method in the base class can use super to call the overridden method, but in a slightly different way.

For example, consider the method writeOutput for the class Student in Listing 8.2. It contains the statement

```
System.out.println("Name: " + getName());
```

to display the name of the Student. Alternatively, you could display the name by calling the method writeOutput of the class Person in Listing 8.1, since the writeOutput method for the class Person will display the person's name. The only problem is that if you use the method name writeOutput within the class Student, it will invoke the method named writeOutput in the class Student. What you need is a way to say "writeOutput() as it is defined in the base class." The way you say that is super.writeOutput(). So an alternative definition of the writeOutput method for the class Student is the following:

Using super as an object calls a base-class method

```
public void writeOutput()
{
    super.writeOutput(); //Display the name
    System.out.println("Student Number: " + studentNumber);
}
```

If you replace the definition of writeOutput in the definition of Student (Listing 8.2) with the preceding definition, the class Student will behave exactly the same as it did before.

RECAP Calling an Overridden Method

Within the definition of a method of a derived class, you can call an overridden method of the base class by prefacing the method name with super and a dot.

SYNTAX

```
super.Overridden_Method_Name(Argument_List)
```

EXAMPLE

```
public void writeOutput()
{
    super.writeOutput(); //Calls writeOutput in the base
                         //class
    System.out.println("Student Number: " + studentNumber);
}
```

PROGRAMMING EXAMPLE: A Derived Class of a Derived Class

You can form a derived class from a derived class. In fact, this is common. For example, we previously derived the class Student (Listing 8.2) from the class Person (Listing 8.1). We now derive a class Undergraduate from Student, as shown in Listing 8.4. Figure 8.4 contains a UML diagram showing the relationship among the classes Person, Student, and Undergraduate.

LISTING 8.4   A Derived Class of a Derived Class

```java
public class Undergradute extends Student
{
    private int level; //1 for freshman, 2 for sophomore
                       //3 for junior, or 4 for senior.
    public Undergraduate()
    {
        super();
        level = 1
    }
    public Undergraduate(String initialName,
                  int initialStudentNumber, int initialLevel)
    {
        super(initialName, initialStudentNumber);
        setLevel(initialLevel); //checks 1 <= initialLevel <= 4
    }
    public void reset(String newName, int newStudentNumber,
                      int newLevel)
    {
        reset(newName, newStudentNumber); //Student's reset
        setLevel(newLevel); //Checks 1 <= newLevel <= 4
    }

    public int getLevel()
    {
        return level;
    }
    public void setLevel(int newLevel)
    {
        if ((1 <= newLevel) && (newLevel <= 4))
            level = newLevel;
        else
        {
            System.out.println("Illegal level!");
            System.exit(0);
        }
    }
    public void writeOutput()
    {
        super.writeOutput();
        System.out.println("StudentLevel: " + level);
    }
    public boolean equals(Undergraduate otherUndergraduate)
    {
        return equals(Student)otherUndergraduate) &&
               (this.level == otherUndergraduate.level);
    }
}
```

FIGURE 8.4 More Details of the UML Class Hierarchy Shown in Figure 8.2

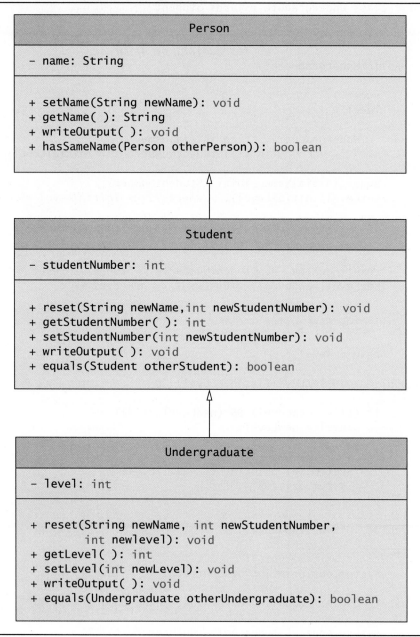

An object of the class Undergraduate has all the public members of the class Student. But Student is already a derived class of Person. This means that an object of the class Undergraduate also has all the public members of the class Person. An object of the class Person has the instance variable name. An object of the class Student has the instance variable studentNumber, and an object of the class Undergraduate has the instance variable level. Although an object of the class Undergraduate does not inherit the instance variables name and studentNumber, since they are private, it can use its inherited accessor and mutator methods to access and change them. In effect, the classes Student and Undergraduate—as well as any other classes derived from either of them—reuse the code given in the definition of the class Person, because they inherit all the public methods of the class Person.

Each of the constructors in the class Undergraduate begins with an invocation of super, which in this context stands for a constructor of the base class Student. But the constructors for the class Student also begin with an invocation of super, which in this case stands for a constructor of the base class Person. Thus, when we use new to invoke a constructor in Undergraduate, constructors for Person and Student are invoked, and then all the code following super in the constructor for Undergraduate is executed.

The classes Student and Undergraduate both define a method named reset. In Student, reset has two parameters, while in Undergraduate, reset has three parameters, so reset is an overloaded name. The reset method in the class Undergraduate, which we reproduce here, begins by invoking reset, passing it only two arguments:

reset is an overloaded method

```java
public void reset(String newName, int newStudentNumber, int
newLevel)
{
    reset(newName, newStudentNumber); //Student's reset
    setLevel(newLevel); //Checks 1 <= newLevel <= 4
}
```

Thus, this invocation is to the method named reset defined in the base class Student, which changes the values of the instance variables name and studentNumber. The Undergraduate reset method then changes the value of the new instance variable level by calling setLevel.

Remember that within the definition of the class Undergraduate, the private instance variables name and studentNumber—of the base classes Person and Student, respectively—cannot be referenced by name, and so a mutator method is needed to change them. The reset method of the class Student is perfect for this purpose.

Because the version of reset defined in the class Undergraduate has a different number of parameters than the version of reset defined in the class Student, there is no conflict in having both versions of reset in the derived class Undergraduate. In other words, we can overload the reset method. In contrast, the definition of the method writeOutput in Undergraduate, which we reproduce here, has exactly the same parameter list as the version of writeOutput in the base class Student:

writeOutput
overrides the
base-class method
having the same
signature

```java
public void writeOutput()
{
    super.writeOutput();
    System.out.println("StudentLevel: " + level);
}
```

Thus, when writeOutput is invoked, Java must decide which definition of writeOutput to use. For an object of the derived class Undergraduate, it uses the version of writeOutput given in the definition of the class Undergraduate. The version in Undergraduate overrides the definition given in the base class Student. To invoke the version of writeOutput defined in Student within the definition of the derived class Undergraduate, you must place super and a dot in front of the method name writeOutput, as shown previously.

Now consider the methods named equals in the classes Student and Undergraduate. They have different parameter lists. The one in the class Student has a parameter of type Student, while the one in the class Undergraduate has a parameter of type Undergraduate. They have the same number of parameters—namely, one—but that one parameter is of a different type in each of the two definitions. Recall that a difference in type is enough to qualify for overloading. To help us analyze the situation, we reproduce the definition of equals within the derived class Undergraduate here:

```java
public boolean equals(Undergraduate otherUndergraduate)
{
    return equals((Student)otherUndergraduate) &&
        (this.level == otherUndergraduate.level);
}
```

VideoNote
Defining classes using
inheritance

Why did we cast otherUndergraduate to Student in the invocation of equals? Because otherwise Java would invoke the definition of equals in the class Undergraduate. That is, this equals method would invoke itself. While a method that invokes itself is perfectly acceptable under certain conditions—as you will see in Chapter 11—it isn't what we want to happen here. By casting the argument from Undergraduate to Student, we cause Java to call Student's equals method. Notice that otherUndergraduate, as an Undergraduate object, has all the behaviors of a Student object, and so will act correctly within Student's equals method. We will elaborate this point in the next section.

Extra code on the
Web

There is nothing unusual about how the class Undergraduate is used, but we have included a simple demonstration program for this class in the file

`UndergraduateDemo.java` as part of the source code for this book that is available on the Web.

Another Way to Define the `equals` Method in `Undergraduate`

The `equals` method in the class `Undergraduate` casts its parameter `otherUndergraduate` from `Undergraduate` to its base class `Student` when it passes it to `Student`'s `equals` method. Another way to force Java to call the definition of `equals` in `Student` is to use `super` and a dot, as follows:

```java
public boolean equals(Undergraduate otherUndergraduate)
{
    return super.equals(otherUndergraduate) &&
           (this.level == otherUndergraduate.level);
}
```

GOTCHA   You Cannot Use Repeated `supers`

As we already noted, within the definition of a method of a derived class, you can call an overridden method of the base class by prefacing the method name with `super` and a dot. However, you cannot repeat the use of `super` to invoke an overridden method from some ancestor class other than a direct parent. Suppose that the class `Student` is derived from the class `Person`, and the class `Undergraduate` is derived from the class `Student`. You might think that you can invoke a method of the class `Person` within the definition of the class `Undergraduate` by using `super.super`, as in

```java
super.super.writeOutput();//ILLEGAL!
```

However, as the comment indicates, it is illegal to have such a train of `supers` in Java. ■

Type Compatibility

Consider the class `Undergraduate` in Listing 8.4. It is a derived class of the class `Student`. In the real world, every undergraduate is also a student. This relationship holds true in our Java example as well. Every object of the class `Undergraduate` is also an object of the class `Student`. Thus, if you have a method that has a formal parameter of type `Student`, the argument in an invocation of this method can be an object of type `Undergraduate`. In this case, the method could use only methods defined in the class `Student`, but every object of the class `Undergraduate` has all these methods.

For example, suppose that the classes `Student` and `Undergraduate` are defined as in Listings 8.2 and 8.4, and consider the following method definition that might occur in some class:

```
public class SomeClass
{
    public static void compareNumbers(Student s1, Student s2)
    {
        if (s1.getStudentNumber() == s2.getStudentNumber())
            System.out.println(s1.getName() + " has the same " +
                                        "number as " + s2.getName());
        else
            System.out.println(s1.getName() + " has a different "+
                                        "number than " + s2.getName());
    }
    . . .
}
```

An object of a derived class can serve as an object of the base class

A program that uses SomeClass might contain the following code:

```
Student studentObject = new Student("Jane Doe", 1234);
Undergraduate undergradObject =
    new Undergraduate("Jack Buck", 1234, 1);
SomeClass.compareNumbers(studentObject, undergradObject);
```

If you look at the heading for the method compareNumbers, you will see that both parameters are of type Student. However, the invocation

```
SomeClass.compareNumbers(studentObject, undergradObject);
```

uses one argument of type Student and one object of type Undergraduate. How can we use an object of type Undergraduate where an argument of type Student is required? The answer is that every object of type Undergraduate is also of type Student. To make the point a little more dramatically, notice that you can reverse the two arguments and the method invocation will still be valid, as shown below:

```
SomeClass.compareNumbers(undergradObject, studentObject);
```

Note that there is no automatic type casting here. An object of the class Undergraduate *is* an object of the class Student, and so it *is* of type Student. It need not be, and is not, type cast to an object of the class Student.

An object can have several types because of inheritance

An object can actually behave as if it has more than two types as a result of inheritance. Recall that the class Undergraduate is a derived class of the class Student and that Student is a derived class of the class Person in Listing 8.1. This means that every object of the class Undergraduate is also an object of type Student as well as an object of type Person. Thus, everything that works for objects of the class Person also works for objects of the class Undergraduate.

For example, suppose that the classes Person and Undergraduate are defined as in Listings 8.1 and 8.4, and consider the following code, which might occur in a program:

```
Person joePerson = new Person("Josephine Student");
System.out.println("Enter name:");
Scanner keyboard = new Scanner(System.in);
String newName = keyboard.nextLine();
Undergraduate someUndergrad =
    new Undergraduate(newName, 222, 3);
if (joePerson.hasSameName(someUndergrad))
    System.out.println("Wow, same names!");
else
    System.out.println("Different names");
```

If you look at the heading for the method hasSameName in Listing 8.1, you will see that it has one parameter, and that parameter is of type Person. However, the call in the preceding if-else statement,

```
joePerson.hasSameName(someUndergrad)
```

is perfectly valid, even though the argument someUndergrad is an object of the class Undergraduate—that is, its type is Undergraduate—but the corresponding parameter in hasSameName is of type Person. Every object of the class Undergraduate is also an object of the class Person.

Even the following invocation is valid:

```
someUndergrad.hasSameName(joePerson)
```

The method hasSameName belongs to Person, but it is inherited by the class Undergraduate. So the Undergraduate object someUndergrad has this method. An object of type Undergraduate is also of type Person. Everything that works for objects of an ancestor class also works for objects of any descendant class. Or, to say this another way, an object of a descendant class can do the same things as an object of an ancestor class. As we have already seen, if class A is derived from class B, and class B is derived from class C, then an object of class A is of type A. It is also of type B, and it is also of type C. This works for any chain of derived classes, no matter how long the chain is.

Because an object of a derived class has the types of all of its ancestor classes in addition to its "own" type, you can assign an object of a class to a variable of any ancestor type, but not the other way around. For example, because Student is a derived class of Person, and Undergraduate is a derived class of Student, the following code is valid:

```
Student s = new Student();
Undergraduate ug = new Undergraduate();
Person p1 = s;
Person p2 = ug;
```

An object of a class can be referenced by a variable of any ancestor type

You can even bypass the variables s and ug and place the new objects directly into the variables p1 and p2, as follows:

```
Person p1 = new Student();
Person p2 = new Undergraduate();
```

However, the following statements are all illegal:

```
Student s = new Person(); //ILLEGAL!
Undergraduate ug = new Person(); //ILLEGAL!
Undergraduate ug2 = new Student(); //ILLEGAL!
```

And if we define p and s as follows:

```
Person p = new Person(); //valid
Student s = new Student(); //valid
```

even the following statements, which may look more innocent, are similarly illegal:

```
Undergraduate ug = p; //ILLEGAL!
Undergraduate ug2 = s; //ILLEGAL!
```

This all makes perfectly good sense. For example, a Student *is a* Person, but a Person is not necessarily a Student. Some programmers find the phrase "is a" to be useful in deciding what types an object can have and what assignments to variables are valid. As another example, if Employee is a derived class of Person, an Employee *is a* Person, so you can assign an Employee object to a variable of type Person. However, a Person *is not necessarily* an Employee, so you cannot assign an object created as just a plain Person to a variable of type Employee.

A Student "is a" Person, but the converse might not be true

REMEMBER Assignment Compatibilities

An object of a derived class has the type of the derived class, but it can be referenced by a variable whose type is any one of its ancestor classes. Thus, you can assign an object of a derived class to a variable of any ancestor type, but not the other way around.

■ PROGRAMMING TIP   Is-a and Has-a Relationships

As we just noted, a Student is a Person, so we made the Student class a derived class of the Person class. This is an example of an is-a relationship between classes. It is one way to make a more complex class out of a simpler class.

Another way is known as the **has-a relationship.** For example, you have a class Date that records a date; you might add a date of enrollment to the Student class by adding an instance variable of type Date to the Student class. In this case we say a Student "has a" Date. As another example, if we have a class MechanicalArm and we are defining a class to simulate a robot, we can give the Robot class an instance variable of type MechanicalArm. In this case we say that a Robot "has a" MechanicalArm.

In most situations you can make your code work with either an "is-a" relationship or a "has-a" relationship. Often, a "has-a" relationship is the better choice. It seems silly to make the Robot class a derived class of the MechanicalArm class, but it can be done. The result would be a poor design, however.

Fortunately, the best programming technique is usually to simply follow what sounds most natural in English. It makes more sense to say "A Robot has a MechanicalArm" than it does to say "A Robot is a MechanicalArm." So it makes better programming sense to have a MechanicalArm as an instance variable of a Robot class.

> If class A has an object of class B as an instance variable, the relationship between A and B is "has a"

You will often encounter the terms *is-a* and *has-a* in the literature on programming techniques.   ■

SELF-TEST QUESTIONS

8. Give a complete definition of a class called TitledPerson, which you derive from the class Person in Listing 8.1. The class TitledPerson has one additional String instance variable for a title, such as Ms., Mr., or The Honorable. The class TitledPerson has two constructors: a default constructor and one that sets both the name and the title. It has a writeOutput method, a reset method, an equals method, an accessor method getTitle that returns the title, and a mutator method setTitle that changes the person's title. For two titled people to be equal, they must have the same name and the same title. You may want to use the class Student in Listing 8.2 as a model.

9. Add a constructor to the class Student that sets the student's name to a given argument string and sets the student's number to zero. Your constructor should invoke another constructor in Student to accomplish this.

10. Rewrite the definition of the method writeOutput for the class Undergraduate in Listing 8.4, using getName and getStudentNumber instead of super.writeOutput. (Most programmers would use the version in Listing 8.4, but you should be able to write either version.)

11. Rewrite the definition of the method reset for the class Undergraduate in Listing 8.4, using setName and setStudentNumber instead of the overloaded reset method name. (Most programmers would use the version in Listing 8.4, but you should be able to write either version.)

12. Can an object be referenced by variables of several different data types?

13. What is the type or types of the variable(s) that can reference the object created in the following statement? (The definition of the class Undergraduate is given in Listing 8.4.)

```
Undergraduate ug = new Undergraduate();
```

14. Describe two uses for the keyword `super`.

15. What is the difference between `this` and `super` when these words are used within a constructor definition as the names of methods that are called?

The Class `Object`

The class `Object` is the ultimate ancestor of all classes

Java has an "Eve" class—that is, a class that is an ancestor of every class. In Java, every class is derived from the class `Object`. If a class C has a different base class B, this base class is derived from `Object`, and so C is a derived class of `Object`. Thus, every object of every class is of type `Object`, as well as being of the type of its class and all its ancestor classes. Even classes that you define yourself without using inheritance are descendant classes of the class `Object`. If you do not make your class a derived class of some class, Java will automatically make it a derived class of `Object`.

The class `Object` allows Java programmers to write Java methods that have a parameter of type `Object` that represents an object of any class whatsoever. You will eventually encounter library methods that accept an argument of type `Object` and hence can be used with an argument that is an object of absolutely any class.

Every class inherits the methods `toString` and `equals` from `Object`

The class `Object` does have some methods that every Java class inherits. For example, every class inherits the methods `equals` and `toString` from some ancestor class, either directly from the class `Object` or from a class that ultimately inherited the methods from the class `Object`. However, the methods `equals` and `toString` inherited from `Object` will not work correctly for almost any class you define. Thus, you need to override the inherited method definitions with new, more appropriate definitions.

Writing a correct version of `equals` is a bit complicated for beginning programmers. The `equals` methods we present in this book will work well in most situations. The next section shows how to write a fully complete and correct definition of `equals`.

The inherited method `toString` takes no arguments. The method `toString` is supposed to return all the data in an object, packaged into a string. However, the inherited version of `toString` is almost always useless, because it will not produce a nice string representation of the data. You need to override the definition of `toString` so it produces an appropriate string for the data in objects of the class being defined.

For example, the following definition of `toString` could be added to the class Student in Listing 8.2:

```java
public String toString()
{
    return "Name: " + getName() +
            "\nStudent number: " + studentNumber;
}
```

The version of the class Student included with the source code for this book, which is available on the Web, includes this toString method, so you can easily try it out.

After adding this toString method to the class Student, we can use it to display output in the following way:

```
Student joe = new Student("Joe Student", 2001);
System.out.println(joe.toString());
```

The output produced would be

```
Name: Joe Student
Student number: 2001
```

The method println that is invoked here has a parameter of type String.

The object System.out has several definitions of println—in other words, println is overloaded. One of these println methods has a parameter of type Object. The definition is equivalent to the following one:

```
public void println(Object theObject)
{
    System.out.println(theObject.toString());
}
```

println is an example of a real-life overloaded method

PROGRAMMING TIP   Define Your Own toString Method Within Typical Classes

Object's toString method will not display any data related to your class. You usually should override toString in the classes that you write. ■

Another method inherited from the class Object is the method clone. This method takes no arguments and returns a copy of the calling object. The returned object is supposed to have data identical to that of the calling object, but it is a different object—an identical twin or a "clone." Like other methods inherited from the class Object, the method clone needs to be redefined (overridden) before it will function properly. However, in the case of the method clone, there are other things you must do as well. A thorough discussion of the method clone is beyond the scope of this text, but some information on this method is given in the section "Privacy Leaks" of Chapter 6 and in Appendix 9 (on the book's Web site).

clone is another method in object

SELF-TEST QUESTIONS

myprogramminglab

16. Consider the code below, which was discussed in the previous section:

```
Student joe = new Student("Joe Student", 2001);
System.out.println(joe.toString());
```

Why is the output on two lines instead of being all on one line?

17. Which of the following lines are legal and which are illegal? The class `Undergraduate` is a derived class of `Student`, and `Student` is a derived class of `Person`.

    a. `Person p1 = new Student();`

    b. `Person p2 = new Undergraduate();`

    c. `Student s1 = new Person();`

    d. `Student s2 = new Undergraduate();`

    e. `Undergraduate ug1 = new Person();`

    f. `Undergraduate ug2 = new Student();`

    g. `Object ob = new Student();`

    h. `Student s3 = new Object();`

A Better equals Method

As we mentioned in the previous section, the class `Object` defines an `equals` method that every class inherits. But most of the time, if you want your class to have an `equals` method that works correctly, you should override `Object`'s definition of `equals` and define your own version. However, we did not, strictly speaking, follow our own advice. The heading for the method `equals` in our definition of the class `Student` given in Listing 8.2 is

```
public boolean equals(Student otherStudent)
```

but the heading for the method `equals` in the class `Object` is

```
public boolean equals(Object otherObject)
```

These two `equals` methods have different parameter types, so we actually have not overridden the definition of `equals`. We have merely overloaded the method. In other words, the class `Student` has both of these methods. For most situations, this will not matter. However, there are cases in which it does matter.

Suppose we use some method—either predefined or programmer defined—that has a parameter of type `Object` named `objectParam` and another parameter `studentParam` of type `Student`. Now suppose the body of this method contains the invocation

```
studentParam.equals(objectParam)
```

If you plug in two arguments of type `Student` for the parameters `objectParam` and `studentParam`, Java will use the definition of `equals` inherited from the class `Object`, not the one we defined for the class `Student`. This means that in some cases, the method `equals` will return the wrong answer.

An equals method that works in most cases

To fix this problem, we need to change the type of the parameter for the equals method in the Student class from Student to Object. A first try might be the following:

```
//First try at an improved equals method
public boolean equals(Object otherObject)
{
    Student otherStudent = (Student)otherObject;
    return this.hasSameName(otherStudent) &&
      (this.studentNumber == otherStudent.studentNumber);
}
```

Note that we need to type cast the parameter otherObject from type Object to type Student. Without the type cast and the variable otherStudent, we would receive a syntax error when we write

```
otherObject.studentNumber
```

because the class Object does not have an instance variable named studentNumber. (Actually, the invocation of hasSameName would likely also cause a syntax error.)

This first try at an improved equals method does override the definition of equals given in the class Object and will work well in almost all cases. However, it still has a shortcoming: Our new definition of equals now allows an argument that can be any object at all. What happens if the method equals is used with an argument that is not a Student? The answer is that a run-time error will occur when the type cast to Student is executed.

We should make our definition work for any object. If the object is not a Student, we simply return false. After all, the method belongs to a Student object, and so if the argument is not a Student, the two objects cannot be considered equal. But how can we tell when the parameter is not of type Student?

> **ASIDE Multiple Inheritance**
>
> Some programming languages—such as C++ — allow one class to be derived from two different base classes. That is, you can derive class C from classes A and B. This feature, known as **multiple inheritance,** is not allowed in Java. In Java, a derived class can have only one base class. You can, however, derive class B from class A and then derive class C from class B, since this is not multiple inheritance.
>
> A derived class can implement any number of **interfaces** in addition to extending any one base class. Interfaces are discussed later in this chapter. This capability gives Java an approximation to multiple inheritance without the complications that arise with multiple base classes.

We can use the instanceof operator to check whether an object is of type Student. The syntax is

The instanceof *operator checks an object's class*

```
Object instanceof Class_Name
```

This expression returns true if *Object* is of type *Class_Name*; otherwise it returns false. So the following will return true if otherObject is of type Student:

```
otherObject instanceof Student
```

Therefore, the equals method should return false if the preceding boolean expression is false.

Our final version of the method equals is shown in Listing 8.5. Note that we have also taken care of one more possible case. The predefined

LISTING 8.5   A Better equals Method for the Class Student

```java
public boolean equals(Object otherObject)
{
    boolean isEqual = false;
    if ((otherObject != null) &&
        (otherObject instanceof Student))
    {
        Student otherStudent = (Student)otherObject;
        isEqual = this.sameName(otherStudent) &&
                    (this.studentNumber ==
                                otherStudent.studentNumber);
    }
    return isEqual;
}
```

constant `null` can be plugged in for a parameter of type `Object`. The Java documentation says that an `equals` method should return false when comparing an object and the value `null`. So that is what we have done.

8.3 POLYMORPHISM

What's in a name? That which we call a rose

By any other name would smell as sweet.

—WILLIAM SHAKESPEARE, *ROMEO AND JULIET*

VideoNote
Exploring polymorphism

Inheritance allows you to define a base class and derive classes from the base class. **Polymorphism** allows you to make changes in the method definition for the derived classes and have those changes apply to the methods written *in the base class.* This all happens automatically in Java, but it is important to understand the process.

Dynamic Binding and Inheritance

Consider a program that uses the Person, Student, and Undergraduate classes as depicted in Figure 8.4. Let's say that we would like to set up a committee that consists of four people that are either students or employees. If we use an array to store the list of committee members, then it makes sense to make the array of type Person so it can accommodate any class derived from it. Here is a possible array declaration:

```java
Person[] people = new Person[4];
```

Next we might add objects to the array that represent members of the committee. In the example below we have added three objects of type Undergraduate and one object of type Student (perhaps we don't know if this person is an undergraduate or graduate):

```
people[0] = new Undergraduate("Cotty, Manny", 4910, 1);
people[1] = new Undergraduate("Kick, Anita", 9931, 2);
people[2] = new Student("DeBanque, Robin", 8812);
people[3] = new Undergraduate("Bugg, June", 9901, 4);
```

In this case we are assigning an object of a derived class (either Student or Undergraduate) to a variable defined as an ancestor of the derived class (Person). This is valid because Person encompasses the derived classes. In other words, Student "is-a" Person and Undergraduate "is-a" Person, so we can assign either one to a variable of type Person.

Next, let's output a report containing information about all of the committee members. The report should be as detailed as possible. For example, if a student is an undergraduate, then the report should contain the student's name, student number, and student level. If the student is of type Student, then the report should contain the name and student number. Similar details would be expected for employees. The writeOutput method contains this detail, but which one is invoked? There are three of them, one defined for Undergraduate, Student, and Person.

If we focus on just people[0], then we can see that it is declared to be an object of type Person. If we invoke:

```
people[0].writeOutput();
```

then it is logical to assume that the writeOutput method defined in the Person object will be invoked. But that is not what happens! Instead, Java recognizes that an object of type Undergraduate is stored in people[0]. As a result, even though people[0] is declared to be of type Person, the method associated with the class used to create the object is invoked. This is called **dynamic binding** or **late binding.**

More precisely, when an overridden method is invoked, its action is the one defined in the class used to create the object using the new operator. It is not determined by the type of the variable naming the object. A variable of any ancestor class can reference an object of a descendant class, but the object always remembers which method actions to use for every method name. The type of the variable does not matter. What matters is the class name when the object was created.

Returning to our report, the code below could be used to generate it:

```
for (Person p : people)
{
    p.writeOutput();
    System.out.println();
}
```

This code would output:

```
Name: Cotty, Manny
Student Number: 4910
Student Level: 1

Name: Kick, Anita
Student Number: 9931
Student Level: 2

Name: DeBanque, Robin
Student Number: 8812

Name: Bugg, June
Student Number: 9901
Student Level: 4
```

A complete program is given in Listing 8.6.

LISTING 8.6 A Demo of Polymorphism *(part 1 of 2)*

```java
public class PolymorphismDemo
{
    public static void main(String[] args)
    {
        Person[] people = new Person[4];
        people[0] = new Undergraduate("Cotty, Manny", 4910, 1);
        people[1] = new Undergraduate("Kick, Anita", 9931, 2);
        people[2] = new Student("DeBanque, Robin", 8812);
        people[3] = new Undergraduate("Bugg, June", 9901, 4);
        for (Person p : people)
        {
            p.writeOutput();
            System.out.println();
        }
    }
}
```

Even though p is of type Person, the writeOutput method associated with Undergraduate or Student is invoked depending upon which class was used to create the object.

Screen Output

```
Name: Cotty, Manny
Student Number: 4910
Student Level: 1

Name: Kick, Anita
Student Number: 9931
Student Level: 2
```

(continued)

LISTING 8.6   A Demo of Polymorphism *(part 2 of 2)*

```
Name: DeBanque, Robin
Student Number: 8812

Name: Bugg, June
Student Number: 9901
Student Level: 4
```

One of the amazing things about polymorphism is it lets us invoke methods that might not even exist yet! For example, assume the program in Listing 8.6 exists and runs with only the Person, Student, and Undergraduate classes defined. At some later date we could write the Employee, Faculty, and Staff classes as depicted in Figure 8.1. Since all of these classes would be derived from the Person class, as long as each implements a writeOutput method then we could add one of these objects to the array and its writeOutput method would be invoked in the for loop. We wouldn't even need to recompile the PolymorphismDemo class in Listing 8.6 to invoke the new methods via dynamic binding.

> **ASIDE Java Assumes Dynamic Binding**
>
> In many other languages, you must specify in advance what methods may need dynamic binding. Java always assumes that dynamic binding will occur. Although making this assumption is less efficient, Java is easier to program and less prone to errors as a result.

> **REMEMBER Objects Know How They Are Supposed to Act**
>
> When an overridden method is invoked, its action is the one defined in the class used to create the object using the new operator. It is not determined by the type of the variable naming the object. A variable of any ancestor class can reference an object of a descendant class, but the object always remembers which method actions to use for every method name. The type of the variable does not matter. What matters is the class name when the object was created. This is because Java uses dynamic binding.

Dynamic Binding with toString

If you include an appropriate toString method in the definition of a class, then you can output an object of the class using System.out.println. For example, in the previous section we described adding a toString method to the Student class:

```java
public String toString()
{
    return "Name: " + getName() +
            "\nStudent number: " + studentNumber;
}
```

For the `Student` object `joe`, we can invoke the method with the statement

```
System.out.println(joe.toString());
```

However, we can get the exact same result without the `toString`:

```
System.out.println(joe);
```

This happens because Java uses dynamic binding with the `toString` method. The various `println` methods that belong to the object `System.out` were written long before we defined the class `Student`. Yet the invocation calls the definition of `toString` in the class `Student`, not the definition of `toString` in the class `Object`, because `joe` references an object of type `Student`. Dynamic binding is what makes this work. Because `System.out.println` invokes `toString` in this manner, always defining a suitable `toString` method for your classes is a good idea.

RECAP **Dynamic Binding and Polymorphism**

With dynamic, or late, binding the definition of a method is not bound to an invocation of the method until run time when the method is called. Polymorphism refers to the ability to associate many meanings to one method name through the dynamic binding mechanism. Thus, polymorphism and dynamic binding are really the same topic.

 SELF-TEST QUESTIONS

18. What is polymorphism?

19. What is dynamic binding? What is late binding? Give an example of each.

20. Is overloading a method name an example of polymorphism?

21. In the following code, will the two invocations of `writeOutput` produce the same output on the screen or not? (The relevant classes are defined in Listings 8.1, 8.2, and 8.4.)

```
Person person = new Student("Sam", 999);
person.writeOutput();
person = new Undergraduate("Sam", 999, 1);
person.writeOutput();
```

22. In the following code, which definition of `writeOutput` is invoked? (The classes are defined in the previous case study.)

```
Undergraduate ug = new Undergraduate("Sam", 999, 1);
Personp = (Person) ug;
p.writeOutput();
```

8.4 INTERFACES AND ABSTRACT CLASSES

Art, it seems to me, should simplify. That, indeed, is very nearly the whole of the higher artistic process; finding what conventions of form and what details one can do without and yet preserve the spirit of the whole . . .

—WILLA SIBERT CATHER, *ON THE ART OF FICTION*

Chapter 5 defined a class interface as the portion of a class that tells a programmer how to use it. In particular, a class interface consists of the headings for the public methods and public named constants of the class, along with any explanatory comments. Knowing only a class's interface—that is, the specifications of its public methods—a programmer can write code that uses the class. The programmer does not need to know anything about the class's implementation.

Until now, we have integrated a class's interface into its definition. Java, however, enables you to write an interface and to store it in its own file, separate from the implementation file. Let's further examine the idea of a class interface and see how this concept translates to a Java interface.

Class Interfaces

In Chapter 1, we imagined a person calling her pets to dinner by whistling. Each animal responded in its own way: Some ran, some flew, and some swam. Let's specify some behaviors for these pets. For example, suppose our pets are able to

- Be named
- Eat
- Respond to a command

We could specify the following method headings for these behaviors:

- ```
  /** Sets a pets name to petName. */

  public void setName(String petName)
  ```

- ```
  /** Returns true if a pet eats the given food.*/

  public boolean eat(String food)
  ```

- ```
  /** Returns a description of a pet's response to the given
  command. */

  public String respond(String command)
  ```

An example of a class interface

These method headings can form a class interface.

Now imagine that each of the three classes Dog, Bird, and Fish implements all of these methods. The objects of these classes then have the same behaviors—that is, each object can be named, can eat, and can respond. The nature of these behaviors, however, can be different among the objects.
  ```

Although dogs, birds, and fish respond to a command, for example, the way they respond differs.

Imagine a Java statement such as

```
String response = myPet.respond("Come!");
```

This statement is legal regardless of whether myPet names a Dog object, a Bird object, or a Fish object. The value of the string response, however, differs according to the type of object that myPet names. We can substitute one type of object for the other with no problem, as long as each of the three classes implements the method respond in its own way. How can we be sure that a class implements certain methods? Read on.

Java Interfaces

A **Java interface** is a program component that contains the headings for a number of public methods. Some interfaces describe all the public methods in a class, while others specify only certain methods. An interface also can define public named constants. In addition, an interface should include comments that describe the methods, so a programmer will have the necessary information to implement them. In this way, a class designer can specify methods for other programmers. In fact, the Java Class Library contains interfaces that are already written for your use, but you can also define your own.

The class interface that we wrote in the previous section is almost in the form necessary for a Java interface. A Java interface begins like a class definition, except that you use the reserved word interface instead of class. That is, an interface begins with

```
public interface Interface_Name
```

rather than

```
public class Class_Name
```

The interface can contain any number of public method headings, each followed by a semicolon. For example, Listing 8.7 contains a Java interface for objects whose methods return their perimeters and areas.

You name and store an interface as you would a class

By convention, an interface name begins with an uppercase letter, just as class names do. You store an interface in its own file, using a name that begins with the name of the interface, followed by .java. For example, the interface in Listing 8.7 is in the file Measurable.java. This interface provides a programmer with a handy summary of the methods' specifications. The programmer should be able to use these methods given only the information in the interface, without looking at the method bodies.

An interface has no instance variables, constructors, or method definitions

An interface does not declare any constructors for a class. Methods within an interface must be public, so you can omit public from their headings. An interface can also define any number of public named constants. It contains no instance variables, however, nor any complete method definitions—that is, methods cannot have bodies.

LISTING 8.7   A Java Interface

```
/**
 An interface for methods that return
 the perimeter and area of an object.
*/
public interface Measurable
{
    /** Returns the perimeter. */
    public double getPerimeter();
    /** Returns the area. */
    public double getArea();
}
```

> Do not forget the semicolons at the end of the method headings.

RECAP Java Interfaces

SYNTAX

```
public interface Interface_Name
{
    Public_Named_Constant_Definitions
    . . .
    Public_Method_Heading_1;
    . . .
    Public_Method_Heading_n;
}
```

EXAMPLE

```
/**
 An interface of static methods to convert measurements
 between feet and inches.
*/
public interface Convertible
{
    public static final int INCHES_PER_FOOT = 12;
    public static double convertToInches(double feet);
    public static double convertToFeet(double inches);
}
```

Implementing an Interface

When you write a class that defines the methods declared in an interface, we say that the class **implements the interface.** A class that implements an interface must define a body for every method that the interface specifies.

A class that
implements an
interface defines
each specified
method

It might also define methods not declared in the interface. That is, an interface need not declare every method defined in a class. In addition, a class can implement more than one interface.

To implement an interface, a class must do two things:

1. Include the phrase

   ```
   implements Interface_Name
   ```

   at the start of the class definition. To implement more than one interface, just list all the interface names, separated by commas, as in

   ```
   implements MyInterface, YourInterface
   ```

2. Define each method declared in the interface(s).

In this way, a programmer can guarantee—and indicate to other programmers—that a class defines certain methods. Additionally, recall that Java does not allow a class to be derived from multiple parent classes. However, a class can implement multiple interfaces. This is a way to capture some of the behavior that would be possible with multiple inheritance.

For example, to implement the interface `Measurable` shown in Listing 8.7, a class `Rectangle` must begin as follows:

```
public class Rectangle implements Measurable
```

The class must also implement the two methods `getPerimeter` and `getArea`. A full definition of the class `Rectangle` is given in Listing 8.8.

Other classes, such as the class `Circle` shown in Listing 8.9, can implement the interface `Measurable`. Notice that `Circle` defines the method `getCircumference` in addition to the methods declared in the interface. It isn't unusual for a class to define two methods that perform the same task. Doing so provides a convenience for programmers who use the class but prefer a more familiar name for a particular method. Notice, however, that `getCircumference` calls `getPerimeter` instead of performing its own calculation. Doing so makes the class easier to maintain. For example, if we ever discovered a problem with the statements in `getPerimeter`, fixing it would also fix `getCircumference`.

REMEMBER Interfaces Help Designers and Programmers

Writing an interface is a way for a class designer to specify methods for another programmer. Implementing an interface is a way for a programmer to guarantee that a class defines certain methods.

LISTING 8.8   An Implementation of the Interface Measurable

```java
/**
A class of rectangles.
*/
public class Rectangle implements Measurable
{
    private double myWidth;
    private double myHeight;

    public Rectangle(double width, double height)
    {
        myWidth = width;
        myHeight = height;
    }
    public double getPerimeter()
    {
        return 2 * (myWidth + myHeight);
    }
    public double getArea()
    {
        return myWidth * myHeight;
    }
}
```

> **REMEMBER Several Classes Can Implement the Same Interface**
>
> Different classes can implement the same interface, perhaps in different
> ways. For example, many classes can implement the interface Measurable
> and provide their own version of the methods getPerimeter and getArea.

An Interface as a Type

An interface is a reference type. Thus, you can write a method that has a
parameter of an interface type, such as a parameter of type Measurable. For
example, suppose that your program defines the following method:

An interface is a reference type

```java
public static void display(Measurable figure)
{
    double perimeter = figure.getPerimeter();
    double area = figure.getArea();
    System.out.println("Perimeter = " + perimeter +
            "; area = " + area);
}
```

Your program can invoke this method, passing it an object of any class that
implements the interface Measurable.

LISTING 8.9 Another Implementation of the Interface
Measurable

```
/**
 A class of circles.
*/
public class Circle implements Measurable
{
    private double myRadius;
    public Circle(double radius)
    {
        myRadius = radius;
    }
    public double getPerimeter()
    {
        return 2 * Math.PI * myRadius;
    }
    public double getCircumference()          This method is not declared
    {                                          in the interface.
        return getPerimeter();
    }                                          Calls another method instead
    public double getArea()                    of repeating its body
    {
        return Math.PI * myRadius * myRadius;
    }
}
```

For instance, your program might contain the following statements:

```
Measurable box = new Rectangle(5.0, 5.0);
Measurable disc = new Circle(5.0);
```

Even though the type of both variables is Measurable, the objects referenced by box and disc have different definitions of getPerimeter and getArea. The variable box references a Rectangle object; disc references a Circle object. Thus, the invocation

```
display(box);
```

displays

```
Perimeter = 20.0; area = 25.0
```

while the invocation

```
display(disc);
```

displays

```
Perimeter = 31.4; area = 78.5
```

The classes Rectangle and Circle implement the same interface, so we are able to substitute an instance of one for an instance of the other when we call the method display. This is another example of polymorphism—the ability to substitute one object for another using dynamic binding. These terms refer to the fact that the method invocation is not bound to the method definition until the program executes.

Objects having the same interface can be used interchangeably

As another example, consider the following code:

```
Measurable m;
Rectangle box = new Rectangle(5.0, 5.0);
m = box;
display(m);
Circle disc = new Circle(5.0);
m = disc;
display(m);
```

The two calls to `display` are identical, and the code within the method `display` is identical in both cases. Thus, the invocations of `getPerimeter` and `getArea` within `display` are identical. Yet these invocations use different definitions for `getPerimeter` and `getArea`, and so the two invocations of `display` produce different output, just as they did in our earlier example.

A variable of an interface type can reference an object of a class that implements the interface, but the object itself always determines which method actions to use for every method name. The type of the variable does not matter. What matters is the class name when the object was created, because Java uses dynamic binding. Not even a type cast will fool Java.

You therefore need to be aware of how dynamic binding interacts with the Java compiler's type checking. For example, consider

```
Measurable m = new Circle(5.0);
```

We can assign an object of type `Circle` to a variable of type `Measurable`, again because `Circle` implements `Measurable`. However, we can use the variable to invoke only a method that is in the interface `Measurable`. Thus, the invocation of `getCircumference` in

```
System.out.println(m.getCircumference()); //ILLEGAL!
```

is illegal, because `getCircumference` is not the name of a method in the `Measurable` interface. In this invocation, the variable m is of type `Measurable`, but the object referenced by m is still an object of type `Circle`. Thus, although the object has the method `getCircumference`, the compiler does not know this! To make the invocation valid, you need a type cast, such as the following:

```
Circle c = (Circle)m;
System.out.println(c.getCircumference());//Legal
```

REMEMBER What Is Legal and What Happens

A variable's type determines what method names can be used, but the object the variable references determines which definition of the method will be used.

VideoNote
Exploring interfaces

> **RECAP Dynamic Binding and Polymorphism Apply to Interfaces**
>
> Dynamic binding applies to interfaces just as it does with classes. The process enables objects of different classes to substitute for one another, if they have the same interface. This ability—called polymorphism—allows different objects to use different method actions for the same method name.

SELF-TEST QUESTIONS

23. Imagine a class `Oval` that defines the methods `getPerimeter` and `getArea` but does not have the clause `implements Measurable`. Could you pass an instance of `Oval` as an argument to the method `display` given in the previous section?

24. Can a class implement more than one interface?

Extending an Interface

Once you have an interface, you can define another interface that builds on, or **extends,** the first one by using a kind of inheritance. Thus, you can create an interface that consists of the methods in an existing interface plus some new methods.

You can define an interface based on another interface

For example, consider the classes of pets we discussed earlier and the following interface:

```
public interface Nameable
{
    public void setName(String petName);
    public String getName();
}
```

We can extend `Nameable` to create the interface `Callable`:

```
public interface Callable extends Nameable
{
    public void come(String petName);
}
```

A class that implements `Callable` must implement the methods `come`, `setName`, and `getName`.

You also can combine several interfaces into a new interface and add even more methods if you like. For example, suppose that in addition to the previous two interfaces, we define the following interfaces:

```
public interface Capable
{
    public void hear();
    public String respond();
}
public interface Trainable extends Callable, Capable
{
    public void sit();
    public String speak();
    public void lieDown();
}
```

A class that implements Trainable must implement the methods setName, getName, come, hear, and respond, as well as the methods sit, speak, and lieDown.

SELF-TEST QUESTIONS

myprogramming**lab**

25. Suppose a class C implements the interface Trainable, as defined in the previous section. Can you pass an instance of C to a method whose parameter is of type Capable?

26. Suppose a class D implements the interfaces Callable and Capable, as defined in the previous section. Can you pass an instance of D to a method whose parameter is of type Trainable?

CASE STUDY Character Graphics

Java has methods to draw graphics on your computer screen. Suppose, however, that the screen on the inexpensive device you are designing for has no graphics capability, allowing only text output. In this case study, we will design three interfaces and three classes that produce graphics on a screen by placing ordinary keyboard characters on each line to draw simple shapes. Our drawings will not be sophisticated, but we will be able to explore the use of interfaces and inheritance in solving a problem.

Let's begin by writing an interface that specifies the methods that our objects should have. Suppose the method drawHere draws the shape beginning at the current line and drawAt draws it after moving a given number of lines down from the current one.

Specify the solution by writing an interface

All shapes have some properties in common. For example, each of the shapes will have an offset telling how far it is indented from the left edge of the screen. We can include set and get methods for this offset. Each shape will also have a size, but the size of some shapes is described by a single number, while the size of others is determined by several numbers. Since the size will be specified according to the kind of shape, it isn't an attribute that all shapes will have in common. Listing 8.10 contains an interface for the methods that all shapes will have.

Suppose we want to draw rectangles and triangles. The size of a rectangle is given as its width and height, each expressed as a number of characters. Because characters are taller than they are wide, a rectangle might look taller than we expect. For example, a 5 by 5 rectangle will not look square on the screen, but will appear as shown in Figure 8.5.

Suppose we decide that a triangle will always point up, with its base at the bottom. After choosing the length of the base, and to make the other sides smooth, the slopes of the sides are limited to what we get by indenting one character per line. So once the base is chosen, we have no choice regarding what the sides of the triangle will be. Figure 8.5 also shows a sample of a triangle.

If we could be content to specify a shape's offset and size in its constructor alone, the interface we wrote in Listing 8.10 would suffice. But suppose that we also want to be able to redefine the size of an existing shape. That is, we want a mutator method. Since the size of a shape depends on the shape being

LISTING 8.10 An Interface for Drawing Shapes Using Keyboard Characters

```java
/**
Interface for simple shapes drawn on
the screen using keyboard characters.
*/
public interface ShapeInterface
{
    /**
    Sets the offset for the shape.
    */
    public void setOffset(int newOffset);
    /**
    Returns the offset for the shape.
    */
    public int getOffset();
    /**
    Draws the shape at lineNumber lines down
    from the current line.
    */
    public void drawAt(int lineNumber);
    /**
    Draws the shape at the current line.
    */
    public void drawHere();
}
```

FIGURE 8.5　A Sample Rectangle and Triangle

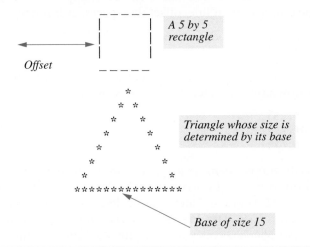

drawn, we will define two more interfaces, one for rectangles and one for triangles. Listing 8.11 contains these interfaces. Note that both of them extend `ShapeInterface`.

LISTING 8.11　Interfaces for Drawing Rectangles and Triangles

```java
/**
Interface for a rectangle to be drawn on the screen.
*/
public interface RectangleInterface extends ShapeInterface
{
    /**
    Sets the rectangle's dimensions.
    */
    public void set(int newHeight, int newWidth);
}
/**
Interface for a triangle to be drawn on the screen.
*/
public interface TriangleInterface extends ShapeInterface
{
    /**
    Sets the triangle's base.
    */
    public void set(int newBase);
}
```

Try writing some code that uses the specifications of your classes

We now have our specifications, so we can try to write some Java statements that use our drawing methods. For example, we could draw an 8 by 4 rectangle on the current line, offset five spaces, as follows:

```java
RectangleInterface box = new Rectangle(5, 8, 4);
box.drawHere();
```

We then could revise the size and indentation of the object box and draw it after moving down on the screen by two lines, as follows:

```java
box.set(5, 5);
box.setOffset(10);
box.drawAt(2);
```

Attributes and methods common to the classes can form a base class

Our specifications seem reasonable, so we'll now go on to some implementation issues. Let's write a base class named ShapeBasics that implements ShapeInterface. Later we can derive the classes Rectangle and Triangle from this base class. We saw that the only common attribute is the offset, so the class ShapeBasics will have only the following instance variable:

```java
private int offset;
```

ShapeBasics is our base class

Our interface specifies the class's methods, so we need only define them and add some appropriate constructors. Listing 8.12 contains a definition for the class ShapeBasics.

LISTING 8.12 **The Base Class** ShapeBasics (*part 1 of 2*)

```java
/**
Class for drawing simple shapes on the screen using keyboard
characters. This class will draw an asterisk on the screen as a
test. It is not intended to create a "real" shape, but rather
to be used as a base class for other classes of shapes.
*/
public class ShapeBasics implements ShapeInterface
{
    private int offset;
    public ShapeBasics()
    {
        offset = 0;
    }
    public ShapeBasics(int theOffset)
    {
        offset = theOffset;
    }
    public void setOffset(int newOffset)
    {
        offset = newOffset;
    }
```

(continued)

LISTING 8.12   The Base Class ShapeBasics *(part 2 of 2)*

```
public int getOffset()
{
    return offset;
}
public void drawAt(int lineNumber)
{
    for (int count = 0; count < lineNumber; count++)
        System.out.println();
    drawHere();
}
public void drawHere()
{
    for (int count = 0; count < offset; count++)
        System.out.print(' ');
    System.out.println('*');
}
}
```

The method drawAt has one parameter of type int, whose value indicates the number of blank lines to be inserted before the drawing of the shape. The shape is drawn by a call to drawHere.

drawAt calls drawHere

The method drawHere indents a number of spaces on the screen equal to the offset and then writes an asterisk on the screen. This simple output is just so you can have something to test. You do not intend to use this version of drawHere in any application. You will override the definition of drawHere when you define classes for rectangles and triangles.

Derived classes must override drawHere

Now we turn our attention to the class for drawing a rectangle. The class, called Rectangle, will be a derived class of the class ShapeBasics. Thus, the class definition will begin with

```
public class Rectangle extends ShapeBasics
```

Since we want our class to implement RectangleInterface, we add an implements clause, as follows:

```
public class Rectangle extends ShapeBasics
    implements RectangleInterface
```

When you have both an extends clause and an implements clause, the extends clause is always first. An easy way to remember the order of these two clauses is to notice that the keywords extends and implements are in alphabetical order.

extends is always before implements

We need to decide what instance variables, if any, to add to those already in the class ShapeBasics. We also need to decide whether to override any method definitions in ShapeBasics. Our class Rectangle will be able to use the instance variable offset in the base class, but we need to have instance variables for the height and the width of the rectangle. Thus, the class definition looks like the following:

```
public class Rectangle extends ShapeBasics
    implements RectangleInterface
{
    private int height;
    private int width;
    <Method definitions>
}
```

Note that we do not list the instance variable offset within Rectangle.

We know that Rectangle needs the usual constructors and a set method for the sides. Rectangle inherits the methods setOffset, getOffset, drawAt, and drawHere from the class ShapeBasics. However, we need to override the definition of the method drawHere so that it does indeed draw a rectangle. Do we need to override the method drawAt? When we look at the method drawAt in Listing 8.12, we see that, as long as drawHere is correctly defined, the method drawAt will work fine for a rectangle or any other shape. Polymorphism will ensure that the correct version of drawHere is called.

Let's look first at a sample constructor, one that sets all instance variables to the values given as its arguments. But one instance variable, namely offset, is a private instance variable of the base class ShapeBasics, so we cannot access it directly by name. However, we can either call the method setOffset or use super to call the base class constructor. We choose the latter, so the definition of this constructor is as follows:

Each constructor in a derived class calls a constructor in the base class ShapeBasics

```
public Rectangle(int theOffset, int theHeight, int theWidth)
{
    super(theOffset);
    height = theHeight;
    width = theWidth;
}
```

The default constructor similarly calls the base class default constructor and sets the rectangle's dimensions to zero. We could omit an explicit call to super in the default constructor, and it would be called automatically anyway, but we leave it in for clarity.

The method set, as specified in RectangleInterface, is straightforward, so let's examine the method drawHere, which depends heavily on the particulars of the shape it is drawing. We can use a technique known as **top-down design.** In this technique, we break down the task to be performed into subtasks. We have the following subtasks:

Algorithm to draw a rectangle

1. Draw the top line.

2. Draw the side lines.

3. Draw the bottom line.

Note that not every way of choosing subtasks will work. You might at first be tempted to draw the sides of the box in two subtasks. However, output must be produced one line after the other, and you are not allowed to back up. Thus, we must draw the two sides together so they will be side by side, as they should be.

The definition of the method drawHere is easy:

```java
public void drawHere()
{
    drawHorizontalLine();
    drawSides();
    drawHorizontalLine();
}
```

Although that was easy, it does postpone most of the work. You still need to define the methods drawHorizontalLine and drawSides. Because these are helping methods, they will be private methods.

Subtasks of drawHere are realized as private methods

The logic for drawHorizontalLine is not complicated, as you can see from the following pseudocode:

Algorithm for drawHorizontalLine

1. Display offset blank spaces.

2. Display width copies of the character '-'.

3. System.out.println();

The task of writing a specified number of blanks is done by another helping method called skipSpaces, which contains a simple loop. The final code for the method drawHorizontalLine is

```java
private void drawHorizontalLine()
{
    skipSpaces(getOffset());
    for (int count = 0; count < width; count++)
        System.out.print('-');
    System.out.println();
}
```

Next we consider the method drawSides. Its task is to draw a shape like the following:

Drawing both sides

Since each line is identical, we can treat the display of one of these lines as a subtask. So the definition of the method drawSides is

```
private void drawSides()
{
    for (int count = 0; count < (height - 2); count++)]
        drawOneLineOfSides();
}
```

Note that we display two fewer lines than the height. The top and bottom horizontal lines account for those extra two units of height.

Just about all that is left to do is to define the helping method drawOne-LineOfSides. Because we already have a method for the subtask of writing spaces, the pseudocode for drawOneLineOfSides turns out to be Java code:

```
skipSpaces(getOffset());
System.out.print('|');
skipSpaces(width - 2);
System.out.println('|');
```

We are basically done. Listing 8.13 gives the complete class definition of Rectangle.

LISTING 8.13   **The Class** Rectangle *(part 1 of 2)*

```
/**
Class for drawing rectangles on the screen using keyboard
characters. Each character is higher than it is wide, so
these rectangles will look taller than you might expect.
Inherits getOffset, setOffset, and drawAt from the class
ShapeBasics.
*/
public class Rectangle extends ShapeBasics
                       implements RectangleInterface
{
    private int height;
    private int width;

    public Rectangle()
    {
        super();
        height = 0;
        width = 0;
    }
    public Rectangle(int theOffset, int theHeight,
                     int theWidth)
    {
        super(theOffset);
        height = theHeight;
        width = theWidth;
    }
```

(continued)

LISTING 8.13   **The Class** Rectangle *(part 2 of 2)*

```java
public void set(int newHeight,int newWidth)
{
    height = newHeight;
    width = newWidth;
}
public void drawHere();
{
    drawHorizontalLine();
    drawSides();
    drawHorizontalLine();
}
private void drawHorizontalLine()
{
    skipSpaces(getOffset());
    for (int count = 0; count < width; count++)
        System.out.print('-');
    System.out.println();
}
private void drawSides()
{
    for (int count = 0; count < (height - 2); count++)
        drawOneLineOfSides();
}
private void drawOneLineOfSides()
{
    skipSpaces(getOffset());
    System.out.print(`|');
    skipSpaces(width - 2);
    System.out.println(`|');
}
//Writes the indicated number of spaces.
private static void skipSpaces(int number)
{
    for (int count = 0; count < number; count++)
        System.out.print(' ');
}
}
}
```

For clarity, the method skipSpaces *was made static because it does not depend on an object.*

Although we will not stop to describe the testing process in this case study, all the methods in the class ShapeBasics, the class Rectangle, and the class Triangle—which we have not yet discussed—need to be tested. Remember, each method should be tested in a program in which it is the only untested method.

Test the methods along the way

Listing 8.14 contains the definition of the class Triangle. We can design this class using the same techniques we used to design the class Rectangle. We will discuss only one part of the method drawHere for which the technical details might not be clear at first. The method drawHere divides its task into

LISTING 8.14   **The Class** Triangle *(part 1 of 2)*

```
/**
 Class for drawing triangles on the screen using keyboard
 characters. A triangle points up. Its size is determined
 by the length of its base, which must be an odd integer.
 Inherits getOffset, setOffset, and drawAt from the class
 ShapeBasics.
*/
public class Triangle extends ShapeBasics
                           implements TriangleInterface
{
    private int base;

    public Triangle()
    {
        super();
        base = 0;
    }
    public Triangle(int theOffset, int theBase)
    {
        super(theOffset);
        base = theBase;
    }
    /** Precondition: newBase is odd. */
    public void set(int newBase)
    {
        base = newBase;
    }
    public void drawHere()
    {
        drawTop();
        drawBase();
    }
    private void drawBase()
    {
        skipSpaces(getOffset());
        for (int count = 0; count < base; count++)
            System.out.print('*');
        System.out.println();
    }
    private void drawTop()
    {
        //startOfLine == number of spaces to the
        //first '*' on a line. Initially set to the
        //number of spaces before the topmost '*'.
        int startOfLine = getOffset() + base / 2;
        skipSpaces(startOfLine);
        System.out.println('*');//top '*'
```

(continued)

LISTING 8.14   The Class `Triangle` *(part 2 of 2)*

```
        int lineCount = base / 2 - 1;//height above base

        //insideWidth == number of spaces between the
        //two '*'s on a line.
        int insideWidth = 1;
        for (int count = 0; count < lineCount; count++)
        {
            //Down one line, so the first '*' is one more
            //space to the left.
            startOfLine --;
            skipSpaces(startOfLine);
            System.out.print.('*');
            skipSpaces(insideWidth);
            System.out.println('*');

            //Down one line, so the inside is 2 spaces wider.
            insideWidth = insideWidth + 2;
        }
    }
    private static void skipSpaces(int number)
    {
        for (int count = 0; count < number; count++)
            System.out.print(' ');
    }
}
```

two subtasks: Draw the inverted V for the top of the triangle, and draw the horizontal line for the bottom of the triangle.

The method `drawTop` draws a shape like the following:

drawTop draws two sides of the triangle

```
            *
          *   *
        *       *
      *           *
    *               *
  *                   *
*                       *
```

Note that the entire shape is offset. The indentation for the wide bottom of the shape is exactly this offset. But going up from bottom to top, each line has a greater indentation. Alternatively, moving down the lines from top to bottom—as the computer must—the indentation decreases by one character per line. So if the indentation for the top of the triangle is given by the value of the `int` variable `startOfLine`, the first indentation can be performed by

```
skipSpaces(startOfLine);
```

We then write a single asterisk.

Loop that draws
two sides without
the asterisk at
their juncture

After writing the asterisk for the first line, we need to write two asterisks for each subsequent line. We write a loop that decreases startOfLine by 1 on each iteration and executes a statement exactly like the previous call to skipSpaces. We then write an asterisk and skip some more spaces before writing the second asterisk. The size of the gap between the two asterisks on a line increases by 2 as we move down from line to line. If this gap is given by the value of the int variable insideWidth, the loop for drawing all of the inverted V except for the top asterisk can be

```java
for (int count = 0; count < lineCount; count++)
{
    startOfLine--;
    skipSpaces(startOfLine);
    System.out.print(*);
    skipSpaces(insideWidth);
    System.out.println(*);
    insideWidth = insideWidth + 2;
}
```

The complete definition of the method drawTop is given in Listing 8.14.

The base of the triangle is a line of asterisks. Ideally, we should use an odd number of asterisks, for otherwise the triangle will look slightly off-balance. However, to keep the class simple, we simply state this as a precondition of Triangle's set method and do not try to enforce it.

The sample application program shown in Listing 8.15 demonstrates our classes by drawing a triangle and a rectangle to form a crude picture of a fir tree.

LISTING 8.15   **A Demonstration of** Triangle **and** Rectangle
(part 1 of 2)

```java
/**
A program that draws a fir tree composed of a triangle and
a rectangle, both drawn using keyboard characters.
*/
public class TreeDemo
{
    public static final int INDENT = 5;
    public static final int TREE_TOP_WIDTH = 21;// must be odd
    public static final int TREE_BOTTOM_WIDTH = 4;
    public static final int TREE_BOTTOM_HEIGHT = 4;

    public static void main(String[] args)
    {
        drawTree(TREE_TOP_WIDTH, TREE_BOTTOM_WIDTH,
                TREE_BOTTOM_HEIGHT);
    }
```

(continued)

LISTING 8.15   A Demonstration of Triangle **and** Rectangle
(part 2 of 2)

```
public static void drawTree(int topWidth, int bottomWidth,
                            int bottomHeight)
{
    System.out.println("    Save the Redwoods!");
    TriangleInterface treeTop = new Triangle(INDENT, topWidth);
    drawTop(treeTop);
    RectangleInterface treeTrunk = new Rectangle(INDENT +
                    (topWidth / 2) - (bottomWidth / 2),
                    bottomHeight, bottomWidth);
    drawTrunk(treeTrunk);
}
private static void drawTop(TriangleInterface treeTop)
{
    treeTop.drawAt(1);
}
private static void drawTrunk(RectangleInterface treeTrunk)
{
    treeTrunk.drawHere(); // or treeTrunk.drawAt(0);
}
}
```

Screen Output

```
    Save the Redwoods!
                 *
             *       *
            *         *
           *           *
          *             *
         *               *
        *                 *
       *                   *
      *                     *
     *                       *
    *                         *
    *************************
             - - - -
             |     |
             |     |
             - - - -
```

SELF-TEST QUESTIONS

27. Is the definition of drawHere given in Listing 8.13 an example of overloading or overriding?

28. Is the definition of drawHere given in Listing 8.14 an example of overloading or overriding?

29. Are the two definitions of the constructors given in Listing 8.14 an example of overloading or overriding?

30. The private method skipSpaces appears in the definitions of both Rectangle (Listing 8.13) and Triangle (Listing 8.14). Can we move this method to the base class ShapeBasics (Listing 8.12) so that both Rectangle and Triangle can inherit it instead of each defining its own copy?

31. Describe the implementation of the method drawHere for a class called Diamond that is derived from the class ShapeBasics. Programming Project 2 at the end of this chapter asks you to actually write this class. (*Hint*: The class Diamond is similar to the class Triangle.)

CASE STUDY The Comparable Interface

Java has many predefined interfaces that are used by many classes. One of them is the Comparable interface, and it is used to impose an ordering upon the objects that implement it. The Comparable interface has only one method heading. The method compareTo must be written for a class to implement the Comparable interface.

```
public int compareTo(Object other);
```

The interface allows you to specify how one object compares to another in terms of when one should "come before" or "come after" or "equal" the other. It is the programmer's responsibility to follow the semantics appropriately. For example, if you define A to come before B, and B to come before C, you shouldn't allow C to come before A.

The compareTo method should return

- a negative number if the calling object "comes before" the parameter other,
- a zero if the calling object "equals" the parameter other,
- and a positive number if the calling object "comes after" the parameter other.

As an example, consider the idiom that one can't compare apples to oranges. Let's show that this idiom doesn't quite apply to Java classes because we can define the compareTo method as we see fit. Our first attempt to define a Fruit class to represent apples and oranges might look like the code in Listing 8.16. This simple class uses a String to store the name of the fruit along with methods to get and set the name. The constructor takes the name of the fruit. This initial attempt does not implement any interfaces.

LISTING 8.16   First Attempt to Define a Fruit Class

```java
public class Fruit
{
    private String fruitName;
    public Fruit()
    {
        fruitName = "";
    }
    public Fruit(String name)
    {
        fruitName = name;
    }
    Public void setName(String name)
    {
        fruitName = name;
    }
    public String getName()
    {
        return fruitName;
    }
}
```

A short demo program is given in Listing 8.17 that attempts to use the Fruit class. In this example we make an array that contains four Fruit objects. Then we try to sort the array using Arrays.sort described in Chapter 7.4.

LISTING 8.17   Program to Sort an Array of Fruit Objects

```java
import java.util.Arrays;
public class FruitDemo
{
    public static void main(String[] args)
    {
        Fruit[] fruits = new Fruit[4];
        fruits[0] = new Fruit("Orange");
        fruits[1] = new Fruit("Apple");
        fruits[2] = new Fruit("Kiwi");
        fruits[3] = new Fruit("Durian");
        Arrays.sort(fruits);
        // Output the sorted array of fruits
        for (Fruit f : fruits)
        {
            System.out.println(f.getName());
        }
    }
}
```

The program in Listing 8.17 will compile and run but produce the following run-time error:

```
Exception in thread "main" java.lang.ClassCastException: Fruit
cannot be cast to java.lang.Comparable
```

This error occurs because Java doesn't know how to compare two instances of the Fruit class to each other to see if one "comes after" the other when attempting to sort the array. More precisely, the Arrays.sort method has been written with the expectation that the objects passed in the array have a compareTo method in accordance with the Comparable interface. Arrays.sort attempts to invoke compareTo on objects in the array (for example, to see if fruits[0] is greater than fruits[1]) so they can be rearranged in sorted order, but since the method doesn't exist there is an error.

The solution is to make sure that the Fruit class implements the Comparable interface with a compareTo method. One way we might compare one fruit to another is to use the lexicographic ordering of the fruit name. Lexicographic ordering is the same as alphabetical ordering when both strings are either all uppercase or all lowercase letters. For example, apples would come before oranges because the word "apple" is lexicographically ordered before "orange." To accomplish this we can use the compareTo method defined for the String class. That is, if we have two strings str1 and str2 then

```
str1.compareTo(str2)
```

will return a negative number if str1 is lexicographically before str2, the value 0 if str1 is equal to str2, and a positive number if str1 is lexicographically after str2. The compareTo method we write for the Fruit class can then return the result of the compareTo method for the names of the fruits being compared. The code in Listing 8.18 contains a version of the Fruit class with these changes highlighted.

LISTING 8.18   A Fruit Class implementing Comparable
                  (part 1 of 2)

```
public class Fruit implements Comparable
{
    private String fruitName;
    public Fruit()
    {
        fruitName = "";
    }
    public Fruit(String name)
    {
        fruitName = name;
    }
```

(continued)

LISTING 8.18   A `Fruit` Class implementing `Comparable`
(part 2 of 2)

```java
public void setName(String name)
{
    fruitName = name;
}
public String getName()
{
    return fruitName;
}
public int compareTo(Object o)
{
    if ((o != null) &&
        (o instanceof Fruit))
    {
        Fruit otherFruit = (Fruit) o;
        return (fruitName.compareTo(otherFruit.fruitName));
    }
    return -1;    // Default if other object is not a Fruit
}
}
```

Now the program in Listing 8.17 will run and produce the output:

```
Apple
Durian
Kiwi
Orange
```

The `Arrays.sort` method is now successful because it can call the `compareTo` method to compare objects in the array and reorder them. To drive home the point that our `compareTo` method is being called from within the `Arrays.sort` method, we can redefine `compareTo` with different criteria to sort fruit. Instead of lexicographic ordering, let's use the length of the fruit name as the comparison metric. Fruit with shorter names will come before fruit with longer names. Below is an alternate definition of the `compareTo` method:

```java
public int compareTo(Object o)
{
    if ((o != null) &&
        (o instanceof Fruit))
    {
        Fruit otherFruit = (Fruit) o;
        if (fruitName.length() >
            otherFruit.fruitName.length())
            return 1;
        else if (fruitName.length() <
                otherFruit.fruitName.length())
```

```
                            return -1;
                else
                            return 0;
        }
        return -1;   // Default if other object is not a Fruit
    }
```

The program in Listing 8.17 will now produce the output:

```
Kiwi
Apple
Orange
Durian
```

The fruits are now sorted in order of shortest word first.

Abstract Classes

When we wrote the class ShapeBasics in Listing 8.12, we did not plan to create objects of the class ShapeBasics. Instead, we designed it as a base class for other classes, such as the class Rectangle in Listing 8.13. Although we do not really need to create objects of the class ShapeBasics, we can do so, as in the following statement:

```
ShapeBasics shapeVariable = new ShapeBasics();
```

To make this statement valid, however, we needed to write a definition for the method drawHere in the class ShapeBasics. The definition that we wrote is just a place holder; all it does is draw a single asterisk, just so something would happen if we invoked it. We never intended to invoke the method drawHere of an object of the base class ShapeBasics. Rather, we planned to use the method drawHere only with objects of derived classes, such as Rectangle and Triangle.

An abstract method has no body

Instead of giving a contrived definition of a method that we plan to override in a derived class, however, we can declare the method to be **abstract,** as follows:

```
public abstract void drawHere();
```

We write the keyword abstract in the method heading, follow the heading with a semicolon, and omit a method body. An abstract method must be overridden by any (nonabstract) derived class and given a definition. Including an abstract method in a class is a way to force a derived class to define a particular method.

Java requires that if a class has at least one abstract method, the class must be declared to be abstract. You do this by including the keyword abstract in the heading of the class definition, as in the following:

An abstract class has at least one abstract method

```
public abstract class ShapeBase

{ ...
```

A class defined in this way is said to be an **abstract class.** If a class is abstract, you cannot create objects of that class; it can be used only as a base class for other classes. For this reason, an abstract class is sometimes called an **abstract base class.**

In Listing 8.19, we have revised the class ShapeBasics as an abstract class and named it ShapeBase. If we had used this abstract class ShapeBase in the previous case study, all of our derived classes would work as before, even though we could not create objects of ShapeBase.

Although the class ShapeBase is abstract, not all of its methods are abstract. All the method definitions, except for the method drawHere, are exactly the same as in our original ShapeBasics. They are full definitions and do not use the keyword abstract. When it makes sense to define a body for a method in an abstract class, it should be given. That way, as much detail as possible is pushed into the abstract class, so that such detail need not be repeated in each derived class.

Why have abstract classes? They simplify your thinking. We have already explained in the case study that we defined the class ShapeBasics so we would not have to duplicate the definitions of methods such as drawAt for every kind of shape. But we also had to write a useless definition for the method drawHere. An abstract class makes it easier to define a base class by relieving you of the obligation to write useless method definitions. If a method will always be overridden, make it an abstract method—and so

> You cannot create an object of an abstract class

LISTING 8.19   **The Abstract Class** ShapeBase

```
/**
 Abstract base class for drawing simple shapes on the screen
 using characters.
*/
public abstract class ShapeBase implements ShapeInterface
{
    private int offset;
    public abstract void drawHere();
```

The rest of the class is identical to **ShapeBasics** *in Listing 8.12, except for the names of the constructors. Only the method* **drawHere** *is abstract. Methods other than* **drawHere** *have bodies and do not have the keyword* **abstract** *in their headings. We repeat one such method here:*

```
    public void drawAt(int lineNumber)
    {
        for (int count = 0; count < lineNumber; count++)
            System.out.println();
        drawHere();
    }
}
```

make the class abstract. An abstract method serves a purpose, even though it is not given a full definition. It serves as a place holder for a method that must be defined in all (nonabstract) derived classes. Note that the method drawAt in Listing 8.19 includes an invocation of the method drawHere. If the abstract method drawHere were omitted, this invocation of drawHere would be illegal.

You might notice that an abstract class is very similar to an interface. Both define methods and you can't make instances of either one. However, you can define default methods for the derived classes in an abstract class and you can only specify the method heading in an interface. Conceptually, an abstract class represents a conceptual view of an abstract entity in the problem you are trying to solve. An interface specifies functionality that a class must support.

REMEMBER An Abstract Class Is a Type

You cannot create an object of an abstract class. For example, given the abstract class ShapeBase as defined in Listing 8.19, the following statement is illegal:

```
ShapeBase f = new ShapeBase(); // ILLEGAL!
```

Nonetheless, it makes perfectly good sense to have a parameter of type ShapeBase. Then an object of any of the descendant classes of ShapeBase can be plugged in for the parameter.

VideoNote
Defining an abstract class

myprogramminglab

SELF-TEST QUESTIONS

32. Is the following valid if ShapeBase is defined as in Listing 8.19?
    ShapeInterface shapeVariable = new ShapeBase();

33. Is the following valid if ShapeBase is defined as in Listing 8.19, and Rectangle is as defined in Listing 8.13 but ShapeBasics is replaced by ShapeBase?

    ShapeBase shapeVariable = new Rectangle();

8.5 GRAPHICS SUPPLEMENT

Good Heavens! For more than forty years I have been speaking prose without knowing it.

—MOLIÈRE, *LE BOURGEOIS GENTILHOMME*

In this section, we explain how you have been using inheritance every time you write the definition of an applet or GUI application. We also describe window events and window listeners in more detail.

The Class `JApplet`

As you can tell from the way we have been writing code for applet classes, an applet is a derived class of the class `JApplet`, as indicated by the first line of an applet class definition. For example:

JApplet is the base class of applets

```
public class LabelDemo extends JApplet
```

The class `JApplet` has methods named `init` and `paint`. So when you define an applet's `init` or `paint` method, you are overriding (redefining) the inherited method. This is why the methods `init` and `paint` can be invoked automatically for you. The details go something like this: Imagine a method named `showApplet`[1] that has a parameter named `anApplet` of type `JApplet`:

```
public void showApplet(JApplet anApplet)
{
    anApplet.init();
    ...
    anApplet.paint();
}
```

The body of the method `showApplet` can include invocations like `anApplet.init()` and `anApplet.paint()`, because the class `JApplet` has methods named `init` and `paint`.

Applets override the methods `init` and `paint`

Thanks to polymorphism, any invocation of the method `showApplet` with your applet class plugged in for the parameter `anApplet` will invoke your definitions of the methods `init` and `paint` that you wrote in your applet. Thus, library classes that were defined before you wrote your applets can be used to run your applet and automatically invoke your definitions of `init` and `paint`.

The Class `JFrame`

In Chapter 2 we described how to build a Java GUI application using the `JFrame` class, but at that point we had not covered enough material about classes and objects to really describe why it worked. At this point we can now delve into these details. The class `JApplet` is used as a base class for applets that will be run from a Web page. To obtain GUIs (windowing interfaces) that can be run as regular Java applications, you use the class `JFrame`, rather than `JApplet`, as the base class. As an example we have rewritten the applet from Listing 6.22 of Chapter 6 by replacing the base class `JApplet` with the base class `JFrame` and making a few other necessary adjustments to accommodate

---

[1] The method name `showApplet` is fictitious and is a stand-in for any method with a parameter of type `JApplet`.

this change. The resulting class, `ButtonDemo`, is shown in Listing 8.20. We have also added a `WindowDestroyer` that is discussed in the next section.

To use the GUI produced by `ButtonDemo`, we need a Java application program, such as the one in Listing 8.21, that creates an object of the class `ButtonDemo`. This simple application program creates an object, named `gui`, of the class `ButtonDemo` and displays the GUI with the following statement:

```
gui.setVisible(true);
```

The class `JFrame`, and hence every class derived from `JFrame`, has a method named `setVisible`. This method takes a boolean argument. If the argument

LISTING 8.20   A Window Interface Derived from `Jframe`
(part 1 of 2)

```
import javax.swing.JButton;
import javax.swing.JFrame;
import java.awt.Container;
import java.awt.event.ActionEvent;
import java.awt.event.ActionListener;

/**
Simple demonstration of putting buttons in a JFrame window.
*/

public class ButtonDemo extends JFrame implements ActionListener
{
    public static final int WIDTH  = 400;
    public static final int HEIGHT = 300;

    public ButtonDemo()
    {
        setSize(WIDTH, HEIGHT);
        WindowDestroyer listener = new WindowDestroyer();
        addWindowListener(listener);

        Container contentPane = getContentPane();
        contentPane.setBackground(Color.WHITE);

        contentPane.setLayout(new FlowLayout());

        JButton sunnyButton = new JButton("Sunny");
        sunnyButton.addActionListener(this);
        contentPane.add(sunnyButton);

        JButton cloudyButton = new JButton("Cloudy");
        cloudyButton.addActionListener(this);
        contentPane.add(cloudyButton);
    }
```

> To compile this class, you should have the class **WindowDestroyer** in the same directory (folder) as this class. The class **WindowDestroyer** is discussed a bit later in this graphics supplement.

(continued)

LISTING 8.20 A Window Interface Derived from Jframe
(part 2 of 2)

```java
    public void actionPerformed(ActionEvent e)
    {
        String actionCommand = e.getActionCommand();
        Container contentPane = getContentPane();

        if (actionCommand.equals("Sunny"))
            contentPane.setBackground(Color.BLUE);
        else if (actionCommand.equals("Cloudy"))
            contentPane.setBackground(Color.GRAY);
        else
            System.out.println("Error in button interface.");
    }
}
```

LISTING 8.21 Running a JFrame **Class from an Application**

```java
public class ShowButtonDemo
{
        public static void main(String[] args)
        {
            ButtonDemo gui = new ButtonDemo();
            gui.setVisible(true);
        }
}
```

Screen Output

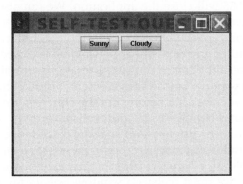

This GUI changes color in reaction to button clicks in the same way as the applet in Listing 6.22.

is true, the GUI is visible. If the argument is false, the GUI is invisible. This setVisible method is the same method that we discussed in the graphics supplement of Chapter 6. Ultimately, labels, buttons, JFrame GUIs, and other components all inherit the method setVisible from a common ancestor class. Inheritance is what gives us this uniform behavior of the method setVisible across a wide range of classes.

Let's return to our GUI class (Listing 8.20) derived from `JFrame` and explain the parts of the code that differ from the corresponding applet code in Chapter 6 (Listing 6.22). The differences are all highlighted. The most conspicuous change is that we have replaced `extends JApplet` with `extends JFrame`, but we have already explained that difference. The other major difference is that the class derived from `JFrame` has no `init` method but does use a constructor. The code that would be placed in the `init` method of an applet is instead placed in the constructor of a class derived from `JFrame`. In a sense there is nothing to explain here. These are all initialization actions, and initialization actions belong in constructors. Applets, which use an `init` method rather than a constructor, are the unusual case.

A GUI derived from `JFrame` sets its initial size by invoking the method `setSize`, as in the following line from Listing 8.20:

```
setSize(WIDTH, HEIGHT);
```

Finally, an applet ends when the Web page displaying it goes away or when you click the close-window button of the applet viewer. (That close-window button you have seen on applets is not an applet close-window button, but is the applet viewer's close-window button.) With `JFrame`, you need to program the GUI's close-window button. We discuss how in the next section.

Window Events and Window Listeners

In Chapter 2 we specified the behavior when the close-window button is clicked with the following statement:

```
setDefaultCloseOperation(EXIT_ON_CLOSE);
```

This is a `JFrame` method that determines the default operation when a window is closed. The constant `EXIT_ON_CLOSE` will close the application. We can also use other constants such as `HIDE_ON_CLOSE` (the default) or `DO_NOTHING_ON_CLOSE`. While this solution is simple and convenient, a more powerful technique is to write our own method that will be invoked when the window is closed. This way we can do anything we like, although in our simple example we will just close the application. The close-window button fires an event, just like the ordinary button object of `JButton` we have seen before. But the close-window button generates a **window event** that is handled by a **window listener.**

You must program the window's close button

The class `WindowAdapter` is a window listener, and so every class derived from the class `WindowAdapter` is a window listener. The class `WindowDestroyer`, given in Listing 8.22, is an example of a window listener. Just as we must register a button object of `JButton`, we must register a window listener for a `JFrame` GUI. We do this by calling the method `addWindowListener`, which is completely analogous to the class `addActionListener` for `JButton` objects. The following code creates and registers a `WindowDestroyer` object as a window listener for our `JFrame` GUI in Listing 8.20:

Clicking the close button generates a window event

```
WindowDestroyer listener = new WindowDestroyer();
addWindowListener(listener);
```

LISTING 8.22   A Listener Class for Window Events from
JFrame GUIs

> The class WindowDestroyer is
> not defined for you in Java. This is
> a class that you, the programmer,
> must define.

```java
import java.awt.event.WindowAdapter;
import java.awt.event.WindowEvent;

/**
If you register an object of this class as a listener to any
object of the class JFrame, the object will end the program
and close the JFrame window if the user clicks the window's
close-window button.
*/
public class WindowDestroyer extends WindowAdapter
{
    public void windowClosing(WindowEven e)
    {
        System.exit(0);
    }
}
```

The class WindowDestroyer is not a class in any of the standard Java libraries. You must define it yourself. However, it is easy to define this class, as shown in Listing 8.22. The method windowClosing responds to the close-window button in a way analogous to how actionPerformed responds to events fired from JButton objects. So when the close-window button is clicked, the JFrame GUI ends, because the method windowClosing invokes System.exit. We discuss window listeners and the classes WindowAdapter and WindowDestroyer more fully in Chapter 13, which is on the Web. Until then, you can simply copy the definition of WindowDestroyer from Listing 8.22 and always include the following lines in the constructors for your JFrame GUIs:

> You must define a class to handle the window event; the class is a window listener

```java
WindowDestroyer listener = new WindowDestroyer();
addWindowListener(listener);
```

GOTCHA   Do Not Confuse JButtons and the Close-Window Button

The close-window button of a JFrame GUI is not a JButton object. A JButton object fires an action event that is handled by an action listener. The close-window button fires a window event that is handled by a window listener, such as WindowDestroyer in Listing 8.22. A JFrame GUI always has a close-window button and may also have button objects of JButton. ■

The ActionListener Interface

We introduced interfaces at the beginning of this chapter, but if you have been reading the graphics supplements, Chapter 6 introduced you to the interface ActionListener. This interface declares only one method heading, namely

```
public void actionPerformed(ActionEvent e)
```

A listener that responds to button clicks in either an applet or a JFrame GUI must be an **action listener**, which simply means that a listener for a button must implement the ActionListener interface.

SELF-TEST QUESTIONS

34. Is WindowDestroyer in any standard Java package (library)?

35. What is the difference between what you can do in an applet's paint method and what you can do in the paint method for a GUI derived from JFrame?

36. A GUI derived from JFrame normally has no init method. In a GUI derived from JFrame, where do you put the code that you would put in the init method of an applet?

What to Do Next

You may, of course, cover the chapters of this book in order. However, if you want to cover more material on GUIs sooner, you can read Chapter 13 next. Chapter 13, which is on the Web, is devoted completely to JFrame GUIs and does not use any material from Chapters 9 through 12. If you prefer to read some of Chapters 9 through 12 before Chapter 13, you can still cover some material on GUIs as you do so. Chapters 9 and 10 have graphics supplements, but they are not required for Chapter 13 or any other part of this book.

CHAPTER SUMMARY

■ A Java interface contains the headings of public methods and the definitions of public named constants. It does not declare constructors or private instance variables.

■ A class that implements an interface must define a body for every method that the interface specifies. It might also define methods not declared in the interface. A class can implement more than one interface.

■ An interface provides a way for a class designer to specify methods for another programmer. By implementing an interface, a programmer can guarantee that a class defines certain methods.

- An interface is a reference type, and so you can declare variables and method parameters as having an interface type.

- You can extend an interface to create an interface that consists of the methods in the existing interface plus some new methods.

- Dynamic, or late, binding is a process that enables objects of different classes to substitute for one another, if they have identical interfaces. This ability—called polymorphism—allows different objects to use different method actions for the same method name.

- A derived class is obtained from a base class by adding instance variables and methods. The derived class inherits all public instance variables and public methods that are in the base class.

- When defining a constructor for a derived class, your definition should first call a constructor of the base class by using super. If you do not make an explicit call, Java will automatically call the default constructor of the base class.

- Within a constructor, this calls a constructor of the same class, but super invokes a constructor of the base class.

- You can redefine a method from a base class so that it has a different definition in the derived class. This is called overriding the method definition.

- When you override a method definition, the new method definition given in the derived class must have the same name, the exact same number and types of parameters, and the same return type as the method in the base class. If the method in the derived class has a different number of parameters or a parameter position of a different type from the method in the base class, the method is overloaded, not overridden.

- Within the definition of a method of a derived class, you can call an overridden method of the base class by prefacing the method name with super and a dot.

- Private instance variables and private methods of a base class cannot be accessed directly by name within a derived class.

- An object of a derived class has the type of the derived class, and it also has the type of the base class. More generally, a derived class has the type of every one of its ancestor classes.

- You can assign an object of a derived class to a variable of any ancestor type, but not the other way around.

- In Java, every class is a descendant of the predefined class Object. So every object of every class is of type Object, as well as the type of its class and any other ancestor classes.

- A class derived from JFrame produces a windowing interface that is similar to an applet but that is used within an ordinary Java application program.

■ You can write a class derived from the class `WindowAdapter` to serve as a window listener that responds to a click of the close-window button in a `JFrame` window.

Exercises

1. Consider a program that will keep track of the items in a school's library. Draw a class hierarchy, including a base class, for the different kinds of items. Be sure to also consider items that cannot be checked out.

2. Implement your base class for the hierarchy from the previous exercise.

3. Draw a hierarchy for the components you might find in a graphical user interface. Note that some components can trigger actions. Some components may have graphics associated with them. Some components can hold other components.

Graphics

4. Suppose we want to implement a drawing program that creates various shapes using keyboard characters. Implement an abstract base class `DrawableShape` that knows the center (two integer values) and the color (a string) of the object. Give appropriate accessor methods for the attributes. You should also have a mutator method that moves the object by a given amount.

5. Create a class `Square` derived from `DrawableShape`, as described in the previous exercise. A `Square` object should know the length of its sides. The class should have an accessor method and a mutator method for this length. It should also have methods for computing the area and perimeter of the square. Although characters are taller than they are wide—so the number of characters in the vertical sides will differ from the number in the horizontal sides—you need not worry about this detail when drawing the square.

6. Create a class `SchoolKid` that is the base class for children at a school. It should have attributes for the child's name and age, the name of the child's teacher, and a greeting. It should have appropriate accessor and mutator methods for each of the attributes.

7. Derive a class `ExaggeratingKid` from `SchoolKid`, as described in the previous exercise. The new class should override the accessor method for the age, reporting the actual age plus 2. It also should override the accessor for the greeting, returning the child's greeting concatenated with the words "I am the best."

8. Create an abstract class `PayCalculator` that has an attribute `payRate` given in dollars per hour. The class should also have a method `computePay(hours)` that returns the pay for a given amount of time.

9. Derive a class `RegularPay` from `PayCalculator`, as described in the previous exercise. It should have a constructor that has a parameter for the pay rate. It should not override any of the methods. Then derive a class `HazardPay` from `PayCalculator` that overrides the `computePay` method. The new method should return the amount returned by the base class method multiplied by 1.5.

10. Create an abstract class `DiscountPolicy`. It should have a single abstract method `computeDiscount` that will return the discount for the purchase of a given number of a single item. The method has two parameters, `count` and `itemCost`.

11. Derive a class `BulkDiscount` from `DiscountPolicy`, as described in the previous exercise. It should have a constructor that has two parameters, `minimum` and `percent`. It should define the method `computeDiscount` so that if the quantity purchased of an item is more than `minimum`, the discount is `percent` percent.

12. Derive a class `BuyNItemsGetOneFree` from `DiscountPolicy`, as described in Exercise 10. The class should have a constructor that has a single parameter n. In addition, the class should define the method `computeDiscount` so that every nth item is free. For example, the following table gives the discount for the purchase of various counts of an item that costs $10, when n is 3:

Count	1	2	3	4	5	6	7
Discount	0	0	10	10	10	20	20

13. Derive a class `CombinedDiscount` from `DiscountPolicy`, as described in Exercise 10. It should have a constructor that has two parameters of type `DiscountPolicy`. It should define the method `computeDiscount` to return the maximum value returned by `computeDiscount` for each of its two private discount policies. The two discount policies are described in Exercises 11 and 12.

14. Define `DiscountPolicy` as an interface instead of the abstract class described in Exercise 10.

15. Create an interface `MessageEncoder` that has a single abstract method `encode(plainText)`, where `plainText` is the message to be encoded. The method will return the encoded message.

16. Create a class `SubstitutionCipher` that implements the interface `MessageEncoder`, as described in the previous exercise. The constructor should have one parameter called `shift`. Define the method `encode` so that each letter is shifted by the value in `shift`. For example, if `shift` is 3, *a* will be replaced by *d*, *b* will be replaced by *e*, *c* will be replaced by *f*, and so on. (*Hint*: You may wish to define a private method that shifts a single character.)

17. Create a class `ShuffleCipher` that implements the interface `MessageEn-coder`, as described in Exercise 15. The constructor should have one parameter called `n`. Define the method `encode` so that the message is shuffled `n` times. To perform one shuffle, split the message in half and then take characters from each half alternately. For example, if the message is `abcdefghi`, the halves are `abcde` and `fghi`. The shuffled message is `afbgchdie`. (*Hint*: You may wish to define a private method that performs one shuffle.)

PROGRAMMING PROJECTS

myprogramminglab

Visit www.myprogramminglab.com to complete many of these Programming Projects online and get instant feedback.

1. Define a class named `Employee` whose objects are records for employees. Derive this class from the class `Person` given in Listing 8.1. An employee record inherits an employee's name from the class `Person`. In addition, an employee record contains an annual salary represented as a single value of type `double`, a hire date that gives the year hired as a single value of type `int`, and an identification number that is a value of type `String`. Give your class a reasonable complement of constructors, accessor methods, and mutator methods, as well as an `equals` method. Write a program to fully test your class definition.

2. Define a class called `Diamond` that is derived from either the class `ShapeBasics` (Listing 8.12) or the abstract class `ShapeBase` (Listing 8.19). A diamond has the same sort of top half as a `Triangle` object, and its bottom half is an inverted version of its top half. Define a utility class having public static methods, such as the method `skipSpaces` and other methods that draw horizontal lines, big V's, and inverted big V's. Recall that Self-Test Question 31 asked you to describe one method in this class.

3. Define two derived classes of the abstract class `ShapeBase` in Listing 8.19. Your two classes will be called `RightArrow` and `LeftArrow`. These classes will be like the classes `Rectangle` and `Triangle`, but they will draw arrows that point right and left, respectively. For example, the following arrow points to the right:

The size of the arrow is determined by two numbers, one for the length of the "tail" and one for the width of the arrowhead. (The width is the length of the vertical base.) The arrow shown here has a length of 16 and a width of 7. The width of the arrowhead cannot be an even number, so your constructors and mutator methods should check to make sure that it is always odd. Write a test program for each class that tests all the methods in the class. You can assume that the width of the base of the arrowhead is at least 3.

4. Define a class named `Doctor` whose objects are records for a clinic's doctors. Derive this class from the class `Person` given in Listing 8.1. A `Doctor` record has the doctor's name—defined in the class `Person`—a specialty as a string (for example Pediatrician, Obstetrician, General Practitioner, and so on), and an office-visit fee (use the type `double`). Give your class a reasonable complement of constructors and accessor methods, and an `equals` method as well. Write a driver program to test all your methods.

5. Define two classes, `Patient` and `Billing`, whose objects are records for a clinic. Derive `Patient` from the class `Person` given in Listing 8.1. A `Patient` record has the patient's name (defined in the class `Person`) and identification number (use the type `String`). A `Billing` object will contain a `Patient` object and a `Doctor` object (from Programming Project 4). Give your classes a reasonable complement of constructors and accessor methods, and an `equals` method as well. First write a driver program to test all your methods, then write a test program that creates at least two patients, at least two doctors, and at least two `Billing` records and then displays the total income from the `Billing` records.

6. Create a base class called `Vehicle` that has the manufacturer's name (type `String`), number of cylinders in the engine (type `int`), and owner (type `Person` given in Listing 8.1). Then create a class called `Truck` that is derived from `Vehicle` and has additional properties: the load capacity in tons (type `double`, since it may contain a fractional part) and towing capacity in tons (type `double`). Give your classes a reasonable complement of constructors and accessor methods, and an `equals` method as well. Write a driver program (no pun intended) that tests all your methods.

VideoNote
Deriving a class from Vehicle

7. Create the classes `RightTriangle` and `Rectangle`, each of which is derived from the abstract class `ShapeBase` in Listing 8.19. Then derive a class `Square` from the class `Rectangle`. Each of these three derived classes will have two additional methods to calculate area and circumference, as well as the inherited methods. Do not forget to override the method `drawHere`. Give your classes a reasonable complement of constructors and accessor methods. The `Square` class should include only one dimension, the side, and should automatically set the height and width to the length of the side. You can use dimensions in terms of the character width and line spacing even though they are undoubtedly unequal, so a square will not look square (just as a `Rectangle` object, as discussed in this chapter, won't look square). Write a driver program that tests all your methods.

8. Create a new class called `Dog` that is derived from the `Pet` class given in Listing 6.1 of Chapter 6. The new class has the additional attributes of

breed (type `String`) and `boosterShot` (type `boolean`), which is true if the pet has had its booster shot and false if not. Give your classes a reasonable complement of constructors and accessor methods. Write a driver program to test all your methods, then write a program that reads in five pets of type `Dog` and displays the name and breed of all dogs that are over two years old and have not had their booster shots.

9. Create an interface `MessageDecoder` that has a single abstract method `decode(cipherText)`, where `cipherText` is the message to be decoded. The method will return the decoded message. Modify the classes `SubstitutionCipher` and `ShuffleCipher`, as described in Exercises 16 and 17, so that they implement `MessageDecoder` as well as the interface `MessageEncoder` that Exercise 15 describes. Finally, write a program that allows a user to encode and decode messages entered on the keyboard.

10. For this Programming Project, start with implementations of the `Person`, `Student`, and `Undergraduate` classes as depicted in Figure 8.4 and the polymorphism demo in Listing 8.6. Define the `Employee`, `Faculty`, and `Staff` classes as depicted in Figure 8.2. The `Employee` class should have instance variables to store the employee ID as an `int` and the employee's department as a `String`. The `Faculty` class should have an instance variable to store the faculty member's title (e.g. "Professor of Computer Science") as a `String`. The `Staff` class should have an instance variable to store the staff member's pay grade (a number from 1 to 20) as an `int`. Every class should have appropriate constructors, accessors, and mutators, along with a `writeOutput` method that outputs all of the instance variable values.

Modify the program in Listing 8.6 to include at least one `Faculty` object and at least one `Staff` object in addition to the `Undergraduate` and `Student` objects. Without modification to the `for` loop, the report should output the name, employee ID, department, and title for the `Faculty` objects, and the name, employee ID, department, and pay grade for the `Staff` objects.

11. Modify the `Student` class in Listing 8.2 so that it implements the `Comparable` interface. Define the `compareTo` method to order `Student` objects based on the value in `studentNumber`. In a `main` method create an array of at least five `Student` objects, sort them using `Arrays.sort`, and output the students. They should be listed by ascending student number. Next, modify the `compareTo` method so it orders `Student` objects based on the lexicographic ordering of the `name` variable. Without modification to the `main` method, the program should now output the students ordered by name.

12. Create an application in a `JFrame` window that uses `JTextField` to get a message and encode or decode it using the classes described in the previous

programming project. Use four buttons to control the kind of cipher used and to specify whether to encode or decode the message. Also, use JText-Field to get the number used in the constructor for the ciphers.

Graphics

13. Enhance the classButtonDemo (Listing 8.20) so that the GUI behaves in all of the following ways: When the GUI first appears, both buttons are visible, but when one button is clicked, that button disappears and only the other button is visible. Thereafter, only one button is visible at a time; when the button is clicked, it disappears and the other button appears. When a button is clicked, the color changes, as in the version in Listing 8.20, and a smiley face appears when sunny is clicked and a frowning face appears when cloudy is clicked. When the program is first run, no face is visible in the GUI. Subsequent faces should replace the previous face. After ten button clicks, the message Only one more click appears. After one more click, the program ends.

Graphics

14. Create an application in a JFrame GUI that will draw a spiral using line segments.

Graphics

The equations for the points on a spiral are

$$x = 250 + k\theta \sin \theta$$

$$y = 250 + k\theta \sin \theta$$

You should draw 150 points. Start θ at 0 and increase it by 0.1 for each new point. Let k be 15. Set the size of the window to 500 by 500.

Answers to Self-Test Questions

1. *Overriding* refers to redefining a base-class method so that it has a different definition in a derived class. *Overloading* refers to giving a method name two definitions that have different parameter lists. In both cases, the methods have the same name. When you *override* a method definition, the new method definition given in the derived class has the exact same name, return type, and number and types of parameters. On the other hand, if the method in the derived class were to have a different number of parameters or a parameter of a different type from the method in the base class, the derived class would have both methods. That would be *overloading*. You can also overload method names in a single class definition without involving a base class.

2. No, a derived class does not inherit the private instance variables of its base class. However, SportsCar can access or change the values of speed, manufacturer, and numberOfCylinders if the base class provides public methods for that purpose.

3. Yes, it will have the methods. A derived class has all the public methods that the base class has, and they perform exactly the same actions in the derived class as they do in the base class. However, the derived class can contain a new overriding definition of a method, and the new definition will replace the old definition—provided it has the same name, return type, and number and types of parameters.

4. No.

5. No.

6. The method hasSameName is not listed in the class diagram for Student. So you follow the arrow to the class diagram for Person. The method has-SameName is in the class diagram for Person. The data type of this method's parameter is Person. But since you know that a Student is a Person, you can pass a Student object to this method as an argument. So the definition used for the method hasSameName is in the class definition of Person.

7. You start at the class diagram for Student. The method setStudentNumber is in the class diagram for Student, so you need look no further. The definition used for the method setStudentNumber is in the class definition of Student.

8.
```java
public class TitledPerson extends Person
{
    private String title;
    public TitledPerson()
    {
        super();
        title = "no title yet";
    }
/* //ALTERNATE DEFINITION OF DEFAULT CONSTRUCTOR:
    public TitledPerson()
    {
        this("no title yet");
    }
*/
    public TitledPerson(String initialName, String initialTitle)
    {
        super(initialName);
        title = initialTitle;
    }
    public void reset(String newName, String newTitle)
    {
        setName(newName);
        title = newTitle;
    }
    public String getTitle()
```

```
        {
            return title;
        }
        public void setTitle(String newTitle)
        {
            title = newTitle;
        }
        public void writeOutput()
        {
            System.out.println("Name: " + getName());
            System.out.println("Title: " + title);
        }
        public boolean equals(TitledPerson otherPerson)
        { // 'this' is optional in the next statement
            return this.sameName(otherPerson) &&
                this.title.equalsIgnoreCase(otherPerson.title);
        }
    }
```

9.
```
    public Student(String initialName)
    {
        this(initialName, 0);
    }
```

10.
```
    public void writeOutput()
    {
        System.out.println("Name:" + getName());
        System.out.println("Student Number: " + getStudentNumber());
        System.out.println("Student Level:" + level);
    }
```

11.
```
    public void reset(String newName, int newStudentNumber,
                      int newLevel)
    {
        setName(newName);
        setStudentNumber(newStudentNumber);
        level = newLevel;
    }
```

12. Yes. If class A is derived from class B, an object of type B can be referenced by a variable of type A and a variable of type B.

13. Variables of the types `Undergraduate`, `Student`, and `Person` can reference this object. (As you will find out soon in this chapter, a variable of type `Object` could also reference this object. `Object` is a predefined Java class that we are about to introduce in the next section.)

14. It is used as the name for a constructor of the base class. (See Listing 8.2.) When used as a receiving object, as in
```
super.writeOutput();
```

super indicates that the method in the base class should be called. In List-ing 8.4, for example, this statement calls the method writeOutput of the base class Student, as opposed to the method writeOutput of the class Undergraduate.

15. The keyword this, when used as a method name, names a constructor in the same class as the one being defined. The keyword super, when used as a method name, names a constructor for the base class of the derived class being defined.

16. Because the value returned by toString includes the new-line character '\n'.

17. a. Valid. A Student is a Person.
    b. Valid. An Undergraduate is a Person.
    c. Illegal. A Person object will not be able to perform all Student actions.
    d. Valid. An Undergraduate is a Student.
    e. Illegal. A Person object will not be able to perform all Undergraduate actions.
    f. Illegal. A Student object will not be able to perform all Undergraduate actions.
    g. Valid. A Student is an Object.
    h. Illegal. An Object object will not be able to perform all Student actions.

18. *Polymorphism* means using the process of dynamic binding to allow objects to behave correctly, regardless of the type of the variable that names them. The meaning of a method name depends on the object named by a variable.

19. *Dynamic binding* and *late binding* are two terms for the same thing (so we will give only one definition and only one example). With dynamic bind-ing, or late binding, the meaning of a method invocation is not bound to its location until you run the program. Java uses dynamic binding. When deciding which definition of a method to use, Java uses the definition in effect when the object was created using the new operator. It does not nec-essarily use the definition that applies to the type of the variable naming the object.

20. This question may not have a definitive answer. In the original definition of *polymorphism*, overloading was considered an example of polymorphism, and some books still use that old definition. In current usage, and in this book, overloading a method name is *not* an example of polymorphism.

21. No, they will produce different output. The first will output the name Sam and the Student Number 9999. The second will output the name Sam, the Student Number 9999, and the Student Level 1.

22. The definition of writeOutput given in Undergraduate is used—not the definition of writeOutput given in Person—because p references an Undergraduate object.

23. No. The class Oval must contain an implements clause stating that it implements Measurable.

24. Yes, a class can implement several interfaces. Simply list the interfaces, separated by commas, after the keyword implements.

25. Yes.

26. No.

27. Overriding.

28. Overriding.

29. Overloading.

30. No. A derived class cannot inherit a private method. We could make this move if we made skipSpaces a public method instead of a private one. A better solution would be to define a utility class having public static methods, like the method skipSpaces and other methods that draw horizontal lines, big V's, and inverted big V's.

31. The method drawHere can call two private methods, drawTop and drawBottom. We can use the method drawTop from Triangle, where the variable base is the width of the diamond. The method drawBottom is like drawTop, but with the following changes: startOfLine begins at the offset, and insideWidth begins at 2 * lineCount – 1; at the end of each iteration, startOfLine increases by 1 and insideWidth decreases by 2. The method skipSpaces is the same as in Triangle.

32. No, it is illegal because ShapeBase in Listing 8.19 is an abstract class.

33. Yes, it is legal.

34. No. You need to define it yourself (or copy it from this text or from the source code for this book that is available on the Web).

35. There is no difference.

36. In the constructor of the GUI derived from JFrame.

Exception Handling 9

9.1 BASIC EXCEPTION HANDLING   658
Exceptions in Java   659
Predefined Exception Classes   669

9.2 DEFINING YOUR OWN EXCEPTION CLASSES   671

9.3 MORE ABOUT EXCEPTION CLASSES   681
Declaring Exceptions (Passing the Buck)   681
Kinds of Exceptions   684
Errors   686

Multiple Throws and Catches   687
The `finally` Block   693
Rethrowing an Exception (*Optional*)   694
Case Study: A Line-Oriented Calculator   695

9.4 GRAPHICS SUPPLEMENT   707
Exceptions in GUIs   707
Programming Example: A `JFrame` GUI Using Exceptions   707

Chapter Summary   711   Programming Projects   715   Answers to Self-Test Questions   720

It's the exception that proves the rule.

—COMMON MAXIM (POSSIBLY A CORRUPTION OF SOMETHING LIKE *IT'S THE EXCEPTION THAT TESTS THE RULE*).

One way to write a program is first to assume that nothing unusual or incorrect will happen. For example, if the program takes an entry from a list, you might assume that the list is not empty. Once you have the program working for the core situation, in which things go as planned, you can then add code to take care of the exceptional cases. Java has a way to reflect this approach in your code. Basically, you write your code as if nothing very unusual will happen. After that, you add code for exceptional cases, using the facilities in Java. This chapter introduces you to these facilities.

OBJECTIVES

After studying this chapter, you should be able to

- Describe the notion of exception handling
- React correctly when certain exceptions occur
- Use Java's exception-handling facilities effectively in your own classes and programs

PREREQUISITES

Section 9.1 of this chapter requires only that you have read Chapters 1 through 6. The remainder of the chapter also requires some material about inheritance in Chapter 8. Arrays are also mentioned, but if you have not read Chapter 7 as yet, you can ignore those occurrences.

9.1 BASIC EXCEPTION HANDLING

Jack, be nimble,
Jack, be quick,
Jack, jump over the candle stick.

—ANONYMOUS

Java provides a way to handle certain kinds of special conditions in your program. This facility enables you to divide a program or method definition into separate sections for the normal case and for the exceptional case. In this way, you treat one larger programming task as two smaller and more easily doable programming tasks.

An **exception** is an object that signals the occurrence of an unusual event during the execution of a program. The process of creating this object—that is, generating an exception—is called **throwing an exception.** You place the code that deals with the exceptional case at another place in your program—perhaps in a separate class or method. The code that detects and deals with the exception is said to **handle the exception.**

An exception signals an unusual event during execution

Using exceptions is perhaps most important when a method has a special case that some programs will treat in one way, but others will treat in another way. As you will see, such a method can throw an exception if the special case occurs. This allows the special case to be handled outside of the method in a way that is appropriate to the situation. For example, if a division by zero occurs in a method, it may turn out that, for some invocations of the method, the program should end, but for other invocations of the method, something else should happen.

Java code can handle an exception that is thrown

Exceptions in Java

Most short programs need very little, if any, exception handling, and the exception handling they do use is often not easy to see in the code. For simplicity, we will use a toy program for our initial example. First we will write the program without using Java's exception-handling facilities, and then we will rewrite it using exception handling.

For this example, suppose that milk is such an important item in our society that people almost never allow themselves to run out of it, but still we would like our programs to accommodate the very unlikely situation of running out of milk. The basic code, which assumes that we do not run out of milk, might be as follows:

```
System.out.println("Enter number of donuts:");
int donutCount = keyboard.nextInt();

System.out.println("Enter number of glasses of milk:");
int milkCount = keyboard.nextInt();

double donutsPerGlass = donutCount / (double)milkCount;
System.out.println(donutCount + " donuts.");
System.out.println(milkCount + " glasses of milk.");
System.out.println("You have " + donutsPerGlass +
                " donuts for each glass of milk.");
```

If the number of glasses of milk entered is zero—that is, if we have no milk—this code will produce a division by zero. To take care of the unlikely scenario in which we run out of milk and get an erroneous division, we can add a test for this unusual situation. The complete program with this added test for the special situation is shown in Listing 9.1.

Now let's revise this program, using Java's exception-handling facilities. A division by zero produces an exception. So instead of avoiding such a division, we can let it occur but react to the resulting exception, as we have done in Listing 9.2. Because this example is so simple, we probably would not actually

LISTING 9.1   One Way to Deal with a Problem Situation

```java
import java.util.Scanner;

public class GotMilk
{
    public static void main(String[] args)
    {
        Scanner keyboard = new Scanner(System.in);

        System.out.println("Enter number of donuts:");
        int donutCount = keyboard.nextInt();

        System.out.println("Enter number of glasses of milk:");
        int milkCount = keyboard.nextInt();

        //Dealing with an unusual event without Java's exception
        //handling features:
        if (milkCount < 1)
        {
            System.out.println("No milk!");
            System.out.println("Go buy some milk.");
        }
        else
        {
            double donutsPerGlass = donutCount / (double)milkCount;
            System.out.println(donutCount + " donuts.");
            System.out.println(milkCount + " glasses of milk.");
            System.out.println("You have " + donutsPerGlass +
                                " donuts for each glass of milk.");
        }
        System.out.println("End of program.");
    }
}
```

Sample Screen Output

```
Enter number of donuts:
2
Enter number of glasses of milk:
0
No milk!
Go buy some milk.
End of program.
```

use exception handling here. The revised program as a whole is certainly not simpler than the original one in Listing 9.1. However, the code between the words try and catch is cleaner than the code used in the original program and hints at the advantage of handling exceptions. A clear organization and structure are essential for large, complex programs.

The code in Listing 9.2 is basically the same as the code in Listing 9.1, except that instead of the big `if-else` statement, this program has the following smaller `if` statement:

```
if (milkCount< 1)
    throw new Exception("Exception: No milk!");
```

This `if` statement says that if we have no milk, the program should do something exceptional. That something exceptional is given after the word

LISTING 9.2 An Example of Exception Handling *(part 1 of 2)*

```
import java.util.Scanner;

public class ExceptionDemo
{
    public static void main(String[] args)
    {
        Scanner keyboard = new Scanner(System.in);

        try
        {
            System.out.println("Enter number of donuts:");
            int donutCount = keyboard.nextInt();

            System.out.println("Enter number of glasses of milk:");
            int milkCount = keyboard.nextInt();

            if (milkCount < 1)
                throw new Exception("Exception: No milk!");

            double donutsPerGlass = donutCount / (double)milkCount;
            System.out.println(donutCount + " donuts.");
            System.out.println(milkCount + " glasses of milk.");
            System.out.println("You have " + donutsPerGlass +
                                    " donuts for each glass of milk.");
        }
        catch(Exception e)
        {
            System.out.println(e.getMessage());
            System.out.println("Go buy some milk.");
        }
        System.out.println("End of program.");
    }
}
```

This program is just a simple example of the basic syntax for exception handling.

try *block*

catch *block*

(continued)

LISTING 9.2 An Example of Exception Handling *(part 2 of 2)*

Sample Screen Output 1

```
Enter number of donuts:
3
Enter number of glasses of milk:
2
3 donuts.
2 glasses of milk.
You have 1.5 donuts for each glass of milk.
End of program.
```

Sample Screen Output 1

```
Enter number of donuts:
2
Enter number of glasses of milk:
0
Exception: No milk!
Go buy some milk.
End of program.
```

catch. The idea is that the normal situation is handled by the code following the word try and that the code following the word catch is used only in exceptional circumstances. Let's look at the details.

The basic way of handling exceptions in Java consists of a try-throw-catch threesome. A try **block** has the syntax

```
try
{
    Code_To_Try
}
```

A try block contains the code for the basic algorithm when everything goes smoothly. It is called a try block because you are not 100 percent sure that all will go smoothly, but you want to give it a try.

If something does go wrong, you want to throw an exception, which is a way of indicating that there is some sort of problem. So the basic outline, when we add a throw **statement,** is as follows:

A try block
detects an
exception

```
try
{
    Code_To_Try
    Possibly_Throw_An_Exception
    More_Code
}
```

The try block in Listing 9.2 has this form and contains the statement

A throw
statement throws
an exception

```
throw new Exception("Exception: No milk!");
```

If this throw statement executes, it creates a new object of the predefined class Exception with the expression

```
new Exception("Exception: No milk!")
```

and **throws** the exception object. The string "Exception: No milk!" is an argument for the constructor of the class Exception. The Exception object created here stores this string in an instance variable of the object so that it can be recovered later.

When an exception is thrown, the code in the surrounding block stops execution, and another portion of code, known as a **catch block,** begins execution. Executing the catch block is called **catching the exception.** When an exception is thrown, it should ultimately be caught by some catch block. In Listing 9.2, the catch block immediately follows the try block.

A catch block
deals with
a particular
exception

The catch block looks a little like a method definition that has a parameter. Although it is not a method definition, a catch block behaves like a method in some ways. It is a separate piece of code that is executed when a program executes a throw statement from within the preceding try block. This throw statement is similar to a method call, but instead of calling a method, it calls the catch block and causes the code in the catch block to be executed.

Let's examine the first line of the catch block in Listing 9.2:

```
catch(Exception e)
```

The identifier e looks like a parameter and acts very much like a parameter. So even though the catch block is not a method, we call this e the **catch-block parameter.** The catch-block parameter gives us a name for the exception that is caught, so that we can write code within the catch block to manipulate the exception object. The most common name for a catch-block parameter is e, but you can use any legal identifier.

When an exception object is thrown, it is plugged in for the catch-block parameter e, and the code in the catch block is executed. So in this case, you can think of e as the name of the exception object that was thrown. Every exception object has a method called getMessage, and unless you provide code specifying otherwise, this method retrieves the string that was given to the exception object by its constructor when the exception was thrown. In our example, the invocation e.getMessage() returns "Exception: No milk!"Thus, when the catch block in Listing 9.2 executes, it writes the following lines to the screen:

An exception's
getMessage
method returns a
description of the
exception

```
Exception: No milk!
Go buy some milk.
```

The class name preceding the catch-block parameter specifies what kind of exception the catch block can catch. The class Exception in our example indicates that this catch block can catch an exception of type Exception. Thus, a thrown exception object must be of type Exception in order for this

Only one catch
block executes
per try block

particular catch block to apply. As you will see, other types of exceptions are possible, and several catch blocks—one for each type of exception to be handled—can follow a try block. Only one of these catch blocks—the one corresponding to the type of exception thrown—can execute, however. The rest are ignored when handling a particular exception. Since all exceptions are of type Exception, the solitary catch block in our example will catch any exception. Although this might sound like a good idea, it generally is not. Several specific catch blocks are usually preferable to one general one.

For the program in Listing 9.2, when the user enters a positive number for the number of glasses of milk, no exception is thrown. The flow of control in this case is shown in Listing 9.3. Listing 9.4 shows the flow of control when an exception is thrown because the user enters zero or a negative number for the number of glasses of milk.

LISTING 9.3 Flow of Control When No Exception Is Thrown

```java
import java.util.Scanner;

public class ExceptionDemo
{
    public static void main(String[] args)
    {
        Scanner keyboard = new Scanner(System.in);

        try
        {
            System.out.println("Enter number of donuts:");
            int donutCount = keyboard.nextInt();

            System.out.println("Enter number of glasses of milk:");
            int milkCount = keyboard.nextInt();
            if (milkCount < 1)
                throw new Exception("Exception: No milk!");

            double donutsPerGlass = donutCount / (double)milkCount;
            System.out.println(donutCount + " donuts.");
            System.out.println(milkCount + " glasses of milk.");
            System.out.println("You have " + donutsPerGlass
                               + " donuts for each glass of milk.");
        }
        catch(Exception e)
        {
            System.out.println(e.getMessage());
            System.out.println("Go buy some milk.");
        }
        System.out.println("End of program.");
    }
}
```

Here we assume that the user enters a positive number for the number of glasses of milk.

milkCount is positive, so an exception is NOT thrown here.

This code is NOT executed.

LISTING 9.4   Flow of Control When an Exception Is Thrown

```
import java.util.Scanner;
public class ExceptionDemo
{
    public static void main(String[] args)
    {
        Scanner keyboard = new Scanner(System.in);
        try
        {
            System.out.println("Enter number of donuts:");
            int donutCount = keyboard.nextInt();

            System.out.println("Enter number of glasses of milk:");
            int milkCount = keyboard.nextInt();

            if (milkCount < 1)
                throw new Exception("Exception: No milk!");

            double donutsPerGlass = donutCount / (double)milkCount;
            System.out.println(donutCount + " donuts.");
            System.out.println(milkCount + " glasses of milk.");
            System.out.println("You have " + donutsPerGlass
                                        + " donuts for each glass of milk.");
        }

        catch(Exception e)
        {
            System.out.println(e.getMessage());
            System.out.println("Go buy some milk.");
        }

        System.out.println("End of program.");
    }
}
```

Here we assume that the user enters zero for the number of glasses of milk, and so an exception is thrown.

`milkCount` *is zero or negative, so an exception IS thrown here.*

This code is NOT executed.

In summary, a `try` block contains some code that can throw an exception. It is able to throw an exception because it either includes a `throw` statement or, as you will see later, invokes another method that contains a `throw` statement. The `throw` statement is normally executed only in exceptional circumstances, but when it is executed, it throws an exception of some exception class. (So far, `Exception` is the only exception class we have discussed, but we will talk about others soon.) When an exception is thrown, execution of the try block ends. All the rest of the code in the try block is ignored, and control passes to a suitable catch block, if one exists. A catch block applies only to an immediately preceding try block. If an exception is thrown and caught, that exception object is plugged in for the catch-block parameter and the statements in the catch block are executed. After the catch-block code is executed, the program proceeds with the code after the last catch block; it does not return to the try block. So none of the try-block code after the statement that threw the exception is executed, as shown in Listing 9.4. (Later, we will discuss what happens when there is no appropriate catch block.)

If an exception occurs within a try block, the rest of the block is ignored

Now let's look at what happens when no exception is thrown in a try block. When the try block executes normally to completion, without throwing an exception, program execution continues with the code after the last catch block. In other words, if no exception is thrown, all associated catch blocks are ignored, as shown in Listing 9.3.

If no exception occurs within a try block, the catch blocks are ignored

This explanation makes it seem as though a try-throw-catch sequence is equivalent to an if-else statement. They are almost equivalent, except for the message carried by the thrown exception. An if-else statement cannot send a message to one of its branches. This may not seem like much of a difference, but as you will see, the ability to send a message gives the exception-handling mechanism more versatility than an if-else statement.

Comparing try-throw-catch and if-else

REMEMBER An Exception Is an Object

A statement, such as

```
throw new Exception("Illegal character.");
```

does not just specify some action that is taken and forgotten. It creates an object that has a message. In this example, the message is "Illegalcharacter."

To see this, note that the previous statement is equivalent to the following:

```
Exception exceptObject = new Exception
    ("Illegal character.");
throw exceptObject;
```

The first of these statements invokes a constructor of the class Exception, creating an object of the class Exception. The second statement throws this exception object. This object and its message are available to a catch block, and so the effect of throwing an exception is more than just a transfer of control to the first statement of a catch block.

RECAP Throwing Exceptions

The `throw` statement throws an exception.

SYNTAX

```
throw new Exception_Class_Name(Possibly_Some_Arguments);
```

A `throw` statement is usually embedded in an `if` statement or an `if-else` statement. A `try` block can contain any number of explicit statements or any number of method invocations that might throw exceptions.

EXAMPLE

```
throw new Exception("Unexpected End of Input.");
```

RECAP Handling Exceptions

The `try` and `catch` statements, used together, are the basic mechanism for handling exceptions.

```
try
{
    Code_To_Try
    Possibly_Throw_An_Exception
    More_Code
}
catch (Exception_Class_NameCatch_Block_Parameter)
{
    Process_Exception_Of_Type_Exception_Class_Name
}
Possibly_Other_Catch_Blocks
```

If an exception is thrown within the `try` block, the rest of the `try` block is ignored and execution continues with the first `catch` block that matches the type of the thrown exception. After the `catch` block is completed, any code after the last `catch` block is executed.

If no exception is thrown in the `try` block, after it completes execution, program execution continues with the code after the last `catch` block. In other words, if no exception is thrown, the `catch` blocks are ignored.

More than one block is allowed for each `try` block, but each `catch` block can handle only one class of exceptions. *Catch_Block_Parameter* is an identifier that serves as a place holder for an exception that might

(continued)

be thrown. When an exception of the class *Exception_Class_Name* is thrown in the preceding `try` block, that exception is plugged in for the *Catch_Block_Parameter*. The code in the `catch` block may refer to the *Catch_Block_Parameter*. A common choice for *Catch_Block_Parameter* is e; however, you may use any legal identifier.

RECAP The `getMessage` **Method**

Every exception object has a `String` instance variable that contains some message, which typically identifies the reason for the exception. For example, if the exception is thrown by the statement

```
throw new Exception(String_Argument);
```

the value of this `String` instance variable is *String_Argument*. If the exception object is called e, the invocation e.`getMessage( )` returns this string.

SELF-TEST QUESTIONS

1. What output is produced by the following code?

   ```
   int waitTime = 46;
   try
   {
       System.out.println("Try block entered.");
       if (waitTime> 30)
           throw new Exception("Time Limit Exceeded.");
       System.out.println("Leaving try block.");
   }
   catch(Exception e)
   {
       System.out.println("Exception: " + e.getMessage());
   }
   System.out.println("After catch block");
   ```

2. What output would the code in the previous question produce if we changed 46 in the first statement to 12?

3. What is an exception? Is it an identifier? A variable? A method? An object? A class? Something else?

4. Is the following statement legal?

   ```
   Exception myException = new Exception("Hi Mom!");
   ```

5. In the code in Listing 9.2, how would the program's behavior change if you were to replace

```
if (milkCount < 1)
    throw new Exception("Exception: No milk!");
```

with the following?

```
if (milkCount < 1)
{
    Exception e = new Exception("Exception: No milk!");
    throw e;
}
```

6. Which part of the code given in Self-Test Question 1 is the statement?

7. What happens when a throw statement is executed? Discuss what happens in general, not simply what happens in the code in Self-Test Question 1 or some other sample code.

8. In the code given in Self-Test Question 1, identify the try block.

9. In the code given in Self-Test Question 1, identify the catch block.

10. In the code given in Self-Test Question 1, identify the catch-block parameter.

11. Would the code given in Self-Test Question 1 perform any differently if the catch block were changed to the following?

```
catch(Exception messenger)
{
    System.out.println("Exception: " +
                        messenger.getMessage());
}
```

12. Write a statement that will throw an exception of type Exception if the value of the String variable named status is "bad". The string recovered by getMessage should be "Exception thrown: Bad Status." You need not write the try block and catch block.

Predefined Exception Classes

When you learn about the methods of predefined classes, you will sometimes be told that they might throw certain types of exceptions. These exceptions are of predefined exception classes within the Java Class Library. If you use one of these methods, you can put the method invocation in a try block and follow it with a catch block to catch the exception. The names of predefined

Java provides
several exception
classes

exceptions are designed to be self-explanatory. Some examples of predefined exception classes are

```
BadStringOperationException
ClassNotFoundException
IOException
NoSuchMethodException
```

When you catch an exception of one of these predefined exception classes, the string returned by the getMessage method will usually provide you with enough information to identify the source of the exception. Thus, if you have a class called SampleClass, and this class has a method called doStuff, which throws exceptions of the class IOException, you might use the following code:

```
SampleClass object = new SampleClass();
try
{
    <Possibly some code>
    object.doStuff(); //may throw IOException
    <Possibly some more code>
}
catch(IOException e)
{
    <Code to deal with the exception, probably including the
     following:>
    System.out.println(e.getMessage());
}
```

If you think that continuing with program execution is infeasible after the exception occurs, the catch block can include a call to System.exit to end the program, as follows:

```
catch(IOException e)
{
    System.out.println(e.getmessage());
    System.out.println("Program aborted");
    System.exit(0);
}
```

VideoNote
**Using predefined exception
classes**

■ PROGRAMMING TIP   Catch Specific Exceptions

You can use the class Exception in a catch block, as we did in our initial examples, but catching a more specific exception, such as IOException, is more useful.   ■

■ PROGRAMMING TIP   Importing Exceptions

Most of the exceptions you will see in this book do not need to be imported, as they are in the package java.lang. Some, however, are in different packages and do need to be imported. For example, the class IOException is in the package java.util. When you examine the documentation for an exception, note which package contains it so you can provide an import statement if necessary.   ■

SELF-TEST QUESTIONS

myprogramminglab

13. Are the following statements legal?

    ```
    IOException sos = new IOException("Hello Houston!");
    throw sos;
    ```

14. Is the following catch block legal?

    ```
    catch(NoSuchMethodException exception)
    {
        System.out.println(exception.getmessage());
        System.exit(0);
    }
    ```

9.2 DEFINING YOUR OWN EXCEPTION CLASSES

I'll make an exception this time.

—MY MOTHER

You can define your own exception classes, but they must be derived classes of some already defined exception class. An exception class can be a derived class of any predefined exception class or of any exception class that you have already successfully defined. Our examples will be derived classes of the class Exception.

When you define an exception class, you typically define only constructors

When defining an exception class, the constructors are the most important and often the only methods, other than those inherited from the base class. For example, Listing 9.5 contains an exception class, called DivideByZeroException, whose only methods are a default constructor and a constructor having one String parameter. For our purposes, that is all we need to define. However, the class does inherit all the methods of the base class Exception. In particular, the class DivideByZeroException inherits the method getMessage, which returns a string message. In the definition of the default constructor, this string message is set by the following statement:

Call the base-class constructor and pass it a message

```
super("Dividing by Zero!");
```

This statement calls a constructor of the base class Exception. As we have already noted, when you pass a string to the constructor of the class Exception, the value of a String instance variable is set. You can recover this value later

LISTING 9.5 A Programmer-Defined Exception Class

```java
public class DivideByZeroException extends Exception
{
    public DivideByZeroException()
    {
        super("Dividing by Zero!");
    }
    public DivideByZeroException(String message)
    {
        super(message);
    }
}
```

You can do more in an exception constructor, but this form is common.

super is an invocation of the constructor for the base class Exception.

by calling the method getMessage, which is an ordinary accessor method of the class Exception and is inherited by the class DivideByZeroException. For example, Listing 9.6 shows a sample program that uses this exception class. The exception is created by the default constructor and then thrown, as follows:

```java
throw new DivideByZeroException();
```

LISTING 9.6 Using a Programmer-Defined Exception Class *(part 1 of 3)*

```java
import java.util.Scanner;
public class DivideByZeroDemo
{
    private int numerator;
    private int denominator;
    private double quotient;

    public static void main(String[] args)
    {
        DivideByZeroDemo oneTime = new DivideByZeroDemo();
        oneTime.doIt();
    }
    public void doIt()
    {
        try
        {
            System.out.println("Enter numerator:");
            Scanner keyboard = new Scanner(System.in);
            numerator = keyboard.nextInt();
```

We will present an improved version of this program later in this chapter.

(continued)

LISTING 9.6 Using a Programmer-Defined Exception Class *(part 2 of 3)*

```
        System.out.println("Enter denominator:");
        denominator = keyboard.nextInt();

        if (denominator == 0)
            throw new DivideByZeroException();

        quotient = numerator / (double)denominator;
        System.out.println(numerator + "/" + denominator +
                            " = " + quotient);
    }
    catch(DivideByZeroException e)
    {
        System.out.println(e.getMessage());
        giveSecondChance();
    }
    System.out.println("End of program.");
}
public void giveSecondChance()
{
    System.out.println("Try again:");
    System.out.println("Enter numerator:");
    Scanner keyboard = new Scanner(System.in);
    numerator = keyboard.nextInt();
    System.out.println("Enter denominator:");
    System.out.println("Be sure the denominator is not zero.");
    denominator = keyboard.nextInt();
```

Sometimes, dealing with an exceptional case without throwing an exception is better.

```
    if (denominator == 0)
    {
        System.out.println("I cannot do division by zero.");
        System.out.println("Since I cannot do what you want,");
        System.out.println("the program will now end.");
        System.exit(0);
    }

    quotient = ((double)numerator) / denominator;
    System.out.println(numerator + "/" + denominator +
                        " = " + quotient);
    }
}
```

(continued)

LISTING 9.6 **Using a Programmer-Defined Exception Class** *(part 3 of 3)*

Sample Screen Output 1

```
Enter numerator:
5
Enter denominator:
10
5/10 = 0.5
End of program.
```

Sample Screen Output 2

```
Enter numerator:
5
Enter denominator:
0
Dividing by Zero!
Try again.
Enter numerator:
5
Enter denominator:
Be sure the denominator is not zero.
10
5/10 = 0.5
End of program.
```

Sample Screen Output 3

```
Enter numerator:
5
Enter denominator:
0
Dividing by Zero!
Try again.
Enter numerator:
5
Enter denominator:
Be sure the denominator is not zero.
0
I cannot do division by zero.
Since I cannot do what you want,
the program will now end.
```

This exception is caught in the catch block, which contains the following statement:

```
System.out.println(e.getMessage());
```

This statement displays the following output on the screen, as shown in the sample screen output of Listing 9.6:

```
Dividing by Zero!
```

The class DivideByZeroException in Listing 9.5 also defines a second constructor. This constructor has one parameter of type String, allowing you to choose any message you like when you throw an exception. If the throw statement in Listing 9.6 was instead

```
throw new DivideByZeroException(
    "Oops. Shouldn't Have Used Zero.");
```

the statement

```
System.out.println(e.getMessage());
```

would have produced the following output to the screen:

```
Oops. Shouldn't Have Used Zero.
```

Notice that the try block in Listing 9.6 contains the normal part of the program. If all goes normally, that is the only code that will be executed, and the output will be like that shown in Sample Screen Output 1. In the exceptional case, when the user enters zero for the denominator, the exception is thrown and then is caught in the catch block. The catch block displays the message of the exception and then calls the method giveSecondChance. The method giveSecondChance gives the user a second chance to enter the input correctly and then carries out the calculation. If the user tries a second time to divide by zero, the method ends the program without throwing an exception. The method giveSecondChanceexists only for this exceptional case. So we have separated the code for the exceptional case of a division by zero into a separate method, where it will not clutter the code for the normal case.

A try block contains the normal case; a catch block deals with the exceptional case

■ PROGRAMMING TIP   Preserve getMessage in Your Own Exception Classes

For all predefined exception classes, the method getMessage will return the string that is passed as an argument to the constructor. (If no argument is passed to the constructor—that is, if you invoke the default constructor—getMessage returns a default string.) For example, suppose the exception is thrown as follows:

```
throw new Exception("This is a big exception!");
```

The value of the `String` instance variable is set to "This is a big exception!" If the exception object is called `e`, the method call `e.getMessage()` returns "This is a big exception!"

You should preserve this behavior of the method `getMessage` in any exception class you define. For example, suppose you define an exception class called `MySpecialException` and throw an exception as follows:

```
throw new MySpecialException("Wow, what an exception!");
```

If `e` is a name for the exception thrown, `e.getMessage()` should return "Wow, what an exception!" To ensure that the exception classes that you define behave in this way, be sure to include a constructor that has a string parameter and whose definition begins with a call to `super`, as illustrated by the following constructor:

```
public MySpecialException(String message)
{
    super(message);
    //There can be more code here, but often there is none.
}
```

The call to `super` is a call to a constructor of the base class. If the base-class constructor handles the message correctly, so will a class defined in this way.

You should also include a default constructor in each exception class. This default constructor should set up a default value to be retrieved by `getMessage`. The constructor's definition should begin with a call to `super`, as illustrated by the following constructor:

```
public MySpecialException()
{
    super("MySpecialException thrown.");
    //There can be more code here, but often there is none.
}
```

If `getMessage` works as we described for the base class, this default constructor will work correctly for the new exception class being defined. ■

REMEMBER Characteristics of Exception Objects

The two most important things about an exception object are

- The object's type—that is, the name of the exception class. The upcoming sections explain why this is important.
- The message that the object carries in an instance variable of type `String`. This string can be recovered by calling the accessor method `getMessage`. The string allows your code to send a message along with an exception object so that the `catch` block can recover the message.

■ PROGRAMMING TIP   When to Define an Exception Class

As a general rule, if you are going to insert a `throw` statement in your code, it is probably best to define your own exception class. That way, when your code catches an exception, your `catch` blocks can tell the difference between your exceptions and exceptions thrown by methods in predefined classes. For example, in Listing 9.6, we used the exception class `DivideByZeroException`, which we defined in Listing 9.5.

Although doing so would not be a good idea, you might be tempted to use the predefined class `Exception` to throw the exception in Listing 9.6, as follows:

```
throw new Exception("Dividing by Zero!");
```

You could then catch this exception with the `catch` block

```
catch(Exception e)
{
    System.out.println(e.getMessage());
    giveSecondChance();
}
```

Although this approach will work for the program in Listing 9.6, it is not the best technique, because the previous `catch` block will catch any exception, such as an `IOException`. An `IOException`, however, might need a different action than the one provided by a call to `giveSecondChance`. Thus, rather than using the class `Exception`to deal with a division by zero, it is better to use the more specialized programmer-defined class `DivideByZeroException`, as we did in Listing 9.6.   ■

RECAP Programmer-Defined Exception Classes

You can define your own exception classes, but every such class must be derived from an existing exception class—either a predefined class or one defined by you.

GUIDELINES

- Use the class `Exception` as the base, if you have no compelling reason to use any other class as the base class.
- You should define at least two constructors, including a default constructor and one that has a single `String` parameter.
- You should start each constructor definition with a call to the constructor of the base class, using `super`. For the default constructor, the call to `super` should have a string argument that indicates what kind of exception it is. For example,

```
super("Tidal Wave Exception thrown!");
```

(continued)

If the constructor has a `String` parameter, the parameter should be the argument in the call to super. For example,

```
super(message);
```

In this way, the string can then be recovered using the getMessage method.

- Your exception class inherits the method getMessage. You should not override it.
- Normally, you do not need to define any other methods, but it is legal to do so.

EXAMPLE

```
public class TidalWaveException extends Exception
{
    public TidalWaveException()
    {
        super("Tidal Wave Exception thrown!");
    }
    public TidalWaveException(String message)
        super(message);
    }
}
```

`super` is a call to the constructor of the base class `Exception`

myprogramminglab

VideoNote
Using your exception classes

SELF-TEST QUESTIONS

15. Define an exception class called `CoreBreachException`. The class should have a default constructor. If an exception is thrown using this zero-argument constructor, getMessage should return "Core Breach! Evacuate Ship!" The class should also define a constructor having a single parameter of type `String`. If an exception is thrown using this constructor, getMessageshould return the value that was used as an argument to the constructor.

16. Repeat the previous question, but instead name the class `MessageTooLongException`. Also, if an exception is thrown using the default constructor, getMessage should return "Message Too Long!"

17. Suppose the exception class `ExerciseException` is defined as follows:

```
public class ExerciseException extends Exception
{
```

```java
    public ExerciseException()
    {
        super("Exercise exception thrown!");
        System.out.println("Exception thrown.");
    }
    public ExerciseException(String message)
    {
        super(message);
        System.out.println("ExerciseException invoked "+
            "with an argument.");
    }
}
```

What output would be produced by the following unlikely code?

```java
ExerciseException e = new ExerciseException("Do Be Do");
System.out.println(e.getMessage());
```

18. Suppose the exception class CrazyException is defined as follows:

```java
public class CrazyException extends Exception
{
    public CrazyException()
    {
        super("Crazy exception thrown!");
        System.out.println("Wow, Crazy exception thrown!");
    }
    public CrazyException(String message)
    {
        super(message);
        System.out.println("Wow, crazy exception thrown with "+
            "an argument!");
    }
    public void crazyMethod()
    {
        System.out.println("Message is " + getMessage());
    }
}
```

What output would be produced by the following unlikely code?

```java
CrazyException exceptionObject = new CrazyException();
System.out.println(exceptionObject.getMessage());
exceptionObject.crazyMethod();
```

19. Suppose the exception class DoubleException is defined as follows:

```java
public class DoubleException extends Exception
{
    public DoubleException()
    {
```

```
                super("Double exception thrown!");
        }
        public DoubleException(String message)
        {
            super(message + " " + message);
        }
    }
```

What output would be produced by the following unlikely code?

```
try
{
    System.out.println("try block entered:");
    int number = 42;
    if (number > 0)
        throw new DoubleException("DoubleException thrown!");
    System.out.println("Leaving try block.");
}
catch(DoubleException exceptionObject)
{
    System.out.println(exceptionObject.getMessage());
}
System.out.println("End of code.");
```

20. Suppose that, in the catch block of the previous question, we change the type DoubleException to Exception. How would this change affect the output?

21. Suppose that, in Self-Test Question 19, we change the value of number from 42 to –99. How would this change affect the output?

22. Although an exception class normally carries only a string message, you can define exception classes to carry a message of any type. You can give your exception class instance variables and methods. For example, objects of the following type can also carry an int "message," as well as a string message:

```
public class IntException extends Exception
{
    private int intMessage;
    public IntException()
    {
        super("IntException thrown!");
    }
    public IntException(String message)
    {
        super(message + " " + message);
    }
    public IntException(int number)
```

```
    {
        super("IntException thrown!");
            intMessage = number;
    }
    public int getNumber()
    {
        returnintMessage;
    }
}
```

What output would be produced by the following unlikely code?

```
IntException e = new IntException(42);
System.out.println(e.getNumber());
System.out.println(e.getMessage());
```

23. Can you derive an exception class from the predefined class `IOException`, or must it be derived from the class `Exception`?

9.3 MORE ABOUT EXCEPTION CLASSES

buck n. 1. A counter or marker formerly passed from one poker player to another to indicate an obligation, especially one's turn to deal. 2. Informal: Obligation to account for something; responsibility: tried to pass the buck . . .

—*THE AMERICAN HERITAGE DICTIONARY OF THE ENGLISH LANGUAGE,* FOURTH EDITION

The buck stops here.

—SIGN ON HARRY S TRUMAN'S DESK WHILE HE WAS PRESIDENT

In this section, we discuss techniques for using exceptions that go beyond the basics but are still fundamental.

Declaring Exceptions (Passing the Buck)

Sometimes it makes sense to delay handling of an exception. For example, you might have a method whose code throws an exception, but you may not want to catch the exception in that method. Perhaps some programs that use the method should simply end if the exception is thrown, and other programs that use the method should do something else. As a result, you would not know what to do about the exception if you caught it inside the method. In these cases, it makes sense not to catch the exception in the method definition, but instead to have any code that uses the method place the method invocation in a `try` block and catch the exception in a `catch` block that follows that `try` block.

A method might not catch an exception that its code throws

If a method does not catch an exception, it must at least warn programmers that any invocation of the method might possibly throw an exception. This warning is called a `throws` **clause**. For example, a method that might throw a

A method that does not handle an exception that it throws must have a throws clause in its heading

DivideByZeroException but that does not catch the exception would have a heading like the following one:

```
public void sampleMethod() throws DivideByZeroException
```

The part throwsDivideByZeroException is a throws clause. It states that an invocation of the method sampleMethod might throw a DivideByZeroException.

Most exceptions that might be thrown when a method is invoked must be accounted for in one of two ways:

- Catch the possible exception in a catch block within the method definition.
- Declare the possible exception by writing a throws clause in the method's heading and let whoever uses the method worry about how to handle the exception.

In any one method, you can mix these two alternatives, catching some exceptions and declaring others in a throws clause.

You already know about handling exceptions in a catch block. The second technique is a form of "passing the buck." For example, suppose methodA has a throws clause as follows:

```
public void methodA() throws DivideByZeroException
```

In this case, methodA is absolved of the responsibility of catching any exceptions of type DivideByZeroException that might occur when methodA is executed. If, however, the definition of methodB includes an invocation of methodA, methodB must deal with the exception. When methodA adds the throws clause, it is "saying" to methodB, "If you invoke me, you must worry about any DivideByZeroException that I throw." In effect, methodA has passed the responsibility ("passed the buck") for any exceptions of type DivideByZeroException from itself to any method that calls it.

A method that can throw several different exceptions has only one throws clause

Of course, if methodA passes the buck to methodB by including a throws clause in its heading, methodB can also pass the buck to whatever method calls it by including the same throws clause in its definition. But in a well-written program, every exception that is thrown should eventually be caught by a catch block in some method that does not pass the buck.

A throws clause can contain more than one exception type. In such cases, you separate the exception types with commas, as follows:

```
public int myMethod() throws IOException, DivideByZeroException
```

If a derived class overrides a base-class method that has a throws clause, you cannot add exceptions to the throws clause of the new overriding method.

REMEMBER Throwing an Exception Can End a Method

If a method throws an exception, and the exception is not caught inside the method, the method invocation ends immediately after the exception is thrown.

So if this method needs to throw an exception that is not already listed in the throws clause of the overridden method in the base class, the overriding method must handle that exception in try-catch blocks. You can, however, declare fewer exceptions in the throws clause of the overriding method.

Listing 9.7 shows a revision of the program in Listing 9.6 so that the normal case is in a method called doNormalCase. This method can throw a

A throws clause in an overriding method can declare fewer, but not more, exceptions than the overridden method declares

LISTING 9.7   Passing the Buck Using a throws Clause

```java
import java.util.Scanner;

public class DoDivision
{
    private int numerator;
    private int denominator;
    private double quotient;

    public static void main(String[] args)
    {
        DoDivision doIt = new DoDivision();
        try
        {
            doIt.doNormalCase();
        }
        catch(DivideByZeroException e)
        {
            System.out.println(e.getMessage());
            doIt.giveSecondChance();
        }
        System.out.println("End of program.");
    }
    public void doNormalCase() throws DivideByZeroException
    {
        System.out.println("Enter numerator:");
        Scanner keyboard = new Scanner(System.in);
        numerator = keyboard.nextInt();
        System.out.println("Enter denominator:");
        denominator = keyboard.nextInt();
        if (denominator == 0)
            throw new DivideByZeroException();

        quotient = numerator / (double)denominator;
        System.out.println(numerator + "/" + denominator +
                           " = " + quotient);
    }
```

The method giveSecondChance *and the input/output samples are identical to those given in Listing 9.6*

DivideByZeroException, but it does not catch it. Thus, we need to declare this possible exception in a throws clause in the heading of the method's definition. If we set up our program in this way, the case in which nothing goes wrong is completely isolated and easy to read. It is not even cluttered by try blocks and catch blocks. However, when the method main calls the method doNormalCase, it must do so within a try block.

RECAP **The throws Clause**

If you define a method that might throw an exception of some particular class, normally you either must catch the exception within a catch block in the method definition or declare the exception class by writing a throws clause in the method's heading.

SYNTAX

```
public Type Method_Name(Parameter_List)
throws List_Of_Exceptions
    Body_Of_Method
```

EXAMPLE

```
public void methodA(int n) throws IOException,
MyException
{
    ...
}
```

REMEMBER **throw Versus throws**

The keyword throw is used to throw an exception, whereas throws is used in a method's heading to declare an exception. Thus, a throw statement throws an exception, but a throws clause declares one.

Kinds of Exceptions

Thus far, we have said that, in most cases, an exception must either be caught in a catch block or be declared in a throws clause in a method's heading. That is the basic rule, but there are exceptions to this rule. (An exception to a rule about exceptions! Seems reasonable enough.) Java has some exceptional exceptions that you do not need to account for in this way—although you can catch them in a catch block if you want to.

All Java exceptions are categorized as either checked or unchecked. A **checked exception** must either be caught in a catch block or declared in a throws clause. Such exceptions often indicate serious problems that likely should lead to program termination. The exceptions `BadStringOperationException`, `ClassNotFoundException`, `IOException`, and `NoSuchMethodException`—mentioned earlier in this chapter—are all checked exceptions in the Java Class Library.

An **unchecked,** or **run-time, exception** need not be caught in a `catch` block or declared in a `throws` clause. These exceptions usually indicate that something is wrong with your code and that you should fix it. Normally, you would not have written a `throw` statement for these exceptions. They are usually thrown during the evaluation of an expression or by a method in predefined classes. For example, if your program attempts to use an array index that is either too small or too large, an `ArrayIndexOutOfBoundsException` occurs. If an arithmetic operation causes a problem, such as a division by zero, an `ArithmeticException` occurs. For such exceptions, you should repair your code, not add a `catch` block. Note that an uncaught run-time exception terminates program execution.

How do you know whether an exception is checked or unchecked? You can consult the documentation for the Java Class Library to learn the exception's base class and from that deduce whether it is checked or unchecked. Figure 9.1 shows the hierarchy of the predefined exception classes. The class `Exception` is the base class of all exceptions. Every exception class is a descendant of the class `Exception`—that is, it is derived either directly from the class `Exception` or from a class that ultimately is derived from the class `Exception`. Classes of unchecked exceptions are derived from the class `RuntimeException`. All other exception classes are of checked exceptions that must be caught.

> Some exceptions do not need to be caught

> All exception classes are derived from the predefined class `Exception`.

FIGURE 9.1 **Hierarchy of the Predefined Exception Classes**

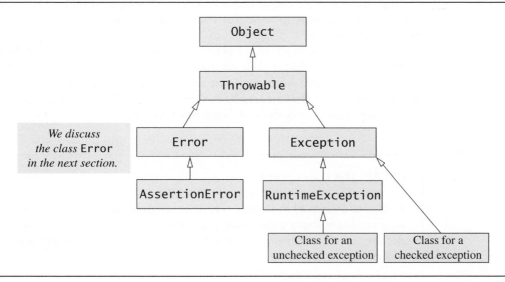

You need not worry too much about which exceptions you do and do not need to catch or declare in a `throws` clause. If you fail to account for some exception that Java requires you to handle, the compiler will tell you about it. You can then either catch it or add it to a `throws` clause.

RECAP Kinds of Exceptions

Every exception class is a descendant class of the class `Exception`. `RuntimeException` is derived from `Exception`, and classes derived from `RuntimeException` or any of its descendants represent unchecked exceptions. Such exceptions do not need to be caught or declared in a `throws` clause of a method's heading. All other exceptions are checked and must be either caught or declared in a `throws` clause.

Errors

An error is not an exception, but is similar to one

An **error** is an object of the class `Error`, which is derived from `Throwable`, as Figure 9.1 indicates. Note that `Throwable` is also the base class of `Exception`. Technically speaking, the class `Error` and its descendant classes are not considered exception classes, because they are not descendants of the class `Exception`. To us, however, they look like exceptions. Objects of the class `Error` are similar to unchecked exceptions in that we need not catch or declare them in a `throws` clause, even though you could. Errors are more or less beyond your control. For example, an `OutOfMemoryError` occurs if your program has run out of memory. This means that you must either revise your program to make it more efficient in its use of memory, change a setting to let Java access more memory, or buy more memory for your computer. Adding a `catch` block will not help in this case.

When we discussed the `assert` operator and assertion checking in Chapter 4, we said that if your program contains an assertion check and the assertion check fails, your program will end with an error message. What actually happens is that an `AssertionError` occurs. As the name suggests, the class `AssertionError` is derived from the class `Error`.

RECAP The Class `Error`

Errors are objects of the class `Error` that are generated when certain abnormal conditions occur. Most programs should not catch them or declare them in a `throws` clause. Errors are technically not exceptions, even though they look like them.

Multiple Throws and Catches

A try block can potentially throw any number of exceptions, which can be of different types. Each catch block can catch exceptions of only one type, but you can catch exceptions of different types by placing more than one catch block after a try block. For example, the program in Listing 9.8

A try block may be followed by several catch blocks

LISTING 9.8 Catching Multiple Exceptions *(part 1 of 2)*

```java
import java.util.Scanner;
```

This is just an example of handling exceptions using two catch *blocks.*

```java
public class TwoCatchesDemo
{
    public static void main(String[] args)
    {
        try
        {
            System.out.println("Enter number of widgets " +
                            "produced:");
            Scanner keyboard = new Scanner(System.in);
            int widgets = keyboard.nextInt();
            if (widgets < 0)
                throw new NegativeNumberException("widgets");

            System.out.println("How many were defective?");
            int defective = keyboard.nextInt();
            if (defective < 0)
                throw new NegativeNumberException("defective " +
                                            "widgets");

            double ratio = exceptionalDivision(widgets,
                                            defective);
            System.out.println("One in every " + ratio +
                            " widgets is defective.");
        }
        catch(DivideByZeroException e)
        {
            System.out.println("Congratulations! A perfect " +
                            "record!");
        }
        catch(NegativeNumberException e)
        {
            System.out.println("Cannot have a negative number of " +
                            e.getMessage());
        }
```

(continued)

LISTING 9.8 Catching Multiple Exceptions *(part 2 of 2)*

```
        System.out.println("End of program.");
    }
    public static double exceptionalDivision(double numerator,
                double denominator) throws DivideByZeroException
    {
        if (denominator == 0)
            throw new DivideByZeroException();
        return numerator / denominator;
    }
}
```

Sample Screen Output 1

```
Enter number of widgets produced:
1000
How many were defective?
500
One in every 2.0 widgets is defective.
End of program.
```

Sample Screen Output 2

```
Enter number of widgets produced:
-10
Cannot have a negative number of widgets
End of program.
```

Sample Screen Output 3

```
Enter number of widgets produced:
1000
How many were defective?
0
Congratulations! A perfect record!
End of program.
```

has two catch blocks after its try block. One catch block is for exceptions of type DivideByZeroException—defined earlier in Listing 9.5—and the second is for exceptions of type NegativeNumberException, which is defined in Listing 9.9.

LISTING 9.9   The Class NegativeNumberException

```
public class NegativeNumberException extends Exception
{
    public NegativeNumberException()
    {
        super("Negative Number Exception!");
    }
    public NegativeNumberException(String message)
    {
        super(message);
    }
}
```

■ **PROGRAMMING TIP**   **Catch the More Specific Exception First**

When catching multiple exceptions, the order of the catch blocks can be important. When an exception is thrown in a try block, the catch blocks are examined in order of appearance. The first block that matches the type of the exception thrown is the one that executes. Thus, the following ordering of catch blocks would not be good:

```
catch(Exception e) //This catch block should not be first.
{
    . . .
}
catch(DivideByZeroException e)
{
    . . .
}
The second catch block can never be reached.
```

With this ordering, the catch block for DivideByZeroException would never be used, because all exceptions are caught by the first catch block. Fortunately, the compiler will probably warn you about this problem.

The correct ordering is to reverse the catch blocks so that the more specific exception comes before its parent exception class, as shown in the following code:

The order of catch blocks matters

```
catch(DivideByZeroException e)
{
    . . .
}
catch(Exception e)
{
    . . .
}
```

■

■ **PROGRAMMING TIP**   User Input

When your program reads input data entered by the user of your program, you likely will need to deal with exceptions. Users can type almost anything as input, unintentionally or not! ■

■ **PROGRAMMING TIP**   Exception Handling and Information Hiding

You know that a method invocation can cause an exception that is declared in the method's `throws` clause. Any time an exception is thrown, regardless of whether you write a `throw` statement or call a method, you handle it in the exact same way: It is either caught in a `catch` block or declared in another `throws` clause. When analyzing a method invocation that might throw an exception, do not think about where in the method definition the `throw` statement is located. It does not matter how the exception is thrown. All that matters is that the method invocation might throw an exception. The exception is handled in the same way no matter what happens inside the method. ■

myprogramminglab   ## SELF-TEST QUESTIONS

24. Correct the following method definition by adding a suitable `throws` clause:

```
public void doStuff(int n)
{
    if (n < 0)
        throw new Exception("Negative number.");
}
```

25. What happens if you invoke a method and it throws a checked exception that it does not catch?

26. Consider an invocation of method A. Suppose that method A calls method B, and method B calls method C. If method C throws an exception that it does not catch itself, where might the exception be caught? In B? In A? Outside of A?

27. What output will be produced by the following code? The definition of the class `NegativeNumberException` is given in the preceding material, but you do not need to look at it to answer this question.

```
try
{
    int n = 7;
    if (n > 0)
        throw new Exception();
    else if (n < 0)
        throw new NegativeNumberException();
    else
        System.out.println("Hello!");
}
catch(NegativeNumberException e)
{
    System.out.println("First catch.");
}
catch(Exception e)
{
    System.out.println("Second catch");
}
System.out.println("End of code");
```

28. Repeat Self-Test Question 27, but change the value of n from 7 to –7.

29. Repeat Self-Test Question 27, but change the value of n from 7 to 0.

30. What output is produced by the following program?

```
public class Question30
{
    public static void main(String[] args)
    {
        Question30 object = new Question30();
        try
        {
            System.out.println("Trying");
            object.sampleMethod();
            System.out.println("Trying after call.");
        }
        catch(Exception e)
        {
            System.out.println("Catching");
            System.out.println(e.getMessage());
        }
    }
    public void sampleMethod() throws Exception
    {
        System.out.println("Starting sampleMethod.");
        throw new Exception("From sampleMethod with love.");
    }
}
```

FAQ When should my code throw an exception?

The use of a throw statement should be reserved for cases in which it is unavoidable. If you are tempted to include a throw statement, think about how you might write your program or class definition without this throw statement. If you can think of an alternative that produces reasonable code, you probably should not throw an exception. But if the way to deal with an exceptional condition depends on how and where a method is invoked, the best approach is to let the programmer who invokes the method handle the exception. In all other situations, it is preferable to avoid throwing exceptions.

Predefined methods often leave exception handling to the programmer invoking the method. When you learn about a predefined method, you may be told that it throws exceptions of certain kinds. You, as the programmer who uses the predefined method, are then expected to handle any exception thrown by the method.

■ PROGRAMMING TIP   Where to Throw an Exception

Thus far, we have used some very simple code to illustrate the basic concepts of exception handling. However, our examples were unrealistically simple. In general, you should separate throwing an exception and catching the exception into separate methods. For example, one method might have the following form:

```java
public void methodA() throws MyException
{
    ...
    throw new MyException("Blah Blah Blah");
    ...
}
```

and some other method—perhaps even in some other class—might be

```java
public void methodB()
{
    ...
    try
    {
        ...
        methodA();
        ...
    }
    catch(MyException e)
    {
        ... //Deal with the exception.
    }
    ...
}
```

The reason for this is related to the previous FAQ on when you should throw an exception. If a method knows how to deal with a certain situation, it likely should do so without throwing an exception. If an exception is thrown by some code within a method—for example, if your method invokes another method that throws an exception—handle it if you can. Otherwise, declare the exception in a `throws` clause in your method, and let a different method contain the `catch` block. ■

VideoNote
Using a throws clause

GOTCHA Nested try-catch Blocks

Although you can place a `try` block and its subsequent `catch` blocks inside a larger `try` block or inside a larger `catch` block, doing so is rarely useful. If you are tempted to nest these blocks, you should at least consider whether there is another way to organize your code. For example, you might eliminate one or more `try` blocks completely, or you could place the inner `try-catch` blocks inside a method definition and invoke that method within the outer `try` block or `catch` block. It is almost always better to avoid nested `try-catch` blocks.

Suppose, however, that you do use nested `try-catch` blocks. If you place a `try` block and its subsequent `catch` blocks inside a larger `try` block, and an exception is thrown in the inner `try` block but is not caught in the inner `catch` blocks, the exception is thrown to the outer `try` block for processing and might be caught in one of the outer `catch` blocks. If you place a `try` block and its subsequent `catch` blocks inside a larger `catch` block, you will need to use different names for the catch-block parameters in the inner and outer blocks, respectively. After all, `try` blocks and `catch` blocks are blocks, so you need to remember how Java handles nested blocks of any kind. ■

The finally Block

You can add a `finally` block after a sequence of `catch` blocks. The code in the `finally` block is executed whether or not an exception is thrown. This block gives you an opportunity to clean up any loose ends that linger as a result of the exception.

A `finally` block always executes

The general syntax is as follows:

```
try
{
    ...
}
Catch_Block(s)
finally
{
    Some_Code //Always executed.
}
```

Possible outcomes
with a finally
block

To see the significance and potential usefulness of a finally block, suppose that the try-catch-finally blocks are inside a method definition. After all, every set of try-catch-finally blocks is inside some method, even if it is only the method main.

One of three possible outcomes will occur when the code in the try-catch-finally blocks is run:

- The try block runs to the end, and no exception is thrown. In this situation, the finally block executes after the try block.
- An exception is thrown within the try block and is caught in a corresponding catch block positioned after the try block. In this case, the finally block executes after the catch block executes.
- An exception is thrown in the try block, but no matching catch block exists to catch the exception. The method invocation ends, and the exception object is thrown to the enclosing method. In this case, the finally block executes before the method ends. Note that you cannot account for this third case simply by placing code after the string of catch blocks.

A catch block
can throw an
exception

At this stage of your programming, you might not have much need for a finally block, but we've included this description of it for completeness. At some point, you may find it useful.

Rethrowing an Exception (*Optional*)

It is legal to throw an exception within a catch block. In rare cases, you may want to catch an exception and then, depending either on the string produced by getMessage or on something else, decide to throw the same or a different exception for handling further up the chain of exception-handling blocks.

SELF-TEST QUESTIONS

31. Can you have a try block and corresponding catch blocks inside another, larger try block?

32. Can you have a try block and corresponding catch blocks inside another, larger catch block?

33. Consider the following program:

```java
public class Question33
{
    public static void main(String[ ] args)
    {
        try
        {
            sampleMethod(99);
        }
```

```
        catch(Exception e)
        {
            System.out.println("Caught in main.");
        }
    }
    public static void sampleMethod(int n) throws Exception
    {
        try
        {
            if (n > 0)throw new Exception();
            else if (n < 0)
                throw new NegativeNumberException();
            else
                System.out.println("No exception.");
            System.out.println("Still in sampleMethod.");
        }
        catch (NegativeNumberException e)
        {
            System.out.println("Caught in sampleMethod.");
        }
        finally
        {
            System.out.println("In finally block.");
        }
        System.out.println("After finally block.");
    }
}
```

a. What output does the program produce?
b. What output would the program produce if the argument to sampleMethod were –99 instead of 99?
c. What output would the program produce if the argument to sampleMethod were 0 instead of 99?

CASE STUDY A Line-Oriented Calculator

We have been asked to write a program that can be used as a calculator, similar to a handheld calculator. The calculator should do addition, subtraction, multiplication, and division. For our initial draft of the program, we won't use a windowing interface, but instead we will use simple line-by-line text input and text output—like the previous programs in this chapter.

Specify the task

We need to specifically define the user interface. Let's tell the user to enter an operation, a space, and a number, all on one line, as in the following example:

    + 3.4

Any extra whitespace before or after the operation or the number is optional. As the user enters more operations and numbers, the program keeps track of the results of the operations performed so far. These results are like the number displayed on a handheld calculator—the running result of the operations. On the screen, it is shown as, for example,

```
updated result = 3.4
```

The user can add, subtract, multiply, and divide, using instructions such as

```
* 3
```

Design the user interface

For example, we might have the following interaction between the user and the program:

```
result = 0
+ 80
result + 80 = 80
updated result = 80
- 2
result - 2 = 78
updated result = 78
e
```

The user's input is shown in color, and the black text is output from the program. The program assumes that the initial "result" is zero. The program echoes the input data and shows the result of each computation. To end a set of calculations, let's ask the user to enter the letter E in either uppercase or lowercase.

Design a class

After our suggested interface is accepted, we can begin designing a class for a calculator. We can give the class a `main` method that is a complete, simple calculator program that adheres to our specifications for a user interface. Later, we can design a more elaborate interface and let the calculator be a bit more powerful. Ultimately, we could give our calculator a windowing interface.

Keep track of the result in an instance variable `result`

Let's maintain the current result in a private instance variable called `result`. The program always adds, subtracts, multiplies, or divides the current result and the number entered. For instance, if the user enters

```
- 9.5
```

and the current value of `result` is 80, the value of `result` is changed to 70.5.

Let's give the class at least the following methods:

- A method `reset` to reset the value of `result` to zero
- A method `evaluate` to calculate the result of one operation
- A method `doCalculation` that performs a series of operations
- An accessor method `getResult` that returns the value of the instance variable `result`
- A mutator method `setResult` that sets the value of `result` to any specified value

Desired methods

The definitions of the methods `reset`, `setResult`, and `getResult` are routine, but the methods `evaluate` and `doCalculation` require a bit of thought. To simplify the first draft of our code, let's assume that everything will go smoothly. That is, nothing unusual will occur to cause an exception. We might note possible exceptions as we think of them, but we will not write any exception-handling code until after the core of the class is designed.

To make our class more versatile, the method `evaluate` can return the result of one operation, rather than updating the instance variable `result` directly. Thus, we can specify the method as follows:

Specification of a method to return the result of one operation

```
/**
Returns n1 op n2,
provided op is one of '+', '-', '*', or '/'.
*/
public double evaluate(char op, double n1, double n2)
```

The heart of the calculator's action is performed by the method `doCalculation`, which we specify as

```
/**
Interacts with the user to perform a series
of calculations and updates result.
*/
public void doCalculation()
```

Specification of a method to return the result of a series of operations

Let's develop `doCalculation` first. The method should repeat the following sequence again and again until the user enters a sentinel such as the letter E:

```
char nextOp = (keyboard.next()).charAt(0);
double nextNumber = keyboard.nextDouble();
result = evaluate(nextOp, result, nextNumber);
```

Here `keyboard.next()` reads the operator as a string, and `charAt(0)` returns it as a character. Also, `nextOp` and `nextNumber` are local variables, while `result` is the instance variable.

We will embed the previous code in a loop within `doCalculation`, as follows:

```
boolean done = false;
while (!done)
{
    char nextOp = (keyboard.next()).charAt(0);
    if ((nextOp == 'e') || (nextOp == 'E'))
        done = true;
    else
    {
        double nextNumber = keyboard.nextDouble();
        result = evaluate(nextOp, result, nextNumber);
        System.out.println("result " + nextOp + " " +
                            nextNumber + " = " + result);
        System.out.println("updated result = " + result);
    }
}
```

The basic logic of the method doCalculation

Next, let's consider the method `evaluate`. We can write a large `switch` statement like the following one:

```
switch (op)
{
    case '+':
        answer = n1 + n2;
        break;
    case '-':
        answer = n1 - n2;
        break;
    case '*':
        answer = n1 * n2;
        break;
    case '/':
        answer = n1 / n2; //Worry about division by zero
        break;
    default: //Worry about illegal characters
}
return answer;
```

The basic logic of the method evaluate

In the first test of our code, we could completely ignore our comments about the things that can be wrong, but to shorten this case study, we will throw some exceptions. We will not, however, handle the exceptions right now. Suppose we include the following code in the preceding case for division:

Do not compare a floating-point number with zero

```
if (n2 == 0.0)
    throw new DivideByZeroException();
```

This approach is conceptually fine, but there is one problem: The numbers involved are of type `double`. Floating-point numbers such as these represent only approximate quantities, so we should not use `==` to test them for exact equality, as we discussed in Chapter 3. The value of n2 might be so close to zero that dividing another number by it would have the same effect as dividing by zero, yet the test would say that it is not equal to zero. We should throw an exception whenever the denominator is very close to zero. How should we define "very close to zero"? We could, for example, consider any quantity less than one ten-thousandth as very close to zero. But we might find later that this value is not the best choice, so instead let's use an instance variable, named `precision`. For now, the definition of `precision` can be

```
private double precision = 0.0001;
```

Thus, the case for division becomes

```
case '/':
    if ( (-precision < n2) && (n2 < precision) )
        throw new DivideByZeroException();
    answer = n1 / n2;
    break;
```

Preventing division by zero or almost zero

Now, what if the user enters some character other than '+', '-', '*', or '/' for the operation? We can throw another exception in the default case of the switch statement, as follows:

Throw an exception if the operator is not recognized

```
default:
    throw new UnknownOpException(op);
```

The DivideByZeroException class was defined in Listing 9.5. UnknownOpException is a new exception class that we need to define. It is similar to other exception classes we have written and is given in Listing 9.10. Note that when the user enters an unknown operator, we want to provide an error message that includes the erroneous character. Thus, our class has a constructor that names the operator as an argument of type char.

LISTING 9.10   The UnknownOpException Class

```java
public class UnknownOpException extends Exception
{
    public UnknownOpException()
    {
        super("UnknownOpException");
    }

    public UnknownOpException(char op)
    {
        super(op + " is an unknown operator.");
    }

    public UnknownOpException(String message)
    {
        super(message);
    }
}
```

The heading of the method doCalculation must include a throws clause for the exception classes UnknownOpException and DivideByZeroException, even though the body of doCalculation does not contain any throw statements. The throws clause is necessary because doCalculation calls the method evaluate, and the method evaluate can throw an UnknownOpException or a DivideByZeroException.

Our first draft can throw exceptions but will not handle them

At this point, we have most of the program written, except for the exception handling. Our preliminary version of the program is shown in Listing 9.11.We can debug and test it before we write the exception-handling portion. As long as the user does not enter an unknown operator or attempt to perform a division by zero, this version will run fine.

LISTING 9.11   **The Unexceptional Cases** *(part 1 of 3)*

> *This version of the program does not handle exceptions and thus is not yet complete. However, it does run and can be used for debugging.*

```java
import java.util.Scanner;
/**
PRELIMINARY VERSION without exception handling.
Simple line-oriented calculator program. The class
can also be used to create other calculator programs.
*/
public class PrelimCalculator
{
    private double result;
    private double precision = 0.0001;
    //Numbers this close to zero are treated as if equal to zero.

    public static void main(String[] args)
                    throws DivideByZeroException,
                           UnknownOpException
    {
        PrelimCalculator clerk = new PrelimCalculator();

        System.out.println("Calculator is on.");
        System.out.print("Format of each line: ");
        System.out.println("operator space number");
        System.out.println("For example: + 3");
        System.out.println("To end, enter the letter e.");
        clerk.doCalculation();

        System.out.println("The final result is " +
                            clerk.resultValue());
        System.out.println("Calculator program ending.");
    }
    public PrelimCalculator()
    {
        result = 0;
    }
    public void reset()
    {
        result = 0;
    }
```

> *The definition of the* **main** *method will change before this case study ends.*

(continued)

LISTING 9.11   **The Unexceptional Cases** *(part 2 of 3)*

> *reset,* `setResult`*, and* `getResult`
> *are not used in this program, but might
> be needed by some other application
> that uses this class.*

```java
public void setResult(double newResult)
{
    result = newResult;
}
public double getResult()
{
    return result;
}
/**
Returns n1 op n2, provided op is one of '+', '-', '*',or '/'.
Any other value of op throws UnknownOpException.
*/
public double evaluate(char op, double n1, double n2)
           throws DivideByZeroException, UnknownOpException
{
    double answer;
    switch (op)
    {
        case '+':
            answer = n1 + n2;
            break;
        case '-':
            answer = n1 - n2;
            break;
        case '*':
            answer = n1 * n2;
            break;
        case '/':
            if ((-precision < n2) && (n2 < precision))
                throw new DivideByZeroException();
            answer = n1 / n2;
            break;
        default:
            throw new UnknownOpException(op);
    }
    return answer;
}
```

(continued)

LISTING 9.11 **The Unexceptional Cases** *(part 3 of 3)*

```java
public void doCalculation() throws DivideByZeroException,
                                    UnknownOpException
{
    Scanner keyboard = new Scanner(System.in);
    boolean done = false;
    result = 0;
    System.out.println("result = " + result);

    while (!done)
    {
        char nextOp = (keyboard.next()).charAt(0);
        if ((nextOp == 'e') || (nextOp == 'E'))
            done = true;
        else
        {
            double nextNumber = keyboard.nextDouble();
            result = evaluate(nextOp, result, nextNumber);
            System.out.println("result " + nextOp + " " +
                                nextNumber + " = " + result);
            System.out.println("updated result = " + result);
        }
    }
}
```

Sample Screen Output

```
Calculator is on.
Format of each line: operator space number
For example: + 3
To end, enter the letter e.
result = 0.0
+ 4
result + 4.0 = 4.0
updated result = 4.0
* 2
result* 2.0 = 8.0
updated result = 8.0
e
The final result is 8.0
Calculator program ending.
```

Once we have debugged the preliminary version of our program, we can add exception handling. The most significant exception is UnknownOpException, so we consider it first. We have already given the definition of the class UnknownOpException, but we have not yet done anything with it, other than to throw it in the method evaluate and to declare it in throws clauses. The method evaluate is invoked by the method doCalculation, and the method doCalculation is invoked by the method main. We have three typical ways of handling the exception:

Our final version adds exception handling

- Catch the exception in the method evaluate.
- Declare the exception UnknownOpException in a throws clause in the method evaluate, and then catch the exception in the method doCalculation.
- Declare the exception UnknownOpException in a throws clause in both the method evaluate and the method doCalculation, and then catch the exception in the method main.

Possible ways to handle an exception due to an unknown operator

The approach we choose depends on what we want to have happen when an exception is thrown. We would use either of the first two ways if we wanted the user to try again to enter the operator. We would use the last way if we wanted to restart the entire calculation. Suppose we decide on this last approach and place the try and catch blocks in the method main. This decision leads us to rewrite main, as shown in Listing 9.12. In doing so, we introduce two new methods, handleUnknownOpException and handleDivideByZeroException. All that is left to do is to define these two methods for handling exceptions.

We handle exceptions in separate methods

If you look at the catch block in the method main, you will see that, when an UnknownOpException is thrown, it is handled by the method handleUnknownOpException. We designed this method to give the user a second chance to enter the calculation, starting from the beginning. If the user enters an unknown operator during this second chance, another UnknownOpException is thrown, but this time it is caught in the method handleUnknownOpException and the program ends. (There are other good ways to handle an UnknownOpException, but this one is satisfactory.) To see the code for this case, look at the catch block in the method handleUnknownOpException in Listing 9.12.

If the user attempts to divide by zero, we will simply end the program. (Perhaps we will do something more elaborate in a future version of this program, but this will do for now.) Thus, the method handleDivideByZeroException is quite simple.

■ **PROGRAMMING TIP**   **Documentation Should Describe Possible Exceptions**

When using classes and methods written by another programmer, you would want documentation that describes the possible exceptions. Such documentation can give you some idea of how to handle these exceptions. Consider this when writing the javadoc comments and other documentation for the code that you write.   ■

LISTING 9.12 The Complete Line-Oriented Calculator
(part 1 of 3)

```java
import java.util.Scanner;
/**
 Simple line-oriented calculator program. The class
 can also be used to create other calculator programs.
*/
public class Calculator
{
    private double result;
    private double precision = 0.0001;
    //Numbers this close to zero are treated as if equal to zero.

    public static void main(String[] args)
    {
        Calculator clerk = new Calculator();

        try
        {
            System.out.println("Calculator is on.");
            System.out.print("Format of each line: ");
            System.out.println("operator space number");
            System.out.println("For example: + 3");
            System.out.println("To end, enter the letter e.");
            clerk.doCalculation();
        }
        catch(UnknownOpException e)
        {
            clerk.handleUnknownOpException(e);
        }
        catch(DivideByZeroException e)
        {
            clerk.handleDivideByZeroException(e);
        }

        System.out.println("The final result is " +
                            clerk.resultValue());
        System.out.println("Calculator program ending.");
    }

    public Calculator()
    {
        result = 0;
    }
```

(continued)

LISTING 9.12 **The Complete Line-Oriented Calculator**
(part 2 of 3)

```java
public void handleDivideByZeroException
                            (DivideByZeroException e)
{
    System.out.println("Dividing by zero.");
    System.out.println("Program aborted");
    System.exit(0);
}
public void handleUnknownOpException(UnknownOpException e)
{
    System.out.println(e.getMessage());
    System.out.println("Try again from the beginning:");

    try
    {
        System.out.print("Format of each line: ");
        System.out.println("operator number");
        System.out.println("For example: + 3");
        System.out.println("To end, enter the letter e.");
        doCalculation();    ◄────────── The first UnknownOpException
    }                                    gives the user another chance.

    catch(UnknownOpException e2)  ◄────  This block catches an
                                         UnknownOpException
                                         if it is thrown a second time.
    {
        System.out.println(e2.getMessage());
        System.out.println("Try again at some other time.");
        System.out.println("Program ending.");
        System.exit(0);
    }
    catch(DivideByZeroException e3)
    {
        handleDivideByZeroException(e3);
    }
}
```

The methods reset, setResult, getResult, evaluate, and doCalculation
are the same as in Listing 9.11.
```java
}
```

(continued)

LISTING 9.12   The Complete Line-Oriented Calculator
(part 3 of 3)

Sample Screen Output

```
Calculator is on.
Format of each line: operator space number
For example: + 3
To end, enter the letter e.
result = 0.0
+ 80
result + 80.0 = 80.0
updated result = 80.0
- 2
result - 2.0 = 78.0
updated result = 78.0
% 4
% is an unknown operator.
Try again from the beginning:
Format of each line is: operator space number
For example: + 3
To end, enter the letter e.
result = 0.0
+ 80
result + 80.0 = 80.0
updated result = 80.0
- 2
result - 2.0 = 78.0
updated result = 78.0
* 0.04
result * 0.04 = 3.12
updated result = 3.12
e
The final result is 3.12
Calculator program ending.
```

SELF-TEST QUESTIONS   myprogramminglab

34. Write an accessor method called `getPrecision` that can be added to the class `Calculator` in Listing 9.12 and that returns the value of the instance variable `precision`. Also, write a mutator method called `setPrecision` that changes the value of the instance variable `precision` to any specified value.

35. What would happen if you ran the program in Listing 9.11 and entered an unknown operator—such as % or #—that the program cannot recognize?

9.4 GRAPHICS SUPPLEMENT

That's an interesting color. What's it called?

—A FRIEND ON SEEING MY NEWLY PAINTED DINING ROOM

In this section we give an example of a `JFrame` GUI that uses exceptions.

Exceptions in GUIs

You could avoid catching any exceptions that methods could throw by declaring all exceptions in `throws` clauses in the methods, including `main`. However, this is not a good programming practice. An uncaught exception in a non-GUI Java application program will end the program with an error message. In either a `JFrame` GUI program or an applet, an uncaught exception does not end the program. However, your GUI may not cope correctly with the exception, or the user may not receive sufficient instructions. Thus, with GUI programs it is even more important to ensure that all checked exceptions that are thrown are eventually caught.

Catching exceptions in a GUI program is important

PROGRAMMING EXAMPLE	A JFrame GUI Using Exceptions

Listing 9.13 contains the definition of a `JFrame` GUI that allows the user to see samples of colors. The user enters the name of the color in a text field and clicks the `ShowColor` button. If the GUI knows about that color, the background changes to the named color. If the GUI does not know about the color, the text field shows the message `UnknownColor` and the background changes to gray.

The user's input string is converted to an object of the class `Color` by the method `getColor`. The method `getColor` throws an exception if it is given a

LISTING 9.13   A `JFrame` **GUI Using Exceptions** *(part 1 of 2)*

```java
import javax.swing.JButton;
import javax.swing.JFrame;
import javax.swing.JTextField;
import java.awt.Color;
import java.awt.Container;
import java.awt.FlowLayout;
import java.awt.Graphics;
import java.awt.event.ActionEvent;
import java.awt.event.ActionListener;
public class ColorDemo extends JFrame implements ActionListener
{
    public static final int WIDTH = 400;
    public static final int HEIGHT = 300;
    public static final int NUMBER_OF_CHAR = 20;

    private JTextField colorName;

    public ColorDemo()
    {
        setSize(WIDTH, HEIGHT);
        WindowDestroyer listener = new WindowDestroyer();
        addWindowListener(listener);

        Container contentPane = getContentPane();
        contentPane.setBackground(Color.GRAY);
        contentPane.setLayout(new FlowLayout());
        JButton showButton = new JButton("Show Color");
        showButton.addActionListener(this);
        contentPane.add(showButton);

        colorName = new JTextField(NUMBER_OF_CHAR);
        contentPane.add(colorName);
    }
    public void actionPerformed(ActionEvent e)
    {
        Container contentPane = getContentPane();

        try
        {
            contentPane.setBackground(
                    getColor(colorName.getText()));
        }
        catch(UnknownColorException exception)
```

(continued)

LISTING 9.13 A JFrame GUI Using Exceptions *(part 2 of 2)*

```java
        {
            colorName.setText("Unknown Color");
            contentPane.setBackground(Color.GRAY);
        }
    }
    public Color getColor(String name) throws UnknownColorException
    {
        if (name.equalsIgnoreCase("RED"))
            return Color.RED;
        else if (name.equalsIgnoreCase("WHITE"))
            return Color.WHITE;
        else if (name.equalsIgnoreCase("BLUE"))
            return Color.BLUE;
        else if (name.equalsIgnoreCase("GREEN"))
            return Color.GREEN;
        else
            throw new UnknownColorException();
    }
}
```

color that it does not recognize, such as Orange. The exception is not caught in the method getColor but is declared in a throws clause. The invocation of the method getColor is in a try block in the method actionPerformed, which also contains the catch block for the exception.

To run the GUI, you need four classes: ColorDemo, given in Listing 9.13; UnknowColorException, given in Listing 9.14; ShowColorDemo, given in Listing 9.15; and WindowDestroyer, given in Listing 8.22 in the previous chapter.

LISTING 9.14 The Class UnknownColorException

```java
public class UnknownColorException extends Exception
{
    public UnknownColorException()
    {
        super("Unknown Color!");
    }
    public UnknownColorException(String message)
    {
        super(message);
    }
}
```

LISTING 9.15 Running the GUI ColorDemo

```
public class ShowColorDemo
{
    public static void main(String[] args)
    {
        ColorDemogui = new ColorDemo( );
        gui.setVisible(true);
    }
}
```

Sample Screen Output

Sample Screen Output

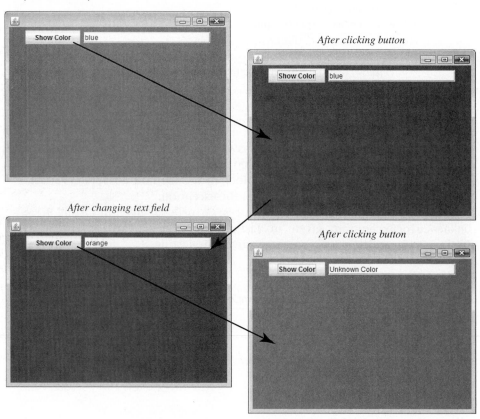

GOTCHA A throws Clause Is Not Allowed in actionPerformed

When you define the method actionPerformed in an action listener class, you cannot add a throws clause. The heading for the method actionPerformed is completely specified for you, and you cannot change it in any way, other than renaming its one parameter. Thus, if you throw an exception in your definition of the method actionPerformed, you need to catch the exception within the method. For example, in Listing 9.13, you must catch the UnknownColorException within the body of actionPerformed.

Similarly, if you were to redefine the method windowClosing in a window listener class, such as WindowDestroyer, you could not add a throws clause to the heading of the method windowClosing. ■

GOTCHA Uncaught Checked Exceptions in a GUI Program

An uncaught checked exception in either an applet or a GUI program that uses JFrame will not end program execution. Although a Java application program that does not have a GUI will end with an error message in such cases, an applet or a GUI program will cause unpredictable results and likely leave the user bewildered. ■

SELF-TEST QUESTIONS

myprogramminglab

36. Rewrite the class ColorDemo in Listing 9.13 so that it is an applet.

37. The try block in Listing 9.13 contains invocations to three methods: SetBackground, getColor, and getText. The one catch block catches an UnknownColorException thrown by the method getColor. Should we have written other catch blocks for exceptions thrown by the other two methods called in the try block?

CHAPTER SUMMARY

- An exception is an object of a class derived from the class Exception. Descendants of the class Error are not exceptions, but they behave like them.

- Exception handling allows you to design and code the normal case for your program separately from the code that handles exceptional situations.

- Java provides predefined exception classes. You can also define your own exception classes.

- Java has two kinds of exceptions: checked and unchecked (run-time). A method that throws a checked exception must either handle it or declare it in a throws clause within its heading. Checked exceptions must be caught eventually. Otherwise, program execution will terminate. Unchecked, or run-time, exceptions need not be caught or declared in a throws clause and usually are not. Unchecked exceptions belong to classes derived from the class RuntimeException. All other exceptions are checked.

■ Certain Java statements themselves might throw an exception. Methods from class libraries might throw exceptions. You can also explicitly throw an exception in your code by using a throw statement.

■ When a method might throw an exception but not catch it, the exception class usually must be listed in a throws clause for the method.

■ An exception is caught in a catch block.

■ A try block is followed by one or more catch blocks. In this case, always list the catch block for a more specific exception class before the catch block for a more general exception class.

■ Every exception has a getMessage method that can be used to recover a description of the caught exception.

■ Do not overuse exceptions.

Exercises

1. Write a program that allows students to schedule appointments at either 1, 2, 3, 4, 5, or 6 o'clock pm. Use an array of six strings to store the names for the time slots. Write a loop that iterates as long as the array has a free space. Within a try block, allow the user to enter a time and a name. If the time is free, put the name in the array. If the time is not free, throw a TimeInUse-Exception. If the time is not valid, throw an InvalidTimeException. Use a catch block for each different kind of exception.

2. Write a program that allows the user to compute the remainder after the division of two integer values. The remainder of x/y is x%y. Catch any exception thrown and allow the user to enter new values.

3. Write an exception class that is appropriate for indicating that a time entered by a user is not valid. The time will be in the format *hour:minute* followed by "am" or "pm."

4. Derive exception classes from the class you wrote in the previous exercise. Each new class should indicate a specific kind of error. For example, InvalidHourException could be used to indicate that the value entered for *hour* was not an integer in the range 1 to 12.

5. Write a class TimeOfDay that uses the exception classes defined in the previous exercise. Give it a method setTimeTo(timeString) that changes the

time if `timeString` corresponds to a valid time of day. If not, it should throw an exception of the appropriate type.

6. Write code that reads a string from the keyboard and uses it to set the variable `myTime` of type `TimeOfDay` from the previous exercise. Use `try-catch` blocks to guarantee that `myTime` is set to a valid time.

7. Create a class `SongCard` that represents a gift card for the purchase of songs online. It should have the following private attributes:

   - `songs`—the number of songs on the card
   - `activated`—true if the card has been activated

   and the following methods:

   - `SongCard(n)`—a constructor for a card with *n* songs.
   - `activate`—activates the gift card. Throws an exception if the card has already been activated.
   - `buyASong`—records the purchase of one song by decreasing the number of songs left for purchase using this card. Throws an exception if the gift card is either completely used or not active.
   - `songsRemaining`—returns the number of songs that can be purchased using the gift card.

8. Create a class `Rational` that represents a rational number. It should have private attributes for

   - The numerator (an integer)
   - The denominator (an integer)

   and the following methods:

   - `Rational(`*numerator, denominator*`)`—a constructor for a rational number.
   - Accessor methods `getNumerator` and `getDenominator` and mutator methods `setNumerator` and `setDenominator` for the numerator and the denominator.

   You should use an exception to guarantee that the denominator is never zero.

9. Revise the class `Rational` described in the previous exercise to use an assertion instead of an exception to guarantee that the denominator is never zero.

10. Suppose that you are going to create an object used to count the number of people in a room. We know that the number of people in the room can never be negative. Create a `RoomCounter` class having three public methods:

    - `addPerson`—adds one person to the room
    - `removePerson`—removes one person from the room
    - `getCount`—returns the number of people in the room

If removePerson would make the number of people less than zero, throw a NegativeCounterException.

11. Revise the class RoomCounter described in the previous exercise to use an assertion instead of an exception to prevent the number of people in the room from becoming negative.

12. Show the modifications needed to add exponentiation to the class Calculator in Listing 9.12. Use ^ to indicate the exponentiation operator and the method Math.pow to perform the computation.

13. Write a class LapTimer that can be used to time the laps in a race. The class should have the following private attributes:

- running—a boolean indication of whether the timer is running
- startTime—the time when the timer started
- lapStart—the timer's value when the current lap started
- lapTime—the elapsed time for the last lap
- totalTime—the total time from the start of the race through the last completed lap
- lapsCompleted—the number of laps completed so far
- lapsInRace—the number of laps in the race

The class should have the following methods:

- LapTimer(*n*)—a constructor for a race having *n* laps.
- start—starts the timer. Throws an exception if the race has already started.
- markLap—marks the end of the current lap and the start of a new lap. Throws an exception if the race is finished.
- getLapTime—returns the time of the last lap. Throws an exception if the first lap has not yet been completed.
- getTotalTime—returns the total time from the start of the race through the last completed lap. Throws an exception if the first lap has not yet been completed.
- getLapsRemaining—returns the number of laps yet to be completed, including the current one.

Express all times in seconds.

To get the current time in milliseconds from some baseline date, invoke

```
Calendar.getInstance().getTimeInMillis()
```

This invocation returns a primitive value of type long. By taking the difference between the returned values of two invocations at two different times, you will know the elapsed time in milliseconds between the invocations. Note that the class Calendar is in the package java.util.

PROGRAMMING PROJECTS

Visit www.myprogramminglab.com to complete many of these Programming Projects online and get instant feedback.

myprogramminglab

1. Use the exception class `MessageTooLongException` of Self-Test Question 16 in a program that asks the user to enter a line of text having no more than 20 characters. If the user enters an acceptable number of characters, the program should display the message, "You entered *x* characters, which is an acceptable length" (with the letter *x* replaced by the actual number of characters). Otherwise, a `MessageTooLongException` should be thrown and caught. In either case, the program should repeatedly ask whether the user wants to enter another line or quit the program.

2. Write a program that converts a time from 24-hour notation to 12-hour notation. The following is a sample interaction between the user and the program:

```
Enter time in 24-hour notation:
13:07
That is the same as
1:07 PM
Again? (y/n)
y
Enter time in 24-hour notation:
10:15
That is the same as
10:15 AM
Again? (y/n)
y
Enter time in 24-hour notation:
10:65
There is no such time as 10:65
Try Again:
Enter time in 24-hour notation:
16:05
That is the same as
4:05 PM
Again? (y/n)
n
End of program
```

Define an exception class called `TimeFormatException`. If the user enters an illegal time, like 10:65, or even gibberish, like 8&*68, your program should throw and handle a `TimeFormatException`.

3. Write a program that uses the class `Calculator` in Listing 9.12 to create a more powerful calculator. This calculator will allow you to save one result in memory and call the result back. The commands the calculator takes are

   - e for end
   - c for clear; sets `result` to zero

- m for save in memory; sets memory equal to result
- r for recall memory; displays the value of memory but does not change result

You should define a derived class of the class Calculator that has one more instance variable for the memory, a new main method that runs the improved calculator, a redefinition of the method handleUnknownOpException, and anything else new or redefined that you need. A sample interaction with the user is shown next. Your program need not produce identical output, but it should be similar and just as clear or even clearer.

```
Calculator on:
result = 0.0
+ 4
result + 4.0 = 4.0
updated result = 4.0
/ 2
result / 2.0 = 2.0
updated result = 2.0
m
result saved in memory
c
result = 0.0
+ 99
result + 99.0 = 99.0
updated result = 99.0
/ 3
result / 3.0 = 33.0
updated result = 33.0
r
recalled memory value = 2.0
result = 33.0
+ 2
result + 2.0 = 35.0
updated result = 35.0
e
End of program
```

4. Write a program that converts dates from numerical month-day format to alphabetic month-day format. For example, input of 1/31 or 01/31 would produce January 31 as output. The dialogue with the user should be similar to that shown in Programming Project 2. You should define two exception classes, one called MonthException and another called DayException. If the user enters anything other than a legal month number (integers from 1 to 12), your program should throw and catch a MonthException. Similarly, if the user enters anything other than a valid day number (integers from 1 to either 29, 30, or 31, depending on the month), your program should throw and catch a DayException. To keep things simple, assume that February always has 28 days.

5. Modify the driver program from Programming Project 6 in Chapter 8 to use three exception classes called `CylinderException`, `LoadException`, and `TowingException`. The number of cylinders must be an integer from 1 to 12, the load capacity must be a number from 1 to 10 (possibly with a fractional part), and the towing capacity must be a number from 1 to 20 (possibly with a fractional part). Anything other than numbers in these ranges should cause your program to throw and catch the appropriate exception. You also need to define the classes `CylinderException`, `LoadException`, and `TowingException`.

6. Define an exception class called `DimensionException` to use in the driver program from Programming Project 7 in Chapter 8. Modify that driver program to throw and catch a `DimensionException` if the user enters something less than or equal to zero for a dimension.

VideoNote
Defining an exception class

7. Write a program to enter employee data, including Social Security number and salary, into an array. The maximum number of employees is 100, but your program should also work for any number of employees less than 100. Your program should use two exception classes, one called `SSNLengthException` for when the Social Security number entered—without dashes or spaces—is not exactly nine characters and the other called `SSNCharacterException` for when any character in the Social Security number is not a digit. When an exception is thrown, the user should be reminded of what she or he entered, told why it is inappropriate, and asked to reenter the data. After all data has been entered, your program should display the records for all employees, with an annotation stating whether the employee's salary is above or below average. You will also need to define the classes `Employee`, `SSNLengthException`, and `SSNCharacterException`. Derive the class `Employee` from the class `Person` in Listing 8.1 of Chapter 8. Among other things, the class `Employee` should have input and output methods, as well as constructors, accessor methods, and mutator methods. Every `Employee` object should record the employee's name (as defined in `Person`), salary, and Social Security number, as well as any other data you need or think is appropriate.

8. A method that returns a special error code can sometimes cause problems. The caller might ignore the error code or treat the error code as a valid return value. In this case it is better to throw an exception instead. The following class maintains an account balance and returns a special error code.

```
public class Account
{
    private double balance;
    public Account()
    {
        balance = 0;
    }
```

```
            public Account(double initialDeposit)
            {
                balance = initialDeposit;
            }
            public double getBalance()
            {
                return balance;
            }
            // returns new balance or -1 if error
            public double deposit(double amount)
            {
                if (amount > 0)
                    balance += amount;
                else
                    return -1;   // Code indicating error
                return balance;
            }
            // returns new balance or -1 if invalid amount
            public double withdraw(double amount)
            {
                if ((amount > balance) || (amount < 0))
                    return -1;
                else
                    balance -= amount;
                return balance;
            }
        }
```

VideoNote
Solution to Project 8

Rewrite the class so that it throws appropriate exceptions instead of returning –1 as an error code. Write test code that attempts to withdraw and deposit invalid amounts and catches the exceptions that are thrown.

9. Revise the class `Calculator` in Listing 9.12 as an applet. Have the user enter input, such as +80, in a text field. Have a button labeled `Update` that causes the applet to perform the indicated operations, such as +80. Another text field contains the result. Also include a `Reset` button that restarts a computation—that is, sets `result` to zero.

Graphics

10. Repeat the previous programming project, but instead of an applet, write an application that implements a GUI.

Graphics

11. Write an application or applet that implements a lap timer using the class `LapTimer` described in Exercise 13. The new lap timer should have two buttons: `Start` and `Lap`, as well as two labels, one for the time of the last lap and the other for the total time of all laps. Your class should create a private instance of `LapTimer`. Any reasonable small number can be used for the number of laps.

Graphics

12. Suppose that you are in charge of customer service for a certain business. As phone calls come in, the name of the caller is recorded and eventually a

service representative returns the call and handles the request. Write a class `ServiceRequests` that keeps track of the names of callers. The class should have the following methods:

- addName(*name*)—adds a name to the list of names. Throws a Service-BackUpException if there is no free space in the list.
- removeName(*name*)—removes a name from the list. Throws a NoService-RequestException if the name is not in the list.
- getName(*i*)—returns the *i*th name in the list.
- getNumber—returns the current number of service requests.

Write a program that uses an object of type `ServiceRequests` to keep track of customers that have called. It should have a loop that, in each iteration, attempts to add a name, remove a name, or print all names. Use an array of size 10 as the list of names.

13. Write an application or applet that implements a trip-time calculator. Define and use a class `TripComputer` to compute the time of a trip. `TripComputer` should have the private attributes

- totalTime—the total time for the trip
- restStopTaken—a boolean flag that indicates whether a rest stop has been taken at the end of the current leg

and the following methods:

- computeLegTime(*distance*, *speed*)—computes the time for a leg of the trip having a given distance in miles and speed in miles per hour. If either the distance or the speed is negative, throws an exception.
- takeRestStop(*time*)—takes a rest stop for the given amount of time. If the time is negative, throws an exception. Also throws an exception if the client code attempts to take two rest stops in a row.
- getTripTime—returns the current total time for the trip.
- Here is one possible configuration of the labels, buttons, and text fields required by the trip-time calculator:

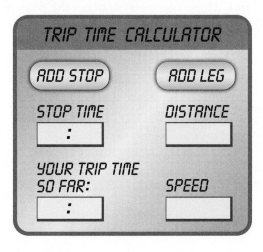

Answers to Self-Test Questions

1. Try block entered.
   Exception: Time Limit Exceeded.
   After catch block.

2. Try block entered.
   Leaving try block.
   After catch block.

3. An exception is an object. For example, in the following code, `Exception` is a constructor for the class `Exception`:

   ```
   throw new Exception("Time Limit Exceeded.");
   ```

   The expression

   ```
   new Exception("Time Limit Exceeded.");
   ```

   creates an exception object.

4. Yes, it is perfectly valid, although it is unlikely that you would ever have a good reason to use it.

5. The behavior would not change. The new code is equivalent to the old code it replaces.

6. ```
   throw new Exception("Time Limit Exceeded.");
   ```

   Note that the following is an `if` statement, not a `throw` statement, even though it contains a `throw` statement:

   ```
   if (waitTime> 30)
       throw new Exception("Time Limit Exceeded.");
   ```

7. When a `throw` statement is executed, the enclosing `try` block ends; no other statements in the `try` block are executed. Control passes to the subsequent `catch` block whose parameter matches the exception object in type. Execution continues with the statements in that `catch` block.

8. ```
   try
   {
       System.out.println("Try block entered.");
       if (waitTime> 30)
           throw new Exception("Time Limit Exceeded.");
       System.out.println("Leaving try block.");
   }
   ```

9. ```
   catch (Exception e)
   {
       System.out.println("Exception: " + e.getMessage());
   }
   ```
   ```

10. `e` is the catch-block parameter.

11. No. The catch-block parameter `e` is just a place holder and can be replaced by any other valid identifier, such as `messenger`.

12. ```
if (status.equals("bad"))
        throw new Exception("Exception thrown: Bad Status.");
```

13. Yes, they are perfectly legal, although you would be more likely to write the following instead:

    ```
    throw new IOException("Hello Houston!");
    ```

    In practice, this `throw` statement would typically be included in some branching statement, such as an `if` statement.

14. Yes, it is legal.

15. ```
public class CoreBreachException extends Exception
{
    public CoreBreachException()
    {
        super("Core Breach! Evacuate Ship!");
    }
    public CoreBreachException(String message)
    {
        super(message);
    }
}
```

16. ```
public class MessageTooLongException extends Exception
{
    public MessageTooLongException()
    {
        super("Message Too Long!");
    }
    public MessageTooLongException(String message)
    {
        super(message);
    }
}
```

17. ```
ExerciseException invoked with an argument.

Do Be Do
```

18. ```
Wow, Crazy exception thrown!
Crazy exception thrown!
Message is Crazy exception thrown!
```
```

19. ```
    try block entered:
    DoubleException thrown! DoubleException thrown!
    End of code.
    ```

20. The output would not change at all. The modified program is completely equivalent to the original program.

21. The output would change to the following:

    ```
    try block entered:
    Leaving try block.
    End of code.
    ```

22. ```
    42
    IntException thrown!
    ```

23. An exception class can be a derived class of any exception class, predefined or programmer defined. In particular, you can derive an exception class from the predefined class IOException.

24. Add the throws clause to the method's heading, as follows:

    ```
    public void doStuff(int n) throws Exception
    ```

25. Since the code evidently has compiled, we must assume that the method declares the exception in a throws clause. If you did not handle the exception by enclosing the method invocation within a try block and writing an appropriate catch block, the method invocation ends immediately after the exception is thrown. If the method invocation is inside a try block, the exception is thrown to a corresponding catch block, if there is one. If there is no catch block that corresponds to the exception, you have an uncaught exception, and the method invocation ends as soon as that exception is thrown.

26. It might be caught either in method B or, if not there, in method A or, if not in A, outside of method A.

27. ```
    Second catch.
    End of code.
    ```

28. ```
    First catch.
    End of code.
    ```

29. ```
    Hello!
    End of code.
    ```

30. ```
    Trying
    Starting sampleMethod.
    Catching
    From sampleMethod with love.
    ```

31. Yes. However, it would probably be better to place the inner `try` and `catch` blocks within a method definition and invoke the method within the larger `try` block.

32. Yes. However, it would probably be better to place the inner `try` and `catch` blocks within a method definition and invoke the method within the larger `catch` block.

33. Output for argument 99 is

    ```
    In finally block.
    Caught in main.
    ```

    Output for argument −99 is

    ```
    Caught in sampleMethod.
    In finally block.
    After finally block.
    ```

    Output for argument 0 is

    ```
    No exception.
    Still in sampleMethod.
    In finally block.
    After finally block.
    ```

34.
    ```
    public double getPrecision()
    {
        return precision;
    }
    public void setPrecision(double newPrecision)
    {
        precision = newPrecision;
    }
    ```

35. The program would end as soon as an `UnknownOpException` was thrown.

36. You need only make the following changes to the class `ColorDemo`: Replace

    ```
    extends JFrame
    ```

    with

    ```
    extends JApplet
    ```

    Replace

    ```
    public ColorDemo()
    ```

    with

    ```
    public void init()
    ```

    Delete the following three lines:

```
        setSize(WIDTH, HEIGHT);
        WindowDestroyer listener = new WindowDestroyer();
        addWindowListener(listener);
```

You do not need the class `WindowDestroyer` for the applet version, but you still need the class `UnknownColorException`. These changes are made to produce the applet file `ColorDemoApplet.java`, available over the Web as part of the source code for this book.

37. No. The method `SetBackground` in the class `Component` does not throw a checked exception. The method `getText`, which is inherited by the class `JTextField` from the class `JTextComponent`, also does not throw a checked exception. Although `getText` can throw a `NullPointerException`, it is a run-time exception that is usually not caught.

Streams and File I/O

10.1 AN OVERVIEW OF STREAMS AND FILE I/O 727

The Concept of a Stream 727
Why Use Files for I/O? 728
Text Files and Binary Files 728

10.2 TEXT-FILE I/O 730

Creating a Text File 730
Appending to a Text File 736
Reading from a Text File 738

10.3 TECHNIQUES FOR ANY FILE 741

The Class `File` 741
Programming Example: Reading a File
  Name from the Keyboard 741
Using Path Names 743
Methods of the Class `File` 744
Defining a Method to Open a Stream 746
Case Study: Processing a Comma-Separated Values
  File 748

10.4 BASIC BINARY-FILE I/O 751

Creating a Binary File 751
Writing Primitive Values to a Binary File 753
Writing Strings to a Binary File 756
Some Details About `writeUTF` 757
Reading from a Binary File 759
The Class `EOFException` 764
Programming Example: Processing a File
  of Binary Data 766

10.5 BINARY-FILE I/O WITH OBJECTS AND ARRAYS 771

Binary-File I/O with Objects of a Class 771
Some Details of Serialization 775
Array Objects in Binary Files 776

10.6 GRAPHICS SUPPLEMENT 779

Programming Example: A `JFrame` GUI for
  Manipulating Files 779

Chapter Summary 786   **Programming Projects** 790   **Answers to Self-Test Questions** 793

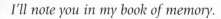

I'll note you in my book of memory.

—WILLIAM SHAKESPEARE, *Henry VI, Part II*

I/O refers to program input and output. Input can be taken from the keyboard or from a file. Similarly, output can be sent to the screen or to a file. In this chapter, we explain how you can write your programs to take input from a file and send output to a file. By doing so, you will be able to retain your data and objects long after your program ends its execution.

OBJECTIVES

After studying this chapter, you should be able to

- Describe the concept of an I/O stream
- Explain the difference between text files and binary files
- Save data, including objects, in a file
- Read data, including objects, from a file

PREREQUISITES

You will need some knowledge of exception handling, as described in Chapter 9, to understand this chapter. Having some knowledge of inheritance will also be helpful. Only Section 10.5 and the Case Study in Section 10.3 of this chapter actually requires that you know about arrays, interfaces, and inheritance (covered in Chapters 7 and 8). You can, of course, skip this section until you learn about these topics. You may cover Section 10.3 after Sections 10.4 and 10.5 if you wish. Many readers may choose to skip the coverage of binary files. Only selected Programming Projects in the rest of this book requires knowledge of anything covered in this chapter.

Details of the prerequisites are as follows:

Section	Prerequisite
10.1 An Overview of Streams and File I/O	Chapters 1 through 6.
10.2 Text-File I/O	Sections 9.1 and 10.1. Also some knowledge of inheritance from Chapter 8.
10.3 Techniques for Any File	Section 10.2 and Chapter7 for the Case Study.
10.4 Basic Binary-File I/O	Sections 9.2 and 10.2. You do not need Section 10.3.

10.5 Binary-File I/O with Objects and Arrays	Section 10.4 and Chapters 7 and 8. You do not need Section 10.3.
10.6 Graphics Supplement	Sections 9.4 and 10.3.

10.1 AN OVERVIEW OF STREAMS AND FILE I/O

Fish say, they have their stream and pond,

But is there anything beyond?

—RUPERT BROOKE, *HEAVEN*

In this section, we give you a general introduction to file I/O. In particular, we explain the difference between text files and binary files. The Java syntax for file I/O statements is given in subsequent sections of this chapter.

The Concept of a Stream

You are already using files to store your Java classes and programs, your music, your pictures, and your videos. You can also use files to store input for a program or to hold output from a program. In Java, file I/O, as well as simple keyboard and screen I/O, is handled by streams. A **stream** is a flow of data. The data might be characters, numbers, or bytes consisting of binary digits. If the data flows *into your program*, the stream is called an **input stream**. If the data flows *out of your program*, the stream is called an **output stream**. For example, if an input stream is connected to the keyboard, the data flows from the keyboard into your program. If an input stream is connected to a file, the data flows from the file into your program. Figure 10.1 illustrates some of these streams.

> Files can store programs, music, pictures, video, and so on

In Java, streams are implemented as objects of special stream classes. Objects of the class Scanner, which we have been using for keyboard input, are input streams. The object System.out is an example of an output stream

> A stream is a flow of data into or out of a program

FIGURE 10.1 **Input and Output Streams**

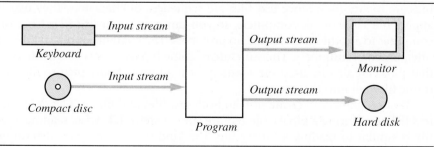

that we have also used. In this chapter, we discuss streams that connect your program to files instead of to the keyboard or display.

RECAP   **Streams**

A stream is an object that either

- Delivers data from your program to a destination, such as a file or the screen, or
- Takes data from a source, such as a file or the keyboard, and delivers the data to your program.

Why Use Files for I/O?

Data in a file remains after program execution ends

The keyboard input and screen output we have used so far deal with temporary data. When the program ends, the data typed at the keyboard and left on the screen go away. Files provide you with a way to store data permanently. The contents of a file remain until a person or program changes the file.

An input file can be used over and over again by different programs, without the need to type the data again for each program. Files also provide you with a convenient way to deal with large quantities of data. When your program takes its input from a large input file, it receives a lot of data without user effort.

Text Files and Binary Files

All of the data in any file is stored as binary digits (bits)—that is, as a long sequence of 0s and 1s. However, in some situations, we do not think of a file's contents as a sequence of binary digits. Instead, we think of them as a sequence of characters. Files that are thought of as sequences of characters, and that have streams and methods to make the binary digits look like characters to your program and your text editor, are called **text files**. All other files are called **binary files**. Each kind of file has its own streams and methods to process them.

Two kinds of files: text files and binary files

Your Java programs are stored in text files. Your music files and picture files are binary files. Since text files are sequences of characters, they usually appear the same on all computers, so you can move your text files from one computer to another with few or no problems. The contents of binary files are often based on numbers. The structure of some binary files is standardized so that they can also be used on a variety of platforms. Many picture files and music files fall into this category.

Java programs can create or read both text files and binary files. Writing a text file and writing a binary file require similar steps. Likewise, reading a text file is similar to reading a binary file. The kind of file, however, determines which classes we use to perform the input and output.

The one big advantage of text files is that you can create, look at, and edit them by using a text editor. You have already done this when writing a Java program. With binary files, all the reading and writing must normally be done by a special program. Some binary files must be read by the same type of computer and with the same programming language that originally created them. However, Java binary files are platform independent; that is, with Java, you can move your binary files from one type of computer to another, and your Java programs will still be able to read the binary files.

Each character in a text file is represented as 1 or 2 bytes, depending on whether the system uses ASCII or Unicode. When a program writes a value to a text file, the number of characters written is the same as if they were written to a display using `System.out.println`. For example, writing the `int` value 12345 to a text file places five characters in the file, as shown in Figure 10.2. In general, writing an integer places between 1 and 11 characters in a text file.

Binary files store all values of the same primitive data in the same format. Each is stored as a sequence of the same number of bytes. For example, all `int` values occupy 4 bytes each in a binary file, as Figure 10.2 also illustrates. A Java program interprets these bytes in very much the same way that it interprets a data item, such as an integer, in the computer's main memory. That is why binary files can be handled so efficiently.

FAQ Should I use a text file or a binary file?

Use a text file if you want a text editor to either create a file that a program will read or read a file that a program created. In other cases, consider a binary file, as it usually occupies less space.

REMEMBER Input and Output Terminology

The word *input* means that data moves into your program, not into the file. The word *output* means that data moves out of your program, not out of the file.

FIGURE 10.2A   Text File and a Binary File Containing the Same Values

A text file

| 1 | 2 | 3 | 4 | 5 | | – | 4 | 0 | 2 | 7 | | 8 | | … |

A binary file

| 12345 | –4072 | 8 | … |

SELF-TEST QUESTIONS

1. Why would anybody write a program that sends its output to a file instead of to the screen?

2. When we discuss input, are we referring to data moving from the program to a file or from a file to the program?

3. What is the difference between a text file and a binary file?

10.2 TEXT-FILE I/O

Proper words in proper places,

make the true definition of a style.

—JONATHAN SWIFT, LETTER TO A YOUNG CLERGYMAN (JANUARY 9,1720)

In this section, we give a description of the most common ways to perform text-file I/O in Java.

Creating a Text File

The class `PrintWriter` in the Java Class Library defines the methods that we will need to create and write to a text file. This class is the preferred one for writing to a text file. It is in the package `java.io`, so we will need to begin our program with an `import` statement. Actually, we will be using other classes as well, so we will import them also, as you will see soon.

Before we can write to a text file, we must connect it to an output stream. That is, we **open** the file. To do this, we need the name of the file as a string. The file has a name like `out.txt` that the operating system uses. We also must declare a variable that we will use to reference the stream associated with the actual file. This variable is called the **stream variable**. Its data type in this case is `PrintWriter`. We open a text file for output by invoking `PrintWriter`'s constructor and passing it the file name as its argument. Since this action can throw an exception, we must place the call to the constructor within a `try` block.

The following statements will open the text file `out.txt` for output:

Opening a file connects it to a stream

```
String fileName = "out.txt";//Could read file name from user
PrintWriter outputStream = null;
try
{
    outputStream = new PrintWriter(fileName);
}
catch(FileNotFoundException e)
{
    System.out.println("Error opening the file " + fileName);
    System.exit(0);
}
```

The class `FileNotFoundException` must also be imported from the package `java.io`.

Note that the name of the file, in this case `out.txt`, is given as a `String` value. Generally, we would read the name of the file instead of using a literal. We pass the file name as an argument to the `PrintWriter` constructor. The result is an object of the class `PrintWriter`, which we assign to our stream variable `outputStream`.

When you connect a file to an output stream in this way, your program always starts with an empty file. If the file `out.txt` already exists, its old contents will be lost. If the file `out.txt` does not exist, a new, empty file named `out.txt` will be created.

Because the `PrintWriter` constructor might throw a `FileNotFoundException` while attempting to open the file, its invocation must appear within a `try` block. Any exception is caught in a `catch` block. If the constructor throws an exception, it does not necessarily mean that the file was not found. After all, if you are creating a new file, it doesn't already exist. In that case, an exception would mean that the file could not be created because, for example, the file name was already being used for a folder (directory) name.

After we open the file—that is, connect the file to the stream—we can write data to it. The method `println` of the class `PrintWriter` works the same for writing to a textfile as the method `System.out.println` works for writing to the screen. `PrintWriter` also has the method `print`, which behaves just like `System.out.print`, except that the output goes to a text file.

Now that the file is open, we always refer to it by using the stream variable, not its name. Our stream variable `outStream` references the output stream—that is, the `PrintWriter` object—that we created, so we will use it when we invoke `println`. Notice that `outStream` is declared outside of the `try` block so that it is available outside of the block. Remember, anything declared in a block—even within a `try` block—is local to the block.

Let's write a couple of lines to the text file. The following statements would come after the previous statements that opened the file:

```
outputStream.println("This is line 1.");
outputStream.println("Here is line 2.");
```

Rather than sending output to a file immediately, `PrintWriter` waits to send a larger packet of data. Thus, the output from a `println` statement, for example, is not sent to the output file right away. Instead, it is saved and placed into an area of memory called a **buffer,** along with the output from other invocations of `print` and `println`. When the buffer is too full to accept more output, its contents are written to the file. Thus, the output from several `println` statements is written at the same time, instead of each time a `println` executes. This technique is called **buffering;** it allows faster file processing.

After we finish writing the entire text file, we disconnect the stream from the file. That is, we **close** the stream connected to the file by writing Closing a file
disconnects it
from a stream

```
outputStream.close();
```

Closing the stream causes the system to release any resources used to connect the stream to the file and to do some other housekeeping. If you do not close a stream, Java will close it for you when the program ends. However, it is safest to close the stream by explicitly calling the method close. Recall that when you write data to a file, the data might not immediately reach its destination. Closing an output stream forces any pending output to be written to the file. If you do not close the stream and your program terminates abnormally, Java might not be able to close it for you, and data can be lost. The sooner you close a stream, the less likely it is that this will happen.

If your program writes to a file and later reads from the same file, it must close the stream after it is through writing to the file and then reopen the file for reading. (Java does have a class that allows a file to be open for both reading and writing, but we will not cover that class in this book.) Note that all stream classes, such as PrintWriter, include a method named close.

The calls to println and close need not be within a try block, as they do not throw exceptions that must be caught. Listing 10.1 contains a simple but complete program that creates a text file from data read from the user. Notice that the lines shown in the resulting text file look just as they would if we wrote them to the screen. We can read this file either by using a text editor or by using another Java program that we will write a little later.

LISTING 10.1   Writing Output to a Text File *(part 1 of 2)*

```java
import java.io.PrintWriter;
import java.io.FileNotFoundException;
import java.util.Scanner;

public class TextFileOutputDemo
{
    public static void main(String[] args)
    {
        String fileName = "out.txt"; //The name could be read from
                                     //the keyboard.
        PrintWriter outputStream = null;
        try
        {
            outputStream = new PrintWriter(fileName};
        }
        catch(FileNotFoundException e)
        {
            System.out.println("Error opening the file" +
                                    fileName);
            System.exit(0);
        }
```

(continued)

LISTING 10.1 **Writing Output to a Text File** *(part 2 of 2)*

```
        System.out.println("Enter three lines of text:");
        Scanner keyboard = new Scanner(System.in);
        for (int count = 1; count <= 3; count++)
        {
            String line = keyboard.nextLine();
            outputStream.println(count + " " + line);
        }
        outputStream.close();
        System.out.println("Those lines were written to " +
                            fileName);
    }
}
```

Sample Screen Output

```
Enter three lines of text:
A tall tree
in a short forest is like
a big fish in a small pond.
Those lines were written to out.txt
```

Resulting file

```
1 A tall tree
2 in a short forest is like
3 a big fish in a small pond.
```
You can use a text editor to read this file.

RECAP **Creating a Text File**

SYNTAX

```
// Open the file PrintWriter
Output_Stream_Name = null;
try
{
    Output_Stream_Name = new PrintWriter(File_Name);
}
catch(FileNotFoundException e)
{
    Statements_Dealing_With_The_Exception
}
```

(continued)

```
// Write the file using statements of either or both of the
// following forms:
Output_Stream_Name.println(...);
Output_Stream_Name.print(...);
// Close the file
Output_Stream_Name.close();
```

EXAMPLE

See Listing 10.1.

■ **PROGRAMMING TIP**   A Program Should Not Be Silent

A program that creates a file should inform the user when it has finished writing the file. Otherwise, you will have written a **silent program,** and the user will wonder whether the program has succeeded or has encountered a problem. This advice applies to both text files and binary files.   ■

REMEMBER A File Has Two Names in a Program

Every file used by a program, whether for input or for output, appears to have two names: the actual file name used by the operating system and the name of the stream that is connected to the file. The file name is used when connecting the file to a stream. The stream name is used thereafter to work with the file. The stream name does not exist after the program ends its execution, but the actual file name persists. Note that, since a stream variable can have aliases, a file actually can have more than two names. However, distinguishing between a file name and a stream name is what is important here.

FAQ What are the rules for naming files?

The rules for how you spell file names depend on your operating system, not on Java. When you pass a file name to a Java constructor for a stream, you are not giving the constructor a Java identifier. You are giving the constructor a string corresponding to the file name. Most common operating systems allow you to use letters, digits, and the dot symbol when spelling file names. Many operating systems allow other characters as well, but letters, digits, and the dot symbol are enough for most purposes. A suffix, such as .txt in out.txt, has no special meaning to a Java program. We are using the suffix to indicate a text file, but that is just a common convention. You can use any file names that are allowed by your operating system, but you should be aware that some operating systems will hide the suffix by default.

GOTCHA   A try Block Is a Block

Look again at the program in Listing 10.1. It is not an accident or a minor stylistic concern that caused us to declare the variable outputStream outside the try block. Suppose we were to move that declaration inside the try block, like this:

```
try
{
    PrintWriter outputStream = new PrintWriter(fileName);
}
```

This replacement looks innocent enough, but it makes outputStream a local variable in the try block. Thus, we would not be able to use outputStream outside the try block. If we did, we would get an error message saying that outputStream is an undefined identifier. ∎

Chapter 8 suggested that you define a method toString in your classes. This method returns a string representation of the data in an instance of the class. The methods print and println of System.out invoke toString automatically when given an object as an argument. This is also true for print and println of an object of PrintWriter.

For example, we could add a toString method to the class Species in Chapter 5. Recall that this class defines three instance variables: name, population, and growthRate. Thus, we could define toString, as follows:

Overriding toString in the class Species

```
public String toString()
{
    return ("Name = " + name + "\n" +
            "Population = " + population + "\n" +
            "Growth rate = " + growthRate + "%");
}
```

Now, if we write the statements

```
Species oneRecord = new Species("Calif. Condor", 27, 0.02);
System.out.println(oneRecord.toString());
```

in a program, they will produce the output

```
Name = Calif. Condor
Population = 27
Growth rate = 0.02%
```

We also know that

```
System.out.println(oneRecord);
```

will invoke automatically, and so it will produce the same output.

The same is true if we were to write to a text file. Either of the statements

```
outputStream.println(oneRecord.toString());
```

or

```
outputStream.println(oneRecord);
```

will write the previously shown output to the text file attached to the stream
`outputStream`.

Extra code on the
Web

The program in the file `TextFileSpeciesOutputDemo`, which is in the
source code available on the book's Web site, illustrates this fact.

■ **PROGRAMMING TIP**   **Define the Method toString for Your
Classes**

Since the methods `print` and `println` automatically invoke the method
`toString`, regardless of whether they belong to the object `System.out` or to
an object of an output stream, it is a good idea to define `toString` for your
classes.   ■

GOTCHA   **Overwriting a File**

When you open a text file or a binary file for output, you always begin with
an empty file. If no existing file has the given name, the constructor that you
invoke will create an empty file with that name. But if an existing file has the
given name, all of its data will be eliminated. Any new output will be written
to this existing file. Section 10.3 shows how to test for the existence of a file so
that you can avoid accidentally overwriting it.   ■

Appending to a Text File

The way we opened a text file for output in Listing 10.1 ensures that we always
begin with an empty file. If the named file already exists, its old contents
will be lost. Sometimes, however, that is not what we want. We may simply
want to add, or **append**, more data to the end of the file. To append program
output to the text file named by the `String` variable `fileName`, we would
connect the file to the stream `outputStream` as follows:

Appending, or
adding, data to
the end of a file

```
outputStream =
    new PrintWriter(new FileOutputStream(fileName, true));
```

Since `PrintWriter` does not have an appropriate constructor for this task, we
need some help from the class `FileOutputStream`, which we must import
from the package java.io. The second argument (`true`) of `FileOutputStream`'s
constructor indicates that we want to add data to the file, if it exists already.
So if the file already exists, its old contents will remain, and the program's
output will be placed after those contents. But if the file does not already
exist, Java will create an empty file of that name and append the output to
the end of this empty file. The effect in this case is the same as in Listing 10.1.

When appending to a text file in this way, we would still use the same `try` and catch blocks as in Listing 10.1. A version of the program in Listing 10.1 that appends to the file `out.txt` is in the program `AppendTextFile.java` included with the source code for this book available on the Web.

Extra code on the Web

RECAP   Opening a Text File for Appending

You can create a stream of the class `PrintWriter` that appends data to the end of an existing text file.

SYNTAX

```
PrintWriter Output_Stream_Name = new PrintWriter(new
FileOutputStream(File_Name, true));
```

EXAMPLE

```
PrintWriter outputStream = new PrintWriter(new
FileOutputStream("out.txt", true));
```

After this statement, you can use the methods `println` and `print` to write to the file, and the new text will be written after the old text in the file. (In practice, you might want to separate the declaration of the stream variable and the invocation of the constructor, as we did in Listing 10.1, so you can handle a `FileNotFoundException` that might be thrown when opening the file.)

SELF-TEST QUESTIONS

myprogramminglab

4. Write some code that will create a stream named `outStream` that is an object of the class `PrintWriter` and that connects this stream to a text file named `sam.txt` so that your program can send output to the file. If the file `sam.txt` does not exist, create a new empty file. However, if a file named `sam.txt` already exists, erase its old contents so the program can start with an empty file with that name.

5. Repeat Question 4, but if the file `sam.txt` exists already, write the new data after the old contents of the file.

6. Repeat Question 4, but read the name of the file from the user.

7. What kind of exception might be thrown by the following statement, and what would be indicated if this exception were thrown?

```
PrintWriter outputStream = new PrintWriter("out.txt");
```

Reading from a Text File

Listing 10.2 contains a simple program that reads data from a text file and writes it to the screen. The file out.txt is a text file that could have been created by either a person using a text editor or a Java program—such as the one in Listing 10.1—using the class PrintWriter. Notice that we use the class

LISTING 10.2   Reading Data from a Text File

```java
import java.util.Scanner;
import java.io.File;
import java.io.FileNotFoundException;

public class TextFileInputDemo
{
    public static void main(String[] args)
    {
        String fileName = "out.txt";
        Scanner inputStream = null;
        System.out.println("The file " + fileName +
                        "\ncontains the following lines:\n");
        try
        {
            inputStream = new Scanner(new File(fileName));
        }
        catch(FileNotFoundException e)
        {
            System.out.println("Error opening the file " +
                                fileName);
            System.exit(0);
        }
        while (inputStream.hasNextLine())
        {
            String line = inputStream.nextLine();
            System.out.println(line);
        }
        inputStream.close();
    }
}
```

Screen Output

```
The file out.txt
contains the following lines;
1 A tall tree
2 in a short forest is like
3 a big fish in a small pond.
```

Scanner, the same class we have been using to read data from the keyboard. Recall that we passed System.in as an argument to Scanner's constructor.

Unfortunately, we cannot pass a file name to Scanner's constructor. Although Scanner does have a constructor that takes a string argument, the string is interpreted as data, and not the name of a file. Scanner, however, does have a constructor that accepts as an argument an instance of another standard class, File, and File has a constructor to which we can pass a file name. (The next section will describe the class File in more detail.) So a statement of the following form will open the file for input:

```
Scanner Stream_Name = new Scanner(new File(File_Name));
```

If your program attempts to open a file for reading, but there is no such file, Scanner's constructor will throw a FileNotFoundException. As you saw earlier in this chapter, a FileNotFoundException is also thrown in certain other situations.

Using Scanner to open a text file for input

Notice that the program in Listing 10.2 has some general similarities to the program in Listing 10.1 that created a text file. Each opens the file using try-catch blocks, does something with the file, and then closes the file. Let's look at the statements in Listing 10.2 that read and display the entire file:

```
while (inputStream.hasNextLine())
{
    String line = inputStream.nextLine();
    System.out.println(line);
}
```

Reading and displaying an entire text file

This loop reads and then displays each line in the file, one at a time, until the end of the file is reached. The screen output shown in Listing 10.2 assumes that the file out.txt is the one we created in Listing 10.1.

All the methods of Scanner that we have used before are still available to us and work in the same way. Some of these methods, including nextLine, are described in Figure 2.7 of Chapter 2. However, we have not used the method hasNextLine before. It returns true if another line in the file is available for input. Figure 10.3 summarizes this method and a few other analogous methods.

RECAP Reading a Text File

SYNTAX

```
// Open the file
Scanner Input_Stream_Name = null;
try
{
    Input_Stream_Name = new Scanner(new File(File_Name));
}
```

(continued)

VideoNote
**Writing and reading a
text file**

```
        catch(FileNotFoundException e)
        {
            Statements_Dealing_With_The_Exception
        }
        // Read the file using statements of the form:
        Input_Stream_Name.Scanner_Method();
        // Close the file
        Input_Stream_Name.close();
```

EXAMPLE

See Listing 10.2

SELF-TEST QUESTIONS

8. Write some code that will create a stream named `textStream` that is an object of the class `PrintWriter` and that connects the stream to a text file named dobedo so that your program can send output to this file.

9. Suppose you run a program that writes to the text file dobedo, using the stream defined in the previous self-test question. Write some code that will create a stream named `inputStream` that can be used to read from this text file in the ways we discussed in this section.

10. What is the type of a value returned by the method `next` in the class Scanner? What is the type of a value returned by the method `nextLine` in the class Scanner?

FIGURE 10.3   Additional Methods in the Class Scanner
(See also Figure 2.7)

Scanner_Object_Name.hasNext() Returns true if more input data is available to be read by the method `next`.
Scanner_Object_Name.hasNextDouble() Returns true if more input data is available to be read by the method `nextDouble`.
Scanner_Object_Name.hasNextInt() Returns true if more input data is available to be read by the method `nextInt`.
Scanner_Object_Name.hasNextLine() Returns true if more input data is available to be read by the method `nextLine`.

10.3 TECHNIQUES FOR ANY FILE

An ounce of prevention is worth a pound of cure.

—COMMON SAYING

This section discusses some techniques that we can use with both text files and binary files, even though our examples here will involve text files. We begin by describing the standard class `File`, which we used in the previous section when reading from a text file.

The Class `File`

The class `File` provides a way to represent file names in a general way. A string such as `"treasure.txt"` might be a file name, but it has only string properties, and Java does not recognize it as a file name. On the other hand, if you pass a file name as a string to the constructor of the class `File`, it produces an object that can be thought of as the name of a file. In other words, it is a system-independent abstraction rather than an actual file. For example, the object

```
new File("treasure.txt")
```

is not simply a string. It is an object that "knows" it is supposed to name a file.

Although some stream classes have constructors that accept a string as the name of a file, some do not. Some stream classes have constructors that accept only a `File` object as an argument. We already saw in the previous section that when reading a text file, we cannot pass the file's name as a string to Scanner's constructor. Instead, we passed it an object of the class `File`. The class `PrintWriter`, which we used to write a text file, has a constructor that accepts a string as the name of a file, as well as a constructor that accepts an instance of `File` to specify a particular file.

A `File` object represents the name of a file

Before we go on to describe some of `File`'s methods, let's look at an example that reads the name of a file from the user. Although our example uses a text file, we can do something similar with binary files.

PROGRAMMING EXAMPLE   Reading a File Name from the Keyboard

Thus far, we have assigned a quoted string to a `String` variable and used it as the file name in our programs. However, you might not know what the file name will be when you write a program, so you may want to have the user enter the file name at the keyboard when the program is run. This task is easy to do. Simply have the program read the file name into the `String` variable. This technique is illustrated in Listing 10.3. That program is just like the one

Let the user enter the file name at the keyboard

in Listing 10.2, but it replaces the assignment to `filename` with statements that read the file name from the keyboard.

LISTING 10.3 Reading a File Name and Then the File

```java
import java.util.Scanner;
import java.io.File;
import java.io.FileNotFoundException;

public class TextFileInputDemo2
{
    public static void main(String[] args)
    {
        System.out.print("Enter file name: ");
        Scanner keyboard = new Scanner(System.in);
        String fileName = keyboard.next();
        Scanner inputStream = null;
        System.out.println("The file " + fileName + "\n" +
                           "contains the following lines:\n");
        try
        {
            inputStream = new Scanner(new File(fileName));
        }
        catch(FileNotFoundException e)
        {
            System.out.println("Error opening the file " +
                               fileName");
            System.exit(0).
        }
        while (inputStream.hasNextLine())
        {
            String line = inputStream.nextLine();
            System.out.println(line);
        }
        inputStream.close();
    }
}
```

Sample Screen Output

```
Enter file name: out.txt
The file out.txt
contains the following lines:
1 A tall tree
2 in a short forest is like
3 a big fish in a small pond.
```

Notice that our new program reads input from two different places. The Scanner object named keyboard is used to read the name of the file from the keyboard. The Scanner object named inputStream is connected to the specified file and is used to read data from that file.

Using Path Names

When writing a file name as an argument to a constructor for opening a file in any of the ways we have discussed, the file is assumed to be in the same directory (folder) as the one in which the program is run. However, we could specify the directory that contains the file, if it is different than the location of the program, by writing a **path name** instead of only the name of the file. A **full path name,** as the name suggests, gives a complete path name, starting from the root directory. A **relative path name** gives the path to the file, starting with the directory containing your program. The way you specify path names depends on your particular operating system, and we will discuss only some of the details here.

A path name specifies the folder containing a file

An example of a typical UNIX path name is

```
/user/smith/homework1/data.txt
```

To create an input stream connected to this file, we would write

```
Scanner inputStream = new Scanner(new
            File("/user/smith/homework1/data.txt"));
```

Windows uses \ instead of / in path names. A typical Windows path name is

```
C:\homework\hw1\data.txt
```

To create an input stream connected to this file, we would write

```
Scanner inputStream = new Scanner(
            new File("C:\\homework\\hw1\\data.txt"));
```

Notice that we must use \\ in place of \, as Java will otherwise interpret a backslash paired with another character—for example, \h—as an escape character.

Although we normally must be careful about using a backslash in a quoted string, this problem does not occur when reading a name from the keyboard. Suppose we run a program like the one in Listing 10.3, and suppose part of the dialogue with the user is as follows:

```
Enter file name:
C:\homework\hw1\data.txt
```

This path name will be understood. The user need not type double backslashes, as in

```
C:\\homework\\hw1\\data.txt
```

In fact, the use of \\ in input might produce an incorrect reading of the file name. When the user enters input at the keyboard, Java "understands" that \h is the backslash character followed by an h and not an escape character, because everything the user types consists of characters.

One way to avoid these escape-character problems altogether is always to use UNIX conventions when writing path names. A Java program will accept a path name written in either Windows or UNIX format, even if it is run on a computer whose operating system does not match the format used. Thus, an alternative way to create an input stream connected to the Windows file

```
C:\homework\hw1\data.txt
```

is the following:

```
Scanner inputStream = new Scanner( new
           File("C:/homework/hw1/data.txt"));
```

Methods of the Class File

You can use methods of the class File to check properties of files. You can check things like whether an existing file either has a specified name or is readable.

Suppose you create a File object and name it fileObject using the following code:

```
File fileObject = new File("treasure.txt");
```

Recall that a File object is not a file. Rather, fileObject is a system-independent abstraction of a file's path name—treasure.txt, in this case.

A File object can check whether a file by that name exists or is readable

After creating fileObject, you can then use the File method exists to test whether any existing file has the name treasure.txt. For example, you can write

```
if (!fileObject.exists())
    System.out.println("No file by that name.")
```

If there already is such a file, you can use the method canRead to see whether the operating system will let you read from the file. For example, you can write

```
if (!fileObject.canRead())
    System.out.println("Not allowed to read from that file.");
```

Files can be tagged as readable or not readable

Most operating systems let you designate some files as not readable or as readable only by certain users. The method canRead provides a good way to check whether you or somebody else has made a file nonreadable—either inadvertently or intentionally.

We could add the following statements to the program shown in Listing 10.3 to check that we have a text file ready as input, right after we read the file's name:

```
File fileObject = new File(fileName);
boolean fileOK = false;
while (!fileOK)
{
    if (!fileObject.exists( ))
        System.out.println("No such file");
    elseif (!fileObject.canRead( ))
            System.out.println("That file is not readable.");
    else
        fileOK = true;
    if (!fileOK)
    {
        System.out.println("Enter file name again:");
        fileName = keyboard.next( );
        fileObject = new File(fileName);
    }
}
```

We have made this change to the program in Listing 10.3 and saved it in the file FileClassDemo.java, which is included in the source code for this book on its Web site.

Extra code on the Web

The method canWrite is similar to canRead, except that the former checks to see whether the operating system will allow you to write to the file. Most operating systems let you designate some files as not writable or as writable only by certain users. Figure 10.4 lists these methods and some others that are in the class File.

RECAP The Class File

The class File represents file names. The constructor for the class File takes a string as an argument and produces an object that can be thought of as the file with that name. You can use the File object and methods of the class File to answer questions such as the following: Does the file exist? Does your program have permission to read the file? Does your program have permission to write to the file? Figure 10.4 summarizes some of the methods for the class File.

EXAMPLE

```
File file Object = new File("stuff.txt");
if (!fileObject.exists())
    System.out.println("There is no file named "+
                        "stuff.txt.");
else if (!fileObject.canRead())
    System.out.println("File stuff.txt is "+
                        "not readable.");
```

FIGURE 10.4   Some Methods in the Class `File`

`public boolean canRead()` Tests whether the program can read from the file.
`public boolean canWrite()` Tests whether the program can write to the file.
`public boolean delete()` Tries to delete the file. Returns true if it was able to delete the file.
`public boolean exists()` Tests whether an existing file has the name used as an argument to the constructor when the `File` object was created.
`public String getName()` Returns the name of the file. (Note that this name is not a path name, just a simple file name.)
`public String getPath()` Returns the path name of the file.
`public long length()` Returns the length of the file, in bytes.

FAQ   What is the difference between a file and a `File` object?

A file is a collection of data stored on a physical device such as a disc.
A `File` object is a system-independent abstraction of a file's path name.

SELF-TEST QUESTION

11. Write a complete Java program that asks the user for a file name, tests whether the file exists, and—if the file does exist—asks the user whether or not it should be deleted and then does as the user requests.

Defining a Method to Open a Stream

Imagine that we want to write a method that opens a file. We will use a text file here and open it for output, but the idea is applicable to any kind of file. Our method has a `String` parameter that represents the file name, which could be either a literal or a string read from the user, as shown earlier. The following method creates an output stream, connects it to the named text file, and returns the stream:

```
public static PrintWriter openOutputTextFile
    (String fileName) throws FileNotFoundException
{
    PrintWriter toFile = new PrintWriter(fileName);
    return toFile;
}
```

We could invoke this method as follows:

```
PrintWriter outputStream = null;
try
{
    outputStream = openOutputTextFile("data.txt");
}
<appropriate catch block(s)>
```

and go on to use `outputStream` to write to the file. A simple program demonstrating this technique is in the file `OpenFileDemo.java` included with the source code for this book available on the Web.

Extra code on the Web

What if we had written the method as a `void` method so that instead of returning an output stream, it had the stream as a parameter? The following method looks reasonable, but it has a problem:

```
// This method does not do what we want it to do.
public static void openFile(String fileName,
    PrintWriter stream) throws FileNotFoundException
{
    stream = new PrintWriter(fileName);
}
```

Let's consider, for example, the following statements that invoke the method:

```
PrintWriter toFile = null;
try
{
    openFile("data.txt", toFile);
}
```

After this code is executed, the value of `toFile` is still `null`. The file that was opened in the method `openFile` went away when the method ended. The problem has to do with how Java handles arguments of a class type. These arguments are passed to the method as memory addresses that cannot be changed. The state of the object at the memory address normally can be changed, but the memory address itself cannot be changed. Thus, you cannot change the value of `toFile`.

This applies only to arguments of methods. If the stream variable is either an instance variable or declared locally within the body of the method, you can open a file and connect it to the stream and this problem will not occur. Once a stream is connected to a file, you can pass the stream variable as an argument to a method, and the method can change the file.

CASE STUDY Processing a Comma-Separated Values File

A **comma-separated values** or **CSV** file is a simple text format used to store a list of records. A comma is used as a delimiter to separate the fields (also referred to as columns) for each record. This format is commonly used to transfer data between a spreadsheet, database, or custom application program. As an example, consider a cash register that saves a log of the day's sales in a CSV file named `Transactions.txt`. The text file contains the following data:

```
SKU,Quantity,Price,Description
4039,50,0.99,SODA
9100,5,9.50,T-SHIRT
1949,30,110.00,JAVA PROGRAMMING TEXTBOOK
5199,25,1.50,COOKIE
```

The first line of the file is a header that identifies the fields. The first field is the SKU, or stock-keeping unit. This is a unique identifier associated with every product sold. The second field is the quantity of the SKU sold in the transaction. The third field is the price of one unit, and the last field is a description of the item sold. For example, the second line of the file indicates that 50 sodas were sold at a price of $0.99 each and the SKU for the soda is 4039.

There are many ways we might process the data, but in this case study we present a simple strategy to read every field in the file, output each transaction in a more English-like format, and compute the total sales for the cash register. The general algorithm is as follows:

1. Read and skip the header line of the file

2. Repeat while we have not reached the end of the file

    a. Read an entire line (one record) from the file as a String

    b. Create an array of strings from the line where `array[0]` is the value of the first field, `array[1]` is the value of the second field, etc.

    c. Convert any numeric fields from the array of strings to the appropriate numeric data type

    d. Process the fields.

Step 2b of the algorithm might seem to be difficult. At this step we have just read a line from the file. For the first line of our example we will have read `"4039,50,0.99,SODA"` into a variable of type `String`. Since a comma is used to separate every field, we could search the string for the first comma, extract the substring from the beginning of the string to the comma to extract the first field, and repeat this process for every successive field. However, the `split` method associated with the `String` class does all this for us and is defined as follows:

```
public String[] split(String delimiter)
```

The method splits the string around matches of `delimiter` and returns an array of the strings separated by `delimiter`. The `delimiter` parameter is interpreted as a regular expression, which is a flexible way to match patterns. For our purposes we will simply use this as a string that contains our delimiter character of a comma. The following example illustrates the `split` method.

```
String line = "4039,50,0.99,SODA"
String[] ary = line.split(",");
System.out.println(ary[0]);          // Outputs 4039
System.out.println(ary[1]);          // Outputs 50
System.out.println(ary[2]);          // Outputs 0.99
System.out.println(ary[3]);          // Outputs SODA
```

Listing 10.4 applies the technique to the sales transaction scenario. All that remains is to read the file, parse the quantity into an integer, parse the price into a double, and add the business logic to compute total sales by accumulating the product of the quantity sold multiplied by the price of the item. In the program, we used `System.out.printf` to format the price and totals with two decimal places.

LISTING 10.4   Processing a Comma-Separated Values File Containing Sales Transactions *(part 1 of 2)*

```
import java.io.FileInputStream;
import java.io.FileNotFoundException;
import java.io.IOException;
import java.io.File;
import java.util.Scanner;
public class TransactionReader
{
public static void main(String[] args)
    {
        String fileName = "Transactions.txt";
        try
        {
        Scanner inputStream = new Scanner(new File(fileName));
        // Skip the header line by reading and ignoring it
        String line = inputStream.nextLine();
        // Total sales
        double total = 0;
        // Read the rest of the file line by line
        while (inputStream.hasNextLine())
        {
            // Contains SKU,Quantity,Price,Description
            line = inputStream.nextLine();
```

(continued)

LISTING 10.4 **Processing a Comma-Separated Values File Containing Sales Transactions** *(part 2 of 2)*

```java
                // Turn the string into an array of strings
                String[] ary = line.split(",");
                // Extract each item into an appropriate
                // variable
                String SKU = ary[0];
                int quantity = Integer.parseInt(ary[1]);
                double price = Double.parseDouble(ary[2]);
                String description = ary[3];
                // Output item
                System.out.printf("Sold %d of %s (SKU: %s) at "+
                    "$%1.2f each.\n",
                    quantity, description, SKU, price);
                // Compute total
                total += quantity * price;
            }
            System.out.printf("Total sales: $%1.2f\n",total);
            inputStream.close( );
        }
        catch(FileNotFoundException e)
        {
            System.out.println("Cannot find file " + fileName);
        }
        catch(IOException e)
        {
            System.out.println("Problem with input from file " +
            fileName);
        }
    }
}
```

Sample Screen Output

```
Sold 50 of SODA (SKU: 4039) at $0.99 each.
Sold 5 of T-SHIRT (SKU: 9100) at $9.50 each.
Sold 30 of JAVA PROGRAMMING TEXTBOOK (SKU: 1949) at
$110.00 each.
Sold 25 of COOKIE (SKU: 5199) at $1.50 each.
Total sales: $3434.50
```

10.4 BASIC BINARY-FILE I/O

The White Rabbit put on his spectacles. "Where shall I begin, please your Majesty" he asked.

"Begin at the beginning," the King said, very gravely, "And go on till you come to the end: then stop."

—LEWIS CARROLL, *ALICE IN WONDERLAND*

We will use the stream classes `ObjectInputStream` and `ObjectOutputStream` to read and write binary files. Each of these classes has methods to read or write data one byte at a time. These streams can also convert numbers and characters to bytes that can be stored in a binary file. They allow your program to be written as if the data placed in the file, or read from the file, were made up not just of bytes but of either items of any of Java's primitive data types—such as `int`, `char`, and `double`—or strings or even objects of classes you define, as well as entire arrays. If you do not need to access your files via a text editor, the easiest and most efficient way to read data from and write data to files is to use `ObjectOutputStream` to write to a binary file and `ObjectInputStream` to read from the binary file.

We begin by creating a binary file, and then discuss how to write primitive-type data and strings to the file. Later, we will investigate using other objects and arrays as data for input and output.

Creating a Binary File

If you want to create a binary file to store values of a primitive type, strings, or other objects, you can use the stream class `ObjectOutputStream`. Listing 10.5 shows a program that writes integers to a binary file. Let's look at the details shown in that program.

Note that the substance of the program is in a `try` block. Any code that does binary-file I/O in the ways we are describing can throw an `IOException`. Your programs can catch any `IOException` that is thrown, so that you get an error message and the program ends normally.

We can create an output stream for the binary file `numbers.dat` as follows:

```
ObjectOutputStream outputStream =
    new ObjectOutputStream(new FileOutputStream
        ("numbers.dat"));
```

As with text files, this process is called opening the (binary) file. If the file `numbers.dat` does not already exist, this statement will create an empty file named `numbers.dat`. If the file `numbers.dat` already exists, this statement will erase the contents of the file, so that the file starts out empty. The situation is basically the same as what happens when opening a text file, except that we're using a different class here.

Note that the constructor for `ObjectOutputStream` cannot take a string argument, but the constructor for `FileOutputStream` can. Moreover, `ObjectOutputStream` does have a constructor that will accept an object of

Opening a binary file for output

LISTING 10.5   Using `ObjectOutputStream` to Write to a File
(part 1 of 2)

```java
import java.io.FileOutputStream;
import java.io.ObjectOutputStream;
import java.io.FileNotFoundException;
import java.io.IOException;
import java.util.Scanner;

public class BinaryOutputDemo
{
    public static void main(String[] args)
    {
        String fileName = "numbers.dat";
        try
        {
            ObjectOutputStream outputStream =
            new ObjectOutputStream(new
                        FileOutputStream(fileName));
            Scanner keyboard = new Scanner(System.in);

            System.out.println("Enter nonnegative integers.");
            System.out.println("Place a negative number at the "+
                                "end.");

            int anInteger;
            do
            {
                anInteger = keyboard.nextInt();
                outputStream.writeInt(anInteger);
            } while (anInteger >= 0);

            System.out.println("Numbers and sentinel value");
            System.out.println("written to the file " + fileName);
            outputStream.close();   ←——— A binary file is closed in the same
        }                                 way as a text file.
        catch(FileNotFoundException e)
        {
            System.out.println("Problem opening the file " +
            fileName);
        }
        catch(IOException e)
        {
            System.out.println("Problem with output to file " +
            fileName);
        }
    }
}
```

(continued)

LISTING 10.5   **Using** `ObjectOutputStream` **to Write to a File** *(part 2 of 2)*

Sample Screen Output

```
Enter nonnegative integers.
Place a negative number at the end.
1 2 3 -1
Number and sentinel value
written to the file numbers.dat
```

The binary file after the program is run: *This file is a binary file. You cannot read this file using a text editor.*

1	2	3	-1

The **-1** *in this file is a sentinel value. Ending a file with a sentinel value is not essential, as you will see later.*

FileOutputStream as its argument. So in much the same way that we passed a File object to the Scanner constructor when we read from a text file, we pass a FileOutputStream object to the constructor of ObjectOutputStream. Note that the ObjectOutputStream constructor can throw an IOException and the FileOutputStream constructor can throw a FileNotFoundException.

Exceptions are possible

Writing Primitive Values to a Binary File

An object of the class ObjectOutputStream does not have a method named println, as objects do when writing to either a text file or the screen. However, it does have a method named writeInt that can write a single int value to a binary file, as well as other output methods that we will discuss shortly. So once we have the stream outputStream of the class ObjectOutputStream connected to a file, we can write integers to the file, as in the following statement from Listing 10.5:

```
outputStream.writeInt(anInteger);
```

The method writeInt can throw an IOException.

Listing 10.5 shows the numbers in the file numbers.dat as if they were written in a human-readable form. That is not how they are actually written, however. A binary file has no lines or other separators between data items. Instead, items are written to the file in binary—each as a sequence of bytes—one immediately after the other. These encoded values typically cannot be read using an editor. Realistically, they will make sense only to another Java program.

You can use a stream from the class ObjectOutputStream to write values of any primitive type. Each primitive data type has a corresponding write method in the class ObjectOutputStream, such as writeLong, writeDouble, writeFloat, and writeChar.

Writing values of any primitive type to a binary file

The method `writeChar` can be used to write a single character. For example, the following would write the character `'A'` to the file connected to the stream named `outputStream`:

```
outputStream.writeChar('A');
```

The method `writeChar` has one possibly surprising property: It expects its argument to be of type `int`. So if you have an argument of type `char`, the `char` value will be type cast to an `int` before it is given to the method `writeChar`. Thus, the previous invocation is equivalent to the following one:

```
outputStream.writeChar((int)'A');
//You can omit the type cast
```

After you finish writing to a binary file, you close it in the same way that you close a text file. Here, the statement

```
outputStream.close();
```

closes the binary file.

Figure 10.5 summarizes some methods in the class `ObjectOutputStream`, including those that we have not discussed as yet. Many of these methods can throw an `IOException`.

RECAP Creating a Binary File

SYNTAX

```
try
{
    // Open the file
    ObjectOutputStream Output_Stream_Name =
        new ObjectOutputStream(new FileOutputStream(File_Name));
    // Write the file using statements of the form:
    Output_Stream_Name.MethodName(Argument); // See Figure 10.5
    // Close the file
    Output_Stream_Name.close();
}
catch(FileNotFoundException e)
{
    Statements_Dealing_With_The_Exception
}
catch(IOException e)
{
    Statements_Dealing_With_The_Exception
}
```

EXAMPLE

See Listing 10.5.

FIGURE 10.5   Some Methods in the Class `ObjectOutputStream` *(part 1 of 2)*

`public ObjectOutputStream(OutputStream streamObject)`
Creates an output stream that is connected to the specified binary file. There is no constructor that takes a file name as an argument. If you want to create a stream by using a file name, you write either

```
new ObjectOutputStream(new FileOutputStream(File_Name))
```

or, using an object of the class `File`,

```
new ObjectOutputStream(new FileOutputStream(
                          new File(File_Name)))
```

Either statement creates a blank file. If there already is a file named *File_Name*, the old contents of the file are lost.

The constructor for `FileOutputStream` can throw a `FileNotFoundException`. If it does not, the constructor for `ObjectOutputStream` can throw an `IOException`.

`public void writeInt(int n) throws IOException`
Writes the `int` value n to the output stream.

`public void writeLong(long n) throws IOException`
Writes the `long` value n to the output stream.

`public void writeDouble(double x) throws IOException`
Writes the `double` value x to the output stream.

`public void writeFloat(float x) throws IOException`
Writes the `float` value x to the output stream.

`public void writeChar(int c) throws IOException`
Writes a `char` value to the output stream. Note that the parameter type of c is `int`. However, Java will automatically convert a `char` value to an `int` value for you. So the following is an acceptable invocation of `writeChar`:

```
outputStream.writeChar('A');
```

`public void writeBoolean(boolean b) throws IOException`
Writes the `boolean` value b to the output stream.

`public void writeUTF(String aString) throws IOException`
Writes the string `aString` to the output stream. UTF refers to a particular method of encoding the string. To read the string back from the file, you should use the method `readUTF` of the class `ObjectInputStream`. These topics are discussed in the next section.

(continued)

FIGURE 10.5 **Some Methods in the Class** `ObjectOutputStream` *(part 2 of 2)*

```
public void writeObject(Object anObject) throws IOException,
            NotSerializableException, InvalidClassException
```
Writes anObject to the output stream. The argument should be an object of a serializable class, a concept discussed later in this chapter. Throws a `NotSerializable-Exception` if the class of anObject is not serializable. Throws an `InvalidClassException` if there is something wrong with the serialization. The method `writeObject` is covered later in this chapter.

```
public void close() throws IOException
```
Closes the stream's connection to a file.

---

myprogramminglab

SELF-TEST QUESTIONS

12. Write some Java code to create an output stream of type `ObjectOutputStream` that is named `to File` and is connected to a binary file named `stuff.data`.

13. Give three statements that will write the values of the three `double` variables x1, x2, and x3 to the file `stuff.data`. Use the stream `toFile` that you created for the previous question.

14. Give a statement that will close the stream `toFile` created for the previous two questions.

15. What import statement(s) do you use when creating a binary file?

Writing Strings to a Binary File

Use `writeUTF` for strings

To write a string to a binary file, we use the method `writeUTF`. For example, if `outputStream` is a stream of type `ObjectOutputStream`, the following will write the string "Hi Mom" to the file connected to that stream:

```
outputStream.writeUTF("Hi Mom");
```

Of course, with any of the write methods, you can use a variable of the appropriate type (in this case, the type `String`) as an argument to the method, instead of using a literal.

You may write output of different types to the same binary file. For example, you may write a combination of `int`, `double`, and `String` values. However, mixing types in a binary file does require special care, so that later the values in the file can be read correctly. In particular, we need to know the order in which the various types appear in the file, because, as you will see, we use a different method to read data of each different type.

FAQ What does UTF stand for?

To write an `int` to a stream of the class `ObjectOutputStream`, you use `writeInt`; to write a `double`, you use `writeDouble`; and so forth. However, to write a string, you use `writeUTF`. There is no method called `writeString` in `ObjectOutputStream`. Why this funny name `writeUTF`? UTF stands for Unicode Text Format. That is not a very descriptive name. Here is the full story:

Recall that Java uses the Unicode character set, which includes many characters used in languages whose character sets are very different from that of English. Most text editors and operating systems use the ASCII character set, which is the character set normally used for English and for typical Java programs. The ASCII character set is a subset of the Unicode character set, so the Unicode character set has many characters you do not need. For English-speaking countries, the Unicode way of encoding characters is not a very efficient scheme. The UTF coding scheme is an alternative scheme that codes all of the Unicode characters but favors the ASCII character set. It does so by giving short, efficient codes for ASCII characters but inefficient codes for the other Unicode characters. However, if you do not use the other Unicode characters, this is a good deal.

Some Details About `writeUTF`

The method `writeInt` writes integers into a file, using the same number of bytes—that is, the same number of 0s and 1s—to store any integer. Similarly, the method `writeLong` uses the same number of bytes to store each value of type `long`. However, these methods use different numbers of bytes. The situation is the same for all the other write methods that write primitive types to binary files. The method `writeUTF`, however, uses varying numbers of bytes to store different strings in a file. Longer strings require more bytes than shorter strings. This condition can present a problem to Java, because data items in a binary file have no separators between them. Java can make this approach work by writing some extra information at the start of each string. This extra information tells how many bytes are used to write the string, so that `readUTF` knows how many bytes to read and convert. (The method `readUTF` will be discussed a little later in this chapter, but as you may have already guessed, it reads a `String` value.)

The situation with `writeUTF` is even a little more complicated than we've just described, however. Notice that we said that the information at the start of the string code in the file tells how many *bytes* to read, *not how many characters are in the string.* These two figures are not the same. With the UTF way of encoding, different characters are encoded in different numbers of bytes. However, all the ASCII characters are stored in just one byte. If you are using only ASCII characters, therefore, this difference is more theoretical than real to you.

Reading from a Binary File

If you write to a binary file by using `ObjectOutputStream`, you can read from that file by using the stream class `ObjectInputStream`. Figure 10.6 gives some of the most commonly used methods for this class. If you compare these methods with the methods for `ObjectOutputStream` given in Figure 10.5, you will see that each output method has a corresponding input method. For example, if you write an integer to a file by using the method `writeInt` of `ObjectOutputStream`, you can read that integer from the file by using the method `readInt` of `ObjectInputStream`. If you write a number to a file by using the method `writeDouble` of `ObjectOutputStream`, you can use the method `readDouble` of `ObjectInputStream` to read it from the file, and so on.

You open a binary file for reading using `ObjectInputStream` in a manner similar to what you have already seen for `ObjectOutputStream`. The program in Listing 10.6 opens a binary file and connects it to a stream named

Opening a binary file for input

`inputStream` as follows:

```
ObjectInputStream inputStream =
    new ObjectInputStream(new FileInputStream(fileName));
```

Note that this statement is like the analogous one in Listing 10.5, except that here we use the classes `ObjectInputStream` and `FileInputStream` instead of `ObjectOutputStream` and `FileOutputStream`, respectively. Once again, the class that defines the methods we need does not have a constructor that accepts a string as an argument. In addition, the constructor for `FileInputStream` can throw a `FileNotFoundException`, which is a kind of `IOException`. If the `FileInputStream` constructor succeeds, the constructor for `ObjectInputStream` can throw a different `IOException`.

`ObjectInputStream` allows you to read input of different types from the same file. So you may read a combination of, for example, `int` values, `double` values, and `String` values. However, if the next data item in the file is not of the type expected by the reading method, the result is likely to be unpleasant. For example, if your program writes an integer using `writeInt`, any program that reads that integer should read it using `readInt`. If you instead use

Reading multiple types

`readLong` or `readDouble`, for example, your program will misbehave in unpredictable ways.

FIGURE 10.6   Some Methods in the Class `ObjectInputStream` *(part 1 of 2)*

`ObjectInputStream(InputStream streamObject)`
Creates an input stream that is connected to the specified binary file. There is no constructor that takes a file name as an argument. If you want to create a stream by using a file name, you use either

   `new ObjectInputStream(new FileInputStream(`*File_Name*`))`

or, using an object of the class `File`,

   `new ObjectInputStream(new FileInputStream(`
                   `new File(`*File_Name*`)))`

   The constructor for `FileInputStream` can throw a `FileNotFoundException`. If it does not, the constructor for `ObjectInputStream` can throw an `IOException`.

`public int readInt() throws EOFException, IOException`
Reads an `int` value from the input stream and returns that `int` value. If `readInt` tries to read a value from the file that was not written by the method `writeInt` of the class `ObjectOutputStream` (or was not written in some equivalent way), problems will occur. If the read goes beyond the end of the file, an `EOFException` is thrown.

`public long readLong() throws EOFException, IOException`
Reads a `long` value from the input stream and returns that `long` value. If `readLong` tries to read a value from the file that was not written by the method `writeLong` of the class `ObjectOutputStream` (or was not written in some equivalent way), problems will occur. If the read goes beyond the end of the file, an `EOFException` is thrown.
   Note that you cannot write an integer using `writeLong` and later read the same integer using `readInt`, or to write an integer using `writeInt` and later read it using `readLong`. Doing so will cause unpredictable results.

`public double readDouble() throws EOFException, IOException`
Reads a `double` value from the input stream and returns that `double` value. If `readDouble` tries to read a value from the file that was not written by the method `writeDouble` of the class `ObjectOutputStream` (or was not written in some equivalent way), problems will occur. If the read goes beyond the end of the file, an `EOFException` is thrown.

`public float readFloat() throws EOFException, IOException`
Reads a `float` value from the input stream and returns that `float` value. If `readFloat` tries to read a value from the file that was not written by the method `writeFloat` of the class `ObjectOutputStream` (or was not written in some equivalent way), problems will occur. If the read goes beyond the end of the file, an `EOFException` is thrown.
   Note that you cannot write a floating-point number using `writeDouble` and later read the same number using `readFloat`, or write a floating-point number using `writeFloat` and later read it using `readDouble`. Doing so will cause unpredictable results, as will other type mismatches, such as writing with `writeInt` and then reading with `readFloat` or `readDouble`. *(continued)*

FIGURE 10.6 **Some Methods in the Class** `ObjectInputStream` *(part 2 of 2)*

`public char readChar() throws EOFException, IOException`
Reads a `char` value from the input stream and returns that `char` value. If `readChar` tries to read a value from the file that was not written by the method `writeChar` of the class `ObjectOutputStream` (or was not written in some equivalent way), problems will occur. If the read goes beyond the end of the file, an `EOFException` is thrown.

`public boolean readBoolean() throws EOFException, IOException`
Reads a `boolean` value from the input stream and returns that `boolean` value. If `readBoolean` tries to read a value from the file that was not written by the method `writeBoolean` of the class `ObjectOutputStream` (or was not written in some equivalent way), problems will occur. If the read goes beyond the end of the file, an `EOFException` is thrown.

`publicString readUTF() throws IOException, UTFDataFormatException`
Reads a `String` value from the input stream and returns that `String` value. If `readUTF` tries to read a value from the file that was not written by the method `writeUTF` of the class `ObjectOutputStream` (or was not written in some equivalent way), problems will occur. One of the exceptions `UTFDataFormatException` or `IOException` can be thrown.

`Object readObject() throws ClassNotFoundException,`
`    InvalidClassException, OptionalDataException, IOException`
Reads an object from the input stream. Throws a `ClassNotFoundException` if the class of a serialized object cannot be found. Throws an `InvalidClassException` if something is wrong with the serializable class. Throws an `OptionalDataException` if a primitive data item, instead of an object, was found in the stream. Throws an `IOException` if there is some other I/O problem. The method `readObject` is covered in Section 10.5.

`public void close() throws IOException`
Closes the stream's connection to a file.

LISTING 10.6 **Using** `ObjectInputStream` **to Read from a File** *(part 1 of 2)*

Assumes the program in Listing 10.4 was already run.

```java
import java.io.FileInputStream;
import java.io.ObjectInputStream;
import java.io.EOFException;
import java.io.FileNotFoundException;
import java.io.IOException;
import java.util.Scanner;
```

(continued)

LISTING 10.6 Using `ObjectInputStream` to Read from a File *(part 2 of 2)*

```java
public class BinaryInputDemo
{
    public static void main(String[] args)
    {
        String fileName = "numbers.dat";
        try
        {
            ObjectInputStream inputStream =
                    new ObjectInputStream(new FileInputStream(fileName));
            System.out.println("Reading the nonnegative integers");
            System.out.println("in the file " + fileName);
            int anInteger = inputStream.(readInt);
            while (anInteger >= 0)
            {
                System.out.ptintln(anInteger);
                anInteger = inputStream.readInt();
            }
            System.out.println("End of reading from file.");
            inputStream.close();
        }
        catch(FileNotFoundException e)
        {
            System.out.println("Problem opening the file " + fileName);
        }
        catch(EOFException e)
        {
            System.out.println("Problem reading the file " + fileName);
            System.out.println("Reached end of the file.");
        }
        catch(IOException e)
        {
            System.out.println("Problem reading the file " + fileName);
        }
    }
}
```

Screen Output

```
Reading the nonnegative integers
in the file number.dat
1
2
3
End of reading from file.
```

Notice that the sentinel value −1 is read from the file but is not displayed on the screen.

RECAP Reading from a Binary File

SYNTAX

```
try
{
    // Open the file
    ObjectInputStream Input_Stream_Name =
            new ObjectInputStream(new FileInputStream
                            (File_Name));
    // Read the file using statements of the form:
    Input_Stream_Name.MethodName(Argument); // See Figure 10.6
    // Close the file
    Input_Stream_Name.close();
}
catch(FileNotFoundException e)
{
    Statements_Dealing_With_The_Exception
}
catch(EOFException e)
{
    Statements_Dealing_With_The_Exception
}
catch(IOException e)
{
    Statements_Dealing_With_The_Exception
}
```

EXAMPLE

See Listing 10.6.

RECAP `FileInputStream` and `FileOutputStream`

In this book, we use the classes `FileInputStream` and `FileOutputStream` for their constructors and nothing else. Each of these two classes has a constructor that takes a file name as an argument. We use these constructors to produce arguments for the constructors for stream classes, such as `ObjectInputStream` and `ObjectOutputStream`, that do not take a file name as an argument. Below are examples of using `FileInputStream` and `FileOutputStream`:

(continued)

```
ObjectInputStream fileInput = new ObjectInputStream(
                    new FileInputStream("rawstuff.dat"));
ObjectOutputStream fileOutput = new ObjectOutputStream(
                    new FileOutputStream("nicestuff.dat"));
```

We used similar statements in Listing 10.6 and Listing 10.5, respectively.

The constructors for `FileInputStream` and `FileOutputStream` can throw an exception in the class `FileNotFoundException`. A `FileNotFoundException` is a kind of `IOException`.

GOTCHA   Using `ObjectInputStream` to Read a Text File

Binary files and text files encode their data in different ways. Thus, a stream that expects to read a binary file, such as a stream in the class `ObjectInputStream`, will have problems reading a text file. If you attempt to read a text file using a stream in the class `ObjectInputStream`, your program will either read "garbage values" or encounter some other error condition. Similarly, if you attempt to use `Scanner` to read a binary file as if it were a text file, you will also get into trouble. ■

SELF-TEST QUESTIONS

myprogramminglab

16. Write some Java code to create an input stream of type `ObjectInputStream` that is named `fromFile` and is connected to a file named `stuff.data`.

17. Give three statements that will read three numbers of type `double` from the file `stuff.data`. Use the stream `fromFile` that you created in the previous question. Declare three variables to hold the three numbers.

18. Give a statement that will close the stream `fromFile` that you created for the previous two questions.

19. Can you use `writeInt` to write a number to a file and then read that number using `readLong`? Can you read that number using `readDouble`?

20. Can you use `readUTF` to read a string from a text file?

21. Write a complete Java program that asks the user for the name of a binary file and writes the first data item in that file to the screen. Assume that the first data item is a string that was written to the file with the method `writeUTF`.

The Class EOFException

An
EOFException
can end a loop

Many of the methods that read from a binary file will throw an EOFException when they try to read beyond the end of a file. As illustrated by the program in Listing 10.7, the class EOFException can be used to test for the end of a file when you are using ObjectInputStream. In that sample program, the statements that read the file are placed within a while loop whose boolean expression is true. Although this loop appears to be "infinite," it does come to an end: When the end of the file is reached, an exception is thrown, ending the entire try block and passing control to the catch block.

LISTING 10.7   Using EOFException *(part 1 of 2)*

Assumes the program in
Listing 10.4 was already
run.

```java
import java.io.FileInputStream;
import java.io.ObjectInputStream;
import java.io.EOFException;
import java.io.FileNotFoundException;
import java.io.IOException;

public class EOFExceptionDemo
{
    public static void main(String[] args)
    {

        String fileName = "numbers.dat";
        try
        {
            ObjectInputStream inputStream =
                new ObjectInputStream(new
                FileInputStream(fileName));
            System.out.println("Reading ALL the integers");
            System.out.printin("in the file " + fileName);
            try
            {
                while (true)         The loop ends when an
                {                    exception is thrown.

                    int anInteger = inputStream.readInt();
                    System.out.println(anInteger);
                }
            }
            catch(EOFException e)
```

(continued)

LISTING 10.7   Using EOFException *(part 2 of 2)*

```
            {
                System.out.println("End of reading from file.");
            }
            inputStream.close();
        }
        catch(FileNotFoundException e)
        {
            System.out.println("Cannot find file " + fileName);
        }
        catch(IOException e)
        {
            System.out.println("Problem with input from file " +
            fileName);
        }
    }
}
```

Screen Output

```
Reading ALL the integers
in the file numbers.dat
1
2
3
-1
End of reading from file.
```

When you use EOFException *to end reading, you can read files that contain any kind of integers, including the* -1 *here, which is treated just like any other integer.*

It is instructive to compare the program in Listing 10.7 with the similar program in Listing 10.6. The one in Listing 10.6 checks for the end of a file by testing for a negative number. This approach is fine, but it means that you cannot store negative numbers in the file, except as a sentinel value. On the other hand, the program in Listing 10.7 uses EOFException to test for the end of a file. Thus, it can handle files that store any kind of integers, including negative integers.

RECAP The EOFException **Class**

When reading primitive data from a binary file using the methods listed in Figure 10.6 for the class ObjectInputStream, if your program attempts to read beyond the end of the file, an EOFException is thrown. This exception can be used to end a loop that reads all the data in a file.

The class EOFException is derived from the class IOException. So every exception of type EOFException is also of type IOException.

■ **PROGRAMMING TIP**   Always Check for the End of a File

Nothing good happens if your program reads beyond the end of a file. Exactly what occurs will depend on the details of your program: It might enter an infinite loop or end abnormally. Always be sure that your program checks for the end of a file and does something appropriate when it reaches that point. Even if you think your program will not read past the end of the file, you should provide for this eventuality, just in case things do not go exactly as you planned. ■

GOTCHA   Checking for the End of a File in the Wrong Way

Different file-reading methods—usually in different classes—check for the end of a file in different ways. Some throw an exception of the class EOFException when they try to read beyond the end of a file. Others return a special value, such as null. When reading from a file, you must be careful to test for the end of a file in the correct way for the method you are using. If you test for the end of a file in the wrong way, one of two things will probably happen: Either your program will go into an unintended infinite loop or it will terminate abnormally.

Not all methods in all classes will throw an EOFException when they try to read beyond the end of a file. For the classes discussed in this book, the rule is as follows: If your program is reading primitive data from a binary file, it will throw an EOFException. If, however, your program is reading from a text file, it will return some special value, such as null, at the end of the file, and no EOFException will be thrown. ■

RECAP Detecting the End of Data in a Binary File

You can read all of the data in a binary file in one of two ways:
- By detecting a sentinel value written at the end of the file
- By catching an EOFException

PROGRAMMING EXAMPLE   Processing a File of Binary Data

Listing 10.8 contains a program that does some simple processing of data. It asks the user for two file names, reads the numbers in the input file, doubles them, and writes the resulting numbers to the output file. This programming task is not very complicated, but it does employ many standard programming

LISTING 10.8   Processing a File of Binary Data *(part 1 of 3)*

```java
import java.io.FileInputStream;
import java.io.FileOutputStream;
import java.io.ObjectInputStream;
import java.io.ObjectOutputStream;
import java.io.EOFException;
import java.io.FileNotFoundException;
import java.io.IOException;
import java.util.Scanner;

public class Doubler
{
    private ObjectInputStream inputStream = null;
    private ObjectOutputStream outputStream = null;

    /**
     Doubles the integers in one file and puts them in another file.
     */
    public static void main(String[] args)
    {
        Doubler twoTimer = new Doubler();
        twoTimer.connectToInputFile();
        twoTimer.connectToOutputFile();
        twoTimer.timesTwo();
        twoTimer.closeFiles();
        System.out.println("Numbers from input file");
        System.out.println("doubled and copied to output file.");
    }
    public void connectToInputFile()
    {
        String inputFileName =
            getFileName("Enter name of input file:");
        try
        {
            inputStream = new ObjectInputStream(
                            new FileInputStream(inputFileName));
        }
        catch(FileNotFoundException e)
        {
            System.out.println("File " + inputFileName +
                            " not found.");
            System.exit(0);
        }
        catch(IOException e)
        {
            System.out.println("Error opening input file" +
                            inputFileName);
```

(continued)

LISTING 10.8   Processing a File of Binary Data *(part 2 of 3)*

```java
            System.exit(0);
        }
    }
    private String getFileName(String prompt)
    {
        String fileName = null;
        System.out.println(prompt);
        Scanner keyboard = new Scanner(System.in);
        fileName = keyboard.next();

        return fileName;
    }
    public void connectToOutputFile()
    {
        String outputFileName =
                        getFileName("Enter name of output file:");
        try
        {
            outputStream = new ObjectOutputStream(
                        new FileOutputStream(outputFileName));
        }
        catch(IOException e)
        {
            System.out.println("Erroropeningoutputfile" +
                                outputFileName);
            System.out.println(e.getMessage());
            System.exit(0);
        }
    }
```

> A class used in a real-life application would usually transform the input data in a more complex way before writing it to the output file. **Such a class likely would have** additional methods.

```java
    public void timesTwo()
    {
        try
        {
            while (true)
            {
                int next = inputStream.readInt();
                outputStream.writeInt(2 * next);
            }
        }
```

(continued)

LISTING 10.8   Processing a File of Binary Data *(part 3 of 3)*

```java
catch(EOFException e)
{
    //Do nothing. This just ends the loop.
}
catch(IOException e)
{
    System.out.println(
                    "Error: reading or writing files.");
    System.out.println(e.getMessage());
    System.exit(0);
}
}
public void closeFiles()
{
    try
    {
        inputStream.close();
        outputStream.close();
    }
    catch(IOException e)
    {
        System.out.println("Error closing files " +
                            e.getMessage());
        System.exit(0);
    }
}
}
```

techniques for handling file I/O. In particular, note that the variables for stream objects connected to the files are instance variables, and note that the task is divided into subtasks assigned to various methods.

We have made the `try` blocks small so that, when an exception is thrown, it is caught in a nearby `catch` block. If we had fewer—and larger—`try` blocks, it would have been harder to decide what part of the code had thrown an exception.

VideoNote
Writing and reading a binary file

GOTCHA   Exceptions, Exceptions, Exceptions

Many situations involving a text file that do not throw exceptions during I/O do throw exceptions when a binary file is involved. So you will need to do more exception handling when working with binary files than when working with text files. For example, closing a text file connected to a stream of type `PrintWriter` does not cause an exception to be thrown. However, closing a binary-file stream of the types we have been discussing can cause an `IOException` to be thrown. When doing binary-file I/O as we have described it, almost anything can cause an exception to be thrown. Also, the methods `writeObject` and `readObject` can throw a long list of exceptions, which you can see by checking Figures 10.5 and 10.6   ■

SELF-TEST QUESTIONS

22. Suppose that you want to create an input stream and connect it to the binary file named `mydata.dat`. Will the following code work? If not how can you write something similar that does work?

    ```
    ObjectInputStream inputStream = new
        ObjectInputStream("mydata.dat");
    ```

23. Does the class `FileInputStream` have a method named `readInt`? Does it have one named `readDouble`? Does it have one named `readUTF`?

24. Does the class `FileOutputStream` have a constructor that accepts a file name as an argument?

25. Does the class `ObjectOutputStream` have a constructor that accepts a file name as an argument?

26. When opening a binary file for output in the ways discussed in this chapter, might an exception be thrown? What kind of exception? What are the answers to these questions if we open a binary file for input instead of for output?

27. Suppose that a binary file contains exactly three numbers written to the file using the method `writeDouble` of the class `ObjectOutputStream`. Suppose further that you write a program to read all three numbers using three invocations of the method `readDouble` of the class `ObjectInputStream`. If your program invokes `readDouble` a fourth time, what will happen?

28. The following code appears in the program in Listing 10.7:

    ```
    try
    {
        while (true)
        {
            int anInteger = inputStream.readInt();
            System.out.println(anInteger);
        }
    }
    catch(EOFException e)
    {
        System.out.println("End of reading from file.");
    }
    ```

    Why doesn't this code really include an infinite loop?

29. Write a complete Java program that will display all the numbers in a binary file named `temperatures.dat` on the screen, one per line. Assume that the entire file was written with the method `writeDouble`.

10.5 BINARY-FILE I/O WITH OBJECTS AND ARRAYS

In this section, we cover I/O for binary files involving objects of a class and arrays, which, you'll recall, are really objects. We will use the classes `ObjectInputStream` and `ObjectOutputStream`.

Binary-File I/O with Objects of a Class

We have seen how to write primitive values and strings to a binary file, and how to read them again. How would we write and read objects other than strings? We could, of course, write an object's instance variables to a file and invent some way to reconstruct the object when we read the file. Since an instance variable could be another object that itself could have an object as an instance variable, however, completing this task sounds formidable.

Fortunately, Java provides a simple way—called **object serialization**—to represent an object as a sequence of bytes that can be written to a binary file. This process will occur automatically for any object that belongs to a class that is **serializable.** Making a class serializable is easy to do. We simply add the two words `implementsSerializable` to the heading of the class definition, as in the following example:

Objects of a serializable class can be written to a binary file

```
public class Species implements Serializable
```

Actually, we do need to worry about some details involving a class's instance variables, but since those details will not be relevant to our example, we will postpone discussing them until the next section. We will also discuss the meaning of serialization at that time.

`Serializable` is an interface in the Java Class Library within the package `java.io`. The interface is empty, so we have no additional methods to implement. Although an empty interface might seem useless, this one tells Java to make the class serializable. We make the interface available to our program by including the following `import` statement:

```
import java.io.Serializable;
```

In Listing 10.9, we have made the class `Species`, which we saw in Listing 5.17 of Chapter 5, serializable and added constructors and a `toString` method. Let's use the class `Species` to illustrate the reading and writing of objects to a binary file.

We can write objects of a serializable class to a binary file by using the method `writeObject` of the class `ObjectOutputStream` and then read those objects from the file by using the method `readObject` of the class `ObjectInputStream`. Listing 10.10 provides an example of this process. To

LISTING 10.9 The Class Species **Serialized for Binary-File I/O**

This is a new, improved definition of the class Species and
replaces the **definition in** Listing 5.19 of Chapter 5.

```java
import java.io.Serializable;
import java.util.Scanner;

/**
Serialized class for data on endangered species.
*/
public class Species implements Serializable
{
    private String name;
    private int population;
    private double growthRate;

    public Species()
    {
        name = null;
        population = 0;
        growthRate = 0;
    }

    public Species(String initialName, int initialPopulation,
                    double initialGrowthRate)
    {
        name = initialName;
        if (initialPopulation >= 0)
            population = initialPopulation;
        else
        {
            System.out.println("ERROR: Negative population.");
            System.exit(0);
        }

        growthRate = initialGrowthRate;
    }
    public String toString()
    {
        return ("Name = " + name + "\n" +
                "Population = " + population + "\n" +
                "Growth rate = " + growthRate + "%");
    }
```

These two words and the **import**
statement make this class serializable.

<Other methods are the same as those in Listing 5.19 of Chapter 5,
but they are not needed for the discussion in this chapter.>

```java
}
```

LISTING 10.10   **File I/O of Class Objects** *(part 1 of 3)*

```java
import java.io.FileInputStream;
import java.io.FileOutputStream;
import java.io.IOException;
import java.io.ObjectInputStream;
import java.io.ObjectOutputStream;

public class ClassObjectIODemo
{
    public static void main(String[]args)
    {
        ObjectOutputStream outputStream = null;
        String fileName = "species.records";

        try
        {
            outputStream = new ObjectOutputStream(
                        new FileOutputStream(fileName));
        }
        catch(IOException e)
        {
            System.out.println("Error opening output file " +
                                fileName + ".");
            System.exit(0);
        }
        Species califCondor =
                new Species("Calif. Condor", 27, 0.02);
        Species blackRhino =
                new Species("Black Rhino", 100, 1.0);
        try
        {
            outputStream.writeObject(califCondor);
            outputStream.writeObject(blackRhino);
            outputStream.Close();
        }
        catch(IOException e)
        {
            System.out.println("Error wring to file " +
                                fileName + ".");
            System.exit(0)
        }

        System.out.println("Records sent to file " +
                            fileName + ".");
        System.out.println(
                "Now let's reopen the file and echo " +
                "the records.");
```

(continued)

LISTING 10.10   File I/O of Class Objects *(part 2 of 3)*

```java
ObjectInputStream inputStream = null;

try
{
    inputStream = new ObjectInputStream(
                    new FileInputStream("species.records"));
}
catch(IOException e)
{
    System.out.println("Error opening input file " +
                            fileName + ".");
    System.exit(0);
}
Species readOne = null, readTwo = null;

try
{
    readOne = (Species)inputStream.readObject();
    readTwo = (Species)inputStream.readObject();
    inputStream.close();
}

catch(Exception e)
{
    System.out.println("Error reading from file " +
                            fileName + ".");
    System.exit(0);
}

System.out.println("The following were read\n" +
                    "from the file " + fileName + ".");
System.out.println(readOne);
System.out.println();
System.out.println(readTwo);

System.out.println("End of program.");
    }
}
```

Notice the type casts.

A separate **catch** *block for each type of exception would be better. We use only one to save space.*

Sample Screen Output

```
Records sent to file species.records.
Now let's reopen the file and echo the records.
The following were read
from the file species.records.
Name = Calif. Condor
Population = 27
Growth rate = 0.02%
```

(continued)

LISTING 10.10   File I/O of Class Objects *(part 3 of 3)*

```
Name = Black Rhino
Population = 100
Growth rate 1.0%
End of program.
```

write an object of the class Species to a binary file, we pass the object as the argument to the method writeObject, as in

```
outputStream.writeObject(oneSpecies);
```

where outputStream is a stream of type ObjectOutputStream and oneSpecies is of type Species.

REMEMBER Writing Objects to a Binary File

You can write objects to a binary file using writeObject only if their class is serializable. When checking the documentation for predefined classes, see whether the class implements Serializable.

An object written to a binary file with the method writeObject can be read by using the method readObject of the stream class ObjectInputStream, as illustrated by the following example taken from Listing 10.10:

readObject recovers an object in a binary file

```
readOne = (Species)inputStream.readObject();
```

Here, inputStream is a stream of type ObjectInputStream that has been connected to a file that was filled with data using writeObject of the class ObjectOutputStream. The data consists of objects of the class Species, and the variable readOne is of type Species. Note that readObject returns its value as an object of type Object. If you want to use it as an object of type Species, you must type cast it to the type Species.

Before we leave this example, let's clarify a potential misconception. The class Species has a method toString. This method is needed so that output to the screen and output to a text file—using println—appears correctly. However, the method toString has nothing to do with object I/O to a binary file. Object I/O with a binary file would work fine even if a class did not override toString.

Some Details of Serialization

Our introduction to serialization in the previous section omitted some details that we must cover now, in order to arrive at a complete definition of a serializable class. Recall that we mentioned that an instance variable could be another object that itself could have an object as an instance variable. In fact, the class Species has a string as an instance variable. When a serializable class has instance variables

Properties of a
serializable class

of a class type, the class for those instance variables should also be serializable, and so on for all levels of instance variables within classes.

Thus, a class is serializable if all of the following are true:

- The class implements the interface `Serializable`.
- Any instance variables of a class type are objects of a serializable class.
- The class's direct super class, if any, is either serializable or defines a default constructor.

For example, the class `Species` implements the interface `Serializable` and has a string as an instance variable. The class `String` is serializable. Since any subclass of a serializable class is serializable, a class derived from `Species` would also be serializable.

What is the effect of making a class serializable? In a sense, there is no direct effect on the class, but there is an effect on how Java performs file I/O with objects of the class. If a class is serializable, Java assigns a **serial number** to each object of the class that it writes to a stream of type `ObjectOutputStream`. If the same object is written to the stream more than once, after the first time, Java writes only the serial number for the object, rather than writing the object's data multiple times. This feature makes file I/O more efficient and reduces the size of the file. When the file is read using a stream of type `ObjectInputStream`, duplicate serial numbers are returned as references to the same object. Note that this condition means that, if two variables contain references to the same object, and you write the objects to the file and later read them from the file, the two objects that are read will be references to the same object. So nothing in the structure of your object data is lost when you write the objects to the file and later read them.

Some classes
aren't serializable
for security
reasons

Serializability sounds great. So why aren't all classes made serializable? In some cases, it is for security reasons. The serial-number system makes it easier for programmers to get access to the object data written to secondary storage. In other cases, writing objects to secondary storage may not make sense, since they would be meaningless when read again later. For example, if the object contains system-dependent data, the data may be meaningless later.

Array Objects in Binary Files

Arrays are
objects, and so
can be written to
a binary file

Since Java treats arrays as objects, you can use `writeObject` to write an entire array to a binary file, and you can use `readObject` to read it from the file. When doing so, if the array has a base type that is a class, the class should be serializable. This means that, if you store all your data for one serializable class in a single array, you can write all your data to a binary file using one invocation of `writeObject`.

For example, suppose that `group` is an array of `Species` objects. If `toFile` is an instance of `ObjectOutputStream` that is associated with a binary file, we can write the array to that file by executing the statement

```
toFile.writeObject(group);
```

After creating the file, we can read the array by using the statement

```
Species[] myArray = (Species[])fromFile.readObject();
```

where `fromFile` is an instance of `ObjectInputStream` that is associated with the file that we just created.

Note that the base-class type, `Species`, is serializable. Note also the type cast when reading the array from the file. Since `readObject` returns its value as an object of type `Object`, it must be type cast to the correct array type, `Species[]` in this case.

Listing 10.11 contains a sample program that writes and reads an array using a binary file. Notice that we declared the arrays `oneArray` and `anotherArray` outside of the `try` blocks so that they exist both outside and

LISTING 10.11   **File I/O of an Array Object** *(part 1 of 2)*

```java
import java.io.FileInputStream;
import java.io.FileOutputStream;
import java.io.IOException;
import java.io.ObjectInputStream;
import java.io.ObjectOutputStream;

public class ArrayIODemo
{
    public static void main(String[] args)
    {
        Species[] oneArray = new Species[2];
        oneArray[0] = new Species("Calif. Condor", 27, 0.02);
        oneArray[1] = new Species("Black Rhino", 100, 1.0);

        String fileName = "array.dat";

        try
        {
            ObjectOutputStream outputStream =
                new ObjectOutputStream(
                    new FileOutputStream(fileName));
            outputStream.writeobject(oneArray);
            outputStream.close();
        }
        catch(IOException e)
        {
            System.out.println("Error writing to file " +
                            fileName + ".");
            System.exit(0);
        }
        System.out.println("Array written to file " +
                        fileName + " and file is closed.");
```

(continued)

LISTING 10.11   File I/O of an Array Object *(part 2 of 2)*

```
System.out.println("Open the file for input and " +
                      "echo the array.")
Species[] anotherArray = null;
try
{
    ObjectInputStream inputStream =
                new objectInputStream(
                      new FileInputStream(fileName));
    anotherArray = (Species[])inputStream.readobject();
    inputStream.close();
}
catch(Exception e)
{
    System.out.println("Error reading file " +
                      fileName + ".");
    System.exit(0);
}
System.out.println("The following were read from " +
                      "the file " + fileName + ":");
for (int i = 0; i < anotherArray.length; i++)
{
    System.out.println(anotherArray[i]);
    System.out.println();
}
System.out.println("End of program.");
    }
}
```

Note the type cast → (points to the ObjectInputStream line)

A separate **catch** *block for each type of exception would be better. We use only one to save space.*

Sample Screen Output

```
Array written to file array.dat and file is closed.
Open the file for input and echo the array.
The following were read from the file array.dat:
Name = Calif. Condor
Population = 27
Growth rate = 0.02%

Name = black Rhino
Population = 100
Growth rate = 1.0%

End of program.
```

inside these blocks. Also note that `anotherArray` is initialized to `null`, not `newSpecies[2]`. Had we allocated a new array here, it would have been replaced by the subsequent call to `readObject`. That is, `readObject` creates a new array; it does not fill an existing one.

VideoNote
Using a binary file of objects and arrays

 SELF-TEST QUESTIONS

myprogramminglab

30. How do you make a class serializable?

31. What is the return type for the method `readObject` of the class `ObjectInputStream`?

32. What exception(s) might be thrown by the method `writeObject` of the class `ObjectOutputStream`? (Consult the documentation for the Java Class Library.)

33. What exception(s) might be thrown by the method `readObject` of the class `ObjectInputStream`? (Consult the documentation for the Java Class Library.)

10.6 GRAPHICS SUPPLEMENT

The "real world" is the only world.

—GRAFFITI

Graphical user interfaces, or GUIs, are not just for cute little demonstrations. GUIs are meant to be interfaces for real application programs. This section provides one small example of a `JFrame` GUI that manipulates files.

| **PROGRAMMING EXAMPLE** | A JFrame GUI for Manipulating Files |

The program in Listing 10.12 uses a `JFrame` to create a GUI that lets you do some housekeeping with your text files. The GUI has three buttons and two text fields. You can type a file name in the indicated text field. If you then click the `Show first line` button, the first line of the file is displayed in the other text field as a reminder of what is in the file. However, if the file does not exist or is not readable, you get a message explaining the situation instead. And if the file is not a text file, you will get gibberish.

LISTING 10.12   A File Organizer GUI *(part 1 of 4)*

```java
import javax.swing.JFrame;
import javax.swing.JButton;
import javax.swing.JFrame;
import javax.swing.JTextField;
import java.awt.Color;
import java.awt.Container;
import java.awt.FlowLayout;
import java.awt.Graphics;
import java.awt.event.ActionEvent;
import java.awt.event.ActionListener;
import java.io.File;
import java.io.FileNotFoundException;
import java.util.Scanner;

public class FileOrganizer extends JFrame implements ActionListener
{
    public static final int WIDTH = 400;
    public static final int HEIGHT = 300;
    public static final int NUMBER_OF_CHAR = 30;

    private JTextField fileNameField;
    private JTextField firstLineField;

    public FileOrganizer()
    {
        setSize(WIDTH, HEIGHT);
        WindowDestroyer listener = new WindowDestroyer();
        addWindowListener(listener);
        Container contentPane = getContentPane();
        contentPane.setLayout(new FlowLayout());

        JButton showButton = new JButton("Show first line");
        showButton.addActionListener(this);
        contentPane.add(showButton);

        JButton removeButton = new JButton("Remove file");
        removeButton.addActionListener(this);
        contentPane.add(removeButton);

        JButton resetButton = new JButton("Reset");
        resetButton.addActionListener(this);
        contentPane.add(resetButton);

        fileNameField = new JTextField(NUMBER_OF_CHAR);
        contentPane.add(fileNameField);
        fileNameField.setText("Enter file name here.");

        firstLineField = new JTextField(NUMBER_OF_CHAR);
        contentPane.add(firstLineField);
    }
```

(continued)

LISTING 10.12   A File Organizer GUI *(part 2 of 4)*

```java
public void actionPerformed(ActionEvent e)
{
    String actionCommand = e.getActionCommand();
    if (actionCommand.equals("Show first line"))
        showFirstLine();
    else if (actionCommand.equals("Remove file"))
            removeFile();
    else if (actionCommand.equals("Reset"))
        resetFields();
    else
        firstLineField.setText("Unexpected error.");
}
private void showFirstLine()
{
    Scanner fileInput = null;
    String fileName = fileNameField.getText();
    File fileObject = new File(fileName);

    if (!fileObject.exists())
        firstLineField.setText("No such file");
    else if (!fileObject.canRead())
        firstLineField.setText("That file is not readable.");
    else
    {
        try
        {
            fileInput = new Scanner(fileObject);
        }
        catch(FileNotFoundException e)
        {
            firstLineField.setText("Error opening the file " +
                                    fileName);
        }
        String firstLine = fileInput.nextLine();
        firstLineField.setText(firstLine);
        fileInput.close();
    }
}
private void resetFields()
{
    fileNameField.setText("Enter file name here.");
    firstLineField.setText("");
}
```

(continued)

LISTING 10.12   A File Organizer GUI *(part 3 of 4)*

```java
    private void removeFile()
    {
        Scanner fileInput = null;
        String firstLine;
        String fileName = fileNameField.getText();
        File fileObject = new File(filename);

        if (!fileObject.exists())
            firstLinefield.setText("No such file");
        else if (!fileObject.canWrite())
            firstLineField.setText("Permission denied.");
        else
        {
            if (fileObject.delete())
                firstLineField.setText("File deleted.");
            else
                firstLineField.setText("Could not delete file.");
        }
    }
    public static void main(String[] args)
    {
        FileOrganizer gui = new FileOrganizer();
        gui.setVisible(true);

    }
}
```

Screen Output Showing GUI's State Initially or After the Reset Button is Clicked

(continued)

LISTING 10.12   **A File Organizer GUI**   *(part 4 of 4)*

Screen Output After Entering the File Name and Clicking the Show first line **Button**

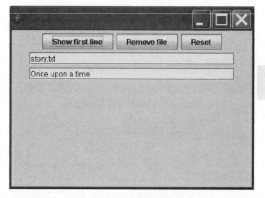

Assumes that the first line in the file is as shown

Screen Output After Entering the Remove line **Button**

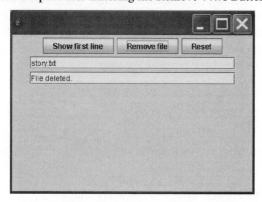

Screen Output After Entering the File Name and Clicking the Show first line **Button**

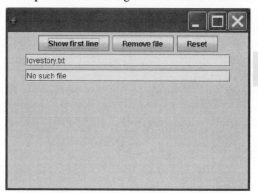

Assumes that the named file does not exist

If you want to delete a file, you type the file name in the text field and click the Remove file button. As long as the file exists and is writable, it is deleted and a confirmation message is displayed. If the file does not exist or is not writable—which normally also means you cannot delete it—an appropriate message appears instead. Finally, the Reset button restores the text fields to their original contents. Let's look at some code.

Within the constructor of our class, we define the three buttons and the two text fields. Having two text fields means that the file name can remain visible while any output is given in the other text field. To differentiate the text fields, we initialize the one for the file name as follows:

```
fileNameField.setText("Enter file name here.");
```

Chapter 13, which is on the Web, shows how to label a text field so that the label is outside the text field rather than in it.

The method actionPerformed identifies the button click and takes the appropriate action by calling one of three private methods within our class. The method showFirstLine retrieves the file name from the text field and, after checking that the file exists and is readable, opens the file for input. The method then reads the first line, displays it in the text field, and finally closes the file. The statements for these latter three steps are

```
String firstLine = fileInput.readLine();
firstLineField.setText(firstLine);
fileInput.close();
```

Before entering another file name, the user should click the Reset button, which sets the two text fields as follows:

```
fileNameField.setText("Enter file name here.");
firstLineField.setText("");
```

The second statement sets the text field contents to the empty string, which sets the field to blank. (The GUI will give correct answers even if the Reset button is not clicked, but the output will be clearer if it is clicked.) These two statements are in the private method resetFields that actionPerformed calls when the Reset button is clicked.

Finally, if the Remove file button is clicked, actionPerformed calls the private method removeFile. After checking that the file exists and is readable, removeFile deletes the file by using the following code:

```
if (fileObject.delete())
    firstLineField.setText("File deleted.");
else
    firstLineField.setText("Could not delete file.");
```

The invocation fileObject.delete() tries to delete the file. If delete is successful, it returns true; otherwise it returns false.

In this example, we have defined a main method within our class to create and display the GUI. Whether you choose to place main within this class or another one depends on the situation and to some extent on personal taste. ▌

SELF-TEST QUESTIONS

myprogramminglab

34. The class FileOrganizer in Listing 10.12 includes a main method that creates and displays a GUI. Is it legal to instead do this within a main method of a separate class without deleting the main method in the class FileOrganizer?

35. In Listing 10.12, could you avoid having to catch exceptions simply by adding a throws clause to all methods that might throw an exception?

GOTCHA   **An Applet Cannot Manipulate Files on Another Computer**

For reasons of security, an applet is limited in what it can do. Since an applet is designed to be embedded in a Web page and run from another computer someplace else on the World Wide Web, the Java designers did not give applets the ability to manipulate files on a remote computer. Hence, you cannot write an applet version of the JFrame GUI in Listing 10.12 that will read and delete files on the computer on which it is viewed. You can, however, write an applet version that, when run with the applet viewer on your own computer, will manipulate files on your computer. In that case, however, you may as well use a JFrame GUI.   ■

 PROGRAMMING TIP   **When to Define GUI Components as Instance Variables**

When GUI components must be available to more than one method within a class, defining them as instance variables is more convenient than passing them as arguments to several methods. In Listing 10.12, for example, two text fields—fileNameField and firstLineField—are created and initialized by the constructor and used in all of the other methods in the class except main. These text fields are defined as instance variables.

However, notice the buttons that the constructor defines. Since they are used only in the constructor, they can be local to that method. Although the method actionPerformed is responsible for a button's action, it does not reference any buttons by name. Instead, an action command is obtained from the action event that is generated when a button is clicked. This action command is dealt with entirely within actionPerformed. There is no reason in this case for the buttons to be instance variables.   ■

CHAPTER SUMMARY

■ Files that are considered to be strings of characters and that look like characters to your program and to a text editor are called text files. All other files are called binary files.

■ Your program can use the class `PrintWriter` to write to a text file and can use the class `Scanner` to read from a text file.

■ When reading from a file, you should always check for the end of a file and do something appropriate if the end of the file is reached. The way you test for the end of a file depends on whether your program is reading from a text file or a binary file.

■ You can read a file name from the keyboard into a variable of type `String` and use that variable in place of a file name.

■ The class `File` can be used to see whether an existing file has a given name. It can also be used to see whether your program is allowed to read the file or write to the file.

■ Your program can use the class `ObjectOutputStream` to write to a binary file and can use the class `ObjectInputStream` to read from a binary file.

■ Your program can use the method `writeObject` of the class `ObjectOutputStream` to write class objects or arrays to a binary file. Objects or arrays can be read from a binary file using the method `readObject` of the class `ObjectInputStream`.

■ In order to use the methods `writeObject` of the class `ObjectOutputStream` and `readObject` of the class `ObjectInputStream`, the class whose objects are written to a binary file must implement the `Serializable` interface.

Exercises

1. Write a program that will write the Gettysburg Address to a text file. Place each sentence on a separate line of the file.

2. Modify the program in the previous exercise so that it reads the name of the file from the keyboard.

3. Write some code that asks the user to enter either of the words append or new. According to the user response, open either an existing text file to which data can be appended or a new, empty text file to which data can be written. In either case, the file's name is a string given by the variable `fileName`.

4. Write a program that will record the purchases made at a store. For each purchase, read from the keyboard an item's name, its price, and the number bought. Compute the cost of the purchase (number bought times price),

and write all this data to a text file. Also, display this information and the current total cost on the screen. After all items have been entered, write the total cost to both the screen and the file. Since we want to remember all purchases made, you should append new data to the end of the file.

5. Modify the class `LapTimer`, as described in Exercise 13 of the previous chapter, as follows:

   - Add an attribute for a file stream to which we can write the times
   - Add a constructor

     `LapTimer(n, person, fileName)`

   for a race having *n* laps. The name of the person and the file to record the times are passed to the constructor as strings. The file should be opened and the name of the person should be written to the file. If the file cannot be opened, throw an exception.

6. Write a class `TelephoneNumber` that will hold a telephone number. An object of this class will have the attributes

   - `areaCode`—a three-digit integer
   - `exchangeCode`—a three-digit integer
   - `number`—a four-digit integer

   and the methods

   - `TelephoneNumber(aString)`—a constructor that creates and returns a new instance of its class, given a string in the form xxx–xxx–xxxx or, if the area code is missing, xxx–xxxx. Throw an exception if the format is not valid. (*Hint*: To simplify the constructor, you can replace each hyphen in the telephone number with a blank. To accept a telephone number containing hyphens, you could process the string one character at a time or learn how to use `Scanner` to read words separated by a character—such as a hyphen—other than whitespace.)
   - `toString`—returns a string in either of the two formats shown previously for the constructor.

   Using a text editor, create a text file of several telephone numbers, using the two formats described previously. Write a program that reads this file, displays the data on the screen, and creates an array whose base type is `TelephoneNumber`. Allow the user to either add or delete one telephone number. Write the modified data on the text file, replacing its original contents. Then read and display the numbers in the modified file.

7. Write a class `ContactInfo` to store contact information for a person. It should have attributes for a person's name, business phone, home phone, cell phone, e-mail address, and home address. It should have a `toString` method that returns this data as a string, making appropriate replacements

for any attributes that do not have values. It should have a constructor `ContactInfo(aString)` that creates and returns a new instance of the class, using data in the string `aString`. The constructor should use a format consistent with what the `toString` method produces.

Using a text editor, create a text file of contact information, as described in the previous paragraph, for several people. Write a program that reads this file, displays the data on the screen, and creates an array whose base type is `ContactInfo`. Allow the user to do one of the following: change some data in one contact, add a contact, or delete a contact. Finally, write over the file with the modified contacts.

8. Write a program that reads every line in a text file, removes the first word from each line, and then writes the resulting lines to a new text file.

9. Repeat the previous exercise, but write the new lines to a new binary file instead of a text file.

10. Write a program that will make a copy of a text file, line by line. Read the name of the existing file and the name of the new file—the copy—from the keyboard. Use the methods of the class `File` to test whether the original file exists and can be read. If not, display an error message and abort the program. Similarly, see whether the name of the new file already exists. If so, display a warning message and allow the user to either abort the program, overwrite the existing file, or enter a new name for the file.

11. Suppose you are given a text file that contains the names of people. Every name in the file consists of a first name and last name. Unfortunately, the programmer who created the file of names had a strange sense of humor and did not guarantee that each name was on a single line of the file. Read this file of names and write them to a new text file, one name per line. For example, if the input file contains

> Bob Jones Fred
> Charles Ed
> Marston
> Jeff
> Williams

the output file should be

> Bob Jones
> Fred Charles
> Ed Marston
> Jeff Williams

12. Suppose that you have a binary file that contains numbers whose type is either `int` or `double`. You don't know the order of the numbers in the file,

but their order is recorded in a string at the beginning of the file. The string is composed of the letters *i* (for int) and *d* (for double) in the order of the types of the subsequent numbers. The string is written using the method writeUTF.

For example, the string "iddiiddd" indicates that the file contains eight values, as follows: one integer, followed by two doubles, followed by two integers, followed by three doubles. Read this binary file and create a new text file of the values, written one to a line.

13. Suppose that we want to store digitized audio information in a binary file. An audio signal typically does not change much from one sample to the next. In this case, less memory is used if we record the change in the data values instead of the actual data values. We will use this idea in the following program.

    Write a program StoreSignal that will read positive integers, each of which must be within 127 of the previous integer, from the keyboard (or from a text file, if you prefer). Write the first integer to a binary file. For each subsequent integer, compute the difference between it and the integer before it, cast the difference to a byte, and write the result to the binary file. When a negative integer is encountered, stop writing the file.

14. Write a program RecoverSignal that will read the binary file written by StoreSignal, as described in the previous exercise. Display the integer values that the data represents on the screen.

15. Even though a binary file is not a text file, it can contain embedded text. To find out if this is the case, write a program that will open a binary file and read it one byte at a time. Display the integer value of each byte as well as the character, if any, that it represents in ASCII.

    Technical details: To convert a byte to a character, use the following code:

    ```
    char[] charArray = Character.toChars(byteValue);
    ```

    The argument byteValue of the method toChars is an int whose value equals that of the byte read from the file. The character represented by the byte is charArray[0]. Since an integer is four bytes, byteValue can represent four ASCII characters. The method toChars tries to convert each of the four bytes to a character and places them into a char array. We are interested in just the character at index 0. If a byte in the file does not correspond to a character, the method will throw an IllegalArgumentException. If the exception is thrown, display only the byte value and continue on to the next byte.

PROGRAMMING PROJECTS

VideoNote
Processing a file

Visit www.myprogramminglab.com to complete many of these Programming Projects online and get instant feedback.

1. Write a program that searches a file of numbers and displays the largest number, the smallest number, and the average of all the numbers in the file. Do not assume that the numbers in the file are in any special order. Your program should obtain the file name from the user. Use either a text file or a binary file. For the text-file version, assume one number per line. For the binary-file version, use numbers of type double that are written using writeDouble.

2. Write a program that reads a file of numbers of type int and writes all the numbers to another file, but without any duplicate numbers. Assume that the numbers in the input file are already ordered from smallest to largest. After the program is run, the new file will contain all the numbers in the original file, but no number will appear more than once in the file. The numbers in the output file should also be sorted from smallest to largest. Your program should obtain both file names from the user. Use either a text file or a binary file. For the text-file version, assume one number per line. For the binary-file version, use numbers of type int that are written using writeInt.

3. Write a program that checks a text file for several formatting and punctuation matters. The program asks for the names of both an input file and an output file. It then copies all the text from the input file to the output file, but with the following two changes: (1) Any string of two or more blank characters is replaced by a single blank; (2) all sentences start with an uppercase letter. All sentences after the first one begin after either a period, a question mark, or an exclamation mark that is followed by one or more whitespace characters.

4. Write a program similar to the one in Listing 10.10 that can write an arbitrary number of Species objects to a binary file. (Species appears in Listing 5.19 of Chapter 5.) Read the file name and the data for the objects from a text file that you create by using a text editor. Then write another program that can search a binary file created by your first program and show the user the data for any requested endangered species. The user gives the file name and then enters the name of the species. The program either displays all the data for that species or gives a message if that species is not in the file. Allow the user to either enter additional species' names or quit.

5. Write a program that reads from a file created by the program in the previous programming project and displays the following information on the screen: the data for the species having the smallest population and the data for the species having the largest population. Do not assume that the objects in the file are in any particular order. The user gives the file name.

6. Programming Project 4 asks you, among other things, to write a program that creates a binary file of objects of the class `Species`. Write a program that reads from a file created by that program and writes the objects to another file after modifying their population figures as they would be in 100 years. Use the method `predictPopulation` of the class `Species`, and assume that you are given each species' growth rate.

7. Text messaging is a popular means of communication. Many abbreviations are in common use but are not appropriate for formal communication. Suppose the abbreviations are stored, one to a line, in a text file named `abbreviations.txt`. For example, the file might contain these lines:

> lol
> :)
> iirc
> 4
> u
> ttfn

Write a program that will read a message from another text file and surround each occurrence of an abbreviation with <> brackets. Write the marked message to a new text file.

For example, if the message to be scanned is

> How are u today? Iirc, this is your first free day. Hope you are having fun! :)

the new text file should contain

> How are <u> today? <Iirc>, this is your first free day. Hope you are having fun! <:)>

8. Modify the `TelephoneNumber` class described in Exercise 6 so that it is serializable. Write a program that creates an array whose base type is `Tele phoneNumber` by reading data from the keyboard. Write the array to a binary file using the method `writeObject`. Then read the data from the file using the method `readObject` and display the information to the screen. Allow the user to change, add, or delete any telephone number until he or she indicates that all changes are complete. Then write the modified telephone numbers to the file, replacing its original contents.

9. Revise the class `Pet`, as shown in Listing 6.1 of Chapter 6, so that it is serializable. Write a program that allows you to write and read objects of type `Pet` to a file. The program should ask the user whether to write to a file or read from a file. In either case, the program next asks for the file name. A user who has asked to write to a file can enter as many records as desired. A user who has asked to read from a file is shown all of the records in the

file. Be sure that the records do not scroll by so quickly that the user cannot read them. (*Hint*: Think of a way to pause the program after a certain number of lines are displayed.)

10. Write a program that reads records of type `Pet` from a file created by the program described in the previous programming project and displays the following information on the screen: the name and weight of the heaviest pet, the name and weight of the lightest pet, the name and age of the youngest pet, and the name and age of the oldest pet.

11. The following is an old word puzzle: "Name a common word, besides tremendous, stupendous, and horrendous, that ends in dous." If you think about this for a while it will probably come to you. However, we can also solve this puzzle by reading a text file of English words and outputting the word if it contains "dous" at the end. The text file "words.txt" contains 87314 English words, including the word that completes the puzzle. This file is available online with the source code for the book. Write a program that reads each word from the text file and outputs only those containing "dous" at the end to solve the puzzle.

VideoNote
Solution to Project 11

12. The UC Irvine Machine Learning repository contains many datasets for conducting computer science research. One dataset is the Haberman's Survival dataset, available at http://archive.ics.uci.edu/ml/datasets/ Haberman's+Survival and also included online with the source code for the book. The file "haberman.data" contains survival data for breast cancer patients in comma-separated value (CSV) format. The first field is the patient's age at the time of surgery, the second field is the year of the surgery, the third field is the number of positive axillary nodes detected, and the fourth field is the survival status. The survival status is 1 if the patient survived 5 years or longer and 2 if the patient died within 5 years.

Write a program that reads the CSV file and calculates the average number of positive axillary nodes detected for patients who survived 5 years or longer, and the average number of positive axillary nodes detected for patients who died within 5 years. A significant difference between the two averages suggests whether or not the number of positive axillary nodes detected can be used to predict survival time. Your program should ignore the age and year fields for each record.

Graphics

13. Repeat any of the previous programming projects using a `JFrame` graphical user interface.

14. Write an application or applet that uses a text field to get the name of a file, reads the file byte by byte, and displays the bytes as characters. (Exercise 15 describes how to convert a byte value to a character.) Display the first 20 characters in a label. If a byte does not correspond to a legal character, display a space instead. Clicking the `Next` button reads and displays the next 20 characters in the file. The GUI might look like the sketch in Figure 10.7.

Graphics

FIGURE 10.7A GUI for Programming Project 14

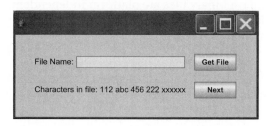

15. Write an application or applet that implements a simple text editor. Use a text field and a button to get the file. Read the entire file as characters and display it in a JTextArea. The user will then be able to make changes in the text area. Use a Save button to get the contents of the text area and write that over the original file.

    Technical Details: Read each line from the file and then display the line in the text area using the method append(aString). The method getText will return all of the text in the text area in a string that then can be written to the file. The following statement will make the text area referenced by editorTextArea scrollable:

    ```
    JScrollPane scrollPane = new
        JScrollPane(editorTextArea);
    ```

    Then add scrollPane to your GUI, just as you would any other component. The text area editorTextArea does not need to be added to the GUI, but it can be used.

Answers to Self-Test Questions

1. If a program sends its output to the screen, the output goes away when (or soon after) the program ends. If your program sends its output to a file, the file will remain after the program has finished running. A program that sends its output to a file has preserved its output for use long after the program ends its execution. The contents of a file remain until a person or program changes the file.

2. From a file to the program.

3. All files contain binary data. Text files can be thought of as a sequence of characters. You can write to and read a text file by using a text editor or your own Java program. All other files are called binary files. Data in these files

cannot conveniently be read using a text editor, but some standard binary files—such as certain music or picture files—can be created and read on any platform. Java binary files are platform independent, but other binary files might depend on the programming language and type of computer used to create them.

4. `PrintWriter outStream = new PrintWriter("sam.txt");`

5. ```
PrintWriter out Stream = new
   PrintWriter(new FileOutputStream("sam.txt", true));
```

6. ```
System.out.print("Enter file name: ");
Scanner keyboard = new Scanner(System.in);
String fileName = keyboard.next();
PrintWriter outStream = new PrintWriter(fileName);
```

7. A `FileNotFoundException` would be thrown if the file could not be opened because, for example, there is already a directory (folder) named `out.txt`. Note that if the file does not exist but can be created, no exception is thrown. If you answered `IOException`, you are not wrong, because a `FileNotFoundException` is an `IOException`. However, the better answer is the more specific exception class, namely, `FileNotFoundException`.

8. `PrintWriter textStream = new PrintWriter("dobedo");`

9. `Scanner inputStream = new Scanner(new File("dobedo"));`

10. Both methods return a value of type `String`.

11. The code for the following program is included with the source code for this book available on the Web:

```
import java.io.File;
import java.util.Scanner;
public class Question11
{
    public static void main(String[] args)
    {
        System.out.print("Enter a file name and I will ");
        System.out.println("tell you whether it exists.");
        Scanner keyboard = new Scanner(System.in);
        String name = keyboard.next();
        File fileObject = new File(name);
        if (fileObject.exists())
        {
            System.out.println("I found the file " + name);
            System.out.println("Delete the file?");
            String ans = keyboard.next();
            if (ans.equalsIgnoreCase("yes"))
```

```
                    {
                        System.out.println("If you delete the file " +
                        name);
                        System.out.println("all data in the file " + "will
                        be lost.");
                        System.out.println("Delete?");
                        ans = keyboard.next();
                        if (ans.equalsIgnoreCase("yes"))
                        {
                            if (fileObject.delete())
                                System.out.println("File deleted.");
                            else
                                System.out.println("Can't delete.");
                        }
                        else
                            System.out.println("File not deleted.");
                    }
                    else
                        System.out.println("File not deleted.");
                }
                else
                        System.out.println("I cannot find " + name);
            }
        }
```

12. ```
    ObjectOutputStream toFile = new ObjectOutputStream(
            new FileOutputStream("stuff.data"));
    ```

13. ```
    toFile.writeDouble(x1);
    toFile.writeDouble(x2);
    toFile.writeDouble(x3);
    ```

14. ```
    toFile.close();
    ```

15. ```
    import java.io.FileOutputStream;
    import java.io.ObjectOutputStream;
    import java.io.FileNotFoundException;
    import java.io.IOException;
    ```

16. ```
    ObjectInputStream fromFile = new ObjectInputStream(
            new FileInputStream("stuff.data"));
    ```

17. ```
    double x1 = fromFile.readDouble();
    double x2 = fromFile.readDouble();
    double x3 = fromFile.readDouble();
    ```

18. ```
    fromFile.close();
    ```

19. No. If a number is written to a file using `writeInt`, it should be read only by `readInt`. If you use `readLong` or `readDouble` to read the number, something will go wrong.
    ```

20. You should not use `readUTF` to read a string from a text file. You should use `readUTF` only to read a string from a binary file. Moreover, the string should have been written to that file using `writeUTF`.

21. The following program is included with the source code for this book available on the Web:

```java
import java.io.FileInputStream;
import java.io.FileNotFoundException;
import java.io.ObjectInputStream;
import java.io.IOException;
import java.util.Scanner;
public class Question21
{
    public static void main(String[] args)
    {
        //To use fileName in a catch block,
        //declare it outside of the try block
        String fileName = null;
        try
        {
            System.out.println("Enter file name:");
            Scanner keyboard = new Scanner(System.in);
            fileName = keyboard.next();
            ObjectInputStream inputStream =
                        new ObjectInputStream(
                        new FileInputStream(fileName));
            System.out.println("The first thing in the file");
            System.out.println(fileName + " is");
            String first = inputStream.readUTF();
            System.out.println(first);
            inputStream.close();
        }
        catch(FileNotFoundException e)
        {
            System.out.println("Problem opening the file "+
                            "fileName);
        }
        catch(EOFException e)
        {
            System.out.println("Unexpected end of file.");
        }
        catch(IOException e)
        {
            System.out.println("Problem with input from "+
                            " file fileName);
        }
    }
}
```

22. It will not work, because no constructor of `ObjectInputStream` has a parameter of type `String`. The correct way to accomplish the desired effect is by using

```
ObjectInputStream inputStream = new ObjectInputStream(
    new FileInputStream("mydata.dat"));
```

23. The class `FileInputStream` does not have any of the methods `readInt`, `readDouble`, or `readUTF`.

24. Yes.

25. No.

26. When opening a binary file for either output or input in the ways discussed in this chapter, a `FileNotFoundException` and other `IOExceptions` can be thrown.

27. An `EOFException` will be thrown.

28. Because when the end of the file is reached, an exception will be thrown, and that will end the entire `try` block.

29. The following program is included with the source code for this book available on the Web:

```java
import java.io.ObjectInputStream;
import java.io.EOFException;
import java.io.IOException;
public class Question29
{
    public static final String FILE_NAME = "temperatures.dat";
    public static void main(String[] args)
    {
        try
        {
            ObjectInputStream inputStream =
                        new ObjectInputStream(
                            new FileInputStream(FILE_NAME));
            System.out.println("Numbersfromthefile " +
                        FILE_NAME + ":");
            try
            {
                while (true)
                {
                    double number = inputStream.readDouble();
                    System.out.println(number);
                }
            }
            catch(EOFException e)
```

```
            {
                //Do nothing
            }
            System.out.println("End of reading from file.");
            inputStream.close();
        }
        catch(IOException e)
        {
            System.out.println("Problem reading from file.");
        }
    }
}
```

30. You add the two words `implementsSerializable` to the heading of the class definition. Any objects that are instance variables of the class must belong to a serializable class.

31. The return type is `Object`, which means that the returned value usually needs to be type cast to its "true" class.

32. `InvalidClassException`, `NotSerializableException`, and `IOException`.

33. `ClassNotFoundException`, `InvalidClassException`, `StreamCorrupted Exception`, `OptionalDataException`, and `IOException`.

34. Yes, it is perfectly legal. Try it.

35. This would not be good style, but in this case it is not even possible. You can add the `throws` clause to the method `showFirstLine` and eliminate the `try` and `catch` blocks in that method. However, you would then have to catch the exception in the method `actionPerformed`. You cannot add a `throws` clause to the method `actionPerformed`. See the Gotcha section at the end of the graphics supplement of Chapter 9 entitled "A throws Clause Is Not Allowed in `actionPerformed`." There are no other `catch` blocks to eliminate.

Recursion 11

11.1 THE BASICS OF RECURSION 800
Case Study: Digits to Words 803
How Recursion Works 808
Infinite Recursion 812
Recursive Methods Versus Iterative Methods 814
Recursive Methods That Return a Value 816

11.2 PROGRAMMING WITH RECURSION 820
Programming Example: Insisting That User Input
Be Correct 820
Case Study: Binary Search 822
Programming Example: Merge Sort—A Recursive
Sorting Method 830

Chapter Summary 834   **Programming Projects** 837   **Answers to Self-Test Questions** 843

There are two kinds of people in the world; those who divide the world into two kinds of people and those who do not.

—ANONYMOUS

Many people believe that you should never define anything in terms of itself. That would be a kind of circularity, they say. However, there are situations in which it is both possible and useful to define a method in terms of itself. If you do it correctly, it need not even be circular. Java permits you to, in some sense, define a method in terms of itself. More precisely, a Java method definition can contain an invocation of the very method being defined. That is, a method can call itself. Such methods are the subject of this chapter.

OBJECTIVES

After studying this chapter, you should be able to

- Describe the concept of recursion
- Use recursion as a programming tool
- Describe and use the recursive form of the binary search algorithm to search an array for a particular element
- Describe and use the merge sort algorithm to sort an array

PREREQUISITES

Most of this chapter requires only Chapters 1 through 6. Only the last two sections of the chapter—the case study "Binary Search" and the programming example "Merge Sort—A Recursive Sorting Method" require knowledge of any additional material. Those two sections require that you know about arrays, which are covered in Chapter 7.

11.1 THE BASICS OF RECURSION

coral n. 2: A piece of coral

—MERRIAM-WEBSTER ONLINE DICTIONARY

The TTP Project

—DILBERT

It often turns out that a natural way to design an algorithm involves using the same algorithm on one or more subcases. For example, the following is an outline of an algorithm for searching for a name in a phone book: Open the phone book to the middle of the book. If the name is on that page, you are done. If the name is alphabetically before that page, search the first half of the book. If the name is alphabetically after that page, search the second half of the book. Searching half of the phone book is a smaller version of the original task of searching the entire phone book.

Whenever an algorithm has one subtask that is a smaller version of the entire algorithm's task, it is said to be **recursive.** You can use a recursive algorithm to write a **recursive method** in Java. A recursive method contains an invocation of itself. That invocation is called a **recursive call,** or **recursive invocation.**

A recursive method calls itself

Of course, you must define a recursive method in the right way, or your Java code will cause problems, but the goal of this chapter is to show you the right way. The general topic of recursive methods is called **recursion.**

We begin with a simple example that illustrates recursion in Java. Given an integer variable num, we would like to output all of the numbers from num down to 1. If num is less than 1, then a newline should be printed. For example, if num is 3, then our program should output:

    321

Such a program can obviously be written with a simple for loop. The for loop is the preferred method for this problem, but we will provide a recursive countDown method to illustrate how recursion works for a simple example. Later in this chapter, we will see other problems for which recursion is the more elegant and preferred solution.

First, consider the simplest instance of our problem. This is usually the case when the inputs to the problem are the simplest or smallest values possible and can generally be solved with a straightforward solution. In our problem, the simplest input possible is when the input num is less than 1. In this case, all we need to do is print a blank line. This case is called a **base case,** or **stopping case**—that is, a case containing no recursive calls. As we will see, when this case occurs recursion will end. Additionally, unless this simple case is made to work correctly, no other case will work correctly.

A base or stopping case must be reached

Code for a method implementing the base case for our countdown problem is simple:

```java
public static void countDown(int num)
{
    if (num <= 0)
    {
        System.out.println();
    }
}
```

This method handles the base case, but not the more interesting case when num is 1 or more. To solve this recursively we have to break the problem up into a smaller version of the same problem. This means rephrasing the problem in terms of a method call back to countDown. Let's say that num equals 3. In other words, we have invoked countDown(3). We want to output "321".

This is the same as outputting "3" followed by "21". But outputting "21" is what countDown(2) should output! Our algorithm to solve this becomes:

- Output 3
- Call countDown(2)—which is responsible for outputting 21

In turn, countDown(2) can repeat the same process:

- Output 2
- Call countDown(1)—which is responsible for outputting 1

In turn, countDown(1) can repeat the same process:

- Output 1
- Call countDown(0)—which is responsible for outputting a newline

When countDown(0) is invoked, this executes the base case which prints a newline and ends the recursive method calls.

For an arbitrary value in num the recursive solution becomes:

- Output num
- Call countDown(num-1)—which is responsible for counting from num-1 to 1

A complete program with the algorithm implemented in Java is shown in Listing 11.1.

LISTING 11.1   Recursive Countdown Method

```java
public class RecursiveCountdown
{
    public static void main(String[] args)
    {
        countDown(3);
    }
    public static void countDown(int num)
    {
        if (num <= 0)
        {
            System.out.println();
        }
        else
        {
            System.out.print(num);
            countDown(num - 1);
        }
    }
}
```

Sample Screen Output

321

FIGURE 11.1 **Recursive Calls for the** countDown **Method**

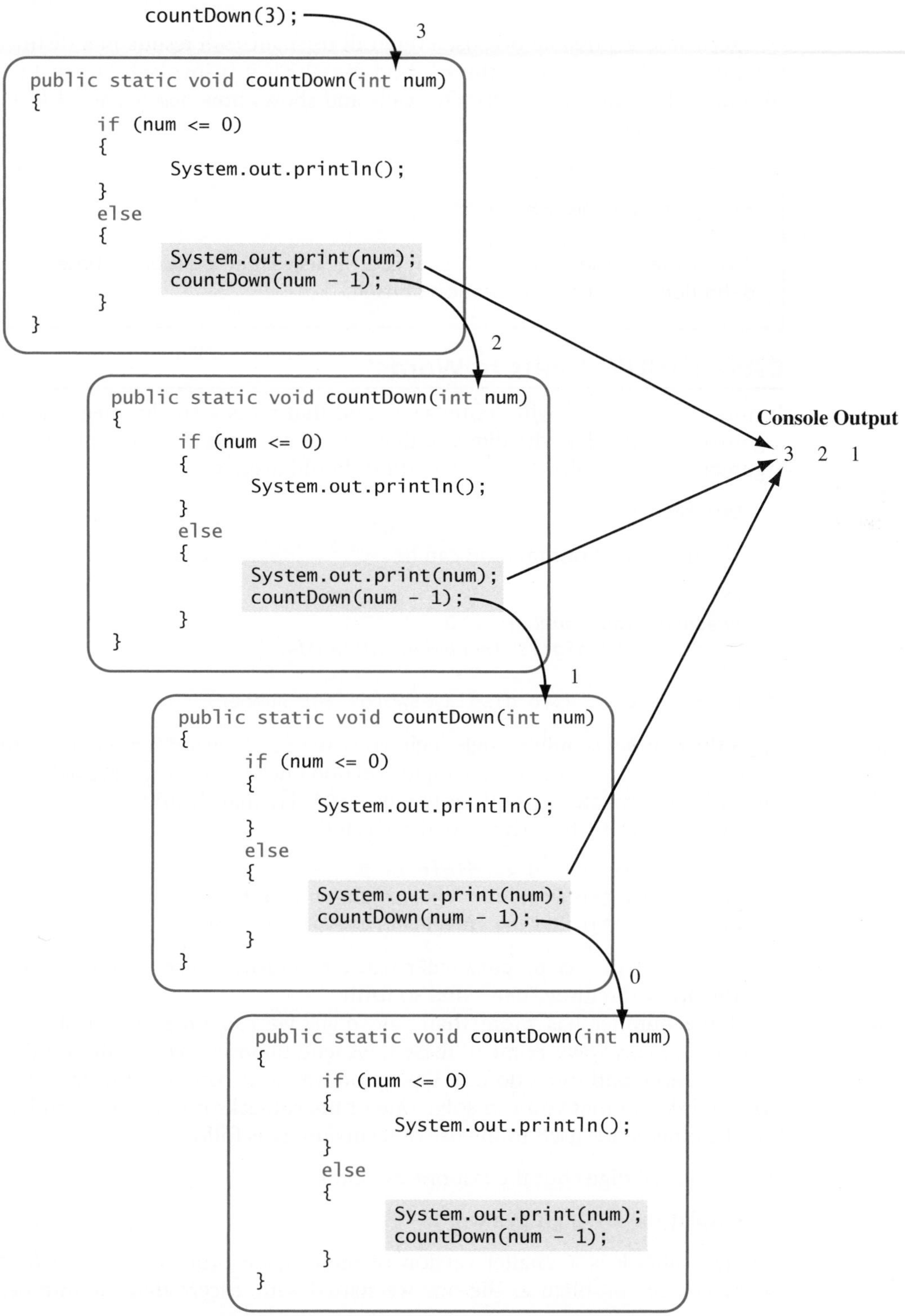

Recursion is possible because every call to countDown results in a distinct variable num that is local to the method for which it is invoked. Figure 11.1 illustrates the sequence of recursive calls and shows how num is passed from one method to the next.

> **RECAP Recursive Methods**
>
> A recursive method calls itself. That is, a recursive method is one whose definition contains an invocation of itself.

CASE STUDY Digits to Words

In this case study, we will define a method that takes a single integer as an argument and displays the digits of that integer as words. For example, if the argument is the number 223, the method should display

```
two two three
```

The heading of our method can be

```
/**
Precondition: number >= 0
Displays the digits in number as words.
*/
public static void displayAsWords(int number)
```

Single digits do not need recursion

If the number is only a single digit, you can use a long switch statement to decide which word to use for the digit; you don't need recursion. Let's delegate this task to a private method, getWordFromDigit, that displayAsWords can call. We can specify this private method as follows:

```
// Precondition: 0 <= digit <= 9
// Returns the word for the argument digit.
private static String getWordFromDigit(int digit)
```

Thus, when digit is 0, getWordFromDigit returns "zero", when digit is 1, the method returns "one", and so forth.

Break the task into subtasks

If the number has more than one digit, we can break our task into subtasks in many ways. Some of these ways lend themselves to a solution that uses recursion, and some do not. One good way to decompose this task into two subtasks, so that you can solve one of the subtasks immediately, and so that the other lends itself to the use of recursion, is as follows:

1. Display all digits but the last one as words.

2. Display the last digit as a word.

The first subtask is a smaller version of the original problem. It is, in fact, the exact same problem as the one we started with, except that the number in question is smaller—in particular, it contains fewer digits. Therefore, you can accomplish the first subtask by calling the very method we are defining. The second subtask is accomplished by a call to the private method `getWordFromDigit`. This scenario suggests the following refinement of our previous two steps:

Algorithm for displayAsWords(number)

1. `displayAsWords(`number after deleting its last digit `)`;

2. `System.out.print(getWordFromDigit(` last digit of `number) + " ");`

How do we remove the last digit of a number so we can perform step 1 yet retain that digit for step 2? Let's consider an example. Suppose we choose a number that has more than one digit, like 987. We need to break this number into two parts, 98 and 7. We can use integer division by 10 to accomplish this task. For example, 987 / 10 is 98, and 987 % 10 is 7. Thus, our algorithm leads us to the following Java code:

A recursive subtask

```
displayAsWords(number / 10);
System.out.print(getWordFromDigit(number % 10) + " ");
```

Using these statements as the body of the method `displayAsWords`, we get the following definition:

```
public static void displayAsWords(int number)
//Not quite right
{
    displayAsWords(number / 10);
    System.out.print(getWordFromDigit(number % 10) + " ");
}
```

A recursive method, but it ignores the one-digit case

As the comment indicates, however, this method will not quite work.

The method is recursive and uses the right basic idea, but it has one big problem: The preceding definition assumes that the argument `number` is more than one digit long. You need to make a special case for numbers that are only one digit long. This observation leads us to revise the method definition as follows:

The correct recursive method

```
public static void displayAsWords(int number)
{
    if (number < 10)
        System.out.print(getWordFromDigit(number) + " ");
    else//number has two or more digits
    {
        displayAsWords(number / 10);
        System.out.print(getWordFromDigit(number % 10) + " ");
    }
}
```

A recursive call must solve a "smaller" problem

The recursive call `displayAsWords(number / 10)` has an argument whose value is smaller than `number`, the argument to the preceding call to `displayAsWords`. It is important that a recursive call within a method solve a "smaller" version of the original problem (using some intuitive notion of "smaller," which we will make clearer before the end of this chapter).

As you will see in the next section, the successful execution of a recursive method, such as `displayAsWords`, requires that the simplest (base) case not involve a recursive call. In the definition of `displayAsWords`, this base case is a one-digit number, which is handled as follows:

One case must not involve recursion

```java
if (number < 10)
    System.out.print(getWordFromDigit(number) + " ");
```

No recursive call occurs in this case.

The definition of the method `displayAsWords` is now complete. Listing 11.2 shows the method embedded in a demonstration program.

LISTING 11.2   A Recursion Program for Digits to Words
(part 1 of 2)

```java
import java.util.Scanner;

public class RecursionDemo
{
    public static void main(String[] args)
    {
        System.out.println("Enter an integer:");
        Scanner keyboard = new Scanner(System.in);
        int number = keyboard.nextInt();
        System.out.println("The digits in that number are:")
        displayAsWords(number);
        System.out.println();

        System.out.println("If you add ten to that number,")
        System.out.println("the digits in the new number are:")
        number = number + 10;
        displayAsWords(number);
        System.out.println();
    }
    /**
    Precondition: number >= 0
    Displays the digits in number as words.
    */
    public static void displayAsWords(int number)
    {
        if (number < 10)
            System.out.print(getWordFromDigit(number) + " ")
```

(continued)

LISTING 11.2   A Demonstration of Recursion *(part 2 of 2)*

```
        else //number has two or more digits
        {
                displayAsWords(number / 10);        ←———— Recursive call
                System.out.print(getWordFromDigit(number) + " ")
        }
    }


    // Precondition: 0 <= digit <= 9
    // Returns the word for the argument digit.
    private static String getWordFromDigit(int digit)
    {
        String result = null;

        switch (digit)
        {
                case 0: result = "zero";  break;
                case 1: result = "one";   break;
                case 2: result = "two";   break;
                case 3: result = "three"; break;
                case 4: result = "four";  break;
                case 5: result = "five";  break;
                case 6: result = "six";   break;
                case 7: result = "seven"; break;
                case 8: result = "eight"; break;
                case 9: result = "nine";  break;
                default:
                    {
                        System.out.println("Fatal Error.");
                        System.exit(0);
                    }
        }
        return result;
    }
}
```

Sample Screen Output

```
Enter an integer:
987
The digits in that number are:
nine eight seven
If you add ten to that number,
the digits in the new number are:
nine nine seven
```

How Recursion Works

Exactly how does the computer handle a recursive call? To see the details, consider the following invocation of the method displayAsWords:

```
displayAsWords(987);
```

Although the definition of displayAsWords in Listing 11.2 contains a recursive call, Java does nothing special to handle this or any other invocation of displayAsWords. The value of the argument 987 is copied into the method's parameter number and the resulting code executes. This code is equivalent to the following:

The effect of the original call to the method

```
{//Code for invocation of displayAsWords(987)
    if (987 < 10)
            System.out.print(getWordFromDigit(987) + " ");
    else//987 has two or more digits
    {
            displayAsWords(987 / 10);
            System.out.print(getWordFromDigit(987 % 10) + " ");
    }
}
```

Because 987 is not less than 10, the compound statement after the else executes. This compound statement starts with the recursive call displayAsWords(987 / 10). The rest of the compound statement cannot execute until this recursive call is completed. Note that this would be true even if the method was calling another method, rather than calling itself recursively. So the execution of the code for displayAsWords(987) is suspended and waits for the execution of displayAsWords (987 / 10) to complete. When execution of the recursive call completes, the suspended computation resumes. That is, the rest of the compound statement executes.

The new recursive invocation, displayAsWords(987 / 10), is handled just like any other method invocation: The value of the argument 987 / 10 is copied into the parameter number, and the resulting code is executed. Since the value of 987 / 10 is 98, the resulting code is equivalent to the following:

The effect of the first recursive call

```
{//Code for invocation of displayAsWords(98)
    if (98 < 10)
        System.out.print(getWordFromDigit(98) + " ");
    else//98 has two or more digits
    {
        displayAsWords(98 / 10);
        System.out.print(getWordFromDigit(98 % 10) + " ");
    }
}
```

Once again, the argument to the method—98 this time—is not less than 10, so the execution of this new code involves a recursive call, namely, displayAsWords(98 / 10). At that point, the preceding computation is suspended and waits for this recursive call to complete. The value of the parameter number is the value of 98 / 10, or 9, and the following code begins execution:

The effect of the second recursive call

```
{//Code for invocation of displayAsWords(9)
    if (9 < 10)
        System.out.print(getWordFromDigit(9) + " ");
    else//9 has two or more digits
    {
        displayAsWords(9 / 10);
        System.out.print(getWordFromDigit(9 % 10) + " ");
    }
}
```

Because 9 is indeed less than 10, only the first part of the if-else statement,

```
System.out.print(getWordFromDigit(9) + " ");
```

is executed. This case is called a **base case,** or **stopping case**—that is, a case containing no recursive calls. A quick look at the definition of the method getWordFromDigit shows that the string "nine" is displayed on the screen. The invocation of displayAsWords(98 / 10) is now complete.

A base or stopping case must be reached

At this point, the suspended computation, shown here, can resume after the position indicated by the arrow:

Continuing execution after the last recursive call finishes

```
{//Code for invocation of displayAsWords(98)
    if (98 < 10)
        System.out.print(getWordFromDigit(98) + " ");
    else //98 has two or more digits
    {
        displayAsWords(98 / 10);  ←——————  Recursive call
        System.out.print(getWordFromDigit(98 % 10) + " ");
    }
}
```

Thus, the statement

```
System.out.print(getWordFromDigit(98 % 10) + " ");
```

executes—causing the string "eight" to be displayed on the screen—and ends the invocation of the recursive call displayAsWords(98).

Stay with us, dear reader! The process is almost over. We have only one more suspended computation waiting to be completed, and it is shown in the code that follows:

Continuing execution after the next-to-last recursive call finishes

```
{//Code for invocation of displayAsWords(987)
    if (987 < 10)
        System.out.print(getWordFromDigit(987) + " ");
    else //987 has two or more digits
    {
        displayAsWords(987 / 10);  ←——————  Recursive call
        System.out.print(getWordFromDigit(98 % 10) + " ");
    }
}
```

The computation resumes after the position indicated by the arrow, and the following code executes:

```
System.out.print(getWordFromDigit(987 % 10) + " ");
```

This statement causes "seven" to be displayed on the screen, and the entire process ends. The sequence of recursive calls is illustrated in Figure 11.2.

FIGURE 11.2 Executing a Recursive Call

`displayAsWords(987)` is equivalent to executing:

```
{//Code for invocation of displayAsWords(987)
    if (987 < 10)
        System.out.print(getWordFromDigit(987) + " ");
    else //987 has two or more digits
    {
        displayAsWords(987 / 10);          Computation waits
                                           here for the completion
        System.out.print(getWordFromDigit(987 % 10) + " ");   of the recursive call.
    }
}
```

`displayAsWords(987/10)` is equivalent to `displayAsWords(98)`, which is equivalent to executing:

```
{//Code for invocation of displayAsWords(98)
    if (98 < 10)
        System.out.print(getWordFromDigit(98) + " ");
    else //98 has two or more digits
    {
        displayAsWords(98 / 10);           Computation waits
                                           here for the completion
        System.out.print(getWordFromDigit(98 % 10) + " ");    of the recursive call.
    }
}
```

`displayAsWords(98/10)` is equivalent to `displayAsWords(9)`, which is equivalent to executing:

```
{//Code for invocation of displayAsWords(9)
    if (9 < 10)
        System.out.print(getWordFromDigit(9) + " ");
    else //9 has two or more digits
    {                                      Another recursive call
                                           does not occur.
        displayAsWords(9 / 10);
        System.out.print(getWordFromDigit(9 % 10) + " ");
    }
}
```

Note that nothing special happens when an invocation of a recursive method executes. Argument values are copied to parameters, and the code in the method definition executes, just as it would for any method invocation.

REMEMBER **Keys to Successful Recursion**

A definition of a method that includes a recursive invocation of the method itself will not behave correctly unless you follow some specific design guidelines. The following rules apply to most cases that involve recursion:

- The heart of the method definition must be an `if-else` statement or some other branching statement that leads to different cases, depending on some property of a parameter of the method.

- One or more of the branches should include a recursive invocation of the method. These recursive invocations must, in some sense, use "smaller" arguments or solve "smaller" versions of the task performed by the method.

- One or more branches must include no recursive invocations. These branches are the base cases, or stopping cases.

VideoNote
Writing `void` methods
that are recursive

RECAP **Base (Stopping) Cases**

Base cases must be designed so that they terminate every chain of recursive calls. A method invocation can produce a recursive invocation of the same method, and that invocation may produce another recursive invocation, and so forth for some number of recursive calls, but every such chain must eventually lead to a base case that ends with no recursive invocation. Otherwise, an invocation of the method might never end (or might not end until the computer runs out of resources).

A typical recursive method definition includes an `if-else` statement or other branching statement that chooses among one or more cases that each include a recursive call of the method and one or more cases that each end the method invocation without any recursive invocation. Every chain of recursive calls must eventually lead to one of those nonrecursive, or base, cases.

The most common way to ensure that a base case is always reached is to make all the recursive invocations of the method use a "smaller" argument. For example, consider the method `displayAsWords` given in Listing 11.2. Its parameter is number, and the parameter to the method's recursive invocation is the smaller value number/10. In this way, the recursive invocations in a chain of recursive calls each have a smaller argument. Because the definition of this method has a base case for any one-digit argument, we know that, eventually, a base case is always reached.

Infinite Recursion

Consider the method displayAsWords defined in the previous section. Suppose we had been careless and had defined it as follows:

```
public static void displayAsWords(int number)//Not quite right
{
    displayAsWords(number / 10);
    System.out.print(getWordFromDigit(number % 10) + " ");
}
```

In fact, we almost did define it this way, until we noticed an omitted case. Suppose, however, that we did not notice the omitted case and used this shorter definition. Let's quickly trace the computation of the recursive call displayAsWords(987).

The method invocation displayAsWords(987) produces the recursive call

displayAsWords(987 / 10),

which is equivalent to displayAsWords(98). The invocation of displayAsWords(98) produces the recursive call

displayAsWords(98 / 10),

which is equivalent to displayAsWords(9). Because our incorrect version of displayAsWords has no special case for one-digit numbers, the invocation of displayAsWords(9) produces the recursive call

displayAsWords(9 / 10),

which is equivalent to displayAsWords(0). The invocation of displayAsWords(0) produces the recursive call

displayAsWords(0 / 10),

which is equivalent to displayAsWords(0).

Now the problem becomes apparent: The invocation of displayAsWords(0) produces another invocation of displayAsWords(0), which produces yet another invocation of displayAsWords(0), and so forth forever—or until your computer runs out of resources. This situation is called **infinite recursion.**

Note that the preceding definition of displayAsWords is incorrect only in the sense that it performs the wrong computation. It is not illegal. The Java compiler will accept this definition of displayAsWords—and any similar recursive method definition that does not have a case to stop the series of recursive calls. However, unless your recursive definition ensures that a base case will, in fact, be reached, you will get an infinite chain of recursive calls, causing your program either to run forever or to end abnormally.

In order for a recursive method definition to work correctly and not produce an infinite chain of recursive calls, there must be one or more cases—the base cases—that, for certain values of the argument(s), will end without producing any recursive call. The correct definition of displayAsWords, given in Listing 11.2, has one base case, which is highlighted in the following code:

```java
public static void displayAsWords(int number)                    ← Base case
{
    if (number < 10)
        System.out.print(getWordFromDigit(number) + " ");
    else //number has two or more digits
        {
            displayAsWords(number / 10);
            System.out.print(getWordFromDigit(number % 10) + " ");
        }
}
```

GOTCHA   Stack Overflow

When a method invocation leads to infinite recursion, your program is likely to end with an error message that mentions a "stack overflow." The term **stack** refers to a data structure that is used to keep track of recursive calls—and other things as well.

The system maintains a record within the computer's memory of each recursive call. You can imagine these records as pieces of paper. The system "stacks" these papers one on top of the other. When this stack becomes too large for it to fit in the available memory, a **stack overflow** occurs.   ■

SELF-TEST QUESTIONS

myprogramminglab

1. What output will be produced by the following code?

```java
public class Question1
{
    public static void main(String[] args)
    {
        methodA(3);
    }
    public static void methodA(int n)
    {
        if (n < 1)
                System.out.println('B');
        else
        {
            methodA(n - 1);
            System.out.println('R');
        }
    }
}
```

B
R
R
R

2. What is the output produced by the following code?

```java
public class Question2
{
    public static void main(String[] args)
    {
        methodB(3);
    }
    public static void methodB(int n)
    {
        if (n < 1)
            System.out.println('B');
        else
        {
            //The following two lines are in the reverse of
            //their order in Self-Test Question 1.
            System.out.println('R');
            methodB(n - 1);
        }
    }
}
```

3. Write a recursive definition for the following method:

```java
/**
Precondition: n >= 1.
Displays the symbol '#' n times on one line
and then advances to the next line.
*/
public static void displaySharps(int n)
```

For example, the call displaySharps(3) is equivalent to

```java
System.out.println("###");
```

If you have trouble writing this method, simplify it so that the output does not advance to the next line. For that simpler case, you need not worry about the distinction between print and println. In the simpler case, you use only print. After doing the simpler case, try to do the exercise as stated.

Recursive Methods Versus Iterative Methods

Any method definition that includes a recursive call can be rewritten so that it accomplishes the same task without using recursion. For example, Listing 11.3 contains a revision of the program in Listing 11.2 in which the definition of displayAsWords does not use recursion. Both versions of displayAsWords perform the exact same action—that is, they write the same output to the screen. As is the case here, the nonrecursive version of a method definition typically involves a loop instead of recursion. A nonrecursive repetitive process is called **iteration**,[1] and a method that implements such a process is called an iterative method.

Processes or methods that involve a loop are said to be iterative

LISTING 11.3 **An Iterative Version of** `displayAsWords`

```
import java.util.scanner;
public class IterativeDemo
{
    public static void main(String[] args)
    <The rest of main is the same as Listing 11.2.>

    /**
    Precondition: number >= 0
    Displays the digits in number as words.
    */
    public static void displayAsWords(int number)
    {
        int divisor = getPowerOfTen(number);
        int next = number;
        while (divisor >= 10)
        {
            System.out.print(getWordFromDigit(next / divisor) +
                            " ");
            next = next % divisor
            divisor = divisor / 10
        }
        System.out.print(getWordFromDigit(next / divisor) + " ");
    }
    // Precondition: n >= 0.
    // Returns 10 raised to the power n.
    private static int getPowerOfTen(int n)
    {
        int result = 1;
        while (n >= 10)
        {
            result = result * 10;
            n = n / 10;
        }
        result result;
    }
    private static String getWordFromDigit(int digit)
    <The rest of getWordFromDigit is the same as in Listing 11.2.>
}
```

Screen Output

> The output is exactly the same as in Listing 11.2.

---

[1] Note that Chapter 4 defines an *iteration* as one repetition of a loop. The term also has the definition we introduce here.

A recursive method uses more storage space than an iterative version of the method, because of the overhead to the system that results from tracking the recursive calls and suspended computations. This overhead can make a recursive method run slower than a corresponding iterative one. Sometimes the extra time necessary for a particular recursive method is so large that recursion should not be used. For example, the Fibonacci numbers introduced in Programming Project 7 at the end of this chapter should never be computed recursively. In other situations, however, recursion is perfectly acceptable and can make your code easier to understand. Indeed, there are times when recursion can be a big aid in terms of program clarity.

Recursive Methods That Return a Value

A recursive method can be a void method, as you have seen, or it can be a method that returns a value. You design a recursive method that returns a value in essentially the same way that you design a recursive void method. That is, you follow the design guidelines given earlier in this chapter on page 761. We can clarify the second guideline so that it accounts for returned values by adding the italicized words in the following:

> One or more of the branches should include a recursive invocation of the method *that leads to the returned value*. These recursive invocations must, in some sense, use "smaller" arguments or solve "smaller" versions of the task performed by the method.

Facts that can be used to solve this problem recursively

The recursive method getNumberOfZeros defined in Listing 11.4 returns a value. It returns the number of zeros in the integer given as an argument. For example, getNumberOfZeros(2030) returns 2, because 2030 contains two zero digits. Let's look at how this method works.

LISTING 11.4   A Recursive Method That Returns a Value
(part 1 of 2)

```
import java.util.Scanner;

public class RecursionDemo2
{
    public static void main(String[] args)
    {
        System.out.println("Enter a nonnegative number:");
        Scanner keyboard = new Scanner(System.in);
        int number = keyboard.nextInt();
        System.out.println(number + " contains " +
                        getNumberOfZeros(number) + " zeros.");
    }
```

(continued)

LISTING 11.4 A Recursive Method That Returns a Value
(part 2 of 2)

```
/**
Precondition: n >=0
Returns the number of zero digits in n.
*/
public static int getNumberOfZeros(int n)
{
    int result;
    if (n == 0)
        result = 1;
    else if (n < 10)
        result = 0; //n has one digit that is not 0
    else if (n % 10 == 0)
        result = getNumberOfZeros(n / 10) + 1;
    else //n % 10 !=0
        result = getNumberOfZeros(n / 10);
    return result;
}
}
```

Sample Screen Output

```
Enter a nonnegative number:
2008
2008 contains 2 zeros.
```

The definition of the method uses the following simple facts:

- If *n* contains only one digit, the number of zero digits in *n* is 1 if *n* is zero and 0 if *n* is not zero.
- If *n* contains two or more digits, let *d* be its last digit and *m* be the integer left after removing the last digit from *n*. The number of zero digits in *n* is the number of zeros in *m* plus 1 if *d* is zero.

For example, the number of zeros in 20030 is the number of zeros in 2003 plus 1 for the last zero. The number of zeros in 20035 is the number of zeros in 2003 without adding anything, because the extra digit is not zero. With this definition in mind, let's go through a simple computation using getNumberOfZeros.

First, consider the simple expression

```
getNumberOfZeros(0)
```

which might occur as the right-hand side of some assignment statement. When the method is called, the value of the parameter n is set equal to 0, and the code in the body of the method definition is executed. Because the value of n is equal to 0, the first case of the multiway if-else statement applies, and the value returned is 1.

Next, consider another simple expression:

```
getNumberOfZeros(5)
```

When the method is called, the value of the parameter n is set equal to 5, and the code in the body of the method definition is executed. Since the value of n is not equal to 0, the first case of the multiway if-else statement does not apply. The value of n is, however, less than 10, so the second branch of the multiway if-else statement applies, and the value returned is 0. As you can see, these two simple cases work out correctly.

Now let's look at an example that involves a recursive call. Consider the expression

```
getNumberOfZeros(50)
```

When the method is called, the value of n is set equal to 50, and the code in the body of the method definition is executed. Since this value of n is not equal to 0 and is not less than 10, neither of the first two branches of the multiway if-else statement applies. 50 % 10 is 0, so the third branch applies. Thus, the value returned is

```
getNumberOfZeros(n / 10) + 1
```

which in this case is equivalent to

```
getNumberOfZeros(50 / 10) + 1
```

which, in turn, is equivalent to

```
getNumberOfZeros(5) + 1
```

We saw earlier that getNumberOfZeros(5) returns 0, so the value returned by getNumberOfZeros(50) is 0 + 1, or 1, which is the correct value.

Larger numbers will produce longer chains of recursive calls. For example, consider the expression

```
getNumberOfZeros(2008)
```

A trace of
recursive calls

The value of this expression is calculated as follows:

```
getNumberOfZeros(2008) is getNumberOfZeros(200) + 0
getNumberOfZeros(200) is getNumberOfZeros(20) + 1
getNumberOfZeros(20) is getNumberOfZeros(2) + 1
getNumberOfZeros(2) is 0 (a base case)
getNumberOfZeros(20) is getNumberOfZeros(2) + 1, which is 0 + 1, or 1
getNumberOfZeros(200) is getNumberOfZeros(20) + 1, which is 1 + 1, or 2
getNumberOfZeros(2008) is getNumberOfZeros(200) + 0, which is 2 + 0,
    or 2
```

Note that when Java reaches the base case, getNumberOfZeros(2), three computations have been suspended. After calculating the value returned for the base case, the most recently suspended computation resumes, yielding the value of getNumberOfZeros(20). After that, each of the other suspended computations resumes and completes in turn. Each computed value is used in another suspended computation, until the computation for the original invocation, getNumberOfZeros(2008), completes. The suspended computations are completed in an order opposite to the order in which they were suspended. The final value returned is 2, which is correct, because 2008 has two zero digits.

VideoNote
**Writing recursive methods
that return a value**

REMEMBER Do Not Confuse Recursion and Overloading

Do not confuse recursion and overloading. When you overload a method name, you are giving two different methods the same name. If the definition of one of these two methods includes a call to the other, that is not recursion. In a recursive method definition, the definition of the method includes a call to the exact same method with the exact same definition, including the same number and types of parameters.

SELF-TEST QUESTIONS

`myprogramminglab`

4. What is the output of the following code?

```java
public class Question4
{
    public static void main(String[] args)
    {
        System.out.println(getMysteryValue(3));
    }
    public static int getMysteryValue(int n)
    {
        if (n <= 1)
            return 1;
        else
            return getMysteryValue(n - 1) + n;
    }
}
```

5. Complete the definition of the following method. Your definition should be recursive. (*Hint*: 10^n is $10^{n-1} * 10$ for $n > 1$.)

```java
/**
Precondition: n >= 0.
Returns 10 to the power n.
*/
public static int computeTenToThe(int n)
```

6. Complete the definition of the following method. Your definition should be recursive. Unlike the method in Question 5, this method does not restrict the sign or value of its argument. You can use the same technique you used for Question 5, but you should have one more recursive case for negative exponents. (*Hints*: 10^n is $1/10^{-n}$ for negative values of n. Also, if n is negative, $-n$ is positive.)

```
/**
Precondition: n can be any int.
Returns 10 to the power n.
*/
public static int computeTenToThe(int n)
```

11.2 PROGRAMMING WITH RECURSION

All short statements about programming techniques are false.

—ANONYMOUS

In this section, we present some programs that illustrate ways to use recursion.

| PROGRAMMING EXAMPLE | Insisting That User Input Be Correct |

The program in Listing 11.5 simply requests a positive integer and then counts down from that integer to zero. The method `getCount` reads the integer from the user. Notice that if the user enters a number that is not positive, the method `getCount` calls itself. This call starts the input process all over again from the beginning. If the user enters another incorrect number, another recursive call occurs, and the input process will start yet again. This procedure is repeated until the user enters a positive integer. Of course, in practice, not many recursive calls would be necessary, but they would take place as often as the user entered bad data. In general, this technique is not recommended because every invalid entry results in a recursive call. If the user kept making invalid entries, this would be similar to infinite recursion and could eventually result in a stack overflow.

LISTING 11.5 Recursion for Starting Over *(part 1 of 2)*

```
import java.util.Scanner;
public class CountDown
{
    private int count;

    public static void main(String[] args)
```

(continued)

LISTING 11.5   **Recursion for Starting Over** *(part 2 of 2)*

```java
    {
        CountDown countDowner = new CountDown();
        countDowner.getCount();
        countDowner.showCountDown();
    }

    public void getCount()
    {
        System.out.println("Enter a positive integer:");
        Scanner keyboard = new Scanner(System.in);
        count = keyboard.nextInt();
        if (count <= 0)
        {
            System.out.println("Input must be positive.");
            System.out.println("Try again.");
            getCount();//start over
        }
    }
    public void showCountDown()
    {
        System.out.println("Counting down:");
        for (int left = count; left >= 0; left--)
            System.out.print(left + ", ");
        System.out.println("Blast Off!");
    }
}
```

Sample Screen Output

```
Enter a positive integer:
0
Input must be positive.
Try again.
Enter a positive integer:
3
Counting down:
3, 2, 1, 0, Blast Off!
```

SELF-TEST QUESTION

myprogramminglab

7. Revise the method getCount in Listing 11.5 so that it is iterative instead of recursive.

VideoNote
**Using recursion to search
and sort an array**

CASE STUDY Binary Search

This case study assumes that you have already covered the basics about arrays given in Chapter 7. We will design a recursive method that tells whether a given number is or is not in an array of integers. If the sought-after number is in the array, the method will also give the index of the number's position in the array.

For example, suppose that the array contains a list of winning lottery tickets and you want to search the list to see whether you are a winner. Suppose another array contains the prize amounts for these tickets in an order that corresponds to the order of the tickets in the first array. Thus, if you know the index of a winning number, you can use this index to locate the amount of your winnings in the second array.

In Chapter 7, the section "Searching an Array" discussed a method for searching an array simply by checking every array position. The method we develop in this case study will be much faster than that simple sequential search. However, for this faster method to work, the array must be sorted. We will assume that the array is already sorted into ascending order and is completely filled. So if the array is named a, we know that

Assume a sorted array

```
a[0] ≤ a[1] ≤ a[2] ≤...≤ a[a.length-1]
```

Recall that the sequential search does not have this requirement.

Specify the method's behavior

Let's design our method to return an integer that gives the index of the sought-after number. If the number is not in the array, the method will return –1. Before we worry about the exact setup of the class and methods and about connecting the method to an array, we first design some pseudocode to solve the search problem.

Because the array is sorted, we can rule out whole sections of the array that could not possibly contain the number we seek. For example, if we are looking for the number 7 and we know that a[5] contains 9, we know, of course, that 7 is not equal to a[5]. But we also know much more: Because the array is sorted, we know that

```
7 < a[5] ≤ a[i] for i ≥ 5
```

So we know that 7 is not equal to a[i] for any value of i that is greater than or equal to 5. Thus, all the elements a[i] for i≥5 need not be searched. We know that the sought-after value 7 is not among them without needing to check them. Similarly, if the sought-after number, 7, were greater than a[5]—for example, if a[5] were 3 instead of 9—we could rule out all the elements a[i] for i ≤5.

First-draft algorithm

Let's express these observations as a first-draft algorithm, after replacing the index 5 in the preceding examples with m:

Algorithm to search a sorted array for the element target (draft 1)

1. m = an index between 0 and (a.length - 1)

2. if (target == a[m])

3.   `return m;`

4. `else if(target < a[m])`

5.   `return` the result of searching `a[0]` through `a[m - 1]`

6. `else if(target > a[m])`

7.   `return` the result of searching `a[m + 1]` through `a[a.length - 1]`

If `a[m]` is not the element we seek, we can ignore one part of the array and search only the other part. Our choice of m affects the size of these two parts. Since we do not know which part contains `a[m]`, we might as well make the two parts as equal in size as we can. To do so, we choose m so that `a[m]` would be at or near the middle of the array. Thus, we replace step 1 of the previous pseudocode with

1. m = approximate midpoint between 0 and (`a.length - 1`)

To clarify our algorithm, we can rename the index m as `mid`.

Notice that each of the two `else-if` cases searches a segment of the array. This search is a smaller version of the very task we are designing. This observation suggests recursion. In fact, the segments of the array can be searched by using recursive calls to the algorithm itself. Although we need to write two recursive calls in our algorithm, only one of them will execute during a given search, because we will be searching only one half of the array. Thus, if `a[mid]` is not the element we seek, we would search either

`a[0]` through `a[mid - 1]`, or

`a[mid + 1]` through `a[a.length - 1]`

There is, however, one complication. (Isn't there always?) To implement these recursive calls, we need more parameters. These recursive calls specify that a subrange of the array is to be searched. In the first case, it is the elements indexed by 0 through `mid - 1`. In the second case, it is the elements indexed by `mid + 1` through `a.length - 1`. Thus, we need two extra parameters to specify the first and last indices of the subrange of the array to be searched. Let's call these extra parameters `first` and `last`, respectively. We now can express the pseudocode more precisely as follows:

Algorithm to search a [first] through a [last] of a sorted array for   Second-draft
the element target (draft 2)   algorithm

1. `mid` = approximate midpoint between `first` and `last`

2. `if(target == a[mid])`

3.   `return mid`

4. `else if(target < a[mid])`

5.   `return` the result of searching `a[first]` through `a[mid - 1]`

6. `else if (target > a[mid])`

7.   `return` the result of searching `a[mid + 1]` through `a[last]`

If we want to search the entire array, we would set `first` equal to 0 and `last` equal to `a.length - 1` initially. But each recursive call will use some other values for `first` and `last`. For example, if the first recursive call made is the one in step 5, it will set `first` equal to 0 and `last` equal to `mid - 1`.

You should always ensure that any recursive algorithm you write will not produce an infinite recursion by checking whether every possible invocation of the algorithm will lead to a base case. Consider the three possibilities in the nested `if-else` statement. In the first case, the sought-after number is found in `a[mid]`, and there is no recursive call, so the process terminates. We have reached the base case. In each of the other two possibilities, a smaller subrange of the array is searched by a recursive call. If the sought-after number is in the array, the algorithm will narrow the range down more and more until it finds the number. But what if the number is not anywhere in the array? Will the resulting series of recursive calls eventually lead to a base case if the number is not in the array? Unfortunately not.

Final algorithm for a binary search

The problem is not hard to fix, however. Note that in each recursive call, either the value of `first` is increased or the value of `last` is decreased. If these two indices ever pass each other in value and `first` actually becomes larger than `last`, we will know that there are no more indices left to check and that the number `target` is not in the array. If we add this test to our pseudocode, we get the following, more complete, pseudocode:

Algorithm to search a [first] through a [last] of a sorted array for the element target (final version)

1. `mid` = approximate midpoint between `first` and `last`

2. `if (first > last)`

3.   `return -1`

4. `else if (target == a[mid])`

5.   `return mid`

6. `else if(target < a[mid])`

7.   `return` the result of searching `a[first]` through `a[mid - 1]`

8. `else if(target > a[mid])`

9.   `return` the result of searching `a[mid + 1]` through `a[last]`

This way of searching an array is called a **binary search**. While searching, the algorithm eliminates one half of the array, then half of what's left, and so on. Figure 11.3 provides an example of how this algorithm works.

FIGURE 11.3 A Binary Search Example

target *is* 33

Eliminate half of the array elements:

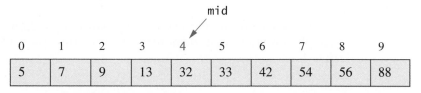

1. mid = (0 + 9)/2 (which is 4).
2. 33 > a[mid] (that is, 33 > a[4]).
3. So if 33 is in the array, 33 is one of
   a[5],a[6],a[7],a[8],a[9].

Eliminate half of the remaining array elements:

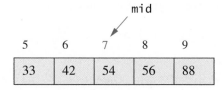

1. mid = (5 + 9)/2 (which is 7).
2. 33 < a[mid] (that is, 33 < a[7]).
3. So if 33 is in the array, 33 is one of
   a[5], a[6].

Eliminate half of the remaining array elements:

1. mid = (5 + 6)/2 (which is 5).
2. 33 equals a[mid], so we found 33 at index 5.

33 *found in* a[5].

Now we need to translate this pseudocode algorithm into Java code. Let's name the method binarySearch and place it in a class called ArraySearcher. The class will have an instance variable to name the array, and the array to be searched will be given that name by the constructor. Since the method binarySearch has extra parameters, the user would always have to set them

The public
method find
calls the
private method
binarySearch

A binary search
is fast

equal to 0 and a.length − 1 in order to specify that the entire array be searched. To avoid the need to worry about this detail, we add the method find, which simply calls the method binarySearch. It allows the user simply to specify the target value and not be concerned about indices. Since the method binarySearch is now just a helping method, we make it a private method.

The final code for the class ArraySearcher is shown in Listing 11.6. A simple program that demonstrates how this class works is given in Listing 11.7.

LISTING 11.6 A Binary Search Class *(part 1 of 2)*

```
/**
Class for searching an already sorted array of integers.
*/
public class ArraySearcher
{
    private int[] a;

    /**
     Precondition: theArray is full and is sorted
     from lowest to highest.
    */
    public ArraySearcher(int[] theArray)
    {
        a = theArray;//a is now another name for theArray.
    }

    /**
     If target is in the array, returns the index of an occurrence
     of target. Returns -1 if target is not in the array.
    */
    public int find(int target)
    {
        return binarySearch(target, 0, a.length - 1);
    }
    //Uses binary search to search for target in a[first] through
    //a[last] inclusive. Returns the index of target if target
    //is found. Returns -1 if target is not found.
    private int binarySearch(int target, int first, int last)
    {
        int result:
        if (first > last)
            result = -1;
        else
        {
```

(continued)

LISTING 11.6 **A Binary Search Class** *(part 2 of 2)*

```java
            int mid = (first + last)/2;
            if (target == a[mid])
                result = mid;
            else if (target < a[mid])
                result = binarySearch(target, first, mid - 1);
            else //(target > a[mid])
                result = binarySearch(target, mid + 1, last);
        }
        return result;
    }
}
```

LISTING 11.7 **A Binary Search Demonstration** *(part 1 of 3)*

```java
import java.util.Scanner;
public class ArraySearcherDemo
{
    public static void main(String[] args)
    {
        int[] anArray = new int[10];
        Scanner keyboard = new Scanner(System.in);
        System.out.println("Enter 10 integers in increasing " +
                           "order,");
        System.out.println("one per line.");
        for (int i = 0; i < 10; i++)
            anArray[i] = keyboard.nextInt();
        System.out.println();

        for (int i = 0; i < 10; i++)
            System.out.print("a[" + i + "]=" + anArray[i] + " ");
        System.out.println();
        System.out.println();

        ArraySearcher finder = new ArraySearcher(anArray);
        String ans;
        do
        {
            System.out.println("Enter a value to search for:");
            int target = keyboard.nextInt();
            int result = finder.find(target);

            if (result < 0)
                System.out.println(target + "is not in the array.");
            else
                System.out.println(target + "is at index" + result);
            System.out.println("Again?");
            ans = keyboard.next();
```

(continued)

LISTING 11.7 **A Binary Search Demonstration** *(part 2 of 3)*

```
        } while (ans.equalsIgnoreCase("yes"));

        System.out.println(
                "May you find what you're searching for.");
    }
}
```

Sample Screen Output

```
Enter 10 integers in increasing order,
one per line.
0
2
4
6
8
10
12
14
16
18
a[0]=0
a[1]=2 a[2]=4 a[3]=6 a[4]=8 a[5]=10 a[6]=12 a[7]=14
a[8]=16 a[9]=18

Enter a value to search for:
14
14 is at index 7
Again?
yes
Enter a value to search for:
0
0 is at index 0
Again?
yes
Enter a value to search for:
2
2 is at index 1
Again?
yes
```

(continued)

LISTING 11.7   A Binary Search Demonstration *(part 3 of 3)*

```
Enter a value to search for:
13
13 is not in the arrray.
Again?
no
May you find what you're searching for.
```

The binary search algorithm is extremely fast. It eliminates about half the array from consideration right at the start. It then eliminates another quarter of the array, then another eighth, and so forth. This process of elimination means that most of the array need not be searched at all, saving a lot of time. For example, for an array with 1000 elements, the binary search will need to compare only about 10 array elements with the target value. By comparison, a simple serial search could possibly compare all 1000 array elements with the target value; on average, it will make about 500 comparisons. Searching an array of 1 million items provides an even more impressive example. A binary search of 1 million items requires at most 20 comparisons, whereas a sequential search of the same array would take, on average, 500,000 comparisons and might even need 1 million comparisons.

■ **PROGRAMMING TIP**   Generalize the Problem

When designing a recursive algorithm, you often need to solve a more general problem than the one you set out to solve. For example, consider the method binarySearch in the previous case study. We designed it to search not only the entire array but also any subrange of the array. This design was necessary to be able to express the recursive subcases. It is often true that, when you are designing a recursive algorithm, you must make the problem a bit more general so that you can easily express the recursive subcases.   ■

■ **SELF-TEST QUESTIONS**   myprogramminglab

8. Will the binary search algorithm work if the array is not sorted?

9. Will the binary search work for an array that has repeated values, or do all the values need to be different?

10. Suppose you want the class ArraySearcher to work for arrays whose values are sorted in descending order instead of ascending order. How would you change the definition of ArraySearcher?

| PROGRAMMING EXAMPLE | Merge Sort—A Recursive Sorting Method |

Some of the most efficient sorting algorithms are easiest to state as recursive algorithms. One such example is the **merge sort** algorithm for sorting an array. In this example, we present a method that implements the merge sort algorithm to sort an array of `int` values from smallest to largest. With minor changes, you can obtain a method to sort an array of items of any type that can be ordered. Some examples of these changes are discussed in the self-test questions.

Merge sort is an example of a divide-and-conquer algorithm. The array to be sorted is divided in half, and the two halves of the array are sorted by recursive calls. That process produces two smaller sorted arrays. The two sorted arrays are then merged to form a single sorted array with all the elements from the two smaller arrays. In outline form, the algorithm is as follows:

Merge sort algorithm to sort the array a

1. If the array a has only one element, do nothing (base case). Otherwise, do the following (recursive case):
2. Copy the first half of the elements in a to a smaller array named `firstHalf`.
3. Copy the rest of the elements in the array a to another smaller array named `lastHalf`.
4. Sort the array `firstHalf` using a recursive call.
5. Sort the array `lastHalf` using a recursive call.
6. Merge the elements in the arrays `firstHalf` and `lastHalf` into the array a.

It is straightforward to implement most of the details of this algorithm as Java code. However, the merging of the two arrays `firstHalf` and `lastHalf` into a single sorted array a does require some explanation.

The basic idea of the merging algorithm is as follows: The arrays `firstHalf` and `lastHalf` are both sorted from smallest to largest. So the smallest element in the array `firstHalf` is `firstHalf[0]`, and the smallest element in the array `lastHalf` is `lastHalf[0]`. Therefore, the smallest of all the elements in both arrays is the smaller of `firstHalf[0]` and `lastHalf[0]`. Move that smallest element to `a[0]`.

Merging two sorted arrays into one sorted array

For example, let's say that the smaller element is `lastHalf[0]`, so that element gets moved to `a[0]`. The smallest of the elements left to move to a is the smaller of `firstHalf[0]` and `lastHalf[1]`. Move that element to `a[1]`, and continue with this process.

The Java code for the merging process will look something like the following:

```
int firstHalfIndex = 0, lastHalfIndex = 0, aIndex = 0;
while (Some_Condition)
{
    if (firstHalf[firstHalfIndex] < lastHalf[lastHalfIndex])
```

```
        {
            a[aIndex] = firstHalf[firstHalfIndex];
            aIndex++;
            firstHalfIndex++;
        }
        else
        {

            a[aIndex] = lastHalf[lastHalfIndex];
            aIndex++;
            lastHalfIndex++;

        }
    }
```

Now, what is the condition for the `while` loop? Note that the loop does not make sense unless both of the arrays `firstHalf` and `lastHalf` have elements left to move. So rather than looping until the array a is full, we must loop until all the elements in one of the arrays `firstHalf` or `lastHalf` have been completely moved to a. Hence, the `while` loop condition can be

```
while ((firstHalfIndex < firstHalf.length) &&
        (lastHalfIndex < lastHalf.length))
```

When this `while` loop ends, one of the arrays `firstHalf` or `lastHalf` has had all of its elements moved to the array a, and the other might have—in fact, probably will have—elements left to move to a. These elements are sorted and are all larger than the elements already moved to a. So all we need to do is move the elements remaining in the array `firstHalf` or `lastHalf` to a.

> After the loop, one array will be entirely moved

Listing 11.8 gives the complete Java implementation of the merge sort algorithm, including the method `merge`. Listing 11.9 contains a demonstration program that uses the `MergeSort` class from Listing 11.8.

LISTING 11.8   The `MergeSort` Class *(part 1 of 3)*

```
/**
Class for sorting an array of integers from smallest to largest
using the merge sort algorithm.
*/
public class MergeSort
{
    /**
    Precondition: Every indexed variable of the array a has a value.
    Postcondition: a[0] <= a[1] <= . . . <= a[a. length - 1].
    */
    public static void sort(int[] a)
    {
        if (a.length >= 2)
```

(continued)

LISTING 11.8 The MergeSort Class *(part 2 of 3)*

```
        {
                int halfLength = a.length / 2;
                int[] firstHalf = new int[halfLength];
                int[] lastHalf = new int[a.length - halfLength];

                divide(a, firstHalf, lastHalf);
                sort(firstHalf);
                sort(lastHalf);
                merge(a, firstHalf, lastHalf);
        }
        //else do nothing. a.length == 1, so a is sorted.
    }
    //Precondition: a.length = firstHalf.length + lastHalf.length.
    //Postcondition: All the elements of a are divided
    //between the arrays firstHalf and lastHalf.
    private static void divide(int[] a, int[] firstHalf,
                                         int[] lastHalf)
    {
        for (int i = 0); i < firstHalf.length; i++)
            firstHalf[i] = a[i];

        for (int i = 0; i < lastHalf.length; i++)
            lastHalf[i] = a[firstHalf.length + i];
    }
    //Precondition: Arrays firstHalf and lastHalf are sorted from
    //smallest to largest; a. length = firstHalf.length +
    //lastHalf.length.
    //Postcondition: Array a contains all the values from firstHalf
    //and lastHalf and is sorted from smallest to largest.
    private static void merge(int[] a, int[] firstHalf,
                                         int[] lastHalf)
    {
        int firstHalfIndex = 0, lastHalfIndex = 0, aIndex = 0;
        while ((firstHalfIndex < firstHalf.length) &&
               (lastHalfIndex < lastHalf.length))
        {
            if (firstHalf[firstHalfIndex] < lastHalf[lastHalfIndex])
            {
                a[aIndex] = firstHalf[firstHalfIndex];
                firstHalfIndex++;
            }
            else
            {
                a[aIndex] = lastHalf[firstHalfIndex];
                lastHalfIndex++;
            }
            aIndex++;
        }
```

(continued)

LISTING 11.8   The `MergeSort` Class *(part 3 of 3)*

```
//At least one of firstHalf and lastHalf has been
//completely copied to a.

//Copy rest of firstHalf, if any.
while (firstHalfIndex < firstHalf.length)
{
    a[aIndex] = firstHalf[firstHalfIndex];
    aIndex++;
    firstHalfIndex++;
}
//Copy rest of lastHalf, if any.
while (lastHalfIndex < lastHalf.length)
{
    a[aIndex] = lastHalf[lastHalfIndex];
    aIndex++;
    lastHalfIndex++;
}
    }
}
```

LISTING 11.9   **Demonstration of the** `MergeSort` Class

```
public class MergeSortDemo
{
    public static void main(String[] args)
    {
        int[] anArray = {7, 5, 11, 2, 16, 4, 18, 14, 12, 30};
        System.out.println("Array values before sorting:");
        for (int i = 0; i < anArray.length; i++)
            System.out.print(anArray[i] + " ");
        System.out.println();

        MergeSort.sort(anArray);

        System.out.println("Array values after sorting:");
        for (int i = 0; i < anArray.length; i++)
            System.out.print(anArray[i] + " ");
        System.out.println();
    }
}
```

Screen Output

```
Array values before sorting:
7 5 11 2 1 4 18 14 12 30
Array values after sorting:
2 4 5 7 11 12 14 16 18 30
```

A merge sort is fast

The merge sort algorithm is much more efficient than the selection sort algorithm we presented in Chapter 7. In fact, there is no sorting algorithm that is "orders of magnitude" more efficient than the merge sort algorithm. The details of what is meant by "orders of magnitude" are beyond the scope of this book, but we can hint at its meaning.

There are algorithms that, in practice, are more efficient than the merge sort algorithm. However, for very large arrays, any of these algorithms (including the merge sort algorithm) are so much faster than the selection sort algorithm that the improvement over selection sort is more dramatic than the differences between these various faster algorithms.

myprogramminglab

SELF-TEST QUESTIONS

11. What Java statement will sort the following array, using the class `MergeSort`?

    ```
    int[] myArray = {9, 22, 3, 2, 87, -17, 12, 14, 33, -2};
    ```

12. How would you change the class `MergeSort` so that it can sort an array of values of type `double` instead of type `int`?

13. How would you change the class `MergeSort` so that it can sort an array of values of type `int` into decreasing order, instead of increasing order?

14. If a value in an array of base type `int` occurs twice—for example, both `b[0]` and `b[5]` are 7—and you sort the array by using the method `MergeSort.sort`, will there be one or two copies of the repeated value after the array is sorted?

CHAPTER SUMMARY

- If a method definition includes an invocation of the method itself, that invocation is known as a recursive call. Recursive calls are legal in Java and can sometimes make a method definition clearer.

- Whenever an algorithm has one subtask that is a smaller version of the entire algorithm's task, you can realize the algorithm as a Java recursive method.

- To avoid infinite recursion, a recursive method definition should contain two kinds of cases: one or more cases that include a recursive call and one or more base (stopping) cases that do not involve any recursive calls.

- Two good examples of recursive algorithms are the binary search algorithm and the merge sort algorithm.

Exercises

1. What output will be produced by the following code?

```java
public class Demo
{
    public static void main(String[] args)
    {
        System.out.println("The output is:");
        foo(23);
        System.out.println();
    }
    public static void foo(int number)
    {
        if (number > 0)
        {
            foo(number / 2);
            System.out.print(number % 2);
        }
    }
}
```

2. What output will be produced by the following code?

```java
public class Demo
{
    public static void main(String[] args)
    {
        System.out.println("The output is:");
        bar(11156);
        System.out.println();
    }
    public static void bar(int number)
    {
        if (number > 0)
        {
            int d = number % 10;
            boolean odd = (number / 10) % 2 == 1;
            bar(number / 10);
            if (odd)
                System.out.print(d / 2 + 5);
            else
                System.out.print(d / 2);
        }
    }
}
```

3. Write a recursive method that will compute the number of odd digits in a number.

4. Write a recursive method that will compute the sum of the digits in a positive number.

5. Complete a recursive definition of the following method:

```
/**
Precondition: n >= 0.
Returns 10 to the power n.
*/
public static int computeTenToThe(int n)
```

Use the following facts about x^n:

$x^n = (x^{n/2})^2$ when n is even and positive
$x^n = x(x^{(n-1)/2})^2$ when n is odd and positive
$x^0 = 1$

6. Write a recursive method that will compute the sum of all the values in an array.

7. Write a recursive method that will find and return the largest value in an array of integers. (*Hint*: Split the array in half and recursively find the largest value in each half. Return the larger of those two values.)

8. Write a recursive ternary search algorithm that splits the array into three parts instead of the two parts used by a binary search.

9. Write a recursive method that will compute cumulative sums in an array. To find the cumulative sums, add to each value in the array the sum of the values that precede it in the array. For example, if the values in the array are [2, 3, 1, 5, 6, 2, 7], the result will be [2, (2) + 3, (2 + 3) + 1, (2 + 3 + 1) + 5, (2 + 3 + 1 + 5) + 6, (2 + 3 + 1 + 5 + 6) + 2, (2 + 3 + 1 + 5 + 6 + 2) + 7] or [2, 5, 6, 11, 17, 19, 26]. (*Hint*: The parenthesized sums in the previous example are the results of a recursive call.)

10. Suppose we want to compute the amount of money in a bank account with compound interest. If the amount of money in the account is m, the amount in the account at the end of the month will be $1.005m$. Write a recursive method that will compute the amount of money in an account after t months with a starting amount of m.

11. Suppose we have a satellite in orbit. To communicate to the satellite, we can send messages composed of two signals: dot and dash. Dot takes 2 microseconds to send, and dash takes 3 microseconds to send. Imagine that we want to know the number of different messages, $M(k)$, that can be sent in k microseconds.

   - If k is 0 or 1, we can send 1 message (the empty message)
   - If k is 2 or 3, we can send 1 message (dot or dash, respectively)

- If k is larger than 3, we know that the message can start with either dot or dash. If the message starts with dot, the number of possible messages is $M(k - 2)$. If the message starts with dash, the number of possible messages is $M(k - 3)$. Therefore the number of messages that can be sent in k microseconds is $M(k - 2) + M(k - 3)$.

Write a program that reads a value of k from the keyboard and displays the value of $M(k)$, which is computed by a recursive method.

12. Write a recursive method that will count the number of vowels in a string. (*Hint*: Each time you make a recursive call, use the `String` method substring to construct a new string consisting of the second through last characters. The final call will be when the string contains no characters.)

13. Write a recursive method that will remove all the vowels from a given string and return what is left as a new string. (*Hint*: Use the + operator to perform string concatenation to construct the string that is returned.)

14. Write a recursive method that will duplicate each character in a string and return the result as a new string. For example, if "book" is the argument, the result would be "bbooookk".

15. Write a recursive method that will reverse the order of the characters in a given string and return the result as a new string. For example, if "book" is the argument, the result would be "koob".

PROGRAMMING PROJECTS

Visit www.myprogramminglab.com to complete many of these Programming Projects online and get instant feedback.   myprogramminglab

1. Write a static recursive method that returns the number of digits in the integer passed to it as an argument of type `int`. Allow for both positive and negative arguments. For example, –120 has three digits. Do not count leading zeros. Embed the method in a program, and test it.

2. Write a static recursive method that returns the sum of the integers in the array of `int` values passed to it as a single argument. You can assume that every indexed variable of the array has a value. Embed the method in a test program.

3. One of the most common examples of recursion is an algorithm to calculate the **factorial** of an integer. The notation $n!$ is used for the factorial of the integer n and is defined as follows:

0! is equal to 1
1! is equal to 1
2! is equal to $2 \times 1 = 2$
3! is equal to $3 \times 2 \times 1 = 6$

4! is equal to $4 \times 3 \times 2 \times 1 = 24$

. . .

$n!$ is equal to $n \times (n - 1) \times (n - 2) \times \ldots \times 3 \times 2 \times 1$

An alternative way to describe the calculation of $n!$ is the recursive formula $n \times (n - 1)!$, plus a base case of $0!$, which is 1. Write a static method that implements this recursive formula for factorials. Place the method in a test program that allows the user to enter values for n until signaling an end to execution.

4. A common example of a recursive formula is one to compute the sum of the first n integers, $1 + 2 + 3 + \ldots + n$. The recursive formula can be expressed as

   `1 + 2 + 3 + ... + n = n + (1 + 2 + 3 + ... + (n - 1))`

   Write a static method that implements this recursive formula to compute the sum of the first n integers. Place the method in a test program that allows the user to enter the values of n until signaling an end to execution. Your method definition should not use a loop to add the first n integers.

5. A **palindrome** is a string that reads the same forward and backward, such as `"radar"`. Write a static recursive method that has one parameter of type `String` and returns true if the argument is a palindrome and false otherwise. Disregard spaces and punctuation marks in the string, and consider upper- and lowercase versions of the same letter to be equal. For example, the following strings should be considered palindromes by your method:

   `"Straw? No, too stupid a fad, I put soot on warts."`
   `"xyzcZYx?"`

   Your method need not check that the string is a correct English phrase or word. Embed the method in a program, and test it. For an additional challenge, use your palindrome-checking method with the file of English words described in Programming Project 11 in Chapter 10 to find the word with the longest palindrome.

6. A **geometric progression** is defined as the product of the first n integers and is denoted as

   $$\text{geometric}(n) = \prod_{i=1}^{n} i$$

   where this notation means to multiply the integers from 1 to n. A **harmonic progression** is defined as the product of the inverses of the first n integers and is denoted as

   $$\text{harmonic}(n) = \prod_{i-1}^{n} \frac{1}{i}$$

Both types of progression have an equivalent recursive definition:

$$\text{geometric}(n) = n \times \prod_{i=1}^{n-1} i$$

$$\text{harmonic}(n) = \frac{1}{n} \times \prod_{i=1}^{n-1} \frac{1}{i}$$

Write static methods that implement these recursive formulas to compute `geometric(n)` and `harmonic(n)`. Do not forget to include a base case, which is not given in these formulas, but which you must determine. Place the methods in a test program that allows the user to compute both `geometric(n)` and `harmonic(n)` for an input integer n. Your program should allow the user to enter another value for n and repeat the calculation until signaling an end to the program. Neither of your methods should use a loop to multiply n numbers.

7. The **Fibonacci sequence** occurs frequently in nature as the growth rate for certain idealized animal populations. The sequence begins with 0 and 1, and each successive Fibonacci number is the sum of the two previous Fibonacci numbers. Hence, the first ten Fibonacci numbers are 0, 1, 1, 2, 3, 5, 8, 13, 21, and 34. The third number in the series is 0 + 1, which is 1; the fourth number is 1 + 1, which is 2; the fifth number is 1 + 2, which is 3; and so on.

Besides describing population growth, the sequence can be used to define the form of a spiral. In addition, the ratios of successive Fibonacci numbers in the sequence approach a constant, approximately 1.618, called the "golden mean." Humans find this ratio so aesthetically pleasing that it is often used to select the length and width ratios of rooms and postcards.

Use a recursive formula to define a static method to compute the nth Fibonacci number, given n as an argument. Your method should not use a loop to compute all the Fibonacci numbers up to the desired one, but should be a simple recursive method. Place this static recursive method in a program that demonstrates how the ratio of Fibonacci numbers converges. Your program will ask the user to specify how many Fibonacci numbers it should calculate. It will then display the Fibonacci numbers, one per line. After the first two lines, it will also display the ratio of the current and previous Fibonacci numbers on each line. (The initial ratios do not make sense.) The output should look something like the following if the user enters 5:

```
Fibonacci #1 = 0
Fibonacci #2 = 1
Fibonacci #3 = 1; 1/1 = 1
Fibonacci #4 = 2; 2/1 = 2
Fibonacci #5 = 3; 3/2 = 1.5
```

8. Imagine a candy bar that has k places where it can be cut. You would like to know how many different sequences of cuts are possible to divide the bar into pieces. For example, if k is 3, you could cut the bar at location 1, then location 2, and finally at location 3. We indicate this sequence of cuts by 123. So if k is 3, we have six ways to divide the bar: 123, 132, 213, 231, 312, or 321. Notice that we have k possibilities for making the first cut. Once we make the first cut we have $k - 1$ places where a cut must be made. Recursively, this can be expressed as

$$C(k) = kC(k - 1)$$

Let's make this a bit more interesting by adding a restriction. You must always cut the leftmost pieces that can be cut. Now if k is 3, we can cut the bar at locations 123, 132, 213, 312, or 321. A cutting sequence of 231 would not be allowed, because after the cut at 2 we would have to make the cut at location 1, since it is the leftmost piece. We still have k possibilities for making the first cut, but now we have to count the number of ways to cut two pieces and multiply. Recursively, this can be expressed as

$$D(k) = \sum_{i=1}^{k} D(i - 1)D(k - i)$$

When k is 3, we would compute

$$D(3) = \sum_{i=1}^{3} D(i - 1)D(3 - i) = D(0)D(2) + D(1)D(1) + D(2)D(0)$$

$$D(2) = \sum_{i=1}^{2} D(i - 1)D(2 - i) = D(0)D(1) + D(1)D(0)$$

$$D(1) = \sum_{i=1}^{1} D(i - 1)D(1 - i) = D(0)D(0)$$

For both recursive formulas, if $k = 0$, there is exactly one way to divide the bar.

Develop a program that will read a value of k from the keyboard and then display $C(k)$ and $D(k)$. ($D(k)$ is interesting because it turns out to be the number of ways that we can parenthesize an arithmetic expression that has k binary operators.)

9. Once upon a time in a kingdom far away, the king hoarded food and the people starved. His adviser recommended that the food stores be used to help the people, but the king refused. One day a small group of rebels attempted to kill the king but were stopped by the adviser. As a reward, the adviser was granted a gift by the king. The adviser asked for a few grains of wheat from the king's stores to be distributed to the people. The number of grains was to be determined by placing them on a chessboard. On the first square of the chessboard, he placed one grain of wheat. He then placed two grains on the second square, four grains on the third square, eight grains on the fourth square, and so forth.

Compute the total number of grains of wheat that were placed on k squares by writing a recursive method getTotalGrains(k, grains). Each time getTotalGrains is called, it "places" grains on a single square; grains is the number of grains of wheat to place on that square. If k is 1, return grains. Otherwise, make a recursive call, where k is reduced by 1 and grains is doubled. The recursive call computes the total number of grains placed in the remaining $k - 1$ squares. To find the total number of grains for all k squares, add the result of the recursive call to grains and return that sum.

10. There are n people in a room, where n is an integer greater than or equal to 2. Each person shakes hands once with every other person. What is the total number of handshakes in the room? Write a recursive method to solve this problem with the following header:

```
public static int handshake(int n)
```

where handshake(n) returns the total number of handshakes for n people in the room. To get you started, if there are only one or two people in the room, then:

```
handshake(1) = 0
handshake(2) = 1
```

11. Given the definition of a 2D array such as the following:

```
String[][] data = {
        {"A","B"},
        {"1","2"},
        {"XX","YY","ZZ"}
    };
```

write a recursive program that outputs all combinations of each subarray in order. In the above example, the desired output (although it doesn't have to be in this order) is:

```
A 1 XX
A 1 YY
A 1 ZZ
A 2 XX
A 2 YY
A 2 ZZ
B 1 XX
B 1 YY
B 1 ZZ
B 2 XX
B 2 YY
B 2 ZZ
```

Your program should work with arbitrarily sized arrays in either dimension. For example, the following data:

```
String[][] data = {
            {"A"},
            {"1"},
            {"2"},
            {"XX","YY"}
        };
```

should output:

```
A 1 2 XX
A 1 2 YY
```

Graphics

VideoNote
Drawing recursively

12. Create an application in a `JFrame` GUI that will draw a fractal curve using line segments. Fractals are recursively defined curves. The curve you will draw is based on a line segment between points p_1 and p_2:

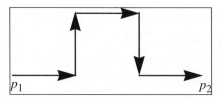

To draw the curve from p_1 to p_2, you first split the segment into thirds. Then add two segments and offset the middle segment to form part of a square, as shown in the following picture:

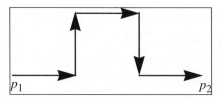

Note that you would not draw the arrowheads, but we use them here to indicate the direction of drawing. If the order of p_1 and p_2 were reversed, the square would be below the original line segment.

This process is recursive and is applied to each of the five new line segments, resulting in the following curve:

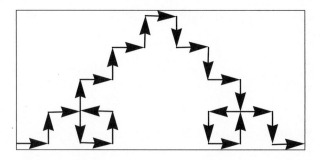

The fractal is given by repeating this recursive process an infinite number of times. Of course, we will not want to do that and will stop the process after a certain number of times.

To draw this curve, use a recursive method drawFractal($p1x$, $p1y$, $p2x$, $p2y$, k). If k is zero, just draw a line from p_1 to p_2. Otherwise, split the line segment into five segments, as described previously, and recursively call drawFractal for each of these five segments. Use $k - 1$ for the last argument in the recursive calls. For convenience, you may assume that the segments are either vertical or horizontal.

The initial call should be drawFractal(50, 800, 779, 800, 5). Set the size of the window to 1000 by 1000.

Answers to Self-Test Questions

1. B
   R
   R
   R

   Note that the 'B' is the first output, not the last output.

2. R
   R
   R
   B

   Note that the 'B' is the last output.

3.
```java
/**
 Precondition: n >= 1.
 Displays the symbol '#' n times on one line
 and then advances to the next line.
*/
public static void displaySharps(int n)
{
    if (n <= 1)
        System.out.println('#');
    else
    {
        System.out.print('#');
        displaySharps(n - 1);
    }
}
```

4. 6

5.
```java
/**
Precondition: n >= 0
Returns 10 to the power n.
*/
public static int computeTenToThe(int n)
{
    if (n <= 0)
        return 1;
    else
        return computeTenToThe(n - 1) * 10;
}
```

6.
```java
/**
Precondition: n can be any int.
Returns 10 to the power n.
*/
public static int computeTenToThe(int n)
{
    if (n == 0)
        return 1;
    else if (n > 0)
        return computeTenToThe(n - 1) * 10;
    else//n < 0
        return 1 / computeTenToThe(-n);
}
```

7.
```java
public void getCount()
{
    System.out.println("Enter a positive integer:");
    Scanner keyboard = new Scanner(System.in);
    int count = keyboard.nextInt();
    while (count <= 0)
    {
        System.out.println("Input must be positive.");
        System.out.println("Try again.");
        count = keyboard.nextInt();
    }
}
```

8. No.

9. The array can have repeated values, as long as the array is sorted.

10. The multiway if-else statement in the method binarySearch needs to have two comparison operators changed so that it reads as follows:

```java
if (target == a[mid])
    result = mid;
else if (target > a[mid])//Changed from <to>
    result = search(target, first, mid - 1);
```

```
else if (target < a[mid])//Changed from > to <
    result = search(target, mid + 1, last);
```

No other changes are needed, but the comments should be revised to reflect the fact that the array is sorted from largest to smallest.

11. MergeSort.sort(myArray);

12. Change the types for the array elements to double. For example, you would replace

```
private static void divide(int[] a, int[] firstHalf,
                           int[] lastHalf)
```

with

```
private static void divide(double[] a,
                           double[] firstHalf,double[] lastHalf)
```

13. Replace the < with > in the following line of the definition of merge:

```
if (firstHalf[firstHalfIndex] < lastHalf[lastHalfIndex])
```

14. If an array of base type int has a value that occurs twice, and you sort the array by using the method MergeSort.sort, the repeated value will occur twice in the sorted array.

Dynamic Data Structures and Generics 12

12.1 ARRAY-BASED DATA STRUCTURES 849
The Class ArrayList 850
Creating an Instance of ArrayList 850
Using the Methods of ArrayList 852
Programming Example: A To-Do List 856
Parameterized Classes and Generic Data Types 859

12.2 THE JAVA COLLECTIONS FRAMEWORK 859
The Collection Interface 860
The Class HashSet 861
The Map Interface 862
The Class HashMap 862

12.3 LINKED DATA STRUCTURES 865
The Class LinkedList 865
Linked Lists 866
Implementing the Operations of a Linked List 869
A Privacy Leak 876
Inner Classes 877
Node Inner Classes 878
Iterators 878
The Java Iterator Interface 890
Exception Handling with Linked Lists 890
Variations on a Linked List 892
Other Linked Data Structures 894

12.4 GENERICS 895
The Basics 895
Programming Example: A Generic Linked List 898

Chapter Summary 903   **Programming Projects** 908   **Answers to Self-Test Questions** 913

All is in flux, nothing stays still.

—HERACLITUS

As Chapter 5 noted, an abstract data type, or ADT, specifies a set of data and the operations on that data. It describes what the operations do but not how to implement them or store the data. Basically, an ADT specifies a particular data organization. You can express the specifications of an ADT by writing a Java interface, as described in Chapter 8. You know that a class can implement an interface in various ways. Thus, you implement an ADT by defining a Java class. In doing so, you use various data structures. A **data structure** is a construct, such as a class or an array, within a programming language.

This chapter focuses on data structures. In particular, we discuss two kinds of data structures whose size can grow or shrink while your program is running. Such structures are said to be **dynamic.** One kind of dynamic structure is based on an array. As an example, we will introduce the class ArrayList, which is available in the Java Class Library. The other kind links its data items to one another, so that one data item "knows" where the next one is. Although there are many different kinds of linked data structures, we will emphasize one simple but useful linked data structure known as a linked list. In the process of covering linked lists, we will introduce inner classes, which are a kind of class definition within another class definition.

Starting with version 5.0, Java allows class definitions to have parameters for the data types they use. These parameters are known as **generic types**. In Section 12.1 we show you how to use one such definition—ArrayList— which is in the Java Class Library. Section 12.3 shows you how to write class definitions that have generic data types.

OBJECTIVES

After studying this chapter, you should be able to

- Define and use an instance of ArrayList
- Describe the general idea of linked data structures and how to implement them in Java
- Manipulate linked lists
- Use inner classes in defining linked data structures
- Describe, create, and use iterators
- Define and use classes that have generic types

PREREQUISITES

You should read Section 12.1 before Section 12.2. Section 12.3 stands on its own but you should read Sections 12.1 through 12.3 before Section 12.4. Chapters 1 through 7 are needed to fully understand this chapter. Some familiarity with basic inheritance and basic exception handling will be helpful. The details are as follows:

Section	Prerequisite
12.1 Array-Based Data Structures	Chapters 1 through 7 and Section 9.1
12.2 The Java Collections Framework	Section 12.1
12.3 Linked Data Structures (excluding "Exception Handling with Linked Lists")	Chapters 1 through 7
The subsection of Section 12.3 entitled "Exception Handling with Linked lists"	Chapters 1 through 7 and Chapter 9
12.4 Generics	Sections 12.1 through 12.3 up to, but not including, "Exception Handling with Linked Lists"

12.1 ARRAY-BASED DATA STRUCTURES

"Well, I'll eat it," said Alice, "and if it makes me grow larger, I can reach the key; and if it makes me grow smaller, I can creep under the door; so either way I'll get into the garden."

—LEWIS CARROLL, *ALICE'S ADVENTURES IN WONDERLAND*

In Java, you can read the length of an array as data when the program is running, but once your program creates an array of that length, it cannot change the length of the array. For example, suppose you write a program to record customer orders for a mail-order house, and suppose you store all the items ordered by one customer in an array `order` of objects of a class called `OrderItem`. You could ask the user for the number of items in an order, store the number in a variable called `numberOfItems`, and then create the array `order`, using the following statement:

An array of a certain size

```java
OrderItem[] order = new OrderItem[numberOfItems];
```

But suppose the customer enters `numberOfItems` items and then decides to order another item? There is no way to actually increase the size of the array `order`. However, we can simulate increasing its size: We create a new and larger array, copy the elements from the original array to the new array, and then rename the new array order. For example, the following statements effectively double the size of our array:

Doubling the size of an array

```
OrderItem[] largerArray = new OrderItem[2 * numberOfItems];
for (int index = 0; index <numberOfItems; index++)
    largerArray[index] = order[index];
order = largerArray;
```

The Class ArrayList

Instead of worrying about changing the size of the array order, we can use an instance of the class ArrayList, which is in the package java.util of the Java Class Library. Such an instance can serve the same purpose as an array, except that it can change in length while the program is running. An ArrayList object could handle the customer's extra order without any problems.

ArrayList versus an array

If we can simply use ArrayList to overcome the main disadvantage of using an array, why did we study arrays? Why don't we always use ArrayList? It often seems that every silver lining has a cloud, and that is true here as well. There are two main drawbacks when using ArrayList:

- Using an instance of ArrayList is less efficient than using an array.
- An instance of ArrayList can store only objects; it cannot contain values of a primitive type, such as int, double, or char.

The implementation of ArrayList uses arrays. In fact, to expand the capacity of its underlying array, it uses the same technique we used to expand our array order. Using ArrayList instead of an array in your program will require more computer time, but that might or might not be significant. You would need to analyze your situation before making a choice. The second drawback can be addressed as follows: Instead of storing int values, for example, you could store Integer values, where Integer is the wrapper class whose objects simulate int values. Automatic boxing and unboxing—as discussed in Chapter 6—makes using a wrapper class convenient. But using one does add to the time overhead of a program.

The ADT list

Note that ArrayList is an implementation of an ADT called a **list**. The ADT list organizes data in the same way that you do when you write a list in everyday life. Lists of tasks, address lists, gift lists, and grocery lists are all examples of familiar lists. In each case, you can add entries to the list—at the beginning, at the end, or between items—delete entries, look at entries, and count entries. These are the same kinds of operations that an object of ArrayList can perform.

Creating an Instance of ArrayList

Using an instance of ArrayList has similarities to using an array, but there are some important differences. First, the definition of the class ArrayList is not provided automatically. The definition is in the package java.util, and any code that uses the class ArrayList must contain the following statement at the start of the file:

```
import java.util.ArrayList;
```

ArrayList is
in the package
java.util

You create and name an instance of `ArrayList` in the same way that you create and name objects of any class, except that you specify the base type using a different notation. For example,

```
ArrayList<String>list = new ArrayList<String>(20);
```

This statement makes `list` the name of an object that stores instances of the class `String`. The type `String` is the base type. An object of the class `ArrayList` stores objects of its base type, just as an array stores items of its base type. The difference here is that the base type of `ArrayList` must be a class type; you cannot use a primitive type, such as `int` or `double`, as the base type.

An object of
ArrayList
stores objects of
a specified base
type

Our object `list` has an **initial capacity** of 20 items. When we say that an `ArrayList` object has an initial capacity, we mean that it has been allocated memory for that many items, but if it needs to hold more items, the system will automatically allocate more memory. By carefully choosing the initial capacity, you can often make your code more efficient. If you choose an initial capacity that is large enough, the system will not need to reallocate memory too often, and as a result, your program should run faster. On the other hand, if you make your initial capacity too large, you will waste storage space. No matter what capacity you choose, it has no effect on how many items an `ArrayList` object can hold. Note that if you omit the initial capacity, you will invoke `ArrayList`'s default constructor, which assumes a capacity of ten.

An object of
ArrayList
can increase its
capacity

RECAP Creating and Naming an Instance of `ArrayList`

An object of the class `ArrayList` is created and named in the same way as any other object, except that you specify a base type.

SYNTAX

```
ArrayList<Base_Type> Variable  =
                    new ArrayList<Base_Type>();
ArrayList<Base_Type> Variable  =
                    new ArrayList<Base_Type>(Capacity);
```

The *Base_Type* must be a class type; it cannot be a primitive type such as `int` or `double`. When a number *Capacity* is given as an argument to the constructor, that number determines the initial capacity of the list. Omitting an argument results in an initial capacity of ten.

EXAMPLES

```
ArrayList<String>aList = new ArrayList<String>();
ArrayList<Double>bList = new ArrayList<Double>(30);
```

■ **PROGRAMMING TIP**   Newer Versions of Java Require the
Base Type Only Once

Prior to JDK version 7, the syntax to create an object of the class `ArrayList` required the base type to be repeated in the constructor.

```
ArrayList<Base_Type> Variable = new ArrayList<Base_Type>();
```

For example:

```
ArrayList<String> aList = new ArrayList<String>();
```

Starting with JDK version 7 the format does not require the base type to be repeated in the constructor. The syntax is:

```
ArrayList<Base_Type> Variable = new ArrayList<>();
```

For example:

```
ArrayList<String> aList = new ArrayList<>();
```

This saves a bit of typing over the old version and can make code more readable for more complex base types. The base type is no longer required in the constructor due to a feature called **type inference**. The compiler is able to infer the base type from the variable declaration. Programmers have been using the earlier format for many years, so you are likely to see it in existing code. For greater compatibility the examples in this book do not use the syntax supported in JDK 7.   ■

Using the Methods of `ArrayList`

An object of `ArrayList` can be used like an array, but you must use methods instead of an array's square-bracket notation. Let's define an array and an object of `ArrayList` and give them the same capacity:

Creating an array and an object of `ArrayList`

```
String[] anArray = new String[20];
ArrayList<String> aList = new ArrayList<String>(20);
```

Objects of `ArrayList` are indexed in the same way as an array: The index of the first item is 0. So if you would use

```
anArray[index] = "Hi Mom!";
```

for the array `anArray`, the analogous statement for the object `aList` would be

An array and an object of `ArrayList` use the same indexing

```
aList.set(index, "Hi Mom!");
```

If you would use

```
String temp = anArray[index];
```

to retrieve an element from the array `anArray`, the analogous statement for `aList` would be

```
String temp = aList.get(index);
```

The two methods set and get give objects of `ArrayList` approximately the same functionality that square brackets give to arrays. However, you need to be aware of one important point: The method invocation

```
aList.set(index, "Hi Mom!");
```

is *not* always completely analogous to

```
anArray[index] = "Hi Mom!";
```

The method set can replace any *existing* element, but you cannot use set to put an element at just any index, as you would with an array. The method set is used to change the value of existing elements, not to set them for the first time.

To set an element for the first time, you use the method add. This method adds elements at index positions 0, 1, 2, and so forth, in that order. An `ArrayList` object must always be filled in this order. The method add has two forms; that is, it is overloaded. When given one argument, add adds an element immediately after the last currently occupied position. Given two arguments, the method adds the element at the indicated position, assuming that the indicated position is not after an unoccupied position. For example, if aList contains five elements, either

```
aList.add("Caboose");
```

or

```
aList.add(5, "Caboose");
```

adds "Caboose" as the sixth—and last—element. But notice that for a list of five items, the statement

```
aList.add(6, "Caboose");
```

would cause an `IndexOutOfBoundsException` exception. Because the list contains five items, the index of the last item is 4. Attempting to add an item at index 6 before placing one at index 5 is illegal.

After adding elements to aList, you also can use add to insert an element before or between existing elements. The statement

```
aList.add(0, "Engine");
```

adds (inserts) a string before all other elements in aList. Existing elements are shifted to make room for the new element. So the original string at index 0 is not replaced, but rather is shifted to index position 1. Likewise,

```
aList.add(4, "BoxCar");
```

inserts "BoxCar" as the element at index 4. Elements at indices before 4 remain in place, while those originally after it are shifted to the next higher index position. When you use the method add to insert a new element at an index position, all the elements that were at that index position or higher have their index increased by 1 so that there is room to insert the new element without losing any of the older elements. Unlike the procedure for inserting into an array, this process happens automatically, and you need not write any extra code to move elements. Clearly, using `ArrayList` is much easier than using an array.

The method `size`

You can find out how many elements have already been added to aList by using the method `size`. The expression `aList.size()` returns the number of elements stored in aList. The indices of these elements range from 0 to `aList.size()` minus 1.

Figure 12.1 describes a selection of the methods in the class `ArrayList`.

FAQ Why are some parameters of type *Base_Type* and others of type `Object`?

Look at the table of methods in Figure 12.1. In some cases, when a parameter is naturally an object of the base type, the parameter type is the base type, but in other cases it is the type `Object`. For example, the method add has a parameter of the base type, but the method `contains` has a parameter of type `Object`. Why the difference in parameter types? For `ArrayList`, it makes sense to add only an element of the base type, so add does not accommodate objects of other types. However, `contains` is more general. Since its parameter's type is `Object`, it can test whether an object of any type is on the list. An object whose type is not the base type cannot possibly be on the list, so if it is passed to `contains`, the method will return false.

RECAP Arrays Versus Objects of the Class `ArrayList`

With arrays, the square brackets and the instance variable `length` are the only tools automatically provided for a programmer. If you want to use arrays for other things, you must write code to manipulate the arrays. `ArrayList`, on the other hand, comes with a large selection of powerful methods that can do many of the things that you must do for yourself when using an array. For example, the class `ArrayList` has a method—add—that inserts a new element between two existing elements.

SELF-TEST QUESTIONS

1. Suppose aList is an object of the class `ArrayList<String>`. How do you add the string `"Hello"` to the end of aList?

FIGURE 12.1   **Some Methods in the Class** ArrayList

public ArrayList<*Base_Type*>(int initialCapacity) Creates an empty list with the specified *Base_Type* and initial capacity. The *Base_Type* must be a class type; it cannot be a primitive type such as int or double. When the list needs to increase its capacity, the capacity doubles.
public ArrayList<*Base_Type*>() Behaves like the previous constructor, but the initial capacity is ten.
public boolean add(*Base_Type* newElement) Adds the specified element to the end of this list and increases the list's size by 1. The capacity of the list is increased if that is required. Returns true if the addition is successful.
public void add(int index, *Base_Type* newElement) Inserts the specified element at the specified index position of this list. Shifts elements at subsequent positions to make room for the new entry by increasing their indices by 1. Increases the list's size by 1. The capacity of the list is increased if that is required. Throws IndexOutOfBoundsException if index < 0 or index > size().
public *Base_Type* get(int index) Returns the element at the position specified by index. Throws IndexOutOfBoundsException if index < 0 or index ≥ size().
public *Base_Type* set(int index, *Base_Type* element) Replaces the element at the position specified by index with the given element. Returns the element that was replaced. Throws IndexOutOfBoundsException if index < 0 or index ≥ size().
public *Base_Type* remove(int index) Removes and returns the element at the specified index. Shifts elements at subsequent positions toward position index by decreasing their indices by 1. Decreases the list's size by 1. Throws IndexOutOfBoundsException if index < 0 or index ≥ size().
public boolean remove(Object element) Removes the first occurrence of element in this list, and shifts elements at subsequent positions toward the removed element by decreasing their indices by 1. Decreases the list's size by 1. Returns true if element was removed; otherwise returns false and does not alter the list.
public void clear() Removes all elements from this list.
public int size() Returns the number of elements in this list.
public boolean contains(Object element) Returns true if element is in this list; otherwise, returns false.
public int indexOf(Object element) Returns the index of the first occurrence of element in this list. Returns –1 if element is not on the list.
public boolean isEmpty() Returns true if this list is empty; otherwise, returns false.

2. Suppose `instruction` is an object of the class `ArrayList<String>` that contains the string "Stop" at index position 5. How do you change the string at index position 5 to "Go"?

3. Can you use the method `set` to place an element in a list at any index you want?

4. Can you use the method `add` to place an element in a list at any index you want?

5. Can you use the method `add` to insert an element at a position for which you cannot use `set`?

6. If `aList` is an object of the class `ArrayList<String>` that contains seven elements, why does `aList.add(7, "Red truck")` place a new string as the eighth element of `aList`?

7. Suppose `aList` is an object of the class `ArrayList<String>` that contains the four strings: "red", "blue", "green", and "yellow". What strings are on the list after `aList.add(2, "orange")` executes?

8. If you create a list using the statement

   `ArrayList<Double> aList = new ArrayList<Double>(20);`

   can the list contain more than 20 elements?

9. Suppose `aList` is an object of the class `ArrayList<String>`. Write Java statements that will display all the elements in `aList` on the screen.

PROGRAMMING EXAMPLE   A To-Do List

Listing 12.1 contains an example of using `ArrayList` to maintain a list of everyday tasks. The user can enter as many tasks as desired, and then the program will display the list.

LISTING 12.1   Using `ArrayList` to Maintain a List (part 1 of 2)

```java
import java.util.ArrayList;
import java.util.Scanner;

public class ArrayListDemo
{
    public static void main(String[] args)
```

(continued)

LISTING 12.1   Using `ArrayList` **to Maintain a List** *(part 2 of 2)*

```java
{
    ArrayList<String> toDoList = new ArrayList<String>();
    System.out.println("Enter items for the list, when "+
                        "prompted.");
    boolean done = false;
    Scanner keyboard = new Scanner(System.in);
    while (!done)
    {
        System.out.println("Type an entry:");
        String entry = keyboard.nextLine( );
        toDoList.add(entry);
        System.out.print("More items for the list? ");
        String ans = keyboard.nextLine( );
        if (!ans.equalsIgnoreCase("yes"))
            done = true;
    }
    System.out.println("The list contains:");
    int listSize = toDoList.size( );
    for (int position = 0; position < listSize;
        position++)
            System.out.println(toDoList.get(position));
}
}
```

Sample Screen Output

```
Enter items for the list, when prompted.
Type an entry:
Buy milk
More items for the list? yes
Type an entry:
Wash car
More items for the list? yes
Type an entry:
Do assignment
More items for the list? no
The list contains:
Buy milk
Wash car
Do assignment
```

■ **PROGRAMMING TIP**   Use a For-Each Loop to Access All
Elements in an Instance of `ArrayList`

The last loop in Listing 12.1, which displays all the elements in an instance of
`ArrayList`, can be replaced by the following for-each loop:

```
for (String element : toDoList)
    System.out.println(element);
```

This loop is much simpler to write than the original one when you want to
access all of the elements in a collection such as an `ArrayList` object.   ■

■ **PROGRAMMING TIP**   Use `trimToSize` to Save Memory

`ArrayList` objects automatically double their capacity when your program
needs them to have additional capacity. However, the new capacity may
be more than your program requires. In such cases, the capacity does not
automatically shrink. If the capacity of your expanded list is much larger
than you need, you can save memory by using
the method `trimToSize`. For example, if `aList` is
an instance of `ArrayList`, the invocation `aList.
trimToSize()` will shrink the capacity of `aList`
down to its actual size, leaving it with no unused
capacity. Normally, you should use `trimToSize`
only when you know that you will not soon need
the extra capacity.   ■

ASIDE **Early Versions of `ArrayList`**

Versions of Java before version 5.0 had
a class named `ArrayList` that was not
parameterized and was used just like any
other class. For example,

```
ArrayList aList = new
            ArrayList(10);
```

This older class is still available in recent
versions of Java and is approximately
equivalent to the class `ArrayList<Object>`.
So the previous line of code is approximately
equivalent to

```
ArrayList<Object>aList = new
ArrayList<Object>(10);
```

The class `ArrayList<Object>` and the
older class `ArrayList` are not completely
equivalent, but for simple applications they
can be considered equivalent. The differences
between these classes become relevant only
when you are dealing with issues related to
type casting or subtyping. This older class is
in the package `java.util`, as is the newer
parameterized `ArrayList`. Knowing about
the older class is relevant if you have a
program written in earlier versions of Java.

GOTCHA   Using an Assignment
Statement to Copy a List

As was true for objects of other classes, as well as
for arrays, you cannot make a copy of an instance
of `ArrayList` by using an assignment statement.
For example, consider the following code:

```
ArrayList<String>aList = new
    ArrayList<String>();
<Some code to fill aList>
ArrayList<String>anotherName = aList;
//Defines an alias
```

This code simply makes `anotherName` another
name for `aList` so that you have two names but
only one list. If you want to make an identical
copy of `aList` so that you have two separate

copies, you use the method `clone`. So instead of the previous assignment statement, you would write

```
ArrayList<String> duplicateList =
    (ArrayList<String>)aList.clone();
```

For lists of objects other than strings, using the method `clone` can be more complicated and can lead to a few pitfalls. Appendix 9, which is on the book's Web site, explains more about this method. ■

Parameterized Classes and Generic Data Types

The class `ArrayList` is a **parameterized class.** That is, it has a parameter, which we have been denoting *Base_Type*, that can be replaced with any class type to obtain a class that stores objects having the specified base type. *Base_ Type* is called a **generic data type.** You already know how to use parameterized classes, since you know how to use `ArrayList`. Section 12.3 will outline how to define such a class yourself.

 SELF-TEST QUESTIONS

10. Can you have a list of `ints`?

11. Suppose `list` is an instance of `ArrayList`. What is the difference between the capacity of `list` and the value of `list.size()`?

12. Suppose `list` is an instance of `ArrayList` that was defined with an initial capacity of 20. Imagine that we add 10 entries to `list`. What will be the values of the elements at indices 10 through 19? Garbage values? A default value? Something else?

12.2 THE JAVA COLLECTIONS FRAMEWORK

What we become depends on what we read after all of the professors have finished with us. The greatest university of all is a collection of books.

—THOMAS CARLYLE

The **Java Collections Framework** is a collection of interfaces and classes that may be used to manipulate groups of objects. The classes implemented in the Java Collections Framework serve as reusable data structures and include algorithms for common tasks such as sorting or searching. The framework uses parameterized classes so you can use them with the classes of your choice. Utilizing the framework can free the programmer from lots of low-level details if they aren't the focus of the program. This section is just enough for you to use a few common components of the Java Collections Framework.

The Collection Interface

The Collection **interface** is the highest level of Java's framework for collection classes and it describes the basic operations that all collection classes should implement. Selected methods for the Collection interface are given in Figure 12.2. The methods support basic operations such as adding, removing, or checking to see if an object exists in the collection. The Collection interface takes a base type that allows you to create a collection of objects of your choice. Note that the toArray method returns an array of type Object. You may need to type cast elements of the array to the appropriate class or abstract data type.

You may have noticed that many of the methods from Figure 12.2 look the same as those in Figure 12.1, the listing of methods for the ArrayList class. This is no coincidence. The ArrayList class implements the Collection interface, so it must have the same methods. Other classes that implement the Collection interface must also have the same methods, but of course the implementation of the methods may differ. Additionally, classes can add their own methods not specified by the interface. For example, the get and set methods for the ArrayList class are specified not in the Collection interface but by a derived interface, List, that in turn is implemented by ArrayList. While these methods provide specialized functionality, an understanding of the Collection interface is enough to give you a basic understanding of how to use any class that implements it.

FIGURE 12.2   Selected Methods in the Collection Interface

public boolean add(*Base_Type* newElement) Adds the specified element to the collection. Returns true if the collection is changed as a result of the call.
public void clear() Removes all of the elements from the collection.
public boolean remove(Object o) Removes a single instance of the specified element from the collection if it is present. Returns true if the collection is changed as a result of the call.
public boolean contains(Object o) Returns true if the specified element is a member of the collection.
public boolean isEmpty() Returns true if the collection is empty.
public int size() Returns the number of elements in the collection.
public Object[] to Array() Returns an array containing all of the elements in the collection. The array is of a type Object so each element may need to be typecast back into the original base type.

The Class HashSet

The HashSet class is used to store a set of objects. Like the ArrayList, the HashSet class also implements the Collection interface. However, the HashSet stores a set rather than a list of items. This means that there can be no duplicate elements, unlike an ArrayList, which can have many duplicates. The class is named HashSet because the algorithm used to implement the set is called a hash table. A description of how the hash table algorithm works is beyond the scope of this text, but in summary it provides a fast and efficient way to look up items. Listing 12.2 demonstrates how to use the HashSet class to store and manage a set of integers. The base type is the wrapper class Integer (described in Section 6.2) rather than int because primitive types are not allowed as a base type. Only objects may be stored in any collection. The example uses only the methods specified in the Collection interface.

The HashSet class stores a set of objects

LISTING 12.2 A HashSet **Demonstration** (*part 1 of 2*)

```java
import java.util.HashSet;
public class HashSetDemo
{
    public static void main(String[] args)
    {
        HashSet<Integer> intSet = new HashSet<Integer>();
        intSet.add(2);
        intSet.add(7);
        intSet.add(7);        ←———————  Ignored since 7 is already in the set
        intSet.add(3);
        printSet(intSet);
        intSet.remove(3);
        printSet(intSet);
        System.out.println("Set contains 2: " +
            intSet.contains(2));
        System.out.println("Set contains 3: " +
            intSet.contains(3));
    }
    public static void printSet(HashSet<Integer> intSet)
    {
        System.out.println("The set contains:");
        for (Object obj : intSet.toArray())
        {
            Integer num = (Integer) obj;
            System.out.println(num.intValue());
        }
    }
}
```

(continued)

LISTING 12.2   A HashSet Demonstration *(part 2 of 2)*

Sample Screen Output

```
The set contains:
2
3
7
The set contains:
2
7
Set contains 2: true
Set contains 3: false
```

The Map Interface

The Map
interface
describes a
mapping from a
key object to a
value object

The Map interface is also a top-level interface in the Java Collection Framework. The Map interface is similar in character to the Collection interface, except that it deals with collections of ordered pairs. Think of the pair as consisting of a key K (to search for) and an associated value V. For example, the key might be a student ID number and the value might be an object storing information about the student (such as the name, major, address, or phone number) associated with that ID number. Selected methods for the Map interface are given in Figure 12.3. The Map interface takes a base type for the key and a base type for the value. Use the put method to add a key/value pair to the collection and the get method to retrieve the value for a given key. Just like the Collection interface, the base types must be objects and cannot be primitive data types.

The Class HashMap

The HashMap
class implements
the Map interface

The HashMap class implements the Map interface and is used to store a map from a key object to a value object. Like the HashSet, the class is called HashMap because it also uses the hash table algorithm. It can be used like a small database and is able to quickly retrieve the value object when given the key object. Listing 12.3 demonstrates how to use the HashMap class to map from the names of mountain peaks to their height in feet. The name of the mountain is the key and the height is the mapped value. The base type of the key is String and the base type of the value is Integer. We must use the wrapper class Integer rather than int because primitive data types are not allowed as a base type. The example uses only the methods specified in the Map interface to add several mappings, look up a mapping, modify a mapping, and remove a mapping.

VideoNote
Walkthrough of the
HashMap **demonstration**

FIGURE 12.3 **Selected Methods in the** Map **Interface**

public *Base_Type_Value* put(*Base_Type_Key* k, *Base_Type_Value* v) Associates the value v with the key k. Returns the previous value for k or null if there was no previous mapping
public *Base_Type_Value* get(Object k) Returns the value mapped to the key k or null if no mapping exists.
public void clear() Removes a single instance of the specified element from the collection if it is present. Returns true if the collection is changed as a result of the call.
public *Base_Type_Value* remove(Object k) Removes the mapping of key k from the map if present. Returns the previous value for the key k or null if there was no previous mapping.
public boolean containsKey(Object k) Returns true if the key k is a key in the map.
public boolean containsValue(Object v) Returns true if the value v is a value in the map.
public boolean isEmpty() Returns true if the map contains no mappings.
public int size() Returns the number of mappings in the map.
public Set *<Base_Type_Key>* keySet() Returns a set containing all of the keys in the map.
public Collection *<Base_Type_Values>* values() Returns a collection containing all of the values in the map.

LISTING 12.3 **A** HashMap **Demonstration** *(part 1 of 2)*

```java
import java.util.HashMap;
public class HashMapDemo
{
    public static void main(String[] args)
    {
        HashMap<String, Integer> mountains =
            new HashMap<String, Integer>();
        mountains.put("Everest", 29029);
        mountains.put("K2", 28251);
        mountains.put("Kangchenjunga", 28169);
        mountains.put("Denali", 20335);
        printMap(mountains);
        System.out.println("Denali in the map: " +
            mountains.containsKey("Denali"));
        System.out.println();
```

(continued)

LISTING 12.3 A HashMap Demonstration *(part 2 of 2)*

```java
        System.out.println("Changing height of Denali.");
        mountains.put("Denali", 20320);
        printMap(mountains);                          <- Overwrites the old
                                                         value for Denali
        System.out.println("Removing Kangchenjunga.");
        mountains.remove("Kangchenjunga");
        printMap(mountains);
    }

    public static void printMap(HashMap<String, Integer> map)
    {
        System.out.println("Map contains:");
        for (String keyMountainName : map.keySet())
        {
            Integer height = map.get(keyMountainName);
            System.out.println(keyMountainName + " --> " +
                height.intValue() + " feet.");
        }
        System.out.println();
    }
}
```

Sample Screen Output

```
Map contains:
K2 --> 28251 feet.
Denali --> 20355 feet.
Kangchenjunga --> 28169 feet.
Everest --> 29029 feet.
Denali in the map: true
Changing height of Denali.
Map contains:
K2 --> 28251 feet.
Denali --> 20320 feet.
Kangchenjunga --> 28169 feet.
Everest --> 29029 feet.
Removing Kangchenjunga.
Map contains:
K2 --> 28251 feet.
Denali --> 20320 feet.
Everest --> 29029 feet.
```

■ **PROGRAMMING TIP**   **Other Classes in the Java Collections Framework**

There are many other methods, classes, and interfaces in the Java Collections Framework. You will be happy to know that the methods specified in either the Collection or Map interfaces provide a uniform interface for all classes in the framework. For example, there is a TreeSet class that stores data in a tree instead of a hash table like the HashSet class. The program in Listing 12.2 will produce identical output if the data type is changed to TreeSet. However, many classes have additional methods specific to the type of data structure or algorithm being implemented. ■

SELF-TEST QUESTIONS

myprogramminglab

13. Define and invoke the constructor for a HashSet variable named colors capable of holding strings.

14. Given the variable colors defined in Question 13, write the code to add "red" and "blue" to the set, output if the set contains "blue", then remove "blue" from the set.

15. Define and invoke the constructor for a HashMap named studentIDs that holds a mapping of integers to strings.

16. Given the variable studentIDs defined in Question 15, write the code to map 5531 to "George", 9102 to "John", and print the name associated with ID 9102.

12.3 LINKED DATA STRUCTURES

Do not mistake the pointing finger for the moon.

—ZEN SAYING

A **linked data structure** is a collection of objects, each of which contains data and a reference to another object in the collection. We will confine most of our discussion of linked data structures to a simple but widely used kind known as a linked list.

A collection of linked objects

The Class LinkedList

Instead of using the class ArrayList and worrying about allocating too much memory, we can use an instance of the class LinkedList, which is also in the package java.util of the Java Class Library. Like ArrayList, LinkedList is another implementation of the ADT list. Although the two classes do not have the same methods, both have the same basic list operations described in Figure 12.1,

The class
LinkedList
implements a list

with the exception of the constructors and the last method, trimToSize. As you will see, LinkedList—as a linked data structure—allocates memory only as needed to accommodate new entries and deallocates memory when an entry is removed.

After importing LinkedList from the package java.util, you create a new instance of LinkedList by invoking its default constructor. For example, the following statement creates myList as a list of strings:

```
LinkedList<String> myList = new LinkedList<String>();
```

You then can go on to use the methods of LinkedList—such as add, set, get, remove, and size—just as you did when using the class ArrayList.

It makes sense to use predefined classes such as LinkedList and ArrayList, since they were written by experts, are well tested, and will save you a lot of work. However, using LinkedList will not teach you how to implement linked data structures in Java. To do that, you need to see a simple example of building at least one linked data structure. A linked list is both a simple and a typical linked data structure. We will construct our own simplified example of a linked list so you can see how linked data structures work.

VideoNote
Using List, ArrayList,
and LinkedList

■ PROGRAMMING TIP   The Interface List

The Java Collections Framework contains the interface List, which specifies the operations for an ADT list. The methods listed in Figure 12.1 are a part of this interface. Both of the classes ArrayList and LinkedList implement the interface List.   ■

myprogramminglab

SELF-TEST QUESTION

17. What changes would you make to the program in Listing 12.1 to use LinkedList instead of ArrayList?

Linked Lists

A linked list links
nodes

A **linked list** is a dynamic data structure that links the items in a list to one another. Figure 12.4 shows a linked list in diagrammatic form. Like all linked data structures, a linked list consists of objects known as **nodes.** In the figure, the nodes are the boxes that are divided in half by a horizontal line. Each node has a place for some data and a place to hold a **link** to another node. The links are shown as arrows that point to the node they "link" to. In Java, the links are implemented as references to a node, and in practice they are instance variables of the node type. However, for your first look at a linked list, you can simply think of the links as arrows. In a linked list, each node contains only one link, and the nodes are arranged one after the other so as to form a list, as in Figure 12.4. In an intuitive sense, you or, more properly, your code moves from node to node, following the links.

FIGURE 12.4   A Linked List

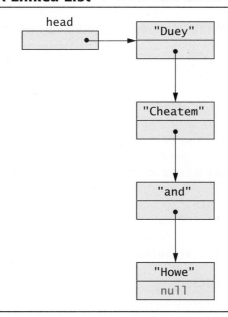

The link marked head is not on the list of nodes; in fact, it is not even a node, but is a link that gets you to the first node. In implementations, head will contain a reference to a node, so head is a variable of the node type. Your program can easily move through the list in order, from the first node to the last node, by following the "arrows."

RECAP Linked List

A linked list is a data structure consisting of objects known as nodes. Each node can contain both data and a reference to one other node so that the nodes link together to form a list, as illustrated in Figure 12.4.

Now let's see exactly how we can implement a linked list in Java. Each node is an object of a class that has two instance variables, one for the data and one for the link. Listing 12.4 gives the definition of a Java class that can serve as the node class for linked lists like the one shown in Figure 12.4. In this case, the data in each node consists of a single String value.[1] As noted in Listing 12.4, we will later make this node class private.

---

[1] Technically speaking, the node does not contain the string, but only a reference to the string, as would be true of any variable of type String. However, for our purposes, we can think of the node as containing the string, since we never use this string reference as an "arrow."

LISTING 12.4 A Node Class

```
public class ListNode
{
    private String data;
    private ListNode link;

    public ListNode()
    {
        link = null;
        data = null;
    }

    public ListNode(String newData, ListNode linkValue)
    {
        data = newData;
        link = linkValue;
    }

    public void setData(String newData)
    {
        data = newData;
    }

    public String getData()
    {
        return data;
    }

    public void setLink(ListNode newLink)
    {
        link = newLink;
    }

    public ListNode getLink()
    {
        return link;
    }
}
```

> Later in this chapter, we will hide this class by making it private.

The class
ListNode

Notice that the link instance variable of the class ListNode in Listing 12.4 is of type ListNode. This relationship sounds circular, and in a sense, it is. However, this kind of class definition is perfectly legal in Java. Recall that a variable of a class type holds a reference to an object of that class. So the link instance variable of an object of the ListNode class will contain a reference to another object of the class ListNode. Thus, as the arrows in the diagram in Figure 12.4 show, each node object of a linked list contains in its link instance variable a reference to another object of the class ListNode; this other object contains a reference to another object of the class ListNode, and so on, until the end of the linked list.

When dealing with a linked list, your code needs to be able to "get to" the first node, and you need some way to detect when the last node is reached. To get to the first node, you use a variable of type ListNode that contains a reference to the first node. As we noted earlier, this variable is not a node on the list. In Figure 12.4, the variable containing a reference to the first node is represented by the box labeled head. The first node in a linked list is called the **head node**, and it is common to use the name head for a variable that contains a reference to this first node. In fact, we call head a **head reference**.

A reference to the head (first) node is called the head reference

In Java, you indicate the end of a linked list by setting the link instance variable of the last node object to null, as shown in Figure 12.4. That way your code can test whether a node is the last node in a linked list by testing whether the node's link instance variable contains null. Recall that you check whether a variable contains null by using the operator ==. In contrast, the data instance variable in Listing 12.4 is of type String, and you normally check two String variables for equality by using the equals method.

Linked lists usually start out empty. Since the variable head is supposed to contain a reference to the first node in a linked list, what value do you give head when there is no first node? You give head the value null in order to indicate an empty list. This technique is traditional and works out nicely for many algorithms that manipulate a linked list.

head is null for an empty list

REMEMBER Use null for the Empty List and to Indicate Its End

The head reference of an empty linked list contains null, as does the link portion of the last node of a nonempty linked list.

Implementing the Operations of a Linked List

Listing 12.5 contains a definition of a linked-list class that uses the node class definition given in Listing 12.4. Note that this new class has only one instance variable, and it is named head. This head instance variable contains a reference to the first node in the linked list, or it contains null if the linked list is empty—that is, when the linked list contains no nodes. The one constructor sets this head instance variable to null, indicating an empty list.

Before we go on to discuss how nodes are added and removed from a linked list, let's suppose that a linked list already has a few nodes and that you want to display the contents of all the nodes to the screen. You can do so by writing the following statements:

```
ListNode position = head;
while (position != null)
{
    System.out.println(position.getData());
    position = position.getLink();
}
```

LISTING 12.5 A Linked-List Class *(part 1 of 2)*

```java
public class StringLinkedList
{
    private ListNode head;
    public StringLinkedList()
    {
        head = null;
    }
    /**
     Displays the data on the list.
    */
    public void showList()
    {
        ListNode position = head;
        while (position != null)
        {
            System.out.println(position.getData());
            position = position.getLink();
        }
    }
    /**
     Returns the number of nodes on the list.
    */
    public int length()
    {
        int count = 0.
        ListNode position = head;
        while (position != null)
        {
            count++;
            position = position.getLink();
        }
        return count;
    }
    /**
     Adds a node containing the data addData at the
     start of the list.
    */
    public void addANodeToStart(String addData)
    {
        head = new ListNode(addData, head);
    }
```

We will give another definition of this class later in this chapter.

(continued)

LISTING 12.5   A Linked-List Class *(part 2 of 2)*

```java
    /**
     Deletes the first node on the list.
    */
    public void deleteHeadNode()
    {
        if (head != null)
            head = head.getLink();
        else
        {
            System.out.println("Deleting from an empty list.");
            System.exit(0);
        }
    }
    /**
     Sees whether target is on the list.
    */
    public boolean onList(String target)
    {
        return find(target) != null;
    }
    //Returns a reference to the first node containing the
    //target data. If target is not on the list, returns null.
    private ListNode find(String target)
    {
        boolean found = false;
        ListNode position = head;
        while ((position != null) && !found)
        {
            String dataAtPosition = position.getData();
            if (dataAtPosition.equals(target))
                found = true;
            else
                position = position.getLink();
        }
        return position
    }
}
```

The variable named `position` contains a reference to one node. Initially, `position` contains the same reference as the `head` instance variable; thus, it starts out positioned at the first node. After we display the data in that node, the reference in `position` changes from one node to the next via the assignment

Stepping through a list

```java
    position = position.getLink();
```

This process is illustrated in Figure 12.5.

FIGURE 12.5   Moving Down a Linked List

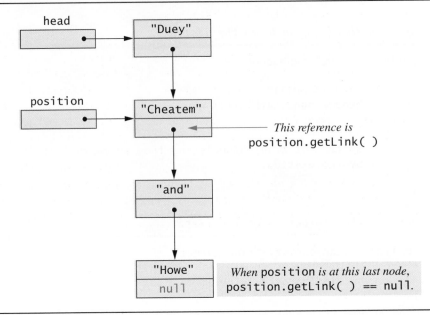

To see that this assignment "moves" the position variable to the next node, note that position contains a reference to the node pointed to by the position arrow in Figure 12.5. So position is a name for that node, and position.link is a name for the link portion of that node. Thus, position.link references the next node. The value of link is produced by calling the accessor method getLink. Therefore, a reference to the next node in the linked list is position.getLink(). You "move" the position variable by giving it the value of position.getLink().

The previous loop continues to move the position variable down the linked list, displaying the data in each node as it goes along. When position reaches the last node, it displays the data in that node and again executes

```
position = position.getLink();
```

If you study Figure 12.5, you will see that position's value is set to null at this point. When this occurs, we want to stop the loop, so we iterate the loop while position is not null.

The method showList contains the loop that we just discussed. The method length uses a similar loop, but instead of displaying the data in each node, length just counts the nodes as the loop moves from node to node. When the loop ends, length returns the number of entries on the list. By the way, a process that moves from node to node in a linked list is said to **traverse** the list. Both showList and length traverse our list.

Next, let's consider how the method addANodeToStart adds a node to the start of the linked list so that the new node becomes the first node of the list.

This operation is performed by the single statement

```
head = new ListNode(addData, head);
```

In other words, the variable head is set equal to a reference to a new node, making the new node the first node in the linked list. To link this new node to the rest of the list, we need only set the link instance variable of the new node equal to a reference to the old first node. But we have already done that: The new node produced by newListNode(addData, head) references the old first node, because head contains a reference to the old first node before it is assigned a reference to the new node. Therefore, everything works out as it should. This process is illustrated in Figure 12.6.

So far, we have added a node only at the start of the linked list. Later, we will discuss adding nodes at other places in a linked list, but the easiest place to add a node is at the start of the list. This is also the easiest place to delete a node.

The method deleteHeadNode removes the first node from the linked list and leaves the head variable referencing the old second node—which is now the first node—in the linked list. We will leave it to you to figure out that the following assignment correctly accomplishes this deletion:

```
head = head.getLink();
```

FIGURE 12.6 Adding a Node at the Start of a Linked List

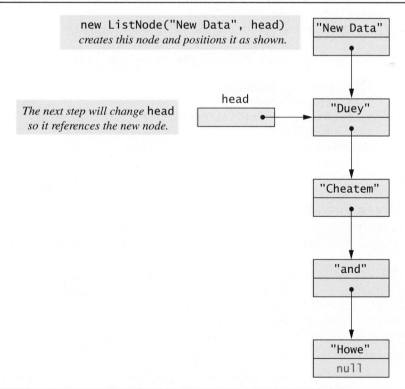

Listing 12.6 contains a simple program that demonstrates the behavior of some of the methods we just discussed.

LISTING 12.6   A Linked-List Demonstration

```java
public class StringLinkedListDemo
{
    public static void main(String[] args)
    {
        StringLinkedList list = new StringLinkedList();
        list.addANodeToStart("One");
        list.addANodeToStart("Two");
        list.addANodeToStart("Three");
        System.out.println("List has " + list.length() +
                            " entries.");
        list.showList();

        if (list.onList("Three"));
            System.out.println("Three is on list.");
        else
            System.out.println("Three is NOT on list.");

        list.deleteHeadNode();

        if (list.onList("Three"));
            System.out.println("Three is on list.");
        else
            System.out.println("Three is NOT on list.");

        list.deleteHeadNode();
        list.deleteHeadNode();
        System.out.println("Start of list:");
        list.showList();
        System.out.println("End of list");
    }
}
```

Screen Output

```
List has 3 entries.
Three
Two
One
Three is on list.
Three is NOT on list.
Start of list:
End of list.
```

FAQ What happens to a deleted node?

When your code deletes a node from a linked list, it removes the linked list's reference to that node. So as far as the linked list is concerned, the node is no longer in the linked list. But you gave no command to destroy the node, so it must be someplace in the computer's memory. If there is no other reference to the deleted node, the storage that it occupies should be made available for other uses. In many programming languages, you, the programmer, must keep track of deleted nodes and give explicit commands to return their memory for recycling to other uses. This process is called **garbage collecting.** In Java, this task is done for you automatically, or, as it is ordinarily phrased, Java has **automatic garbage collection.**

GOTCHA   NullPointerException

You have undoubtedly received the message `NullPointerException` at some time when you have run a program. (If you have not received the message, congratulations! You are an exceptionally careful programmer.) The message `NullPointerException` indicates that your code tried to use a variable of a class type to reference an object, but the variable contains `null`. That is, the variable does not contain a reference to any object. This message may make more sense to you now. In our nodes, we used `null` to indicate that a link instance variable contains no reference. So a value of `null` indicates no object reference, and that is why the exception is called `NullPointerException`.

A `NullPointerException` is one of the exceptions that you do not need to catch in a `catch` block or declare in a `throws` clause. Instead, it indicates that you need to fix your code. ■

REMEMBER Most Nodes Have No Name

The variable head contains a reference to the first node in a linked list. So head can be used as a name for the first node. However, the other nodes in the linked list have no named variable that contains a reference to any of them, so the rest of the nodes in the linked list are nameless. The only way to name one of them is via some indirect reference, like head.getLink(), or by using another variable of type ListNode, such as the local variable position in the method showList (Listing 12.5).

SELF-TEST QUESTIONS

18. How do you mark the end of a linked list?

19. Assume that the variable head is supposed to contain a reference to the first node in a linked list and that the linked list is empty. What value should head have?

20. Write a definition of a method isEmpty for the class StringLinkedList that returns true if the list is empty, that is, if it has no nodes.

21. What output is produced by the following code?

```
StringLinkedList list = new StringLinkedList();
list.addANodeToStart("A");
list.addANodeToStart("B");
list.addANodeToStart("C");
list.showList();
```

A Privacy Leak

The point made in this section is important but a bit subtle. It will help you to understand this section if you first review Section 6.5 in Chapter 6. There we said that a privacy problem can arise in any situation in which a method returns a reference to a private instance variable of a class type. The private restriction on the instance variable could be defeated easily if it names an object that has a set method. Getting a reference to such an object could allow a programmer to change the private instance variables of the object.

Consider the method getLink in the class ListNode (Listing 12.4). It returns a value of type ListNode. That is, it returns a reference to a ListNode object, that is, a node. Moreover, ListNode has public set methods that can damage the contents of a node. Thus, getLink can cause a privacy leak.

On the other hand, the method getData in the class ListNode causes no privacy leak, but only because the class String has no set methods. The class String is a special case. If the data were of another class type, getData could produce a privacy leak.

If the class ListNode is used only in the definition of the class StringLinkedList and classes like it, there is no privacy leak. This is the because no public method in the class StringLinkedList returns a reference to a node. Although the return type of the method find is ListNode, it is a private method. If the method find were public, a privacy leak would result. Therefore, note that making find private is not simply a minor stylistic point.

Although there is no problem with the class definition of ListNode when it is used in a class definition like StringLinkedList, we cannot guarantee that the class ListNode will be used only in this way. You can fix this privacy-

LISTING 12.9   A Linked List with an Iterator *(part 2 of 4)*

```java
/**
 Sets iterator to beginning of list.
*/
public void resetIteration()
{
    current = head;
    previous = null;
}
/**
 Returns true if iteration is not finished.
*/
public boolean moreToIterate()
{
    return current != null;
}
/**
 Advances iterator to next node.
*/
public void goToNext()
{
    if (current != null)
    {
        previous = current;
        current = current.link;
    }
    else if (head != null)
    {
        System.out.println(
            "Iterated too many times or uninitialized
            iteration.");
        System.exit(0);
    }
    else
    {
        System.out.println("Iterating with an empty list.");
        System.exit(0);
    }
}
/**
 Returns the data at the current node.
*/
public String getDataAtCurrent()
{
    String result = null;
    if (current != null)
        result = current.data;
```

(continued)

LISTING 12.9 A Linked List with an Iterator *(part 3 of 4)*

```java
        else
        {
            System.out.println(
                    "Getting data when current is not at any node.");
            System.exit(0);
        }
        return result;
    }
    /**
     Replaces the data at the current node.
     /*
    public void setDataAtCurrent(String newData)
    {
        if (current != null)
        {
            current.data = newData;
        }
        else
        {
            System.out.println(
                    "Setting data when current is not at any node.");
            System.exit(0);
        }
    }
    /**
     Inserts a new node containing newData after the current node.
     The current node is the same after invocation as it is before.
     Precondition: List is not empty; current node is not
     beyond the entire list.
     */
    public void insertNodeAfterCurrent(String newData)
    {
        ListNode newNode = new LisNode();
        newNode.data = newData;
        if (current != null)
        {
            newNode.link = current.link;
            current.link = newNode;
        }

        else if (head != null)
        {
            System.out.println(
                    "Inserting when iterator is past all " +
                    "nodes or is not initialized.");
            System.exit(0);
        }
```

(continued)

LISTING 12.9   A Linked List with an Iterator *(part 4 of 4)*

```
    else
    {
        System.out.println(
                "Using insertNodeAfterCurrent with empty list.";
        System.exit(0);
        }
    }
    /**
    Deletes the current node. After the invocation,
    the current node is either the node after the
    deleted node or null if there is no next node.
    */
    public void deleteCurrentNode()
    {
        if ((current != null) && (previous == null))
        {
            previous.link = current.link;
            current = current.link;
        }
        else if ((current != null) && (previous == null))
        {//At head node
            head = current.link;
            current = head;
        }
        else //current==null
        {
            System.out.println(
                "Deleting with uninitialized current or an empty " +
                "list.");
            System.exit(0);
        }
    }
```
<The methods length, onList, find, and showList, as well as the
private inner class ListNode are the same as in Listing 12.7.>
<The method toArray is the same as in Listing 12.8.>
```
}
```

deleteHeadNode *is no longer needed, since
you have* deleteCurrentNode, *but if you
want to retain* deleteHeadNode, *it must
be redefined to account for* current *and*
previous.

Instance variables
current and
previous

The method
goToNext

An internal
iterator

An external
iterator

In addition to the instance variables head and current, we have added an instance variable named previous. The idea is that, as the reference current moves down the linked list, the reference previous follows behind by one node. This setup gives us a way to reference the node before the one named by current. Since the links in the linked list all move in one direction, we need the node previous so that we can do something equivalent to backing up one node.

The method resetIteration starts current at the beginning of the linked list by giving it a reference to the first (head) node, as follows:

```
current = head;
```

ASIDE Internal and External Iterators

The class StringLinkedListWithIterator (Listing 12.9) uses the instance variable current of type ListNode as an iterator to step through the nodes of the linked list one after the other. An iterator defined within the linked-list class in this way is known as an **internal iterator.**

If you copy the values in a linked list to an array via the method toArray, you can use a variable of type int as an iterator on the array. The int variable holds one index of the array and thus specifies one element of the array and one data item of the linked list. If the int variable is named position and the array is named a, the iterator position specifies the element a[position]. To move to the next item, simply increase the value of position by 1. An iterator that is defined outside the linked list, such as the int variable position, is known as an **external iterator.** Note that the important thing is not that the array is outside the linked list, but that the int variable position, which is the iterator, is outside the linked list. To better understand this point, note that the int variable position is also an external iterator for the array.

You can have several external iterators at one time, each at a different position within the same list. This is not possible with internal iterators, which is a distinct disadvantage.

It is possible to define an external iterator that works directly with the linked list, rather than with an array of the linked-list data. However, that technique is a bit more complicated, and we will not go into it in this text.

Because the instance variable previous has no previous node to reference, it is simply given the value null by the resetIteration method.

The method goToNext moves the iterator to the next node, as follows:

```
previous = current;
current = current.link;
```

This process is illustrated in Figure 12.7. In the goToNext method, the last two clauses of the multibranch if-else statement simply produce an error message when the method goToNext is used in a situation where using it does not make sense.

The method moreToIterate returns true as long as current is not equal to null, that is, as long as current contains a reference to some node. This result makes sense most of the time, but why does the method return true when current contains a reference to the last node? When current references the last node, your program cannot tell that it is at the last node until it invokes goToNext one more time, at which point current is set to null. Study Figure 12.7 or the definition of goToNext to see how this process works. When current is equal to null, moreToIterate returns false, indicating that the entire list has been traversed.

Now that our linked list has an iterator, our code has a way to reference any node in the linked list. The current instance variable can hold a reference to any one node; that one node is known as the **node at the iterator.** The method insertAfterIterator inserts a new node after the node at the iterator (at current). This process

FIGURE 12.7 The Effect of goToNext on a Linked List

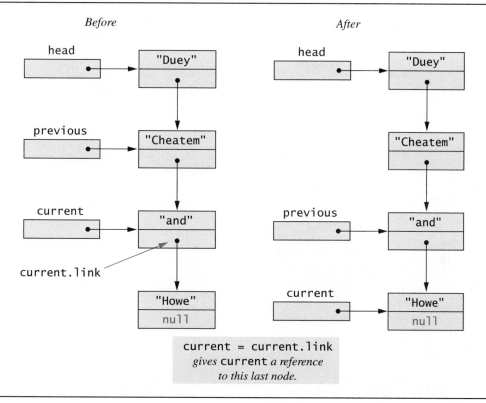

$$current = current.link$$
gives current *a reference*
to this last node.

is illustrated in Figure 12.8. The method deleteCurrentNode deletes the node at the iterator. This process is illustrated in Figure 12.9.

> The method moreToIterate

The other methods in the class StringLinkedListWithIterator (Listing 12.9) are fairly straightforward, and we will leave it up to you to read their definitions and see how they work.

> Inserting and deleting items within a list

SELF-TEST QUESTIONS

22. What is an inner class?

23. Why does the definition of the inner class ListNode in Listing 12.7 not have the accessor and mutator methods getLink, setLink, getData, and setData, as the class definition ListNode in Listing 12.4 does?

24. What is an iterator for a collection of items, such as an array or a linked list?

FIGURE 12.8 **Adding a Node to a Linked List, Using** `insertAfterIterator`

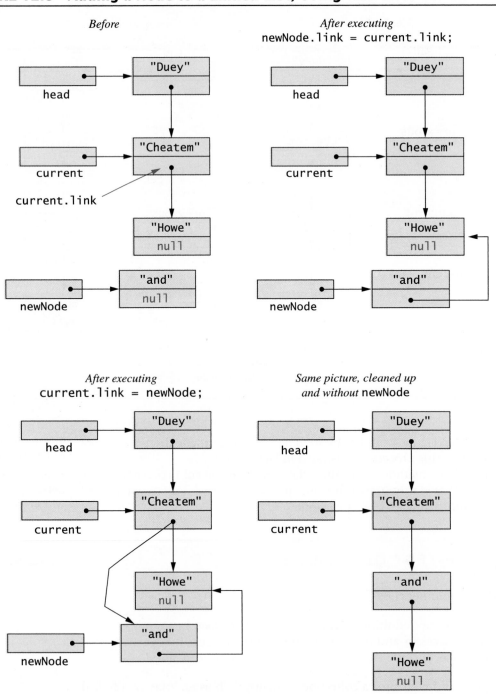

FIGURE 12.9   **Deleting a Node**

Before

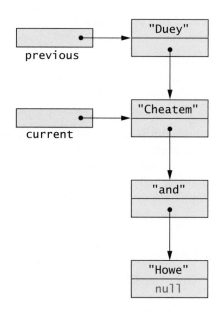

After executing
`previous.link = current.link;`

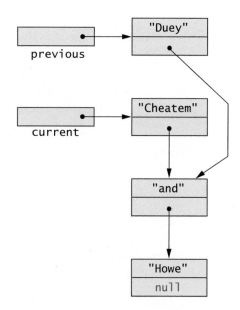

After executing
`current = current.link;`

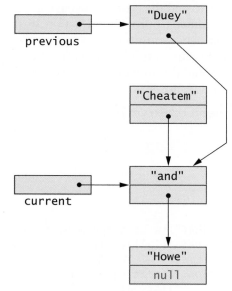

*Same picture, cleaned up
and without the deleted node*

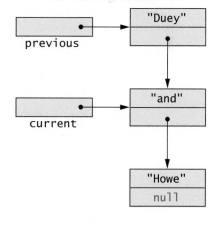

The Java `Iterator` Interface

The standard
interface
`Iterator`

Our introduction to iterators defined them as variables that enable you to step through a collection of items. However, Java formally considers an iterator to be an object, not simply a variable. The interface named `Iterator` in the package `java.util` stipulates how Java would like an iterator to behave. The interface specifies the following three methods:

- `hasNext`—returns true if the iteration has another element to return.
- `next`—returns the next element in the iteration.
- `remove`—removes from the collection the element returned most recently by the invocation `next()`.

Our iterators do not satisfy this interface, but it is easy to define classes that use our iterators and that do satisfy this interface. The `Iterator` interface also uses exception handling, but that use is not difficult to understand. Appendix 8, which is on the book's Web site, briefly describes the `Iterator` interface. Exercise 16 at the end of this chapter asks you to define a linked-list class that satisfies this interface.

Exception Handling with Linked Lists

As you may have guessed, you need to have read Chapter 9, on exception handling, before reading this section.

Consider the class `StringLinkedListWithIterator` in Listing 12.9. We defined the methods for that class such that whenever something went wrong, the method sent an error message to the screen and ended the program. However, it may not always be necessary to end the program when something unusual happens. To allow the programmer to provide an action in these unusual situations, it would make more sense to throw an exception and let the programmer decide how to handle the situation. The programmer can still decide to end the program but instead could do something else. For example, you could rewrite the method goToNext as follows:

```java
public void goToNext() throws LinkedListException
{
    if (current != null)
    {
        previous = current;
        current = current.link;
    }
    else if (head != null)
        throw new LinkedListException("Iterated too many times"
                                + " or uninitialized iteration.");
    else
        throw new LinkedListException("Iterating an empty "+
                                "list.");
}
```

LISTING 12.10   **The LinkedListException Class**

```java
public class LinkedListException extends Exception
{
    public LinkedListException()
    {
        super("Linked List Exception");
    }
    public LinkedListException(String message)
    {
        super(message);
    }
}
```

In this version, we have replaced each of the branches that end the program with a branch that throws an exception. The exception class `LinkedListException` can be a routine exception class, as shown in Listing 12.10.

You can use an exception thrown during an iteration for a number of different purposes. One possibility is to check for the end of a linked list. For example, suppose that the version of `StringLinkedListWithIterator` that throws exceptions is named `StringLinkedListWithIterator2`. The following code removes all nodes that contain a given string (`badString`) from a linked list, throwing an exception if it attempts to read past the end of the list:

```java
StringLinkedListWithIterator2 list =
        new StringLinkedListWithIterator2();
String badString;
<Some code to fill the linked list and set the variable badString.>
list.resetIteration();
try
{
    while (list.length() >= 0)
    {
        if (badString.equals(list.getDataAtCurrent()))
            list.deleteCurrentNode();
        else
            list.goToNext();
    }
}
catch(LinkedListException e)
{
    if (e.getMessage().equals("Iterating an empty list."))
    {//This should never happen, but
     //the catch block is compulsory.
        System.out.println("Fatal Error.");
        System.exit(0);
    }
}
System.out.println("List cleaned of bad strings.");
```

This use of an exception to test for the end of a list may seem a bit strange at first, but similar uses of exceptions do occur in Java programming. For example, Java requires something like this when checking for the end of a binary file. Of course, there are many other uses for the `LinkedListException` class.

The self-test questions that follow ask you to rewrite more of the methods in `StringLinkedListWithIterator` so that they throw exceptions in unusual or error situations.

SELF-TEST QUESTIONS

25. Redefine the method `getDataAtCurrent` in `StringLinkedListWith Iterator` (Listing 12.9) so that it throws an exception instead of ending the program when something unusual happens.

26. Repeat Question 25 for the method `setDataAtCurrent`.

27. Repeat Question 25 for the method `insertNodeAfterCurrent`.

28. Repeat Question 25 for the method `deleteCurrentNode`.

Variations on a Linked List

The study of data structures is a large topic, with many good books on the subject. In this book, we want to introduce you to all aspects of programming, and therefore we cannot go into the topic of linked data structures in exhaustive detail. Instead, we will give you an informal introduction to a few important linked data structures, beginning with some other kinds of linked lists that link their nodes in different ways.

You can have a linked list of any kind of data. Just replace the type `String` in the definition of the node class (and other corresponding places) with the data type you want to use. You can even have a linked list of objects of different kinds by replacing the type `String` in the node definition (and other corresponding places) with the type `Object`, as shown in the following code:

A list node having `Object` data

```
private class ListNode
{
    private Object data;
    private ListNode link;
    public ListNode()
    {
        link = null;
        data = null;
    }
    public ListNode(Object newData, ListNode linkValue)
```

```
    {
        data = newData;
        link = linkValue;
    }
}
```

Because an object of any class type is also of type `Object`, you can store any kinds of objects in a linked list with nodes of this kind.

Instead of using `Object` as the data type of the list items, you can use a generic data type. Section 12.3 of this chapter will show you how. By using a generic data type, you restrict the objects in the linked list to having the same data type.

Sometimes it is handy to have a reference to the last node in a linked list. This last node is often called the **tail node** of the list, so the linked-list definition might begin as follows:

The last node in a linked list is its tail node

```
public class StringLinkedListWithTail
{
    private ListNode head;
    private ListNode tail;
    . . .
```

The constructors and methods must be modified to accommodate the new reference, `tail`, but the details of doing so are routine.

You have seen that the link portion of the last node in a linked list contains `null`. In a **circular linked list,** this link is instead a reference to the first node. Thus, no link in a circular linked list is `null`. Such a linked list still has a beginning and an end, as well as an external reference to either its first node or its last node. Figure 12.10 illustrates a circular linked list that has an external reference, `tail`, to its last node. Note that `tail.link` is then a reference to the list's first node.

A linked list can be circular

An ordinary linked list allows you to follow its links and move down the list in only one direction. A **doubly linked list** has two links in each node: one link is a reference to the next node and one is a reference to the previous node. Figure 12.11 illustrates a doubly linked list.

A linked list can be doubly linked

FIGURE 12.10 A Circular Linked List

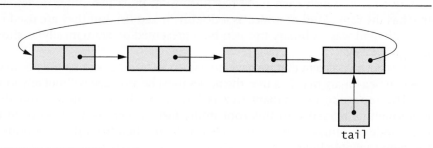

tail

FIGURE 12.11 A Doubly Linked List

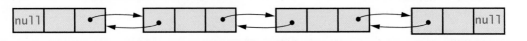

The node class for a doubly linked list can begin as follows:

```
private class ListNode
{
    private Object data;
    private ListNode next;
    private ListNode previous;
    . . .
```

The constructors and some of the methods in the doubly linked list class will have somewhat different definitions than those in the singly linked case in order to accommodate the extra link.

A **circular doubly linked list** is also possible. In this structure, the previous link of the first node references the last node and the next link of the last node references the first node.

Other Linked Data Structures

We have discussed a few kinds of linked lists as examples of linked data structures. Here are several more linked data structures that you will surely encounter in later studies.

The ADT stack

A **stack** is an ADT whose implementation is not necessarily a linked data structure, but it can be implemented as one. A stack organizes its data so that items are removed in the reverse of the order in which they were inserted. So if you insert "one", then "two", and then "three" into a stack and then remove them, they will come out in the order "three", then "two", and finally "one". A linked list that inserts and deletes only at the beginning of the list—such as the one in Listing 12.5—behaves like a stack, and so can be an implementation of a stack.

Another common and powerful data structure is a **tree**. In a tree, each node leads to several other nodes. The most common form of a tree is a

A binary tree

binary tree, in which each node has links to at most two other nodes. This tree has the same kind of nodes as a doubly linked list, but they are used in a very different way. A binary tree can be represented diagramatically as shown in Figure 12.12.

It is not an accident that we have no references leading back up the tree in our diagram of a binary tree. In a tree, the nodes must be arranged without any loops.

The top node in a binary tree is known as the **root node**, and there is normally a reference to this root node, just as there is a reference to the head node of a linked list. Every node can be reached from the root node by following suitable links.

FIGURE 12.12 A Binary Tree

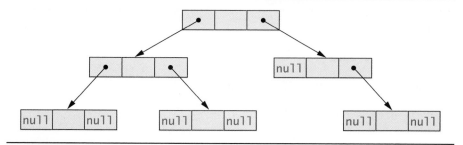

12.4 GENERICS

generic adj. 1. Relating to or descriptive of an entire group or class; general.

—THE AMERICAN HERITAGE DICTIONARY OF THE ENGLISH LANGUAGE, FOURTH EDITION*

As we mentioned earlier, beginning with version 5.0, Java allows class definitions to include parameters for data types. These parameters are called **generics.** This section gives a brief introduction to this topic. Programming with generics can be subtle and requires care. To do serious programming with generics, you may want to consult a more advanced text.

The Basics

Classes and methods can use a **type parameter** instead of a specific data type. When Generics allows you to parameterize a data type using such a class or method, a programmer plugs in any class type for the type parameter to produce a specific class type or method for that particular instance. For example, Listing 12.11 shows a very simple class definition that uses a type parameter T. Notice the angle bracket notation around T in the class heading. You can use any nonkeyword identifier for the type parameter; you need not use T. However, by convention, type parameters start with an uppercase letter, and there seems to be a tradition of using a single letter for these parameters. Starting with an uppercase letter makes sense, since only a class type may be plugged in for the type parameter. The tradition of using a single letter is not as compelling.

Generics allows you to parameterize a data type

When writing a class or method that uses a type parameter, you can use the parameter almost anywhere that you can use a class type. For example, the class Sample in Listing 12.11 uses T as the data type of the instance variable data, the method parameter newValue, and the return type of the method getData. You cannot, however, use a type parameter to create a new object. So even though data is of type T in the class Sample, you cannot write

```
data = new T(); //Illegal!
```

> ### LISTING 12.11   A Class Definition That Uses a Type Parameter
>
> ```
> public class Sample<T>
> {
>     private T data;
>
>     public void setData(T newValue)
>     {
>         data = newValue;
>     }
>
>     public T getData()
>     {
>         return data;
>     }
> }
> ```

Moreover, you cannot use a type parameter when allocating memory for an array. Although you can declare an array by writing a statement such as

```
T[] anArray; //Valid declaration of an array
```

you cannot write

```
anArray = new T[20]; //Illegal!
```


GOTCHA   **You Cannot Use a Type Parameter Everywhere You Can Use a Type Name**

Within the definition of a parameterized class definition, there are places where a type name is allowed but a type parameter is not. You cannot use a type parameter in simple expressions that use new to create a new object or to allocate memory for an array. For example, the following expressions are illegal within the definition of a parameterized class definition whose type parameter is T:

```
new T(); //Illegal!
new T[20]; //Illegal!
```
■

A class definition that uses a type parameter is stored in a file and compiled just like any other class. For example, the parameterized class shown in Listing 12.11 would be stored in a file named Sample.java.

Once the parameterized class is compiled, it can be used like any other class, except that when using it in your code, you must specify a class type to replace the type parameter. For example, the class Sample from Listing 12.11 could be used as follows:

```
Sample<String> sample1 = new Sample<String>();
sample1.setData("Hello");
Sample<Species> sample2 = new Sample<Species>();
Species creature = new Species();
... <Some code to set the data for the object creature>
sample1.setData(creature);
```

Notice the angle bracket notation for the actual class type that replaces the type parameter. The class Species could be as defined in Chapter 5, but the details do not matter; it could be any class you define.

You should now realize that the class ArrayList, which we discussed at the beginning of this chapter, is a parameterized class. Recall that we created an instance of ArrayList by writing, for example,

```
ArrayList<String> list = new ArrayList<String>(20);
```

Here String replaces the type parameter in the definition of the class.

RECAP Class Definitions Having a Type Parameter

You can define classes that use a parameter instead of an actual class type. You write the type parameter within angle brackets right after the class name in the heading of the class definition. You can use any nonkeyword identifier for the type parameter, but by convention, the type parameter starts with an uppercase letter.

You use the type parameter within the class definition in the same way that you would use an actual class type, except that you cannot use it in conjunction with new.

EXAMPLE

See Listing 12.11.

RECAP Using a Class Whose Definition Has a Type Parameter

You create an object of a parameterized class in the same way that you create an object of any other class, except that you specify an actual class type, rather than the type parameter, within angle brackets after the class name.

EXAMPLE

```
Sample<String> anObject = new Sample<String>();
anObject.setData("Hello");
```

GOTCHA   You Cannot Plug in a Primitive Type for a Type Parameter

When you create an object of a class that has a type parameter, you cannot plug in a primitive type, such as int, double, or char. For example, the following statement will cause a syntax error:

```
ArrayList<int> aList = new ArrayList<int>(20); //Illegal!
```

The type plugged in for a type parameter must be a class type.   ■

■ PROGRAMMING TIP   Compile with the -Xlint Option

There are many pitfalls that you can encounter when using type parameters. If you compile with the -Xlint option, you will receive more informative diagnostics of any problems or potential problems in your code. For example, the class Sample in Listing 12.11 should be compiled as follows:

```
javac -Xlint Sample.java
```

If you are using an integrated development environment, or IDE, to compile your programs, check your documentation to see how to set a compiler option.

When compiling with the -Xlint option, you will get more warnings than you would otherwise get. A warning is not an error, and if the compiler gives only warnings and no error message, the class has compiled and can be used. However, in most cases be sure you understand the warning and feel confident that it does not indicate a problem, or else change your code to eliminate the warning.   ■

PROGRAMMING EXAMPLE   A Generic Linked List

Let's revise the definition of the linked-list class that appears in Listing 12.7 to use a type parameter, E, instead of the type String as the type of data stored on the list. Listing 12.12 shows the result of this revision.

Notice that the constructor heading looks just as it would in a nonparameterized class. It does not include <E>, the type parameter within angle brackets, after the constructor's name. This is counterintuitive to many people. While a constructor—like any other method in the class—can use the type parameter within its body, its heading does not include the type parameter.

Likewise, the inner class ListNode does not have <E> after its name in its heading, but ListNode does uses the type parameter E within its definition. These are correct as shown, however, because ListNode is an inner class and can access the type parameter of its outer class.

LISTING 12.12   A Generic Linked-List Class *(part 1 of 2)*

```
import java.util.ArrayList;
public class LinkedList2<E>
{
    private ListNode head;
    public LinkedList2( )
    {
        head = null;
    }
    public void showList( )
    {
        ListNode position = head;
        while (position != null)
        {
            System.out.println(position.getData( ));
            position = position.getLink( );
        }
    }
    public int length( )
    {
        int count = 0;
        ListNode position = head;
        while (position != null)
        {
            count++;
            position = position.getLink( );
        }
        return count;
    }
    public void addANodeToStart(E addData)
    {
        head = new ListNode(addData, head);
    }
    public void deleteHeadNode( )
    {
        if (head != null)
        {
            head = head.getLink( );
        }
        else
        {
            System.out.println("Deleting from an empty list.");
            System.exit(0);
        }
    }
    public boolean onList(E target)
    {
        return find(target) != null;
    }
```

Constructor headings do not include the type parameter.

(continued)

LISTING 12.12 A Generic Linked-List Class *(part 2 of 2)*

```java
    private ListNode find(E target)
    {
        boolean found = false;
        ListNode position = head;
        while (position != null)
        {
            E dataAtPosition = position.getData();
            if (dataAtPosition.equals(target))
                found = true;
            else
                position = position.getLink();
        }
        return position;
    }
    private ArrayList<E> toArrayList()
    {
        ArrayList<E> list = new ArrayList<E>(length());
        ListNode position = head;
        while (position != null)
        {
            list.add(position.data);
            position = position.link;
        }
        return list;
    }
    private class ListNode          ◄──────   The inner class heading
    {                               ◄──                 has no type parameter.
        private E data;
        private ListNode link;
        public ListNode()
        {
            link = null;
            data = null;
        }
        public ListNode(E newData, ListNode linkValue)
        {
            data = newData;                           However, the type parameter
            link = linkValue;                         is used within the definition of
        }                                             the inner class.
        public E getData()
        {
            return data;
        }
        public ListNode getLink()
        {
            return link;
        }
    }
}
```

The linked-list class in Listing 12.7 can have a method named toArray—shown in Listing 12.8—that returns an array containing the same data as the linked list. However, our generic version of a linked list cannot implement this same method. If we were to translate toArray in Listing 12.8 so that we could include it in our generic linked list in Listing 12.12, it would begin as follows:

```
public E[] toArray()
{
    E[] anArray = new E[length()]; //Illegal
...
```

As the comment indicates, the expression new E[length()] is not allowed. You cannot include the type parameter in certain situations, and this, unfortunately, is one of them. Thus, you simply cannot have the method toArray in the generic linked list. Instead, Listing 12.12 defines the method toArrayList, which returns an instance of the class ArrayList. Note that its definition contains a loop like the one in toArray.

VideoNote
Creating classes that use generics

Listing 12.13 contains a simple example of using our parameterized linked list.

LISTING 12.13   Using the Generic Linked list

```
public class LinkedList2Demo
{
    public static void main(String[] args)
    {
        LinkedList2<String> stringList = new LinkedList2<String>( );
        stringList.addANodeToStart("Hello");
        stringList.addANodeToStart("Good-bye");
        stringList.showList( );
        LinkedList2<Integer> numberList = new LinkedList2<Integer>( );
        for (int i = 0; i < 5; i++)
            numberList.addANodeToStart(i);
        numberList.deleteHeadNode();
        numberList.showList( );
    }
}
```

Screen Output

```
Good-bye
Hello
3
2
1
0
```

GOTCHA   A Constructor Name in a Generic Class Has No Type Parameter

The class name in a parameterized class definition has a type parameter attached—for example, LinkedList<E> in Listing 12.12. This can mislead you into thinking you need to use the type parameter in the heading of the constructor definition, but that is not the case. For example, you use

```
public LinkedList()
```

instead of

```
public LinkedList<E>() //Illegal
```

However, you can use a type parameter, such as E, within the body of the constructor's definition. ∎

FAQ Can a class definition have more than one type parameter?

Yes, you can define a class with more than one type parameter. To do so, you write the type parameters one after the other, separated by commas, with one pair of angle brackets. For example, the class Pair could begin as follows:

```
public class Pair<S, T>
```

You would use S and T within the definition of Pair as you would actual data types. This class allows you to create pairs of objects that have different data types.

REMEMBER An Inner Class Has Access to the Type Parameter of Its Outer Class

An inner class can access the type parameter of its outer class. In Listing 12.12, for example, the definition of the inner class ListNode uses the type parameter E, which is the type parameter of its outer class LinkedList, even though ListNode does not have <E> after its name in its heading.

∎ PROGRAMMING TIP   Defining Type Parameters in an Inner Class

An inner class can define its own type parameters, but they must be distinct from any defined in the outer class. For example, we could define the outer and inner classes in Listing 12.12 as follows:

```java
public class LinkedList<E>
{
    private ListNode<E> head;
    ...
    private class ListNode<T>
    {
        private T data;
        private ListNode<T> link;
        ...
        public ListNode (T newData, ListNode<T> linkValue)
        {...
        }
    }
}
```

Notice how the inner class `ListNode` uses `T` consistently as its type parameter and the outer class `LinkedList` has `E` as its type parameter. When `ListNode` is used as a data type within this outer class, it is written as `ListNode<E>`, not `ListNode<T>`. Also, note that we have no reason to give `ListNode` its own type parameter in this example, other than to show the syntax you would use if you wanted to do so. ■

 ## SELF-TEST QUESTIONS

myprogramminglab

29. Revise the definition of the class `ListNode` in Listing 12.4 so that it uses a type parameter instead of the type `String`. Note that the class is, and should remain, public. Rename the class to `ListNode2`.

30. Using the definition of the `ListNode2` class from the previous question, how would you create a `ListNode2` object named `node` that stores a value of type `Integer`?

CHAPTER SUMMARY

■ `ArrayList` is a class in the Java Class Library. Instances of `ArrayList` can be thought of as arrays that can grow in length. You create and name such instances in the same way as any other object except that you specify their base type.

■ `ArrayList` has powerful methods that can do many of the things you must do for yourself when using an array.

■ The Java Collections Framework is a collection of interfaces and classes that may be used to manipulate collections of objects in a consistent way.

■ The HashSet class is part of the Java Collections Framework and may be used to efficiently implement a set.

- The HashMap class is part of the Java Collections Framework and may be used to map from one value to another.

- A linked list is a data structure consisting of objects known as nodes, such that each node contains both data and a reference to one other node. In this way, the nodes link together to form a list.

- You can make a linked data structure, such as a linked list, self-contained by making the node class an inner class of the linked-list class.

- A variable or object that allows you to step through a collection of data items, such as an array or a linked list, one item at a time is called an iterator.

- You can define a class that uses a parameter instead of an actual class type. You write the type parameter within angle brackets right after the class name in the heading of the class definition.

- The code that creates an object of a parameterized class replaces the type parameter with an actual class type, retaining the angle brackets.

- The standard classes `ArrayList` and `LinkedList` are parameterized classes.

Exercises

1. Repeat Exercise 2 in Chapter 7, but use an instance of `ArrayList` instead of an array. Do not read the number of values, but continue to read values until the user enters a negative value.

2. Repeat Exercise 3 in Chapter 7, but use an instance of `ArrayList` instead of an array. Do not read the number of families, but read data for families until the user enters the word done.

3. Repeat Exercise 5 in Chapter 7, but use an instance of `ArrayList` instead of an array.

4. Repeat Exercises 6 and 7 in Chapter 7, but use an instance of `ArrayList` instead of an array. We will no longer need to know the maximum number of sales, so the methods will change to reflect this.

5. Write a static method `removeDuplicates(ArrayList<Character> data)` that will remove any duplicates of characters in the object data. Always keep the first copy of a character and remove subsequent ones.

6. Write a static method

   ```
   getCommonStrings(ArrayList<String> list1,
       ArrayList<String> list2)
   ```

   that returns a new instance of `ArrayList` containing all of the strings common to both list1 and list2.

7. Write a program that will read sentences from a text file, placing each sentence in its own instance of `ArrayList`. (You will create a sentence object by adding words to it one at a time as they are read.) When a sentence has been completely read, add the sentence to another instance of `ArrayList`. Once you have read the entire file, you will have an instance of `ArrayList` that contains several instances of `ArrayList`, one for each sentence read. Now ask the user to enter a sentence number and a word number. Display the word that occurs in the given position. If the sentence number or word number is not valid, provide an appropriate error message.

8. Repeat Exercise 12 in Chapter 7, but use an instance of `ArrayList` instead of an array. Make the following slight changes to the methods to reflect that an `ArrayList` object can grow in size:

   - Change the constructor's parameter from the maximum degree to the desired degree.
   - The method `setConstant` might need to add zero-valued coefficients before a_i. For example, if $a_0 = 3$, $a_1 = 5$, $a_2 = 0$, $a_3 = 2$, $a_4 = 0$, and $a_5 = 0$, the polynomial would be of degree 3, since the last nonzero constant is a_3. The invocation `setConstant(8, 15)` would need to set a_6 and a_7 to 0 and a_8 to 15.

9. Write a program that will read a text file that contains an unknown number of movie review scores. Read the scores as `Double` values and put them in an instance of `ArrayList`. Compute the average score.

10. Revise the class `StringLinkedList` in Listing 12.5 so that it can add and remove items from the end of the list.

11. Suppose we would like to create a data structure for holding numbers that can be accessed either in the order that they were added or in sorted order. We need nodes having two references. If you follow one trail of references, you get the items in the order they were added. If you follow the other trail of references, you get the items in numeric order. Create a class `DualNode` that would support such a data structure. Do not write the data structure itself.

12. Draw a picture of an initially empty data structure, as described in the previous exercise, after adding the numbers 2, 8, 4, and 6, in this order.

13. Write some code that will use an iterator to duplicate every item in an instance of `StringLinkedListWithIterator` in Listing 12.9. For example, if the list contains "a", "b", and "c", after the code runs, it will contain "a", "a", "b", "b", "c", and "c".

14. Write some code that will use an iterator to move the first item in an instance of `StringLinkedListWithIterator` (Listing 12.9) to the end of the

list. For example, if the list contains "a", "b", "c", and "d", after the code runs, it will contain "b", "c", "d", and "a".

15. Write some code that will use an iterator to interchange the items in every pair of items in an instance of `StringLinkedListWithIterator` in Listing 12.9. For example, if the list contains "a", "b", "c", "d", "e", and "f", after the code runs, it will contain "b", "a", "d", "c", "f", and "e". You can assume that the list contains an even number of strings.

16. The class `StringLinkedListWithIterator` (Listing 12.9) is its own iterator, but it does not quite implement the Java `Iterator` interface. Redefine the class `StringLinkedListWithIterator` so that it implements the `Iterator` interface. This interface declares the methods `next`, `remove`, and `hasNext` as follows:

```
/**
Returns the next element on the list.
Throws a NoSuchElementException if there is
no next element to return.
*/
public E next() throws NoSuchElementException
/**
Removes the last element that was returned most recently
by the invocation next().
Throws an IllegalStateException if the method next has
not yet been called or if the method remove has already
been called after the last call to the method next.
*/
public void remove() throws IllegalStateException
/**
Returns true if there is at least one more element for
the method next to return. Otherwise, returns false.
*/
public boolean hasNext()
```

Notice the generic data type E in the specification of the method `next`.

If you follow the instructions in this question carefully, you do not need to know what an interface is, although knowing what one is may make you feel more comfortable. Interfaces are covered in Chapter 8.

Begin the class definition with

```
import java.util.Iterator;
public class StringLinkedListWithIterator2
    implements Iterator<String>
{
    private ListNode head;
    private ListNode current;
```

```
        private ListNode previous; //follows current
        private ListNodetwoBack; //follows previous
        private booleanremoveSinceNext;//true if the method
        //remove has been called since the last call of
        //the method next. Also true if next has not
        //been called at all.
        public StringLinkedListWithIterator2()
        {
            head = null;
            current = null;
            previous = null;
            twoBack = null;
            removeSinceNext = true;
        }
```

The rest of the definition is like the one in Listing 12.9, except that you add the method definitions specified by Iterator, make a small change to the method resetIteration so that the new instance variable twoBack is reset, and omit the methods deleteCurrentNode, goToNext, and moreToIterate, which become redundant.

(*Hints*:

- Despite its pretentious-sounding details, this exercise is fairly easy. The three method definitions you need to add are easy to implement using the methods we have.
- Note that the method hasNext and the method moreToIterate in Listing 12.9 are not exactly the same.
- The exception classes mentioned are all predefined, and you should not define them. These particular exceptions do not need to be caught or declared in a throws clause. The Iterator interface says that the method remove throws an UnsupportedOperationException if the remove method is not supported. However, your method remove has no need ever to throw this exception.)

17. Write a program that creates two instances of the generic class LinkedList given in Listing 12.12. The first instance is stadiumNames and will hold items of type String. The second instance is gameRevenue and will hold items of type Double. Within a loop, read data for the ball games played during a season. The data for a game consists of a stadium name and the amount of money made for that game. Add the game data to stadiumNames and gameRevenue. Since more than one game could be played at a particular stadium, stadiumNames might have duplicate entries. After reading the data for all of the games, read a stadium name and display the total amount of money made for all the games at that stadium.

PROGRAMMING PROJECTS

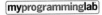

Visit www.myprogramminglab.com to complete many of these Programming Projects online and get instant feedback.

1. Revise the method `selectionSort` within the class `ArraySorter`, as shown in Listing 7.10 of Chapter 7, so that it sorts the strings in an instance of the class `ArrayList<String>` into lexicographic order instead of sorting the integers in an array into ascending order. For words, lexicographic order reduces to alphabetic order if all the words are in either lowercase or uppercase letters. You can compare two strings to see which is lexicographically first by using the `String` method `compareTo`, as described in Figure 2.5 of Chapter 2.

2. Repeat the previous programming project, but instead write a method `bubbleSort` that performs a bubble sort, as described in Programming Project 4 of Chapter 7.

3. Repeat Programming Project 1, but instead write a method `insertionSort` that performs an insertion sort, as described in Programming Project 5 of Chapter 7.

4. Write a program that creates `Pet` objects from data read from the keyboard. Store these objects into an instance of `ArrayList`. Then sort the `Pet` objects into alphabetic order by pet name, and finally display the data in the sorted `Pet` objects on the screen. The class `Pet` is given in Chapter 6, Listing 6.1.

5. Repeat the previous programming project, but sort the `Pet` objects by pet weight instead of by name. After displaying the sorted data on the screen, write the number and percentage of pets that are under 5 pounds, the number and percentage of pets that are 5 to 10 pounds, and the number and percentage of pets that are over 10 pounds.

6. Repeat the previous programming project, but read the input data from a file and send the output to another file. If you have covered binary files, use binary files; otherwise, use text files. Read the file names from the user.

7. Use the class `ClassObjectIODemo` shown in Listing 10.10 of Chapter 10 to create a file of `Species` objects. The class `Species` is given in Chapter 10, Listing 10.9. Then write a program that reads the `Species` objects from the file you created into an instance of `ArrayList`, sorts these instances alphabetically by `Species` name, and then writes the sorted data to both the screen and a file. Read all file names from the user.

8. Define a variation on `StringLinkedListSelfContained` from Listing 12.7 that stores objects of type `Species`, rather than of type `String`. Write a program that uses that linked-list class to create a linked list of `Species` objects, asks the user to enter a `Species` name, and then searches the linked list and displays one of the following messages, depending on whether the name is or is not on the list:

Species *Species_Name* is one of the
Number_Of_Species_Names_On_List species on the list.
The data for *Species_Name* is as follows:
Data_For_Species_Name

or

Species *Species_Name* is not a species on the list.

The user can enter more Species names until indicating an end to the program. The class Species is given in Listing 5.19 of Chapter 5. (If you prefer, you can use the serialized version of Species in Listing 10.9 of Chapter 10.)

9. Repeat the previous programming project, but read the input data from a file and send the output to another file. If you have covered binary files, use binary files; otherwise, use text files. Read the file names from the user.

10. Define a variation on StringLinkedListSelfContained from Listing 12.7 that stores objects of type Employee, rather than objects of type String. Write a program that uses this linked-list class to create a linked list of Employee objects, asks the user to enter an employee's Social Security number, and then searches the linked list and displays the data for the corresponding employee. If no such employee exists, display a message that says so. The user can enter more Social Security numbers until indicating an end to the program. The class Employee is described in Programming Project 7 of Chapter 9. If you have not already done that project, you will need to define the class Employee as described there.

11. Repeat the previous programming project, but read the input data from a file and send the output to another file. If you have covered binary files, use binary files; otherwise, use text files. Read the file names from the user.

12. Write a parameterized class definition for a doubly linked list that has a parameter for the type of data stored in a node. Make the node class an inner class. Choosing which methods to define is part of this project. Also, write a program to thoroughly test your class definition.

VideoNote
Defining a circular linked list

13. Create an application that will keep track of several groups of strings. Each string will be a member of exactly one group. We would like to be able to see whether two strings are in the same group as well as perform a union of two groups.

Use a linked structure to represent a group of strings. Each node in the structure contains a string and a reference to another node in the group. For example, the group {"a", "b", "d", "e"} is represented by the following structure:

One string in each group—"d" in our example—is in a node that has a null reference. That is, it does not reference any other node in the structure. This string is the **representative string** of the group.

Create the class GroupHolder to represent all of the groups and to perform operations on them. It should have the private instance variable items to hold the nodes that belong to all of the groups. The nodes within each group are linked together as described previously. Make items an instance of ArrayList whose base type is GroupNode, where GroupNode is a private inner class of GroupHolder. GroupNode has the following private instance variables:

- data—a string
- link—a reference to another node in the group, or null

Define the following methods in the class GroupHolder:

- addItem(s)— adds a string s to an empty group. First search items for s; if you find s, do nothing; if you do not find s, create a new GroupNode object that has s as its string and null as its link and add it to items. The new group will contain only the item s.
- getRepresentative(s)—returns the representative string for the group containing s. To find the representative string, search items for s. If you do not find s, return null. If you find s, follow links until you find a null reference. The string in that node is the representative string for the group.
- getAllRepresentatives—returns an instance of ArrayList that contains the representative strings of all the groups in this instance of GroupHolder. (A representative string is in an instance of GroupNode that contains a null reference.)
- inSameGroup(s1, s2)—returns true if the representative string for s1 and the representative string for s2 are the same and not null, in which case the strings s1 and s2 are in the same group.
- union(s1, s2)—forms the union of the groups to which s1 and s2 belong. (*Hint*: Find the representative strings for s1 and s2. If they are different and neither is null, make the link of the node containing s1's representative string reference the node for s2's representative string.)

For example, suppose that we call addItem with each of the following strings as an argument: "a","b","c","d","e","f","g", and "h". Next, let's form groups by using these union operations:

union("a", "d"), union("b", "d"), union("e", "b"),
union("h", "f")

We will have four groups–{"a", "b", "d", "e"}, {"c"}, {"f", "h"}, and {"g"}—represented by the following structure:

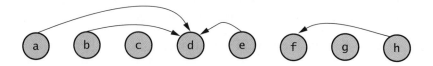

The representative strings for these four groups are "d","c","f", and "g", respectively. Now the operation inSameSet("a", "e") would return true because both getRepresentative("a") and getRepresentative("e") return d. Also, inSameSet("a", "f") would return false because getRepresentative("a") returns d and getRepresentative("f") returns f. The operation union("a", "f") would make the node containing the representative string of the group to which "a" belongs—which is "d"— reference the node containing the representative string of the group to which "f" belongs, which is "f". This reference would be represented by an arrow from "d" to "f" in the previous diagram.

Your application should create an instance of GroupHolder and allow the user to add an arbitrary number of strings, each to its own group. It should then perform an arbitrary number of union operations to form several groups. Finally, it should demonstrate the other operations.

14. For this project, we will create a data structure known as a **queue**. A queue can be thought of as a line. Items are added at the end of the line and are taken from the front of the line. You will create a class LinkedQueue based on one of the linked-list classes given in this chapter. It should have private attributes for

   - front—a reference to the first node in the linked list of queue items
   - count—the number of items in the queue

   and the following operations:

   - addToQueue(item)—adds item to the end of the queue. (Add it at the end of the linked list.)
   - removeFromQueue()—removes the first item from the queue and returns it. If the queue is empty, returns null
   - isEmpty—returns true if the queue contains no items; otherwise, returns false.

   Create a program that demonstrates the methods of the LinkedQueue class.

15. Repeat the previous programming project, but use a circular linked list to implement the queue. Recall from Figure 12.10 that a circular linked list has one external reference, which is to the list's last node.

16. Suppose that we would like to perform a bird survey to count the number of birds of each species in an area. Create a class BirdSurvey that is like one of the linked-list classes given in this chapter. (The linked list you use will affect what your new class can do, so give some thought to your choice.) Modify the inner node class to add room for a count.

    BirdSurvey should have the following operations:

    - add(bird)—adds the bird species bird to the end of the list, if it is not already there, and sets its count to 1; otherwise, adds 1 to the count for bird.
    - getCount(bird)—returns the count associated with the species bird. If bird is not on the list, returns zero.
    - getReport—displays the name and count for each bird species on the list.

    Write a program that uses BirdSurvey to record the data from a recent bird survey. Use a loop to read bird names until done is entered. Display a report when finished.

VideoNote
Solution to Project 17

17. Consider a text file of names, with one name per line, that has been compiled from several different sources. A sample is shown below:

    ```
    Brooke Trout
    Dinah Soars
    Jed Dye
    Brooke Trout
    Jed Dye
    Paige Turner
    ```

    There are duplicate names in the file. We would like to generate an invitation list but don't want to send multiple invitations to the same person. Write a program that eliminates the duplicate names by using a HashSet. Read each name from the file, add it to the HashSet, and then output all names in the HashSet to generate the invitation list without duplicates.

18. Write a program that uses a HashMap to compute a histogram of positive numbers entered by the user. The HashMap's key should be the number that is entered, and the value should be a counter of the number of times the key has been entered so far. Use -1 as a sentinel value to signal the end of user input. For example, if the user inputs:

    ```
    5
    12
    3
    5
    5
    3
    21
    -1
    ```

Then the program should output the following (not necessarily in this order):

```
The number 3 occurs 2 times.
The number 5 occurs 3 times.
The number 12 occurs 1 times.
The number 21 occurs 1 times.
```

Answers to Self-Test Questions

1. `aList.add("Hello");`

2. `aList.set(5, "Go");`

3. No. The index for `set` must be greater than or equal to 0 and less than the size of the list. Thus, you can replace any existing element, but you cannot place a new element at any higher index. That is, you cannot add an element beyond the last-used index. This situation is unlike that of an array. If an array is partially filled to index 10, you can add an element at index 20, as long as the array is that large.

4. No. The index for `add` must be greater than or equal to 0 and less than or equal to the size of the list. Thus, you can insert an element at any index that is currently holding an element, and you can insert an element immediately after the last element, but you cannot insert an element at any higher index.

5. Yes. The method `add` can add an element right after the last element on the list, that is, at index `size()`. However, the index position for `set` must be less than `size()`.

6. The seven elements of `aList` are at indices 0 through 6. A new element added at index 7 is the eighth element and is at the end of the list.

7. `"red"`, `"blue"`, `"orange"`, `"green"`, `"yellow"`

8. Yes. The list can contain more than 20 elements. The argument to the constructor merely gives the initial memory allocation for the list. More memory is automatically allocated when it is needed.

9. ```
   for (int index = 0; index < aList.size(); index++)
       System.out.println(aList.get(index));
   ```

10. No, you cannot have an instance of `ArrayList` that has the base type `int`. However, you can have one that has the base type `Integer`, and thanks to automatic boxing and unboxing, it can be used as if it were a list of `int`s.

11. The method invocation `list.size()` returns the number of elements currently in `list`. The capacity of `list`, however, is the number of elements for which memory has been allocated.
   ```

12. The new elements at indices 10 through 19 will have `null` for their values.

13. `HashSet<String> colors = new HashSet<String>();`

14. `colors.add("red");colors.add("blue");System.out.`
    `println(colors.contains("blue"));colors.remove("blue");`

15. `HashMap<Integer, String> studentids =`
    `    new HashMap<Integer, String>();`

16. `studentIDs.put(5531, "George");`
    `studentIDs.put(9102, "John");`
    `System.out.println(studentIDs.get(9102));`

17. Replace `ArrayList` with `LinkedList` in the `import` statement and twice in the statement that invokes the constructor.

18. You indicate the end of a linked list by setting the `link` instance variable of the last node to `null`.

19. `head` should have the value `null`.

20.
```
public boolean isEmpty()
{
    return length() == 0;
}
```
or
```
public boolean isEmpty()
{
    return head == null;
}
```

Since the first version invokes another method and the second one does not, the second method will execute faster.

21. C
    B
    A

22. An inner class is a class defined within the definition of another class.

23. They are not needed, because the methods in the linked-list class have access to the instance variables `data` and `link` of the nodes.

24. Any variable that allows you to step through the collection one item at a time, such that each item is visited exactly once in one full iteration cycle. Each item can have its data read and, if the data items allow it, can have the data changed. For example, an `int` variable that holds an index value can serve as an iterator for an array. To go to the next item in the array, your code needs only to increase the value of the `int` variable by 1.

```
25. public String getDataAtCurrent() throws LinkedListException
    {
        if (current != null)
            return current.data;
        else
            throw new LinkedListException("Attempted data " +
            "access when current is not at any node.");
    }


26. public void setDataAtCurrent(String newData)
        throws LinkedListException
    {
        if (current != null)
            current.data = newData;
        else
            throw new LinkedListException("Attempted data " +
                "change when current is not at any node.");
    }


27. public void insertNodeAfterCurrent(String newData)
        throws LinkedListException
    {
        ListNode newNode = new ListNode();
        newNode.data = newData;
        if (current != null)
        {
            newNode.link = current.link;
            current.link = newNode;
        }
        else if (head != null)
        {
            throw new LinkedListException("Inserting when " +
                "iterator is past all nodes or " +
                "is not initialized.");
        }
        else
        {
            throw new LinkedListException("Attempted insertion " +
                                        "into an empty list.");
        }
    }


28. public void deleteCurrentNode()
        throws LinkedListException
    {
        if ((current != null) && (previous != null))
        {
            previous.link = current.link;
            current = current.link;
```

```
        }
        else if ((current != null) && (previous == null))
            { //At head node
            head = current.link;
            current = head;
        }
        else//current == null
        {
            throw new LinkedListException("Attempted deletion " +
            "from an empty list, or current is not initialized.");
        }
    }
```

29. The complete definition is given as the class `ListNode2` in the source code available on the Web.

```java
public class ListNode2<E>
{
    private E data;
    private ListNode2<E> link;
    public ListNode2()
    {
        link = null;
        data = null;
    }
    public ListNode2(E newData, ListNode2<E>linkValue)
    {
        data = newData;
        link = linkValue;
    }
    public void setData(E newData)
    {
        data = newData;
    }
    public E getData()
    {
        return data;
    }
    public void setLink(ListNode2<E>newLink)
    {
        link = newLink;
    }
    public ListNode2<E> getLink()
    {
        return link;
    }
}
```

30. `ListNode2<Integer> node = new ListNode2<Integer>();`

Getting Java

A number of Java compilers and integrated development environments (IDEs) are available free of charge for various operating systems. The following list provides links to a selection of these resources.

- **The Java SE Development Kit (JDK)**
  Available from Oracle, the JDK for Linux, Solaris, and Windows includes the Java Runtime Environment (JRE) and command-line tools that you can use to write applications and applets.

  `http://www.oracle.com/technetwork/java/index.html`

- **BlueJ**
  BlueJ is an IDE developed at a university. It was created specifically for beginning Java students and is available for MacOS, Windows, and other systems at

  `www.bluej.org/download/download.html`

  BlueJ requires that you already have Java installed. Windows users should download and install the JDK from Oracle, as described previously. MacOS users will already have Java installed by default.

- **Eclipse**
  Eclipse is an open-source IDE for Linux, MacOS, and Windows that is available at

  `www.eclipse.org/downloads/`

  Eclipse requires that you already have Java installed. Linux and Windows users should download and install the appropriate JDK from Sun, as described previously. MacOS users will already have Java installed by default.

- **NetBeans**
  NetBeans is an open-source IDE for Linux, MacOS, Solaris, and Windows that is available at

  `www.netbeans.info/downloads/index.php`

  The website has a link to download the IDE by itself, in which case you must already have Java installed. Alternately, there is a link to download the IDE bundled with the JDK. MacOS users will already have Java installed by default.

Installation instructions for each of these resources are available at the given URLs.

Running Applets

As you know, applets are Java programs that are run from a Web page. The document that defines any Web page is written in HTML, which is a language designed for this purpose. Chapter 14, which is available on the book's Web site, provides some details about writing an HTML document. However, we can also use the Java tool `appletviewer` to run our applet. This tool requires a simple HTML document that we can write without looking at the details given in Chapter 14. Note that if you are using an IDE, you likely can run an applet without any reference to HTML. As we mentioned in Chapter 1, a typical IDE has a menu command such as Run Applet or something similar.

After you have written an applet, you should compile it. Recall from Chapter 1 that if your applet code is in the file `MyApplet.java`, for example, compiling this file produces another file—`MyApplet.class`—that contains the bytecode for the applet.

Next, to run the applet using `appletviewer`, you need to create another file for a simple HTML document. Its contents have the following form:

```
<applet code = "Applet_Name.class"
width = Applet_Width height = Applet_Height>
</applet>
```

So for our `MyApplet` example, our HTML file could contain

```
<applet code = "MyApplet.class" width = 400 height = 400>
</applet>
```

The number of lines we use for the HTML is irrelevant. The name of the HTML file should be `Applet_Name.html`, in this case, `MyApplet.html`.

Now we are ready to run the applet using the command

```
appletviewer MyApplet.html
```

RECAP Using `appletviewer` to Run an Applet

To run an applet that is in the file *Applet_Name*`.java`, you take the following steps:

- Create a file named *Applet_Name*.`html` that contains the following code:
  applet code = "*Applet_Name*.class"

  width = *Applet_Width* height = *Applet_Height*>

  </applet>
- Give the following commands at your computer's command line:

  javac *Applet_Name*.java

  appletviewer *Applet_Name*.html

Protected and Package Modifiers

In this text, we always use the modifiers `public` and `private` before instance variables and method definitions. Normally, these are the only modifiers you need, but there are two other possibilities that fall between the two extremes of `public` and `private`. In this appendix, we discuss the modifier `protected` as well as the restriction that applies when you use no modifier at all.

If a method or instance variable is modified by `protected` rather than `public` or `private`, it can be accessed directly by name within

- Its own class definition
- Any descendant class
- Any method definition for any class in the same package

That is the extent of the access; the protected method or instance variable cannot be accessed by name within any other classes. Thus, if a method is marked `protected` in class A, and class B is derived from class A, the method can be called inside any method definition in class B. However, in a class that is not in the same package as class A and is not derived from class A, the protected method behaves as if it were private.

The modifier `protected` imposes a peculiar sort of restriction, since it allows direct access to any programmer who is willing to go through the bother of defining a suitable derived class. Thus, it is like saying, "I'll make it difficult for you to use this item, but I will not forbid you to use it." In practice, instance variables should never be marked `protected`; they should be private. However, you can have protected accessor and mutator methods for such instance variables.

If you want an access level that is not public but not as restrictive as private access, an alternative is possible and often preferable. You may have noticed that if you forget to place one of the modifiers `public` or `private` before an instance variable or method definition, your class definition will still compile. In such cases, the instance variable or method can be accessed by name within the definition of any class that is in the same package. It cannot, however, be accessed by name outside of the package. This type of access is called **package access,** or **default access.** You use package access when you have a package of cooperating classes that act as a single encapsulated unit. Note that package access is more restricted than protected access and that it gives more control to the programmer defining the classes. If you control the package directory, you control who is allowed package access.

The DecimalFormat Class

The class `DecimalFormat` is in the Java Class Library within the package `java.text`. Thus, you make it available to a Java program by including the following import statement at the beginning of a program:

```
import java.text.DecimalFormat;
```

You can use this class to convert decimal numbers to formatted strings that can be displayed on the screen or written to a text file. Although the class defines a number of different methods, this appendix describes only one of them, namely, the method `format`. Complete documentation for the class `DecimalFormat` is available on the Oracle Web site.

The general approach to using the method `format` requires you to create a `String` pattern that describes the desired format for decimal numbers. For example, the pattern `"00.000"` means that there will be two digits before the decimal point and three digits after the decimal point. If the value of the number is not consistent with the specified format pattern, the format will be violated so that no digits are lost on the left of the decimal point. For example, the pattern `"00.000"` asks for only two digits before the decimal point, but the value 123.456 will be formatted as 123.456. Note, however, that the fractional portion is rounded when the pattern specifies fewer digits than are available in the actual number. So, using the same pattern, the value 12.3456 will be formatted as 12.346.

Once you have a pattern, you then create an object of the class `DecimalFormat` by writing a statement of the following form:

SYNTAX:

```
DecimalFormat Decimal_Format_Object_Name =
DecimalFormat(Pattern);
```

EXAMPLE:

```
DecimalFormat formattingObject = new DecimalFormat("00.000");
```

You then can use the method `format` to convert a value of type `double` to a corresponding numeral `String`, as follows:

SYNTAX:

Decimal_Format_Object_Name.format(*Double_Expression*)

The method returns a string that corresponds to *Double_Expression*.

EXAMPLE:

```
System.out.println(formattingObject.format(12.3456));
```

If the object formattingObject is created with the pattern "00.000", as in our previous example, the output produced by the foregoing println statement is 12.346.

Note that the method format returns a string that is an object of the class StringBuffer, not String. StringBuffer is similar to String but has methods that can modify the value of its instances.

Other Pattern Symbols

You can also create patterns such as "#0.##0", in which the character '0' stands for a compulsory digit and the character '#' stands for an optional digit. If '#' corresponds to a leading or trailing zero, the zero is omitted from the resulting string. For example, the statements

```
DecimalFormat formattingObject = new DecimalFormat("#0.0#");
System.out.println(formattingObject.format(3.5));
```

display 3.5, whereas

```
DecimalFormat formattingObject = new DecimalFormat("00.00");
System.out.println(formattingObject.format(3.5));
```

display 03.50.

The character '%' placed at the end of a pattern indicates that the number is to be expressed as a percentage. The '%' causes the number to be multiplied by 100 and have a percent sign (%) appended to it. For example, the statements

```
DecimalFormat formattingObject = new DecimalFormat("##0.0%");
System.out.println(formattingObject.format(0.1234));
```

display 12.3%.

You can place a dollar sign and/or commas into a pattern to format currency or large values. These two characters appear unchanged in the locations specified by the pattern. Figure A4.1 includes some examples of such patterns.

Figure A4.1   Some Results of Formatting Decimal Numbers

Value	3.5	3.5	1234.5678	123.45	12345.670	12345.678
Pattern	#0.0#	00.00	##.##	00000.000	###,###.###	$###,###.00
Result	3.5	03.50	1234.57	00123.450	12,345.67	$12,345.68

Figure A4.2   Some Results of Formatting Decimal Numbers Using the Same E-Notation Pattern

Value	0.12345	12345	123456	1234.567
Pattern	##0.##E0	##0.##E0	##0.##E0	##0.##E0
Result	123.45E-3	12.345E3	123.46E3	1.2346E3

You can specify that a value be displayed using E-notation by including an 'E' in the pattern string. For example, the pattern "00.###E0" approximates the specification of two digits before the decimal point, three or fewer digits after the decimal point, and at least one digit after the E, as in 12.346E1. The exact details of what string is produced are a bit more involved. When the number of digits before and after the decimal point satisfies certain constraints, the exponent is a multiple of 3, a notation used by engineers. To see how E-notation patterns work, you should play with a few cases. In any event, do not count on a very precisely specified number of significant digits. Figure A4.2 shows the results of formatting some values using E-notation.

Listing A4.1 contains a program that demonstrates some patterns and their effect.

LISTING A4.1   A Demonstration of the DecimalFormat Class *(part 1 of 2)*

```java
import java.text.DecimalFormat;
public class DecimalFormatDemo
{
    public static void main(String[] args)
    {
        DecimalFormat twoDigitsPastPoint = new DecimalFormat("0.00");
        DecimalFormat threeDigitsPastPoint =
                new DecimalFormat("00.000");

        double d = 12.3456789;
        System.out.println(twoDigitsPastPoint.format(d));
        System.out.println(threeDigitsPastPoint.format(d));

        double money = 12.8;
        System.out.println("$" + twoDigitsPastPoint.format(money));
        String numberString = twoDigitsPastPoint.format(money);
        System.out.println(numberString);

        DecimalFormat percent = new DecimalFormat("0.00%");
        double fraction = 0.734;
        System.out.println(percent.format(fraction));
```

(continued)

LISTING A4.1 **A Demonstration of the DecimalFormat Class** *(part 2 of 2)*

```
        //1 or 2 digits before decimal point:
        DecimalFormat eNotation1 = new DecimalFormat("#0.###E0");
        //2 digits before decimal point:
        DecimalFormat eNotation2 = new DecimalFormat("00.###E0");
        double number = 123.456;
        System.out.println(eNotation1.format(number));
        System.out.println(eNotation2.format(number));

        double small = 0.0000123456;
        System.out.println(eNotation1.format(small));
        System.out.println(eNotation2.format(small));
    }
}
```

Screen Output

```
12.35
12.346
$12.80
12.80
73.40%
1.2346E2
12.346E1
12.346E 6
12.346E 6
```

Javadoc **5**

The Java language comes with a program named javadoc that will automatically generate HTML documents that describe your classes. This documentation tells somebody who uses your program or class what she or he needs to know in order to use it but omits all the implementation details, such as the bodies of all method definitions (both public and private), all information about private methods, and all private instance variables.

Javadoc is normally used on packages, although it can also be used on single classes. Packages are discussed in Chapter 6. You need to have access to an HTML browser (a Web browser) so that you can view the documents produced by javadoc. However, you do not need to know very much HTML in order to use javadoc.

In this appendix, we will first discuss how you should comment your classes so that you can get the most value out of javadoc. We will then discuss the details of how you run the javadoc program.

Commenting Classes for Use with javadoc

To get a useful javadoc document, you must write your comments in a particular way. javadoc extracts these comments, along with the heading for your class and the headings for all public methods and public instance variables. No method bodies and no private items are extracted.

For javadoc to extract a comment, the comment must

- Immediately precede a public class definition, public method definition, or other public item
- Begin with /** and end with */

We will call such comments **javadoc comments.** Note that both comments beginning with // and comments preceding any private items will not be extracted.

Within a javadoc comment, you can use **tags** to identify and describe such things as the method's parameters and return values. The following shows the syntax of some of the tags allowed:

```
@param Parameter_Name  Parameter_Description
@return Description_Of_Value_Returned
@throws Exception_Type  Explanation
```

Each tag begins with the symbol @ and begins a new line within the comment. When used, these three tags must appear in the order given here. You can omit any tag that is not relevant, and you can also use a tag more than once if needed.

For example, the following method has a valid javadoc comment:

```
/**
Computes the total cost of multiple identical items.
@param number number of items purchased
@param price cost of one item
@return total cost of all items at given price per item
*/
public static double computeCost(int number, double price)
{
    return number * price;
}
```

The documentation that javadoc prepares from this comment appears as follows:

ComputeCost
public static double **computeCost**(int number, double price)
   Computes the total cost of multiple identical items.
   Parameters:
      number - number of items purchased
      price - cost of one item
   Returns:
      total cost of all items at given price per item

You can also insert HTML commands in your comments so that you gain more control over javadoc, but that is not necessary and may not even be desirable. HTML commands can clutter the comments, making them harder to read when you look at the source code. Chapter 14, which is on the Web, contains more about HTML than you need to know for this purpose.

To save space, the javadoc comments given in this book do not include tags or HTML commands.

Running javadoc

You run javadoc on an entire package. However, if you want to run it on a single class, you can make the class into a package simply by inserting the following at the start of the file for the class:

```
package Package_Name;
```

Remember that the package name should describe a relative path name for the directory or folder containing the files in the package.

To run javadoc, you must be in the folder (directory) that contains the package folder for which you want to generate documentation, not in the package folder itself. Then all you need to do is give the following command:

```
javadoc -d Document_Folder Package_Name
```

Document_Folder is the name of the folder in which you want javadoc to place the HTML documents it produces.

The code on the book's Web site contains a package named javadocsample, which contains the two classes Person and Student from Chapter 8. It also contains the result of running the following command:

```
javadoc -d javadocsampledocs javadocsample
```

You can include an option on the command line that tells javadoc to include live links to standard classes and methods within the documentation. The syntax is as follows:

```
javadoc -link Link_To -d Document_Directory Package_Name
```

Link_To is either a path to your local version of the Java documentation or the URL of the standard Java documentation on the Oracle Web site.

Differences Between C++ and Java

This appendix is for readers who have had significant programming experience with either C or C++. Other readers can ignore this appendix.

Java and C++ appear to be very similar, but they have more differences than a casual examination of the two languages might lead you to believe. We will not describe all of the differences in this appendix, but we will go over a few similarities and differences in order to help you make the transition from C++ (or C) to Java.

Primitive Types

Java has most of the same basic primitive types as C and C++ (`int`, `short`, `long`, `float`, `double`, and `char`), but Java adds the types `byte` and `boolean`. The Java type `boolean` corresponds to the C++ type `bool`. Java has no type named `long double`. Unlike C and C++, in Java the size, in bytes, of a value for some specific primitive type is fully specified and is not implementation dependent. See Chapter 2 for details.

Strings

Unlike some versions of C and C++, in Java strings are not special kinds of arrays of characters. Java has a class `String` that serves as a predefined type. `String` is somewhat similar to the class `String` in recent versions of C++. (Coverage of the `String` class starts in Chapter 2.)

Flow of Control

Control structures (`if-else`, `switch`, `while`, `do-while`, and `for`) are the same in Java as in C and C++. However, there are some differences in Java that can affect your use of control structures. Specifically, Java has no comma operator; the type `boolean` in Java is not a numeric type, nor can its values be type cast to a numeric type; and the assignment operator is better behaved in Java than in C and C++. We discuss each of these differences briefly below.

Java does not have the comma operator. However, the `for` statement in Java has been defined so as to allow the use of the comma, as in the following code:

```
for (int n = 1, product = 1; n < = 10; n++)

    product = product * n;
```

This "comma operator" can be used only in a for statement.

In Java, the type boolean has the two values, true and false, which cannot be interpreted as numeric values, even with a type cast.

A classic error in C and C++ is to use = in place of ==, as in the following code:

```
if (n = 42)

    . . .
```

In C and C++, the expression n = 42 returns the value 42, which either is or will be converted to a boolean value, depending on what version of C or C++ you are using. In Java, n = 42 also returns the value 42, but in Java, 42 is not of type boolean, nor will it convert to type boolean. So in Java, this mistake will produce a compiler error message.

Testing for Equality

Testing objects of a class type for equality can be troublesome in Java. With values of a primitive type, the == operator tests for equality, as you might expect. However, when you use == to compare two objects of a class type, the addresses of the objects are compared instead of their data. Java classes often define a method called equals to test objects for our intuitive idea of equality. You cannot overload the == operator (or any operator) in Java.

main Method (Function) and Other Methods

Functions are called **methods** in Java. The main method serves the same purpose in Java as the main function in C and C++. In Java, the main method heading is always as follows:

```
public static void main(String[] Parameter_Name)
```

In Java, all methods are defined inside of a class, as is code of any kind.

Files and Including Files

Java does not have an #include directive, but it does have an import statement that allows you to import either a class or an entire package (library) for use in a class.

The general layout of a Java program consists of a number of classes, each in a file by itself. If all the classes are in the same folder (directory), Java will automatically find the class (file) it needs when it needs it. The import statement also makes it possible to combine classes (files) from different folders. See Section 6.7 in Chapter 6 for more details.

In Java, a class must be in a file that has the same name as the class, but with the suffix `.java`. For example, a class named `MyClass` must be in a file named `MyClass.java`. The compiled version of the class will be placed in a file named `MyClass.class`.

Class and Method (Function) Definitions

In Java, all methods must be defined in some class. Additionally, a class definition can be fully defined in one file. Java has no required header, or `.h`, file, as do C and C++. In particular, all method definitions are given in their entirety in their class definition. See Chapter 5 for more details. Java does provide for an interface, which is similar in form to a header file in C and C++ but serves a different purpose. Chapter 8 introduces Java interfaces.

No Pointer Types in Java

There are no pointer types in Java. Java does have pointers; in fact, all objects are named by means of pointers. However, the pointers are called *references*, and they are handled automatically. For example, a variable of type `String` will contain a reference (pointer) to a string, but there is no type for a pointer to a `String`. See Section 5.3 in Chapter 5 for more details.

Method (Function) Parameters

Strictly speaking, Java has only one mechanism for parameter passing, namely, call-by-value. In practice, however, Java's parameter-passing mechanism behaves one way for primitive types—such as `int`, `double`, and `char`—and another way for class types.

For primitive types, the call-by-value parameter-passing mechanism behaves as C and C++ programmers would expect. That is, the parameter contains the value of its corresponding argument. But Java parameters of a class type contain a reference to the class object that is passed. This allows a method (function) to change the data in the object, and so some people consider this mechanism to be a call-by-reference mechanism. It does not satisfy the most common definition of *call-by-reference*, but when doing most simple tasks, it behaves very much like call-by-reference. See Chapter 5 for more details.

Arrays

Java arrays are very much like C or C++ arrays, but there are some differences, and Java arrays are better behaved. An array in Java "knows" its range. If a is an array, the instance variable `a.length` contains an integer equal to the number of elements that the array can hold. Java ensures that the values of array indices (subscripts) are valid, and an exception is thrown if your code attempts to use an array index that is out of range. See Chapter 7 for more details.

Garbage Collection

Memory management and garbage collection are automatic in Java. Java uses the new operator to create and allocate memory for a new object of a class type. This is the only way to explicitly allocate memory. Additionally, Java provides automatic garbage collection, relieving the programmer from this responsibility. Memory leaks, which can be a problem in C and C++, are not an issue in Java.

Other Comparisons

- Comments in Java and C++ are essentially the same.
- There are no global variables in Java.
- Java has no typedef.
- Java has no structures or unions.
- You can overload method (function) names in Java, as you can in C++, but you cannot overload operators in Java.
- Java has no multiple inheritance, but interfaces provide much of the functionality of multiple inheritance. See Chapter 8 for more details on interfaces.
- Java has no templates, but it does have generics in their place. See Chapter 12 for an introduction to generics.
- In Java, a class can have a constructor with a parameter of the same type as the class, but this constructor has no special status, unlike a copy constructor in C++.
- Java has no destructors.

Unicode Character Codes

The printable characters shown are a subset of the Unicode character set known as the ASCII character set. The numbering is the same whether the characters are considered to be members of the Unicode character set or members of the ASCII character set. (Character number 32 is the blank.)

32		56	8	80	P	104	h
33	!	57	9	81	Q	105	i
34	"	58	:	82	R	106	j
35	#	59	;	83	S	107	k
36	$	60	<	84	T	108	l
37	%	61	=	85	U	109	m
38	&	62	>	86	V	110	n
39	'	63	?	87	W	111	o
40	(	64	@	88	X	112	p
41	)	65	A	89	Y	113	q
42	*	66	B	90	Z	114	r
43	+	67	C	91	[	115	s
44	,	68	D	92	\	116	t
45	–	69	E	93	]	117	u
46	.	70	F	94	^	118	v
47	/	71	G	95	_	119	w
48	0	72	H	96	`	120	x
49	1	73	I	97	a	121	y
50	2	74	J	98	b	122	z
51	3	75	K	99	c	123	{
52	4	76	L	100	d	124		
53	5	77	M	101	e	125	}
54	6	78	N	102	f	126	~
55	7	79	O	103	g		

Index

SYMBOLS

' ', single quotes for characters,
52–53

!, not (logical) operator, 148–150

!=, not equal to operator, 145

" ", double quotes, 16, 82–83,
88

  printed statements, 16

  string value, 82–83, 88

"##" whitespace delimiter,
99–100

$, special symbol, 53

%, remainder (modulus) operator,
70

%c, character format specifier, 102

%d, decimal format specifier,
101–102

%e, exponential floating-point
format specifier, 102

%f, floating-point format specifier, 101–102

%s, string format specifier, 102

&&, and (logical) operator,
146–148

( ), parentheses, 16–18, 71–73,
84

  arithmetic expressions, 71–73

  arguments, 16–18, 84

*, multiplication operator, 56, 69

--, decrement operator, 79–80

-, minus (dash) symbol, 56,
69–71, 320–321

  number sign (unary) operator,
70–71

  subtraction (binary) operator,
56, 69, 71

  UML private notation,
320–321

,, comma operator, 220

., dot notation, 16–18, 84–85,
282–283

  instance variables, 282–283

  invoking (calling) methods,
16–18, 84–85, 282

/* */, comments, 104, 106

/** */, comments, 104–106

/, division operator, 69–70

//, comments, 104, 106

;, semicolons, 17, 201, 218–219

  end of instructions, 17

  loop body, 201, 218–219

[ ], brackets for arrays, 482,
485–486, 535–536, 538

\", escape character, 88–89

\', escape character, 88–89

\\, double slash, 88–89,
743–744

  escape character, 88–89

  path names, 743–744

\, single slash for path names,
743–744

'\n', end of line character, 95,
98–99

\n, newline escape character,
88–89

\r, carriage return escape
character, 88–89

\t, tab escape character, 88–89

_, underscore character, 53–54, 63

{ }, braces, 14–15, 50, 106–107,
140–142, 156–157, 199–201,
272, 286–287

  blocks, 286–287

  loop body, 199–201

  if-else statements, 140–142,
156–157

indentation, programming
style, 106–107, 140,
156–157

  methods, 14–15, 272

  variable declaration, 50,
286–287

||, or (logical) operator, 147–
148

+, plus symbol, 56, 69, 70–71,
82–83, 320–321

  addition (binary) operator,
56, 69, 71

  concatenation operator,
82–83

  number sign (unary) operator,
70–71

  UML public notation,
320–321

++, increment operator, 79–80

<, less than operator, 145

<=, less than or equal to operator,
145

=, assignment operator, 55–56,
72–73, 146, 508–511

==, equality operator, 145–146,
150–152, 326–330, 508–511

>, greater than operator, 145

>=, greater than or equal to
operator, 139–140, 145

.class bytecode ending, 20

.java file ending, 19–20

A

Abstract classes, interfaces and,
636–638

Abstract data type (ADT), 319

Abstraction, *see* Information
hiding

Accessor (get) methods, 302–305

Action event and listeners, 450

ActionListener interface, 644

actionPerformed method, 451–453, 711

Actual parameters, 288

Addition operator +, 56, 69, 71

Address, main memory, 3–4

ADT stack, 894

Algorithms, 25–26, 206–209, 230, 410–411, 526–527, 529–531, 624–626, 830–831
  interchange sorting, 526–527
  interfaces, 624–626
  loops, 206–209, 230
  merge sort, 830–831
  programming use of, 25–26, 207
  sorting arrays, 526–527, 529–531, 830–831
  writing methods, 410–411

Alphabetical order, strings, 154

American Standard Code for Information Interchange (ASCII), 67, 89

Ancestor class, *see* Base class

Appending (adding) to text files, 736–737

Applets, 13–14, 30–32, 37–38, 110–113, 241–247, 346–355, 447–467, 548–556, 918–919
  buttons, 447–461
  class methods and parameters, 346–356
  content pane, 353–355
  conversion to application, 110–113
  event handlers, 449–453
  Graphics class methods, 346–351, 553–556
  init method, 352–353, 455
  Internet use of, 13–14
  Java programs, 13–14, 30–32, 37–38, 918–919
  labels added to, 352–355
  listener objects handlers, 449–453

multifaced (looping and branching), 241–247, 348–351
  named constants in, 110
  paint method, 32, 352
  polygons, drawing, 553–556
  programming style rules, 110
  running (executing), 37–38, 918–919
  text areas, 548–552

Appletviewer, 37–38, 918–919

Applications, 13–19, 30, 110–126
  conversion from applet to, 110–113
  dialog windows, 113–126
  graphical user interface (GUI), 110–126
  Java computer programs, 13–19, 30
  JFrame class, 110–114
  JOptionPane class, 113–122
  windowing, 110–126

Arcs drawn in graphics programs, 35–37

Arguments, 16–18, 287–292, 340–343, 503–505
  array methods and, 503–505
  braces ( ) for Java methods, 16–18
  class type variables and, 340–343
  indexed variables as, 503–505
  methods and, 16–18, 84, 503–508
  parameters, 287–292, 340–343, 505–507
  primitive type variables and, 287–292

Arithmetic operators, 56–57, 68–81
  addition operator +, 56, 69, 71
  assignment operators combined with, 72–73
  assignment statements and, 56–57, 68–81
  binary, 70
  decrement operator --, 79–80
  division operator /, 69–70

expressions and, 56–57, 68–81
  increment operator ++, 79–80
  multiplication operator *, 56, 69
  number signs + −, 70–71
  operands, 98
  parentheses ( ) for, 71–73
  precedence rules, 71–72
  remainder (modulus) operator %, 70
  spacing, 71
  subtraction operator −, 56, 69, 71
  unary, 70
  variable values and, 56–57, 80

Array-based data structures, 849–859
  assignment statements for, 858–859
  copying, 858–859
  for-each loop (statement) for, 858
  instantiation, 850–852
  list, 850
  methods, 852–855
  parameterized class, as a, 859

ArrayList class, 850–859

Arrays, 479–573, 776–779, 822–834
  accessing, 482–484
  arguments and, 503–508
  assignment operator = and, 508–511
  binary files and, 776–779
  brackets [ ] for, 482, 485–486, 535–536, 538
  classes and, 495–503, 515–525
  creating, 482–484, 533–536
  declaring, 485–488, 533–536
  elements, 482–488
  equality operator == and, 508–511
  graphic applications, 548–556
  index (subscript), 482–483, 487
  indexed variables, 482–488, 491–493, 503–505

initializing, 494–495
`length` instance variable for, 488–490, 539
loops and, 490, 502, 535–536
methods and, 503–508, 511–515
multidimensional, 532–548
naming, 487–488
objects, 776–779
parameters, 505–507
partially filled, 523–524
programming with, 515–525
ragged, 540–542
recursion and, 822–834
returning, 511–513
searching, 531, 822–829
sorting, 525–531, 830–834
strings and, 516
subscript (index), 482–483, 487
ASCII characters, 67, 89, 729, 932
Assembly language, 7
Assertion checks, 239–240
Assignment operator =, 55–56, 72–73, 146, 508–511
Assignment statements, 55–81, 87, 508–511, 858–859
arithmetic operators and, 56–57, 68–81
array-based data structures, 858–859
arrays and, 508–511
assignment operator =, 55–56, 72–73, 508–511
constants (literals) and, 60–63
data type compatibilities, 63–64
decrement operator --, 79–80
expression values, 55–56
floating-point numbers and, 60–62
increment operator ++, 79–80
input/output (I/O) using, 58–60
primitive data types and, 57
simple input using, 58–59
simple screen output using, 60
`String` variables and, 87
type casting, 65–67

variable declarations, 57–58
variable values, 55–81
Auxiliary (secondary) memory, 3, 5

B

Base (stopping) case, 801–802, 809, 811
Base class (superclass), 579, 584–585, 589–591
class definition, 579
constructors, 589–591
inheritance and, 579, 584–585, 590
`private` instance variables and methods of, 584–585
Binary files, 728–729, 751–779
array objects and, 776–779
class objects and, 771–776
end of file errors, 766
`EOFException` class, 764–765
exceptions in, 764–766, 769–770
`ObjectInputStream` class, 751–758
`ObjectOuputStream` class, 758–763
objects and, 771–779
primitive data values, 729, 753–756
reading from, 758–766
storage in, 728–729
strings, writing to, 756–757
`writeInt` method, 753–757
`writeUTF` method, 757–758
writing (creating), 751–758
Binary operators, 70. *See also* Arithmetic operators
Binary search, 822–829
Binary trees, 894–895
BlueJ, 917
Body, Java methods, 16, 373
`boolean` data type, 52
Boolean expressions, 53, 139–142, 145–152, 166–172, 227–229
and (logical) operator, &&, 146–148
boolean operators, 145–151

boolean variables, 167–168, 227–229
comparison operators, 145–146
data types, 53, 166–172
equality operator, ==, 145–146, 150–152
floating-point comparisons, 146
greater than operator, >, 145
greater than or equal to operator, >=, 139–140, 145
`if-else` statements, 139–142, 145–152, 167–168
input/output (I/O) of values, 171–172
less than operator, <, 145
less than or equal to operator, <=, 145
logical operators, 146–150
loop iteration and, 227–229
not (logical) operator, !, 148–150
not equal to operator, !=, 145
or (logical) operator, ||, 147–148
precedence rules, 168–171
short-circuit evaluation, 170–171
string comparisons, 150–152
`true-false` statements, 167–172
value, 53, 171–172
boolean-valued methods, 334–336
Bottom-up testing, 418
Boxing, wrapper classes, 404
Branching statements, 137–194
`boolean` expressions, 166–174
`break`, 173–177
dialog windows using, 184–186
graphics applications, 180–186
`if-else`, 138–166
indentation { }, 140–142, 156–157
operator precedence, 168–169
`switch`, 173–180

break loop (statement), 232–234
break statement, 173–177
Buffering, 731
Buttons, 447–461, 639–644, 707–711
   ActionListener interface, 644
   actionPerformed method, 451–453, 711
   applets for, 447–461
   color, 707–711
   event handlers, 449–453
   exception handling applications, 707–711
   graphical user interface (GUI) for, 449–461, 639–644, 707–711
   icons, 456–458
   interface applications, 640–642, 644
   listener objects handlers, 449–453
   visibility of, 458–461
   window events and listeners, 642–644
byte data type, 52
Byte.parseByte method, 123
Bytecode, 9–11
Bytes, main memory, 3–5

C

C++ compared to Java, 928–931
Call-by-value parameters, 288–289
Calling methods, *see* Invoking (calling) methods
Canvas, 37
Case labels, switch statements, 173, 175
catch block, 663–664, 687–688, 692–694
ceil (rounding up) method, 401–402
Central processing unit (CPU), 3
char data type, 50–52, 60, 64, 67
Character class, 406–407
Character set, 89
Characters, 50–53, 67, 102
   char data type, 50–52, 64, 67

data types, 52–53
   format specifier %c, 102
   integer relations, 67
   single quotes ' ' for, 52–53
   type casting, 67
   variable declaration, 50–51
Checked exceptions, 684–685
Child class, *see* Derived classes
Circles drawn in graphics programs, 34–35
Circular linked list, 893
Class data types, 51, 322–334, 338–346, 771–776
   arguments and, 340–343
   assignment statements for, 323
   binary files and, 771–776
   equality operator == with, 326–330
   equals method for, 327–331
   memory addresses in, 323–327
   naming objects, 322–334, 338–346
   objects, 322–334, 338–346, 771–776
   parameters of, 338–345
   primitive type variables compared to, 343–345
   reference types and, 322–327
   variables, 51, 322–334, 338–346
Class interfaces, 611–612
Class loader, 11
Class path base directories, 443–446
Class path variables, 443–446
Classes, 19–22, 81–90, 261–372, 389–408, 441–446, 495–503, 515–525, 576–606, 669–678, 877–878
   .class bytecode ending, 20
   .java file ending, 19–20
   accessor (get) methods, 302–305
   arrays in, 495–503, 515–525
   base (superclass), 579, 584–585, 590
   blocks, 286–287

boolean-valued methods, 334–336
class Object, 602–603
compiling, 19–20
definition, 576–584
derived (subclass), 578–582, 589–597
encapsulation, 316–321
equals method for, 327–331
exception, 669–678
file compilation, 265
graphic applications, 346–356
Graphics, 346–351
hierarchy, 578–579, 586–588
implementation, 265–266, 300–302, 306–310, 317
information hiding, 294–321
inheritance, 24–25, 576–606
inner, 877–878
instance variables, 266–268, 282–283, 297–300
instantiation of, 264–265
interface, 317
Java programs, 19–21
javadoc program documentation, 319–320
linked structures, 877–878
local variables, 272, 284–286
main method for, 20, 268, 271
memory addresses and, 322–327
methods and, 261–372
methods calling methods, 310–315
mutator (set) methods, 302–305
objects and, 22–24, 263–265, 282–283, 321–348
overriding methods, 582–584
packages, 441–446
parameters, 287–293, 338–345
predefined exception, 669–671
private modifier, 296–299, 315, 320–321
programmer-defined exception, 671–678

programming and, 22–24, 515–525
public modifier, 296–299, 320–321
reference type variables, 322–334
regression testing, 336–338
return statements, 273–278
running (executing), 20–21
static methods, 389–408
static variables, 389–390
String, 80–91
this keyword, 282–283
unit testing, 336–338
Universal Modeling Language (UML) class diagrams, 264, 320–321, 586–588, 594
variable declaration, 266–268, 272, 284–287, 298–300
variables, 287–293, 322–324, 343–346
void method for, 270–273, 276–277
well-encapsulated, 317–319
wrapper, 403–408
writing, 19
clone method, 859
Code, 8
Collection interface, 860
Color, 180–186, 707–710
addition to graphics, 180–186, 707–711
getColor method, 707–709
setColor method, 182–183
sample choices, 707–711
UnknownColorException class, 709–710
Comma-separated values (CSV), 748–750
Comments, 104–106, 294–295
information hiding, 294–295
postcondition comments, 294–295
precondition comments, 294–295
programming style, 104–106
Comparable interface, 632–636
compareTo method, 152–154
Compiler checks, 416–417

Compilers, 8–10
Compiling Java programs, 19–20
Compound statements, 140–145
Computer systems, 2–12
class loader, 11
compilers, 8–10
hardware, 3–5
interpreter, 8–10
Java bytecode and, 9–11
languages for, 7–11
memory, 3–5
personal (PC), 3
processor (CPU), 3
programs, 6–7
software, 3, 6–7
Concatenation operator +, 82–83
Conditional operators, 165–166
Constants (literals), 60–63, 81–82, 107–110
char data type, 60
floating-point numbers, 60–62
graphics applet, 110
named, 62–63, 107–110
programming style and, 107–110
String class type, 81–82
Constructors, 375–389, 422–423, 584, 589–591
base class, 589–591
calling (invoking) methods from, 384–387, 584
calling (invoking) other constructors from, 387–389
default, 380, 383–384
defining, 375–384
derived class, 589–591
inheritance and, 584, 589–591
new operator for, 375, 380–383
overloading, 422–423
returning a reference, 380–381
set methods compared to, 375–379
super keyword, 589–591
this keyword, 387–389, 591

UML class diagrams for, 376, 384
Content pane, 353–355
continue loop (statement), 234
Control-C forced ending, 210
Coordinate system, graphics programs, 33–34
Count-controlled loops, 225
Counting, positions in strings, 84
Crashing, computer programs, 118

D

Data storage, 3–5, 16–17, 48–80
data types, 16–17, 50–53
directories, 5
expressions, 17, 48–80
files, 5
folders, 5
Java application programs, 14–16
memory and, 3–5
variables, 16, 48–80
Data structures, 847–916
array-based, 849–859
dynamic, 847–916
generics, 895–903
Java Collections Framework, 859–865
linked, 865–895
parameterized classes, 859, 895–903
Data types, 16–17, 50–53, 63–64, 179–180, 423–425, 597–600, 859, 895–903
assignment statement compatibilities, 63–64
automatic type conversion, 423–425
boolean values, 53
boolean, 52
byte, 52, 64
char, 50–52, 64, 67
characters, 52–53, 67
class, 51
double, 50–52, 63–66
enumeration, 179–180

Data types (*continued*)
  expressions and, 17, 65–67
  float, 52, 64
  floating-point numbers, 52
  generics, 859, 895–903
  inheritance compatibility,
    597–600
  int, 16–17, 50–52, 63–67
  integers, 50, 52, 65–67
  long, 52, 64
  overloading and, 423–425
  parameters as, 895–903
  primitive, 51–52
  short, 52, 64
  single quotes ' ' for, 52–53
  type casting, 65–67
  variables as, 16, 50–53
Debugging, 27–28, 235–241
  assertion checks, 239–240
  code correction, 235–236
  DEBUG flag, 238
  gotchas, 28
  hidden error, 28
  infinite loops, 235–236
  logic error, 27
  loop error, 235–241
  off-by-one error, 236–237
  syntax error, 27
  tracing variables, 237–238
DecimalFormat class, 921–924
Declaration, 50–51, 57–58, 219–
    220, 266–268, 272, 284–287,
    298–300, 485–488, 533–536,
    681–684
  arrays, 485–488, 533–536
  braces { } and, 50, 286–287
  exceptions, 681–684
  for loop (statement),
    219–220
  methods for, 266–268, 272,
    284–287, 298–300
  multidimensional arrays,
    533–536
  throws clause, 681–684
  variables, 50–51, 57–58,
    219–220, 266–268, 272,
    284–287, 298–300
Decomposition of method code,
    415–416

Decrement operator --, 79–80
Default access, 920
default case, 173, 176–177
Default constructors, 380,
    383–384
Delimiters, input changes,
    99–100
Derived classes (subclass),
    578–582, 589–597
  calling overridden methods,
    591–592
  class definition, 578–582
  constructors, 589–591
  derived classes of, 592–597
  inheritance and, 578–582,
    589–597
Dialog windows, 113–126,
    184–186
  branch statements for,
    184–186
  graphical user interface (GUI),
    115–126, 184–186
  Integer class, 117–118
  integers, 117–120
  JOptionPane classr, 113–122
  multiple line output, 124–126
  parseInt method, 123
  reading input (data), 123–124
  setSize method, 113–117
  string conversion and storage,
    117–120, 123–124
  string input/output (I/O),
    116–120, 123–124
  Swing package, 116
  yes-or-no buttons, 184–186
Directories, 5, 443–446
Division operator /, 69–70
double data type, 50–52, 63–66
Double.parseDouble method,
    123
Doubly linked list, 893–894
do-while loop (statement),
    200–205
drawArc method, 35–37
Drawing shapes, 34–37,
    241–247, 553–556, 619–636
  graphics programs, 34–37,
    241–247, 553–556
  interfaces, 619–636

drawOval method, 34–35
drawPolygon method, 553–556
drawPolyline method, 553–556
drawString method, 246
Driver programs, 411–414
Dynamic data structures, 847–
    916. *See also* Data structures

E

e (exponent) notation, 61. *See
    also* Floating-point numbers
Eclipse, 917
Empty statements, 218
Empty strings, 82
Encapsulation, 23, 316–321
  information hiding, 316–321
  javadoc program documenta-
    tion, 319–320
  programming use of, 23
End of line character '\n', 95,
    98–99
Enumeration, 179–180, 439–
    441, 542
EOFException class, 764–765
Equality operator ==, 145–146,
    150–152, 326–330, 508–511
  arrays and, 508–511
  class type variables and,
    326–330
  if-else statements using,
    145–146
  strings and, 150–152
equals method, 150–152,
    327–331, 603–606
  class type variables and,
    327–331
  inheritance and, 603–606
  strings and, 150–152
EqualsIgnoreCase method,
    152–154
Error class, 686
Errors, 27–28, 218–219,
    235–241, 686, 766,
    813–814. *See also* Debugging
  assertion checks for, 239–240
  end of file, 766
  exception handling, 686
  hidden, 28
  infinite loops, 219, 235–236

infinite recursion, 813–814
logic, 27
loop, 218–219, 235–241
off-by-one, 236–237
semicolon ; placement,
  218–219
stack overflow, 813–814
syntax, 27
tracing variables for, 237–238
Escape sequences (characters),
  88–89
Event handlers, 449–453
Events, 449
Exception handling, 657–724,
  764–766, 769–770, 890–892
binary files, 764–766,
  769–770
catch block, 663–664,
  687–688, 692–694
checked exceptions, 684–685
code (handling), 659,
  667–668
declaring exceptions, 681–684
errors, 686
finally block, 693–694
graphic applications, 707–711
information hiding and, 690
Java, 659–669
linked structures, 890–892
multiple throws and catches,
  687–690
nested try-catch blocks, 693
predefined classes, 669–671
programmer-defined classes,
  671–678
rethrowing an exception, 694
separate methods for, 692–
  693, 703
throw statement, 663,
  665–666, 692–693
throwing exceptions, 659–669
throws clause, 681–684
try block, 664–666
try-throw-catch sequence,
  666
unchecked (run-time)
  exceptions, 685
exit method, 165–166
Expressions, 17, 55–81

arithmetic operators in,
  56–57, 68–81
assignment statements and,
  55–64
constants (literals) and, 60–63
data storage, 17
data types and, 17, 65–67
floating-point numbers and,
  60–62
named constants, 62–63,
  107–109
parentheses ( ) for, 71–72
spacing, 71
type casting, 65–67
values, 55–56
variables and, 48–81
Extending interfaces, 618–619

F

Field (number of spaces), 101
Figure size and position, 32–34
File class, 741–746
file names, 741–744
path names, 743–744
methods of, 744–746
File I/O, 725–798
binary files, 728–729,
  751–779
comma-separated values
  (CSV), 748–750
File class, 741–746
graphics application, 779–785
methods for, 744–747
overwriting, 736
path names, 743–744
reading data, 738–743,
  758–766
silent programs, 734
streams and, 725–798
text files, 728–740
use of, 728
writeInt method, 753–757
writeUTF method, 757–758
writing data, 730–736,
  743–744, 751–758
Files, 5, 265, 728–740, 751–779
auxiliary memory, 5
binary, 728–729, 751–779
class compilation, 265

naming, 731, 734
text, 728–740
fillOval method, 34–35
fillPolygon method, 553–556
final modifier, 583–584
final statement, 62
finally block, 693–694
Firing and event, 449
float data type, 52
Float.parseFloat method, 123
Floating-point numbers, 52,
  60–64, 68–70, 101–102, 146
arithmetic operators and,
  68–70
assignment compatibility,
  63–64
assignment operators and,
  60–62
boolean expressions == and
  !=, 146
comparison of, 146
constants, 60–62
data types, 52
double data type, 50–52,
  63–64
e (exponent) notation, 61
exponential format specifier
  %e, 102
float data type, 52
format specifier %f, 101–102
imprecision of, 62
floor (rounding down) method,
  401–402
Folders, auxiliary memory, 5
for-each loop (statement), 222,
  858
for loop (statement), 213–221,
  490, 502, 535–536
arrays and, 490, 502,
  535–536
comma operator ,, 220
semantic, 217
semicolons ;, 218–219
syntax, 214–217
variables declared in,
  219–220
Formal parameters, 287, 292.
  See also Parameters
Format specifiers %, 101–102

Formatted output, 101–102
Full path name, 743
Functions, *see* Methods

G

Garbage collection, 875
Generic data types, 859
Generics, parameter types,
  895–903
get (accessor) methods,
  302–305
getColor method, 707–709
getContentPane() method,
  353–354
getText method, 551–552
Global variables, *see* Static
  variables
Graphical user interface (GUI),
  110–126, 449–461, 639–644,
  707–711, 779–785
  ActionListener interface,
    644
  buttons, 449–461, 639–644,
    707–711
  dialog windows (boxes),
    115–126
  event handlers, 449–453
  exception handling, 707–711
  file manipulation, 779–785
  instance variables for, 785
  interface applications,
    640–642, 644
  JFrame class, 110–114, 639–
    644, 707–709, 779–785
  JOptionPane class, 113–122
  listener objects handlers,
    449–453
  string input/output (I/O),
    116–120, 123–124
  Swing package, 116
  UnknownColorException
    class, 709–710
  window events and listeners,
    642–644
Graphics, 30–38, 109–126,
  180–186, 241–247, 346–356,
  447–461, 548–556, 619–636,
  638–644, 707–711, 779–785
  arcs, 35–37

branch statements for,
  180–186, 241–247
buttons, 447–461639–644,
  707–711
canvas, 37
class methods and parameters,
  346–356
color, 180–186, 707–710
conversion from applet to application, 110–113
coordinate system for, 33–34
dialog windows (boxes),
  113–126, 184–186
drawArc method, 35–37
drawing shapes, 34–37, 241–
  247, 553–556, 619–636
drawOval method, 34–35
drawPolygon method,
  553–556
drawPolyline method,
  553–556
drawString method, 246
exception handling for,
  707–711
figure size and position,
  32–34
file I/O for, 779–785
fillOval method, 34–35
fillPolygon method,
  553–556
getText method, 551–552
graphical user interface (GUI),
  110–126, 449, 639–644,
  707–711, 779–785
Graphics class, 346–351,
  553–556
icons, 456–458
init method, 352–353
interfaces for, 619–636,
  639–642, 644
JApplet class, 639
Java programs for, 30–38
JFrame class, 110–114, 639–
  644, 707–709, 779–785
JOptionPane class, 113–122,
  184–186
JTextArea class, 551–552
JTextField class, 551–552
labels, 352–355, 461

looping for, 241–247
multifaced (looping and
  branching) applets,
  241–247, 348–351
ovals and circles, 34–35
paint method, 32, 352
pixels, 32–33
polygons, 553–556
polylines, 553–556
programming style, 109–126
programs, 30–38
sequences, 241–247
setColor class, 181–184
setText method, 551–552
setVisible method,
  458–461
text areas, 548–552
text fields, 548, 551–552
visibility of components,
  458–461
windowing, 110–126
Greater than or equal to symbol
  >=, 139–140, 145

H

Handling exceptions (code), 659,
  667–668
Hardware, computer systems,
  3–5
Has-a relationships, 600–601
HashMap class, 862–864
HashSet class, 861–862
Head node (reference), 869
Heading, void methods, 272
Hidden error, 28
High-level language, 7–8

I

Icons, buttons with, 456–458
Identifiers, 53–55
if statements, 143–144
if-else statements, 138–168
  boolean expressions, 139–142,
    145–152, 167–168
  boolean operators, 151
  boolean variables, 167–168
  compareTo method, 152–154
  compound statements,
    140–145

conditional operators, 165–166

equality operator ==, 150–152

greater than or equal to symbol >=, 139–140

indentation braces { }, 140–142, 156–157

lexicographic order, 153–154

logical operators, 146–150

multibranch, 157–166

nested, 155–157

semantics of, 142–143

string comparisons, 150–155

imageIcon method, 456–457

Implementation, 265–266, 613–615, 869–876

classes, 265–266

interfaces, 613–615

linked structures, 869–876

import statement, 16–17, 58–59, 442–443

Importing packages, 442–443

Increment operator ++, 79–80

Indentation, 106–107, 140–142, 155–157

braces { }, 106–107, 140–142, 156–157

if-else statements, 140–142, 155–157

nesting statements without braces, 155–157

programming style, 106–107

Index (subscript), 482–483, 487, 491–493

arrays, 482–483, 487, 491–493

invalid (out of bounds), 491–493

zero value of, 482–483, 493

Indexed variables, 482–488, 503–505

accessing arrays, 482–484

arguments, as, 503–505

brackets [ ] for, 482, 485–486

creating arrays, 482–486

declaring arrays, 485–488

methods and, 503–505

Infinite loops, 209–210, 218–219, 235–236

code correction for, 235–236

control-C forced ending, 210

iteration and, 209–210

semicolon ; placement, 218–219

Infinite recursion, 812–814

Information hiding, 294–321, 690

abstract data type (ADT), 319

accessor (get) methods, 302–305

class definition and, 435–439

class implementation and, 300–302, 306–310, 317

class interface, 317

encapsulation, 316–321

exception handling and, 690

instance variables and, 297–300

methods calling methods, 310–315

methods for, 294–316, 435–439

mutator (set) methods, 302–305

postcondition comments, 294–295

precondition comments, 294–295

privacy leaks, 435–439

private modifier, 296–299, 315, 320–321

public modifier, 296–299, 320–321

well-encapsulated class, 317–319

Inheritance, 24–25, 576–609

base class (superclass), 579, 584–585, 590

class definition, 576–584

class hierarchy, 578–579, 586–588

constructors and, 584, 589–591

derived classes (subclass), 578–582, 589–597

dynamic binding and, 606–609

equals method, 603–606

final modifier, 583–584

has-a relationships, 600–601

is-a relationships, 580–581

methods and, 582–585, 602–606

Object class, 602–603

overriding methods, 582–584, 591–592

polymorphism and, 606–609

private instance variables and methods, 584–585

programming use of, 24–25, 589–606

super keyword, 589–591, 597

this keyword, 591

toString method, 602–603

type compatibility, 597–600

UML diagrams for, 586–588, 594

init method, 352–353, 445

Initializing arrays, 494–495

Inner classes, 877–878

Input data streams, 727–729, 738–744

keyboard input, 741–744

path names, 743–744

reading data, 738–743

text files, 738–743

Input/output (I/O), 58–60, 91–103, 116–126, 171–172, 409–415. *See also* File I/O

assignment statements used for, 58–60

boolean values, 171–172

conversion of strings to integers, 116–120, 123–124

delimiters, 94, 99–100

dialog windows, 116–126

double quotes " " for, 91–92

format specifiers %, 101–102

formatted output, 101–102

formatting output, 409–415

graphical user interface (GUI), 116–124

keyboard input, 94–100

multiple line output, 124–126

next methods, 94–96

print statement, 92–93

Input/output (I/O) (*continued*)
  printf statement, 101–102
  println statement used for,
    92–93
  screen output, 60, 91–93
  strings used for, 91–103,
    116–120, 123–124
  writing methods and,
    409–415
Instance variables, 266–268,
  282–283, 297–300, 320–321,
  488–490, 584–585, 785
  arrays and, 488–490
  dot notation ., 282–283
  GUI components as, 785
  information hiding, 297–300
  inheritance and, 584–585
  length, 488–490
  object member data, 266–268
  private modifier, 297–300,
    584–585
  this keyword, 282–283
  UML class diagram notation
    for, 320–321
Instantiation, 264–265,
  850–852
int data type, 16–17, 50, 52, 58,
  63–67, 117–119
Int.parseInt method, 123
Integer class, 117–118,
  404–405, 407
Integers, 50, 52, 63–67, 101–102,
  117–120
  assignment compatibility,
    63–64
  byte data type, 52
  character relations, 67
  data types, 50, 52
  decimal format specifier %d,
    101–102
  graphical user interface (GUI),
    117–120
  int data type, 50, 52, 58,
    63–67, 117–119
  long data type, 52
  short data type, 52
  string conversion and storage,
    117–120
  type casting, 65–67

Integrated development
  environment (IDE), 20
Interfaces, 317, 611–642, 644
  abstract classes, 636–638
  ActionListener interface,
    644
  algorithms for, 624–626
  class, 611–612
  Comparable, 632–636
  extending, 618–619
  graphic applications, 619–
    636, 639–642, 644
  implementing, 613–615
  Java, 612–613
  methods specified using,
    614–615
  reference types, as, 615–618
Interpreters, computer systems,
  8–10
Invalid (out of bounds) index,
  491–493
Invoking methods, 16–18,
  83–84, 269–271, 282–283,
  287–293, 310–315, 391–392,
  397–398, 808–811
  arguments ( ), 16–18, 84
  dot (call) notation ., 16–18,
    84–85, 282–283
  instance variables and,
    282–283
  methods calling methods,
    310–315
  parameters and, 287–293
  recursion, 808–811
  returning values, 269–271
  static, 391–392, 397–398
  String class, 83–84
  this keyword, 282–283
Is-a relationships, 580–581
Iterations, 196–197, 200, 225–
  229, 814–816, 878–890
  ask before, 225–226
  boolean variables for,
    227–229
  control in programming,
    225–229
  count-controlled loops, 225
  linked structures and,
    878–890

  loop body, 196–197
  recursive methods compared
    to, 814–816
  sentinel values, 226–227
  while loops, 197, 200
  zero, 200
Iterator interface, 890

J

JApplet class, 639
Java Class Library, 530–531
Java Collections Framework,
  859–865
  Collection interface, 860
  HashMap class, 862–864
  HashSet class, 861–862
  Map interface, 862
java execute command, 20
Java programs, 9–21, 30–38,
  196–222, 319–320, 539–540,
  612–613, 659–669, 728–729,
  771–772, 917–931
  applets, 13–14, 30–32,
    918–919
  applications, 13–19
  bytecode, 9–11
  C++ compared to, 928–931
  class loader for, 11
  classes, 19–21
  compiling, 19–20
  DecimalFormat class,
    921–924
  documentation, 320–321,
    925–927
  exception handling, 659–669
  graphics, 30–38
  integrated development envi-
    ronment (IDE), 20
  interfaces, 612–613
  interpreter for, 9–10
  javadoc, 319–320, 925–927
  language history, 12–13
  looping statements, 196–222
  methods { }, 14–18
  multidimensional arrays,
    539–540
  object serialization, 771–772
  packages, 14, 920
  protected modifiers, 920

resources, 917
running, 20–21
syntax, 17
text file storage of, 728–729
writing, 19
Java SE Development Kit (JDK), 917
Java virtual machine (JVM), 9
javac compile command, 20
javadoc program documentation, 319–320, 925–927
JFrame class, 110–114, 639–644, 707–709, 779–785
JLabel class, 355
JOptionPane class, 113–122
JTextArea class, 551–552
JTextField class, 551–552

K

Keyboard input, 94–100, 741–744
delimiters, 94, 99–100
end of line character '\n', 95, 98–99
file names, 741–744
next methods, 94–96
path names, 743–744
Scanner class, 94–98
Keywords, 54, 282–283, 387–389, 589–592, 597
calling overridden methods, 591–592, 597
constructors and, 387–389, 589–591, 597
instance variables and, 282–283
super, 589–592, 597
this, 282–283, 387–389, 597

L

Labels added to graphics applets, 352–355
Language, 7–11, 12–13, 17
assembly, 7
class loader, 11
compilers, 8–10
computer systems, 7–11
high-level, 7–8
history of Java, 12–13

interpreters, 8–10
Java bytecode, 9–11
low-level, 7
machine, 7
syntax, 17
length instance variable, 488–490, 539
Lexicographic order, if-else statement strings, 153–154
Linked structures, 865–895
ADT stack, 894
binary trees,, 894–895
circular, 893
doubly, 893–894
exception handling, 890–892
head node (reference), 869
implementation of, 869–876
inner classes, 877–878
iterators, 878–890
LinkedList class, 865–895
List interface, 866
nodes, 866–869, 875, 878, 893
object data in, 892–893
privacy leaks, 876–877
tail node, 893
trees, 894–895
LinkedList class, 865–895
List interface, 866
Listener objects handlers, 449–453
Lists, 850. *See also* Array-based data structures; Linked structures
Local variables, 272, 284–286
Locations, main memory,4–5
Logic error, 27
Logical operators, 146–150
long data type, 52
Long.parseLong method, 123
Loops, 195–259, 490, 502, 535–536
algorithms for, 206–209
arrays and, 490, 502, 535–536
body, 196–197, 223
boolean variables for, 227–229
brace { } positions, 199–201
break statement, 232–234

comparison of, 221–222
continue statement, 234
count-controlled, 225
do-while statement, 200–205
ending, 227–229, 232–234
errors, 218–219, 235–241
for statement, 213–221, 490, 502, 535–536
for-each statement, 222
graphics application, 241–247
infinite, 209–210, 218–219, 235–236
initializing statements, 224–225
iterations, 196–197, 200, 225–229
Java statements, 196–222
nested, 211–213
programming, 210, 221–239
semicolons ;, 201, 218–219
while statement, 197–200, 211–213
Low-level language, 7

M

Machine language, 7
Main memory, 3–4
main method, 15, 20, 268, 271, 397–400, 507–508
Map interface, 862
Math class, 400–403
Megapixels, 33
Memory, 3–5, 323–327
address, 3–4, 323–327
auxiliary, 3, 5
bytes, 3–5
class type variables and, 323–327
computer systems, 3–5
data storage, 3–5
directories, 5
files, 5
folders, 5
locations, 4–5
main, 3–4
random access (RAM), 3
secondary, 3
zero and one states, 5

Merge sort, 830–834

Methods, 14–18, 20, 22–23, 83–86, 94–98, 112–113, 117–124, 261–372, 373–478, 503–508, 511–515, 582–585, 602–606, 744–747, 801–820, 852–855

accessor (`get`), 302–305

action performing, 269–271

arguments ( ), 16–18, 84, 503–508

`ArrayList` class, 852–855

arrays and, 503–508, 511–515

body, 16, 272

`boolean`-valued, 334–336

braces { }, 14–15, 272

calling other methods, 310–315

classes and, 261–372

class-type variables, 327–331, 334–336

constructors, 375–389, 422–423

converting strings to numbers, 117–120, 123–124

data structures, 852–855

data types, 16–17

dialog windows, 117–124

dot (call) notation ., 16–18, 84–85, 282–283

end of instructions ;, 17

enumeration, 439–441

`equals`, 327–331, 603–606

`File` class, 744–746

file I/O, 744–747

`final` modifier, 583–584

graphical user interface (GUI), 112–113, 117–124

graphics applications, 112–113, 117–124, 447–461

headings, 272, 292–293

indexed variables as arguments, 503–505

information hiding, 294–316, 435–439

inheritance and, 582–585, 602–606

invoking (calling), 16–18, 118, 269–271, 282–283,

287–293, 384–387, 808–811

Java application programs, 14–18

`JOptionPane` class, 117–124

keyboard input, 94–98

local variables, 272, 284–286

`main`, 15, 20, 268, 271, 397–400, 507–508

`math` class, 400–403

mutator (`set`), 302–305

naming, 275, 425

object-oriented programming (OOP), 22–23

objects, 16, 373–478

overloading, 420–434

overriding, 582–584, 591–592

parameters of, 287–293, 228–345

`parseInt`, 123–124

primitive type variables, 287–293, 343–345

`private` instance variables and, 584–585

reading data, 17, 123–124

recursive, 801–820

`return` statements, 273–278

returning value, 269–271, 273–275, 816–820

running Java classes, 20

`Scanner` class, 94–98

`setSize`, 112–113

signature, 422

statements " ", 16

`static`, 389–408

streams and, 746–747

`String` class, 83–86

stub, 418

testing, 411–415, 418

`this` keyword, 282–283

`toString`, 602–603

UML class diagram notation for, 320–321

variable declaration, 266–268, 272, 284–287, 298–300

`void`, 270–273, 276–278

writing, 409–420

Multibranch `if-else` statements, 157–166

Multidimensional arrays, 532–548

brackets [ ] for, 535–536, 538

declaring and creating, 533–536

enumeration for, 542

`for` loop (statement), 535–536

Java representation of, 539–540

`length` instance variable for, 539

named constants for, 543–548

parameters, 536–538

ragged, 540–542

return types, 536–538

two-dimensional, 532–535, 539–540

Multifaced (looping and branching) applets, 241–247

Multiplication operator *, 56, 69

Mutator (`set`) methods, 302–305

Mutually exclusive statements, 158

N

Named constants, 62–63, 107–109, 532–548

Naming, 50, 53–55, 103–104, 275, 425, 446, 487–488, 731, 734, 741–744

arrays, 487–488

clashes, 446

`File` class, 741–744

files, 731, 734, 741–744

keyboard input, 741–744

methods, 275, 425

packages for organization of, 446

path names, 743–744

variables, 50, 53–55, 103–104

Negative test, 337

Nested statements, 155–157, 211–213, 693

`if-else`, 155–157

indentation for, 156–157

loops, 211–213
try-catch blocks, 693
while, 211–213
NetBeans, 917
new operator, 58–59, 375,
380–383
Newline escape character \n,
88–89
next() method, 94–97
nextBoolean method, 172
nextDouble() method, 94, 96
nextInt() method, 94–96
nextLine() method, 94–97
Nodes, 866–869, 875, 878, 893
null statements, 218, 417,
518–519
NullPointerException
message, 875
numberOfInvocations
statement, 390

O

Object class, 602–603
ObjectInputStream class,
751–758
Object-oriented programming
(OOP), 21–26
algorithms, 25–26
classes and, 22–24
encapsulation, 23
inheritance, 24–25
methods and, 22–23
object attributes, 22
polymorphism, 23–24
ObjectOuputStream class,
758–763
Objects, 8, 16, 22–24, 263–268,
282–283, 287–293, 321–348,
373–478, 771–779, 892–893
attributes, 22, 264
arrays, 776–779
binary files and, 771–779
boolean-valued methods,
334–336
class type variables, 322–334,
338–346, 771–776
classes and, 22–24, 263–265,
282–283, 321–346
code, 8

constructors, 375–389,
422–423
equals method for, 327–331
graphics applications, 346–
348, 447–461
Graphics class, 346–348
information hiding, 435–439
instance variables, 266–268
instantiation of, 264–265
linked structures with,
892–893
members, 265–266
memory addresses and,
322–327
methods and, 16, 373–478
naming, 321–346
new operator, 268
packages, 441–446
parameter passing methods,
287–293, 340–345
primitive type variables,
343–345, 343–345
reference type variables,
322–334
regression testing, 336–338
representation of, 263–264
serialization, 771–772
static methods, 389–408
Off-by-one error, 236–237
Operands, 98
Operating system (OS), 7
Operator precedence, 168–169
Out of bounds (invalid) index,
491–493
Output, *see* File I/O; Input/output
(I/O)
Output data streams, 727–737,
751–758
appending (adding) to files,
736–737
binary files, 751–758
buffering, 731
closing (disconnecting) from
files, 731–732
flow of, 727–729
opening (connecting) to files,
730–731
primitive data types, 753–756
strings, 756–757

text files, 730–737
writing (creating) to files,
730–736, 751–758
Ovals drawn in graphics
programs, 34–35
Overloading, 420–434, 583, 819
automatic type conversion,
423–425
constructors, 422–423
methods, 420–434
naming methods and, 425
overriding compared to, 583
recursion compared to, 819
return data types, 426
signature, 422
Overriding methods, 582–584,
591–592, 597
calling (invoking), 591–592,
597
class and method definitions,
582–584
final modifier, 583–584
super keyword, 591–592, 597

P

Packages, 14, 116, 441–446, 920
access (default), 920
class path base directories,
443–446
class path variables, 443–446
classes, 441–446
graphics application, 116
importing, 442–443
Java programs, 14, 116, 920
naming clashes and, 446
paint method, 32, 352
Parameterized classes, 859,
895–903
Parameters, 287–293, 338–345,
505–507, 536–538, 895–903
actual, 288
arguments and, 287–292,
340–343, 505–507
arrays, 505–507, 536–538
call-by-value, 288–289
class type variables, 338–345
data structures and, 895–903
formal, 287, 292
generics, 895–903

Parameters (*continued*)
headings and, 292–293
inner class access, 902–903
method invocation and, 287–293
multidimensional arrays, 536–538
passing methods, 287–293, 340–345
primitive type variables, 287–293, 343–345
type casting, 290
types, 895–903
Parentheses ( ), arithmetic expressions, 71–73
parse string conversion methods, 123
Partially filled arrays, 523–524
Path names, 743–744
Personal computer (PC), 3
Pictures (icons), 456–460
Pixels, 32–33
Polygons, drawing graphics, 553–556
Polylines, drawing graphics, 553–556
Polymorphism, 606–610
dynamic binding and, 606–610
inheritance and, 606–609
toString method, 609–610
Polymorphism, programming use of, 23–24
Postcondition comments, 294–295
Postfix form, variables, 80
Precedence rules, 71–72, 168–171
arithmetic expressions, 71–72
boolean expressions, 168–171
Precondition comments, 294–295
Predefined exception classes, 669–671
Prefix form, variables, 80
Primitive data types, 51–52, 57, 287–293, 343–345, 403–408, 729, 753–756
assignment statements and, 57

binary files, 729, 753–756
boxing, 404
call-by-value methods, 288–289
Character class, 406–407
class type variables compared to, 343–345
Integer class, 404–405, 407
parameters, 287–293
static methods for, 403–408
String class, 405–406, 408
unboxing, 404–405
variables, 51–52, 287–293
wrapper classes and, 403–408
writing to binary files, 753–756
print statement, 92–93
println statement, 92–93
Privacy leaks, 435–439, 514, 876–877
private modifier, 296–300, 315, 320–321, 920
inheritance and, 584–585
instance variables, 297–300, 584–585
information hiding and, 296–300, 315
methods, 315, 584–585
protected modifier and, 920
UML class diagram notation for, 320–321
Programmer-defined exception classes, 671–678
Programming, 21–29, 53–55, 103–126, 140, 153–157, 210, 221–239, 515–525, 589–606, 820–834. *See also* Debugging
algorithms, 25–26
arrays and, 515–525
binary search, 822–829
boolean variables for, 227–229
break statement, 232–234
case sensitivity, 53–55, 153–154
classes and, 22–24, 515–525
comments, 104–106
continue statement, 234
debugging, 27–28

documentation, 103–109
encapsulation, 23
ending loops, 227–229, 232–234
errors, 27–28, 235–241
graphics applications, 109–126
indentation braces { }, 106–107, 140, 156–157
inheritance, 24–25, 589–606
initializing statements, 224–225
input/output (I/O), 116–126
iteration control, 225–229
lexicographic order, 153–154
loops, 210, 221–239
merge sort, 830–834
methods, 22–23, 113–122
named constants, 107–109
naming variables, 103–104
nested structure, 107
null statements, 518–519
object-oriented (OOP), 21–26
partially filled arrays, 523–524
polymorphism, 23–24
programming use of, 24–25, 589–606
recursion for, 820–834
restarting input process, 820–821
software reuse, 28–29
stopping infinite loops, 210
string order, 153–154
testing for errors, 27–28
Programs, 6–21, 30–38, 104–106, 118
applets, 13–14, 30–32, 37–38
applications, 13–19
classes, 19–21
code, 8, 104–106
compilers, 8–10
computer systems, 6–7
crashing, 118
executing, 6
graphics application, 30–38
interpreters, 8–10
Java, 12–21, 30–38
languages, 7–13, 17

operating system (OS), 7
running, 6, 20–21
self-documenting, 104–106
software, 6–7
`protected` modifier, 920
Pseudocode, 25–26
`public` modifier, 296–299,
320–321, 920
information hiding and,
296–299
`protected` modifier and, 920
UML class diagram notation
for, 320–321
`public static final` statement, 62–63

R

Ragged arrays, 540–542
Random access memory (RAM),
3
`random` method, 402–403
Reading data, 738–743, 758–766
binary files, 758–766
`EOFException` class, 764–765
keyboard input, 741–734
naming files, 741–734
`ObjectOuputStream` class,
758–763
text files, 738–740
Recursion, 800–845
arrays and, 822–834
base (stopping) case for,
801–802, 809, 811
binary search using, 822–829
calling (invoking) methods,
808–811
infinite, 812–814
iterative methods compared
to, 814–816
merge sort using, 830–834
overloading compared to, 819
programming with, 820–834
recursive methods, 801–820
restarting input process,
820–821
returning values, 816–820
stack overflow, 813–814
Reference types, 322–327,
380–381

class type variables as,
322–327
constructors for, 380–381
interfaces as, 615–618
memory addresses as,
323–327
object naming, 322–327
returning, 380–381
variables, 322–327
Regression testing, 336–338
Relative path name, 743
Remainder (modulus) operator
%, 70
Reserved words, 54
Return data types, 426
`return` statements, 273–278
Returning values, 269–271,
273–278, 380–381, 511–513,
536–538, 816–820
arrays, 511–513, 536–538
methods, 269–271, 273–278,
816–820
multidimensional arrays,
536–538
recursive methods, 816–820
references, 380–381
Running (executing) Java programs, 20–21
Run-time (unchecked)
exceptions, 685

S

Scanner class, 94–98
Scientific notation, 60
Screen output, 60, 91–93
Searching arrays, 531, 822–829
binary, 822–829
sequential, 531
Secondary (auxiliary) memory, 3
Selection sort, 525–529
Self-documenting programs,
104–106
Sequential search, 531
Serialization of objects, 771–772
`set` (mutator) methods, 302–305
`setBackground` method, 354
`setColor` method, 182–183
`setSize` method, 113–117
`setText` method, 551–552

`setVisible` method, 458–461
`short` data type, 52
`Short.parseShort` method, 123
Short-circuit evaluation, 170–171
`showInputDialog` method, 117
`showMessageDialog` method,
119
Signature, 422
Silent programs, 734
Software, computer programs, 3,
6–7
Software reuse, 28–29
Sorting arrays, 525–531, 830–
834
algorithms, 526–527, 529–
531, 830–831
interchange sorting algorithm,
526–527
Java Class Library for,
530–531
merge sort, 830–834
recursion for, 830–834
selection sort, 525–529
Source code, 8
Spacing, arithmetic expressions,
71
Stack overflow, 813–814
Statements, 16, 55–81, 87, 137–
194, 195–259, 239–240
assertion, 239–240
assignment, 55–81, 87
branching, 137–194
`break`, 232–234
`continue`, 234
do-`while` statement, 200–205
empty, 218
`for`, 213–221
`for-each`, 222
`if-else`, 138–166
initializing, 224–225
loops, 195–259
mutually exclusive, 158
nested, 155–157, 211–213
null, 218
quotes " " for Java methods,
16
`switch`, 173–180
`while` statement, 197–200,
211–213

Static methods, 389–408
  boxing, 404
  `ceil` (rounding up) method,
    401–402
  `Character` class, 406–407
  class (static) variables,
    389–390
  combinations of classes with,
    392–394
  `floor` (rounding down)
    method, 401–402
  `Integer` class, 404–405, 407
  invoking (calling), 391–392,
    397–398
  `main` method, 15, 20, 268,
    271, 397–400
  `Math` class, 400–403
  non-static methods combined
    with, 394–396
  primitive types and, 403–408
  `random` method, 402–403
  `String` class, 405–406, 408
  subtasks for, 397–398
  unboxing, 404–405
  wrapper classes, 403–408
Static variables, global variables
  as, 286
Stopping (base) case, 801–802,
  809, 811
Stream variable, 730
Streams, 725–798
  binary files, 728–729,
    751–779
  comma-separated values
    (CSV), 748–750
  file I/O and, 725–798
  input data, 727–729
  methods for opening,
    746–747
  `ObjectInputStream` class,
    758–763
  `ObjectOuputStream` class,
    758–763
  opening, 746–747
  output data, 727–737
  text files, 728–740
`String` class, 80–91, 405–406,
  408
String comparisons, 150–155

Strings, 81–103, 116–120,
  123–124, 150–154, 516,
  756–757
  arguments ( ), 84
  arrays and, 516
  assignment statements for,
    87
  binary files, writing to,
    756–757
  `compareTo` method,
    152–154
  comparison of, 150–152
  concatenation operator +,
    82–83
  constants, 81–82
  conversion and storage as
    integers, 117–120, 123
  counting positions, 84
  dialog window construction,
    116–120, 123–124
  empty, 82
  equality operator ==, 150–152
  `equals` method, 150–152
  `EqualsIgnoreCase` method,
    152–154
  escape characters, 88–89
  format specifier %s, 102
  graphical user interface (GUI),
    116–120, 123–124
  `if-else` statements,
    150–154
  index value, 88
  input/output (I/O) using,
    91–103, 116–120,
    123–134
  lexicographic order of,
    153–154
  methods, 83–86
  multiple output, 124
  `parseInt` method, 123
  processing, 85–87
  `String` class, 80–91, 116
  substring, 84–85
  Unicode character set, 89
  value " ", 82–83, 88
  variables, 81–82
  whitespace characters in,
    84–85
Stub methods, 418

Subscript (index), arrays,
  482–483, 487
Subscripted variables, *see* Indexed
  variables
Substring, 84–85
Subtasks, 397–398, 415–416
  method decomposition,
    415–416
  static methods, 397–398
Subtraction operator –,
  56, 69, 71
`super` keyword, 589–592, 597
Swing package, 116, 456
`switch` statements, 173–180
  `break` statement, 173–177
  case labels, 173, 175
  `default` case, 173, 176–177
  enumeration, 179–180
  string expressions, 176–177
Syntactic variables, 51
Syntax, 17
Syntax error, 27, 146
`System.exit` statement,
  120–121
`System.out.println`
  statements, 16

T

Tail node, 893
Testing, 27–28, 411–415, 418.
  See also Debugging
  bottom-up, 418
  methods, 411–415, 418
  programs, 27–28
  stubs, 418
Text areas, 548–552
Text fields, 548, 551–552
Text files, 728–740
  appending (adding) to,
    736–737
  ASCII characters for, 729
  Java program storage in,
    728–729
  reading from, 738–740
  `try` blocks and, 732, 735
  Unicode characters for, 729
  writing (creating), 730–736
`this` keyword, 282–283,
  387–389, 591

throw statement, 663, 665–666, 692–693
Throwing exceptions, 659–669
throws clause, 681–684
toString method, 602–603, 609–610
Tracing variables, 237–238
Trees, linked structures, 894–895
true-false statements, 167–172
  boolean expressions, 168–172
  boolean variables, 167–168
  input/output (I/O) of values, 171–172
  precedence rules, 168–171
  short-circuit evaluation, 170–171
Truncating values, 66
try blocks, 664–666, 687–689, 728–740
try-throw-catch sequence, 666
Two-dimensional arrays, 532–535
Type casting, 65–67, 290, 404–405
  boxing, 404
  changing values using, 65
  character and integer relations, 67
  data types and, 65–67
  parameters, 290
  truncating values using, 66
  unboxing, 404–405

U

Unary operators, 70
Unboxing, wrapper classes, 404–405
Unchecked (run-time) exceptions, 685
Unicode character set, 67, 89, 729, 932
Uninitialized variables, 57
Unit testing, 336–338
Universal Modeling Language (UML) class diagrams, 264, 320–321, 376, 384, 586–588, 594

UnknownColorException class, 709–710
User, 14

V

Values, 49, 53, 55–64, 82–83, 88, 171–172. *See also* Assignment statements
  boolean, 53, 171–172
  expressions, 55–64
  input/output (I/O) of, 171–172
  invalid (out of bounds), 88
  strings " ", 82–83, 88
  variables, 49, 55–64
Variables, 16, 48–82, 103–104, 167–168, 219–220, 237–238, 266–268, 272, 284–287, 298–300, 322–334, 338–346, 443–446, 482–488, 491–493, 503–505
  arithmetic operators and, 56–57, 80
  array elements, 482–488
  assignment statements and, 55–81, 168
  blocks, 286–287
  boolean, 167–168
  braces { } and declaration of, 50, 286–287
  class path, 443–446
  class type, 322–334, 338–346
  classes and, 266–268, 272, 284–287, 298–300
  data storage, 16, 49
  data types, 16–17, 50–53
  declaration, 50–51, 57–58, 219–220, 266–268, 272, 284–287, 298–300
  expressions and, 55–81
  identifiers, 53–55
  indexed, 482–488, 491–493, 503–505
  instance, 266–268, 298–300
  Java case sensitivity, 53–55
  local, 272, 284–286
  loops and, 219–220, 237–238
  methods and, 266–268, 272, 284–287, 298–300

naming, 50, 53–55, 103–104
object naming, 322–334, 338–346
parameters of, 287–293, 228–345
primitive type, 51–52, 287–293, 343–345
programming style, 103–104
reference type, 322–334
static, 389–390
String, 81–82
syntactic, 51
tracing, 237–238
true-false statements, 167–168
type casting, 65–67
uninitialized, 57
value, 49, 55–64, 80, 167–168
Virtual machines, 9
Visibility of graphic components, 458–461
void methods 270–273, 276–278
Volatile information, 3

W

Well-encapsulated class, 317–319
while loop (statement), 197–200, 211–213
Whitespace, 84–85, 99–100
  characters, 84–85
  delimiter "##", 99–100
Window events and listeners, 642–644
Windowing, 110–126. *See also* Dialog windows; Graphical user interface (GUI)
Wrapper classes, 403–408
writeInt method, 753–757
writeUTF method, 757–758
Writing data, 409–420, 730–736, 743–744, 751–758
  algorithms for, 410–411
  binary files, 751–758
  bottom-up testing, 418
  compiler checks, 416–417
  decomposition, 415–416
  driver programs, 411–414

Writing data (*continued*)
    files, 730–736, 743–744,
      751–758
    formatting output, 409–415
    methods, 409–420
    null statement, 417
    ObjectInputStream class,
      751–758
    path names, 743–744

    primitive data values, 729,
      753–756
    strings, 756–757
    stub methods, 418
    testing, 411–415, 418
    text files, 730–736
    writeInt method, 753–757
    writeUTF method, 757–758
Writing Java programs, 19

Y

Yes-or-no dialog boxes, 184–186

Z

Zero and one states of memory,
    5
Zero index values, 482–483,
    493